# Microprocessor Microcomputer and Their Applications

## Third Edition

# Microprocessor Microcomputer and Their Applications

## Third Edition

A.K. Mukhopadhyay

# Alpha Science International Ltd.
Oxford, U.K.

**Professor Ashok Kumar Mukhopadhyay**
Sir R.B. Ghosh Professor in Electrical Engineering
Department of Applied Physics
University College of Technology
Calcutta University, Kolkata, India

Copyright © 1996, 1999, 2007
Second Edition 1999
First Reprint 2001
Second Reprint 2005
Third Edition 2007

Alpha Science International Ltd.
7200 The Quorum, Oxford Business Park North
Garsington Road, Oxford OX4 2JZ, U.K.

**www.alphasci.com**

ISBN-13: 978-1-84265-345-6
ISBN-10: 1-84265-345-8

Printed in India

To
**Indrani**

# Preface to the Third Edition

After the publication of the second edition, I received a lot of interesting feedback from several subject experts and eminent scholars from different parts of the country and abroad. Some suggested to add one chapter on "Embedded System" which I found almost necessary. Considering their views, the text has been revised providing a new chapter "Introduction to Embedded System".

An embedded system is a large or small computer system which is a piece of equipment or another computer system It performs some tasks useful to the product, equipment or system. It is a computer system and it is programmed to perform a particular task. This task may be very simple or very complex but it is not a relevant distinction. It is known that all computers are programmed to perform tasks. However an embedded system is programmed to perform its task from the time when it is powered up and continues to act till it is shut down. Its programming is permanently stored and it cannot be changed till the original programmer so desires.

Earlier 8 and 16 bit processors were universal computing engine found in all smart products, but today these are used in the kingdom of deeply embedded applications. Embedded computer systems constitute the widest possible use of computer systems; it includes all computers other than those specifically intended as general-purpose computers. As an example, an embedded system for controlling reactive power using Intel 8051 based Microcontroller has been developed and presented.

In this chapter features and examples of Embedded system and its characteristics have been added. To express the clear idea of working of an embedded system, a detailed example of Static VAR controller has been given which controls the power factor of a transmission-distribution system at the receiving end. Load bus voltage control Philosophy, together with system hardware and software have been presented.

In corporating the new chapter on embedded system, I feel that the readers will get a clear understanding of the gradual development of microprocessor system starting from INTEL 8085 to the Pentium processor to the Embedded system. I would be eager to receive suggestions for further improvement of the book.

In revising the book, I received tremendous encouragement and support from Mr. N.K. Mehra of M/s Narosa Publishing House for which I am grateful to him.

A.K. MUKHOPADHYAY

# Preface to the First Edition

The twentieth century may be regarded as the century of the scientists and technologists since during this century, the scientific and technological development has reached its extreme. Among the wonderful inventions, mention may be made of the most exciting technological development of the microprocessor and microcomputer first developed in 1971 when a group of scientists of BUSICOM of Japan and the INTEL CORPORATION of USA were engaged in developing a desk calculator. From the moment of its creation in early seventies, microprocessor has revolutionised the field of digital electronics. It has already made an impact on the way of present life and it has been felt deeply that, it will affect on the life of the future generation too.

Since the advent of microprocessor, its application to the field of measurement, protection and control of different electrical and mechanical systems has rapidly been in progress because of its various advantages over the existing methods. The microprocessor is cheaper, physically smaller, easier to protect from environmental hazards, more reliable and it consumes less power than other systems. The development of the microprocessor has made it possible to build up a great deal of intelligence into many instruments and systems. It may be possible to perform with software many tasks that are difficult, if not impossible to perform with the hardware. Since major tasks can be performed by the software execution, it becomes more reliable and versatile in use in the related fields. Inspired from these important exciting features of the microprocessor, an attempt has been made to prepare this volume for engineers and technologists.

Rather than covering the entire spectrum of microprocessors, focus has been made on the most widely used device, the INTEL 8085/8085A though a survey has been made on the device based on INTEL 8751, 8086/8088/80386, ZILOG Z80/Z800/Z80000, MOTOROLA MC 6809/ 68701 etc. Besides, an introduction to the bit-slice processor along with its design features has been added. Although any microprocessor based system requires understanding of both software and hardware, a major burden from hardware may be shifted to the software. Hence software has been emphasised in the book so that one can cope up with the rapid expansion of the field of microprocessor. The subject matter has been presented in a logical manner so that the reader can apply them directly to the laboratory or engineering problems.

In preparing the manuscript, the author acknowledges with thanks, the help he received from different technical reports, manuals, charts, diagrams and mnemonics of INTEL CORPORATION of USA and ZILOG Inc. In preparing this volume, the author received encouragement from his friends, colleagues and students for which he is grateful to them. His special thanks go to Sri S.Sengupta and Sm. M. Mitra of the Department of Applied Physics, Calcutta University for their continuous assistance and discussions. The author is indebted to Sri Arabinda Das and Sri U.K.Gayen for the help they extended during preparation of the manuscript. He also acknowledges the help he received from Sri P. Mandal and Sm. I. Raychaudhari. The author is grateful to Professor D.K. Basu, Secretary, Department of Science and Technology, Government of West Bengal for the encouragement received during preparation of the manuscript. He is grateful to his wife Sm. Indrani Mukhopadhyay for constant inspiration during the preparation of the book. The author is eager to receive suggestions for the future development of the book.

A. K. MUKHOPADHYAY

# Contents

# 1. Microprocessor—A physical system

Microprocessor is one of the most exciting technological development of the present century. From the moment of very creation in early seventies, it has created revolution in the field of digital electronics. It has made an impact on the way of present life and it has been felt deeply that it will affect on the life of the future generation too. Microprocessor, a large scale integrated circuit, was first developed in 1971 when a group of scientists of BUSI COM of Japan and the INTEL CORPORATION of USA were engaged in developing a desk calculator. The responsibility of complex hardware being gradually transferred to software, the concept of programmable Integrated Circuits has been developed. Microprocessor is nothing but a large scale integrated circuit (IC) using large scale integration in metal oxide semiconductor (MOS) technology. The first microprocessor, 4-bit 4004 was introduced by Intel Corporation USA in 1971. Very soon, the 4-bit microprocessor was followed by 8-bit processors viz. INTEL 8080, 8085 and 8085A, zilog Z-80, MOTOROLA 6800, Mos Tech 6502 and 16-bit processors viz. Intel 8086 and 8088, Motorola 68000, Z 800, TMS 9900 etc. Today 32 bit microprocessors (80386, Z80000, MC68030) are also available.

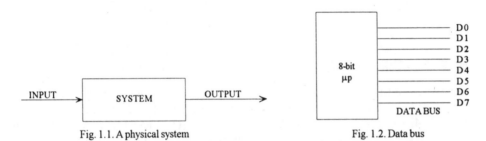

Fig. 1.1. A physical system                    Fig. 1.2. Data bus

Any physical system (Fig. 1.1) receives an input signal and outputs another—the characteristics being dependent on the internal behaviour of the system. The microprocessor may also be considered as one of the systems whose internal behaviour is created by the program stored. But a microprocessor cannot recognise analog signal and accepts only binary inputs. The signal is fed through a DATA BUS as shown in Fig. 1.2 consisting of 8 conductors for an 8-bit processor, each bit of the signal being carried by one conductor. Hence there are $2^8$ or 256 possible combinations of different input data that can be conveyed through DATA BUS. In order to convey analog signal of the outside world to the microprocessor, the signal may be converted to 8-bit digital signal using Analog to Digital Converter (ADC) and the digital signal is introduced to the microprocessor through Input ports and DATA BUS as shown in Fig. 1.3. The DATA BUS is bi-directional and the ADC may be replaced by a magnetic Tape, Punch Card or Key board etc. as input devices.

After receiving the digital signal, the microprocessor performs its task and the results so obtained are brought out through DATA BUS to output Port. Any microprocessor compatible Digital to Analog converter (DAC) converts the digital signal to the analog signal (Fig. 1.4).

Input data received by the microprocessor may not always be required for processing immediately. Hence it becomes essential to store the data in some device (Fig. 1.5). Usually the information received by the microprocessor (data and instruction) is stored in the microprocessor memory called the DATA MEMORY, READ/WRITE MEMORY or more popularly as RANDOM ACCESS MEMORY (RAM). It may be mentioned at this stage that the process of storing data in memory is the WRITE OPERATION and the process of retrieval of Data from memory is known as the READ OPERATION. A RAM contains a large number of memory locations. For a RAM of capacity 4 Kilo byte, the number of memory locations are 4096. For microprocessor's execution, users' program (popularly known as the SOFTWARE) is required and generally the SOFTWARE and the DATA are stored in different memory locations sequentially. The microprocessor during operation (termed as execution) follows the SOFTWARE step by step and computes the results.

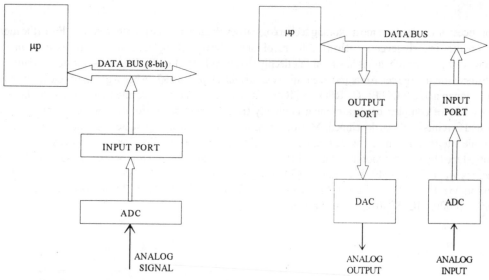

Fig. 1.3. INPUT PORT and DATA BUS       Fig. 1.4. Data bus with I/O Device

Each memory location has a name designated by a four HEXADECIMAL digit-number. Decimal numbers are formed with ten digits—0 through 9. Similarly HEXADECIMAL (HEX.) numbers are formed with sixteen digits viz. 0, 1, 2, 3, 4, 5, 6, 7, 8, 9, A(10), B(11), C(12), D(13), E(14), and F(15). A decimal number $X_4 X_3 X_2 X_1$ means $10^3 X_4 + 10^2 X_3 + 10^1 X_2 + 10^0 X_1$. Similarly the HEXADECIMAL number $X_4 X_3 X_2 X_1$ H means $16^3 X_4 + 16^2 X_3 + 16^1 X_2 + 16^0 X_1$. As an illustration, $9A5B\ H = 9 \times 16^3 + 10 \times 16^2 + 5 \times 16^1 + 11 \times 16^0 = 39415$ (DEC). $FFFF\ H = 15 \times 16^3 + 15 \times 16^2 + 15 \times 16^1 + 15 \times 16^0 = 65535$ (DEC).

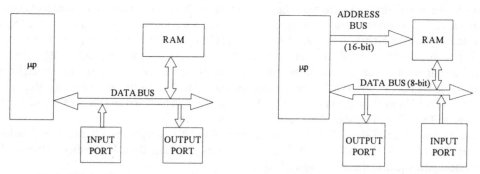

Fig. 1.5. Storing Data in memory       Fig. 1.6. Data and address Bus

Thus in order to store a program or data, it is essential to identify the particular address of the memory location of the RAM and the task is performed by an ADDRESS BUS consisting of 16 conductors as shown in Figs. 1.6 and 1.7. In some microprocessor system, 8 conductors of DATA BUS are combined with another 8 conductors to form a 16-bit ADDRESS BUS where lower part of the BUS (AD0 - AD7) acts as the DATA BUS whereas the complete bus (AD0 - AD7 and A8 - A15) acts as an ADDRESS BUS.

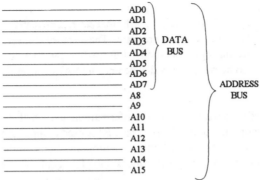

Fig. 1.7. Address Bus

In order to operate a microprocessor, besides RAM, another type of memory is required which is programmed by the manufacturer or used to store useful programs permanently. This type of memory is known as READ ONLY MEMORY or in short ROM which can only be read and never be written during execution of a program. It may be noted that the program stored in ROM can not be changed by the user. The program in ROM may be stored using special devices. In the microprocessor system, in addition to the DATA BUS and ADDRESS BUS, one more bus is connected. This bus is known as CONTROL BUS used for timing and control function. A clock pulse generator is always associated with the microprocessor system and the microprocessor maintains time synchronism by the clock pulse through the control Bus.

The organisation of a microcomputer or a microprocessor system is shown in Fig. 1.8 from which it is clear that the microprocessor system contains four essential units viz. the Central Processing Unit (CPU), the memory units, the input unit and the output unit. An Arithmetic and Logic Unit and a Control unit are combined into one called the Central Processing Unit and a microprocessor is nothing but a CPU for a microcomputer, available in the form of an integrated circuit (IC). When the CPU is associated with the memory unit and the Input/Output (I/O) devices, the combined system is known as a microcomputer or a microprocessor system.

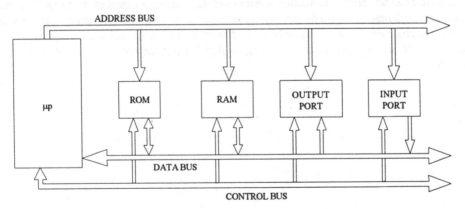

Fig. 1.8. Organisation of a Microcomputer

The ALU is that part of the computer in which arithmetic and logic operations are performed on data coming from either the memory or the Input unit. Results of the operations performed by the ALU can either be stored into memory unit or transferred to the output unit. An overview of different units of a microcomputer has been given below though they have been discussed in more details in Chapter 2.

## MEMORY UNIT

The memory unit stores groups of binary digits (words) that can represent instructions (Program) to be performed by the CPU and the data to be operated by the program. The memory also serves as the storage for intermediate and final results of arithmetic and logic operations. Information can be written into the memory from the ALU or the input unit and can also be stored from the memory into ALU or into the output unit.

## INPUT UNIT

The input unit consists of all the devices used to take informations and data that are external to the microcomputer and put them into the memory unit or the ALU. This unit is used to input data into the ALU or memory from an external device during or prior to the execution of a program. Some of the common input devices are keyboard, teletype-writer, punched card, magnetic tape, analog to digital converter (ADC) etc.

## OUTPUT UNIT

Output unit consists of the devices used to transfer data and information from the microcomputer to the "Outside world". The output devices are directed by the control unit and can receive data from memory or the ALU, which are then put into appropriate form for external use. Examples of common output devices are LED displays, printers, cathode-ray-tube displays, digital to analog converters (DAC) etc.

The ALU and control units combined into one unit is called the central processing unit (CPU). ALU performs the arithmetic and logic operations as directed by the control unit.

## CONTROL UNIT

The function of the control unit is to direct the operation of all the other units by providing timing and control signals. The control unit fetches an instruction from memory by sending an address and a READ command to the memory unit. The instruction word stored at the memory location is then transferred to the control unit. This instruction is then decoded by logic circuitry in the control unit to determine the steps of the execution of the instructions. The control unit generates the necessary signals for executing the instructions.

The microprocessors and microcomputers are increasingly finding wider applications in almost every sphere of life. There are different varieties of microprocessors with different operational characteristics. A particular type is selected considering the required characteristics of the system design and system economy. Some typical applications of microprocessors are Toys and Games, Intelligent household equipments, Intelligent Terminals and Instruments, Office processing, Decision making, Design, Control, Instrumentation, Automation, Communication, Robotics etc.

# 2. The Microprocessor System

Although a Microprocessor is basically a low cost computer, it is not widely used in Mathematical calculations, though not impossible. Rather, it is extremely helpful in system monitoring, control and protection. One single microprocessor may be used as a power line monitor to measure voltage, current, phase difference, power, power factor, volt-ampere demand, Maximum demand, frequency, speed etc. The same microprocessor may well be used for position control, speed control of motors, starting and protection of electrical appliances. It is used in Railway signaling, Telephone industry, Accountancy, robotics etc.

A microprocessor system may be broadly divided into three functional blocks, the Central Processing Unit (CPU), Memory and Input/output (I/O) ports as shown in Fig. 2.1.

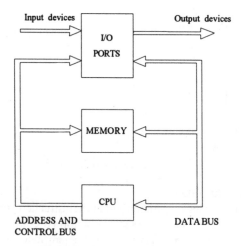

Fig. 2.1. A microprocessor system

## 2.1 CENTRAL PROCESSING UNIT (CPU)

The Central Processing Unit is the most important and active part of a microprocessor. An 8-bit CPU is normally called a general purpose microprocessor. It is available generally as a 40 pin IC package. By "8-bit CPU", it is meant that its data-length is 8-bit wide and generally it possesses an address bus of 16-bit.

The CPU fetches instructions from the memory, decodes into minute steps required for execution, generates control signals accordingly and finally executes the instruction. This process is repeated till the whole program is executed. During the execution of an instruction, the CPU may take data from the memory or the input ports or may store the same into the memory or give out data through the output ports in accordance with the program. The input-output devices practically communicate with the outer world.

A CPU may be divided into following five functional sections:

(i)   Arithmetic and Logic section,
(ii)  General purpose Registers,
(iii) Control Registers,
(iv)  Instruction Register and Decoder and
(v)   Timing and control Unit.

There are a large number of manufacturers having their own varieties of microprocessors. All of them are not identical in architecture and organisation but they may have common features and functional similarities. Fig.2.2 describes the generalised architecture of a CPU based on 8085.

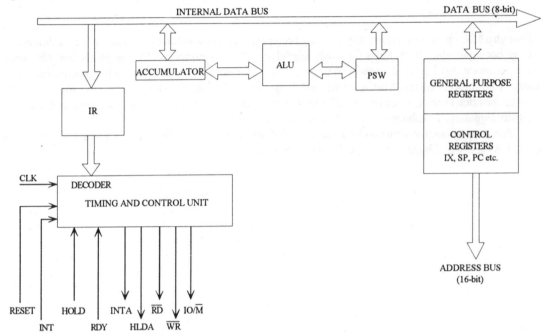

Fig. 2.2. Architecture of a microprocessor

## 2.2 ARITHMETIC-LOGIC SECTION

This section performs arithmetic and logic operation part of the instruction. Primarily the binary numbers are intended to be operated, though some microprocessor may perform operations on BCD and ASCII numbers. This unit has three prominent members: Accumulator (ACC), Program Status Word (PSW) and Arithmetic Logic Unit (ALU). The functions of this section are completely governed by the timing and control unit. In 8-bit microprocessors, 8-bit numbers are dealt with. Hence the numerical computations are slowly performed with respect to the higher bit systems. To speed up the computational work, advanced hardware like pipelining, increased numbers of registers and circuitries for direct multiplication and division etc. are associated.

## 2.3 ACCUMULATOR

The Accumulator (ACC or simply A) is an 8-bit special register or temporary location which is used in various Arithmetic and Logical operations. For example, during the addition of two 8-bit integers, one of the operands must be put in the Accumulator. The other may be kept in the memory or in one of the other registers. The results of the Arithmetical or Logical operations performed by the ALU are stored in the Accumulator. The Accumulator also usually serves as one input to the ALU as shown in Fig.2.3. In microprocessor, all input/output data pass through the Accumulator in general. Thus this is a KEY REGISTER whose size is equal to the size of the data word.

X-Register is a temporary register meant for holding one of the two operands during addition and subtraction. Microcomputers do not have multiplication and division operations as hardware features. They are performed by softwares. However, microprocessors capable of performing hardware multiplication and division usually have a third register called the MQ register.

In some microprocessors, there are more than one accumulators whereas in some CPU, there is no accumulator at all where the general purpose registers (sometimes even the memory locations also) have the capability of the accumulator.

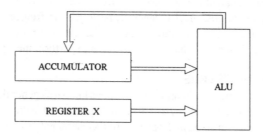

Fig. 2.3. The Accumulator

## 2.4 STATUS REGISTERS

The status register is also a special register where the conditions and states of the recent arithmetic or logic operations are stored. It is also called Flag Register or condition code Register. Informations like Parity, Carry Auxiliary Carry, Zero, Sign, Overflow, Interrupt Mask, Interrupt Request etc. are stored in the different bit-positions of this register. These informations are vital in many arithmetic operations and are often used to decide the conditional branching of proper steps. Though in 8-bit microprocessor, the status Register is also of 8-bit length, but all of the 8-bits may not have status informations. Sometimes, some of these bits may be used as temporary locations, used in computation, debugging etc. Conditional jump instructions are based upon these flags.

The Parity flag signifies the parity of the contents of the ACC. The contents of the status register is called the PROGRAM STATUS WORD (PSW) and the register itself is called PSW REGISTER. The flag register holds one-bit indicators that represent the state of conditions inside the CPU. The common conditions are Zero, Carry, Sign, Parity and Auxiliary Carry. If the result of the last operation remains zero, zero flag will be set (i.e. $Z=1$). Similarly if the last operation generates a carry, the carry flag will be set (i.e. $CY=1$). For example, if the contents of Acc. and Reg. B be 10 H and 12 H respectively and if the content of Reg. B be compared with that of Acc., the carry flag will be set. If the result of the last operation be negative, sign bit will be set. Similarly, if the result has even parity, the Parity flag is set ($P=1$) and if it be in odd parity, the flag is reset ($P=0$). Also, if the instruction causes a carry out of the last significant digits (D3 in ACC.) in the resulting value, Auxiliary carry (AC) flag will be set. Otherwise, it remains in the reset condition.

An example of PSW based conditional jump instruction is "Jump on carry to execute from memory location 0123H or JC 0123," meaning that if carry flag is set, jump to execute the program stored at memory location on 0123H onwards.

Overflow occurs when the result of any operation exceeds the length of the ACC. However, all of these flags are not available in all microprocessors. Normally some of these flags constitute the PSW register and rest of the bits of PSW are either of "don't care" states or intended to be used as temporary locations. Sometimes some of these flags may form another special register parallel to PSW.

## 2.5 ALU

This is the actual circuitry which performs arithmetic and logic operations. Often ALU uses the content of ACC as the first operand and stores the results in the ACC. It can operate on the carry bit. The ALU of some microprocessor may operate on any bit of the contents of its register or even those of memory locations. However, in 8-bit microprocessors, the ALU is intended to perform operations on 8-bit binary numbers. Sometimes it may operate on BCD and ASCII numbers and even on a string also. However, in double byte handling, microprocessors take the lower byte first to or from the memory or register in general. The speed of execution of a microprocessor largely depends on the operation of ALU.

Among the arithmetic operations, ADDITION, SUBTRACTION, INCREMENT, DECREMENT, COMPARISON etc. are generally available. INCLUSIVE-OR, EXCLUSIVE-OR, AND and COMPLEMENT etc. are the most common logic operations, an ALU generally performs. Shifting or rotation of the ACC contents to right or left is also possible by the ALU. Sometimes, ALU may have the facility of correcting Decimal or ASCII operation from the binary ones. Some ALU has also hardwares to perform multiplication and division.

## 2.6 GENERAL PURPOSE REGISTERS

Generally microprocessors have numbers of temporary locations known as general purpose registers (GPR) or Scratch Pad Registers. These are used generally as the second operands of arithmetic and logic operations and for storing the intermediate results. In some microprocessors, General purpose Registers are so versatile and powerful that these may be used as a full fledged accumulators. Execution with these registers requires less time in comparison to deal with memory locations. Hence, efficient programs use these registers as much as possible.

An instruction "SUB C" means to subtract the content of register C from the content of ACC and generally the result is available in ACC. An instruction "MOV R,A" means that register R shall copy the content of ACC.

Sometimes these registers are named as A,B,C,D etc. or sometimes as R0, R1, R2 etc. Some microprocessors have no registers of these kind at all where a certain space of the temporary memory (RAM) locations are used as GPR. These RAM spaces can be selected by the program. Sometimes this type of GPR is helpful for efficient programming.

## 2.7 CONTROL REGISTERS

There are a number of special registers which are used to perform some special functions like the selection of modes and controlling programs, memory spaces, interrupts, timers, USART etc. Both ACC and PSW may also be thought of as control registers. The commonly available control registers are: Program counter (PC), Stack pointer (SP), Index Register (IX), program status word Register (PSW), Data Pointer (DP), Timer controller (TCON), Timer Mode selector (TMOD), Interrupt Mask or Interrupt Priority selector etc. Different microprocessors have different varieties of these registers. Some of the most common control registers have been briefly described as follows.

## 2.8 PROGRAM COUNTER (PC)

Generally the program counter is a 16-bit register. It keeps track of the program. The programs or the instructions to be executed are stored sequentially in the memory. PC contains the address (of the memory-location) of the next instruction. In simple type of microprocessors, when the execution of the present instruction is completed, the instruction stored in the location pointed by PC is fetched into Instruction Register for decoding followed by execution. Instruction register is another special register to be discussed separately. Whenever an instruction is fetched, the PC is updated to the next instruction and this process is continued until the power supply is off or the microprocessor is disturbed anyway by 'HOLD', 'WAIT', 'HALT' or other operations.

Sometimes, the PC is first updated to fetch the next instruction and sometimes reverse is the operation depending on the variety of microprocessors. When the execution of the present instruction is going on, in some cases, fetching of next instruction and updating of PC may also be performed simultaneously, the phenomena being known as 'parallel running' or 'pipelining'. In this case, a number of instruction registers (normally called instruction queue) store sequentially the instructions to be decoded and executed.

## 2.9 STACK POINTER (SP)

The stack pointer (SP) is also a 16-bit register in general for an 8-bit microprocessor. It contains the address of the top of the stack which is a selected space of the memory where data may be stored in 'last in first out' (LIFO) basis similar to stack books, one upon the other, in a book case where the available on is on the top, stored last. By using 'PUSH' instruction, a data in a register or memory location may be stacked and a 'POP' instruction unstacks a data from the stack to a register or memory location. After 'PUSH' and 'POP' instructions, the SP is updated to point at the current top of the stack.

In case of 'CALL' instruction or 'interrupt request', the PC is stored in the stack and loaded by the new address of the subprogram or interrupt-vectored address of memory whereas when a 'RETURN' instruction is executed, the PC is re-loaded by the address stored in the stack and execution of program is started accordingly.

It is interesting to note that the address of the top of stack may go down in some microprocessors and go up in some others while executing a 'PUSH' operation. Registers related to the address of memory locations like stack pointer, program counter, Index Register, segment Register, Page Index Register, Base Pointer, Data pointer etc. may be shorter than 16-bit in length for an 8-bit microprocessor depending upon the type of microprocessors. In some microprocessors, more than one SP may be available. Often one byte and sometimes more than one byte of data may be stacked up.

## 2.10 INDEX REGISTER (IX)
Index registers are used for addressing. The contents of index register are added to the memory address, the sum being the actual address of the data or the effective address. If the contents of index registers are changed, the effective address is also changed. Data can be transferred from one memory to another memory location by using index register or memory address registers. Some microcomputers have auto indexing capability where the index register is automatically incremented or decremented each time it is used. It may be mentioned here that at the time of using index register, it must contain code to indicate whether indexing is being used. In some microcomputers, there may be more than one index register.

In some other types of microcomputer, the index register is used like an address register where the length of the index register is sufficient to hold a complete memory address.

It may be mentioned here that the index register is simply not for indirect memory address. Typically, index register implies an index (or offset) over a base register. More details of index register and its operation have been added in Chapter 13.

## 2.11 INSTRUCTION REGISTER (IR) AND DECODER
The instruction register is a control register of 8-bit in length for an 8-bit microprocessor. The instruction to be executed is first fetched into this register. The decoder unit decodes it into the minute steps for execution. The control unit generates necessary signals to perform these minute steps of execution. In simple microprocessors, the decoding, execution and control units are combined into one control unit. But in some powerful microprocessors, these units may be functionally independent. In these cases, there are a number of instruction registers forming an instruction queue where the fetching, decoding and execution of instructions are performed in parallel within the same clock cycle. This type of hardware is called the pipeline hardware.

## 2.12 TIMING AND CONTROL UNIT
This unit controls all the internal and external units of a microprocessor system. It makes the instruction to be fetched into the IR from the memory using PC and decodes the instruction and then controls the necessary internal and external units to realise the decoded instruction to be executed. This operation is continued in a cyclic order so long as the power is on. It also checks an input to the CPU that can directly alter the sequence of operation at the hardware level. This types of input signals are termed as INTERRUPTS. The INTERRUPT acts like a buzzer causing the processor to halt its normal operation and respond to the input. Interrupts are obviously useful for handling inputs/outputs. The timing and control unit checks whether any external or internal interrupt has occurred and if any interrupt be requested, it stops executing its normal program and starts executing the requested program. It also keeps an eye on whether the bus is requested externally and when requested, it stops execution of the current program and makes the address and data bus floating. This unit has a number of external inputs and outputs known as control bus. These are Clock input, Clock output, Reset in, Reset out, Interrupt

in, Interrupt out, Wait in, Hold in, Hold acknowledge/out, Ready in, Synchronisation out, Read out, Write out, I/O request, Memory request etc. All of them are not available in all microprocessors. These differ according to the types of microprocessors. Some of the most common features of these are described below:

## 2.13 THE CLOCK
Some microprocessors have on-chip internal clock generator whose frequency is controlled by an external crystal only. Where this facility is not available, an external clock is needed to be fed into the clock input. Some of the microprocessors have internal divider which reduces the external or on-chip clock frequency and the resulting frequency is used by the CPU. Normally, this type of microprocessors possesses a clock output also. Popular 8-bit microprocessors normally use a clock of frequency ranging from 3 MHz to 10 MHz.

## 2.14 RESET
Reset input normally forces all the control registers to a predetermined state. The PC is reset to zero in many processors so that the microprocessor starts executing the program stored in memory location zero. In some microprocessors, the reset address could be different from zero.

## 2.15 INTERRUPT
When an interrupt input is active, the CPU stops executing the current program, the PC is stored in the stack and loaded with the vectored address of the interrupt. The CPU then starts executing from this vectored address prefixed by the manufacturer for the particular interrupt input. Normally, there are more than one interrupt inputs. Some of these interrupts can be disabled by means of software. These types of interrupts are called maskable interrupts. The other types, which are not maskable, can be disabled with external hardware. Often there are facilities to give priority among these interrupts. When priority is given and if one interrupt is accepted, an interrupt of higher priority only can cause another level of interruption. But the unmaskable interrupts, since they possess the topmost priority unconditionally, can cause the interruption at any time. Interrupts may be both edge triggered or level-triggered. However, these types of interrupts are called external hardware interrupts.

There may have internal hardware interrupts in some processors. Sometimes, the CPU has on-chip timer, USART etc. which possess interrupt facility and these types of interrupts are internally requested. There are another type of interrupts called software interrupts. These are nothing but some vectored 'CALL' instructions.

When a 'RETURN' instruction is executed during an interrupt service routine, the PC is loaded by the contents in the stack and the CPU starts executing the main-program. Sometimes, the return from a CALL may be a different instruction from the return from an interrupt. Often there is an interrupt acknowledge output for hand shaking purpose.

## 2.16 HOLD
During the HOLD state, the peripheral devices can gain control of the data and address buses for transferring data to or from the memory. This mode of operation is known as DIRECT MEMORY ACCESS (DMA). Modern microcomputers have direct link between the memory and the input/output section and thus data can be transferred to or from peripherals without intervention by the control section. In DMA, data transfer speed is limited by the memory access time whereas the data transfer through program require several instruction cycles. DMA is used with high speed peripherals like magnetic disk, communication lines or CRT display.

When a "HOLD" input is initialised, the CPU stops execution, remains in No-Operation mode and the address and data bus become floating. At this time, the I/O port has direct access to the memory. Often there is an output called HOLD ACKNOWLEDGE. When the CPU is in the hold state, this output becomes active. If an I/O port or an external device wants direct memory access, it sends signals to the hold input and when the CPU goes into the hold state, the CPU sends the signal through its hold acknowledge output so that the I/O port or the external device can understand that the CPU accepts the hold request and the bus is free to be used. This type of communication (request and acknowledge) is called handshaking. A slower device is required to be interfaced in handshaking mode.

## 2.17 READ AND WRITE

The CPU uses these two outputs to communicate with the I/O ports and the memory. When a data is required to be fetched from the memory or an input port, the respective port or memory is first enabled, then READ output becomes active and the port or the memory gives data to the data bus. The CPU then receives that data and stops READ signaling. In a similar manner, the CPU 'WRITE's data into a memory location or an output port. Sometimes READ (RD) and WRITE (WR) signals are combined into a single signal commonly known as R/W signal.

## 2.18 IOR AND MR

When the CPU requires to communicate with an I/O port, the IOR output becomes active and when the CPU addresses a memory location, the MR output becomes active. Sometimes, these two outputs are combined into IO/$\overline{M}$ output. These outputs along with the higher bits of the address bus are used to select any particular memory device, I/O port or external device for communication with CPU.

Some Microprocessors do not have any distinct I/O facility, and no output like IOR or IO/$\overline{M}$ is necessarily available. The CPU treats all the interfaces as the memory locations. Hence an I/O port is assumed in such cases as a memory location. These types of I/O ports are called Memory Mapped I/O. The microprocessors which recognise the significance of I/O facility, may be interfaced with I/O ports in the I/O mode. These types of I/O ports are called I/O Mapped I/O ports.

## 2.19 ADDRESS LATCH ENABLE

This is a special output. Some microprocessors have data bus multiplexed with the lower half of the address bus and when the common bus contains the address, the address latch enable (ALE) output becomes active so that an external latching device may latch the address. Thus this output helps to demultiplex the address bus from the common data and address bus. Before each of the fetching or RD/WR operations, this output becomes active along with the address in common bus.

# 3. The 8085A Microprocessor

It has been pointed out earlier that the first general purpose microprocessor 8080, an 8-bit CPU, was introduced by INTEL. It was followed by a variety of microprocessor by different manufacturers. In this section, an improved version viz. 8085A based microprocessor will be discussed briefly as an example.

## 3.1 ARCHITECTURE AND ORGANISATION OF 8085A

The architecture of the 8085A is simple, though not the simplest one. Fig 3.1(a) describes the block diagram of the architecture of 8085A and more detailed architecture has been given in Fig. 3.1(b) followed by a brief description of its different parts.

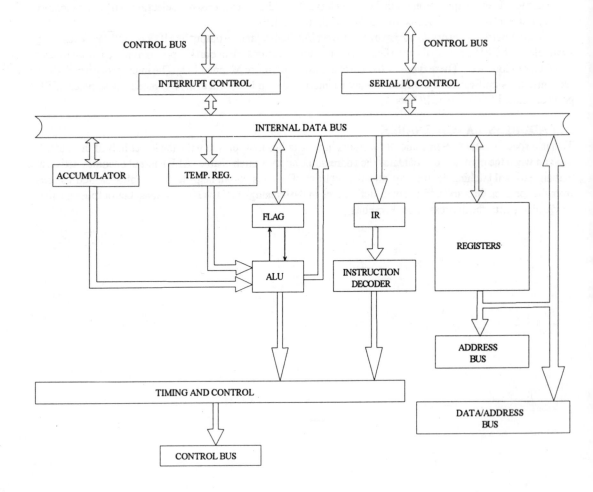

Fig. 3.1. (a) Block diagram of the architecture of INTEL 8085A

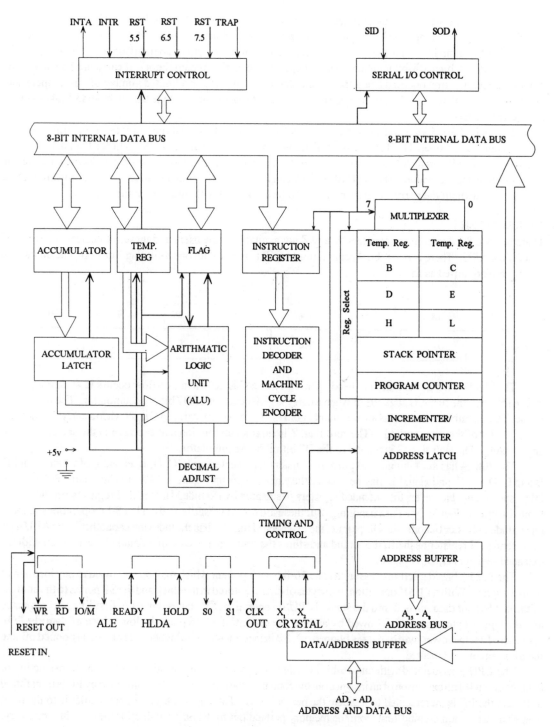

Fig. 3.1. (b) Architecture of INTEL 8085A

## 3.2 THE ALU

8085A has a simple 8-bit ALU and it functions in coordination with the Accumulator and Accumulator Latch, Temporary Register, Flag Flip-Flop (or PSW), and decimal adjust circuitry. It can perform increment or decrement of one binary on an 8- or 16-bit number, addition, subtraction, comparison and AND, OR, XOR operations on two binary 8-bit numbers, the first operand being the Accumulator. It can compliment an 8-bit binary number, the first operand being the Accumulator. It can perform a limited number of 16-bit operations using two 8-bit registers as a 16-bit extended register pairs. In case of double byte handling, 8085A takes always the lower byte first.

The ALU of 8085A generally takes the Accumulator as the first operand and stores the result of an operation in the Accumulator also. The Temporary register is used to receive and hold the data for the ALU from the internal bus. The Decimal Adjust Circuitry converts the result of a binary addition on two decimal numbers in the respective decimal value. The ALU of 8085A can also rotate the content of Accumulator towards left or right with or without the carry. The carry may also be associated with addition or subtraction.

## 3.3 REGISTERS

There are two 8-bit temporary registers W and Z not available to the users and these are dedicated to be used only by the ALU. There is one 8-bit Accumulator (ACC) together with one 8-bit flag flip-flop. The bit pattern of flags are organised as follows:

| D7 | D6 | D5 | D4 | D3 | D2 | D1 | D0 |
|----|----|----|----|----|----|----|----|
| S | Z | | AC | | P | | C |

The bits D1, D3 and D5 are not used. The carry flag C is set when overflow occurs in an operation. It is also set when the result is negative or when a carry is generated out of D7 bit of accumulator. The parity flag P is set if the accumulator contains an even number of 1's. The auxiliary carry, AC is set when a carry is generated out of D3 bit of the Accumulator. The zero flag, Z is set if an instruction makes a zero in the accumulator or any register. The sign flag, S is a copy of the D7 bit of the Accumulator.

The 8085A has six 8-bit general purpose registers represented by B, C, D, E, H and L of which A and F, B and C, D and E, and H and L may be used as the extended 16-bit registers PSW, register pairs BC, DE and HL respectively. However, the extended registers designated by extended B, D and H registers provide some limited scope of double byte data handling. But these are not so versatile as found in 8-bit operations. 8085A has no index register but only the HL pair i.e. the extended H register has the indexing capability. The ALU uses the extended H register as the first operand and stores the result in it in case of a double byte addition with the extended registers B, D, H or SP.

The 8085A based microprocessor has one 16-bit stack pointer which may be initialised to any location of memory space. With a PUSH operation, two bytes of data are stored in the stack and the SP points to the address of the last byte of data pushed into the stack. In PUSH operation, SP comes down i.e. first SP is decremented and the higher byte is pushed followed by another decrement of SP to push the lower byte of data. In POP operation, first the lower byte of data is popped off, SP is incremented, the higher byte of data is popped off and the SP is again incremented.

The CPU is associated with one 16-bit PC which always points to the address of the next instruction or data. At the end of an execution of an instruction, the content of the memory location indicated by PC is transferred to IR and the PC is incremented to indicate the next address. There is one 8-bit IR, not available to the user, where an instruction coming first from the memory pointed out by PC is available for the decoding circuitry.

## 3.4 TIMING AND CONTROL UNIT

The 8085A has an on-chip generator controlled either by an external crystal or a suitable LC or RC network. It has an internal divider which makes the clock frequency to one half of that of the clock and uses this halved frequency. It is intended to be operated by an external crystal of frequency ranging from 1 MHz to 10 MHz. It has a clock output which gives out the internal clock frequency.

Intel 8085A microprocessor is associated with a RESET input and RESET output. Reset input is active low. After a RESET, the program is started from the memory location 0000 H.

It has serial input SID and serial output SOD whose functions, since associated with RIM and SIM instructions, will be stated with the description of interrupts.

Two status outputs S0 and S1 associated with it signify the states of the CPU as described in Table 3.1. It has three outputs $\overline{RD}$, $\overline{WR}$ and IO/$\overline{M}$ to control the external units. 8085A has the lower half of the address bus multiplexed with the 8-bit data bus. When the address is available in the common data and address bus, ALE output becomes active to latch the lower half of the address. It has a 16-bit address bus, the higher half of the address bus being separate and demultiplexed. During input output operations, the higher half of the address bus copies the lower half of the address bus.

Table 3.1

| S1 | S0 | STATES |
|----|----|--------|
| 0 | 0 | HALT |
| 0 | 1 | WRITE |
| 1 | 0 | READ |
| 1 | 1 | FETCH |

The processor has a READY INPUT which when asserted low, the CPU goes into the WAIT state until the READY becomes high. The READY signal must be synchronised with the processor clock. Sometimes the ready signal needs to be kept inactive for several cycles. This state is helpful for interfacing with slow devices and memory. It may be noted that an WAIT output (Pin 24) and a READY input (Pin 23) are used to add extra clock periods to the basic machine cycle in order to access slow memories. Memories with slower access time can be interfaced by using READY line. If the ready line is not sufficiently high (at least 128 ns), the CPU will enter into an WAIT state for one clock cycle and will automatically extend all other control signals.

INTEL 8085A has also a HOLD input which when asserted high, the CPU goes into the HOLD state outputting hold acknowledge signal through HLDA making the address, data and control bus floating. This state is released and the CPU returns to its normal execution if HOLD attains a low state. In this way DMA operation may be carried out.

During HOLD state, the peripheral devices gain control over the data and address buses for data exchange with memory, the operation being known as DMA. DMA is used with high speed peripherals since in data transfer between peripheral and memory, control section of the processor can not make any intervention.

A software HALT instruction 'HLT' makes an identical situation which is released by RESET, HOLD (temporary and as the HOLD goes low, the CPU goes again into HLT-state) or by interrupt request (if the interrupts are enabled by 'EI' instruction).

The 8085A has five external hardware Interrupts INTR, RST 5.5, RST 6.5, RST 7.5 and TRAP. The TRAP is unmaskable, always remains enabled and gets top priority. The priority of these interrupts increases in the ascending order viz. INTR, RST 5.5, RST 6.5, RST 7.5 and TRAP. Interrupts besides TRAP are enabled by Enable Interrupt Instruction EI and disabled by Disable Interrupt Instruction DI. When an interrupt is requested being enabled and unmasked, INTA (interrupt acknowledge) output becomes active and the CPU is vectored to execute programs from respective vectored address of the interrupt. When an interrupt occurs, all the maskable interrupts are disabled until the CPU executes an EI (enable interrupt) instruction again. Moreover, on being interrupted, PC is saved into the stack and loaded with the vectored address of the interrupt service routine. When a return instruction RET is executed, PC pops the previous address from the stack and the CPU returns to execute the main program. The vectored addresses for different interrupts are shown in Table 3.2:

**Table 3.2**

| Interrupt | Address |
|-----------|---------|
| TRAP      | 0024 H  |
| RST 5.5   | 002C H  |
| RST 6.5   | 0034 H  |
| RST 7.5   | 003C H  |

When INTR is requested, an external hardware connected to the data bus delivers the restart instructions according to which the CPU is vectored as:

| RST-0 | ; | 0000H | RST-1 | ; | 0008H | RST-2 | ; | 0010H | RST-3 | ; | 0018H |
|-------|---|-------|-------|---|-------|-------|---|-------|-------|---|-------|
| RST-4 | ; | 0020H | RST-5 | ; | 0028H | RST-6 | ; | 0030H | RST-7 | ; | 0038H |

Interrupts except the TRAP are disabled either by DI instruction, or by a RESET, or by the acknowledge of an interrupt request.

By masking, the interrupts are selectively disabled or enabled. Masking is done by "SIM" (set interrupt mask) instruction. Before this instruction, the ACC. is loaded with the keyword according to the following format:
RST 7.5, 6.5 AND 5.5 FORMAT :

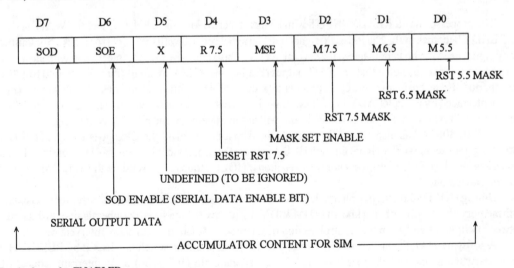

BITS : 0 - 2  ⇒ 0 :  ENABLED
             ⇒ 1 :  DISABLED
BIT   : 3    ⇒ 1 :  BITS 0 - 2 EFFECTIVE
BIT   : 4    ⇒ 0 :  RST 7.5 SET    ⎫  ADDITIONAL CONTROL
             ⇒ 1 :  RST 7.5 RESET ⎭  FOR RST 7.5
BIT   : 5    ⇒      : IGNORED
BIT   : 6    ⇒ 1 :  D7 IS OUTPUT THROUGH SOD WHERE D7 CONTENTS SERIAL DATA
             ⇒ 0 :  D7 IS IGNORED

The interrupts whether masked or unmasked, enabled or disabled requested or not requested, may always be read by 'READ INTERRUPT MASK (RIM)' instruction. This instruction is associated with SID inputs. When RIM instruction is executed, the Accumulator contents a keyword as per following format:

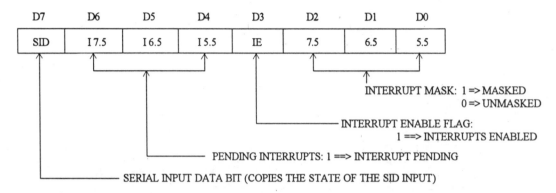

It is important to note that the SID input and SOD output along with RIM and SIM instructions may eliminate the use of any external USART, since they are capable of being used for serial communications.

There are two different types of inputs in the restart Interrupts. RST 5.5 and RST 6.5 are high level - sensitive like INTR and are recognised with the same timing as INTR whereas RST 7.5 is rising edge sensitive. For RST 7.5, only a pulse is required to set an internal flip-flop which remains set until the request is serviced. Then it is reset automatically. This flip-flop may also be reset by using the SIM instruction or by issuing a RESET IN to the 8085A. The RST 7.5 internal flip-flop will be set by a pulse on the RST 7.5 pin even when the RST 7.5 interrupt is masked out. The status of three RST interrupt masks can only be affected by the SIM instruction and RESET IN. Software examples using interrupt have been shown in Chapter 11.

## 3.5 PIN CONFIGURATION OF 8085A

The pin configuration of an INTEL 8085A CPU is described in Fig.3.2.

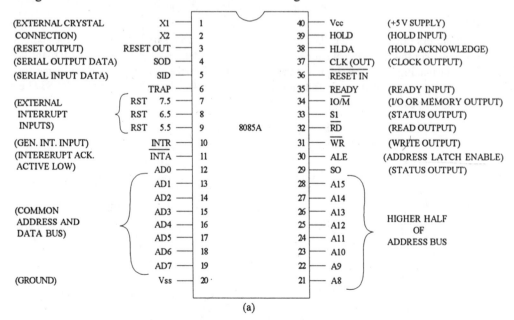

(a)

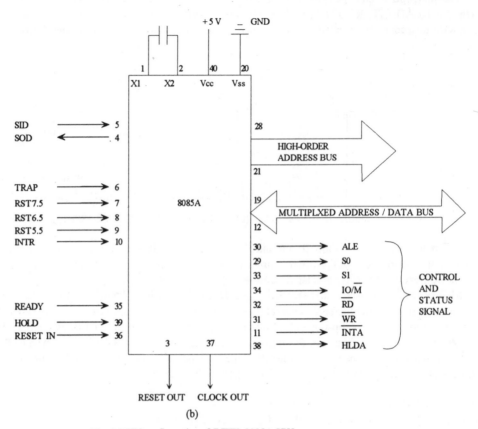

Fig. 3.2 PIN configuration of INTEL 8085A CPU

## 3.6 INTERFACE

Since the address (lower 8-bit) and data bus are common, it is necessary to demultiplex the address from the common bus. For this, an external latch is connected with the data bus along with the ALE to the latch enable input as shown in Fig. 3.3. The outputs of the latch together with the eight higher address connectors form the address bus. Any octal latch can perform this demultiplexing. Octal Latches like 8212, 74LS373 etc. may be used for this purpose.

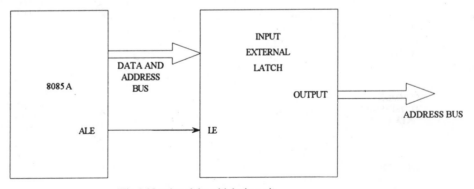

Fig. 3.3 Latch and demultiplexing unit

For chip selection, the higher bits of the address bus are decoded. The decoded output is further gated by IO/$\overline{\text{M}}$ signal to obtain the chip-select lines for different I/O ports and fed to the chip Enable input of the respective devices as shown schematically in Fig. 3.4.

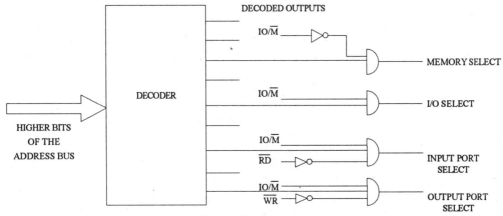

Fig. 3.4. Chip select unit

For simplicity of Interfacing, INTEL designed some dedicated peripherals like RAM, I/O port and Timer chip 8155, EPROM and I/O port chip 8255 etc. These chips are extremely helpful for 8085A CPU because they possess the necessary demultiplexing and decoding circuitry and hence they can be directly attached requiring less number of external components.

A large number of general purpose interfacing chips are available for making large and powerful processors. Among them, the chips for I/O ports, timers, keyboard and display, CRT display, video controller, floppy disc controller, DMA controller, USART etc. are extensively used. A detailed discussion on interfacing will be added in Chapters 6 to 9. Fig 3.5 shows the organisation of a small 8085A based practical system.

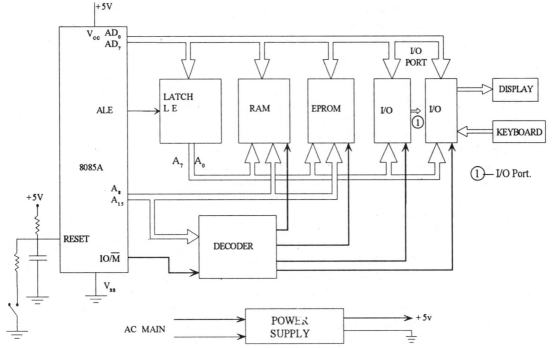

Fig. 3.5. Organisation of an 8085A based microprocessor system.

# 4. INTEL 8085 Assembly Language Programming

A program is a sequence of discrete instructions to be executed in achieving the objective of the user. The program and data are fed into the micro-computer through INPUT UNITS such as key board, tape recorder, tele-type writer, card recorder, etc. and the program is stored in the memory of the microcomputer. Since the computer recognises only the binary numbers (viz. 0 and 1), it is difficult for a programmer to write a program in machine language in binary form. Hence the microcomputer instructions are written in a short form either by using Hex code (taking 4 bits at a time) or by using Mnemonics (name based code).

Suppose a certain data is stored through INPUT UNIT to the Accumulator (Acc. or A) and it is required to transfer the same to some memory location whose address is 4080 (Hex.). The statement required in our language is "Store Data from the Accumulator to the memory location 4080 (Hex)", the corresponding statement in mnemonics being "STA 4080 (Hex)". For 8085 CPU based microcomputer, the same statement in Hex code becomes "32 80 40". But if one attempts to write the instructions in binary code, it will assume the form

00110010      10000000      01000000

The utility of using the Hex code or the Mnemonic code can easily be understood from what has been said above. A source program written in the mnemonic code is called the ASSEMBLY LANGUAGE PROGRAM and the software which translates the source program written in Assembly Language into the machine language is called an ASSEMBLER.

In general, a program written in Hex code, (or Mnemonic code) is fed through the input system associated with the translator which translates the program into the machine language and the microcomputer instructions, data and the intermediate results are stored in the memory in suitable encoded form. The CPU of a microcomputer comprises of the ALU and the control unit. The Arithmetic and the Logical parts of computation are performed inside the ALU which contains the necessary hardware. The interpretations of the individual instructions, instruction sequences and the decision making activities are performed by the control unit.

The results of computations are made available to the outside world through output unit such as line printer, tele-type-writer, CRT, DA card or seven segment display unit etc.

In order to write an effective program for a microcomputer, it is necessary to know its logical organisation and to identify the parts of the machine that are accessible to the programmer. It has been pointed out in earlier chapters that in INTEL 8085 microprocessor, the CPU has an 8-bit Accumulator (Acc.) and six other general purpose registers B,C,D,E, H, L, occasionally known as SCRATCH PAD REGISTERS. Each of the registers can handle 8-bit numbers. These six registers can also be combined into three register pairs viz. BC, DE and HL for 16 bit operation. In this microprocessor, there are two 16-bit registers, the PROGRAM COUNTER and the STACK POINTER. A FLAG REGISTER along side the Accumulator has 5-bits named Z,C,S,P and AC.

As discussed earlier, the READ ONLY MEMORY (ROM) and the RANDOM ACCESS MEMORY (RAM) togather form the total working storage of the machine. The CPU communicates with the memory and INPUT OUTPUT (I/O) PORTS by specifying the address.

Basically the microprocessor must receive data from the outside world, processes the data and sends the results back to the outside world. The microprocessor itself simply performs certain specified actions in response to certain binary inputs. The inputs those cause the microprocessor to perform specified actions are called Instructions. The series of actions that causes the microprocessor to perform a complete task is called PROGRAM, and the collection of instructions that the microprocessor recognises is its INSTRUCTION SET. The microprocessor receives instructions and data in the same form. Both are binary numbers stored in its memory and are brought into the CPU on the data bus.

Now consider the Assembly Language Program:

```
LDA   4000 H      GET  OPERAND  1
MOV   C,A         MOVE OPERAND 1 TO REG.C
LDA   4001 H      GET  OPERAND  2
ADD   C           ADD OPERANDS
STA   4002 H      STORE RESULTS
HLT               STOP
```

In the above program, five instructions of Intel 8080/8085 have been used. The instructions are LDA, MOV, ADD, STA and HLT. Let us examine the program step by step.

Step 1. LDA 4000H

This instruction loads the accumulator with the content of memory location 4000H (16-bit address). LDA requires three words of program memory, and 13 clock cycles.

Step 2. MOV C,A

This instruction loads register C with the contents of accumulator. It requires one word of program memory.

Step 3. LDA 4001H

This instruction is similar to Step 1

Step 4. ADD C

This instruction adds the content of accumulator with that of register C and keeps the results in accumulator. This instruction requires one word of program memory.

Step 5. STA 4002H

This instruction stores the result in memory location 4002H. It requires three words of program memory.

Step 6. HLT

This instruction indicates the end of the program.

The program can be assembled as follows:

| MEMORY ADDRESS (HEXA DECIMAL) | INSTRUCTION (MNEMONICS) | MEMORY CONTENTS (HEXA DECIMAL) |
|---|---|---|
| 2000 | LDA 4000 | 3A |
| 2001 | | 00 |
| 2002 | | 40 |
| 2003 | MOV C,A | 4F |
| 2004 | LDA 4001 | 3A |
| 2005 | | 01 |
| 2006 | | 40 |
| 2007 | ADD C | 81 |
| 2008 | STA 4002 | 32 |
| 2009 | | 02 |
| 200A | | 40 |
| 200B | HLT | 76 |

If 06 H and 04 H are the contents of memory locations 4000 H and 4001 H, the results after execution of the program will be 0A H and the result will be stored in memory location 4002 H. The addition program may be traced stepwise as under:

|  | DATA MEMORY | REGISTERS | FLAGS |
|---|---|---|---|
| Initial conditions | 4000   06 <br> 4001   04 <br> 4002   AB | PC   2000 | |
| After first Instruction | 4000   06 <br> 4001   04 <br> 4002   AB | PC   2003 <br> A   06 | NO FLAG AFFECTED |
| After second Instruction | 4000   06 <br> 4001   04 <br> 4002   AB | PC   2004 <br> A   06 <br> C   06 | NO FLAG AFFECTED |
| After thrid Instruction | 4000   06 <br> 4001   04 <br> 4002   AB | PC   2007 <br> A   04 <br> C   06 | NO FLAG AFFECTED |
| After forth Instruction | 4000   06 <br> 4001   04 <br> 4002   AB | PC   2008 <br> A   0A <br> C   06 | NO FLAG AFFECTED |
| After fifth instruction | 4000   06 <br> 4001   04 <br> 4002   0A | PC   200B <br> A   0A <br> C   06 | NO FLAG AFFECTED |

The steps can be explained by a flowchart (discussed in chapter 11) in the following manner:

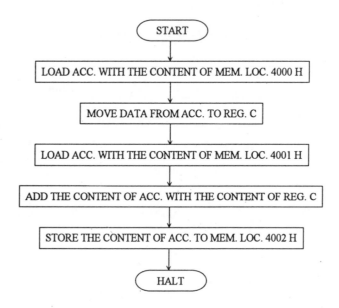

## 4.1 INSTRUCTION SET FOR 8085/8085A

In order to develop the system software, a proper understanding of the instruction set is essential. For INTEL 8085/ 8085A CPU, there are 80 different instructions grouped into eleven different sets. They are DATA

MOVEMENT instruction, INCREMENT /DECREMENT instructions, ROTATE/ SHIFT instructions, SET COMPLEMENT and DECIMAL ADJUSTMENT instructions, MATHEMATICAL/ LOGICAL instructions, AND/OR/EXCLUSIVE-OR instructions, JUMP / CALL / RESTART instructions, CONDITIONAL JUMP / CALL / RESTART instructions, INTERRUPT /HALT / NO OPERATION instructions, INPUT / OUTPUT instructions and INTERRUPT-MASK SERIAL I/O instructions. Instructions under different sets have been classified in the following table:

**Table 4.1**

| INSTRUCTION SET | MNEMONICS |
|---|---|
| 1. DATA MOVEMENT OR DATA TRANSFER. | MOV, LDA, STA, LDAX, STAX, LHLD, SHLD, MVI, LXI, XCHG, SPHL, PUSH, POP, XTHL. |
| 2. INCREMENT/DECREMENT. | INR, DCR, INX, DCX. |
| 3. ROTATE/SHIFT | RAL, RAR, RLC, RRC. |
| 4. SET/COMPLEMENT/ DECIMEL ADJUST | STC, CMC, CMA, DAA. |
| 5. MATHEMATICAL/LOGICAL | ADD,ADC,DAD,ACI,SUB,SBB,SUI,SBI,CMP,CPI. |
| 6. AND/OR/EXCLUSIVE-OR | ANA,ANI,ORA,ORI,XRA,XRI. |
| 7. JUMP/CALL/RESTART | JMP,PCHL,CALL,RET,RST. |
| 8. CONDITIONAL JUMP/ CALL/RETURN | JC,JNC,NZ,JNZ,JP,JM,JPO,JPE,CC,CNC,CNZ,CP CM, CPO, CPE, RC, RNC, RZ, RNZ, RP, RM, RPO, RPE. |
| 9. INTERRUPT HALT/ NO – OPERATION. | EI, DI, HLT, NOP. |
| 10. INPUT/OUTPUT | IN, OUT. |
| 11. INTERRUPT MASK- SERIAL I/O. | SIM, RIM. |

## 4.2 DATA MOVEMENT INSTRUCTIONS

MOV is a very common instruction to transfer data from ACC to a register, register to ACC, ACC and any register to a memory location and vice-versa. For example, MOV A,B means to transfer or move data stored in Reg. B to ACC and not from ACC to Reg. B. Similarly MOV M,C indicates the movement of data from Reg. C to the memory location. It may be mentioned here that for moving DATA from or to any memory location, it is essential to specify in the program, the memory address wherefrom the data is to be transferred or where the data is to be stored. The specification of the memory address is made by loading the respective address of the memory in the HL register pair to be explained later on. If the data transfer is performed among the Acc. and registers., 4'clock periods are consumed by using MOV instruction whereas 7 clock cycles are assigned if the data transfer is performed between the memory and accumulator or a register. The data movement instructions LDA and STA are used to load data to the accumulator from the specified location $A_4$ $A_3$ $A_2$ $A_1$ (Hex) and to store data from accumulator to the memory location $A_4$ $A_3$ $A_2$ $A_1$ (Hex) respectively. These instructions consume 13 clock periods affecting no flags. The instruction "LDA 8040" and "STA 0041" indicate loading of data stored in location 4080H (and not 8040) to the accumulator and storing of data present in the accumulator to the memory location whose address is 4100 H.

EXAMPLE 1: Develop a program to transfer data stored in mem. loc. 4125(hex) to the accumulator,

| MEM.LOC. | MNEMONICS | HEX. CODE | CLOCK CYCLES | DESCRIPTION |
|---|---|---|---|---|
| 4080 | LDA $A_4$ $A_3$ $A_2$ $A_1$ | 3A 25 41 | 13 | MOVE DATA TO ACC. FROM MEM.LOC. 4125 (HEX) |
| 4083 | HLT | 76 | 5 | HALT UNTIL INTERRUPT. |

In the above example, the program is loaded in RAM locations 4080 through 4083 and an instruction HLT has been used in order to terminate the program until the processor receives some interrupt signal to follow the interrupt service routine to be discussed later on.

EXAMPLE 2: Develop a program to store data to the mem.loc. 4200H from the accumulator.

| MEM.LOC. | MNEMONICS | HEX. CODE | CLOCK CYCLES | DESCRIPTION |
|---|---|---|---|---|
| 4100 | STA 4200 H | 32  00  42 | 13 | STORE DATA FROM ACC. TO MEM.LOC. 4200 (HEX) |
| 4103 | HLT | 76 | 5 | HALT UNTIL INTERRUPT. |

Sometimes, it is required to load the Accumulator from memory locations whose address is stored in the Reg. B and Reg. C. Since the memory address is a 16 bit number, the most significant part of the address is kept in Reg. B and the least significant number in Reg. C. Often it is required to transfer data from the Accumulator to the memory location whose address is stored in Reg. B and Reg. C. The instructions used in these cases would be LDAX B and STAX B respectively. Similarly LDAX D signifies to load data to A from memory location whose address is contained in Reg. D and Reg.E. In the same way STAX D means to store data from A to memory location (DE) i.e., the memory location whose address is contained in Register pair DE.

For directly introducing data to ACC or any Register or Memory, move immediate (MVI) instruction may be used keeping in mind that it is essential to specify memory address if any data is to be stored directly to the memory location. There is provision to introduce data to two registers at a time when they are used as register pair. In that case 'LXI' instruction is to be used. For example MVI B 12 H means to introduce 12 H in register B, LXI B $D_4$ $D_3$ $D_2$ $D_1$ indicates the loading of Reg.B and Reg. C with data $D_4$ $D_3$ and $D_2$ $D_1$ respectively, LXI H 4080 means to load Reg. H with 40H and Reg. L with 80 H. It may be mentioned here that at the time of using B,C or D,E or H,L registers as register pairs, Reg. C or E or L should be loaded with data first before loading Reg. B or D or H. If we want to load 4080H in HL Reg. pair, the corresponding program will be as follows:

| MEM.LOC. | MNEMONICS | HEX. CODE | CLOCK CYCLES | DESCRIPTION |
|---|---|---|---|---|
| 4180 | LXI H | 21 | 10 | LOAD 40 H TO REG. H AND 80 H TO REG. L. |
| 4081 | 80 | 80 | - | DATA (80) |
| 4082 | 40 | 40 | - | DATA (40) |

The same technique may be applied for loading Register pairs BC and DE. It may be mentioned here that LXI H is a very useful instruction used to address the memory location. For storing data $D_4$ $D_3$ $D_2$ $D_1$ (hex) in the stack pointer, the instruction LXI SP $D_4$ $D_3$ $D_2$ $D_1$ may be used which is helpful to initialise the topmost memory address of the stack in INTEL 8085 CPU.

EXAMPLE 3 : Store data B3 H to memory location 45 39 (hex).

| MEM.LOC. | MNEMONICS | HEX. CODE | CLOCK CYCLES | DESCRIPTION |
|---|---|---|---|---|
| 4180 | LXI H 4539 H | 21  39  45 | 10 | INITIALISE MEM.LOC. 4539 H THROUGH HL PAIR. |
| 4083 | MVI M B3 H | 36  B3 | 10 | MOVE B3 H IN MEMORY. |
| 4085 | HLT | 76 | 5 | STOP |

EXAMPLE 4 : Use LDAX to load data 89 H to Acc. stored in the memory location 4125 (hex).

| MEM.LOC. | MNEMONICS | HEX. CODE | CLOCK CYCLES | DESCRIPTION |
|---|---|---|---|---|
| 4080 | LXI H 4125 H | 21 25 41 | 10 | INITIALISE MEM. LOC. 4125 H THROUGH HL PAIR |
| 4083 | MVI M 89 H | 36 89 | 10 | MOVE 89 H TO M |
| 4085 | MVI B 41 H | 06 41 | 7 | MOVE 41 H TO REG B. |
| 4087 | MVI C 25 H | 0E 25 | 7 | MOVE 25 H TO REG C. |
| 4089 | LDAX B | 0A | 7 | LOAD ACC FROM MEM. LOC. (BC) |
| 408A | HLT | 76 | 5 | STOP |

RESULTS: Data 89 H stored in memory location 4125 H is transferred to the accumulator.

EXAMPLE 5: Use STAX to store data from Acc. to the memory address 412A (hex).

| MEM.LOC. | MNEMONICS | HEX. CODE | CLOCK CYCLES | DESCRIPTION |
|---|---|---|---|---|
| 4100 | MVI A B0 H | 3E B0 | 7 | B0 H $\longrightarrow$ ACC. |
| 4102 | MVI D 41 H | 16 41 | 7 | 41 H $\longrightarrow$ REG.D |
| 4104 | MVI E 2A H | IE 2A | 7 | 2A H $\longrightarrow$ REG.E |
| 4106 | STAX D | 12 | 7 | (ACC.) $\longrightarrow$ MEM. LOC.(DE) |
| 4107 | HLT | 76 | 5 | HALT |

RESULTS: The data B0 H stored in Acc. is transferred to the memory location 412A (hex).

EXAMPLE 6: Exchange data stored in Reg.D with H and data in Reg. E with L.

| MEM.LOC. | MNEMONICS | HEX. CODE | DESCRIPTION |
|---|---|---|---|
| 4500 | MVI D 01 H | 16 01 | 01 H $\longrightarrow$ REG. D |
| 4502 | MVI E 02 H | IE 02 | 02 H $\longrightarrow$ REG. E |
| 4504 | MVI H 03 H | 26 03 | 03 H $\longrightarrow$ REG. H |
| 4506 | MVI L 04 H | 2E 04 | 04 H $\longrightarrow$ REG. L |
| 4508 | XCHG | EB | (DE) $\rightleftharpoons$ (HL) |
| 4509 | HLT | 76 | STOP |

## 4.3 PUSH AND POP

PUSH instruction is generally used to protect the content of any register pair to the stack before calling a sub program. The main program may involve various registers and accumulator which are used again in the sub program. Hence to protect the contents of registers and accumulator, PUSH instruction is used. PUSH B indicates the transfer of data from Reg. B to Loc. (SP-1) and Reg. C to Loc. (SP-2) where Loc. (SP-1) indicates the memory location whose address is (content of SP-1). Similarly PUSH D or PUSH H mean to transfer data stored in Reg. D and E or Reg. H and L to the stack respectively. The instruction PUSH PSW transfers data from the Acc. and Flag to Loc. (SP-1) and Loc. (SP-2) respectively.

POP instruction is opposite to PUSH instruction and is used to transfer data back to the original registers or accumulator. This instruction is used before returning to the main program at the end of a subroutine. POP B, POP D, POP H, and POP PSW are used to transfer data to Reg. B and C, Reg. D and E, Reg. H and L, and accumulator and flag respectively from the stack. It should be noted at this stage that the PUSH and POP operations should be used maintaining a specific order where the stack pointer moves in LIFO order. If PUSH B, PUSH D, PUSH H and PUSH PSW be used sequentially in a program, POP instruction must be used in the sequential order POP PSW, POP H, POP D and POP B. XTHL is an instruction of the data transfer group which is used to exchange data in Reg. H with Loc (SP-1) and data in Reg. L with Loc (SP).

## 4.4 INCREMENT AND DECREMENT INSTRUCTIONS

It has been pointed out earlier that the Increment / Decrement Instructions are INR, DCR, INX and DCX of which the first two instructions are used to increase or decrease the data stored in a register or Acc. by one whereas the other two are meant for increasing or decreasing the content of a register pair by one. For example, INR B means the increment of the content of the Reg. B by one and DCR C indicates the decrement of the content of Reg.C by one. Similarly if it is required to increase the content of Reg. pair BC or to decrease the content of the Reg. pair DE by one, instructions INX B or DCX D may be used.

## 4.5 ROTATE AND SHIFT INSTRUCTIONS

These types of instructions include RAL, RAR, RLC and RRC. The significance of the instructions may well be explained with the help of Fig.4.1.

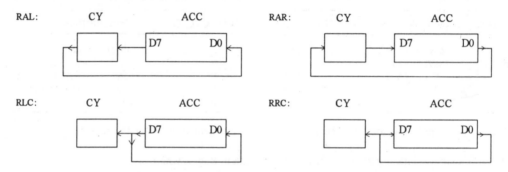

Fig. 4.1 Rotate and Shift instructions

The instruction RAL menas to rotate carry and accumulator towards left, i.e. the content of carry occupies the least significant (LSB) position of the Acc., pushing the content of Acc. towards left so that the most significant bit (MSB) of Acc. can enter into carry. Similarly by instruction RAR, the content of carry and Acc, can be shifted by one bit position towards right so that the LSB enters into carry and the content of carry flag occupies the MSB position of the Acc. The instruction RLC is different from RAL in the sense that MSB of Acc. is stored at the carry as well as the LSB position of Acc shifting the other bits of Acc. by one bit position towards left. Similarly by RRC, bit D0 of Acc. is stored both at carry and MSB position of Acc. shifting the other bits by one bit position towards right. Assuming the data A6 H stored in Acc and carry flag is set at zero, bit positions after different rotate instructions have been presented as under:

|       | CY | D7 |   | ACC |   |   |   | D0 |   |   |
|-------|----|----|---|-----|---|---|---|----|---|---|
|       | 0  | 1  | 0 | 1   | 0 | 0 | 1 | 1  | 0 | = A6 H = 166 Dec. in Acc. |
|       | CY | D7 |   | ACC |   |   |   | D0 |   |   |
| RAL : | 1  | 0  | 1 | 0   | 0 | 1 | 1 | 0  | 0 | = 4C H = 76 Dec. in Acc. |
|       | CY | D7 |   | ACC |   |   |   | D0 |   |   |
| RLC : | 1  | 0  | 1 | 0   | 0 | 1 | 1 | 0  | 1 | = 4D H = 77 Dec. in Acc. |

|  | CY | D7 |  |  | ACC |  |  | D0 |  |
|---|---|---|---|---|---|---|---|---|---|

RAR :  | 0 | | 0 | 1 | 0 | 1 | 0 | 0 | 1 | 1 | = 53 H = 83 Dec. in Acc.

|  | CY | D7 |  |  | ACC |  |  | D0 |  |
|---|---|---|---|---|---|---|---|---|---|

RRC :  | 0 | | 0 | 1 | 0 | 1 | 0 | 0 | 1 | 1 | = 53 H = 83 Dec. in Acc.

It may be noted that RAL multiplies the content of Acc by two whereas RAR divides the same by two. In the above example, the content of Acc after RAR instructions is 53 H (half of A6 H ). After RAL operation, the content of Acc becomes 4C H (76 dec.) but carry flag becomes high indicating overflow of data beyond 255 Dec. Thus considering carry, the results become 332 Dec which is double of 166 Dec.

EXAMPLE 7: Store data AB H in mem. loc. 4100 H, split the data in the form of 0A H and 0B H and store them in mem. locs. 4101 H and 4102 H respectively.

| MEM.LOC. | MNEMONICS | OPCODE | DESCRIPTION |
|---|---|---|---|
| 4200 | LXI  H 4100 | 21  00  41 | INITIALISE MEM. LOC. 4100 H |
| 4203 | MVI  M AB | 36  AB | STORE DATA AB  H IN 4100 H |
| 4205 | MOV A, M | 7E | MOVE (4100) TO REG B. |
| 4206 | MOV B, A | 47 | MOVE (ACC) TO REG B. |
| 4207 | ANI  F0 | E6  F0 | AND F0 H WITH (ACC) & KEEP THE RESULT IN ACC |
| 4209 | RRC | 0F | ROTATE DATA IN ACC TO RIGHT AND LSB TO CY (RESULT IS 55 H) |
| 420A | RRC | 0F | ROTATE DATA IN ACC TO RIGHT AND LSB TO CY (RESULT IS 2A H) |
| 420B | RRC | 0F | ROTATE DATA IN ACC TO RIGHT AND LSB TO CY (RESULT IS 15 H) |
| 420C | RRC | 0F | ROTATE DATA IN ACC TO RIGHT AND LSB TO CY (RESULT IS 0A H) |
| 420D | INX  H | 23 | INCREMENT MEM.ADD.TO 4101 H |
| 420E | MOV M, A | 77 | STORE (ACC) IN 4101 H |
| 420F | MOV A, B | 78 | STORE (REG.B) TO ACC |
| 4210 | ANI  0F | E6  0F | AND 0F H WITH (ACC) & KEEP THE RESULT IN ACC |
| 4212 | INX  H | 23 | INCREMENT MEM ADDRESS TO 4102 H |
| 4213 | MOV M, A | 77 | MOVE (ACC) TO 4102 H |
| 4214 | HLT | 76 | HALT UNTIL INTERRUPT |

The results of execution are 0A and 0B as contents of mem. locs. 4101 H and 4102 H respectively. It may be noted that AB AND F0 = A0 ; AB AND 0F = 0B. Since RRC rotates the content of Acc to the right and LSB to carry and MSB position, the following pattern of bit movement will take place in four RRC operations:

|  |  | D7 |  |  | ACC |  |  | D0 |  |
|---|---|---|---|---|---|---|---|---|---|

| 1 | 0 | 1 | 0 | 0 | 0 | 0 | 0 | = A0 H

|  | CY | D7 |  |  | ACC |  |  | D0 |  |
|---|---|---|---|---|---|---|---|---|---|

First RRC operation :  | 0 | | 0 | 1 | 0 | 1 | 0 | 0 | 0 | 0 | = 50 H

| | CY | D7 | | ACC | | | | D0 | |
|---|---|---|---|---|---|---|---|---|---|
| Second RRC operation : | 0 | 0 | 0 | 1 | 0 | 1 | 0 | 0 | 0 | = 28 H |

| | CY | D7 | | ACC | | | | D0 | |
|---|---|---|---|---|---|---|---|---|---|
| Third RRC operation : | 0 | 0 | 0 | 0 | 1 | 0 | 1 | 0 | 0 | = 14 H |

| | CY | D7 | | ACC | | | | D0 | |
|---|---|---|---|---|---|---|---|---|---|
| Fourth RRC operation : | 0 | 0 | 0 | 0 | 0 | 1 | 0 | 1 | 0 | = 0A H |

## 4.6 SET, COMPLIMENT AND DECIMAL ADJUSTMENT INSTRUCTIONS

STC, CMC, CMA and DAA instructions come under this category. Instruction STC is used to set carry to 1 whereas CMC is used to complement the carry. The use of STC and CMC together clears carry, i.e. the carry is set to zero. If it be required to complement the content to Acc, CMA may be used. For instance, if the data stored in the Acc be AB H, after following the instruction CMA, the content of Acc changes as under :

| | | D7 | | | | | | | D0 |
|---|---|---|---|---|---|---|---|---|---|
| AB H | = | 1 | 0 | 1 | 0 | 1 | 0 | 1 | 1 |

| | | D7 | | | | | | | D0 |
|---|---|---|---|---|---|---|---|---|---|
| Complement of AB H = | | 0 | 1 | 0 | 1 | 0 | 1 | 0 | 0 | = 54 H. |

DAA is an instruction to Decimal Adjust in addition to convert the content of Acc. into decimal number after the binary addition of two decimal numbers. Generally this instruction should follow the ADD instruction. If the content of Acc be 0B H, DAA results in 12 (decimal) in Acc.

EXAMPLE 8: Add two decimal numbers 75 and 15 and find the results in decimal form.

| MEM.LOC. | MNEMONICS | OPCODE | DESCRIPTION |
|---|---|---|---|
| 4080 | MVI  A  75 | 3E  75 | 75 H ⟶ ACC. |
| 4082 | MVI  B  15 | 06  15 | 15 H ⟶ REG. B |
| 4084 | ADD  B | 80 | (REG.B) + (ACC.) ==> ACC. |
| 4085 | DAA | 27 | DECIMAL ADJUST (ACC.) |
| 4086 | MOV  B,A | 47 | (ACC.) ⟶ REG.B |
| 4087 | HLT | 76 | STOP. |

In this program, 75 H and 15 H will be added and the results will be 8A in Acc. after ADD B operation. Then by DAA operation, the least significant part of hex. number will be added with 6 for decimal adjust and the resulted carry, if there by any, will be stored in the Auxiliary carry leaving the decimal adjusted number in the Acc. The content of Auxiliary carry will then be added with the most significant part in Acc. The result 90 will be stored in Reg. B after execution of the program.

Instead, if the decimal numbers to be added be 75 and 25, the results after ADD B operation will be 9A. The DAA instruction will add 6 with A to store zero in Acc. and 1 in the Auxiliary carry which in turn will be added to 9 to yield A. For decimal adjust of the most significant part, 6 will be added to A to obtain 10 of which zero will be stored as the most significant part in Acc and 1 will be kept at the carry. After execution of the program, 00 will be obtained in Reg. B whereas 01 will be stored in the carry and the results will become 100.

## 4.7 ADD, SUBTRACT AND COMPARE INSTRUCTIONS

ADD instruction is used to add the content of any register or memory with that of the accumulator and the result of addition is stored in the Acc. ADD B indicates the addition of the content of Reg B with that of the Acc and the result is stored in Acc. But before using this instruction, the memory location should be specified if one of the data to be added be kept in the memory.

EXAMPLE 9: Store data 24 H and 39 H in mem. locs. 4080 H and 4081 H respectively. Add them and store the results in the mem.loc.4082 H.

| MEM.LOC. | MNEMONICS | OPCODE | DESCRIPTION |
|---|---|---|---|
| 4100 | LXI H 4080H | 21 80 40 | MEM. LOC.——>4080 H |
| 4103 | MVI M 24 | 36 24 | 24 H——>M |
| 4105 | INX H | 23 | NEXT MEM.LOC. |
| 4106 | MVI M 39 | 36 39 | 39 H——>M |
| 4108 | MOV A,M | 7E | (4081 H)——>ACC. |
| 4109 | DCX H | 2B | MEM. LOC. 4080H. |
| 410A | ADD M | 86 | (ACC.) + (4080 H)——> ACC. |
| 410B | INX H | 23 | NEXT MEM. LOC. |
| 410C | INX H | 23 | NEXT MEM. LOC. |
| 410D | MOV M,A | 77 | (ACC.)——>M |
| 410E | HLT | 76 | HALT |

If the results stored in carry flag and content of any register or memory are to be added with the content of the Acc, the instruction ADC should be used. In adding two 8-bit numbers, if there be any overflow, the carry flag will be affected and to get the complete result, this instruction may be useful.

EXAMPLE 10: Add two numbers F0 H and 2A H. Store the results in the mem. loc. 4100 H and 4101 H.

| MEM. LOC. | MNEMONICS | HEX CODE | DESCRIPTION |
|---|---|---|---|
| 4200 | MVI A F0 | 3E F0 | F0 H——>ACC. |
| 4202 | MVI B 2A | 06 2A | 2A H——>REG. B |
| 4204 | ADD B | 80 | (ACC.) + (REG.B)——>ACC. |
| 4205 | LXI H 4101 | 21 01 41 | M——>4101H |
| 4208 | MOV M, A | 77 | (ACC)——>M |
| 4209 | MVI A 00 | 3E 00 | ACC.——>00H |
| 420B | MVI B 00 | 06 00 | REG. B——>00H |
| 420D | ADC B | 88 | (ACC.) + (REG B) + (CY)——>ACC. |
| 420E | DCX H | 2B | M——>4100H |
| 420F | MOV M, A | 77 | (ACC.)——>M |
| 4210 | HLT | 76 | HALT |

The result of addition viz. 011A H will be available in the mem. locs. 4100 H and 4101 H where contents of 4100 H and 4101 H will be 01 H and 1A H respectively.

For addition of certain data directly with the content of Acc., ADI instruction will be used where the results will obviously be stored in Acc. Sometimes it is required to add certain data and the content of carry flag together with the content of Acc. In that case, ACI may be the proper instruction.

For addition of 16-bit numbers, addition of the contents of the register pairs becomes necessary for which the most suitable instructions are DAD B, DAD H, DAD D and DAD SP. DAD B represent the addition of (BC) with (HL) and the results are stored in (HL). Similar is the case with DAD D. DAD H simply means to add the content of HL pair with that of HL itself and the results are obtained in HL. If the content of the stack pointer (SP) is required to be added with that stored in HL, DAD SP instruction may be used.

EXAMPLE 11: Add F1B2 H with 213C H and store the result in the Mem. Loc. 4090, 4091 and 4092 H.

| MEM LOC | MNEMONICS | OPCODE | DESCRIPTION |
|---------|-----------|--------|-------------|
| 4200 | LXI   H  F1B2 H | 21  B2  FF | LOAD FIB2 H IN REG. PAIR HL |
| 4203 | XCHG | EB | (DE) $\rightleftharpoons$ (HL) |
| 4204 | LXI   H  213C H | 21  3C  21 | LOAD 213C H IN REG. PAIR HL |
| 4207 | DAD  D | 19 | (DE) + (HL)——→ HL |
| 4208 | SHLD 4092 | 22  92  40 | (REG.H)——→ 4093H, (REG,L)——→4092 |
| 420B | LXI   H  4093 H | 21  93  40 | M——→4093H |
| 420E | MOV  B,M | 46 | (M)——→ REG. B |
| 420F | DCX  H | 2B | PREVIOUS M |
| 4210 | DCX  H | 2B | PREVIOUS M |
| 4211 | MOV  M,B | 70 | (REG.B)——→M |
| 4212 | MVI   A  00 | 3E  00 | 00 H——→ ACC. |
| 4214 | MVI   B  00 | 06  00 | 00 H——→REG. B |
| 4216 | ADC  B | 88 | (CY) + (REG.B) + (ACC.)——→ACC. |
| 4217 | DCX  H | 2B | PREVIOUS M |
| 4218 | MOV  M, A | 27 | (ACC.) ——→ M |
| 4219 | HLT | 76 | HALT |

The results of addition will be stored as 01 H in Mem. Loc. 4090, 12 H in 4091 and EE in 4092 H respectively.

For direct subtraction of the content of any register or memory from that of the Acc, SUB instruction is used. For example, SUB C indicates subtraction of register C from Acc and the result is stored in Acc. For subtraction of any data from the content of Acc and for subtraction of carry and any data from the content of Acc, there exist the instruction SUI and SBI.

SUI 45 H indicates the subtraction of 45 H from Acc., SBI 45 H presents the subtraction of 45 H and the content of carry flag together from Acc, the result being obtained from Acc in both of the cases. For subtraction of the content of any register or memory and that stored in the carry flag from Acc, the use of SBB may be made. SBB D indicates the mathematical operation (ACC) - (Reg D) - (Carry flag) and the result is kept stored in Acc.

CMP is an extremely useful logical operation in CPU 8085/ 8085A by means of which the content of any register or memory can be compared with that in Acc. CMP actually means to subtract content of any register or memory from that stored in Acc without keeping the results in Acc. This instruction affects all flags. CMP B indicates a subtraction from the content of Acc of the content of reg. B without having any mathematical result in Acc. This instruction is a decision making instruction by means of which a decision regarding equality or inequality can be taken. Generally a JUMP instruction follows CMP. Similarly CPI $D_2D_1$ describes the subtraction of $D_2D_1$ (Hex) from Acc. without putting the result in Acc.

## 4.8 AND, OR AND EXCLUSIVE-OR INSTRUCTIONS

AND is a logical operation and it requires that all input conditions must be simultaneously there for the output to be true. Considering

$$45  H = 0100  0101   \text{and}   AD  H = 1010  1101$$
$$45  H  AND  AD  H = 00000101 = 05  H$$

In a CPU based on 8085, ANA instruction is used to AND the content of any register or memory with Acc putting the result in Acc. It should be noted here that ANA A clears the carry flags. In order to AND any hex. data directly with Acc., ANI instruction followed by the data to be added is used.

The OR instruction indicates that atleast one input condition must be true. Result of 45 H OR AD H is 1110 1101 (=ED H). In the CPU 8085/8085A, ORA instruction is used to OR the content of any register or memory with that stored in Acc and the result of operation is obtained from Acc. In order to OR a hex number with Acc directly, ORI followed by the data is to be used. Like ANA A instruction, ORA A indicates the clearing of the carry flag.

The output of EX-OR operation of two numbers A and B is true only when either A or B but not both is true. 45 H EX-OR AD H gives 1 1 1 0 1 0 0 0 = E8 H. The XRA instruction is used to find the result of EXCLUSIVE -OR operation of the content of any register or memory with Acc. keeping the result in Acc. It may be noted that the instruction XRA A is used to clear Accumulator only. In order to EX-OR any Hex. number directly with Acc., XRI instruction may used.

## 4.9 JUMP, CALL AND RESTART INSTRUCTIONS

In programming, often it becomes necessary to jump to some other location of the program. For repeatation of certain function, jumping is necessary and the execution is performed by JMP instruction followed by the memory address where to be jumped. Sometimes, the instruction PCHL is used for jumping to the memory location whose address is contained in HL pair. Hence this instruction must come after LXI H instruction.

CALL and RETURN are two extremely useful instructions for calling a subroutine from the main program and coming back to the main program. CALL instruction is used in the main program whereas RET is used at the end of the subroutine. CALL $A_4 A_3 A_2 A_1$ means to move PC to Loc. (SP-1) and Loc. (SP-2) and jump to location $A_4 A_3 A_2 A_1$ (Hex.). On the other hand, RET indicates the movement of Loc. (SP + 1) and Loc. (SP) to PC.

In INTEL 8085/8085A, there are eight different restart instructions listed below:

Table 4.2
Restart Instructions

| RESTART INSTRUCTION | OPCODE | DESCRIPTION |
|---|---|---|
| RST 0 | C7 | MOVE PC TO LOC. (SP-1) AND LOC. (SP-2) AND JUMP TO LOC. 0000 H. |
| RST 1 | CF | MOVE PC TO LOC. (SP-1) AND LOC. (SP-2) AND JUMP TO LOC. 0008 H. |
| RST 2 | D7 | MOVE PC TO LOC. (SP-1) AND LOC. (SP-2) AND JUMP TO LOC. 0010 H. |
| RST 3 | DF | MOVE PC TO LOC. (SP-1) AND LOC. (SP-2) AND JUMP TO LOC. 0018 H. |
| RST 4 | E7 | MOVE PC TO LOC. (SP-1) AND LOC. (SP-2) AND JUMP TO LOC. 0020 H. |
| RST 5 | EF | MOVE PC TO LOC. (SP-1) AND LOC. (SP-2) AND JUMP TO LOC. 0028 H. |
| RST 6 | F7 | MOVE PC TO LOC. (SP-1) AND LOC. (SP-2) AND JUMP TO LOC. 0030 H. |
| RST 7 | FF | MOVE PC TO LOC. (SP-1) AND LOC. (SP-2) AND JUMP TO LOC. 0038 H. |

## 4.10 CONDITIONAL JUMP, CALL AND RETURN

After a comparison between or subtraction of two Data X and Y, the first Data being stored in the Acc. and second one in any one of the registers or memory, different mathematical conditions may be obtained affecting carry flag. They are :

i)   If $X > Y$, carry flag remains reset at zero.
ii)  If $X < Y$, carry flag is set at 1.
iii) If $X = Y$, the result becomes zero and zero flag is set at 1.
iv)  If $X \neq Y$, the result becomes non zero and zero flag remains reset at zero.

Also MSB of the result may or may not be zero or it may be one. In many cases, the result may have odd or even number of 1's. In such cases, different jump instructions may be used followed by the memory location of the destination. They are tabulated as under:

**Table 4.3 Conditional Jump Instructions**

| MNEMONICS | OPCODE | DESCRIPTION |
|---|---|---|
| i)   JC  4253 H | DA  53  42 | IF CY.=1, JUMP TO LOC. 4253 H |
| ii)  JNC  4253 H | D2  53  42 | IF CY.=0, JUMP TO LOC. 4253 H |
| iii)  JZ  4253 H | CA  53  42 | IF RESULT IS ZERO (CZ=1), JUMP TO LOC. 4253 H |
| iv) JNZ  4253 H | C2  53  42 | IF RESULT IS NOT ZERO (CZ=0), JUMP TO LOC. 4253 H |
| v)   JP  4253 H | F2  53  42 | IF MSB OF RESULT IS ONE (S=0), JUMP TO LOC. 4253 H |
| vi)  JM  4253 H | FA  53  42 | IF MSB OF RESULT IS ONE (S=1), JUMP TO LOC. 4253 H |
| vii) JPO  4253 H | E2  53  42 | IF RESULT HAS ODD NUMBER OF 1's (P=0), JUMP TO LOC. 4253 H |
| viii) JPE  4253 H | EA  53  42 | IF RESULT HAS EVEN NUMBER OF 1's (P=1), JUMP TO LOC. 4253 H |

(* MEM. LOC.——>4253 H)
These instructions are used to form loops in different programs.

## 4.11 LOOPS IN PROGRAMS

Computers are particularly suitable for jobs requiring repetitive operations. Suppose it is required to add N number (N < FF H) arranged sequentially from memory address 4300 H onwards. This can be done by using the Loop Technique where certain instructions involving that for addition are executed N times to produce the required sum. The program is as follows:

| MEM.LOC. | LABEL | MNEMONICS | HEX.CODE | DESCRIPTION |
|---|---|---|---|---|
| 4080 | | LHI  H  4300 | 21  00  43 | INITIALISE MEM.LOC. 4300 H |
| 4383 | | MVI  B  N | 06  N | STORE DATA N IN REG.B |
| 4085 | | MVI  A  00 | 3E  00 | CLEAR ACCUMULATOR |
| 4087 | LOOP | ADD  M | 86 | ADD (4300 H) WITH (ACC.) |
| 4088 | | INX  H | 23 | INCREMENT HL PAIR TO NEXT MEM. LOC. |
| 4089 | | DCR  B | 05 | DECREMENT (REG. B) |
| 408A | | JNZ  LOOP | C2  87  40 | JUMP TO 4087 IF THE RESULT IS NOT ZERO ( i.e. content of Reg. B = 0 ⁄) |
| 408D | | RST  1 | CF | STOP OTHERWISE. |

The N numbers of data are to be stored from 4300 H onward in RAM locations. The flow chart of the above program is given in Fig. 4.2, the detailed technique of developing the flow chart being discussed in Chapter 11.

It may be seen from the above program that, each time addition is executed, there is different address in the HL Register pair, so that the next data can be added to the last sum accumulated in Acc. Register B has been used as the loop counter and it is decremented by one in each cycle adding one data to the Accumulator. The JNZ loop instruction checks for a zero in Reg. B and sends the program control back to ADD instruction until the loop count reaches zero as shown in the flow diagram of Fig. 4.2.

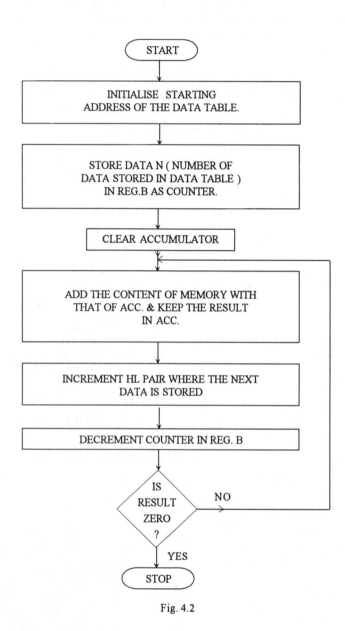

Fig. 4.2

## 4.12 USES OF SUBROUTINES

In designing a nontrivial program, it may so happen that one operation is to be used at different places within the program operating on different parameters. This can be done either by writing the same set of instructions at each of these points in the program where the operation is used, or by writing the set of instructions once at some other memory locations and calling it at the points in the program where the operation is required. This latter concept is called a SUBROUTINE. A Subroutine is a program that defines a particular operation and it can be used at any point in a program by the CALL instruction followed by the starting address of the subroutine.

The subroutine must have a RETURN instruction at the end of it so that after executing it, the control would come back to the main program at the point, it left the same, i.e., just after the call instruction, and continue to execute the remaining part of the main program.

In calculating the expression

$$V = P*Q + R*S$$

where P, Q, R and S are Hex. numbers and V < FF H, the multiplication is to be done twice. To avoid repetition of the same set of instructions in a program, a separate program may be developed for the multiplication for calling it whenever necessary. The program may be developed as under:

**Main Program**

| MEM.LOC. | MNEMONICS | OPCODE | DESCRIPTION |
|---|---|---|---|
| 4081 | LXI H  ADDRESS OF  P | 21  00  41 | INITIALISE ADDRESS 4100 H (WHERE THE DATA P IS STORED). |
| 4084 | LXI D  ADDRESS OF  Q | 11  01  41 | INITIALISE ADDRESS 4101 H (WHERE THE DATA 1 IS STORED). |
| 4087 | CALL    MULTI | CD 00  47 | CALL SUBROUTINE ' MULTI ' |
| 408A | STA 4104 | 32  04  41 | STORE DATA P*Q FROM ACC.TO 4140 H |
| 408D | LXI H  ADDRESS OF  R | 21  02  41 | INITIALISE ADDRESS 4102 H (WHERE THE DATA R IS STORED). |
| 4090 | LXI D  ADDRESS OF  S | 11  03  41 | INITIALISE ADDRESS 4103 H (WHERE THE DATA S IS STORED). |
| 4093 | CALL    MULTI | CD 00  47 | CALL SUBROUTINE ' MULTI ' |
| 4096 | MOV B, A | 47 | TRANSFER R*S IN ACC. TO REG. B |
| 4097 | LDA A 4104 | 3A  04  41 | LOAD DATA TO ACC. FROM 4104 WHERE P*Q WERE STORED). |
| 409A | ADD B | 80 | ADD (REG. B) WITH (ACC.) |
| 409B | LXI H  4104 | 21  04  41 | INITIALISE 4104 H |
| 409E | MOV M, A | 77 | TRANSFER (ACC.) TO 4104 H. |
| 409F | HLT | 76 | HALT |

It may be noted that the four numbers are to be kept in Mem. Locs. 4100 through 4103 and the result will be obtained in the Mem. Loc. 4104 H.

**Subroutine MULTI**

| MEM.LOC. | MNEMONICS | LABEL | OPCODE | DESCRIPTION |
|---|---|---|---|---|
| 4700 | MOV C,M | | 4E | TRANSFER THE FIRST NUMBER OF THE PRODUCT IN REG.C FROM THE MEMORY |
| 4701 | XCHG | | EB | EXCHANGE (HL) AND  (DE). |
| 4702 | MOV B,M | | 46 | TRANSFER SECOND NUMBER OF THE PRODUCT IN REG.B FROM THE MEMORY |
| 4703 | XCHG | | EB | EXCHANGE (HL) AND (DE.) |
| 4704 | MVI  A 00 | | 3E 00 | CLEAR ACC. |
| 4706 | ADD  C | LOOP | 81 | ADD (REG. C) WITH (ACC.) |
| 4707 | DCR  B | | 1D | DECREMENT  REG. B. |
| 4708 | JNZ  LOOP | | C2 06 47 | IF THE CONTENT OF REG. B IS NOT ZERO, GO TO LOOP. |
| 470B | RET | | C9 | OTHERWISE, RETURN. |

**Flow Chart of the Main Program**

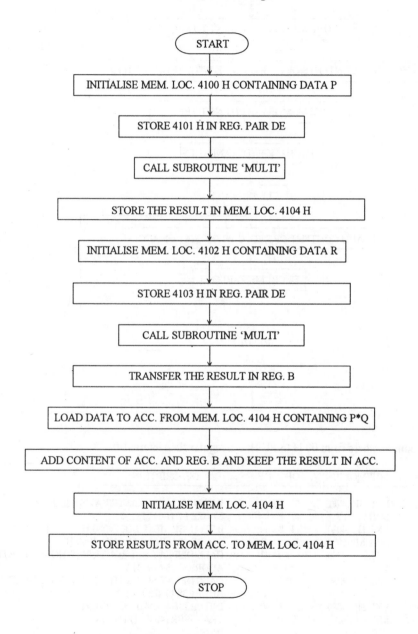

**Sub-Program 'MULTI'**

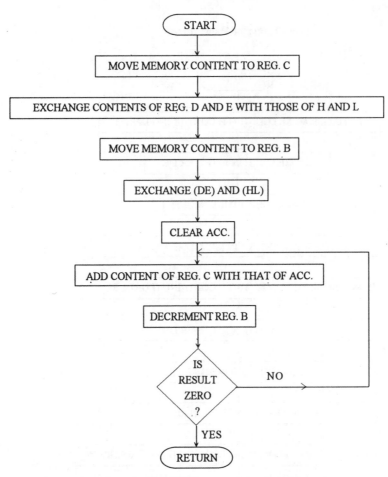

EXAMPLE 1 3:   Count numbers from 00 H to FE H at a regular time interval.

| MEM.LOC. | MNEMONICS | OPCODE | DESCRIPTION |
|---|---|---|---|
| 414D | LXI SP 47FF | 31 FF 47 | DEFINE STACK POINTER AT 47FF H. |
| 4150 | MVI C FF | 0E FF | STORE FF H IN FEG. C |
| 4152 | LXI H 4080 | 21 80 40 | INITIALISE MEM. LOC. 4080 H. |
| 4155 | MVI M 00 | 36 00 | STORE 00 H IN MEM. LOC. 4080 H |
| 4157 | CALL 4200 | CD 00 42 | CALL DISPLAY SUBROUTINE (WHOSE STARTING ADDRESS IS 4200 H.) |
| 415A | CALL 4230 | CD 30 42 | CALL DELAY SUBROUTINE (WHOSE STARTING ADDRESS IS 4230 H.) |
| 415D | LXI H 4080 | 21 80 40 | INITIALISE MEM. LOC. 4080 H |
| 4160 | MOV A, M | 7E | TRANSFER (4080 H) TO ACC. |
| 4161 | INR A | 3C | INCREMENT (ACC.) |
| 4162 | CMP C | B9 | COMPARE REG. C WITH ACC. |
| 4163 | JZ 4150 | CA 50 41 | IF THE RESULT BE ZERO, JUMP TO MEM. LOC. 4150 H. |
| 4166 | MOV M, A | 77 | OTHERWISE, MOVE DATA OF ACC. TO MEM. LOC. 4080 H. |
| 4167 | JMP 4157 | C3 57 41 | JUMP TO MEM. LOC. 4157 H. & CONTINUE. |

If the program be executed, counting will be started and the display will be found in either of the status field or address field or data field of the key board depending on the DISPLAY subroutine after a regular time interval depending on the DELAY subroutine. The system will count from 00 H to FE H at a regular time interval and repeat the cycle of operation continuously. In all microcomputers DISPLAY subroutine supplied by the manufacturer is stored in the EPROM. Sometimes it becomes necessary to develop a new subroutine using the stored EPROM program to fit the same to the main program. The subroutine DISPLAY will be discussed in chapter 11.

In the main program, a DELAY subroutine whose starting address is 4230 H has been used. The DELAY subroutine may be developed in different ways. The purpose of this subroutine is to engage the CPU otherwise without disturbing the main program. An illustrative example of the DELAY subroutine has been discussed in example 14.

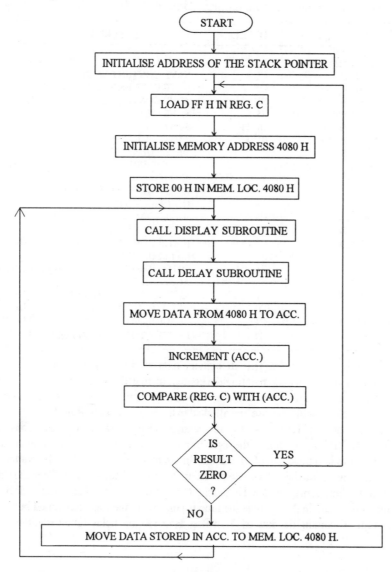

Fig. 4.3 Flow chart

The logic corresponding to the software example 13 can be explained by a sequential flow chart shown in Fig. 4.3. Initially, a data FF H has been stored in Reg. C and storing 00 H in Mem. Loc. 4080 H, the content of 4080 H has been displayed with the help of a DISPLAY SUBROUTINE followed by a DELAY SUBROUTINE to sustend the display. Then the content of 4080 H has been transferred to Acc. and the content of Acc. has been incremented by 1 followed by a comparison with the content of Reg. C. If (Acc.)<(Reg.C), the function of the microcomputer is to transfer the content of Acc. to Mem. Loc. 4080 H and continue to perform the cyclic operation of display and delay. But at (Acc.)=(Reg.C) i.e. when the result of comparison between (Acc.) and (Reg.C) becomes equal to zero, data FF H is again stored in Reg. C and the counting is started from 00 H again.

## 4.13  DELAY SUBROUTINE

EXAMPLE 14.  Develop a DELAY subroutine having starting address 422D H.

| MEM. LOC. | MNEMONICS | OPCODE | DESCRIPTION |
|---|---|---|---|
| 422D | LXI   SP 47FF | 31  FF 47 | INITIALISE STACK POINTER AT 47FF H. |
| 4230 | PUSH B | C5 | SAVE CONTENT OF REG. PAIR BC IN STACK. |
| 4231 | PUSH D | D5 | SAVE CONTENT OF REG. PAIR DE IN STACK. |
| 4232 | PUSH H | E5 | SAVE CONTENT OF REG. PAIR HL IN STACK. |
| 4233 | PUSH PSW | F5 | SAVE CONTENT OF ACC. & FLAG IN STACK. |
| 4234 | MVI   D  FF | 16  FF | STORE FF IN REG. D. |
| 4236 | MVI   B  FF | 06  FF | STORE FF IN REG. B. |
| 4238 | DCR   B | 05 | DECREMENT (REG. B) |
| 4239 | JZ   4241 H | CA 41  42 | IF THE RESULT BE ZERO, JUMP TO MEM.LOC. 4241 H. |
| 423C | NOP | 00 | OTHERWISE NO OPERATION. |
| 423D | NOP | 00 | NO OPERATION. |
| 423E | JMP 4238 | C3  38  42 | JUMP TO MEM.LOC. 4238 (HEX). |
| 4241 | DCR   D | 15 | DECREMENT REG. D |
| 4242 | JNZ 4236 | C2  36  42 | IF THE RESULT BE NON ZERO JUMP TO MEM.LOC. 4236 (HEX) |
| 4245 | POP PSW | F1 | OTHERWISE RETURN DATA FROM STACK TO ACC. AND FLAG. |
| 4246 | POP   H | E1 | RETURN DATA FROM STACK TO HL PAIR. |
| 4247 | POP   D | D1 | RETURN DATA FROM STACK TO DE PAIR. |
| 4248 | POP   B | C1 | RETURN DATA FROM STACK TO BC PAIR. |
| 4249 | RET | C9 | RETURN TO THE MAIN PROGRAM. |

From the flow chart shown in fig. 4.4., it is clear that after saving data of different registers, Acc. and Flag, FF H is stored both in Reg.D and B, then decrementing the content of Reg.B, its data has been examined for zero by a decision block. Considering the two probabilities viz. result ≠0 and =0, the microprocessor has been instructed for no operation twice in the former case and allowed to decrement data of Reg. B by 1 and continue the cycle of operation. If the content of Reg. B is zero, the content in Reg.D has been decremented by 1 and tested whether the content of Reg. D is zero or not. If the result be not equal to zero, the task of the microprocessor is to store FF H in Reg. B and follow the cycle of operation. In the other case i.e., when the content of Reg. D is zero, the data stored in the stack are to be returned to different Registers, Acc and Flag. Then the subroutine is completed by the RET statement. It may be noted here that the microprocessor is engaged in decrementing the content of Reg. B and D only and in doing so, some time is consumed, the time consumed being the time of delay in the main program. Changing the data FF H in Reg. B and D, the delay time be adjusted.

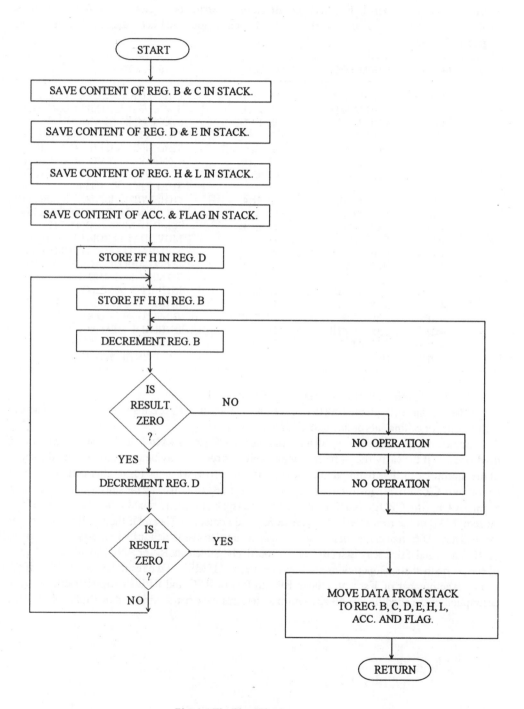

Fig. 4.4 The Flow Chart

Example 15. Two numbers $D_2D_1$ and $D'_2 D'_1$ are stored in Mem. Loc. $A_4A_3A_2A_1$ and Acc. respectively. Develop a software in order to store 00 H or 01 H or 10 H in mem. loc. 4321 according as $D_2D_1$ is equal to, less than or greater than $D'_2 D'_1$.

| MEM. LOC. | MNEMONICS | OPCODE | DESCRIPTION |
|---|---|---|---|
| 4500 | LXI  H  4321 | 21  21  43 | INITIALISE MEM. LOC. 4321 H. |
| 4503 | MVI  M $D_2D_1$ | 36. $D_2D_1$ | STORE $D_2D_1$ H IN MEM. LOC. 4321 H. |
| 4505 | MVI  A $D'_2D'_1$ | 3E $D'_2D'_1$ | STORE $D'_2D'_1$ IN ACC. |
| 4507 | MOV C, A | 4F | TRANSFER $D_2D_1$ FROM ACC. TO REG.C |
| 4508 | MOV B, M | 46 | TRANSFER (4321 H) TO REG.B |
| 4509 | CMP  B | B8 | COMPARE DATA OF REG.B WITH (ACC.). |
| 450A | JNZ  4515 | C2  15  45 | IF THE RESULT BE NON ZERO, JUMP TO THE MEM.LOC. 4515 H. |
| 450D | LXI  H  4321 | 21  21  43 | OTHERWISE,  INITIALISE MEM.LOC. 4321H. |
| 4510 | MVI  M  00 | 36  00 | STORE 00 H IN MEM. LOC. 4321 H |
| 4512 | JMP  4527 | C3  27  45 | JUMO TO MEM.LOC. 4527 H |
| 4515 | MOV A,C | 79 | MOVE DATA FROM REG.C TO ACC. |
| 4516 | SUB B | 90 | SUBTRACT (REG.B) FROM (ACC) |
| 4517 | JNC  4522 | D2  22  45 | IF NO CARRY FLAG BE AFFECTED, JUMP TO MEM. LOC. 4522 H |
| 451A | LXI  H  4321 | 21  21  43 | INITIALISE MEM. LOC. 4321 H |
| 451D | MVI  M  10 | 36  10 | STORE 10 H IN MEM. LOC. 4321 H |
| 451F | JMP  4527 | C3  27  45 | JUMP TO MEM. LOC. 4527 H |
| 4522 | LXI  H  4321 | 21  21  43 | INITILAISE MEM. LOC. 4321 H |
| 4525 | MVI  M  01 | 36  01 | STORE 01 H IN MEM.LOC. 4321 H |
| 4527 | HLT | 76 | HALT UNTIL INTERRUPT |

The corresponding flow chart has been presented in Fig. 4.5.

It has already been pointed out that for calling a subroutine, CALL instruction is used. There are different instructions for calling subroutine under different conditions.

Sometimes, it is required to call a subroutine if the Carry is set to 1. In that case, instruction CC may be used whereas if the carry flag is reset at zero, CNC instruction may be used followed by the starting address of the subroutine. If it is required to call different subroutines when the result after certain instruction be zero or non zero, CZ and CNZ instructions may be used obviously followed by the starting address of the subroutine. Similarly CP, CM, CPO and CPE are the instructions for calling conditional subroutine if the MSB of the result be zero, MSB of the result be 1, if the result has odd number of 1's and if the result has even number of 1's respectively. Different conditional return statement are also available for INTEL 8085 CPU. Instructions RC or RNC are used if the carry is set to 1 or 0 respectively. Statement RZ or RNZ should be applied if the results of certain mathematical operations are zero or nonzero. If MSB of the result be zero and 1 or if the result has odd or even number of 1's, instructions RP and RM or RPO and RPE should respectively be used. Brief description of the conditional call and return statements have been tabulated in Table 4.4 for convenience.

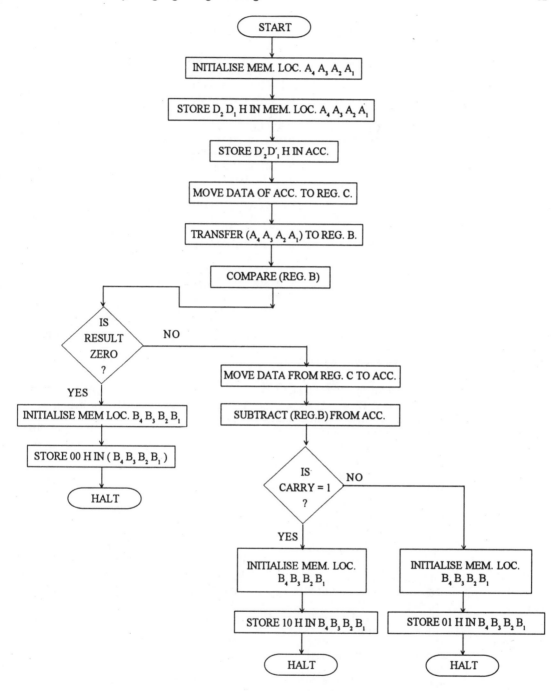

Fig. 4.5 Flow-Chart

Table 4.4. Conditional CALL and RETURN

| MNEMONICS | OPCODE | DESCRIPTION |
|---|---|---|
| CC    4253 H | DC 53 42 | IF CY = 1, CALL  SUBROUTINE AT 4253 H |
| CNC 4253 H | D4 53 42 | IF CY = 0, CALL SUBROUTINE AT 4253 H |
| CZ    4253 H | CC 53 42 | IF THE RESULT BE ZERO, CALL  SUBROUTINE AT 4253 H |
| CNZ 4253 H | C4 53 42 | IF RESULT BE NOT ZERO, CALL SUBROUTINE AT 4253 H |
| CP    4253 H | F4 53 42 | IF MSB OF THE RESULT IS ZERO, CALL SUBROUTINE AT 4253 H |
| CM   4253 H | FC 53 42 | IF MSB OF THE RESULT BE ONE, CALL SUBROUTINE AT 4253 H |
| CPO 4253 H | E4 53 42 | IF THE RESULT HAS ODD NUMBER OF 1'S CALL SUBROUTINE AT 4253 H |
| CPE  4253 H | EC 53 42 | IF THE RESULT HAS EVEN NUMBER OF 1'S CALL SUBROUTINE AT 4253 H |
| RC | D8 | IF CY = 1,RETURN |
| RNC | D0 | IF CY = 0,RETURN. |
| RZ | C8 | IF RESULT BE NONZERO,RETURN. |
| RNZ | C0 | IF RESULT BE ZERO,RETURN |
| RP | F0 | IF MSB OF RESULT BE ZERO, RETURN |
| RM | F8 | IF MSB OF RESULT BE ONE, RETURN. |
| RPO | E0 | IF THE RESULT HAS ODD NUMBER OF 1'S, RETURN |
| RPE | E8 | IF THE RESULT HAS EVEN NUMBER  OF 1'S, RETURN |

** Starting address of the subroutine has been assumed at 4253 H

EXAMPLE 16: Develop a program to store $00$ H, $01$ H and $10$ H in mem. loc. $A_4 A_3 A_2 A_1$ according as $D_2 D_1 = D_2' D_1'$, $D_2 D_1 < D_2' D_1'$ and $D_2 D_1 > D_2' D_1'$ using conditional CALL and RETURN instructions.

| LABEL | MEM. LOC. | MNEMONICS | OPCODE |
|---|---|---|---|
| | 4200 | MVI  A  $D_2 D_1$ | 3E  $D_2 D_1$ |
| | 4202 | MOV  B, A | 47 |
| | 4203 | MVI  C  $D_2' D_1'$ | 0E  $D_2' D_1'$ |
| | 4205 | CMP  C | B9 |
| | 4206 | JNZ    420D | C2  0D 42 |
| | 4209 | CZ    SUBR I | CC  00  41 |
| | 420C | HLT | 76 |
| | 420D | MOV  A, B | 78 |
| | 420E | SUB   C | 91 |
| | 420F | JC     4216 | DA 16 42 |
| | 4212 | CNC  SUBR III | D4  0C 41 |
| | 4215 | HALT | 76 |
| | 4216 | CALL SUBR II | CD 06 41 |
| | 4219 | HALT | 76 |
| SUBR I | 4100 | LXI   H  4500H | 21  00  45 |
| | 4103 | MVI  M  00H | 36  00 |
| | 4105 | RET | C9 |
| SUBR II | 4106 | LXI   H  4500H | 21  00  45 |
| | 4109 | MVI  M  01H | 36  01 |
| | 410B | RET | C9 |
| SUBR  III | 410C | LXI   H  4500H | 21  00  45 |
| | 410F | MVI  M  10H | 36  10 |
| | 4111 | RET | C9 |

The input/output interrupt and interrupt mask serial input/output instructions will be explained in chpater 8.

## 4.14  INSTRUCTION MODES

All the instructions described above may be classified into five different modes as:

| INSTRUCTION MODES | MNEMONICS |
|---|---|
| 1.  Direct addressing mode | LDA, STA |
| 2.  Inherent or register addressing mode. | MOV R, R;  ADD C |
| 3.  Index addressing or indirect addressing mode. | MOV R, M;  LDAX B,  LDAX D,  STAX D |
| 4.  Immediate addressing mode | LXI H,  MVI R,  ADI |
| 5.  Implicit addressing mode | CMA, RLC, RRC |

In data addressing mode, the address of the operand (data) is explicitly specified within the instruction itself. All such instructions are three byte long (e.g. LDA 85 40 or STA A2 41).

When the operands for any operation are in general purpose registers (B,C,D,E,H and L), only the registers be specified as the address of the operands. Such instructions are said to be the register addressing mode. These are single byte instructions.

In register indirect addressing mode, the contents of the specified registers are assumed to be the address of the operand. Here instead of specifying a register, a register-pair (B-C, D-E or H-L) is specified to contain the 16-bit address of the operand. For example,

| | |
|---|---|
| MOV A,M | Move content of memory location (whose address is in H-L pair) to Acc. |
| LDAX B/D | Load Acc. with the content of the memory location whose address is in the register pair (B-C or D-E) only. |
| STAX B/D | Store contents of Acc to the memory location whose address is in the register pair (B-C or D-E) only. |

In immediate addressing mode, the operand is specified within the instruction itself. Here one or two bytes within the instructions are used to specify the data itself. Examples are:

| | |
|---|---|
| LXI H 4080 | Load immediate the H-L pair with 4080 (here lower byte 80 is written first) |
| MVI A  05 | Move 05 immediate to Acc |
| ADI  02 | Add immediate 02 with (Acc). |

In implicit addressing mode, the instructions operate on the operand which is assumed to be in the accumulator. Hence the address of the operand need not be specified. Examples are :-

| | |
|---|---|
| CMA | Compliment the content of Acc. |
| RLC | Rotate the content of Acc left by one position. |
| RRC | Rotate the content of Acc right by one position. |

## 4.15  INSTRUCTION BYTES

Any instruction word of a computer has two parts, the OPCODE part and the ADDRESS part. Instruction in 8085 can be one, two or three byte long. The first byte always contains the operation code, also abbreviated as OPCODE, for the instruction. In case of multiple byte instructions, the address of the instruction always refers to the first byte. The other bytes may contain either data or address. When 16-bit address or data is used, the least significant part occupies the second byte and most significant half occupies the third byte of a three byte instruction.

EXAMPLES :

(i) *Single Byte Instructions*

| OPCODE | D7 | D6 | D5 | D4 | D3 | D2 | D1 | D0 | MNEMONICS |
|--------|----|----|----|----|----|----|----|----|-----------|
| 78 | 0 | 1 | 1 | 1 | 1 | 0 | 0 | 0 | MOV A,B |

Typical examples are PUSH, INR A, ADD B, RET etc.

(ii) *Two Byte Instructions*

| OPCODE | D7 | D6 | D5 | D4 | D3 | D2 | D1 | D0 | MNEMONICS |
|--------|----|----|----|----|----|----|----|----|-----------|
| 3E | 0 | 0 | 1 | 1 | 1 | 1 | 1 | 0 | MVI A |

| OPERAND | D7 | D6 | D5 | D4 | D3 | D2 | D1 | D0 | |
|---------|----|----|----|----|----|----|----|----|--|
| 01 | 0 | 0 | 0 | 0 | 0 | 0 | 0 | 1 | |

Typcial examples are ADI 05, SUBI 02, ACI EF, OUT 04, IN 02 etc.

(iii) *Three Byte Instructions*

| OPCODE | D7 | D6 | D5 | D4 | D3 | D2 | D1 | D0 | MNEMONICS |
|--------|----|----|----|----|----|----|----|----|-----------|
| 21 | 0 | 0 | 1 | 0 | 0 | 0 | 0 | 1 | LXI H |

| LOWER ADDR OR OPERAND 1 | D7 | D6 | D5 | D4 | D3 | D2 | D1 | D0 | |
|---------|----|----|----|----|----|----|----|----|--|
| 80 | 1 | 0 | 0 | 0 | 0 | 0 | 0 | 0 | 80 |

| HIGHER ADDR OR OPERAND 2 | D7 | D6 | D5 | D4 | D3 | D2 | D1 | D0 | |
|---------|----|----|----|----|----|----|----|----|--|
| 40 | 0 | 1 | 0 | 0 | 0 | 0 | 0 | 0 | 40 |

Typical examples are LXI SP 47FF, JZ 4080, JMP 4085, CALL 4255 etc. Some more illustrations on software development have been added in Chapter 11.

# 5. Memories

There are a large variety of memory devices like memory chip, floppy disc, magnetic tape, optical disc and tape, paper tape, punch cards etc. But for a microprocessor system, only the memory chips and floppy discs are popular, though costlier, reasons being their compactness in size, high storage capacity, speed in operation, simplicity in interfacing and reliability in performance.

The memory of a microcomputer is the space where program and data are stored before execution and computation. During execution, the control section may store temporary information if there be any, in the memory, which is the most effective part of a computer and it is equivalent to thousands of registers.

Memory may be of two kinds—semiconductor and the magnetic. The semiconductor memory is faster, economical, smaller in size and lighter. It consumes comparatively less power. The latest generation of computers uses semiconductor memories. A typical microcomputer has a semiconductor memories of upto 65536 memory locations each capable of storing one byte of informations. But the memory size cannot be limited to 65536 bytes since more expansion facilities are available.

Magnetic memories, though cheaper, are slower as compared to semiconductor memories and used as the secondary memories of a computer for bulk storage of data and information.

It may be mentioned here that any operation such as punching, converting etc. which does not involve the main computer, is the off-line mode of operation in which the peripheral equipments are not under the control of CPU. Card-to-tape conversion using auxiliary equipment and similar other processing which take place independently of the CPU are the off-line processing. Similarly, a storage device not under control of CPU is the off-line storage.

The computer operation in which input data are fed to the computer directly from observing Instruments or other input equipments and this computational results are obtained during the progress of the event, is the on-line operation. In on-line storage, the storage is controlled by the CPU of the computer. A magnetic disc directly connected with CPU, thereby increasing the memory capacity of the computer, is called on-line disc file.

## 5.1 SEMICONDUCTOR MEMORIES

These memories can be divided into two main categories : volatile and non-volatile. Volatile memories retain their data only as long as power remains on whereas a non-volatile memory retains its data even after the withdrawal of power.

### 5.1.1 RAM (RANDOM ACCESS OR READ/WRITE MEMORY)

There are two important types of memories — RAM and ROM. RAM is the Random Access Memory or Read/Write memory and the ROM, the Read Only Memory. These memories can again be subdivided into different types. Volatile RAM losses its memory when the power is turned off. Hence battery back up is necessary to retain the informations stored in RAM. There are again two types of RAMs —Static and Dynamic. Static RAM remains active so long the power is on. But a dynamic RAM losses its contents in a very short time even if the power is on. Their memory cells are basically charge storage capacitors with driver transistors. The presence or absence of charge in capacitor is interpreted by the RAM's sense line as a logical 1 or 0. The natural tendency of the charge is to distribute itself into a lower energy state configuration. However, dynamic RAM requires periodic charge refreshing to maintain data storage. Thus it becomes essential to implement added circuitry to refresh dynamic RAM. Generally dynamic RAM has to be periodically refreshed after every 2 milliseconds. The refreshing procedure may sometimes make the RAM unavailable for writing and reading. The integrated RAM or iRAM has removed this disadvantages providing all of the complex refresh circuitry on chip simplifying the system design involving small memories in microprocessor. For large storage requirement, LSI dynamic memory controllers reduce the refresh requirement to a minimum by offering a monolithic controller solution. However dynamic RAM is preferred for large size of memory. For medium size of memory, Static RAM proves to be the best.

The static RAM stores logical 0 and 1 using traditional filp-flop logic gate configuration. It is faster requiring no refreshing circuitry. After addressing a static RAM, the logical bits are stored in the memory with a very brief delay.

**iRAM**: iRAM is an integrated RAM. It possesses the design simplicity of static RAM and higher capacity and other advantages of a dynamic RAM. The iRAM chip looks like a static RAM but it has dynamic RAM density characteristics. iRAM requires no refreshing circuitry.

### 5.1.2 ROM (READ ONLY MEMORY)
ROM is similar to RAM in that a Computer addresses it and then retrieves data stored at that address. ROM includes no mechanism for altering the data stored at that address, hence the name Read only memory. The contents of ROM are stored permanently by the manufacturers. The user can not write into a ROM or change the content of ROM. Hence ROM is the program storage and RAM, the data storage.

For storing users' program permanently, another type of ROM, Called PROM is available. PROM is programmable ROM. Its contents are the users' permanent programs. The program can be stored in PROM by the user utilising PROM programmer. Read only type of memories may also be of some other types viz. EPROM (erasable PROM), EEPROM (Electrically Erasable PROM) etc. EPROM is erasable by ultraviolet light and hence it is not suitable for on board programming and erasing. But it is cheaper and equally suitable for applications where alteration of the program is less frequent. 2716 of 2 K byte, 2764 of 8K byte, 27256 of 32K byte etc. are some examples of popular EPROM.

EEPROM (occasionally Known as E$^2$PROM) is electrically erasable and hence inherently possesses the on-board programming and erasing facilities. Moreover, the programming and erasing time is typically 10 ms, whereas 50 ms is required to program a byte in EPROM. Besides, a single byte of data may be altered or erased in EEPROM but in EPROM, all the locations in the chip are erased at a time. Hence EEPROM is referred in the applications where the permanent programs are frequently needed to be updated on board. However, there exists another type of electrically erasable PROM called Flash memory introduced by Intel Which is 'all-bit' erasable at a time.

### 5.2 NON-VOLATILE RAM
A non-volatile RAM is actually a combination of a static RAM and EEPROM into a single chip. Its operation is similar to a RAM. When power is off, the contents of RAM are transferred to EEPROM by a signal STORE. Another signal RECALL transfers data from EEPROM back into the RAM. X2201 is a non-volatile RAM containing 1K-byte RAM and 1K-byte EEPROM, the time of transfer from RAM to EEPROM and Vice-Versa is only 4 milli seconds. Intel 2004 is also a non-volatile RAM of storage capacity 512 x 8- bits, time of transfer being 10 milliseconds. A list of commonly used memory chips with the memory size in the parenthesis have been shown in Table 5.1.

**Table 5.1 List of Memory Chips**

| STATIC RAM | DYNAMIC RAM | EPROM | EEPROM | FLASH MEMORY | BUBBLE MEMORY |
|---|---|---|---|---|---|
| 6116  (2k)<br>6264  (8k)<br>34256 (32k) | 2118<br>2164 | 2716  (2k)<br>2732  (4k)<br>2764  (8k)<br>27256(32k) | 2815  (2k)<br>2816  (2k)<br>2817  (2k) | 2816  (2k)<br>27F64 (8k)<br>28F256(32k) | 7110<br>7114<br>7230<br>7242 |

## 5.3 PIN CONFIGURATION OF RAM, EPROM AND EEPROM

Pin configuration of a typical RAM (2116), EPROM (2716) and EEPROM (2816) each having a storage capacity of 2k-bytes is shown in Fig. 5.1. Intel 2716 is a 16,384 -bit ultraviolet erasable and electrically programmable read only memory (EPROM). It operates from a +5 V power supply, has a static standby mode and possesses the features of fast single address programming. It is fast in action, simple and economical. For its standby mode, power consumption is reduced without increasing access time.

Intel 2816 is a 16,384-bit electrically erasable, programmable read only memory (EEPROM). It can be easily erased and programmed on byte basis. A chip-erase function is also provided. Its operating voltage is +5V in the read mode, writing and erasing being accomplished by providing 21 V supply. 2816 has very fast access speed and it is compatible with high performance microprocessors. Its high access speed allows practically zero wait operation in large system configuration. Electrically erase and write capability make 2816 ideal for a wide variety of applications. Any byte of 2816 can be erased or written in 10 milli-seconds without affecting the data in any other byte.

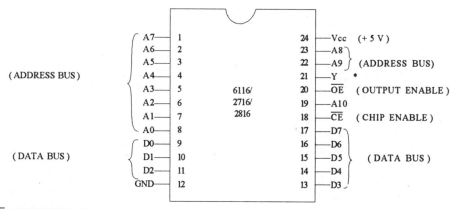

\* WE, WRITE ENABLE FOR 6116,
 Vpp, PROGRAMMING SUPPLY FOR 2716 AND 2816.

Fig. 5.1. Pin configuration of RAM 6116, EPROM 2716 and EEPROM 2816

Considering that a small system decodes its A15, A14, A13 bits for chip - select purpose, each one of the decoded lines is capable of addressing 8192 or 8k locations of memory. If the decoded lines corresponding to A15 = 1, A14 = 0 and A13 = 0 be connected to the $\overline{CE}$ of a 6116 RAM of 2K locations, these locations of 6116 may be addressed by 8000 to 87FF or 8800 to 8FFF or 9000 to 97FF etc. Since A11 and A12 are not used, the non - uniqueness of the address results in. It may be noted that the decoded line must be active low. $\overline{RD}$ may be connected to $\overline{OE}$ and $\overline{WR}$ may be connected to $\overline{WE}$ along with the connections of respective address and data buses.

Intel 2186 (Fig. 5.2) is a 8192 word by 8-bit-integrated RAM (iRAM). Integrated refresh control provides static RAM characteristics at a low cost. It is fully compatible with EPROM and static RAM. It is particularly suitable for microprocessor application.

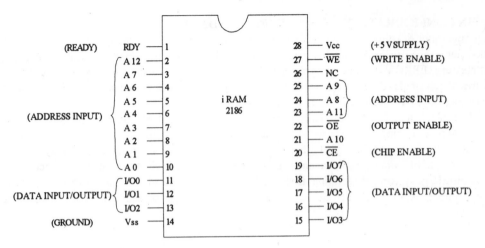

Fig. 5.2. Pin configuration of iRAM 2186

## 5.4 DYNAMIC RAM

Pin configuration of 2118, dynamic RAM introduced by Intel is shown in Fig. 5.3. Intel 2118 (Fig. 5.3), a 16,384 word by 1-bit dynamic MOS RAM, works on + 5V supply. It has high storage density, high reliability and capability of high performance. It uses a single transistor dynamic storage cell and advanced circuitry for high speed with low power dissipation. Multiplexing the 14 address bits into 7 address input pins converts 2118 to a industry standard 16-Pin DIP. The two 7-bit address words are latched into the 2118 by two TTL clocks, ROM address strobe ($\overline{RAS}$) and column address strobe ($\overline{CAS}$). The three state output is controlled by $\overline{CAS}$. After Read–Modify–Write cycle, data is latched on the output by holding $\overline{CAS}$ low. The data out pin is returned to the high impedence state by returning $\overline{CAS}$ to a high state. The hidden refresh feature allows $\overline{CAS}$ to be in low state to maintain latched data while $\overline{RAS}$ is used to execute $\overline{RAS}$–only refresh cycles. The single transistor storage cell requires refreshing for data retention which is performed by $\overline{RAS}$– only refresh cycles, hidden refresh cycles or normal read or write cycles on the 128 address combinations of A0 through A6 during 2-milliseconds time. A write cycle refreshes stored data on all bits of the selected row except the bit which is addressed.

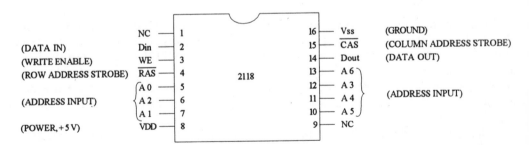

Fig. 5.3 Pin configuration of INTEL 2118

The 2164 A (Fig. 5.4) is another dynamic RAM presented by intel and it is a 65,536 word by 1-bit N channel MOS dynamic RAM suitable for high system performance and reliability. It is widely used as mainframe memory, buffer memory, microprocessor memory, peripheral storage and graphic terminals. Multiplexing the 16 address bits into 8 address input pins makes 2164 A to achieve high packing density. The 16 Pin DIP provides for high system bit densities. Two 8-bit TTL level address segments are latched into 2164A by two TTL clocks, $\overline{RAS}$

and $\overline{CAS}$. The three state TTL compatible data output is controlled by $\overline{CAS}$. After Read-modify-write cycle, data is held on the data output pin by holding $\overline{CAS}$ low. The data output is returned to a high impedence state by returning $\overline{CAS}$ high. Hidden refresh capability allows the device to maintain data at the output by holding $\overline{CAS}$ low and $\overline{RAS}$ is used to execute $\overline{RAS}$–only refresh cycles. Refreshing is accomplished by $\overline{RAS}$–only cycles, hidden refresh cycles or normal read or write cycles on the 128 combinations of addresses A0 through A6 during 2 – milliseconds time.

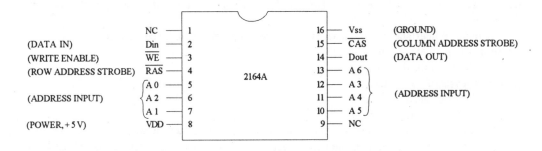

Fig. 5.4 Pin configuration of DYNAMIC RAM 2164A

## 5.5 MEMORY MAP

Memory maps are lists of memory assignment made in the design. Memory mapping prevents interference between different routines from one another, helps in determining the numbers of memory needed, simplifies the process of data handling and helps in finding tables, temporary storage and subroutines. Understanding of the Memory Map is important in software development.

The allocation of addresses to memory chip and I/O devices depends on the architecture of the particular microprocessor. In some microprocessors, there exists only one address space treating I/O devices as memory locations. In some others, two different address spaces are provided, one for the memory and other for the I/O devices and their sizes are different. Thus there exists two different methods of mapping memory addresses into I/O devices - (1) the memory mapped I/O scheme and the I/O mapped I/O scheme. These schemes are discussed in Chapter 6.

# 6. Interfacing the Microprocessors

Interfacing is one of the most important features in designing and understanding a microprocessor based system. Indeed, the interfacing circuitry shapes the overall performances of the microprocessor systems. An introductory feature of the practical and simple interfacing techniques in connection with an 8085 CPU has been shown in chapter 3.

In order to interface any two devices, the following points are to be considered :

(a) Speed of operations of the devices,

(b) Logic levels of the devices,

(c) Power levels of the devices,

(d) Data forms of the devices and

(e) Control bus functions of the devices.

The differences present with reference to the above mentioned facts between the two devices are adjusted by the interfacing circuitry. For example, if it be required to interface an I/O device whose logic level is 0-50V with a microprocessor, it requires to connect the same through a level shifter which shifts 0-5 V microprocessor level to 0-50V or vice-versa. If this particular I/O device accepts a serial form of data, the interfacing circuitry must include the circuitry for 'parallel - in' and 'serial - out' operations. Again, if this device be a slower one, it may be required to connect and operate the same via interrupt lines of the microprocessor.

## 6.1 SPEED

There may be two modes of operation of the interfacing device-Synchronous and Asynchronous. If the speeds of two interfacing devices are compatible, the synchronous operations between them are always possible. This operation inherently gains the highest speed. Incompatibility in speed demands synchronous operation between two devices. Hence the timing parameters are important for interfacing as well as trouble shooting of microprocessors.

In this chapter, the timing parameters have been discussed separately in details.

The synchronous operation is performed by direct addressing the interfacing devices using control lines like $\overline{RD}$, $\overline{WR}$, ALE, IO/$\overline{M}$ etc. The interfaced devices are selected and commanded to read or write operations. In this case, the interfacing circuitry is simple. Normally, the memory chips, I/O ports, A/D, D/A etc. are interfaced in this manner.

Generally, the slower devices are interfaced to operate in asynchronous mode in two different ways, viz, by handshaking and by polling. Handshaking is a hardware based approach where one device addresses the other one and waits till the other one responds giving out the respective acknowledge signal. The slower devices like printer, recorder etc. are generally operated in this way.

'Polling' is a software based approach to asynchronous operation of any slower device. Normally, the microprocessor or the CPU checks continuously whether a particular signal is asserted, when it takes the necessary decisions. Thus the CPU looses its valuable time though the polling techniques may drastically reduce and simplify the interfacing circuitries. A hardware approach to polling may also be performed where the interfacing circuitry checks the signal continuouly and when the respective signal occurs, the interfacing circuit communicates with the microprocessor through the interrupt line. In this method, the CPU may reduce the loss of time inherent in software polling.

## 6.2 LEVEL

In many practical systems, it is seen that there is difference in the logic levels between the microprocessor and its interfacing devices. This problem is solved by the level-shifter. A level-shifter is a voltage/current amplifier or attenuator which converts one level to a desired one. These types of voltage / current shifters are also used to eliminate the power differences between the devices. A current amplifier of this type is generally known as a buffer. To interface a floppy disc, a printer, a recorder or a relay etc., the use of shifters becomes necessary.

## 6.3 DATA FORM

Different devices may be made active through different formats of data. For example, a magnetic tape, a floppy or a printer communicates through serial data link while a memory chip, analog-to-digital or digital-to-analog converter accepts parallel form of data. The serial and parallel data may be of various forms. Hence interfacing circuitry becomes necessary to convert analog singal to microprocessor compatible digital signal to be used by the interfaced devices. Always the CPU or the microprocessor may take part in this conversion through its software resulting in a reduction and simplicity of the interfacing circuitries although requiring some CPU time. The different forms of data will be discussed in chapter 7.

## 6.4 CONTROL BUS FUNCTION

Sometimes there may be a difference in the functions of the available control lines of the microprocessor and its interfacing devices. These differences are eliminated out or the problems due to these differences are solved by the interfacing circuits. A latch is such an interfacing circuit. A latch is a temporary storage device suitable for storing binary information between a processor and input-output devices. A latch is a flip-flop having two stable states. It remains in one of these states until triggered into the other.

The latch may be of different types. IC 7475 and 74LS375 are 4-bit (quad) bistable latches, 5477 is a 4-bit latch, 74100 and 74166 are 8-bit bistable and dual 4-bit latches whereas 74259 and 74779 are 8-bit addressable and quad S-R latches respectively.

An n-bit latch is a parallel combination of n-number of flip-flops that stores a binary word of n-bit length. The n-bit binary word is transferred to the latch in parallel simultaneously. It may be clocked or unclocked.

Computers use thousands of flip-flops and for co-ordination of over all action, a square wave signal, called the 'clock' is sent to each flip-flop. This signal prevents the flip-flops from changing the containing state until the required time is consumed. In microcomputers, an output port operates differently from imput port because, the output data must be held for the peripherals.

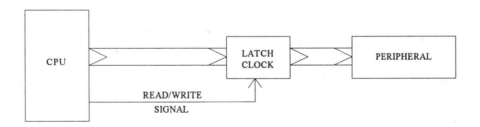

Fig. 6.1. A single output port

All CPU operations send data to the same port, since there are no address connections. In a single output port (fig. 6.1), a READ/WRITE signal latches the data. The data outputs remain the same as the inputs when the clock is active. When the clock is inactive, the outputs retain the values already stored in them. The data must remain stable for minimum intervals before and after the clock transition. The latch must be activated on the proper transition of the READ/WRITE signal. Several peripherals may be handled by the port having the same word length as the CPU. If there be more than one peripherals (Fig. 6.2), the data intended for peripheral 1 is placed in the two least significant bits and so on. The same signal latches all the data.

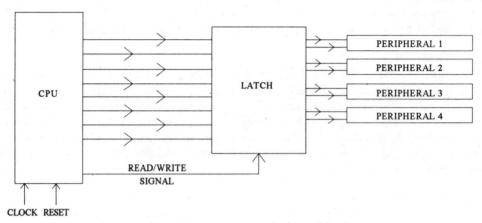

Fig. 6.2. Output port connected to four peripherals

In a processor, having more than one I/O units, busing structure combined with memory sections is necessary. The input busing structure must allow the address input port to control the data bus without interfacing whereas, the output busing structure must latch the contents of the data bus into the address output port. In fig. 6.3, a tristate input busing structure using control signals to enable the ports has been shown. In fig. 6.4 an output busing struture has been shown that uses control signal to clock latches.

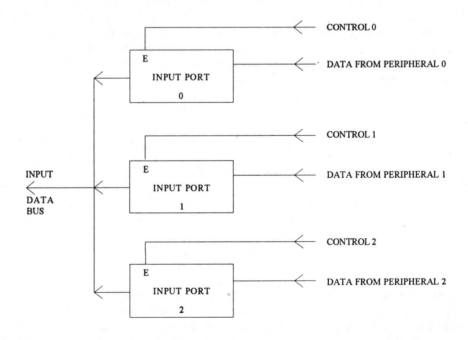

Fig. 6.3. Input busing structure

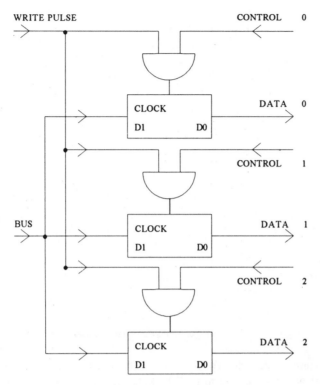

Fig. 6.4. Output busing structure

The 7475 is a 4-bit bi-stable latch used as temporary storage for binary information between processor and I/O or indicator unit. The pin configuration of 7475 is given in fig 6.5 where information present in data input is transferred to output when the Enable is high and the output is followed by the input till the Enable remains

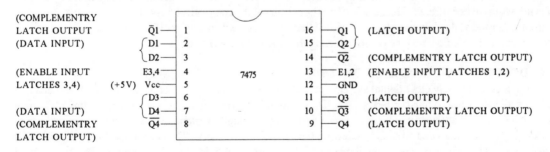

Fig. 6.5. Pin configuration of 7475

high. When the Enable goes low, the former data input is retained at output until again the enable is made high. Chip 7475 has no chip select input and possesses only the latch inputs. Hence it is required to decode the chip select line with the $\overline{WR}$ line and then to feed the resulting control pulse to the latch inputs. Though the procedure is simple, many complications may arise in practical cases due to the incompatibility of the functions of the control lines of the microprocessors and its interfacing devices. To solve these problems, there are a number of standard bus schemes for interfacing like GPIB, RS-232. Discussions of standard interfaces have been made in following few chapters.

## 6.5 BUS-DEMULTIPLEXING

To interface a device, one of the most important requirements is to make the address, data and control bus ready to be used. Sometimes, it is seen that more than one lines of the same bus or different buses are multiplexed in a time-sharing mode when it is necessary to demultiplex them for making ready to be used. As for example, the lower half of the address bus of the 8085 CPU is multiplexed with the data bus and in order to demultiplex them, a control line ALE is available. An actual latch may be used to demultiplex the lower half of the address from the data lines utilising the scheme shown in Fig. 6.6.

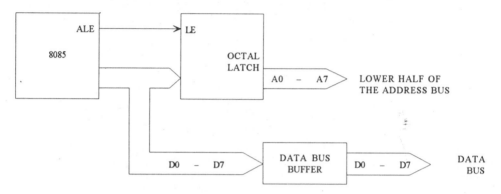

Fig. 6.6. Demultiplexing of address from the DATA BUS for 8085

In this case, the common data address bus is connected to the data inputs of an octal latch while the ALE (Address Latch Enable) line is connected to the LE (Latch Enable) of the latch where outputs give the demultiplexed lower half of the address.

From the timing diagram of 8085, it is apparent that when the address is present in the common data bus, no control signal except the ALE is asserted and when a control signal like $\overline{RD}$ or $\overline{WR}$ is asserted, the data bus always contains the data only. Hence, the common data and address bus may effectively be considered as the data bus. Moreover, since the data bus may be required to be connected to a large number of interfacing devices, it is necessary to be buffered. Hence, a buffer is connected to the common address and data bus and the buffer outputs are used as the data bus. It may be noted that the associated data bus buffer must be bi-directional and the direction of data flow may be controled using the $\overline{WR}$ and /or $\overline{RD}$ lines.

## 6.6. DECODER AND ADDRESS DECODING

Microprocessor like any other digital system accepts only the logical 0 and 1 for its operation. But it is not at all convenient to work on binaries by the user. Thus a suitable interfacing device is necessary to convert decimal and alphabetical characters into binary forms required by the digital system. The encoding is the process of generating binary codes and an encoder executes the conversion to binary. The decoding is the reverse process of encoding. The different decoders available are IC 7441, 7441, 7445, 7445, 74445 which are BCD to Decimal decoders whereas IC 7446, 7447, 7448, 7449, 74246, 74247, 74248, 74249 are BCD to 7 segment decoders. IC 74147 is a decimal to BCD encoder and 74148 and 74348 are octal to binary encoders.

Decoder is used for expansion of systems, memory components and selection of chips. The chip selection is made by decoding the address bus. Generally some of the bits of of the address bus are decoded and the decoded outputs along with the control lines like IO/$\overline{M}$, $\overline{RD}$ or $\overline{WR}$ etc. are used to select chip. For the devices like memory chips, the higher bits of address bus are decoded while for the devices like I/O ports, the lower bits are decoded. In fig 6.7, the higher four bits of the address bus A15 to A12 are decoded into sixteen outputs S0 to S15, the Hex members in the parenthesis being the respective address of the decoded lines.

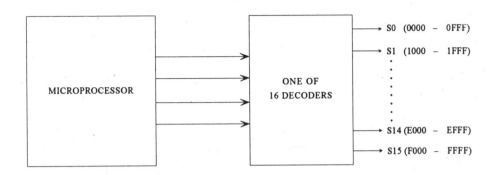

Fig. 6.7. Address decoding of microprocessor

Now, if a memory chip be enabled or selected, say, by S1, the addresses of the memory locations are from 1000 to 1FFF whereas if the I/O port be connected to S1, any address between 1000 to 1FFF will select the respective I/O port. In the first case, the address of each individual memory location may be unique whereas in the second case, the adress of the I/O port is non-unique. Further, in the first case too, if the number of memory locations is less than 0FFF H (or 4K' byte), the address of each individual memory location is nonunique.

However in simple small low cost systems, the address bus is directly used as the chip-selection line. This method of chip selection is known as linear selection technique. Though it is simple requiring no other circuitries for decoding or chip selection, it is inherently associated with a lot of problems.

However, the decoded outputs are often 'AND'ed with the $\overline{RD}$, $\overline{WR}$, $\overline{MRQ}$ or $\overline{IORQ}$ signals to obtain the actual chip-selection signals. Otherwise, the operations of memories may be disturbed by the I/O mapped I/O ports.

Intel 8205 is a high speed 1 out of a 8 binary decoder. It can be used for expansion of systems utilising I/O ports and memory components. It has active low chip select input. The pin configuration of IC 8205 is shown in fig 6.8 and the truth table for gate enable has been given in the table 6.1.

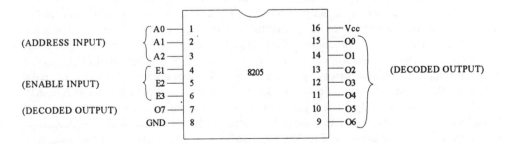

Fig. 6.8. Pin configuration of INTEL 8205 decoder

Table 6.1. Truth Table

| ADDRESS | | | ENABLE | | | OUTPUTS | | | | | | | |
|---|---|---|---|---|---|---|---|---|---|---|---|---|---|
| A0 | A1 | A2 | E1 | E2 | E3 | O0 | O1 | O2 | O3 | O4 | O5 | O6 | O7 |
| 0 | 0 | 0 | 0 | 0 | 1 | 0 | 1 | 1 | 1 | 1 | 1 | 1 | 1 |
| 1 | 0 | 0 | 0 | 0 | 1 | 1 | 0 | 1 | 1 | 1 | 1 | 1 | 1 |
| 0 | 1 | 0 | 0 | 0 | 1 | 1 | 1 | 0 | 1 | 1 | 1 | 1 | 1 |
| 1 | 1 | 0 | 0 | 0 | 1 | 1 | 1 | 1 | 0 | 1 | 1 | 1 | 1 |
| 0 | 0 | 1 | 0 | 0 | 1 | 1 | 1 | 1 | 1 | 0 | 1 | 1 | 1 |
| 1 | 0 | 1 | 0 | 0 | 1 | 1 | 1 | 1 | 1 | 1 | 0 | 1 | 1 |
| 0 | 1 | 1 | 0 | 0 | 1 | 1 | 1 | 1 | 1 | 1 | 1 | 0 | 1 |
| 1 | 1 | 1 | 0 | 0 | 1 | 1 | 1 | 1 | 1 | 1 | 1 | 1 | 0 |
| x | x | x | 0 | 0 | 0 | 1 | 1 | 1 | 1 | 1 | 1 | 1 | 1 |
| x | x | x | 1 | 0 | 0 | 1 | 1 | 1 | 1 | 1 | 1 | 1 | 1 |
| x | x | x | 0 | 1 | 0 | 1 | 1 | 1 | 1 | 1 | 1 | 1 | 1 |
| x | x | x | 1 | 1 | 0 | 1 | 1 | 1 | 1 | 1 | 1 | 1 | 1 |
| x | x | x | 1 | 0 | 1 | 1 | 1 | 1 | 1 | 1 | 1 | 1 | 1 |
| x | x | x | 0 | 1 | 1 | 1 | 1 | 1 | 1 | 1 | 1 | 1 | 1 |
| x | x | x | 1 | 1 | 1 | 1 | 1 | 1 | 1 | 1 | 1 | 1 | 1 |

The 8205 decoder is a standard 16-pin dual-in-line package having three enable inputs, three address inputs and eight decoded outputs. It accepts three-bit binary input and creates exclusive output. The three Enable inputs make system expansion easy. When 8205 is enabled, one of the eight outputs goes low and a single row of memory system is selected. One decoder can drive eight decoders for arbitrary memory expansion and thus large system can be used by cascading 8205. From the truth table, it is clear that, for an input '1 0 1', output pin O5 remains low, keeping all other output pins high.

The 8205 decoder is versatile in application with microprocessor system. The major functions are :

1. Decoding of I/O ports from the address bus.
2. Generation of chip select signals to select memory device.
3. Selection of machine state
4. Interfacing maximum of 24K memories with microprocessor

In 8085 based microcomputer, each memory or I/O chip is enabled by a signal coming from the 8205 address decoder. An array of 82055 can be used to create a simple interface to 24K memory system. The memory devices may be ROM or RAM having 1K storage capacity. 8308 and 8102 are the devices typically used for this application. This type of memory device has ten address inputs and an active-low chip select (CS). The lower address bits A0 to A9 come from the microprocessor and they are bussed to all memory elements. Chip select to enable a specific device or groups of devices comes from the array of 82055. The output of 8205 is active low so that it is directly compatible with the memory components. The CPU issues an address to identify a specific memory location where the 'Write' or 'Read' of data is required. The most significant address bits A10-A14 are decoded by 8205. An active low chip select is generated to enable a specific memory device. The least significant address bits A0-A9 identify a specific location within the selected device. Thus all address throughout the entire memory array are exclusive in nature. 32K Memory Interface using 8205 has been shown in fig. 6.9.

In 8085, each memory and I/O chip is generally enabled by a signal coming from 8205 address decoder. Different chip enable outputs and the corresponding address space over which it is active along with the selected device have been shown in Table 6.2.

### Table 6.2  Decoder 8205 chip enables

| CHIP SELECT OUTPUT | MEMORY ADDRESS SPACE | SELECT DEVICE |
|---|---|---|
| CS0 | 0000-07FF | 8755/8355  MONITOR ROM ( 2K) |
| CS1 | 0800-0FFF | 8755/8355  EXPANSION ROM  (2K) |
| CS2 | 1000-17FF | 6116/RAM  (2K) |
| CS3 | 1800-1FFF | 3279 (KEY BOARD/DISPLAY CTRL  (2K) |
| CS4 | 2000-27FF | BASIC RAM  (2K) |
| CS5 | 2800-2FFF | Expansion RAM (2K) |
| CS6 | 3000-37FF | Expansion RAM (2K) |
| CS7 | 3800-3FFF | Expansion RAM (2K) |

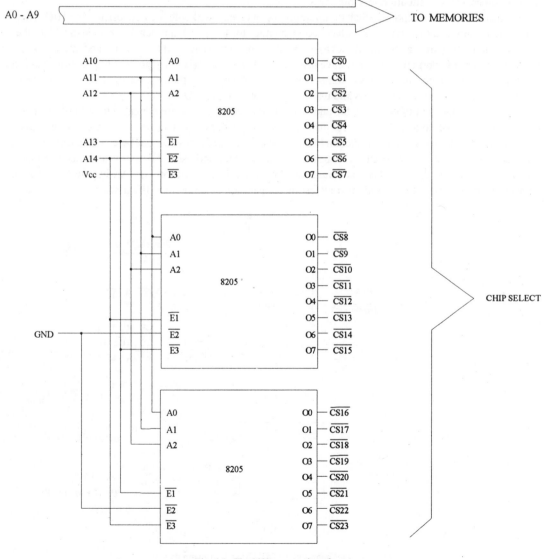

Fig. 6.9.  The 32K memory interface

## 6.7 MAPPING

The microprocessor may treat the I/O ports in two ways—(1) as the normal I/O ports and (2) as a memory location. When the microprocessor uses the I/O ports as normal I/O ports, the respective I/O ports are called normal I/O ports. But when an I/O port is used as a memory location, the respective I/O port is called a Memory Mapped I/O port. In case of a normal I/O port, the instructions like IN or OUT etc. are useful whereas in case of a memory mapped I/O port, these instructions have no meaning at all. Since the memory mapped I/O ports are effectively memory locations to the microprocessors, the data is taken in or given out from or to the I/O port exactly as loading or storing data from or to a memory location. The mapping of I/O ports are practically performed by interfacing techniques. In case of a normal I/O port, the chip selection line is ANDed with the IOR (I/O Request) signal whereas it is ANDed with the MR (Memory Request) signal for a memory mapped I/O port. The memory mapping of I/O ports are used to reduce and simplify the decoding or interfacing circuitries in small expensive system. This becomes a forced situation in some cases.

It has already been mentioned that, the microprocessors are of two kinds-memory oriented and I/O oriented. The memory oriented microprocessors have no read entity for I/O ports and they have no instruction like IN or OUT. Hence they treat all the interfaces as the memory locations only. But the I/O oriented microprocessors have the normal I/O port facility. They have instructions like IN or OUT, they possess the control signals like IOR or MR or IO/$\overline{\text{M}}$ etc. and they may address memory or I/O explicitly though even in these microprocessors, it is possible to ignore the I/O signals and use only memory mapped I/O.

In memory mapped I/O scheme, the addresses in one address space are allocated to both of the memory chips and I/O devices and all data transfer instructions of the processor can be used for transferring data from I/O devices and Vice-versa. The instruction MOV C, M in Intel 8085, transfers one byte of data from a memory location of an input device to register C depending on whether the address in HL pair is assigned to a memory location or to an input device. This is advantageous from the view point of software development since all data transfer instructions can be utilised for transferring data between memory and I/O devices.

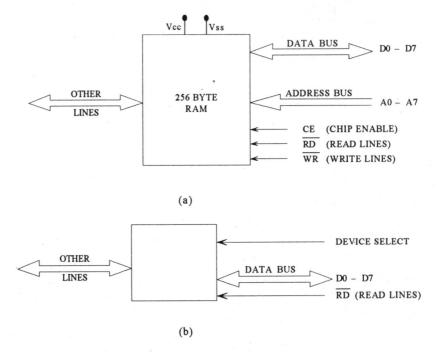

(a)

(b)

Fig. 6.10. (a) Organisation of a RAM and (b) an input device

In a microprocessor provided with 16-bit parallel address and 8-bit parallel data transfer, the address space is 64 KB wide. If it is required to interface two RAM chips of 256 bytes each (Fig. 6.10a) with two input devices (fig. 6.10b), the address space can be partitioned in several ways. For selecting one out of 512 bytes, 9-bits are required and from these 9-bits, one bit may be used for selecting one of the two chips, other 8 bits being kept aside for selecting one of 256 bytes. Also two bits are required for selecting one of the two input devices. The address assignment format may be of the form:

| 15 | 14 | 13 | 12 | 11 | 10 | 9 | 8 | 7 | 6 | 5 | 4 | 3 | 2 | 1 | 0 |
|----|----|----|----|----|----|----|----|----|----|----|----|----|----|----|----|
| I1 | I2 | X | X | X | X | X | C | M | M | M | M | M | M | M | M |

where M and C stand for memory and chip selection, I stands for input device and x stands for unused bit position.

Assuming tri-state operation of memories and input device, if the data and address buses of the processor be connected to those of memory and input devices, the device selection signals for memory and I/O device may be generated as shown in Fig. 6.11 (a).

It may be noted here that, the use of unutilised address bits can not increase the memory capacity beyond 16 K in the above mentioned scheme. Thus this scheme is suitable for small systems only.

Through I/O mapped I/O scheme, memory capacity may be improved.

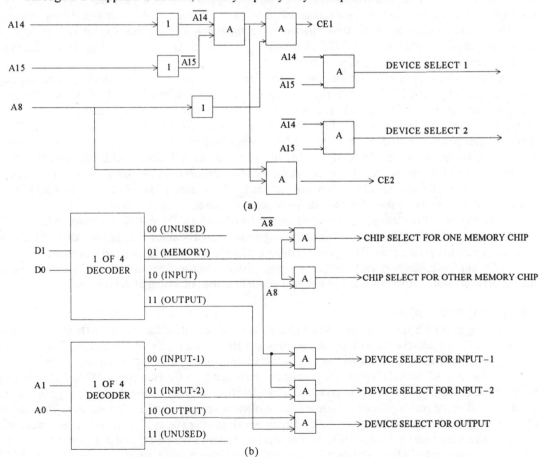

(a)

(b)

Fig. 6.11. (a) Generation of chip select signal and (b) Generation of Chip and I/O Device select signal

Through the scheme shown in Fig. 6.11 (b), 512 bytes of RAM (Fig. 6.10a), two input (6.10b) and one output devices may be interfaced to a Microprocessor. It is assumed that the microprocessor provides a 2-bit code to indicate an I/O operation. The memory can be assigned by the first 512 address in the memory address space, the input device by addresses 0 and 1 and the output device by address 2. It may be noted that address 0, 1 and 2 are overlapping with the memory address. It is further assumed in the scheme that code of 01, 10 and 11 are sent out for addressing memory, input and output devices respectively. Now if IO/$\overline{\text{M}}$ signal sent by the processor designates I/O device and memory device when high and low respectively, D1 -D0 decoder will not be required. In this scheme, the processor need not provide two separate signals to distinguish between input and output devices. In Intel 8085, the processor provides an IO/$\overline{\text{M}}$ signal for enabling I/O or memory devices. For an I/O device, the address is duplicated on A8 - A15 and AD0 - AD7. Any of these 8-bit addresses may be used as an address space for input and output devices. Thus a total of 256 input and 256 output devices can be addressed by 8085. The selection between an input and an output devices having the same address must be done using $\overline{\text{RD}}$ or $\overline{\text{WR}}$ signals.

Thus it is evident that for a small system, memory mapped I/O is sufficient but for a larger system, I/O mapped I/O is preferable.

## 6.8 TIMING PARAMETERS

One of the most important and critical objects for interfacing problems of a microprocessor is the timing relationship. If two devices are not speed compatible, they may, sometimes, work correctly and sometimes may not. Hence, one should compare the timing parameters of the microprocessor and its interfacing devices. As an example, the timing parameters of INTEL 8085A along with its READ and WRITE cycle waveforms are given in Table 6.3 and Figs. 6.12 and 6.13. respectively.

In Table 6.3 it may be observed that the minimum and maximum times for the clock cycle period Tcyc of 8085A are 320 ns and 2000 ns respectively. Hence, it is evident that 8085 A CPU works with the clock frequency varying from 500 Hz to 3.125 MHz. It may be remembered that the frequency generated by the external crystal and the internal clock circuitry is divided by 2 internally to be used as the working clock frequency. Thus for the proper operation of 8085 A, 1 MHz to 6.25 MHz crystal is necessary. Considering the timing waveform for the READ operation, when AD0 to AD7 and A8 to A15 contain the full address, ALE falls and after a delay $t_{LC}$, the $\overline{\text{RD}}$ signal becomes active. Hence the address decoding circuits must be speedy enough to give out the decoded output (i.e. the chip-select signal) within the time $t_{LC}$. The minimum time for $t_{LC}$ is 130 ns for 8085 A, and hence the propagation delay of the decoding circuitries should be less than 130 ns.

Moreover, after the $\overline{\text{RD}}$ signal being active, the combined bus i.e. AD0 to AD7, goes into the DATA - IN state in a time $t_{RD}$. Thus within this time, the interfacing device should be able to access the address and deliver the data outputs to the data bus. These considerations are highly important in the interfacing tasks.

In Conclusion, it may be stated that "the access time of the interfacing device must be less than the response time of the processor". A violation to this rule may result in a malfunctioning of the system.

## 6.9 READ OPERATION

At the starting of the READ operation, A8 to A15 contain the upper half of the address, AD0 to AD7 contain the lower half of the address, the ALE signal goes high and after a time $t_{LL}$, the ALE goes low. Then in a time $t_{LC}$ after the falling edge of ALE, the $\overline{\text{RD}}$ signal is active while in time $t_{LA}$ after the falling edge of the ALE, the combined bus (i.e. AD0 to AD7) goes into the tristate. Note that $t_{LA} > t_{LC}$. However, AD0 to AD7 remain in tristate during a time $t_{RD}$ and then these go into DATA - IN state. At time $t_{CC}$ after the falling edge of the $\overline{\text{RD}}$ signal, the $\overline{\text{RD}}$ signal goes high and this is used as a command to complete the READ operation. The data bus (AD0 to AD7) then becomes floating again, the ALE becomes high after a delay $t_{CL}$, A8 to A15 change to contain the next address in a time $t_{CA}$, while AD0 to AD7 hold the next address in a time $t_{RAE}$. It is important to note that after the end command of $\overline{\text{RD}}$, the data bus remains still in input state during a time $t_{RDH}$. In this way, the READ operation is completed.

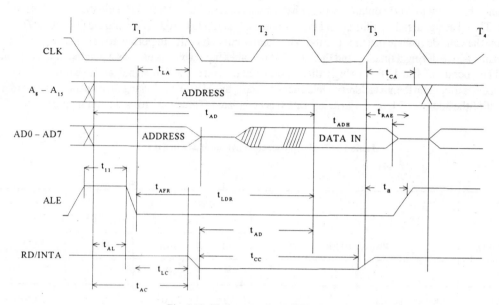

Fig. 6.12. Timing waveform of READ operation

## 6.10 WRITE OPERATION

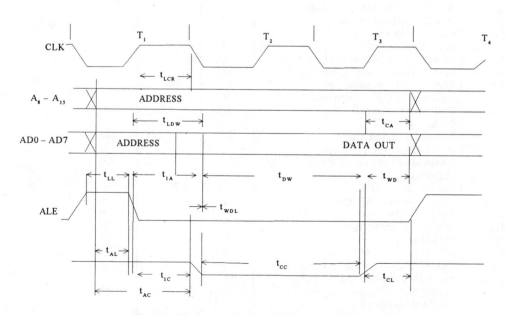

Fig. 6.13. Timing waveform for WRITE OPERATION of 8085A

The WRITE operation is performed in a similar way to the READ operation. As the ALE signal goes high, the common bus AD0 to AD7 contain the lower half of the address while A8 to A15 hold the upper half of the address. The ALE signal falls in time $t_{LL}$ and then in a time $t_{LA}$, the AD0 to AD7 enter into the DATA-OUT state outputting the valid data while in a time $t_{LC}$, the WR signal occurs. It is also important to note that $t_{LA} < t_{LC}$. The WR remains active during a time $t_{CC}$ and then the WR becomes high which is used as a command to complete the WRITE operation. The ALE goes high after a time $t_{CL}$ at the end of the WR signal, and in a time $t_{CA}$, the A8 to A15 changes to contain the next address while after a time $t_{WD}$, the AD0 to AD7 change to hold the corresponding lower half of the address. Thus, the write operation is completed. Table 6.3. gives the timing parameters.

**Table 6.3. Timing parameters (All units are in ns)**

| SYMBOL | PARAMETER | 8085 A* | | 8085A-2* (PRELIMINARY) | |
|---|---|---|---|---|---|
| | | MIN | MAX. | MIN. | MAX. |
| 1 | 2 | 3 | 4 | 5 | 6 |
| TCYC | CLK Cycle Period | 320 | 2000 | 200 | 2000 |
| T1 | CLK Low Time (Standard CLK Loading) | .80 | | 40 | |
| T2 | CLK High Time (Standard CLK Loading) | 120 | | 70 | |
| Tr, Tf | CLK Rise and Fall time | | 30 | | 30 |
| TXKR | X1 Rising to CLK Rising | 30 | 120 | 30 | 100 |
| TXKF | X1 Rising to CLK Falling | 30 | 150 | 30 | 110 |
| TAC | A8-A15 Valid to leading edge of control | 270 | | 115 | |
| TACL | A0-A7 Valid to leading edge of control | 240 | | 115 | |
| TAD | A0-A15 Valid to valid data in | | 575 | | 350 |
| TAFR | Adress float after leading edges of READ (INTA) | | 00 | | 00 |
| TAL | A8-A15 Valid before trailing edge of ALE | 115 | | 50 | |
| TALL | A0-A7 Valid before trailing edge of ALE | 90 | | 50 | |
| TARY | READY Valid from address valid | | 220 | | 100 |
| TCA | Address (A8-A15) Valid after control | 120 | | 60 | |
| TCC | Width of control low (RD, WR, INTA) edge of ALE | 400 | | 230 | |
| TCL | Trailing edge of control to leading edge of ALE | 50 | | 25 | |
| TDW | Data valid to trailing edge of WRITE | 420 | | 230 | |
| THABE | HLDA to bus enable | | 210 | | 150 |
| TABF | Bus float after HLDA | | 210 | | 150 |
| THACK | HLDA valid to trailing edge of CLK | 110 | | 40 | |
| THDH | HOLD hold time | 00 | | 00 | |
| THDS | HOLD setup time to trailing edge of CLK | 170 | | 120 | |
| TINH | INTR Hold time | 00 | | 00 | |
| TINS | XINTR, RST and TRAP setup time to fallilng edge of CLK | 160 | | 150 | |
| TLA | Adress Hold time after ALE | 100 | | 50 | |
| TLC | Trailing edge of ALE to leading edge of control | 130 | | 60 | |

| 1 | 2 | 3 | 4 | 5 | 6 |
|---|---|---|---|---|---|
| TFCK | ALE low during CLK high | 100 | | 50 | |
| TLDR | ALE to valid data during read | | 460 | | 270 |
| TKDW | ALE to valid data during write | | 200 | | 120 |
| TLL | ALE width | 140 | | 80 | |
| TLRY | ALE to READY stable | | 110 | | 30 |
| TRAE | Trailing edge of $\overline{READ}$ to re-enabling of address | 150 | | 90 | |
| TRD | $\overline{READ}$ (or $\overline{INTA}$) to valid data | | 300 | | 150 |
| TRV | Control trailing edge to leading edge of next control | 400 | | 200 | |
| TRDH | Data hold time after $\overline{READ}$, $\overline{INTA}$ | 00 | | 00 | |
| TRYH | READY hold time | 00 | | 00 | |
| TRYS | READY setup time to leading edge of CLK | 110 | | 100 | |
| TWD | Data valid after trailing edge of $\overline{WRITE}$ | 100 | | 60 | |
| TWDL | Leading edge of $\overline{WRITE}$ to data valid | | 40 | | 20 |

From Table 6.3, clock cycle period of 8085 has minimum and maximum limits as

$$T_{min} = 320 \text{ ns}$$

and

$$T_{max} = 2000 \text{ ns.}$$

From data sheet of Intel 8085A, the minimum and maximum frequencies are given by

$$f_{min} = 500 \text{ KHz}$$

and

$$f_{max} = 3.125 \text{ MHz.}$$

Therefore,

$$T_{min} = \frac{1}{f_{max}} = \frac{1}{3.125} \times 10^{-6} = 320 \text{ ns}$$

and

$$T_{max} = \frac{1}{f_{min}} = \frac{1}{500} \times 10^{-3} = 2000 \text{ ns}$$

Again, of $f_{min} = 500$ KHz and $f_{max} = 5$ MHz,

$$T_{min} = \frac{1}{5} \times 10^{-6} = 200 \text{ ns}$$

and

$$T_{max} = \frac{1}{500} \times 10^{-3} = 2000 \text{ ns}$$

as shown in Table 6.3.

## 6.11 WAIT STATE

To understand the WAIT state, the following diagram of READ operation with and without a WAIT state may be carefully observed.

In T1 of the clock cycle, address and data bus hold the address and ALE pulse is occurred. In T2 of the clock cycle, the RD signal becomes active and the data bus goes into the DATA IN state. Here the CPU also checks whether the RDY input is low and if low, the CPU enters into a 'WAIT' state for one clock cycle keeping the data in the data bus, higher half of the address in A8 to A15 and the RD output low. Now, if the RDY is low during the TWAIT cycle, the CPU enters into another wait state of one clock i.e. another TWAIT is inserted. When the RDY becomes high in a TWAIT state, the CPU enters into the T3 of the clock cycle when the RD signal is high and the present READ operation is completed. It is important to note that to be recognized, the RDY should be low at the time TRYS before the rising edge of the clock pulse of TWAIT. This feature of 8085 permits the interfacing of a slower device with it, and for this purpose one method is to connect the RDY input to a monostable multivibrator triggered by the chip select pulse for a particular slower speed device. Another way is to use an acknowledge output of a slower speed device. These acknowledge output should be low during the time of address-access and data delivery of the device and is connected to the RDY of the processor to make the CPU wait till the data is available.

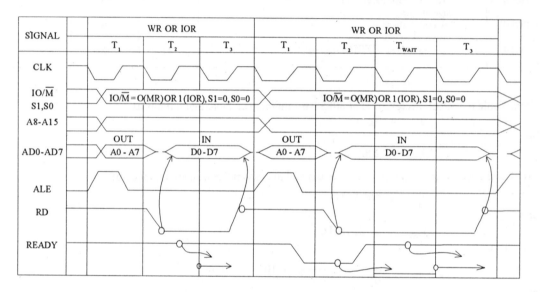

Fig. 6.14 Timing waveform for READ operation with and without a WAIT state for 8085A

## 6.12 HOLD STATES

The HLD input, if made high, requests the CPU to go into the HOLD state when the CPU makes the address, data and control buses floating so that these may be used by an external device or system. On completion of the use of the buses for the current operation, if the HOLD request occurs, the CPU sends a Hold Acknowledge HLDA output and floats the buses at the end of the T3 of the clock cycle. If the current operation needs more than three clock cycles, the operations of the subsequent cycles are performed within the CPU after the buses floated. When the HLDA is sent out, the current operation being completed, the CPU remains idle till the HOLD input goes low. The CPU then starts again with T1 of the clock cycle of the next operation.

The facility of HOLD state may be used in various applications. One of these applications is the Direct Memory Access or DMA operation. DMA is used when quicker communication of data to or from the memory is required since a CPU communicates a data to or from the memory from or to an external device by subsequent one READ and one WRITE operations. So, the respective external device sends HOLD request, the processor floats the address, data and control buses and the external device obtains the possession of all the three buses while it communicates a block of data to or from the memory. When the data transfer is complete, the external device makes the HOLD input low and the CPU starts with the next machine cycle.

## 6.13 HALT STATE

When the Halt instruction HLT is executed, the 8085 A will enter into a 'HALT' state after T2 of the next clock cycle. The processor is stopped here, and the address and the data buses are floated. There are three ways to exit from a HALT state. These are: (i) by resetting the CPU, (ii) by a HOLD request, and (iii) by an interrupt request.

A low on the RESET-IN resets the entire system and loads the program counter by zero. But in a halt state, if a HOLD request is occurred, the processor goes into the HOLD state and remains in this state until the hold input goes low when the CPU re-enters into the HALT state again. An interrupt request can also make the CPU free from the halt state if the interrupt is unmasked and enabled previously.

## 6.14 INTERRUPT STATE

When an interrupt request is occurred, a flag corresponding to the interrupt is set and the CPU on completion of the present instruction, checks whether an interrupt flag is set. If a flag is found set, the CPU resets the interrupt enable flip-flop and sends out the INTA output, then the program counter is saved in the stack and loaded with the vectored address and thus an interrupt state is started. This state continues until the interrupt service routine ends with the return instruction RET. In execution of a RET instruction, the program counter pops out the return address from the stack. It may be remembered that interrupts are disabled by (i) resetting the CPU, (ii) acknowledging a valid interrupt, and (iii) executing a Disable Interrupt (DI) instruction.

# 7. Input-Output Devices

## 7.1 I/O PORTS

I/O ports are extremely important interfacing devices. A large number of devices may directly be connected to the I/O ports without any special interfacing circuitry. It is a frequent practice to connect the keyboard display, relay, printer, A/D converter, D/A converter etc. directly to the I/O ports. A latch may be used as the output port while a tristate buffer may be used as an input port. One of the most widely used programmable peripheral interface chips introduced by INTEL is 8255.

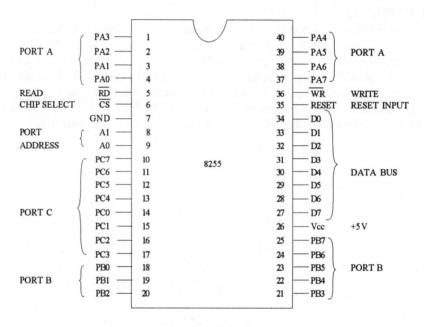

Fig. 7.1. Pin configuration of 8255 PPI

The programmable peripheral interface chip 8255, a highly versatile device has three 8-bit I/O ports : PA, PB and PC, port-C being constituted of two 4-bit I/O ports-PCH and PCL. Hence, these ports may be used as three 8-bit I/O ports, two 12-bit I/O ports or two 8-bit and two 4-bit I/O ports and these ports are programmed by storing control word in the 'control word register' or CWR. The ports and the CWR are selected by A0 and A1 as follows:

**Table 7.1. Ports and control word register CWR**

| A1 | A0 | Selection |
|----|----|-----------|
| 0 | 0 | PA |
| 0 | 1 | PB |
| 1 | 0 | PC |
| 1 | 1 | CWR |

The CWR can only be written and never be read. 8255 may be operated in three modes; Mode-O (Basic I/O Ports), Mode-1 (Strobed I/O Ports) and Mode-2 (Bi-directional Bus). The control word format for the mode selection and port- configurations may be described as under:

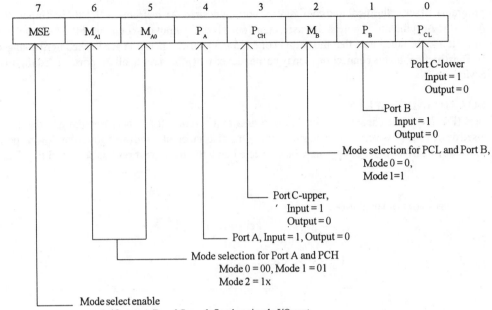

(PA, PB, PCH, PCL : Input = I, Output = O)

| Control Word Bits | | | | | | | | Control Word | PA | PCH | PB | PCL |
|---|---|---|---|---|---|---|---|---|---|---|---|---|
| 7 | 6 | 5 | 4 | 3 | 2 | 1 | 0 | | | | | |
| 1 | 0 | 0 | 0 | 0 | 0 | 0 | 0 | 80 | O | O | O | O |
| 1 | 0 | 0 | 0 | 0 | 0 | 0 | 1 | 81 | O | O | O | I |
| 1 | 0 | 0 | 0 | 0 | 0 | 1 | 0 | 82 | O | O | I | O |
| 1 | 0 | 0 | 0 | 0 | 0 | 1 | 1 | 83 | O | O | I | I |
| 1 | 0 | 0 | 0 | 1 | 0 | 0 | 0 | 88 | O | I | O | O |
| 1 | 0 | 0 | 0 | 1 | 0 | 0 | 1 | 89 | O | I | O | I |
| 1 | 0 | 0 | 0 | 1 | 0 | 1 | 0 | 8A | O | I | I | O |
| 1 | 0 | 0 | 1 | 1 | 0 | 1 | 1 | 9B | I | I | I | I |
| 1 | 0 | 0 | 1 | 0 | 0 | 0 | 0 | 90 | I | O | O | O |
| 1 | 0 | 0 | 1 | 0 | 0 | 0 | 1 | 91 | I | O | O | I |

(PA, PB, PCH, PCL : Input = I, Output = O)

Consider that a small system decodes A7, A6 and A5 of an 8085A CPU. The Decoded line is ANDed with IO/$\overline{M}$ of 8085 and resulting output is connected to the $\overline{CS}$ of an 8255 while $\overline{RD}$, $\overline{WR}$, RESET, A1, A0 and data bus are connected accordingly. If the decoded line of the address be active for A7=1, A6= 0 and A5= 0, then respective port address of PA, PB, PC and CWR are 80, 81, 82 and 83.

If one likes to use the ports in mode - 0 as

PA : Input,
PB : Output,
PCH : Output and
PCL : Input,

the required control word is 91H and hence the program may be developed as :

MVI A 91 H
OUT   83

This program will select the mode and configure the ports as desired. An instruction 'IN 80' will input data from part-A into the Accumulator whereas the instruction 'out 81' will output the contents of the Accumulator through Port B. It may be noted here that the outputs of 8255 in mode-O operation are latched until changed by a next OUT instruction. In this connection, it may be mentioned that after a reset, all the ports are configured as inputs in Mode-0.

## 7.2 KEY BOARD AND DISPLAY

The key board (Fig.7.3) is the cheapest device to insert data to a system. It is highly popular and the  most commonly used device due to its versatility and simplicity. One of its inherent disadvantages is the slower speed of operation.  A key board or a set of keys may be connected directly to an input port as shown in Fig. 7.2.

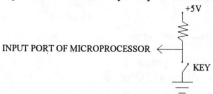

Fig. 7.2. Key board connection

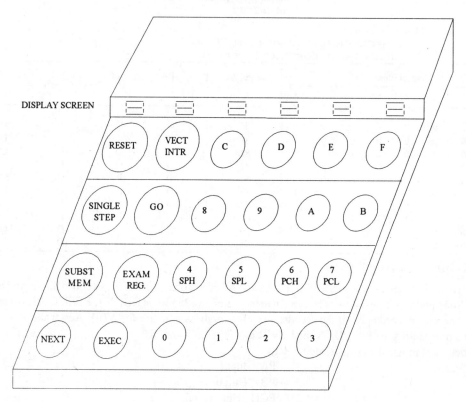

Fig. 7.3. Key board and Display screen

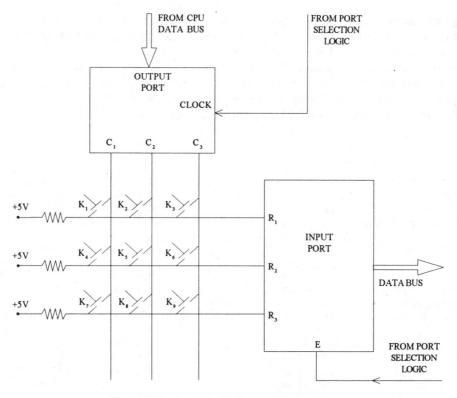

Fig. 7.4 (a) Key board interfaced with microcomputer

However, the inherent bouncing problem may be solved by additional hardware or by a software approach. But for a large number of keys, this type of interfacing is not suitable due to the requirement of a large number of input ports. For this, some of the output lines are scanned sequentially, taking one high or low at a time and are connected in such a way that one of the scanned output line is connected to one side of the keys in a column and the other sides of the keys in a row are connected to one input line as shown in Fig.7.4(a) In this matrix array of keys, the product of used input and output numbers is equal to the maximum possible number of usable keys.

## 7.3 SEVEN SEGMENT DISPLAY AND KEY BOARD INTERFACE

There are a large variety of displays like CRT display, vedeo display, Dot-Matrix LED/LCD display, seven segment display etc. The seven segment LED/LCD displays are the simplest and cheapest among them. The seven segment display pattern is shown in Fig.7.4(b).

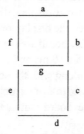

Fig. 7.4. (b) Seven segment display

The segments are nemed as a, b, c, d, e, f, g and h as shown in Fig.7.4(b). These displays of the LED type may be both common cathode and common anode types. These are capable of display digits and some characters of both upper and lower cases. Generally these displays are connected to operate in multiplex to save power, since one of the segments may require 15 mA for continuous glow. Moreover, the multiplexed circuitry is necessarily associated with the least number of output lines of the microprocessor. While discussing various techniques of interfacing of the Key board and display, a description of widely used Key board and display controller chip 8279 introduced by INTEL corporation has been discussed.

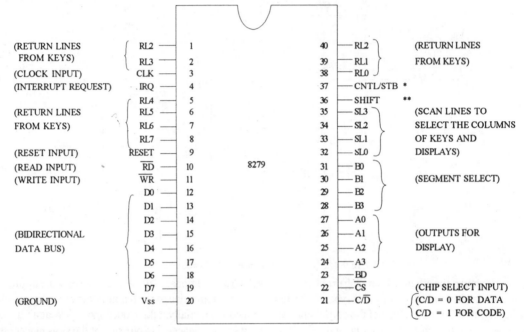

\* CONTROL/STROBED MODE INPUT
\*\* SHIFT INPUT STORED ALONG WITH CNTL/STB AND KEY CODE ON A KEY CLOSURE

Fig. 7.5. Pin configuration of INTEL 8279.

The 8279 has a 16 byte display RAM where codes for the characters are to be loaded. An 8-byte of first in first out (FIFO) RAM is also available to store the encoded return lines along with the scanning outputs which are decoded to scan the displays and the rows of the keys. It has a control register and a status register. The control register may be written or the status register may be read when C/D is high while the FIFO RAM of the display RAM may be read or written when C/D is low. After the 8279 is initialised by storing the control words in the control register, the segment codes for the characters to be displayed are stored in the display RAM. Once it has been loaded, the processor needs no attention to keep the display refreshed. The 8279 keeps the display on continuously in a multiplexed mode. The rows of the Key board are read by return lines RL0 to RL7. When a key is closed, the debouncing circuitry of 8279 waits for 10 ms and checks whether the key is still closed. If found closed, the code for the respective key is stored along with the scanning code in the FIFO RAM and high level is sent out through IRQ. Normally IRQ is connected to an interrupt output of the microprocessor similar to RST-5.5 of 8085A. Then the CPU will vector to the keyboard routine where the date from the FIFO RAM is read.

The 8279 is initialised by a number of control words. One of the useful control word formats for keyboard display mode set is as under:

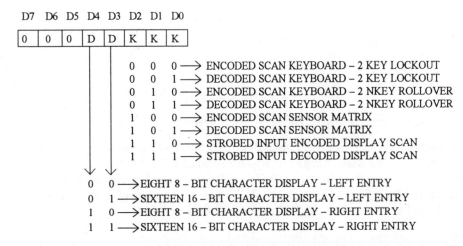

| D7 | D6 | D5 | D4 | D3 | D2 | D1 | D0 |
|----|----|----|----|----|----|----|----|
| 0 | 0 | 0 | D | D | K | K | K |

0  0  0 ⟶ ENCODED SCAN KEYBOARD – 2 KEY LOCKOUT
0  0  1 ⟶ DECODED SCAN KEYBOARD – 2 KEY LOCKOUT
0  1  0 ⟶ ENCODED SCAN KEYBOARD – 2 NKEY ROLLOVER
0  1  1 ⟶ DECODED SCAN KEYBOARD – 2 NKEY ROLLOVER
1  0  0 ⟶ ENCODED SCAN SENSOR MATRIX
1  0  1 ⟶ DECODED SCAN SENSOR MATRIX
1  1  0 ⟶ STROBED INPUT ENCODED DISPLAY SCAN
1  1  1 ⟶ STROBED INPUT DECODED DISPLAY SCAN

0   0 ⟶ EIGHT 8 – BIT CHARACTER DISPLAY – LEFT ENTRY
0   1 ⟶ SIXTEEN 16 – BIT CHARACTER DISPLAY – LEFT ENTRY
1   0 ⟶ EIGHT 8 – BIT CHARACTER DISPLAY – RIGHT ENTRY
1   1 ⟶ SIXTEEN 16 – BIT CHARACTER DISPLAY – RIGHT ENTRY

Here 'encoded' and 'decoded' refer to the scan lines SL0 to SL3. These lines are decoded by an external decoder chip to obtain 16 scanning lines in the encoded mode. But in Decoded mode, only 4 scan lines viz. SL0 to SL3 are available. Left entry or right entry refer to which direction display will be entered. A calculator uses the left entry mode on pressing a key. Here the situation is identical. Two key lock out means that if two keys are pressed simultaneously, the last key release will be entered first. In N key roll-over mode, keys are entered in an order in which they are pressed. Different control formats for writing the display RAM, blank display and reading FIFO are as under:

Control word format for writing the display RAM:

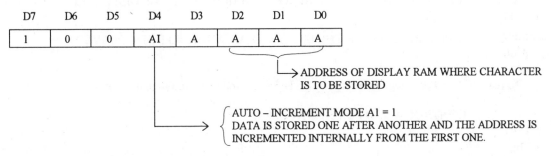

| D7 | D6 | D5 | D4 | D3 | D2 | D1 | D0 |
|----|----|----|----|----|----|----|----|
| 1 | 0 | 0 | AI | A | A | A | A |

⟶ ADDRESS OF DISPLAY RAM WHERE CHARACTER IS TO BE STORED

⟶ AUTO – INCREMENT MODE A1 = 1
DATA IS STORED ONE AFTER ANOTHER AND THE ADDRESS IS INCREMENTED INTERNALLY FROM THE FIRST ONE.

Control word format for blank display :

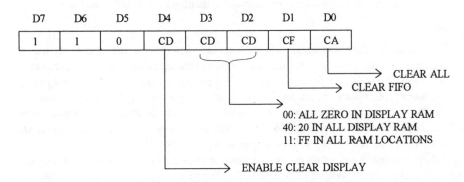

| D7 | D6 | D5 | D4 | D3 | D2 | D1 | D0 |
|----|----|----|----|----|----|----|----|
| 1 | 1 | 0 | CD | CD | CD | CF | CA |

⟶ CLEAR ALL
⟶ CLEAR FIFO

00: ALL ZERO IN DISPLAY RAM
40: 20 IN ALL DISPLAY RAM
11: FF IN ALL RAM LOCATIONS

⟶ ENABLE CLEAR DISPLAY

Control word for reading FIFO:

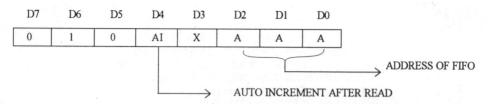

If an 8085 A be interfaced with 8279 where A7, A6 and A5 are decoded for chip selection, the decoded line for A7=0, A6=1 and A5=0 is ANDed with IO/$\overline{M}$ and the result is supplied to CS of 8279 with CD connected to A0 of 8085A, then FIFO and display RAM may be addressed with 40 while the control and status registers may be addressed with 41. If IRQ of 8279 be connected to RST 5.5 of 8085A along with the connection of RESET, CLK, WR, RD, DATA BUS accordingly, 8279 may be initialised by the following software:

```
MVIA 00    :  KEYBOARD/DISPLAY MODE WORD FOR ENCODED SCAN KEY BOARD
OUT 41        -2 KEY LOCK OUT, EIGHT 8-BIT CHARACTER DISPLAY-LEFT ENTRY

MVIA 90    :  FIRST LOCATION OF RAM IS ADDRESSED TO WRITE CODE FOR
OUT  41       CHARACTERS TO BE DISPLED IN AUTO INCREMENT WAY

MVI A CC   :  DISPLAY BLANK COMMAND
OUT  41

MVI A XY1  :  XY1, THE CODE FOR THE FIRST CHARACTER TO BE DISPLAYED
OUT 40

MVI A XY2  :  XY2, THE CODE FOR THE SECOND CHARACTER TO BE DISPLAYED
OUT  40

MVI A XY8  :  XY8, THE CODE FOR THE EIGHTH CHARACTER TO BE DISPLAYED
OUT  40
```

To read the FIFO on being interrupted by RST- 5.5, the following sotfware may be used :

```
MVI A 40   :  CONTROL WORD FOR FIFO ACCESS.
OUT 41
IN   40
```

In Chapter 11, the codes for different characters and their use in display have been discussed.

## 7.4 D/A CONVERTER

A microprocessor receives the analog data through an A/D converter and delivers the analog data via a D/A converter. By a D/A converter, a digital data is converted into its proportional analog value. It is inverse in function to an A/D converter. A/D and D/A converters are the key-devices for microprocessor to deal with the analog world. Resolution, monotonicity, non-linearity, offset, accuracy and output setting times are important parameters of a D/A converter. Resolution is determined by the number of bites to the inputs of D/A converters and may be expressed by the ratio directly or in percentage of one LSB to total number of input states. Sometimes resolution may be expresed by the corresponding voltage change in the output due to a change of LSB in the inputs. A converter is said to be monolithic if it does not miss any step or steps backward when stepped through its entire range by a converter. Off set is the output voltage corresponding to a zero digital input. Non-linearity is the difference between the actual output and the ideal straight line output for all possible input. Output settling time is required to settle the output to a stable state after an input is changed to another one.

The D/A converter may be interfaced with the microprocessor through a latch directly. It may also be interfaced through the output ports. There are a large number of D/A converters available from different manufacturers. Among them, DAC 0800, DAC 0808, MC 1408, DAC 08C etc., are popular 8 bit D/A converters.

### 7.4.1 DAC 0800

The DAC 0800 is a simple monolithic, 8-bit high speed digital to analog converter chip. Its operating voltage is $\pm 4.5$ V to $\pm 18$ V supply, reference voltage being 10 V. The pin configuration and interfacing circuitry have been shown in Fig. 7.6 where pins 5 to 12 are for digital inputs to be connected with a port of microprocessor.

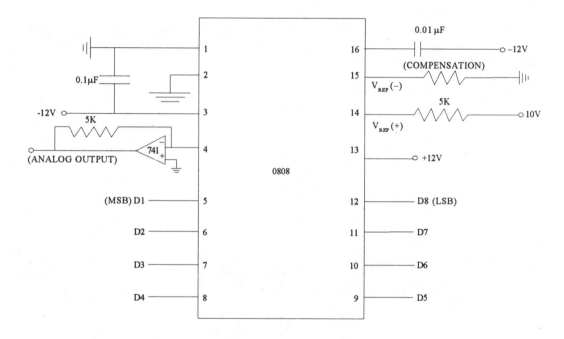

Fig. 7.6. Pin configuration of DAC 0800

### 7.4.2 DAC 0808

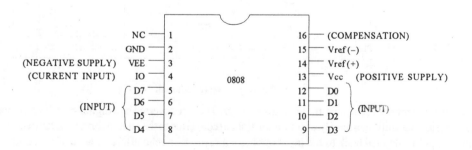

Fig. 7.7. Pin configuration of DAC 0808

The DAC 0808 is an 8-bit D/A Converter with settling time of 150 ns, dissipating 33 mW with +5 V supply. No reference current timing is necessary for most applications since full scale output current is typically ± 1 LSB of (255 Iref/256). Relative accuracy being better then ± 19 %, it ensures 8-bit monotonicity and linearity while zero input output current is typically less than 40 μA for Iref ≥ 2 mA. It operates with a power supply from ± 4.5 V to ± 18 V, the supply current being independent of the bit-codes.

The DAC 0808 may be interfaced with a microprocessor directly through a latch. It may also be interfaced connecting the inputs directly to an output port. When the microprocessor outputs a data through the respective latch of the output port, after the settling time, the output comes out as proportional current through I/O. This current output may be converted into a proportional voltage by a current to voltage converter using a single op-amp along with the necessary buffers.

### 7.4.3 DIGITAL VOICE COMMUNICATION

The D/A converters may be used in system control or instrumentation, music synthesis, speech synthesis, waveform synthesis, digital voice communications, plotters, CRT monitors etc. The schematic diagram of an audio reverve/echo unit is shown in Fig.7.8.

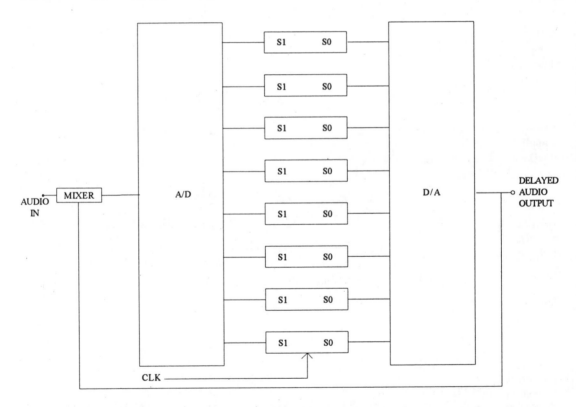

Fig. 7.8. Audio reverve / echo unit

In an audio reverve/echo unit, the analog audio signal being converted into digital from, is supplied to a long series-in series-out shift register whose outputs are again converted to the analog form to obtain a delayed output and this output is also fed back to the input to obtain a reverve or echo effect. The delay is controlled by the clock pulse. A microprocessor may control the clock pulse along with alternations of the feed backs and gains of the mixer / amplifier for several of this units collectively and may perform as a funny sound generating system.

In digital voice communication, a very simple scheme is to convert the audio signal into a digital form and then to transmit as shown is Fig. 7.9.

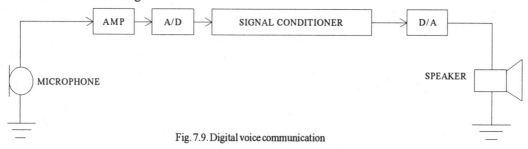

Fig. 7.9. Digital voice communication

The voice is converted into electrical signal by a microphone being amplified and converted into a digital form by an A/D converter and then transmitted. At the receiver end, it is reconverted into the analog form and played on a speaker to obtain the original voice. In this system, the transmission noise is theoretically eliminated. For a number of these systems, a microprocessor may perform the necessary control jobs.

## 7.5 A/D CONVERTER

Analog to digital ( A/D ) converter is the key - device through which a microprocessor receives the analog data for manipulation as required. There are a large number of techniques to convert and analog data into a digital one like parallel comparator technique, single slope integration, dual slope integration, charge balance method, upcounter and D/A method, up-down counter technique, successive approximation method etc. The A/D converters based on successive approximation or up-down converter technique or parallel comparator technique etc. being very fast in conversion with appreciable accuracy and cost effectiveness, are generally preferred in the applications where speed is a critical factor. But when the accuracy becomes the most important parameter, an A/D converter, based on the 'Dual slope - Integration' may be used. Bit - length, conversion time, resolution and accuracy are the main parameters of an A/D converter.

An A/D converter may be interfaced with a microprocessor directly by connecting date bus, output enable etc. (of the A/D converter) to the data bus, address decoded chip select line etc. of the microprocessor. But the most frequent practice is to connect the device to the I/O ports which produces simplicity in interfacing. There are a large variety of A/D converter chips available by different manufacturers. ADC 0800, ADC 0804, ADC 0809, etc. are some examples of the popular A/D converter chips. A brief description of ADC 0808 chip is as under:

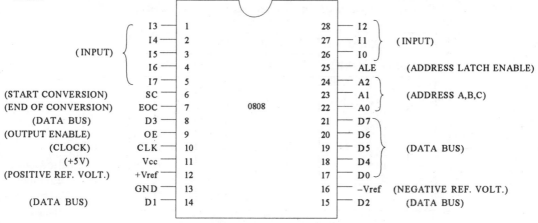

Fig. 7.10. Pin configuration of ADC 0808

The ADC 0808 is an 8 bit A/D converter with 8 multiplexed inputs selected by the address bus A0 to A2. It is a highly versatile device based upon successive approximation technique with typical conversion time of 100 μs with an error of ± 1 LSB, consuming only 15 mW. It is easy to use and simple to interface having TTL compatible outputs. It may be used in a very wide range of applications like data acquisition system, microprocessor based instrumentation, control, etc. It operates with a single + 5V supply and the input range is 0-5V. To operate an ADC 0808, the address for the desired channel of inputs is sent to the address lines first. After 50 ns, the ALE line is made high. After another 2.5 μs, the SC line is made high and then low. When the EOC line goes high, data can be read from the outputs of the device. This device may directly be interfaced with the microprocessor using some special circuitry or it may be interfaced through I/O ports. In order to obtain a continuous conversion mode, the end of conversion (EOC) line may be fed to start conversion (SC) line. In an ADC 0808, the null balance is automatically adjusted. In digital voice communication, digital audio echo system, speech recognition, microprocessor based intelligent instruments, highly versatile measuring instruments, microprocessor based controllers, toys and games etc., ADC may be successfully applied.

### 7.5.1 ADC 0809

The ADC 0809 data acquisition component is a monolithic CMOS device with an 8-bit analog to digital converter, 8 channel multiplexer and microprocessor compatible control logic (Fig. 7.11). The 8 bit A/D converter uses successive approximation as the conversion technique. The converter features a high impedance chopper stabilized comparator, a 256 R voltage divider with analog switch tree and a successive approximation register. The 8 channel multiplexer can directly access any of 8 single ended analog signal.

The device eliminates the requirements for external zero and full scale adjustment. Easy interfacing to microprocessor is provided by the latched and decoding multiplexer address inputs and latched TTL TRI - STATE output.

The ADC 0809 offers high speed, high accuracy, minimal temperature dependence, excellent long time accuracy and repeatability and consumes minimal power. These features make this device ideally suited to application in process and machine control.

The schematic diagram of an 8 bit microprocessor compatible A/D converter based on 0809 with 8 channel multiplexer is shown in Fig. 7.11, the detailed circuit configuration being shown in Fig 7.12. The device contains an 8 channel single ended analog signal multiplexer. A particular input channel is selected by using the address decoder. Table 7.2 shows the input states for the address lines to select any channel. The address is latched into the decoder on the low to high transition of the ALE signal.

**Table 7.2. Input state for the address lines for channel selection**

| SELECTED | ADDRESS LINES | | |
|---|---|---|---|
| ANALOG CHANNEL | C or A0 | B or A1 | A or A2 |
| IN 0 | L | L | L |
| IN 1 | L | L | H |
| IN 2 | L | H | L |
| IN 3 | L | H | H |
| IN 4 | H | L | L |
| IN 5 | H | L | H |
| IN 6 | H | H | L |
| IN 7 | H | H | H |

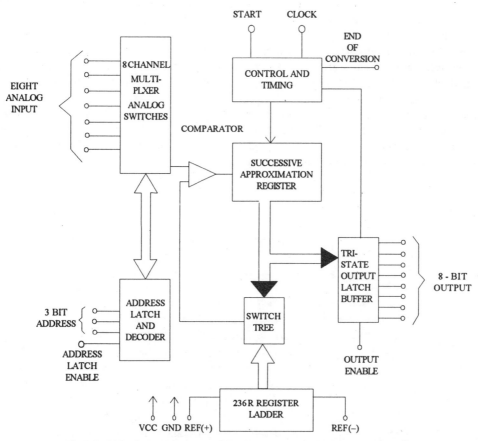

Fig. 7.11. 8-bit microprocesor compatible A/D convertor with 8 - channel multiplexer

## 7.5.2 CONVERTER CHARACTERISTICS

Heart of this single chip data acquisition system is its 8 bit analog to digital converter. The converter is designed to give fast, accurate and repeatable conversation over a wide range of temperatures. The converter is partitioned into three major sections- the 256 R ladder network, the successive approximation register and the comparator. The converter's digital outputs are positive. The 256 R ladder network approach has been chosen over the R/2R ladder because of its inherent monotonicity which confirms no missing digital codes. Monotonicity is particularly important in closed loop feedback control systems in order to avoid oscillations. Additionally, the 256 R network dose not cause load variations on the reference voltage. The bottom resistor and the top registor of the ladder network are not of the same value. The difference in these resistors causes the output characteristics to be symmetrical with the zero and full scale points of the transfer curve. The first output transition occurs when the analog signal has reached + 1/2 LSB and succeeding output transitions occur every 1 LSB later up to full scale. The successive approximation register (SAR) performs eight iterations to approximate the input voltage. For any SAR type converter, n iterations are required for an n bit converter. In the ADC 0809, the approximation technique is extended to 8 bits using the 256 R network.

## Functional Description

The A/D converter's SAR is reset on the position edge of the start conversion (SC) pulse. Conversion starts on the falling edge of the start conversion pulse. A conversion in process is interrupted by the receipt of a new start conversion pulse. Continuous conversion may be accomplished by typing the EOC output to the SC input. If used in this mode, an external start conversion pulse should be applied after power up. EOC will go low between 0 and 8 clock pulses after rising edge of start conversion.

Most important section of the A/D converter is the comparator. It is the section which is responsible for the ultimate accuracy of the entire converter. It is also the comparator drift which has the greatest influence on the repeatability of the device. A chopper stabilised comparator provides the most effective method of satisfying all the converter requirements.

The chopper stabilised comparator converts DC input signal into an AC. This signal is then fed through a high gain AC amplifier and the DC level restarter. This technique limits the drift component of the amplifier since the drift is a dc component which is not passed by the ac amplifier. This makes the entire A/D converter extremely insensitive to temperature, long term drift and input offset errors.

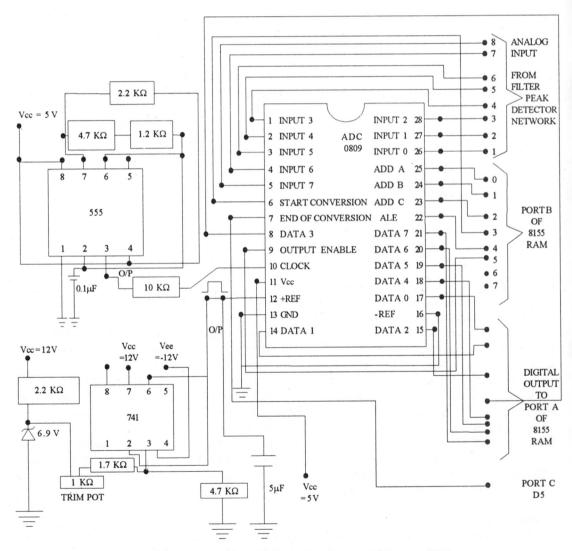

Fig. 7.12. Detailed circuit configuration of Multichannel ADC based on 0809

## 7.6 STANDARD PERIPHERALS

For simplicity of interfacing, different manufacturers produce a large number of standard peripheral devices. These are versatile in operation, simple in interfacing and of great help to a system designer. In the next chapter, some of these peripherals will be discussed in details. Some of the popular peripherals are listed below:

INTEL:

8205  Decoder

8212  IO/LATCH

8224  CLOCK GENERATOR

8251  Universal Sub-synchronous Asynchronous Receiver

8253  Programmable Internal Timer/Counter

8255  Programmable Peripheral Interface, PPI

8257  DMA Controller

8259  Programmable Interrupt Controller

8271  Floppy Disc controller

8275  CRT Controller

8279  Key board and display controller.

# 8. Serial Interface Techniques

## 8.1 INTRODUCTION

There are some devices (like typewriter, video display monitor, floppy disc, cassette tape etc.) to or from which data in serial form may be accessible. For data transmission through a longer distance, the serial form of data is necessary. Moreover to reduce the number of connecting lines, the serial form is preferred. In serial form of communication, both commands and data are transmitted through one line; sometimes unidirectionally and sometimes bi-directionally. Serial transmission, though slower in speed, requires less number of transmission lines. If associated with multiplexed form, it may be possible to communicate a number of systems simultaneously through a single line.

Communications between a microprocessor system and a peripheral may be (i) Simplex, (ii) Half duplex and (iii) Full duplex. In simplex type of communication, data is transmitted unidirectionally whereas in half duplex type, communication is bi-directional (though unidirectional at a time), while the full duplex communications are directed both ways simultaneously. For data communication, it is a practice to use 7-bit ASCII code for characters assigning the 8-bit as parity, though 8-bit ASCII code is also used in many systems.

For different peripherals to be interfaced with a microprocessor system with minimal efforts, a number of serial interfacing devices like INTEL 8251, Zilog Z-80-SIO, Motorola MC 6850 ACIA, MOS Tech. Inc. 6551 ACIA etc. have been developed. These are highly versatile in use and simple to interface.

The data formats for serial communication have also been developed in different ways considering the advantages and requirement for the system. Different standards for serial communications have also been developed for simplicity and universality for interfacing. Among them, RS 232C gains wide acceptance as standard for interfacing format.

## 8.2 PROTOCOLS FOR SYNCHRONOUS SERIAL COMMUNICATION

There are many formats and protocols for synchronous serial communication. In these schemes, the receiver and transmitter are locked from the starting. Out of the different protocols, the IMB's binary synchronous protocol or BISYNC is widely used. A more efficient and popular method is to use SDLC protocol. In BISYNC, continuous 1's are sent during idle state. Further to commence start, the transmitter sends the previously selected 'SYNC' character which is used by the receiver to synchronise its clock with that of the transmitter. Start of Header (SOH) character indicates that, a header along with labels, control codes etc. is active. A start-of-text (STX) indicates a start of a 256-byte of data and an end of text (ETX) indicates an end of a block of characters.

INTEL 8251 (USART) supports a BISYNC communication in its synchronous mode and uses the SYNC. character for synchronisation. It is also capable of generating the required BISYNC handshaking signals.

Since BISYNC uses the bytes SOH, STX, ETX etc. as a part of the message, the BISYNC protocol is called the 'byte-controlled protocol'.

## 8.3 IBM's SYSCHRONOUS DATA LINK CONTROL (SDLC)

Synchronous Data Link Control (SDLC) introduced by IBM is a bit-oriented protocol for synchronous serial communications. In this format, message is determined by the number and position of the bits transmitted. Messages are sent in frames which are constituted by fields. Between successive messages, a continuous set of 1's are transmitted. The start of message is determined by a specific bit pattern known as the 'beginning flag'. It is followed by an 8-bit address of the receiving station, which in turn is followed by an 8-bit control word. Then the information field becomes active and a 16-bit cyclic character is sent for the receiver to check the errors. The frame ends with an ending flag pattern. The message format of SDLC is given as under:

⟵————————————————— FRAME —————————————————⟶

| BEGINNING FLAG 01111110 8 BITS | ADDRESS 8 BITS | CONTROL 8 BITS | INFORMATION ANY NO. OF BITS | FRAME CHECK 16 BITS | ENDING FLAG 01111110 8 BITS |

Fig. 8.1 SDLC Message Format

The SDLC system uses full duplex communication. When an error occurs, the receiver requests the transmitter to send the data again. Intel 8273 SDLC is a suitable interfacing device for microprocessor system.

### 8.3.1 BIT–FORMAT

For serial communication and storage, data bit may be represented in different ways in various formats. As for example, a high state of a bit may not always be a high in the transmission line or in the storage during a certain period, but it may be represented by a wave of a particular frequency. Different formats of a bit have certain advantages and disadvantages. Hence, the selection of proper bit format is important.

To select the proper bit format, the parameters considered, are performance under speed variations, performance under noise variations, self-clocking facility, case of implementation, maximum baud rate etc. Situation may arise when the baud rate may change unexpectedly and transmission line or source may be noise-corrupted. Available self-clocking facility may solve the problem to a desired level. But to make a reliable system, it may often be seen that the implementation technique is tough and costly reducing the baud rate (number of bits transmitted per second). Some of the important bit formats have been discussed in the following few articles.

### 8.3.2 NON-RETURN TO ZERO-FORMAT

In this format, one bit is valid for one clock cycle (rather one baud cycle) and the next one, during the next clock cycle. It gives sufficiently fast rate of transmission, the baud rate exceeding even one million. It shows satisfactory performance under speed and noise variations and the implementation technique is quite simple. The only disadvantage in this technique is that the format does not include the self-clocking facility requiring clock pulses along with the data.

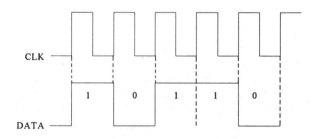

Fig. 8.2. Non-return to zero format

### 8.3.3 PHASE ENCODING FORMAT

This format is similar to the non-return to zero format with a difference that in non-return to zero format, the transition of states for the transmission line occurs at the start of a baud-cycle and the state during the whole baud cycle is represented by a bit whereas in phase encoding format, the transition occurs at the middle of baud cycle and a transition of state indicates a change of bit-states. Hence the implementation of Phase Encoding Format results in a slower baud rate in comparison to a non return-to-zero format. But the phase encoding format is self clocked and it is not used if a baud-rate exceeds 1500.

### 8.3.4 DOUBLE FREQUENCY FORMAT

In this format, a high pulse is used to initiate the start of a bit while the low one indicates the stall of the bit. The presence of this bit means '1', the absence of it being '0'. The next pulse indicates the commencement of the next bit-start. This format is self-clocked. Though a moderately good performance is seen in speed variations, the performance under noise condition is not so good. Maximum baud rate is normally taken to be around 800 only.

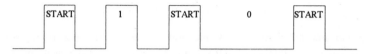

Fig. 8.3 Double frequency format

### 8.3.5 MANCHESTER CODING FORMAT

Manchester coding format is self-clocked possessing excellent performance under noise and speed changes. The baud rate may be as high as 1500. In this format, a bit starts with a low state and then a high state shows '1' and a low state indicates '0'.

Fig. 8.4 Manchester coding format

### 8.3.6 PULSE WIDTH MODULATION FORMAT

This is another self-clocked format, in which, a bit starts with a high state and ends when low. The state between a start and an end indicates a bit. This format is simple, shows good performance under speed variation and possesses moderately good performance in noisy conditions allowing a baud-rate up to 1500.

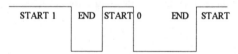

Fig. 8.5. Pulse width modulation format

### 8.3.7 KANSAS CITY STANDARD

Kansas City Standard is a popular format. In standard 300-baud version, eight cycles of 2400 Hz and four cycles of 1200 Hz represent '1' and '0' respectively. The Kansas City Standard specifies for serial data recording that, a leader should be of 30 sec. of 2400 Hz and each data character should consist of one '0' stop bit, 8-data bits including parity and two '1' stop bits, while the blocks of data should be separated by 5 sec. leaders of 2400 Hz.

This form is self-clocked, shows excellent performances under noise and speed variations and is easier to implement. Normally for a baud-rate over 1200, it is not used. However the Kansas city standard is widely used in serial data recording on audio cassette tapes.

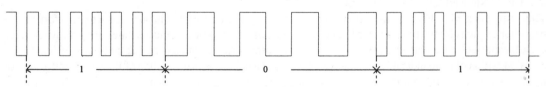

Fig. 8.6. Kansas city standard

## 8.3.8 SERIAL COMMUNICATION STANDARDS

The serial data communication includes transmission, reception, recording and retrieving of serial data. Different systems use different types of bit formats, character formats and message formats.

Some of the EIA standards available are RS-232 C, RS-422, RS-423 etc. Though RS-232 C is widely accepted, RS-422 and RS-423 are the improved versions of RS-232 C. The RS-232 C specifies the voltage level of the communication signal with respect to the ground while RS-422 uses low impedance differential signals carried by a pair of twisted wire where the differential noise may induce at a minimum. RS-422 achieves the maximum baud rate whereas RS-423 uses a low impedance signal ended driver and coaxial cables.

Sometimes for a long distance communication, telephone lines are used. A modulator or demodulator or MODEM sends and receives telephone compatible signals. Sometimes the microwave links are also used for communications. The equipments viz. the MODEM, microwave links and similar other units are known as Data Communication Equipments or DCE. The terminals and microprocessor systems which receive or send the serial data are called Data Terminal Equipments or DTE.

As a standard format for interfacing, RS-232 C has been described in the following article.

## 8.4 RS-232C

This standard defines the handshaking of data signals equipped in a 25 pin-connector. The pin configuration and functions of the 25 pins are given in the following table. A simple system normally uses pins 1 through 8 along with 20th pin only.

| PINS | USUAL NAMES | RS-232 NAMES | DESCRIPTION |
|------|-------------|--------------|-------------|
| 01 | — | AA | PROTECTIVE GROUND |
| 02 | TXD | BA | TRANSMIT DATA |
| 03 | RXD | BB | RECEIVED DATA |
| 04 | RTS | CA | REQUEST TO SEND |
| 05 | CTS | CB | CLEAR TO SEND |
| 06 | DSR | CC | DATA SET RELAY |
| 07 | GND | AB | SIGNAL GROUND (COMMON RETURN) |
| 08 | CD | CF | RECEIVE LINE SIGNAL DETECTOR |
| 09 | — | — | RESERVE FOR DATA SET LISTING |
| 10 | — | — | RESERVE FOR DATA SET LISTING |
| 11 | — | — | UNASSIGNED |
| 12 | — | SCF | SECONDARY RECEIVE LINE SIGNAL DETECTOR |
| 13 | — | SCB | SECONDARY CLEAR TO SEND |
| 14 | — | SBA | SECONDARY TRANSMIT DATA |
| 15 | — | DB | TRANSMISSION SIGNAL ELEMENT TIMING (DCE SOURCE) |
| 16 | — | SBB | SECONDARY RECEIVE DATA |
| 17 | — | DD | RECEIVE SIGNAL ELEMENT TIMING (DCE SOURCE) |
| 18 | — | — | UNASSIGNED |
| 19 | — | SCA | SECONDARY REQUEST TO SEND |
| 20 | DTR | CD | DATA TERMINAL RELAY |
| 21 | — | CG | SIGNAL QUALITY DETECTOR |
| 22 | — | CE | RING INDICATOR |
| 23 | — | CH/CI | DATA SIGNAL RATE SELECTOR (DTE/DCE SOURCE) |
| 24 | — | DA | TRANSMIT SIGNAL ELEMENT TIMING (DTE SOURCE) |
| 25 | — | — | UNASSIGNED |

After the terminal power is turned on, it sends DTR to the MODEM which responds by DSR to indicate that it is ready. The MODEM at the microprocessor end is then dialed. The MODEM responds with a 2225 KHz carrier frequency. When the MODEM, connected to the terminal end receives this carrier, asserts a carrier detect (CD) to the terminal which, then sends the request-to-send (RTS) to the MODEM. After a proper time, the MODEM responds with the clear-to-send (CTS) signal. The terminal then sends the serial data on its TXD output. Similar procedure is followed for receiving data. However, each one of the outputs should be connected to the proper input as shown in Fig.8.7. The cross-connections required are known as null **MODEM**. In this case a logic high means a voltage between - 3V and - 15V on load while a logic low is a voltage level between + 3V and + 15V under load. Typical voltages used are +10V or +12V. To reduce cross-talk between adjacent wires, the rates of rise time or fall time must be limited to 30 volt per micro second. RS-232C specifies the maximum distances as 15 m for a maximum baud rate 20,000. With lower baud rates, wires of even 1000 m are generally used.

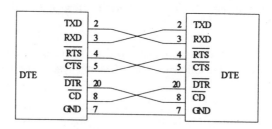

Fig. 8.7. Null MODEM for connecting two DTE in RS-232C

## 8.5 UNIVERSAL SYNCHRONOUS ASYNCHRONOUS RECEIVER TRANSMITTER (USART)

Among the serial interfacing devices, Universal Synchronous Asynchronous Receiver Transmitter or USART is extremely helpful to interface a serial access device and to communicate in serial form. Intel 8251 is a popular USART which is a 28-Pin package. The pin configuration of 8251 has been described in Fig. 8.8.

| (DATA BUS LINES) | D2 | 1 | | 28 | D1 | (DATA BUS LINES) |
| | D3 | 2 | | 27 | D0 | |
| (RECEIVER INPUT) | (RXD) | 3 | | 26 | Vcc | |
| GND | | 4 | | 25 | RXC | (RECEIVER CLOCK) |
| | D4 | 5 | | 24 | $\overline{DTR}$ | (DATA TERMINAL READY) |
| (DATA BUS LINES) | D5 | 6 | INTEL | 23 | $\overline{RTS}$ | (REQUEST TO SEND) |
| | D6 | 7 | 8251 | 22 | $\overline{DSR}$ | (DATA SET READY) |
| | D7 | 8 | USART | 21 | RESET | |
| (TRANSMITTER CLOCK) | $\overline{TXC}$ | 9 | | 20 | CLK | |
| (WRITE) | $\overline{WR}$ | 10 | | 19 | TXD | (TRANSMITTER OUTPUT) |
| (CHIP SELECT) | $\overline{CS}$ | 11 | | 18 | TXE | (TRANSMITTER EMPTY) |
| (CONTROL / DATA) | $C/\overline{D}$ | 12 | | 17 | $\overline{CTS}$ | (CLEAR TO SEND) |
| (READ) | $\overline{RD}$ | 13 | | 16 | SYNDET/BD | (SYNC DETECT/BREAK DETECT) |
| (RECEIVER READY) | RXRDY | 14 | | 15 | TXRDY | (TRANSMITTER READY) |

Fig. 8.8. Pin configuration of INTEL 8251 USART

USART 8251 may be operated in both Synchronous and Asynchronous modes. It is a full duplex double buffered transmitter and receiver. It has facilities of automatic synchronous insertion, false start bit detection, bread detection etc. Error detection facility for parity, over run and framing are also available. RESET, $\overline{RD}$, $\overline{WR}$ and DATA BUS of USART 8251 are connected to the respective pins of CPU, C/$\overline{D}$ may be connected to AO of the address bus while $\overline{CS}$ is connected to the respective chip selection line. 8251 is double-buffered since both transmitter and receiver have two buffers, one holding the data received or to be transmitted, while the other engaged in shifting operation for reception or transmission. If an 8251 be interfaced with 8085 CPU in I/O mapping chip selection line active (i.e. A7 = 1, A6 =0, A5 =0), the address of transmit/receive data buffer and the control/ status register will be 80 and 81 respectively. Thus the data holding buffers are addressed by 80 whereas the control and status registers are addressed by 81.

To operate USART, first the device is to be initialised by loading the mode word followed by the insertion of the command word in the control register which can only be written. The status register can be read and can not be written. The Status Word Format for USART is as under:

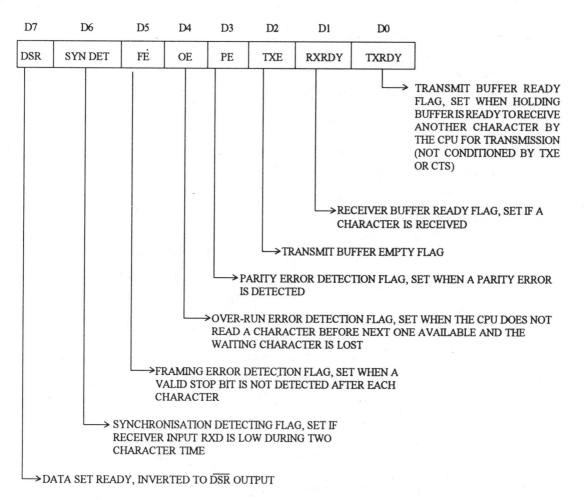

| D7 | D6 | D5 | D4 | D3 | D2 | D1 | D0 |
|-----|---------|-----|-----|-----|-----|-------|-------|
| DSR | SYN DET | FE | OE | PE | TXE | RXRDY | TXRDY |

TRANSMIT BUFFER READY FLAG, SET WHEN HOLDING BUFFER IS READY TO RECEIVE ANOTHER CHARACTER BY THE CPU FOR TRANSMISSION (NOT CONDITIONED BY TXE OR CTS)

RECEIVER BUFFER READY FLAG, SET IF A CHARACTER IS RECEIVED

TRANSMIT BUFFER EMPTY FLAG

PARITY ERROR DETECTION FLAG, SET WHEN A PARITY ERROR IS DETECTED

OVER-RUN ERROR DETECTION FLAG, SET WHEN THE CPU DOES NOT READ A CHARACTER BEFORE NEXT ONE AVAILABLE AND THE WAITING CHARACTER IS LOST

FRAMING ERROR DETECTION FLAG, SET WHEN A VALID STOP BIT IS NOT DETECTED AFTER EACH CHARACTER

SYNCHRONISATION DETECTING FLAG, SET IF RECEIVER INPUT RXD IS LOW DURING TWO CHARACTER TIME

DATA SET READY, INVERTED TO $\overline{DSR}$ OUTPUT

The format for mode word is as follows :

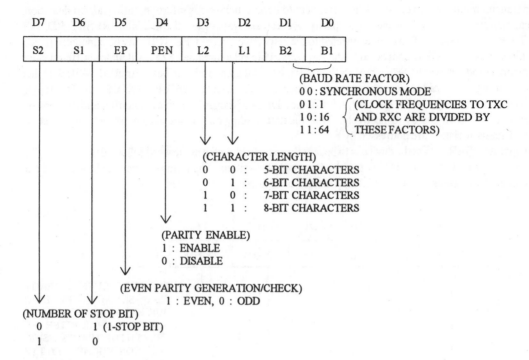

The format for COMMAND WORD is given below :

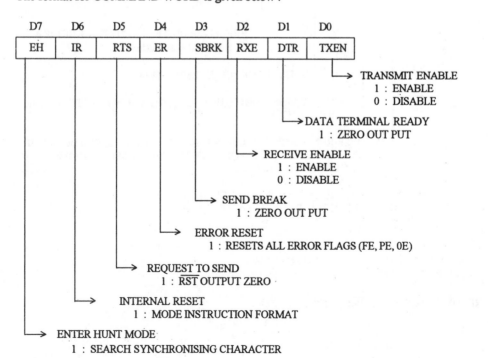

To operate the USART, first the mode word is stored in the control register, and then the command words are given to control the transmission and reception. Sometimes, TXRDY and RXRDY are tied to the interrupts of the CPU, which is then interrupted whenever the reception of a character is complete. Accordingly, the CPU stores the received data in the memory or loads another data to the transmit buffer.

Sometimes, the status word is read by the CPU and in accordance with the respective flag status, the CPU takes decision and does not use the interrupts, the technique being known as 'polling'. In this technique of interfacing, the CPU is involved with the transmit-receive operation while in the interrupt-driver mode, the CPU may perform anything else while transmit-receive operations are carried on by the USART. Sometimes without using an USART, in case of simple systems having slow communication, the CPU may be used to simulate the functions of an USART. The technique is equally effective as one of polling method based on USART.

The synchronous mode of operation of an USART achieves the highest speed in serial communications. In asynchronous mode, at least one start bit and one stop bit are required at the beginning and end of each character and an 8-bit data requires at least 10 bits to be communicated. Hence, 20% of the time is wasted. But, in synchronous mode, no start or stop bit is required and the transmitter and receiver use the same clock starting simultaneously. Locking of receiver and transmitter is performed together as described earlier in this chapter. Timing diagrams for WRITE and READ operations of USART (8251) are shown in Fig. 8.9.

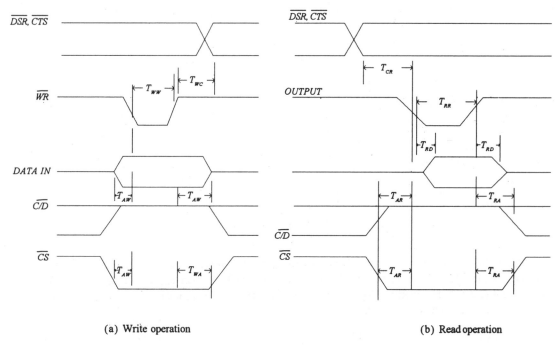

(a) Write operation          (b) Read operation

Fig. 8.9. Timing diagram of USART 8251

## 8.6 TELEPHONE LINES

Using a telephone line, it is possible to send the data to a longer distance with a simple and cheap interfacing circuitry. A number of microprocessor systems may communicate with one at a remote place. In fact, data is inserted into the line by mechanical connections or by feeding an audio sound to the microphone and similarly data may be obtained by tapping or trapping the ear-phone sounds.

It may be  noted that the voltage or current pulse type signals cannot be used in communication through the telephone lines. The baud width of the standard phone lines is about 3 KHz only. Hence a pulse will be distorted beyond recognition by the low-pass filter-action of the lines. So, a digital data is sent through the usual phone lines in the form of: (i) Amplitude Modulation, (ii) Phase shift modulation and (iii) Frequency shift Keying (FSK)

In the amplitude modulation, the presence of the carrier frequency indicates '1' and its absence means a '0'. In phase shift modulation, the phase of a constant frequency carrier is shifted by $180^{\circ}$ to indicate a change from 0 to 1 or 1 to 0.  The overall scheme of interfacing a telephone line is shown in Fig. 8.10.

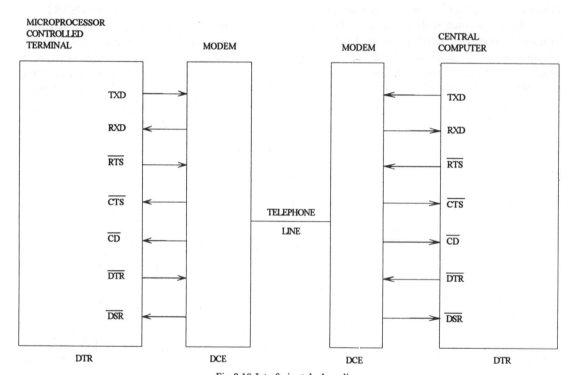

Fig. 8.10. Interfacing telephone line

MODEM  can  communicate  in  full duplex mode and for this purpose four frequencies are used.  In 'originate' mode, a MODEM uses 1270 Hz for '1' and 1070 Hz for '0' while in 'answer' mode, 2225 Hz indicates a logical high and 2025 Hz signifies a logical low. The associated interfacing and implementation techniques are simple and cheap though highly effective.

### 8.7 TELETYPES

Generally teletypes are interfaced using current signals. This gives a better performance in noisy conditions.  A 20 mA or a 60 μA current indicates 1 and 0 current indicates a zero. Teletypes send data at the rate of 300 baud or less though 110 baud rate is very common.

By using two independent current loops, a teletype may be interfaced in full duplex mode. However, one may use RS-232C scheme or any other form of serial communication method or Intel 8251 USART. Using a single current loop, a teletype may be interfaced in half duplex way.

To interface a teletype to an Intel 8085 based system, the SOD and SID pins of the CPU may be used, through which the use of interfacing device like Intel 8251 USART may be eliminated.

## 8.8 AUDIO CASSETTE TAPES

To store bulk data, Audio Cassette Tapes may be used. However with noise and speed variations, its operation is not so efficient. In practice, they are not used as record copies for long time storage. But still it is popular, since in developing a large program for a system, this method of storage may be of great help.

Ordinary audio cassette recorder may be used for storage. The microphone input is connected to an output port while the speaker output of the recorder is clipped to 5V microprocessor compatible output connected to an input port. The Kansas city standard is an widely used recording scheme for audio cassette recorder.

Since a cassette recorder uses a small d.c. shunt motor having a practically constant speed characteristics, the microprocessor is capable of measuring the width and number of pulses by polling the input connected to the speaker- output of the cassette recorder. Thus the interfacing technique is quite simple. Ofcourse a much complicated circuitry may be associated for reliability in long duration storage and good performance under noise and speed variations.

## 8.9 DISC SYSTEMS

In Disc system, massive amounts of data can be stored. The tape systems whether magnetic, paper or optical type, are not so fast in comparison to the disc systems. Moreover, the cost per bit is relatively smaller in disc systems.

There are three types of disc systems available viz. floppy disc, hard disc and optical disc. A 14 inch hard disc may store even 100 M bytes of data with a readout speed of 5 M bytes / sec whereas an optical disc of the same size may contain a bulk of data more than ten times, but the readout speed is only 150 K bytes/ sec, a speed at least three times faster than the floppy disc (8 inch size) which may contain about only one M bytes of data. The floppy discs are relatively inexpensive, simple to interface and hence they are widely used.

## 8.10 FLOPPY DISCS

Floppy discs are made of nylon sheets enclosed in protective envelops. The common sizes available are of 8, 5.25 and 3.5 inches. The protective envelop is square shaped as shown in Fig. 8.11.

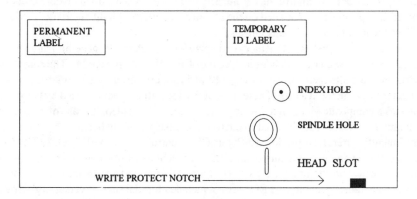

Fig. 8.11. Floppy disc

When a disc is inserted in a drive unit, a spindle clamps in the centre hole and spins the disc at a constant speed of 360 rpm in most cases. The read/write head is positioned for the desired track correctly by a stepper motor and made touched to the disc through the head slot. The single sided drive records data on only one side of the disc whereas the double sided drive uses two heads to read/write both the sides of the disc. The write protect notch on the disc envelop is used to protect the stored data from being written over.

Data is recorded in concentric circular tracks. The number of tracks per side are 77, 40 and 80 for 8, 5.25, and 3.5 inch discs respectively. The start of a track is determined by two methods viz. hard sectoring and soft sectoring. In widely used soft sectoring method, the disc contains only one hole near the centre, called index hole. A photodetector senses this hole and the corresponding position of a track in contact with the head in the start position of the track.

One of the bit formats in recording a disc is the double frequency format, F2F format or FM (Frequency modulated) format. In this format, there is a clock pulse at the start of bit. Recording a disc using this format is called the single density recording. The MFM (Modified frequency Modulation) format is obtained by deleting the clock-pulse and using the bit pulse (preset for only '1') at the centre of the clock period. The resulting format is identical to the Manchester coding format. In this format, double the amount of data may be recorded on a disc in comparison to the recording by F2F format. Recording a disc using MFM is called double density recording.

There are various formats of recording data on a disc for both single density and double density methods. The error detection techniques are also different. Most of the error detection techniques use the CRC (Cyclic redundancy character) methods. After recording, the recorded data is read for checking whether the data is recorded properly. Whenever the error is read, detection technique is used to check whether the data is correctly read. If error is found in writing or reading, several attempts are made repeatedly to obtain a correct one and if all the attempts are failed, the 'error' is shown on the screen.

The floppy disc drive unit is interfaced with a Floppy Disc controller chip like Intel 8272. To use a floppy disc, it requires a long series of commands for the disc controller chip on a bit-by-bit basis which is very tedious and time consuming. To overcome the difficulty, a number of software packages are available. One such package, DOS (Disc operating system) is very simple requiring only a few high level commands for its use.

## 8.11 VIDEO MONITORS

For display of characters or figures video monitors are used. An electron beam is projected on the screen as a very narrow pencil which appears like a dot on the screen. The screen is divided into a large number of horizontal lines and each line consists of a large number of dots. In some TV system, there are 625 horizontal lines and a line consists of 820 dots. The horizontal and vertical deflection circuits make the beam scan along the lines sequentially from top to bottom. By controlling the intensity of the beam, each individual dot may be made bright or dark. Characters and graphs are generated on the screen as a pattern of light and dark. A video set, a TV or even an oscilloscope may be used for this purpose.

The interfacing circuitry consists of a memory or display RAM, a character generator and a complete video generator. The CPU writes the character codes in ASCII or EBCDIC into the RAM. The character generator connects the character codes into their corresponding dot matrix pattern normally a 7x9 matrix, in a series of '1's and '0's for character to character in a line. These rows of the dot matrix codes are used by the video generator to connect them into a composite video signal which is fed to the TV or video. In case of an oscilloscope, the output of the character generator may be used to control the intensity of the beam.

A number of manufacturers have produced different CRT controller IC's like INTEL 8275, Motorola 6845 etc. which contain different amount of required circuits. 8275 contains a row counter programmable for 1 to 64 rows, a character counter programmable for 1 to 80 characters/ row and a scan line counter for 1 to 16 scan lines/ character. The character generator EPROM is not included for the sake of versatility. However, it has 80 byte buffer characters for the row to be displayed currently and 80 byte buffers for the character to be displayed in the next row. The 8279 produces vertical and horizontal synchronous signals, but external circuitry is required for timing of these signals.

# 9. Controlling and Peripheral Devices

There are certain devices which are used in special circumstances like emergency call up, synchronised action etc. These devices are interfaced using the CPU control lines like INT, HOLD, WAIT etc. When the CPU is interrupted, it gives up the current program and executes the interrupt service routine first and then if directed, returns to the main program. In WAIT state, the CPU holds all the three buses (address, data and control) constant and does not proceed so long as WAIT request is valid. In HOLD state, the CPU first completes the use of the buses necessary for the current instruction and then gives up the control over all the buses. Thus the normal flow of execution is interfered by the interfaced devices so that some special task may be performed.

There are some devices which may be interfaced in some other ways apart from control mode. For example, a key board may be connected to an input port which is polled time to time to check whether a key is pressed. Thus the microprocessor looses its valuable time. Hence, a key board may be connected in an interrupt driven mode so that whenever a key is pressed, the CPU is interrupted to insert the keyed data. In this way, the microprocessor can save the loss of time due to polling or checking. Of course, all the interfaces in control driven mode can be interfaced in other ways using polling and handshaking techniques at the cost of some delay not always desirable.

When an interfacing device uses a common memory along with the CPU, the 'WAIT STATE is necessary for the access of the common memory which is being used by the device. Some times an interfacing device may require a direct access to the memory when the 'HOLD-STATE' is required for the CPU. In may occasions, the control access interface mode becomes essential to meet the demand of practical situation. Some control access interfacing devices have been described in this chapter.

## 9.1 TIMER/COUNTER

The time counting, often required in on-line application, may be performed using CPU itself resulting in a loss of execution time for the CPU, which may not always be permissible. In such a case, a parallel counter is necessary to be interfaced in the interrupt mode. Different manufactures have produced a large variety of versatile Timer / Counter packaged in a single chip. These chips are quite versatile and powerful and are not only used as timers, but also used as general purpose counters. In timer mode, pulse width, phase difference etc. can be measured while in counter mode, it is possible to count frequency, pulses, objects etc. with a timer / counter chip. One of the most popular timer/ counter chips viz, Intel 8253 programmable internal Timer is described briefly.

8253 has three independent, programmable, 16-bit binary / BCD down counters for the pulses of 0 to 2 MHz. Each counter has separate clock input and gate along with the output. It has a control register to select and operate the timers. The INTEL 8253 is simple to interface. Its pin configuration is shown in Fig. 9.1.

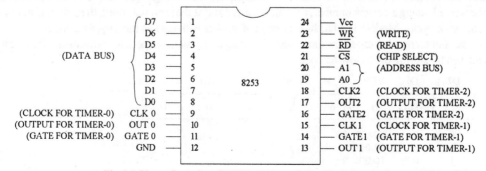

Fig. 9.1. Pin configuration of INTEL 8253 programmable timer

Data bus, address bus and $\overline{RD}$-$\overline{WR}$ are connected with the corresponding lines of CPU. If for a system, an 8253 is interfaced in I/O mapping and chip select line be taken for A7 = 1, A6 = 0, the address of T0 (timer-0), T1, T2 and CWR (control word register) will be 80, 81, 82 and 83 respectively. Now, if T0 is intended to be used by the CPU in interrupt access mode, the output of T0 may be connected to the INT - input of the CPU. In this case, the CLK - 0 or the clock of input T0 should be supplied with clock frequency less than 2 MHz. Each counter of 8253 is individually programmed by storing a control word in the CWR. The control word format is :

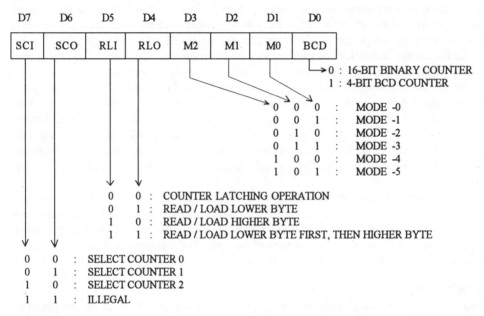

| D7 | D6 | D5 | D4 | D3 | D2 | D1 | D0 |
|-----|-----|-----|-----|-----|-----|-----|-----|
| SCI | SCO | RLI | RLO | M2 | M1 | M0 | BCD |

0 : 16-BIT BINARY COUNTER
1 : 4-BIT BCD COUNTER

| 0 | 0 | 0 | : | MODE -0 |
| 0 | 0 | 1 | : | MODE -1 |
| 0 | 1 | 0 | : | MODE -2 |
| 0 | 1 | 1 | : | MODE -3 |
| 1 | 0 | 0 | : | MODE -4 |
| 1 | 0 | 1 | : | MODE -5 |

| 0 | 0 | : | COUNTER LATCHING OPERATION |
| 0 | 1 | : | READ / LOAD LOWER BYTE |
| 1 | 0 | : | READ / LOAD HIGHER BYTE |
| 1 | 1 | : | READ / LOAD LOWER BYTE FIRST, THEN HIGHER BYTE |

| 0 | 0 | : | SELECT COUNTER 0 |
| 0 | 1 | : | SELECT COUNTER 1 |
| 1 | 0 | : | SELECT COUNTER 2 |
| 1 | 1 | : | ILLEGAL |

There are six modes of operations of 8253, selected by assigning M2 - M1 - M0 in the control word format. In Mode-0 (i.e., 'interrupt on terminal count' mode), the output remains low initially. If the count value be loaded, count is started and at the terminal count, the output becomes high till the count value is further loaded when the output goes low and the count is started. Mode-1 is a programmable retriggerable one-shot where the output goes low on the count following the rising edge of the gate. At terminal count, the output goes high again. Mode-2 is a rate generator where the output remains high normally and goes low for one clock period only. Count is started on loading the count value if gate is high. Mode-3 is a square wave generator. During one half of the count number time, the output of the timer remains high and during the next half, it remains low. If the count number be odd, (say N), for (N+1)/2 count time, the output becomes high again. Mode-4 is a software triggered strobe where loading a current number, a count is started and at the terminal count, the output gives a low pulse for one clock cycle. Mode-5 is a hardware triggered strobes with gate as the triggering input.

The counter may be read at any time. While counting is on, latching operation is necessary for reading which is achieved by storing the following code :

| D7 | D6 | D5 | D4 | D3 | D2 | D1 | D0 |
|-----|-----|-----|-----|-----|-----|-----|-----|
| SCI | SCO | 0 | 0 | 0 | 0 | 0 | 0 |

| 0 | 0 | : | TIMER | 0 |
| 0 | 1 | : | TIMER | 1 |
| 1 | 0 | : | TIMER | 2 |

where SCI-SCO specify the timer.

## 9.2 INTERRUPT CONTROLLER

Interrupt access interfaces are necessary in order to save time, normally lost in polling. For this, a number of interrupts are required though a microprocessor chip usually contains only a few interrupt inputs. To solve this problem, different manufacturers produced different types of interrupt controllers through which a number of separate interrupts are turned into one interrupt input of the microprocessor. Pin configuration of INTEL 8259 interrupt controller has been described in fig 9.2

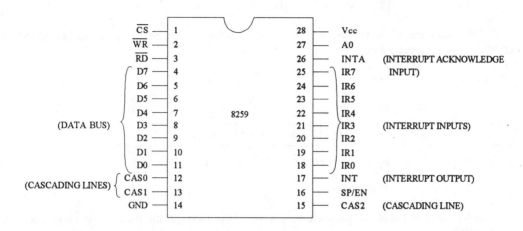

Fig. 9.2. Pin Configuration of INTEL 8259

iNTEL intended to use this interrupt controller with 8080, 8085, 8086 and 8088 families of microprocessors. However, it may be used with any type of microprocessors with the introduction of simple extra circuitries. It is an 8-level priority controller having facility of extending upto 64-level in cascaded form. Along with full programmable masking capability, it may be operated in various modes.

To use INTEL 8259, it must be remembered that this chip is intended to be used with INTR of 8085. If interrupt signal be asserted on the INTR input of 8085 (or 8086), $\overline{\text{INTA}}$ Pulse is sent out, CPU receives the RST instruction from the data bus and sends another $\overline{\text{INTA}}$ Pulse. Then receiving the lower byte of the base address of the interrupts, it delivers $\overline{\text{INTA}}$ pulse, and finally receives the higher byte of the address and delivers $\overline{\text{INTA}}$ signals. The designer must be careful not to permit any other interfacing devices to respond to these repeated INTA signals. To operate 8259, the chip needs 'Initialise Command Word' (ICW). For an 8085 system with simplified non cascaded configuration (single 8259), the following two initialise command words ICW1 and ICW2 may be used:

**ICW1:**

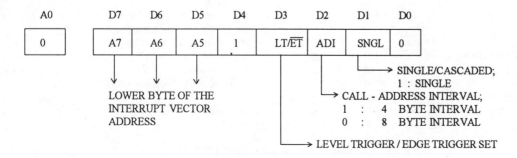

## ICW2:

| A0 | | D7 | D6 | D5 | D4 | D3 | D2 | D1 | D0 |
|----|---|----|----|----|----|----|----|----|----|
| 1 | | A15 | A14 | A13 | A12 | A11 | A10 | A9 | A8 |

where　A15 - A8　:　HIGHER BYTE OF THE INTERRUPT VECTOR ADDRESS
　　　　A0　　　:　THE A0 PIN OR 27TH PIN OF 8259

After initialisation, the masking to the interrupts may be set by giving an 'operational command word' or OCW, one such command word being,

## OCW1:

| A0 | | D7 | D6 | D5 | D4 | D3 | D2 | D1 | D0 |
|----|---|----|----|----|----|----|----|----|----|
| 1 | | M7 | M6 | M5 | M4 | M3 | M2 | M1 | M0 |

where,　$M_i$　=　INTERRUPT MASK FLAG OF THE i-TH INTERRUPT,
　　　　1　　:　MASK SET
　　　　0　　:　MASK RESET

In this simplified mode of operation, the priority of the interrupts are fixed in ascending order from IR0 through IR7.

To interface 8259, $\overline{RD}$, $\overline{WR}$, $\overline{INTA}$, Ao and DATA Bus are connected accordingly and INT of 8259 is connected to the INTR of 8085. In order to use a decoded line when A7 = 1, A6 = 0 and A5 = 0 for the chip select input of 8259 in I/O mapping, addresses for the $\overline{ICW1}$ register and ICW2 (or OCW1) register are 80 and 81 respectively. To use single 8259, one may connect $\overline{SP/EN}$ to + 5V, keeping CAS0-CAS2 open. CAS0 - CAS2 along with $\overline{SP/EN}$ are used in cascading mode where interrupts may be used upto 64-level.

## 9.3 DMA CONTROLLER

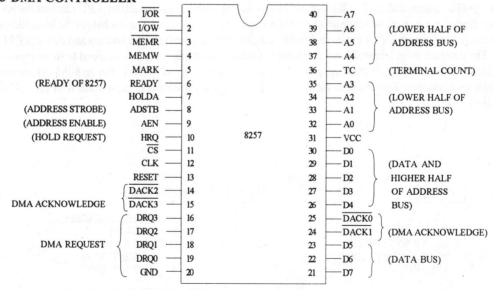

Fig. 9.3. Pin configuration of DMA controller INTEL 8257

The direct access controllers are specifically designed to simplify the transfer of data at high speed for the microprocessor system. Its primary function is to generate, upon request by a peripheral, a sequential addressing to the memory in order to allow the peripheral to write or read directly to or from the memory. Using the 'HOLD' function of the CPU, the possession of the system bus is accomplished. It also maintains the count of the required DMA cycles. A widely used popular DMA controller chip, the Intel 8257 has been described in Fig. 9.3.

On getting DMA request signal through DRQ input, 8257 acknowledges the input according to the priority basis and gives out the HOLD request to the CPU. On getting the hold acknowledge signal, it acquires the control of the system bus and generates necessary WRITE/READ pulses and addresses. The lower half of the address is directly given out through A0 to A7 while the higher half is given out through the data bus (D0 - D7) along with the latching pulse ADSTB. The address enable AEN may be used also to disable the system bus. The priority of the channels, if not programmed differently, is in descending order from DRQ0 to DRQ3. It is important to note that A0, A1, A2 and A3 are bi-directional and are used also to address the control registers of 8257.

For each channel, there exist one 16 bit address register and one 16 bit terminal count register (14 lower significant bit for count value and 2 most significant bits to indicate Read/Write). Besides, there are one '8-bit status register' and one '8-bit mode-set register'. The terminal count register and the address register are enabled when A3 = 0 whereas A3 = 1 enables the status (read only) and the mode-set register (write only). Further A0 = 0 is used for mode set register, status and the address-registers while A0 = 1 is necessary for the terminal count registers. A2 and A1 select the channel. Channels 0, 1, 2 and 3 are to be selected by storing 00, 01, 10 and 11 in A2 A1. Also 00 in A2A1 selects mode-set register and the status. Thus in the beginning, the address register of a channel is loaded sequentially by the lower half and higher half of the address. Next in a similar way, the terminal count is written and finally the mode set register is initialised. To write the most significant byte into the terminal count register, it is required to use D7 = 0 and D6 = 1 while in case of read, D7 = 1 and D6 = 0 are necessary. The mode set register format is :

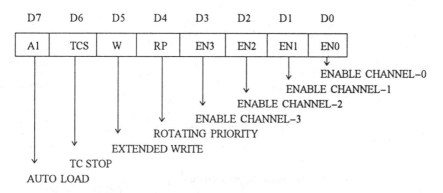

TC may be used as a flag to indicate an end of the DMA operation for the channel currently being serviced. The status when assigned with similar tasks, the format assumes the form :

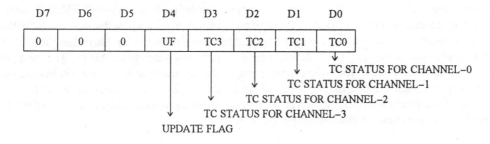

In order to interface an 8257 to an 8085 system, the data bus, address bus, $\overline{RD}$, $\overline{WR}$ and HLDA are to be connected accordingly between them. HRQ of 8257 may be connected to RST-6.5 (if not already engaged). For chip select, a decoded line for A7 = 1, A6 = 0 and A5 = 0 are taken in I/O mapping. An 8212 is also connected to the data bus of 8257 to hold the higher half of the address and its outputs are connected correspondingly to the higher half of the address bus. It is enabled by AEN and latched by ADSTB. The address of the mode set register (and the status) is 88. In order to write the address and terminal count registers of channel - 2, the corresponding addresses will be 84 and 85. It may be remembered that to write the terminal count register, the lower 8-bits are loaded first followed by the loading of higher 6-bits along with D6 = 1 and D7 = 0. The sequential loading of 8-bits of both address and the terminal counts are to be positioned correctly in the 16-bit registers of the address and the terminal counts.

## 9.4 SINGLE STEP LOGIC

Single stepper is a simple interfacing device used in debugging a program in microprocessor trainer kits in order to allow the microprocessor to perform only one instruction on pressing the 'single step' key. After the execution of each instruction, it is possible to examine the registers, memories, status, accumulator, PC, SP, stack etc. The buses and the control lines of different interfaces may also be examined to detect a fault in the system.

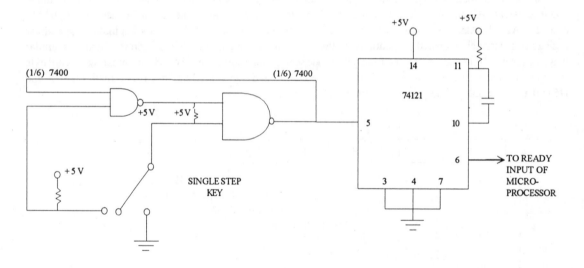

Fig. 9.4. Single stepper interface

There are different methods to perform the single step or double step operations, a simple and inexpensive method being described in Fig. 9.4. The READY line of the CPU is used to insert wait state as long as required. Two NAND gates are used to debounce the single step key, a spring loaded push-button switch. When the switch is pressed, a monostable multivibrator (74121) is triggered and produces a pulse whose duration is smaller than the time necessary to execute an instruction requiring the latest number of clock Cycles. On getting the READY signal, the CPU will start execution but in the T2 cycle of the next instruction, since the READY will be low again, the CPU will enter into WAIT state. Thus with every pressing of the key, only one instruction will be executed.

This technique of single stepping may be used with the CPU 8085, Z-80 etc. But if there be no READY input, this circuit is not directly interfaced. However, it is possible to use a similar circuitry or a modified version of it with any CPU in accordance with available pin functions.

# 10. Some Useful I/O Devices

## 10.1 INTRODUCTION

In the field of on-line monitory, control of power apparatus and systems and in designing protective systems, microprocessor has gained popularity because of its compactness, intelligence and reliability. In developing expert Instrumentation or control or protective system, proper interphasing arrangement should be made with the real system. Since the microprocessor accepts a voltage signal of magnitude +5V, signals from the real system should be converted to microprocessor compatible voltage signal. Some special types of I/O devices become advantageous for interfacing the microprocessor with the on-line real system. Some examples of such devices are the zero crossing detector (ZCD), the peak detector (PD) and the opto-isolator etc.

Zero crossing detector detectes the zero crossing of sinusoidal waveform at the rising and falling instants and synchronises microprocessor software with the sinusoid. For example, to trigger a thyristor, the trigger angle is to be calculated with reference to the zero crossing of the sinusoid at the rising and falling edges. ZCD converts the positive half of the ac waveform to a rectangular waveform and outputs low during the negative half cycle. The microprocessor, receiving the signal from ZCD through I/O ports, detects the rising and falling moments of ac waveform through software and controls the equipment according to the given software.

Peak detecter is useful in the operations with ac voltage or fluctuating d/c voltage. The magnitude of the a/c waveform varies instantaneously and the average and rms values of ac voltage are proportional to the peak value of the ac waveform. The peak detecter outputs positive peak value of ac voltage and conveys the same to microprocessor through A to D converter.

Optocoupler circuitry is extremely helpful to isolate optically the microprocessor with the power circuit. It provides protection to the microprocessor and stops reverse flow of power to the microprocessor. These devices along with some special purpose I/O devices have been discussed in this chapter.

## 10.2 ZERO CROSSING DETECTOR (ZCD)

Zero Crossing Detector is an useful input device. Zero of the a.c. wave is sensed by ZCD, the output of which being a square wave. Output square wave is achieved by the method of voltage comparison using an operational amplifier (LM 339). The system connection is shown in Fig. 10.1. The basis seven is grounded which acts as the reference. When input becomes equal to the reference voltage, square wave output is available. If the reference voltage is zero, square wave output is available starting at zero instant. In case of an operational amplifier, there is no feedback and hence the square wave is available due to saturation. The supply voltage is 5 V to make it compatible with I/O ports of the microcomputer.

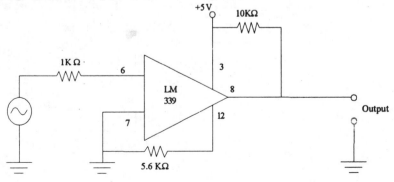

Fig. 10.1. Zero Crossing Detector (ZCD) circuit.

## 10.3 PEAK DETECTOR

Peak detector outputs the peak value of an alternating waveform. Further, a conventional voltmeter cannot be used to measure these non-sinusoidal waveforms (viz. square, triangular, sawtooth and pulse waves etc.) because it is designed to measure the rms value of the pure sine wave. One possible solution to this problem is to measure the peak values of the non-sinusoidal waveforms.

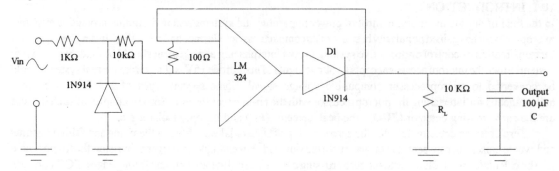

Fig. 10.2. Peak Detecter

Fig. 10.2 shows a peak detector that measures the positive peak values of the square wave input during the positive half-cycle of Vin, output of the OPAMP drives D1 on charging capacitor C to the positive value $V_p$ of the input voltage Vin. Thus when D1 is forward biased, OP-AMP operates as a voltage follower. On the other hand, voltage across C is retained. The only discharge path for C is through $R_L$. Since the input bias current $I_B$ is negligible, for proper operation of the circuit, charging time constant ($CR_d$) and discharging time constant ($CR_L$) must satisfy the following conditions:

$$C_{RD} \leq C_{RL} \quad i.e., \quad C_{RD} \leq (0.1)T$$

where    $R_d$ = resistance of the forward biased diode D1
$T$ = time period of the input waveform and $CR_L \geq 10\ T$, where $R_L$ is the load resistor.

## 10.4 OPTO-COUPLER

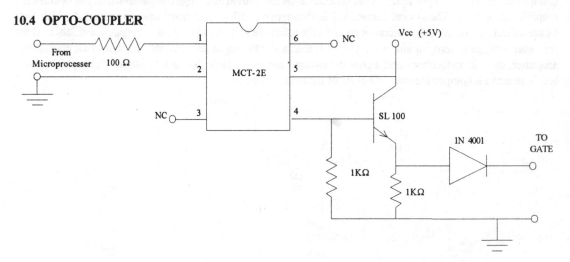

Fig. 10.3 Opto-coupler circuit

An opto-coupler (Fig. 10.3) is an useful interfacing device. It isolates the circuit employing different voltage level from the microcomputer circuit. It contains a light emitting diode (LED) and a transistor. The microprocessor sends a control signal to LED. The light emitted by LED causes photo transistor, connected in the control circuit, to conduct.

The gate circuit of the power SCR is connected to the emitter of a transistor (SL 100). Assuming that there is no radiant excitation, minority carriers are generated thermally and the electrons crossing from the base to the collector as well as the holes crossing from the collector to the base, constitute the reverse saturation collector current. With the signal obtained from output of microprocessor across pins 1 and 2 of chip MCT2E, the in-built LED glows, the photosensitive base of thyristor connected across pins 5 and 6 is activated and the gate receives a supply from emitter of the transistor (SL 100). Instantaneously, SCR is turned on. Thus, opto-coupler isolates high voltage power circuits from low voltage sophisticated triggering circuits.

## 10.5 RELAY

Relay is one of the most important interfacing devices commonly used in system protection. It is a simple but versatile device. Generally a relay is directly connected to an output port of the microprocessor.

Magnetic relay is frequently used as a simple and cheap device for bilateral potential-free switch. However, it requires much current to be triggered and hence a current buffer is connected to it as shown in Fig. 10.4.

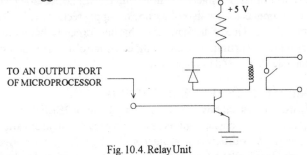

Fig. 10.4. Relay Unit

The connection details are so simple that it requires no explanation to understand the interfacing technique. It may be noted that the reverse biased diode is necessary to protect the system from inductive kick back of the relay coil.

There are a number of solid state relays made of power BJT. VMOS, TRIAC, SCR, SUS, SBS, GTO etc. These devices are sometimes switched by pulse transformer, LASCR or suitable opto-couplers to obtain a very high isolation of the high power lines with the microprocessor.

· As an example of the applications of the relays, a practical system of controlling a temperature bath is shown in fig. 10.5 in block diagram.

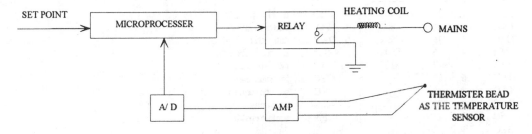

Fig. 10.5. Temperature bath

A thermistor  bead or any suitable element may be used to sense the temperature of the bath whose temperature is needed to be controlled.  The output of the sensor is converted into a temperature proportional voltage by a suitable amplifying circuitries, the voltage being converted into the digital form by an A/D converter. The microprocessor receives the output of the A/D converter and compares with the set-point inserted by the keyboard or a thumb wheel switch and triggers the relay to drive the heater coil so that the temperature of the bath remains effectively very close to the set point.

## 10.6  PARALLEL COMMUNICATION BUS STANDARD

For communication to  different interfacing units or  to  another  microprocessor system,  parallel bus is used usually.  The functions of different lines of a communication bus may differ and hence to maintain a conformity among various systems, a number of standard bus  configurations are suggested.  Among them, S-100, INTEL Multibus, GPIB etc. are important, though GPIB is widely used.

Format of the S-100 bus was developed by MIT Inc. for their ALTAIR Microcomputer based on 8080 microprocessor which contains a chassis with a power supply, a CPU card and slots to insert other PC boards like memory card, floppy controller card etc.  These cards are connected in S-100 bus format.  A 100-pin edge connector is used to insert the cards with 50 pins on each side of the board.

INTEL MULTIBUS is an industrial bus standard used to connect RAM, ROM or I/O boards within a microprocessor system.  This format is designed for an 86-pin edge connector along with an optional 60 pin edge connector.  The 86-pin edge connnector consists of the power supply section, a 20-bit address bus, a 16 bit data bus, and an extensive control bus.  One of the features of this bus format is that more than one CPU cards may be connected to form a multiprocessor unit.  To transfer the bus-control to a CPU board in priority basis, suitable bus-controller IC like Intel 8218 or 8288 may be used.

## 10.7  GENERAL PURPOSE INTERFACE BUS (GPIB)

GPIB is the most widely used industrial bus format popularly know as IEEE-488 or HPIB (Hewlette packard Interface Bus).  It is frequently used to connect another microprocessor system or various interfaces like printers, display monitors, tape recorders or different instruments like digital voltmeter, frequency counter, function generator.  It was developed by Hewlette Packard and accepted as standard by the IEEE.

The standard describes three types of devices which may be interfaced to GPIB.  One of them is a 'listener' which receives data, (eg, a printer, a display monitor etc.) other being a 'talker' which sends the data (eg, a tape recorder, a digital voltmeter etc.).  A device may be a combination of talker and a listener (eg, a microprocessor system, a programmable DVM.).  The third one is a 'controller' which determines who talks and who listens on the bus.

GPIB has eight bi-directional data lines, eight control lines, ground and shield connections.  The data lines transfer data, addresses, commands and status bytes among 8 to 15 instruments or units.  Pin configuration of the GPIB connector is shown in Fig. 10.6.

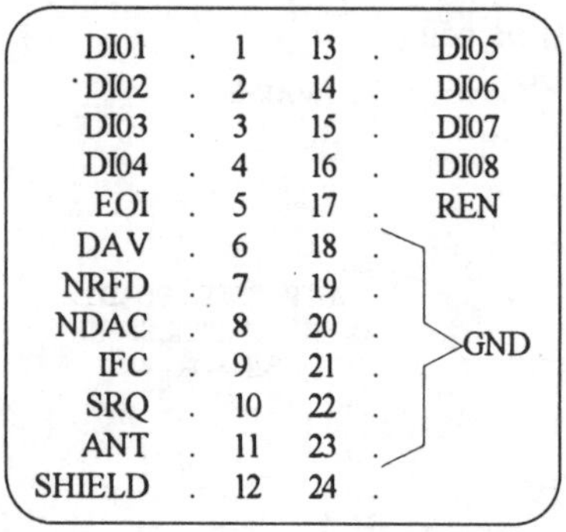

| | | | | | | |
|---|---|---|---|---|---|---|
| DI01 | . | 1 | 13 | . | DI05 | DIO : data in/out |
| DI02 | . | 2 | 14 | . | DI06 | EOI : end or identify |
| DI03 | . | 3 | 15 | . | DI07 | DAV : data valid |
| DI04 | . | 4 | 16 | . | DI08 | NRFD : not ready for data |
| EOI | . | 5 | 17 | . | REN | NDAC : not data accepted |
| DAV | . | 6 | 18 | . | | IFC : interface clear |
| NRFD | . | 7 | 19 | . | | SRQ : service request |
| NDAC | . | 8 | 20 | . | GND | ATN : attention |
| IFC | . | 9 | 21 | . | | REN : remote enable |
| SRQ | . | 10 | 22 | . | | |
| ANT | . | 11 | 23 | . | | |
| SHIELD | . | 12 | 24 | . | | |

Fig. 10.6. GPIB converter

The control unit sends command-address codes along with the data through data lines in accordance with a format shown in Table 10.1 to a talker or listener. The 8th bit of these words is of 'don't care' type and 7th and 6th bits specify the command while bits 5th through 1st, give address of the talker or listener. These codes are only valid where ATN line is low. It may be noted that no connecting unit can be addressed by 1 FC.

Table 10.1 Command address code format in GPIB

| D8 | D7 | D6 | D5 | D4 | D3 | D2 | D1 | Description |
|----|----|----|----|----|----|----|----|-------------|
| X | 0 | 0 | 0 | B4 | B3 | B2 | B1 | Universal commands |
| X | 0 | 1 | A5 | A4 | A3 | A2 | A1 | Listen addresses |
| X | 0 | 1 | 1 | 1 | 1 | 1 | 1 | Unlisten command |
| X | 1 | 0 | A5 | A4 | A3 | A2 | A1 | Talk addresses |
| X | 1 | 0 | 1 | 1 | 1 | 1 | 1 | Untalk command |
| X | 1 | 1 | A5 | A4 | A3 | A2 | A1 | Secondary commands |
| X | 1 | 1 | 1 | 1 | 1 | 1 | 1 | Ignored |

A listener is enabled when controller sends listening command with the respective address along with ATN being low. When the data transfer is complete, listener is turned off by controller with the unlisten command and talker is also turned off by the untalk command.

GPIB has five Bus Management lines viz. IFC, ATM, SRQ, REN and EOI. In addition, it has three Handshake lines DAV, NRFD and NDAC. These eight lines form the control bus. First the controller sends an IFC signal to set all the instruments on the bus, and with an interval, the controller goes on checking the SRQ line. When a unit requires to communicate with the other, it sends SRQ signals asserting low. The controller polls each device till it finds the device requesting service. The controller then makes ATN low, sends the address command for the proper listener, then sends the talk address command to the desired talker and makes ATN high. The talker then raises the DAV line, sends data to the data bus and the listener, on getting DAV high, makes NDAC low and receives the data from the data bus. When the listener receiver data, it makes NDAC high. Thus the talker and listener continue to communicate data by DAV and NDAC handshaking. When the data transfer is complete, the talker sends EOI signal when the controller sends, inturn, the unlisten and untalk commands.

INTEL 8292 is a GPIB controller with which CPU 8085 may be connected while the 6800 and other similar CPU may be connected with MC 68488 general purpose interface adapter. Using this bus format, several instruments may be connected to intelligent systems.

## 10.8 MULTI TALKER-LISTENER

Interface capabilities and bus structure of GPIB have been shown in Fig. 10.9 which explains multiple talker-multiple listener mode. The system consists of Data transfer line, Data transfer control line and General interface management line. Eight lines are used for bi-directional transfer of coded messages. There can be either commands or data from devices and are organised as a sequence of 8-bits.

In Data transfer control lines, 3 lines are used to manage the asynchronous transfer of information on the preceeding 8 lines between one 'talker' and one or more 'listener' devices.

General management line consisting of 5-lines indicates the nature of information (either address or data) on the previous lines and executes some special functions which permit expansion of the capabilities of the interface system.

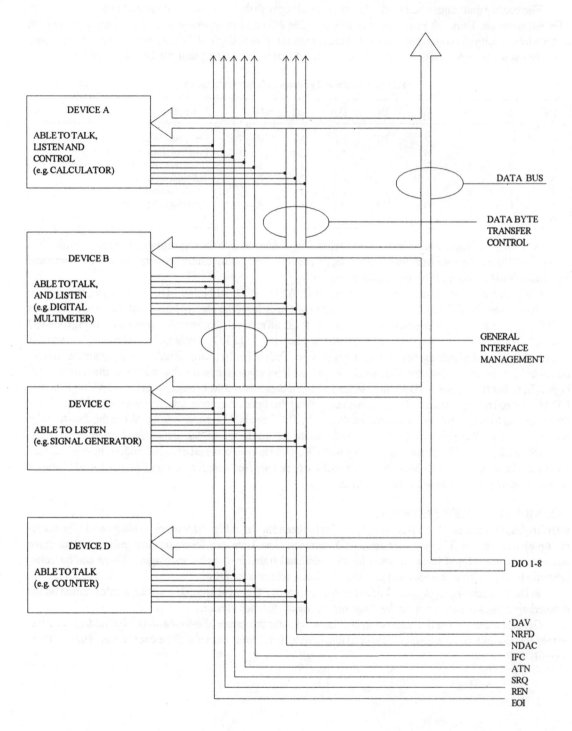

Fig. 10.7. Interface capabilities and bus structure of GPIB

### 10.9 PRINTER

A printer is a device to write output on a plain paper by the microprocessor system. In graphic mode, it may draw figures also. There are many types of printers based on different printing techniques. These are thermal type, Impact type, Dot Matrix type etc.

The dot matrix printers are equally suitable to print a character or to draw a graphic pattern. There are generally six rows and seven, eight or nine columns of dots on the head of a printer. These dots may be generated using different technical procedures. The CPU sends codes to print different dots to make a character or figure. Indeed the instructions necessary to use a printer depend on the manufacture.

To interface a printer, a parallel or a series bus may be used. A printer may also be connected to GPIB parallel bus format or RS - 232C serial bus format. However, many printers support the 'centronics parallel' connectors for interfacing . The pin functions (36-pin connector format) of the centronics bus is given in Table 10.2.

**Table 10.2. Centronix Parallel Signals**

| Pin No. | Signal | Direction |
|---|---|---|
| 1 | Strobe | IN |
| 2 | Data 1 | IN |
| 3 | Data 2 | IN |
| 4 | Data 3 | IN |
| 5 | Data 4 | IN |
| 6 | Data 5 | IN |
| 7 | Data 6 | IN |
| 8 | Data 7 | IN |
| 9 | Data 8 | IN |
| 10 | ACK (Acknowledge) | OUT |
| 11 | BUSY | OUT |
| 12 | PE (Page End) | OUT |
| 13 | PHI (pulled high internally) | |
| 14 | Auto feed | IN |
| 31 | Init (initialise) | IN |
| 32 | Error | OUT |
| 36 | Select | IN |
| 15, 16, 19-30 | GND | |

Data are supplied to pins 2 through 9 and the storbe line is pulsed low. If the printer is not busy, it acknowledges the receipt of the data and stores in its internal buffer. It will print a line of characters if a code LINE READ is instructed to it. Normally, a printer uses the standard ASCII codes to print a letter, number or character. Although the original standard ASCII codes were deviced for decimal numbers 0 to 127, some of the printers may modify it to a range of 0-225. In order to extend the range beyond 225, 'Escape' code ESC is used.

Printers have their own control codes in order to obtain its various features like single strike, emphasized double strike, enlarged character, italics, graphic characters, New-letter quality (NLQ) prints etc.

### 10.10 SIXTEEN CHANNEL MULTIPLEXER (1H6116)

When the number of input signals multiply, it becomes difficult to access the signals through ADC and I/O Ports. In that case multiplexer may be used to eliminate the complexity of the input device.

The 1H6116 is a CMOS monolithic, one out of 16-multiplexers and is a plug in replacement for the DG506. Four in binary decoding is used so that the 16-channels can be controlled by 4-storbe inputs, additionally a 5th input is provided to use as a system enable. If the enable input is 0V, none of the channels can be turned on. When the enable input is high (5V), the channels are sequenced with the 4 line storebe inputs. The 4 strobe inputs are controlled by TTL logic or CMOS logic elements, a '0' corresponding to any voltage less than 0.8V and an "1" corresponding to a voltage greater than 3V. However the enable input 18 must be taken to 5V to enable the system and less than 0.8V to disable the system. Pin Configuration of 1H6116 is shown in Fig. 10.8 and the Truth table in Table 10.3.

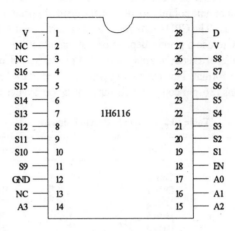

Fig. 10.8. Pin configuration of 1H6116

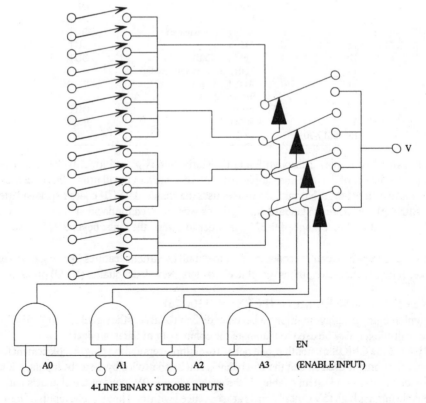

Fig. 10.9. Functional diagram

**Table 10.3. Truth Table of 1H6116**

| $A_3$ | $A_2$ | $A_1$ | $A_0$ | EN | ON SWITCH |
|-------|-------|-------|-------|-----|-----------|
| X | X | X | X | 0 | NONE |
| 0 | 0 | 0 | 0 | 1 | 1 |
| 0 | 0 | 0 | 1 | 1 | 2 |
| 0 | 0 | 1 | 0 | 1 | 3 |
| 0 | 0 | 1 | 1 | 1 | 4 |
| 0 | 1 | 0 | 0 | 1 | 5 |
| 0 | 1 | 0 | 1 | 1 | 6 |
| 0 | 1 | 1 | 0 | 1 | 7 |
| 0 | 1 | 1 | 1 | 1 | 8 |
| 1 | 0 | 0 | 0 | 1 | 9 |
| 1 | 0 | 0 | 1 | 1 | 10 |
| 1 | 0 | 1 | 0 | 1 | 11 |
| 1 | 0 | 1 | 1 | 1 | 12 |
| 1 | 1 | 0 | 0 | 1 | 13 |
| 1 | 1 | 0 | 1 | 1 | 14 |
| 1 | 1 | 1 | 0 | 1 | 15 |
| 1 | 1 | 1 | 1 | 1 | 16 |

Logic "1" $\longrightarrow$ $V_{AH}$ = 3.0V
Logic "0" $\longrightarrow$ $V_{AL}$ = 0.8V

The circuit diagram for obtaining 1 out of 32 channel multiplexer using two 1H6116 is shown in Fig. 10.10 and the corresponding decoded Truth Table has been presented in Table 10.4.

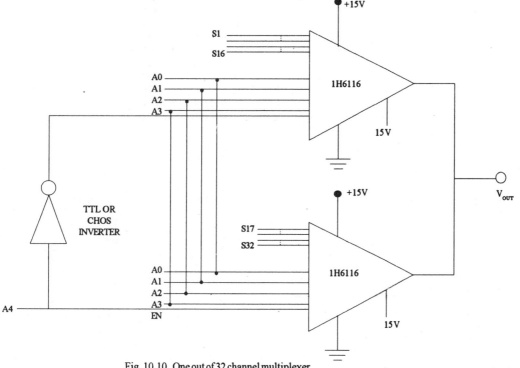

Fig. 10.10. One out of 32 channel multiplexer

Table 10.4. Decode truth table

| A4 | A3 | A2 | A1 | A0 | ON SWITCH |
|----|----|----|----|----|-----------|
| 0 | 0 | 0 | 0 | 0 | S1 |
| 0 | 0 | 0 | 0 | 1 | S2 |
| 0 | 0 | 0 | 1 | 0 | S3 |
| 0 | 0 | 0 | 1 | 1 | S4 |
| 0 | 0 | 1 | 0 | 0 | S5 |
| 0 | 0 | 1 | 0 | 1 | S6 |
| 0 | 0 | 1 | 1 | 0 | S7 |
| 0 | 0 | 1 | 1 | 1 | S8 |
| 0 | 1 | 0 | 0 | 0 | S9 |
| 0 | 1 | 0 | 0 | 1 | S10 |
| 0 | 1 | 0 | 1 | 0 | S11 |
| 0 | 1 | 0 | 1 | 1 | S12 |
| 0 | 1 | 1 | 0 | 0 | S13 |
| 0 | 1 | 1 | 0 | 1 | S14 |
| 0 | 1 | 1 | 1 | 0 | S15 |
| 0 | 1 | 1 | 1 | 1 | S16 |
| 1 | 0 | 0 | 0 | 0 | S17 |
| 1 | 0 | 0 | 0 | 1 | S18 |
| 1 | 0 | 0 | 1 | 0 | S19 |
| 1 | 0 | 0 | 1 | 1 | S20 |
| 1 | 0 | 1 | 0 | 0 | S21 |
| 1 | 0 | 1 | 0 | 1 | S22 |
| 1 | 0 | 1 | 1 | 0 | S23 |
| 1 | 0 | 1 | 1 | 1 | S24 |
| 1 | 1 | 0 | 0 | 0 | S25 |
| 1 | 1 | 0 | 0 | 1 | S26 |
| 1 | 1 | 0 | 1 | 0 | S27 |
| 1 | 1 | 0 | 1 | 1 | S28 |
| 1 | 1 | 1 | 0 | 0 | S29 |
| 1 | 1 | 1 | 0 | 1 | S30 |
| 1 | 1 | 1 | 1 | 0 | S31 |
| 1 | 1 | 1 | 1 | 1 | S32 |

# 11. Programming a Microprocessor

## 11.1 WRITING A PROGRAM

To develop a program, it is necessary to write the main steps of the job to be performed. Then it is essential to arrange the steps in a FLOW DIAGRAM representation of execution. In this diagram the flow of execution is indicated by arrow marks. The technique of flow diagram representation of softwares has been discussed below:

Starting of flow diagram is indicated by a small circle whereas the end is shown by a deformed circle. START and END may be written within the respective symbols.

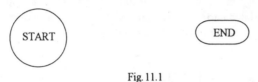

Fig. 11.1

It is often required to write some assignment statements after the START and these are written normally in a parallelogram whereas a rectangle may contain any statements in general. The statement may be written in ASSEMBLY language, MNEMONICS or in simple spoken language. The flow may be branched and the branching is done with respect to some condition. For example the statement "IS A EQUAL TO B ?" has two answers. If the condition is satisfied, it is considered as YES state and if not, a NO state. According to the YES or NO state, the flow is branched and this conditions are written in a rhombus as shown in Fig. 11.2. A typical

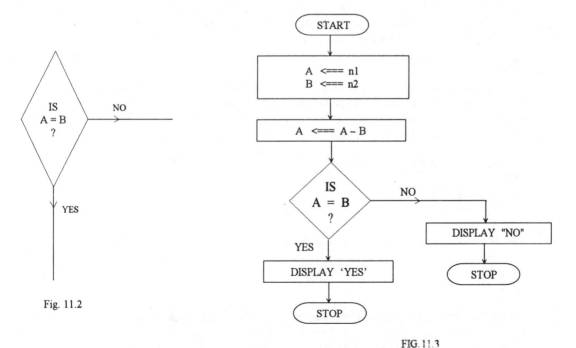

Fig. 11.2

FIG. 11.3

Flow Diagram is presented in Fig. 11.3.

Flow diagram representation is necessary for two reasons: it increases clarity of the program and simplifies translation of program into mnemonic codes of a microprocessor. To translate the flow diagram into mnemonic code, one may attempt to translate step by step, the different boxes of the diagram. It becomes helpful to write a program into five columns viz.

ADDRESS          LABELS          OPCODES          MNEMONICS          COMMENTS

The mnemonics are first written along with the comments, if necessary, for any particular instruction or step. Labels are necessary to indicate the jumping points and to refer a program or subprogram. Each of the programs or the subprograms should start with an identifying label. A label may be considered as a name of a program or of a stage of the program. It may be a collection of a few letters in upper case including numbers. After the program has been translated into the mnemonic codes, one may code the mnemonics using an opcode table given in the appendices. Proper allotment of memory address of different instructions completes the writing of the program.

## 11.2 DISPLAY TECHNIQUES FOR INTEL 8279

The capabilities and methods to display using an 8279 peripheral chip are quite versatile and elaborate as have already been described in INTERFACE section of the book. Codes for different numbers and characters are usually stored in EPROM in a system. Hence one needs to break up a Hexadecimal number into two digits and the codes corresponding to the digits are fetched from the table and stored sequentially in the display RAM of 8279.

For this, it may be necessary to use three subprograms of which one may be for breaking up of a number into two digits and storing them sequentially into the memory locations, say from 4040 to 4047. The subprogram may be labelled as SPLIT. The second subprogram may be labelled as CODE used to fetch the codes for the digits stored in the memory (4040 to 4047) from the look up table already stored in the EPROM by the system designer. The codes thus fetched from 4040 to 4047 respectively may be stored into the memory locations, say from 4040 to 4047. The third subprogram DISP will store the display codes (from 4040 to 4047) into the display RAM of 8279.

It is important to note that FF is a code for a blank character in the system we have used but one may find this code to be 00 in another system. To store a display code into one particular position of the display, the command 8X may be used where X indicates the position number starting from zero. In order to blank the 5th position, the following program may be used :

```
MVI A, 85 ; COMMAND TO STORE IN THE 5-TH POSITION
OUT 01
MVI A FF ; CODE FOR A BLANK.
OUT 00
```

To blank all the 8-characters, the code CC, CD or CF may be used as :

```
MVI A, CD
OUT 01
```

Code 9X may be used in place of 8X to write in one specific position of the display and after the command 9X has been used, all subsequent codes are stored in the successive positions of the display RAM in increasing order of positions which is called AUTOINCREMENTING property. The same technique can not be followed using command 8X.

Seven segment display pattern depends on the hardware implementation of the microprocessor system. A typical seven segment display pattern of the microcomputer used in this chapter has been presented in the following Table:

| d | c | b | a | h | g | f | e | OPCODE | DISPLAY PATTERN |
|---|---|---|---|---|---|---|---|--------|-----------------|
| 1 | 0 | 0 | 1 | 1 | 1 | 1 | 1 | 9F | 1 |
| 0 | 1 | 0 | 0 | 1 | 0 | 1 | 0 | 4A | 2 |
| 0 | 0 | 0 | 0 | 1 | 0 | 1 | 1 | 0B | 3 |
| 1 | 0 | 1 | 1 | 1 | 0 | 0 | 1 | BA | 4 |
| 0 | 0 | 1 | 0 | 1 | 0 | 0 | 1 | 29 | 5 |
| 0 | 0 | 1 | 0 | 1 | 0 | 0 | 0 | 28 | 6 |
| 0 | 0 | 0 | 0 | 1 | 1 | 1 | 1 | 0F | 7 |
| 0 | 0 | 0 | 0 | 1 | 0 | 0 | 0 | 08 | 8 |
| 1 | 0 | 0 | 0 | 1 | 0 | 0 | 1 | 89 | 9 |
| 1 | 0 | 0 | 0 | 1 | 1 | 0 | 0 | 8C | A |
| 0 | 0 | 1 | 1 | 1 | 0 | 0 | 0 | 38 | B |
| 0 | 1 | 1 | 0 | 1 | 1 | 0 | 0 | 6C | C |
| 0 | 0 | 0 | 1 | 1 | 0 | 1 | 0 | 1A | D |
| 0 | 1 | 1 | 0 | 1 | 0 | 0 | 0 | 68 | E |
| 1 | 1 | 1 | 0 | 1 | 0 | 0 | 0 | E8 | F |
| 0 | 0 | 1 | 0 | 1 | 0 | 0 | 0 | 28 | G |
| 1 | 0 | 0 | 1 | 1 | 0 | 0 | 0 | 98 | H |
| 0 | 0 | 0 | 1· | 1 | 1 | 1 | 0 | 1E | J |
| 0 | 1 | 1 | 1 | 1 | 1 | 0 | 0 | 7C | L |
| 0 | 0 | 0 | 0 | 1 | 1 | 0 | 0 | 0C | O |
| 1 | 1 | 0 | 0 | 1 | 0 | 0 | 0 | C8 | P |
| 0 | 0 | 1 | 0 | 1 | 0 | 0 | 1 | 29 | S |
| 0 | 0 | 0 | 1 | 1 | 1 | 0 | 0 | 1C | U |
| 1 | 0 | 0 | 0 | 1 | 1 | 0 | 0 | 8C | ⊓ |
| 1 | 0 | 1 | 1 | 1 | 0 | 1 | 0 | BA | ⊓ |
| 0 | 1 | 1 | 1 | 1 | 0 | 1 | 1 | 7B | = |
| 0 | 1 | 1 | 0 | 1 | 0 | 1 | 1 | 6B | = |
| 1 | 0 | 0 | 1 | 1 | 1 | 0 | 0 | 9C | ‖ |
| 0 | 0 | 1 | 1 | 1 | 0 | 0 | 0 | 38 | h |

## 11.3 PROGRAM EXAMPLES

*Problem 1*

Insert two Hex data in two consecutive memory locations 4080 H and 4081 H. Add them, split the result and store them in memory locations 4104 H and 4105 H. Store carry in the memory location 4103 H if there be any. Display the results on the display screen of the key board.

*Solution*

INPUT : 4080 H and 4081 H

OUTPUT : 4103 H, 4104 H, 4105 H and on the display screen.

In developing the program, initially two data (in Hex) have been stored in mem. locs. 4080 H and 4081 H. First data is brought to ACC. and the content of ACC. has been added to the content stored in mem. loc. 4081 H, the result being kept in ACC. Then the result has been transferred to mem. loc. 4082 H. Then clearing ACC. and Reg. B, the contents of Reg. B and carry have been added to the content of ACC. Carry bit may be set due to overflow in addition. The result is then transferred to Reg. C. Then clearing carry flag, the content of mem. loc. 4082 H has been tranferred to ACC again and copied in Reg. B. ACC. content being ANDed with F0 H, four lower bits have been made zero and using four RRC (Rotate A right, LSB to carry) operations, the upper and lower four bits have been interchanged to make the upper four bits zero. The result being stored in mem.

loc. 4104 H, the content of Reg. B has been moved to ACC., ANDed with 0F H and the result has been kept in mem. loc. 4105 H. Then the content of Reg. C has been transferred to mem. loc. 4103 H and calling the DISPLAY SUBROUTINE stored in EPROM (which is readily available in every microcomputer kit), result has been displayed on the display screen.

If 75 H and 39 H be the data stored in mem. locs. 4080 H and 4081 H, the result will be:

| INPUT | OUTPUT | ON DISPLAY SCREEN |
|---|---|---|
| 4080 H: 75 H | 4103 H: 01 H | 0108 |
| 4081 H: 93 H | 4104 H: 00 H | |
| | 4105 H: 08 H | |

With inputs 20 H and A5 H in 4080 H and 4081 H respectively, the contents of the mem. locs. 4103 H, 4104 H and 4105 H will be 00 H, 0C H and 05 H respectively and display screen will show the result 00C5 H.

It may be noted that the procedure is not the only way to add two hex. numbers. The assembly language program along with flowchart has been presented as under :

**THE PROGRAM**

| MEM. LOC. | OP-CODE | | | MNEMONIC | | | COMMENTS |
|---|---|---|---|---|---|---|---|
| 4200 | 21 | 80 | 40 | LXI | H | 4080 | INITIALISE MEM. LOCATION 4080 H |
| 4203 | 36 | D$_2$D$_1$ | | MVI | M | D$_2$D$_1$ | MOVE DATA D$_2$D$_1$ TO MEM. LOC. 4080 H |
| 4205 | 23 | | | INX | H | | INITIALISE NEXT MEM. LOC. 4031 H |
| 4206 | 36 | D$_4$D$_3$ | | MVI | M | D$_4$D$_3$ | MOVE DATA D$_4$D$_3$ TO MEM. LOC. 4081 H |
| 4208 | 2B | | | DCX | H | | DECREMENT HL PAIR (INITIALISE 4080 H) |
| 4209 | 7E | | | MOV | A,M | | MOVE DATA FROM MEMORY TO ACC. |
| 420A | 23 | | | INX | H | | INCREMENT HL PAIR TO 4081 H |
| 420B | 86 | | | ADD | M | | ADD (MEM.) WITH (ACC.), PUT RESULT IN ACC. |
| 420C | 23 | | | INX | H | | INCREMENT (HL) PAIR AT 4082 H |
| 420D | 77 | | | MOV | M,A | | MOVE DATA FROM ACC. TO MEM. |
| 420E | 3E | 00 | | MVI | A | 00 | MOVE IMMEDIATE 00 H TO ACC. |
| 4210 | 06 | 00 | | MVI | B | 00 | MOVE IMMEDIATE 00 H TO REG. B |
| 4212 | 88 | | | ADC | B | | ADD (CARRY) & (REG. B) TO (ACC.) |
| 4213 | 4F | | | MOV | C,A | | MOVE DATA FROM ACC. TO REG. C |
| 4214 | 37 | | | STC | | | SET CARRY BIT TO 1 |
| 4215 | 3F | | | CMC | | | COMPLEMENT CARRY |
| 4216 | 7E | | | MOV | A,M | | MOVE DATA FROM MEM. TO ACC. |
| 4217 | 47 | | | MOV | B,A | | MOVE DATA FROM ACC. TO REG. B |
| 4218 | E6 | F0 | | ANI | F0 | | ADD F0 H WITH A, PUT RESULT IN ACC. |
| 421A | 0F | | | RRC | | | ROTATE (ACC.) RIGHT, LSB TO CARRY |
| 421B | 0F | | | RRC | | | ROTATE (ACC.) RIGHT, LSB TO CARRY |
| 421C | 0F | | | RRC | | | ROTATE (ACC.) RIGHT, LSB TO CARRY |
| 421D | 0F | | | RRC | | | ROTATE (ACC.) RIGHT, LSB TO CARRY |
| 421E | 21 | 04 | 41 | LXI | H | 4104 | INITIALISE MEM. LOC. 4104 H |
| 4221 | 77 | | | MOV | M,A | | MOVE DATA FROM ACC. TO MEM. |
| 4222 | 78 | | | MOV | A,B | | MOVE DATA FROM REG. B TO ACC. |
| 4223 | E6 | 0F | | ANI | 0F | | AND 0F H WITH (ACC.), STORE RESULTS IN ACC. |
| 4225 | 23 | | | INX | H | | INCREMENT HL PAIR |
| 4226 | 77 | | | MOV | M,A | | MOVE DATA FROM ACC. TO MEM. |
| 4227 | 2B | | | DCX | H | | DECREMENT HL PAIR |
| 4228 | 2B | | | DCX | H | | DECREMENT HL PAIR |
| 4229 | 71 | | | MOV | M,C | | MOVE DATA FROM REG. C TO MEMORY |
| 422A | 2B | | | DCX | H | | DECREMENT HL PAIR |
| 422B | 36 | 00 | | MVI | M | 00 | MOVE 00 H TO MEMORY DIRECTLY |
| 422D | 3E | 01 | | MVI | A | 01 | INITIALISATION FOR DISPLAY POSITION |
| 422F | 06 | 00 | | MVI | B | 00 | ON THE DISPLAY SCREEN |

| MEM. LOC. | OP-CODE | | | MNEMONIC | | | COMMENTS |
|---|---|---|---|---|---|---|---|
| 4231 | 21 | 02 | 41 | LXI | H | 4102 | INITIALISATION FOR THE STARTING ADDRESS OF DATA STORED FOR DISPLAY |
| 4234 | CD | 83 | 02 | CALL | 0283 | | CALL DISPLAY SUBROUTINE (ADDRESS 0283 H) |
| 4237 | C3 | 31 | 42 | JMP | 4231 | | JUMP TO ADDRESS 4231 H |

In developing program, it has been assumed that the microprocessor has been provided with a display screen along with a key board and the screen has been divided into three different fields, viz. STATUS, ADDRESS and DATA FIELDS (Fig. 11.5). Fig. 11.6 shows the necessary flowchart.

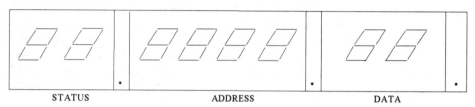

STATUS   ADDRESS   DATA

Fig. 11.5. Display fields

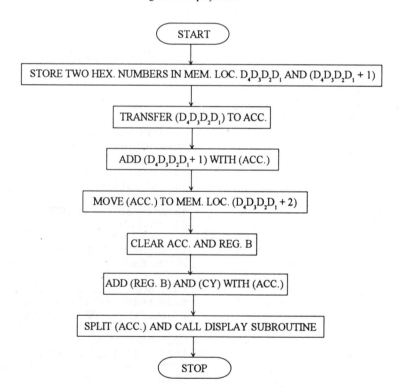

START

STORE TWO HEX. NUMBERS IN MEM. LOC. $D_4D_3D_2D_1$ AND $(D_4D_3D_2D_1 + 1)$

TRANSFER $(D_4D_3D_2D_1)$ TO ACC.

ADD $(D_4D_3D_2D_1 + 1)$ WITH (ACC.)

MOVE (ACC.) TO MEM. LOC. $(D_4D_3D_2D_1 + 2)$

CLEAR ACC. AND REG. B

ADD (REG. B) AND (CY) WITH (ACC.)

SPLIT (ACC.) AND CALL DISPLAY SUBROUTINE

STOP

Fig. 11.6. Flow chart for addition of two hex. numbers

Display field may be selected using words MVI A 00/01/02 respectively. A 'dot' may or may not be displayed according to the necessity at the end of each field using the words MVI B 01 or MVI B 00 respectively.

*Problem 2*

Select maximum from an array of numbers and display the same.

An array of ten hex data has been stored in mem. locs. 4130 H to 4139 H at random. The aim is to select the maximum from the array. The program has been started from mem. loc. 4100 H. The philosophy of developing of program is as under :

Starting address of array, viz. 4130 H is initialised first and the content of it has been transferred to ACC., the size of data reduced by '1' (9 H in this case) being stored in Reg. B as counter. Then the content of next location of the data table being transferred to Reg. C, the same has been compared to the content of Acc. If no carry flag be affected i.e., if carry remains low, the content of Reg. B has been decremented by one. Provided the content of Reg. B is not zero, the processor again brings the content of next mem. loc. of data table to Acc. and followes the same operation of comparison. During comparison, if carry flag be affected, the content of Reg. C will be greater than that of Acc. and in such case, the content of Reg. C is to be transferred to Acc. and the procedure of comparison of the next data from data table is performed after transferring the same in Reg. C with the content of Acc. In this way the maximum number can be obtained in Acc. when the comparison with all data in data Table will be over. In the program, the result of Acc. has been splitted and stored in mem. locs. 413A H and 413B H respectivelly. Then following the display subrouting, the maximum data has been displayed on the screen of the keyboard.

| INPUT | : DATA (HEX) |
|---|---|
| 4130 H | 10  06  13 |
| 4133 H | 09  0A  11 |
| 4336 H | 14  05  02 |
| 4139 H | 01 |

| OUTPUT | : 413A H | 01 H |
|---|---|---|
| | 413B H | 04 H |

ON DISPLAY SCREEN  :  14

**THE PROGRAM**

| MEM. LOC. | OPCODE | MNEMONIC | COMMENTS |
|---|---|---|---|
| 4100 | 21  30  41 | LXI   H   4130 | INITIALISE STARTING ADDRESS 4130 H OF THE ARRAY OF NUMBERS |
| 4103 | 06  09 | MVI   B   09 | MOVE DATA 09 TO REG. B AS THE LENGTH OF THE ARRAY TO BE SEARCHED |
| 4105 | 7E | MOV   A,M | TRANSFER MEMORY CONTENT TO ACC. |
| 4106  LOOP1 | 23 | INX   H | INCREMENT HL PAIR |
| 4107 | 4E | MOV   C,M | TRANSFER MEMORY CONTENT TO REG. C |
| 4108 | B9 | CMP   C | COMPARE (REG. C) WITH (ACC.) |
| 4109 | D2  0D  41 | JNC   LOOP2 | IF CARRY BIT IS 0, JUMP TO LOOP2 |
| 410C | 79 | MOV   A,C | MOVE (REG. C) TO ACC. IF CARRY BIT BE 1 |
| 410D  LOOP2 | 05 | DCR   B | DECREMENT (REG. B) |
| 410E | C2  06  41 | JNZ   LOOP1 | IF RESULT IS NOT ZERO, JUMP TO LOOP1 |
| 411] | 23 | INX   H | OTHERWISE, INCREMENT HL PAIR |
| 4112 | 77 | MOV   M,A | MOVE MEMORY CONTENT TO ACC. |
| 4113 | 21  3A  41 | LXI   H   413A | INITIALISATION FOR CALLING 'SPLIT' |
| 4116 | 56 | MOV   D,M | MOVE DATA FROM MEM. LOC. 413A TO REG. D |
| 4117 | CD  00  42 | CALL   SPLIT | CALL SUB ROUTINE 'SPLIT' TO SPLIT THE MAXIMUM NUMBER & STORE THEM IN MEM. LOC. 4113 AND 4114 H. |
| 411A | 3E  02 | MVI   A   02 | INITIALISE ACC. TO SELECT DISPLAY FIELD |
| 411C | 06  00 | MVI   B   00 | INITIALISE REG. B FOR DISPLAY WITHOUT DECIMAL DOT |
| 411E | 21  13  42 | LXI   H   4213 | INITIALISE STARTING ADDRESS OF THE MEM. LOC. CONTAINING THE SPLITED DATA. |
| 4121 | CD  83  02 | CALL   0283 | CALL 'DISPLAY' SUBROUTINE STORED IN EPROM |
| 4124 | 76 | HLT | HALT UNTIL INTERRUPTED |

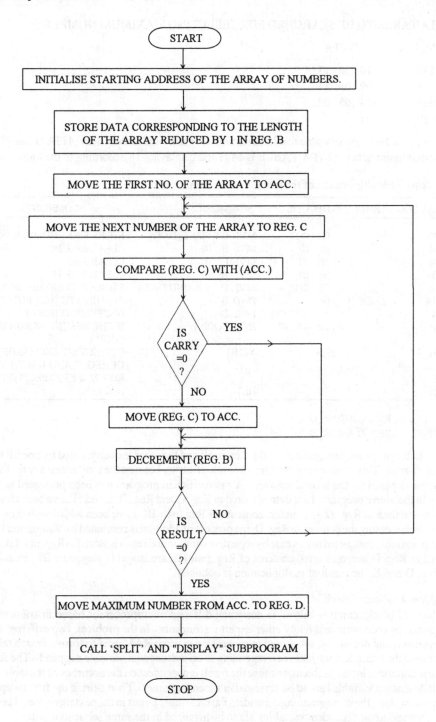

Fig. 11.7. Flow chart for selecting maximum from an array of numbers

DATA TABLE TO BE SEARCHED FOR SELECTING MAXIMUM NUMBER :

MEM. LOC.        DATA

| | |
|---|---|
| 4130 | 10  06  13 |
| 4133 | 09  0A  11 |
| 4336 | 14  05  02 |
| 4139 | 01 |

Execution of above programme results in storing 01 H and 04 H in mem. locs. 413A H and 413B H respectively since maximum data in DATA TABLE is 14 H and displaying 14 according to the Flow Chart (Fig.11.7)

*Problems* 3 : Multiplication of the two 8-bit Hex data.

| MEM. LOC. | LABEL | OPCODE | MNEMONICS | COMMENTS |
|---|---|---|---|---|
| 4240 | | 0E $D_2D_1$ | MVI  C   FIRST  DATA | STORE FIRST NUMBER IN REG. C |
| 4242 | | 06  00 | MVI  B   00 | CLEAR REG. B |
| 4244 | | 2E  00 | MVI  L   00 | CLEAR REG. L |
| 4246 | | 26  00 | MVI  H   00 | CLEAR REG. H |
| 4248 | | 16  $D_4D_3$ | MVI  D   SECOND DATA | STORE SECOND NUMBER IN REG. D |
| 424A | LOOP  1 | 09 | DAD  B | ADD (BC) TO (HL), PUT THE RESULT IN HL |
| 424B | | 15 | DCR  D | DECREMENT (REG. D) |
| 424C | | C2  4A  42 | JNZ  LOOP 1 | IF THE RESULT BE NON ZERO, GO TO LOOP 1 |
| 424F | | EB | XCHG | OTHERWISE, EXCHANGE THE CONTENTS OF REG. H AND L WITH THOSE OF REG. D & E RESPECTIVELY |
| 4250 | | 76 | HLT | HALT |

INPUT    :   REG. C AND REG. D
OUTPUT  :   REG. D AND REG. E

In this program, one number is added by itself and the other is decremented by one till the second number becomes zero. This is not an efficient way of multiplication because the time necessary for the execution of this program depends on the second number. A more efficient program has been presented in Section 11.5.

In the above program, first data is stored in Reg. C and Reg. B, L and H have been cleared. Then storing the second data in Reg. D as counter, contents of Reg. pair BC have been added with those of Reg. pair HL. Then decrementing the counter in Reg. D, the process of addition is continued till the counter becomes zero. The multiplication is completed in this case by repetitive addition and result is stored in Reg. pair HL. When the counter stored in Reg. D becomes zero, contents of Reg. pair HL are stored in Reg. pair DE. Examining the contents of Reg. D and E, the result of multiplication is obtained.

*Problem* 4 : Block Search.

Problem of block search is helpful in designing different microprocessor based instruments, viz. Voltmeter, Ammeter, Speedometer and many other expert instruments. In the problem, two different types of variables, independent and dependent, are stored in succession in some RAM area to form a search table. The task is to determine the dependent variable corresponding to an independent variable supplied. The formation of search table is important in this problem, because the result is dependent on the accuracy of the table. To form the table, the independent variables are to be arranged in ascending order. Then storing the first independent variable in some mem. loc., the corresponding dependent variable must be put in the next mem. loc. The other independent and corresponding dependent variables are to be arranged in the same sequential order.

The philosophy of block search is to store an independent variable in some memory location (say, 4080 H). The corresponding dependent variable is to be searched. In the program, the length of search table (number of independent variables included in the table) is stored in Reg. B as counter. Then the content of mem. loc.

4080 H has been transferred to Reg. C and mem. loc. corresponding to the first independent variable has been initialised. The content of this mem. loc. being transferred to Acc. is compared with the content (supplied independent variable) of Reg. C. If the result is not zero, the counter (content of Reg. B) is to be decremented and the next independent variable is brought to Acc. for comparison with the content of Reg. C. The procedure is followed till no matching is obtained. The matching is obtained when the results of comparison between (Acc.) and (Reg. C) is zero. In this condition, the processor collects the data of the next mem. loc. of the search table, stores the same in Reg. B and displays the result on the display screen of the keyboard.

**THE PROGRAM**

| MEM. LOC. | LABEL | OP-CODE | | | MNEMONICS | | | COMMENTS |
|---|---|---|---|---|---|---|---|---|
| 4300 | | 21 | 80 | 40 | LXI | H | 4080 | INITIALISE MEM. LOC. 4080 H WHERE THE PARTICULAR INDEPENDENT DATA IS STORED FOR TABLE SEARCHING. |
| 4303 | | 4E | | | MOV | C,M | | MOVE DATA FROM (MEM.) TO REG. C. |
| 4304 | | 06 | 0A | | MVI | B | 0A | MOVE DATA CORRESPONDING TO THE LENGTH OF THE SEARCH TABLE IN REG. B. |
| 4306 | | 21 | 37 | 43 | LXI | H | 4337 | INITIALISE STARTING ADDRESS OF THE SEARCH TABLE. |
| 4309 | LOOP 1 | 7E | | | MOV | A,M | | MOVE THE FIRST DATA FROM THE SEARCH TABLE TO ACC. |
| 430A | | B9 | | | CMP | C | | COMPARE THE CONTENT OF REG. C WITH THAT OF (ACC). |
| 430B | | CA | 18 | 43 | JZ | LOOP 2 | | JUMP ON ZERO TO MEM. LOC. 4318 H. |
| 430E | | 05 | | | DCR | B | | DECREMENT THE CONTENT OF REG. B. |
| 430F | | C2 | 13 | 43 | JNZ | LOOP 4 | | JUMP ON NO ZERO TO LOOP 4 |
| 4312 | | 76 | | | HLT | | | OTHERWISE HALT |
| 4313 | LOOP 4 | 23 | | | INX | H | | INCREMENT HL REGISTER-PAIR. |
| 4314 | | 23 | | | INX | H | | INCREMENT HL REGISTER-PAIR. |
| 4315 | | C2 | 09 | 43 | JMP | LOOP 1 | | JUMP TO MEM. LOC. 4309 H |
| 4318 | LOOP 2 | 23 | | | INX | H | | INCREMENT HL REGISTER PAIR. |
| 4319 | | 46 | | | MOV | B,M | | MOVE DATA FROM MEMORY TO REG. B |
| 431A | | CD | 00 | 44 | CALL | SPLIT | | CALL SUB ROUTINE 'SPLIT' |
| 431D | LOOP 3 | CD | 00 | 43 | CALL | DISPLAY | | CALL SUB-ROUTINE 'DISPLAY' |
| 4320 | | C3 | 1D | 43 | JMP | LOOP3 | | JUMP TO MEM. LOC. 431D. |

**Search Table**

| MEM. LOC. | INDEPENDENT DATA | DEPENDENT DATA |
|---|---|---|
| 4337 | 01 | 11 |
| 4339 | 02 | 22 |
| 433B | 03 | 33 |
| 433D | 04 | 44 |
| 433F | 05 | 55 |
| 4341 | 06 | 66 |
| 4343 | 07 | 77 |
| 4345 | 08 | 88 |
| 4347 | 09 | 99 |
| 4349 | 0A | 10 |

| | | | |
|---|---|---|---|
| INPUT | : | ANY ONE DATA FROM 01 H TO 0A H IS TO BE STORED IN MEM. LOC. 4080 H | |
| OUTPUT | : | ON THE DISPLAY SCREEN | |

| | | INPUT | OUTPUT | INPUT | OUTPUT |
|---|---|---|---|---|---|
| RESULT | : | INPUT | OUTPUT | INPUT | OUTPUT |
| | | 05 H | 55 H | 09 H | 99 H |

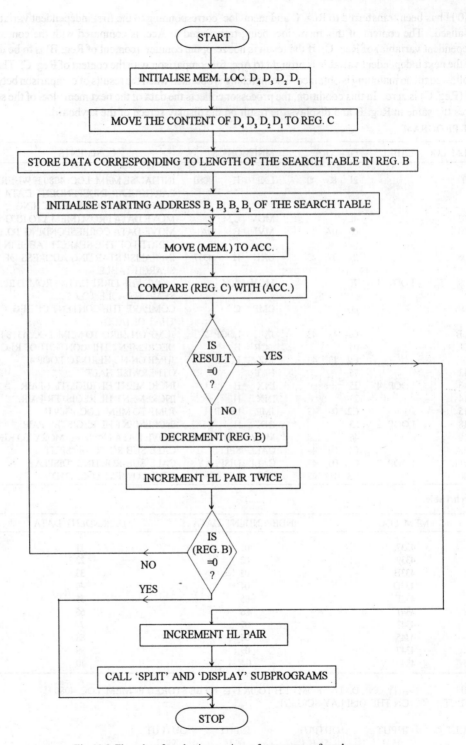

Fig. 11.8. Flow chart for selecting maximum from an array of numbers

## 11.4 DEVELOPING SUBPROGRAM

It is very helpful to develop the Subprograms according to the requirements of different jobs and some of this subprograms are often seen to be very useful in various types of jobs. Some of these are display, block move, searching, sorting, square wave generation, triangular wave generation, pulse count,different numerical computation etc. One may develop one's own subprograms from the idea gained from examples already shown. Some of these types of subprograms are developed below:

### SUBPROGRAM 1

'BCD' : This program converts a 14-bit hexadecimal number into a 4-digit Binary Coded Decimal value (packed). It is useful to remember that 270F H = 9999 (Decimal).

INPUT : A 14 - bit binary number into HL Reg.
OUTPUT : A 4 - digit BCD equivalent into HL Reg.
AFFECTS : A, PSW, C, D, E.

| MEM. LOC. | LABEL | OP-CODE | | | MNEMONICS |
|-----------|-------|---------|----|----|-----------|
| 2000 | BCD | 0E | 10 | | MVI C, 10 |
| 2002 | | 11 | 00 | 00 | LXI D, 00 00 |
| 2005 | LOOP | AF | | | XRA A |
| 2006 | | 29 | | | DAD H |
| 2007 | | 7B | | | MOV A,E |
| 2008 | | 8F | | | ADC A |
| 2009 | | 27 | | | DAA |
| 200A | | 5F | | | MOV E,A |
| 200B | | 7A | | | MOV A,D |
| 200C | | 8F | | | ADC A |
| 200D | | 27 | | | DAA |
| 200E | | 57 | | | MOV D,A |
| 200F | | 0D | | | DCR C |
| 2010 | | C2 | 05 | 20 | JNZ LOOP |
| 2013 | | EB | | | XCHG |
| 2014 | | C9 | | | RET. |

### SUBPROGRAM 2

'HEX' : This programe converts a 4 -digit BCD number in HL into a 16-bit binary in HL.

INPUT : A 14 - bit binary number into HL Reg.
OUTPUT : A 4 - digit BCD equivalent into HL Reg.
AFFECTS : A, PSW, C, D, E.

| MEM. LOC. | LABEL | OP-CODE | | | MNEMONICS |
|-----------|-------|---------|----|----|-----------|
| 2000 | HEX | 11 | 00 | 00 | LXI D, 00 00 |
| 2003 | | D5 | | | PUSH D |
| 2004 | | 0E | 04 | | MVI C, 04 |
| 2006 | LOOP | AF | | | XRA A |
| 2007 | | 29 | | | DAD H |
| 2008 | | 17 | | | RAL |
| 2009 | | 29 | | | DAD H |
| 200A | | 17 | | | RAL |
| 200B | | 29 | | | DAD H |
| 200C | | 17 | | | RAL |
| 200D | | 29 | | | DAD H |

| MEM. LOC. | LABEL | OP-CODE | | | MNEMONICS | |
|-----------|-------|---------|---|---|-----------|---|
| 200E | | 17 | | | RAL | |
| 200F | | E3 | | | XTHL | |
| 2010 | | 29 | | | DAD | H |
| 2011 | | 54 | | | MOV | D,H |
| 2012 | | 5D | | | MOV | E,L |
| 2013 | | 29 | | | DAD | H |
| 2014 | | 29 | | | DAD | H |
| 2015 | | 19 | | | DAD | D |
| 2016 | | 5F | | | MOV | E,A |
| 2017 | | 16 | 00 | | MVI | D, 00 |
| 2019 | | 19 | | | DAD | D |
| 201A | | E3 | | | XTHL | |
| 201B | | 0D | | | DCR | C |
| 201C | | C2 | 06 | 20 | JNZ | LOOP |
| 201F | | E1 | | | POP | H |
| 2020 | | C9 | | | RET. | |

SUBPROGRAM 3

'MULT' : This program multiplies an 8-bit binary number in Reg.H by an 8-bit binary number in Reg. L. The result is in HL.

INPUT       :   Two 8-bit binary number in H and L.
OUTPUT    :   16-bit result in HL
AFFECTS   :   A,C,D,E,F.

| MEM. LOC. | LABEL | OP-CODE | | | MNEMONICS | | |
|-----------|-------|---------|---|---|-----------|---|---|
| 2000 | MULT | 7C | | | MOV | A, | H |
| 2001 | | 26 | 00 | | MVI | H | 00 |
| 2003 | | E5 | | | PUSH | H | |
| 2004 | | D1 | | | POP | D | |
| 2005 | | 6C | | | MOV | L,H | |
| 2006 | | 0E | 08 | | MVI | C, | 08 |
| 2008 | LOOP | B7 | | | ORA | A | |
| 2009 | | 1F | | | RAR | | |
| 200A | | D2 | 0E | 20 | JNC | REPT | |
| 200D | | 19 | | | DAD | D | |
| 200E | REPT | EB | | | XCHG | | |
| 200F | | 29 | | | DAD | H | |
| 2010 | | EB | | | XCHG | | |
| 2011 | | 0D | | | DCR | C | |
| 2012 | | C2 | 08 | 20 | JNZ | LOOP | |
| 2015 | | C9 | | | RET | | |

SUBPROGRAM 4

'DIV' : This program divides a 16-bit binary number in HL by an 8-bit binary number in Reg. D. The integer part of the result is in HL and the fraction part in Reg. D.

INPUT       :   A 16-bit binary number in HL and an 8-bit binary number in Reg. D
OUTPUT    :   The result in HL (integer part) and in Reg. D (fraction part).
AFFECTS   :   A,B,C,D,E.

| MEM. LOC. | LABEL | OP-CODE | | | MNEMONICS | |
|-----------|-------|---------|---|---|-----------|---|
| 2000 | DIV | 01 | 00 | 00 | LXI | B, 0000 |
| 2003 | | C5 | | | PUSH | B |
| 2004 | | 1E | 18 | | MVI | E, 18 |
| 2006 | LOOP | 29 | | | DAD | H |
| 2007 | | 78 | | | MOV | A,B |
| 2008 | | 17 | | | RAL | |
| 2009 | | 47 | | | MOV | B,A |
| 200A | | E3 | | | XTHL | |
| 200B | | 29 | | | DAD | H |
| 200C | | 79 | | | MOV | A,C |
| 200D | | 17 | | | RAL | |
| 200E | | 4F | | | MOV | C,A |
| 200F | | 78 | | | MOV | A,B |
| 2010 | | 92 | | | SUB | D |
| 2011 | | D2 | 16 | 20 | JNC | REPT |
| 2014 | | 2C | | | INR | L |
| 2015 | | 47 | | | MOV | B,A |
| 2016 | REPT | E3 | | | XTHL | |
| 2017 | | 1D | | | DCR | E |
| 2018 | | C2 | 06 | 20 | JNZ | LOOP |
| 201B | | E1 | | | POP | H |
| 201C | | 55 | | | MOV | D,L |
| 201D | | 61 | | | MOV | H,C |
| 201E | | C9 | | | RET | |

## 11.5  SPACE AND SPEED

A program should be compact and well structured. It assures the efficiency both in space and speed. A compact program uses reduced number of instructions whereas a structured program uses a well arranged form of data. instruction and execution plan. Compactness generally increase speed and decreases space area of memory. It increases clarity of program and helps to develop a powerful and completed software. Sometimes the structure may disturb compactness where requirement influences the program pattern.

Use of subprograms may increase compactness but a large number of subprograms may decrease the speed of execution. Similarly repeatative use of jumps may also reduce the speed of execution. Selection of instructions and plans of execution require reasonably high depth of system programming, operating system, formal language, Automata, Data structure, Data based systems, Information retrieval, Operation research, Pattern recognition and even Artificial intelligence, However, these subjects are developed for High Level Language based computers and moreover, those are major and difficult part of computer science and technology. So, often the techniques in these subjects are not directly applicable but always the ideas behind the techniques in them are directly applicable. To reduce the RAM space requirement, constants should be as small in number as possible and variables should be such that a number of variables may be stored in a common location. It is also preferable to use the registers as much as possible instead of using memory locations. To facilitate a programmer, some manufacturers provide a large number of registers. Some of them use a space of the RAM as a bank of registers. However, use of these memory space as the registers slows down to some extent and so, some manufacuters provide a large number of registers along with the facility of banks of registers in the RAM space. Stacking of a large number of registers or location increases the overall time of execution of the program and seriously disturbs the compactness of the program. Bank switchability provides a better solution. In place of stacking, if the banks of registers be switched on, both speed and compactness increase greatly. This phenomenon is called Context Switching. 6800, 6801, 6809, 6502, 8748, 8751 etc. have the facility of context switching.

## 11.6 DATA STRUCTURE

Array of data is the simplest form of structure. Normally these data are associated with the positional indices and the position may be in an n-dimensional space. Practically, the data is stored sequentially and the positional indices are not stored but assumed always. Hence a very simple indexed addressing mode of instruction may deal with them. Stack is a sequential array in LAST IN FIRST OUT basis whereas a queue is also a sequential array in FIRST IN FIRST OUT basis. So one index pointer based instructions are quite sufficient to handle them. Moreover, for these purpose, generally a stack pointer is given. But for a queue, no 'Queue Pointer' is formed in the architecture of the microprocessor. However two index pointers may be quite sufficient to handle them. Of course one index pointer based relative addessing mode instruction is sufficent enough to deal with any queue.

In an array, increase or decrease of the size is not generally permitted. For a variable size of array, the linked list is the suitable structure where the previous one and the next one are indicated along with the data. The indexed indirect or the indirect indexed instruction are very convenient to deal with them.

Trees and graphs are generally constructed and dealt with by conditional jumps and calls or returns. Some CPU possesses very helpful instructions to deal with SEARCHING, SORTING, TABLES, STRINGS and FILES. However subprograms may also be used to tackle with them.

## 11.7 SYSTEM PROGRAMMING

This is an elaborate subject of software and a simple idea is given only in this chapter. When a microprocessor system is switched on, it starts executing its system programming software. A monitor is a simple and basic program for all microprocessor system being executed just after the system power is switched on. For example, the monitor of a trainer kit displays the manufacturer's name and checks whether any key is pressed and branch, according to the pressed key. Sometimes the user may have had the facility to write program in mnemonic codes in place of writing those in the machine code or Hex code. This program in mnemonic code or a modified version of the mnemonic code is called the assembly language program. An assembler program converts this mnemonics into their respective Hex codes.

Sometimes the user's program may require debugging and at the time of debugging, some instructions may be required to be deleted from or inserted into the program. This is done by Editor Programs. Sometimes the user may write his program in high level language. An interpreter program converts each high level instruction into a specific set of machine code, executes it and similarly interpretes the next one. A compiler program reads the entire program of the user and converts them all into executable machine codes or hex codes and then starts execution. Compilers are more powerful, versatile and fast in comparison to interpreters. Debugging and editing become convenient through compilers.

Many systems employ an operating system which governs the disc recording, documentation, multi-processing etc. The simpler and popular one is the Disk Operating System or DOS available on PC. The comparatively powerful ones are UNIX, XENIX etc.

## 11.8 SOME MORE PROGRAM DEVELOPMENT

1. TRANSFER A BLOCK OF DATA STORED IN THE MEM. LOC. STARTING FROM 4300 H TO MEM. LOCS. STARTING FROM 4400 H.

| MEM. LOC. | LABEL | MNEMONICS | | OPCODE | | COMMENTS |
|---|---|---|---|---|---|---|
| 4500 | START | MVI B | FF | 06 | FF H | STORE FF (SIZE OF DATA TO BE MOVED) IN REG. B |
| 4502 | | LXI H | 4300 | 21 | 00 43 | INITIALISE STARTING ADDRESS (4300 H) OF THE BLOCK TO BE MOVED |
| 4505 | | LXI D | 4400 | 11 | 00 44 | STORE DESTINATION ADDRESS (4400 H) IN DE REG. PAIR |
| 4508 | LOOP | MOV A,M | | 7E | | MOVE (4300 H) TO ACC. |
| 4509 | | XCHG | | EB | | EXCHANGE (DE) WITH (HL) |
| 450A | | MOV M,A | | 77 | | MOVE (ACC.) TO MEM. LOC. 4400 H |
| 450B | | XCHG | | EB | | EXCHANGE (DE) WITH (HL) |

| MEM. LOC. | LABEL | MNEMONICS | OPCODE | COMMENTS |
|-----------|-------|-----------|--------|----------|
| 450C | | INX H | 23 | INCREMENT (HL) |
| 450D | | INX D | 13 | INCREMENT (DE) |
| 450E | | DCR B | 05 | DECREMENT (REG. B) |
| 450F | | JNZ LOOP | C2 08 45 | JUMP ON NO ZERO TO LOOP |
| 4512 | | HLT | 76 | OTHERWISE, HALT. |

INPUT : STORE DATA TO BE TRANSFERRED FROM 4300 H TO 43FE H
OUTPUT : DATA WILL BE TRANSFERRED SERIALLY FROM 4400 H TO 44FE H.

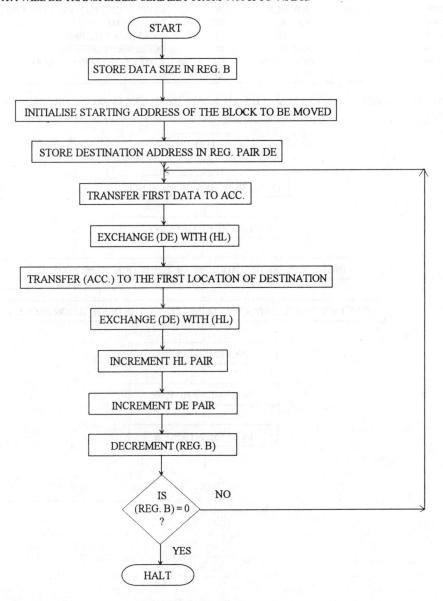

Fig. 11.9. Flowchart

## 2.  STORE  A  BLOCK  OF  DATA  IN  THE  MEM. LOC.  STARTING  FROM  4300 H  TO  43FE H EACH  BEING  INCREMENTED  BY  01 H.

| MEM. LOC. | LABEL | MNEMONICS | OPCODE | COMMENTS |
|---|---|---|---|---|
| 4600 | START | MVI  A  01 | 3E  01 | STORE 01 (STARTING DATA TO BE STORED) IN ACC. |
| 4602 | | MVI  B  FF | 06  FF | STORE FF H (THE SIZE OF DATA TO BE STORED) IN REG. B |
| 4604 | | LXI  H  4300 | 21  00  43 | INITIALISE THE STARTING ADDRESS OF THE BLOCK TO BE STORED |
| 4607 | LOOP | MOV M,A | 77 | MOVE (ACC.) TO MEM. LOC. 4300 H |
| 4608 | | INR  A | 3C | INCREMENT (ACC.) |
| 4609 | | INX  H | 23 | INCREMENT HL PAIR |
| 460A | | DCR  B | 05 | DECREMENT (REG. B) |
| 460B | | JNZ  LOOP | C2  07  46 | JUMP ON NO ZERO TO LOOP |
| 460E | | HLT | 76 | HALT |

OUTPUT:  ALL HEX NUMBERS FROM 01 H TO FF H WILL BE STORED IN ASCENDING ORDER FROM 4300H TO 43FE H.

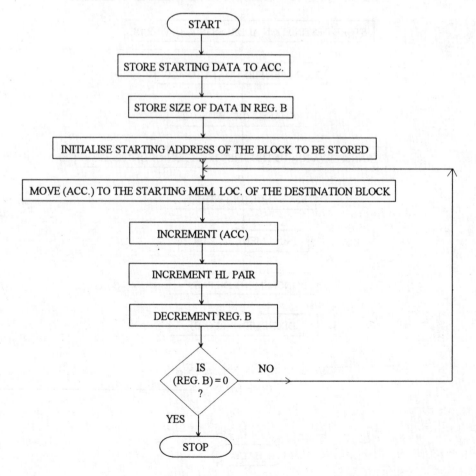

Fig. 11.10. Flow chart

### 3. READ THE FOLLOWING SOFTWARE AND STATE THE CONTENTS OF THE MEMORY LOCATIONS 4200 H TO 4204 H.

| MEM. LOC. | OPCODE | | | MNEMONICS | | | COMMENTS |
|---|---|---|---|---|---|---|---|
| 4600 | 31 | FF | 47 | LXI | SP | 47FF H | DEFINE THE STACK POINTER AT THE MEMORY LOCATION 47FF H. |
| 4603 | 06 | 05 | | MVI | B | 05 H | STORE 05 H IN REG. B |
| 4605 | 21 | 00 | 42 | LXI | H | 4200 H | IDENTIFY THE MEM. LOC. 4200 H THROUGH THE HL REG. PAIR. |
| 4608 | 70 | | | MOV | M,B | | MOVE (REG. B) TO MEM. LOC. |
| 4609 | 3A | 00 | 42 | LDA | 4200 H | | LOAD ACC. WITH DATA STORED IN THE MEM. LOC. 4200 H |
| 460C | 0F | | | RRC | | | ROTATE (CY) AND (ACC.) RIGHT (CONTENT OF ACC. $\longrightarrow$ 82 H ) |
| 460D | 32 | 01 | 42 | STA | 4210 H | | STORE (ACC.) TO MEM. LOC. 4201 H |
| 4610 | 16 | 42 | | MVI | D | 42 H | STORE 42 H IN REG. D |
| 4612 | 1E | 01 | | MVI | E | 01 H | STORE 01 H IN REG. E |
| 4614 | 1A | | | LDAX | D | | LOAD DATA TO ACC. FROM MEM. LOC. 4201 H WHICH IS THE CONTAINT OF REG. PAIR DE |
| 4615 | 07 | | | RLC | | | ROTATE (ACC.) LEFT AND MSB TO CY |
| 4616 | 07 | | | RLC | | | ROTATE (ACC.) LEFT AND MSB TO CY |
| 4617 | 06 | 42 | | MVI | B | 42 H | STORE 42 H IN REG. B |
| 4619 | 0E | 02 | | MVI | C | 02 H | STORE 02 H IN REG. C |
| 461B | 02 | | | STAX | B | | STORE DATA FROM ACC. TO MEM. LOC. 4202 H WHICH IS THE CONTENT OF REG. PAIR BC |
| 461C | 2A | 01 | 42 | LHLD | | 4201 H | LOAD DATA TO REG. H AND REG. L FROM MEM. LOC. 4202 H AND 4201 H RESPECTIVELY |
| 461F | EB | | | XCHG | | | EXCHANGE DATA IN REG. D WITH REG. H AND DATA IN REG. E WITH REG. L. |
| 4620 | 14 | | | INR | D | | INCREMENT (REG. D) |
| 4621 | 21 | 03 | 42 | LXI | H | 4203 H | INITIALISE MEM. LOC. 4203 H |
| 4624 | 72 | | | MOV | M,D | | MOVE (REG. D) TO MEMORY |
| 4625 | 1D | | | DCR | E | | DECREMENT (REG. E) |
| 4626 | 23 | | | INX | H | | INCREMENT (HL REG. PAIR) |
| 4627 | 73 | | | MOV | M,E | | MOVE (REG. E) TO MEMORY |
| 4628 | 76 | | | HLT | | | HALT |

OUTPUT : MEM. LOC. 4200 H    05 H
                 4201 H    82 H
                 4202 H    0A H
                 4203 H    0B H
                 4204 H    81 H

### 4. ADD N NUMBER OF DATA STORED FROM MEMORY LOCATION 4600 H AND PRESERVE THE RESULTS IN MEMORY LOCATIONS 4610 H AND 4611 H.

| LABEL | MEM. LOC. | MNEMONICS | | | OPCODE | | | COMMENTS |
|---|---|---|---|---|---|---|---|---|
| | 4500 | LXI | SP | 47FF H | 31 | FF | 47 | INITIALISE STACK POINTER TO THE MEMORY LOCATION 47FF H |
| START | 4503 | XRA | A | | AF | | | CLEAR CARRY AND ACC. |
| | 4504 | MVI | B | 05 H | 06 | 05 | | STORE SIZE OF DATA IN REG. B |
| | 4506 | LXI | D | 0000 H | 11 | 00 | 00 | CLEAR REG. PAIR DE. |
| | 4509 | LXI | H | 4600 H | 21 | 00 | 46 | INITIALISE MEMORY LOCATION 4600 H, THE STARTING ADDRESS OF FIRST DATA |
| | 450C | MOV | C,M | | 4E | | | TRANSFER CONTENT OF MEMORY TO REG.C |
| REPT | 450D | ADD | C | | 81 | | | ADD (REG. C) WITH (ACC.) |
| | 450E | MOV | C,A | | 4F | | | TRANSFER (ACC.) TO REG. C |
| | 450F | MVI | A | 00 | 3E | 00 | | CLEAR ACC. |

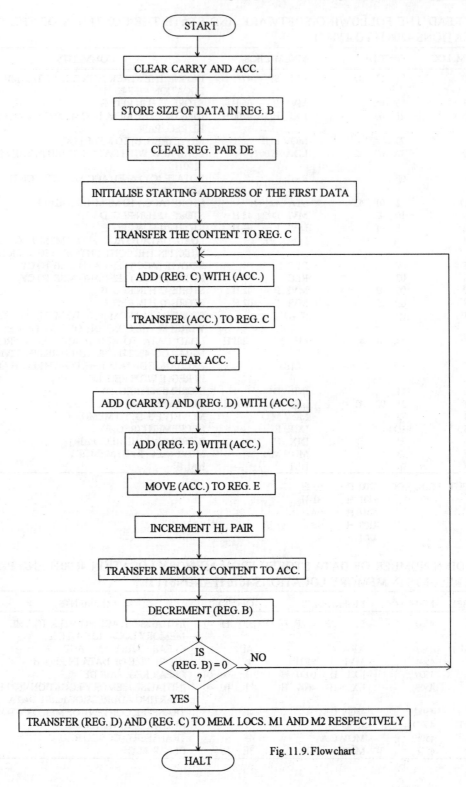

START

CLEAR CARRY AND ACC.

STORE SIZE OF DATA IN REG. B

CLEAR REG. PAIR DE

INITIALISE STARTING ADDRESS OF THE FIRST DATA

TRANSFER THE CONTENT TO REG. C

ADD (REG. C) WITH (ACC.)

TRANSFER (ACC.) TO REG. C

CLEAR ACC.

ADD (CARRY) AND (REG. D) WITH (ACC.)

ADD (REG. E) WITH (ACC.)

MOVE (ACC.) TO REG. E

INCREMENT HL PAIR

TRANSFER MEMORY CONTENT TO ACC.

DECREMENT (REG. B)

IS (REG. B) = 0 ?        NO

YES

TRANSFER (REG. D) AND (REG. C) TO MEM. LOCS. M1 AND M2 RESPECTIVELY

HALT

Fig. 11.9. Flowchart

| LABEL | MEM. LOC. | MNEMONICS | | OPCODE | | | COMMENTS |
|-------|-----------|-----------|--|--------|--|--|----------|
| | 4511 | ADC D | | 8A | | | ADD (CY.) AND (REG. D) WITH (ACC.) |
| | 4512 | ADD E | | 83 | | | ADD (REG. E) WITH (ACC.) |
| | 4513 | MOV E,A | | 5F | | | MOVE THE RESULT TO REG. E. |
| | 4514 | INX H | | 23 | | | INCREMENT HL-PAIR |
| | 4515 | MOV A,M | | 7E | | | TRANSFER THE CONTENT OF THE MEM. LOC. TO ACC. |
| | 4516 | DCR B | | 05 | | | DECREMENT (REG. B). |
| | 4517 | JNZ REPT | | C2 | 0D | 45 | JUMP ON NO ZERO TO 'REPT' |
| | 451A | LXI H 4610 H | | 21 | 10 | 46 | OTHERWISE, INITIALISE MEM. LOC. 4610 H |
| | 451D | MOV M,E | | 73 | | | MOVE (REG. E) TO MEMORY. |
| | 451E | INX H | | 23 | | | INCREMENT HL PAIR |
| | 451F | MOV M,C | | 71 | | | MOVE (REG. C) TO THE MEMORY |
| | 4520 | HLT | | 76 | | | HALT. |

NOTE : THE PROGRAM IS VALID FOR N NUMBERS OF DATA, THE VALUE OF N BEING THE CONTENT OF REG. B IN MEM. LOC. 4504 H.

DATA INPUT : FROM MEM. LOC. 4600 H TO 4604 H
OUTPUT : MEM. LOC. 4610 H AND 4611 H

## 5. ARRANGE THE GIVEN N NUMBERS STORED IN A BLOCK OF MEMORY LOCATIONS IN
## (i) ASCENDING ORDER
## (ii) DESCENDING ORDER

| MEM. LOC. | LABEL | MNEMONICS | | OPCODE | | | COMMENTS |
|-----------|-------|-----------|--|--------|--|--|----------|
| 4300 | | LXI SP 47FF H | | 31 | FF | 47 | INITIALISE STACK POINTER TO THE MEMORY LOCATION 47FF H |
| 4303 | REPT1 | MVI B 10 H | | 06 | 10 | | STORE 10 H (NO. OF DATA) IN REG. B |
| 4305 | | LXI H 4100 H | | 21 | 00 | 41 | INITIALISE STARTING ADDRESS OF DATA |
| 4308 | REPT2 | MOV A,M | | 7E | | | TRANSFER THE MEMORY CONTENT TO ACC. |
| 4309 | | MOV D,A | | 57 | | | PRESERVE THE DATA IN REG. D |
| 430A | | INX H | | 23 | | | INCREMENT HL PAIR |
| 430B | | SUB M | | 96 | | | SUBTRACT MEMORY CONTENT FROM (ACC.) |
| 430C | | JNC NEXT 2 | | D2 | 19 | 43 | IF THERE BE NO CARRY, JUMP TO NEXT 2 |
| 430F | | STC | | 37 | | | OTHERWISE, SET CARRY |
| 4310 | | CMC | | 3F | | | COMPLEMENT CARRY |
| 4311 | | DCR B | | 05 | | | DECREMENT (REG. B) |
| 4312 | | JZ NEXT 1 | | CA | 18 | 43 | IF THE RESULT BE ZERO, JUMP TO NEXT1 |
| 4315 | | JMP REPT2 | | C3 | 08 | 43 | OTHERWISE, JUMP TO REPT2 |
| 4318 | NEXT1 | HLT | | 76 | | | HALT. |
| 4319 | NEXT2 | MOV C,M | | 4E | | | MOVE THE MEMORY CONTENT TO REG. C. |
| 431A | | MOV M,D | | 72 | | | MOVE THE CONTENT OF REG. D TO THE SAME MEMORY LOCATION. |
| 431B | | DCX H | | 2B | | | DECREMENT HL PAIR |
| 431C | | MOV M,C | | 71 | | | MOVE (REG. C) TO THE MEM. LOC. |
| 431D | | JMP REPT1 | | C3 | 03 | 43 | JUMP TO START. |

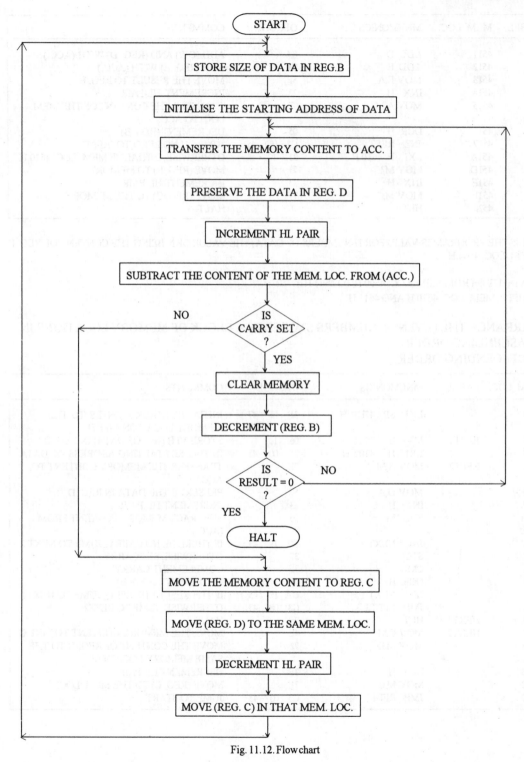

Fig. 11.12. Flowchart

|  DATA  INPUT  |  |  |  OUTPUT (RESULTS)  |  |
|---|---|---|---|---|
| MEM.LOC. | DATA | | MEM.LOC. | DATA |
| 4100 | FF | | 4100 | 01 |
| 4101 | 23 | | 4101 | 05 |
| 4102 | 95 | | 4102 | 08 |
| 4103 | C2 | | 4103 | 10 |
| 4104 | 86 | | 4104 | 23 |
| 4105 | 01 | | 4105 | 35 |
| 4106 | 35 | | 4106 | 86 |
| 4107 | 05 | | 4107 | 95 |
| 4108 | 08 | | 4108 | C2 |
| 4109 | 10 | | 4109 | FF |

(iii)  The software for obtaining the data in descending order is exactly the same as (i) with the only exception that in mem. loc. 430C H, JNC (D2) instruction is to be replaced by JC(DA).  Input will remain unaltered and the data in descending order will be arranged from mem. loc. 4100 H through 4109 H.

*Note*:  The maximum permissible data to be arranged in this program is FF.  If the length of data exceeds FF, MVI B in mem. loc. 4303 H is to be replaced by LXI B followed by a 16-bit data and DCR B is to be changed by DCX B.

## 6. DIVISION OF SIXTEEN BIT NUMBER WITH AN EIGHT BIT NUMBER

| LABEL | MEM. LOC. | OPCODE | | | MNEMONICS | COMMENTS |
|---|---|---|---|---|---|---|
| | 4200 | 21 | 90 | 40 | LXI  H  4090H | INITIALISE MEM. LOC. 4090H |
| | 4203 | 36 | 02 | | MVI M  DIVISOR | STORE DIVISOR IN 4090 H |
| | 4205 | 46 | | | MOV B,  M | MOVE THE CONTENT OF MEMORY TO REG. B |
| | 4206 | 21 | 68 | 34 | LXI  H  DIVIDEND | LOAD 16-BIT DIVIDEND IN REG. PAIR HL |
| | 4209 | 78 | | | MOV A,  B | MOVE (REG. B) IN ACC. |
| | 420A | FE | 00 | | CPI  00H | COMPARE 00H WITH  (ACC.) |
| | 420C | CA | 27 | 42 | JZ   NEXT2 | JUMP TO NEXT2 IF THE RESULT IS ZERO |
| | 420F | 7C | | | MOV A,H | OTHERWISE, MOVE (REG. H) TO ACC. |
| | 4210 | FE | 00 | | CPI  00H | COMPARE 00H WITH (ACC.) |
| | 4212 | C2 | 33 | 42 | JNZ  NEXT1 | JUMP TO NEXT1 IF RESULT BE NOT ZERO |
| | 4215 | 7D | | | MOV A,L | OTHERWISE, MOVE (REG. L) TO ACC |
| | 4216 | FE | 00 | | CPI  00H | COMPARE 00H WITH (ACC.) |
| | 4218 | C2 | 33 | 42 | JNZ  NEXT1 | JUMP TO NEXT1 IF RESULT IS NOT ZERO |
| | 421B | 21 | 80 | 40 | LXI  H  4080H | OTHERWISE, INITIALISE MEM. LOC. 4080 H |
| | 421E | 36′ | 00 | | MVI  M  00H | STORE 00 H IN THE MEMORY |
| | 4220 | 23 | | | INX  H | INCREMENT HL PAIR |
| | 4221 | 36 | 00 | | MVI  M  00H | STORE 00 H IN THE MEMORY |
| | 4223 | 23 | | | INX  H | INCREMENT HL PAIR |
| | 4224 | 36 | 00 | | MVI  M  00H | STORE 00 H IN THE MEMORY |
| | 4226 | 76 | | | HLT | HALT |

| LABEL | MEM. LOC. | OPCODE | | | MNEMONICS | | COMMENTS |
|-------|-----------|--------|----|----|-----------|------|----------|
| NEXT2: | 4227 | 21 | 80 | 40 | LXI H | 4080H | INITIALISE MEM. LOC. 4080 H |
| | 422A | 36 | 0E | | MVI M | 0E H | STORE 0E H IN THE MEMORY |
| | 422C | 23 | | | INX H | | INCREMENT HL PAIR |
| | 422D | 36 | 0E | | MVI M | IE H | STORE 0E H IN THE MEMORY |
| | 422F | 23 | | | INX H | | INCREMENT HL PAIR |
| | 4230 | 36 | 0E | | MVI M | 0E H | STORE 0E H IN THE MEMORY |
| | 4232 | 76 | | | HLT | | HALT |
| NEXT1: | 4233 | CD | 05 | 41 | CALL DIV | | CALL SUBPROGRAM 'DIV' |
| | 4236 | 76 | | | HLT | | HALT |

SUBROUTINE DIV:

| LABEL | MEM.LOC | OPCODE | | | MNEMONICS | | COMMENTS |
|-------|---------|--------|----|----|-----------|------|----------|
| DIV | 4105 | 11 | 00 | 00 | LXI D | 0000H | CLEAR DE REG. PAIR |
| | 4108 | 48 | | | MOV C, B | | MOVE (REG. B) TO REG. C |
| AGAIN: | 4109 | 2B | | | DCX H | | DECREMENT (HL) PAIR |
| | 410A | 05 | | | DCR B | | DECREMERNT (REG. B) |
| | 410B | C2 | 09 | 41 | JNZ AGAIN | | JUMP ON NO ZERO TO AGAIN |
| | 410E | 13 | | | INX D | | OTHERWISE, INCREMENT (DE) REG. PAIR |
| | 410F | 7C | | | MOV A, H | | MOVE (REG. H) TO ACC. |
| | 4110 | 41 | | | MOV B, C | | MOVE (REG. C) TO REG. B |
| | 4111 | FE | 00 | | CPI 00 H | | COMPARE 00 H WITH (ACC.) |
| | 4113 | C2 | 09 | 41 | JNZ AGAIN | | JUMP ON NO ZERO TO 'AGAIN' |
| MORE: | 4116 | 7D | | | MOV A,L | | OTHERWISE, MOVE (REG. L) TO ACC. |
| | 4117 | 41 | | | MOV B,C | | MOVE (REG. C) TO REG. B |
| | 4118 | 90 | | | SUB B | | SUBTRACT (REG.B) FROM (ACC.) |
| | 4119 | CA | 24 | 41 | JZ REPT1 | | JUMP ON ZERO TO REEPT1 |
| | 411C | DA | 2F | 41 | JC REPT2 | | JUMP ON CARRY TO REPT2 |
| | 411F | 6F | | | MOV L,A | | OTHERWISE, MOV (ACC.) TO REG. L |
| | 4120 | 13 | | | INX D | | INCREMENT (DE REG. PAIR) |
| | 4121 | C3 | 16 | 41 | JMP MORE | | JUMP TO 'MORE' |
| REPT1: | 4124 | 13 | | | INX D | | INCREMENT (DE REG. PAIR) |
| | 4125 | 21 | 80 | 40 | LXI H 4080H | | INITIALISE MEM. LOC. 4080 H |
| | 4128 | 72 | | | MOV M,D | | STORE (REG. D) TO MEMORY |
| | 4129 | 23 | | | INX H | | INCREMENT HL REG. PAIR |
| | 412A | 73 | | | MOV M,E | | STORE (REG. E) TO MEMORY |
| | 412B | 23 | | | INX H | | INCREMENT HL PAIR |
| | 412C | 36 | 00 | | MVI M 00H | | STORE 00 H IN MEMORY |
| | 412E | C9 | | | RET | | RETURN |
| REPT2: | 412F | 37 | | | STC | | SET CARRY |
| | 4130 | 3F | | | CMC | | COMPLEMENT CARRY |
| | 4131 | 45 | | | MOV B,L | | MOVE (REG. L) TO REG. B |
| | 4132 | 21 | 80 | 40 | LXI H 4080H | | INITIALISE MEM. LOC. 4080 H |
| | 4135 | 72 | | | MOV M,D | | MOVE (REG. L) TO REG. B. |
| | 4136 | 23 | | | INX H | | INCREMENT HL PAIR |
| | 4137 | 73 | | | MOV M,E | | MOVE (REG. E) TO MEMORY |
| | 4138 | 23 | | | INX H | | INCREMENT HL    PAIR |
| | 4139 | 70 | | | MOV M,B | | MOVE (REG. B) TO MEMORY |
| | 413A | C9 | | | RET | | RETURN |

INPUT:  16-BIT DIVIDEND IN HL REG. PAIR, 8-BIT DIVISOR IN REG. B

OUTPUT:  QUOTIENT IN MEM. LOCS, 4080 H AND 4081 H, REMAINDER IN MEM. LOC. 4082  H

VERIFICATION:

| DIVIDEND (HL) | DIVISOR (REG. B) | QUOTIENT (4080 H) | (4081 H) | REMAINDER (4082 H) |
|---|---|---|---|---|
| 2468 H | 02 H | 12 H | 34 H | 00 H |
| 2469 H | 02 H | 12 H | 34 H | 01 H |
| FFFF H | 0F H | 11 H | 11 H | 00 H |
| FFFE H | 0F H | 11 H | 10 H | 0E H |
| FFFF H | FF H | 01 H | 01 H | 00 H |
| 1234 H | 10 H | 01 H | 23 H | 04 H |

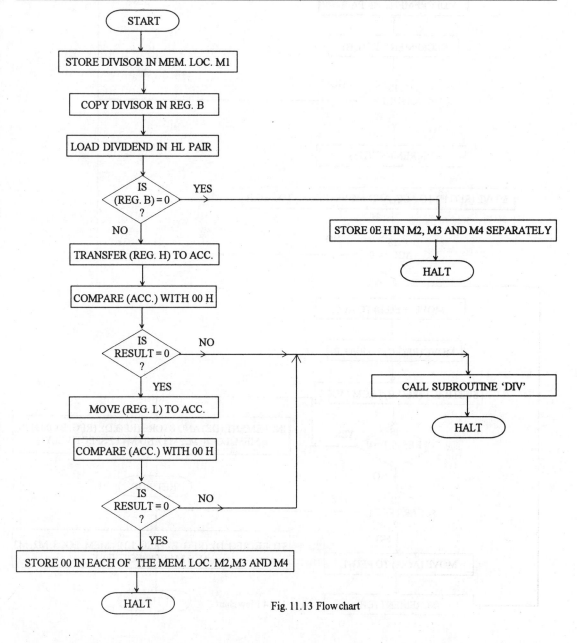

Fig. 11.13 Flowchart

SUBROUTINE : 'DIV'

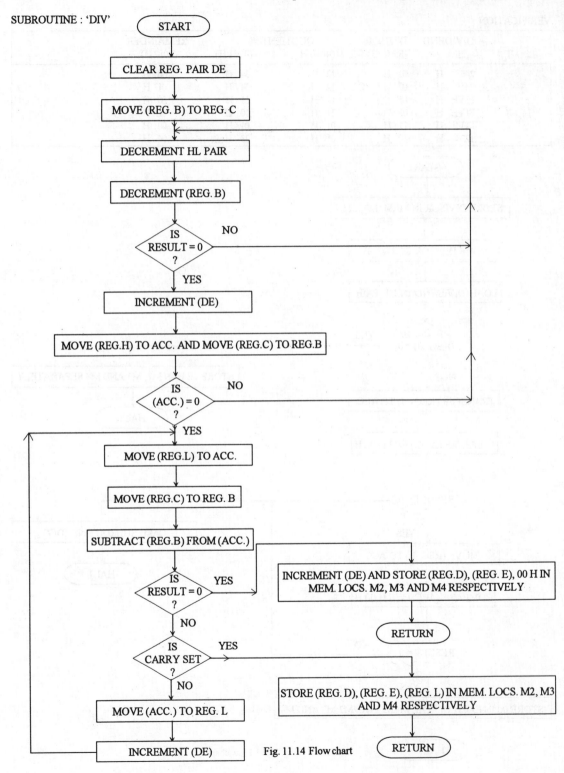

Fig. 11.14 Flow chart

## 7. FIND THE SQUARE ROOT OF AN INTEGER.

Let $X$ be the initial guess value for the square root of N.

Then $\quad X^2 \;=\; N$

or, $\qquad 2X^2 \;=\; N + X^2$

or, $\qquad X^2 \;=\; (N + X^2)\,/\,2$

or, $\qquad X_n \;=\; (X + N/X)/2$

where $X_n$ is the new iteration of $X$.

Also if $\quad X \;=\; X_n$

$$\sqrt{N} \;=\; (X_n + N/X_n)/2$$
$$\;=\; (X_n + R\,/\,X_n + X_n)\,/\,2$$
$$\;=\; X_n + (R/X_n)\,/\,2$$

where $R$ is the remainder.

Hence the nearest value of $\sqrt{N}$ becomes $X_n$ and fractional part be $(R/X_n)\,/2$.

| LABEL | MEM.LOC. | OPCODE | | | MNEMONICS | | | COMMENTS |
|-------|----------|--------|----|----|-----------|------|-------|----------|
| | 4500 | 31 | FF | 47 | LXI | SP | 47FFH | DEFINE STACK POINTER 47FF H |
| | 4503 | 21 | 90 | 40 | LXI | H | 4090H | INITIALISE MEM. LOC. FOR INITIAL GUESS VALUE OF ROOT OF N |
| | 4506 | 36 | 04 | | MVI | M | X | STORE GUESS VALUE (X) IN MEM. LOC. |
| LOOP | 4508 | 46 | | | MOV | B,M | | MOVE X TO REG. B |
| | 4509 | 21 | 16 | 00 | LXI | H | N | LOAD THE NO. N IN HL PAIR WHOSE SQUARE ROOT IS REQUIRED |
| | 450C | CD | 05 | 41 | CALL | DIV | | CALL SUBROUTINE DIV, KEEP QUOTIENT IN 4080 H AND 4081 H, REMAINDER IN 4082 H |
| | 450F | 21 | 81 | 40 | LXI | H | 4081H | INITIALISE MEM. LOC. 4081H |
| | 4512 | 7E | | | MOV | A,M | | TRANSFER (4081 H) TO ACC. |
| | 4513 | 21 | 90 | 40 | LXI | H | 4090H | INITIALISE MEM. LOC. CONTAINING X |
| | 4516 | 46 | | | MOV | B,M | | TRANSFER X TO REG. B |
| | 4517 | 86 | | | ADD | M | | COMPUTE (N/X+X) |
| | 4518 | 0F | | | RRC | | | PERFORM RRC OPERATION |
| | 4519 | E6 | 7F | | ANI | 7FH | | REMOVE MSB TO COMPUTE INTEGER PART OF (N/X+X)/2 = Xn |
| | 451B | 4F | | | MOV | C,A | | STORE THE RESULT IN REG.C |
| | 451C | BE | | | CMP | M | | COMPARE Xn WITH X |
| | 451D | CA | 29 | 45 | JZ | NEXT1 | | IF THE RESULT IS ZERO ,JUMP TO NEXT 1 |
| | 4520 | 21 | 90 | 40 | LXI | H | 4090H | OTHERWISE, INITIALISE THE MEM. LOC. FOR X |
| | 4523 | 71 | | | MOV | M,C | | KEEP Xn IN THE MEM. LOC. |
| | 4524 | 37 | | | STC | | | SET CARRY |
| | 4525 | 3F | | | CMC | | | CLEAR CARRY |
| | 4526 | C3 | 08 | 45 | JMP | LOOP | | JUMP TO LOOP |
| NEXT 1 | 4529 | 21 | 90 | 40 | LXI | H | 4090H | INITIALISE MEM. LOC. FOR X |
| | 452C | 71 | | | MOV | M,C | | KEEP Xn THERE |
| | 452D | 46 | | | MOV | B, M | | TRANSFER Xn TO REG. B |
| | 452E | 21 | 16 | 00 | LXI | H | N | STORE N IN HL PAIR |
| | 4531 | CD | 05 | 41 | CALL | DIV | | CALL DIV |
| | 4534 | 21 | 82 | 40 | LXI | H | 4082H | INITIALISE MEM. LOC. FOR REMAINDER, R |
| | 4537 | 7E | | | MOV | A,M | | TRANSFER R IN ACC. |
| | 4538 | FE | 00 | | CPI | 00 | | COMPARE R WITH 00 H |
| | 453A | C2 | 46 | 45 | JNZ | NEXT2 | | IF THE RESULT IS NOT ZERO. JUMP TO NEXT 2 |
| | 453D | 21 | 91 | 40 | LXI | H | 4091 | INITIALISE MEM. LOC. 4091 H |
| | 4540 | 36 | 00 | | MVI | M | 00 | STORE 00 H THERE |
| | 4542 | 23 | | | INX | H | | INCREMENT HL PAIR |
| | 4543 | 36 | 00 | | MVI | M | 00 | STORE 00 H THERE |

| LABEL | MEM.LOC. | OPCODE | | | MNEMONICS | | COMMENTS |
|---|---|---|---|---|---|---|---|
| | 4545 | 76 | | | HLT | | HALT |
| NEXT 2 | 4546 | CD | 4D | 43 | CALL | NEW | CALL SUBROUTINE 'NEW' |
| | 4549 | 21 | 81 | 40 | LXI | H    4081H | INITIALISE MEM. LOC. 4081 H |
| | 454C | 7E | | | MOV | A, M | MOVE (4081 H) TO ACC. |
| | 454D | 21 | 91 | 40 | LXI | H    4091H | INITIALISE MEM. LOC. 4091 H |
| | 4550 | 77 | | | MOV | M, A | MOVE (ACC.) TO MEM. LOC. 4091 H |
| | 4551 | 21 | 82 | 40 | LXI | H    4082H | INITIALISE MEM. LOC. 4082 H |
| | 4554 | 7E | | | MOV | A, M | MOVE (4082H) TO ACC. |
| | 4555 | FE | 00 | | CPI | 00 | COMPARE (ACC.) WITH 00H |
| | 4557 | CA | 66 | 45 | JZ | NEXT 3 | IF THE RESULT BE ZERO, JUMP TO NEXT 3 |
| | 455A | CD | 4D | 43 | CALL | NEW | CALL SUBROUTINE 'NEW' |
| | 455D | 21 | 81 | 40 | LXI | H    4081H | INITIALISE THE MEM. LOC. 4081H |
| | 4560 | 7E | | | MOV | A, M | MOVE (4081 H) TO ACC. |
| | 4561 | 21 | 92 | 40 | LXI | H    4092H | INITIALISE THE MEM. LOC. 4092 H |
| | 4564 | 77 | | | MOV | M, A | MOVE (ACC.) TO MEM. LOC. 4092 H |
| | 4565 | 76 | | | HLT | | HALT |
| NEXT 3 | 4566 | 21 | 92 | 40 | LXI | H    4092H | INITIALISE MEM. LOC.4092 H |
| | 4569 | 36 | 00 | | MVI | M    00H | STORE 00 H THERE |
| | 456B | 76 | | | HLT | | HALT |

SUBROUTINE NEW

| LABEL | MEM. LOC. | OPCODE | | | MNEMONICS | | COMMENTS |
|---|---|---|---|---|---|---|---|
| NEW | 434D | 06 | 08 | | MVI | B    08 | LOAD 08 H IN REG. B |
| | 434F | 16 | 00 | | MVI | D    00 | STORE 00 H IN REG. D |
| | 4351 | 21 | 82 | 40 | LXI | H    4082H | INITIALISE MEM. LOC. 4082 H |
| | 4354 | 5E | | | MOV | E, M | MOVE (4082 H) TO REG. E |
| | 4355 | 21 | 00 | 00 | LXI | H    0000H | STORE 00 H IN EACH OF REG. H & L |
| ADD | 4358 | 19 | | | DAD | D | ADD (DE) WITH (HL) AND KEEP RESULTS IN HL |
| | 4359 | 05 | | | DCR | B | DECREMENT (REG. B) |
| | 435A | C2 | 58 | 43 | JNZ | ADD | IF THE RESULT IS NOT ZERO, JUMP TO 'ADD' |
| | 435D | EB | | | XCHG | | EXCHANGE (DE) WITH (HL) |
| | 435E | 7A | | | MOV | A,D | MOVE (REG. D) TO ACC. |
| | 435F | FE | 00 | | CPI | 00 | COMPARE (ACC.) WITH 00H |
| | 4361 | CA | 6D | 43 | JZ | THERE | JUMP ON ZERO TO 'THERE' |
| HERE | 4364 | 21 | 90 | 40 | LXI | H    4090H | INITIALISE 4090 H |
| | 4367 | 46 | | | MOV | B,M | MOVE (4090 H) TO REG. B |
| | 4368 | EB | | | XCHG | | EXCHANGE (DE) WITH (HL) |
| | 4369 | CD | 05 | 41 | CALL | DIV | CALL SUBROUTINE 'DIV' |
| | 436C | C9 | | | RET | | RETURN |
| THERE | 436D | 7B | | | MOV | A, E | MOVE (REG. E) TO ACC. |
| | 436E | 21 | 90 | 40 | LXI | H    4090H | INITIALISE MEM. LOC. 4090 H |
| | 4371 | BE | | | CMP | M | COMPARE (ACC.) WITH (MEM. LOC. 4090 H) |
| | 4372 | DA | 78 | 43 | JC | GO | IF CY SET, JUMP TO 'GO |
| | 4375 | C3 | 64 | 43 | JMP | HERE | OTHERWISE, JUMP 'HERE' |
| GO | 4378 | 37 | | | STC | | SET CY |
| | 4379 | 3F | | | CMC | | COMPLEMENT CY |
| | 437A | 21 | 81 | 40 | LXI | H    4081H | INITIALISE MEM. LOC. 4081 H |
| | 437D | 36 | 00 | | MVI | M    00 | STORE 00 H IN MEMORY |
| | 437F | C9 | | | RET | | RETURN |

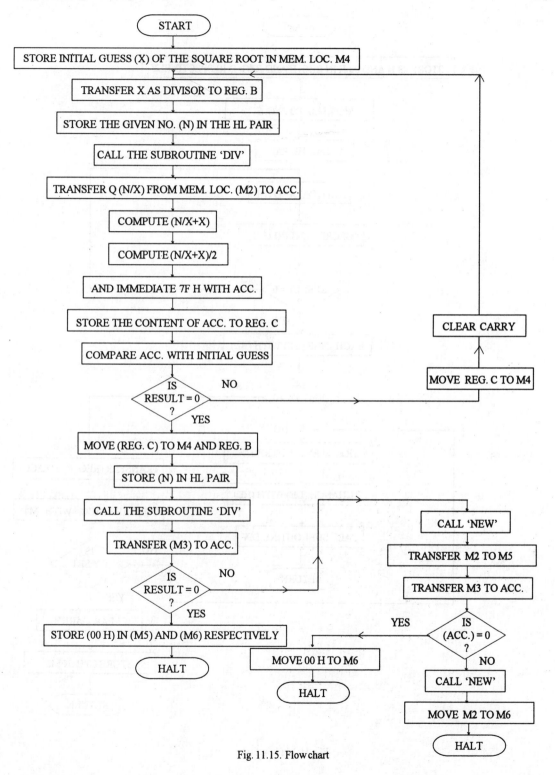

Fig. 11.15. Flow chart

Subroutine NEW :

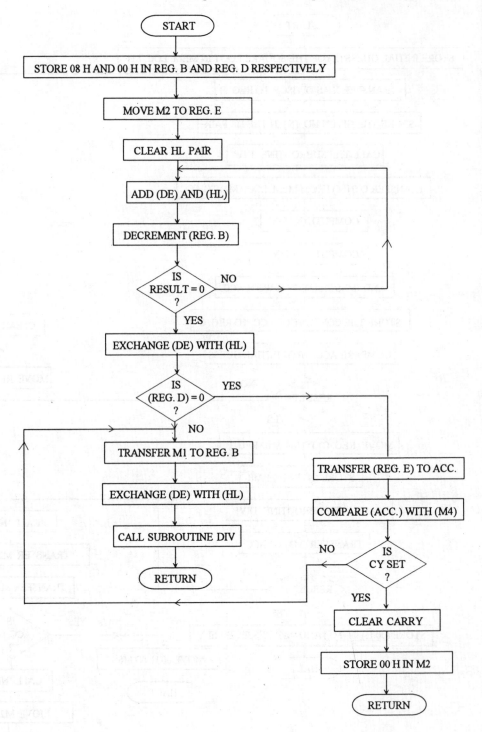

Fig. 11.16 Flowchart

## 8. DEVELOPED THE SOFTWARE FOR A DIGITAL CLOCK

| LABEL | MEM. LOC. | OPCODE | | | MNEMONICS | | | COMMENTS |
|---|---|---|---|---|---|---|---|---|
| | 44FD | 31 | FF | 47 | LXI | SP | 47FF | INITIALISE STACK POINTER |
| START | 4500 | 21 | FF | 40 | LXI | H | 40FF | INITIALISE THE MEM.LOC.40FF H CONTAINING 'HOUR' COUNT |
| NEXT | 4503 | 7E | | | MOV | A,M | | MOVE THE MEM.CONTENT TO ACC. |
| | 4504 | 4E | | | MOV | C,M | | MOVE THE MEM.CONTENT TO REG. C |
| | 4505 | FE | 0A | | CPI | 0A | H | COMPARE 0A H WITH (ACC.) |
| | 4507 | CA | 17 | 45 | JZ | REPT1 | | JUMP ON ZERO TO 'REPT1' |
| | 450A | CD | 50 | 44 | CALL | SPLIT | | CALL SUBPROGRAM 'SPLIT' TO SPLIT THE CONTENT OF 40FF H |
| | 450D | CD | 00 | 42 | CALL | MINSEC | | CALL SUBPROGRAM 'MINSEC' |
| | 4510 | 21 | FF | 40 | LXI | H | 40FF | INITIALISE THE MEM. LOC. 40FF H |
| | 4513 | 34 | | | INR | M | | INCREMENT (MEMORY) |
| | 4514 | C3 | 03 | 45 | JMP | NEXT | | JUMP TO NEXT |
| REPT1 | 4517 | 21 | FF | 40 | LXI | H | 40FF | INITIALISE THE MEM. LOC.40FF H |
| | 451A | 36 | 10 | | MVI | M | 10H | STORE DATA 10 H IN MEMORY |
| REPT3 | 451C | 7E | | | MOV | A,M | | TRANSFER THE MEM. CONTENT TO |
| | 451D | 4E | | | MOV | C,M | | ACC. AND REG. C |
| | 451E | FE | 1A | | CPI | 1A | H | COMPARE 1A H WITH (ACC.) |
| | 4520 | CA | 30 | 45 | JZ | REPT2 | | JUMP ON ZERO TO REPT2 |
| | 4523 | CD | 50 | 44 | CALL | SPLIT | | CALL 'SPLIT' |
| | 4526 | CD | 00 | 42 | CALL | MINSEC | | CALL 'MINSEC' |
| | 4529 | 21 | FF | 40 | LXI | H | 40FF | INITIALISE THE MEM. LOC. 40FF H |
| | 452C | 34 | | | INR | M | | INCREMENT (MEMORY) |
| | 452D | C3 | 1C | 45 | JMP | REPT3 | | JUMP TO REPT3 |
| REPT2 | 4530 | 21 | FF | 40 | LXI | H | 40FF | INITIALISE M |
| | 4533 | 36 | 20 | | MVI | M | 20 H | STORE 20 H IN MEMORY |
| REEPT5 | 4535 | 7E | | | MOV | A,M | | TRANSFER (MEM) TO ACC. |
| | 4536 | 4E | | | MOV | C,M | | TRANSFER (MEM) TO REG. C |
| | 4537 | FE | 24 | | CPI | 24 | H | COMPARE 24 H WITH (ACC.) |
| | 4539 | CA | 49 | 45 | JZ | REPT4 | | JUMP ON ZERO TO REPT4 |
| | 453C | CD | 50 | 44 | CALL | SPLIT | | CALL 'SPLIT' |
| | 453F | CD | 00 | 42 | CALL | MINSEC | | CALL 'MINSEC' |
| | 4542 | 21 | FF | 40 | LXI | H | 40FF | INITIALISE MEM. 40FFH |
| | 4545 | 34 | | | INR | M | | INCREMENT (M) |
| | 4546 | C3 | 35 | 45 | JMP | REPT5 | | JUMP TO REPT5 |
| REPT4 | 4549 | 21 | FF | 40 | LXI | H | 40FF | INITIALISE MEM. LOC. |
| | 454C | 36 | 00 | | MVI | M | 00 | STORE 00 H IN MEMORY |
| | 454E | C3 | 00 | 45 | JMP | START | | JUMP START |
| DISP | 4400 | 3E | 02 | | MVI | A | 02 | INITIALISE DATA FIELD OF |
| | 4402 | 06 | 00 | | MVI | B | 00 | DISPLAY AVOIDING DOT |
| | 4404 | 21 | 06 | 41 | LXI | H | 4106 | INITIALISE MEM. LOC. FOR SEC. DATA |
| | 4407 | CD | 83 | 02 | CALL | BDP | | CALL BDP SUBROUTINE FOR BASIC DISPLAY STORED IN EPROM |
| | 440A | 3E | 01 | | MVI | A | 01 | INITIALISE ADDRESS FIELD OF |
| | 440C | 06, | 00 | | MVI | B | 00 | DISPLAY |
| | 440E | 21 | 02 | 41 | LXI | H | 4102 | INITIALISE MEM. LOC. FOR MIN DATA |
| | 4411 | CD | 83 | 02 | CALL | BDP | | CALL BASIC DISPLAY SUBROUTINE FROM EPROM |
| | 4414 | 3E | 00 | | MVI | A | 00 | INITIALISE STATUS FIELD OF |

| LABEL | MEM. LOC. | OPCODE | | | MNEMONICS | | | COMMENTS |
|-------|-----------|--------|---|---|-----------|---|---|----------|
| | 4416 | 06 | 00 | | MVI | B | 00 | DISPLAY AVOIDING DOT. |
| | 4418 | 21 | 00 | 41 | LXI | H | 4100 | INITIALISE MEM. LOC. FOR HOUR DATA |
| | 441B | CD | 83 | 02 | CALL | BDP | | CALL BASIC DISPLAY SUBPROGRAM FROM EPROM |
| | 441E | C9 | | | RET | | | RETURN |
| SPLIT | 4450 | 79 | | | MOV | A,C | | TRANSFER THE CONTENT OF REG. C TO ACC. |
| | 4451 | E6 | F0 | | ANI | F0 | | AND F0 H TO ACC. |
| | 4453 | 0F | | | RRC | | | ROTATE ACC. RIGHT, LSB TO CARRY |
| | 4454 | 0F | | | RRC | | | ROTATE ACC. RIGHT, LBS TO CARRY |
| | 4455 | 0F | | | RRC | | | ROTATE ACC. RIGHT, LBS TO CARRY |
| | 4456 | 0F | | | RRC | | | ROTATE ACC. RIGHT, LSB TO CARRY |
| | 4457 | 21 | 00 | 41 | LXI H 4100 H | | | INITIALISE MEM. LOC 4100 H |
| | 445A | 77 | | | MOV | M,A | | MOVE (ACC.) TO MEMORY |
| | 445B | 71 | | | MOV | A,C | | MOVE (REG. C) TO ACC. |
| | 445C | E6 | 0F | | ANI | 0F | | AND 0F H WITH (ACC. ) |
| | 446E | 23 | | | INX | H | | INCREMENT HL PAIR |
| | 446F | 77 | | | MOV | M,A | | MOVE (ACC.) TO MEMORY |
| | 4470 | C9 | | | RET | | | RETURN |
| DLY | 4430 | D5 | | | PUSH | D | | PUSH THE CONTENT OF REG. D AND E TO STACK |
| | 4431 | 16 | FF | | MVI | D | FF | STORE FF H IN REG. D |
| NEXT 1 | 4433 | 1E | FF | | MVI | E | FF | STORE FF H IN REG. E |
| NEXT 2 | 4435 | 00 | | | NOP | | | NO OPERATION |
| | 4436 | 00 | | | NOP | | | NO OPERATION |
| | 4437 | 00 | | | NOP | | | NO OPERATION |
| | 4438 | 00 | | | NOP | | | NO OPERATION |
| | 4434 | 52 | | | MOV | D, D | | PRESERVE THE CONTENT OF REG. D |
| | 443A | 5B | | | MOV | E, E | | PRESERVE THE CONTENT OF REG. E |
| | 443B | 1D | | | DCR | E | | DECREMENT THE CONTENT OF REG. E |
| | 443C | C2 | 33 | 44 | JNZ | NEXT 2 | | JUMP ON NO ZERO TO NEXT 2 |
| | 443F | 15 | | | DCR | D | | OTHERWISE, DECREMENT THE CONTENT OF REG. D |
| | 4440 | C2 | 31 | 44 | JNZ | NEXT1 | | JUMP ON NO ZERO TO NEXT1 |
| | 4443 | D1 | | | POP | D | | TRANSFER THE CONTENTS TO REG. D AND E FROM STACK |
| | 4444 | C9 | | | RET | | | RETURN |
| MIMSEC | 4200 | CD | 00 | 44 | CALL | DISP | | CALL DISP SUBROUTINE |
| | 4203 | CD | 30 | 44 | CALL | DLY | | CALL DLY FOR 1 SECOND |
| | 4206 | 21 | 07 | 41 | LXI | H | 4107 | INITIALISE MEMORY LOC CORRESPONDING TO LEAST SIGNIFICANT PART OF SEC. COUNT |
| | 4209 | 34 | | | INR | M | | INCREMENT (MEMORY) |
| | 420A | 7E | | | MOV | A,M | | MOVE (MEMORY ) TO ACC. |
| | 420B | FE | 0A | | CPI | 0A | | COMPARE 0A H WITH (ACC.) |
| | 420D | C2 | 00 | 42 | JNZ | MINSEC | | JUMP ON NO ZERO TO MINSEC |
| | 4210 | 36 | 00 | | MVI | M | 00 | OTHERWISE, LOAD 00 H IN MEMORY |

| LABEL | MEM. LOC. | OPCODE | | | MNEMONICS | | COMMENTS |
|-------|-----------|--------|---|---|-----------|---|----------|
| | 4212 | 2B | | | DCX | H | DECREMENT (HL) |
| | 4213 | 34 | | | INR | M | INCREMENT (MEMORY) |
| | 4214 | 7E | | | MOV | A,M | TRANSFER (MEMORY) TO ACC. |
| | 4215 | FE | 06 | | CPI | 06 H | COMPARE 06 H WITH (ACC.) |
| | 4217 | C2 | 00 | 42 | JNZ | MINSEC | JUMP ON NO ZERO TO MINSEC |
| | 421A | 36 | 00 | | MVI | M 00 | OTHERWISE, LOAD 00 H IN MEMORY |
| | 421C | 2B | | | DCX | H | DECREMENT (HL) |
| | 421D | 2B | | | DCX | H | DECREMENT (HL) |
| | 421E | 2B | | | DCX | H | DECREMENT (HL) |
| | 421F | 34 | | | INR | M | INCREMENT (MEMORY) |
| | 4220 | 7E | | | MOV | A,M | TRANSFER (MEMORY) TO ACC. |
| | 4221 | FE | 0A | | CPI | 0A H | COMPARE 0A H WITH (ACC.) |
| | 4223 | C2 | 00 | 42 | JNZ | MINSEC | JUMP ON NO ZERO TO MINSEC |
| | 4226 | 36 | 00 | | MVI | M 00 | OTHERWISE, LOAD 00 H IN MEMORY |
| | 4228 | 2B | | | DCX | H | DECREMENT (HL) |
| | 4229 | 34 | | | INR | M | INCREMENT (MEMORY) |
| | 422A | 7E | | | MOV | A,M | TRANSFER (MEMORY) TO ACC. |
| | 422B | FE | 06 | | CPI | 06 | COMPARE 06 H WITH (ACC.) |
| | 422D | C2 | 00 | 42 | JNZ | MINSEC | JUMP ON NO ZERO TO MINSEC |
| | 4230 | 36 | 00 | | MVI | M 00 | OTHERWISE, LOAD 00 H IN MEMORY |
| | 4232 | C9 | | | RET | | RETURN |

| INPUT : | MEM. LOC. | 40FF H | : | 8-BIT DATA CORRESPONDING TO THE PRESENT 'HOUR RANGING' FROM 00 TO 23 |
|---------|-----------|--------|---|------|
| | | 4102 H | : | MOST SIGNIFICANT HALF OF PRESENT MINUTE READING |
| | | 4103 H | : | LEAST SIGNIFICANT HALF OF PRESENT 'MINUTE READING' |
| | | 4104 H | : | 15 ; FOR BLANK DISPLAY |
| | | 4105 H | : | 15 ; FOR BLANK DISPLAY |
| | | 4106 H | : | MOST SIGNIFICANT HALF OF PRESENT 'SECOND READING' |
| | | 4107 H | : | LEAST SIGNIFICANT HALF OF PRESENT 'SECOND READING' |

Note : TO START THE CLOCK AT 11 HOURS 35 MINUTES 46 SECONDS, THE INPUT WILL BE AS FOLLOWS :

| | HOUR | MIN | | | | SEC | |
|---|------|-----|---|---|---|-----|---|
| MEM. LOC. | 40FF | 4102 | 4103 | 4104 | 4105 | 4106 | 4107 |
| DATA | 11 | 03 | 05 | 15 | 15 | 04 | 06 |

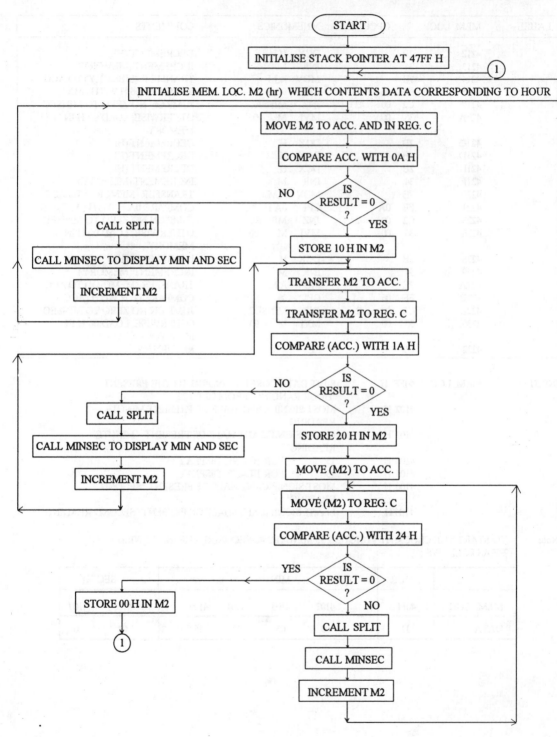

Fig. 11.17 Flowchart

Subroutine 'MINSEC' :

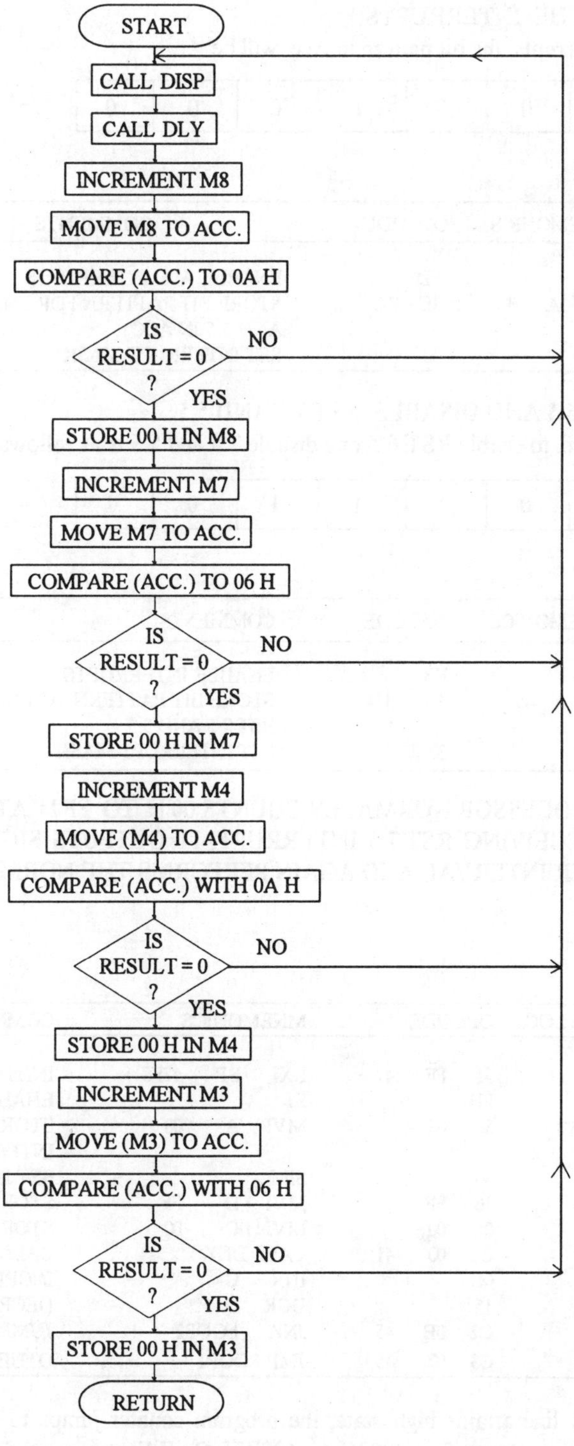

```
                    ( START )
                        │
                 ┌─────────────┐
                 │  CALL DISP  │
                 └─────────────┘
                        │
                 ┌─────────────┐
                 │  CALL DLY   │
                 └─────────────┘
                        │
                 ┌─────────────┐
                 │ INCREMENT M8│
                 └─────────────┘
                        │
                 ┌──────────────────┐
                 │ MOVE M8 TO ACC.  │
                 └──────────────────┘
                        │
              ┌────────────────────────┐
              │ COMPARE (ACC.) TO 0A H │
              └────────────────────────┘
                        │
                      ╱IS╲        NO
                   ╱ RESULT=0 ╲ ──────────►
                      ╲  ?  ╱
                        │ YES
                 ┌──────────────────┐
                 │ STORE 00 H IN M8 │
                 └──────────────────┘
                        │
                 ┌─────────────┐
                 │ INCREMENT M7│
                 └─────────────┘
                        │
                 ┌──────────────────┐
                 │ MOVE M7 TO ACC.  │
                 └──────────────────┘
                        │
              ┌────────────────────────┐
              │ COMPARE (ACC.) TO 06 H │
              └────────────────────────┘
                        │
                      ╱IS╲        NO
                   ╱ RESULT=0 ╲ ──────────►
                      ╲  ?  ╱
                        │ YES
                 ┌──────────────────┐
                 │ STORE 00 H IN M7 │
                 └──────────────────┘
                        │
                 ┌─────────────┐
                 │ INCREMENT M4│
                 └─────────────┘
                        │
                 ┌──────────────────┐
                 │ MOVE (M4) TO ACC.│
                 └──────────────────┘
                        │
              ┌──────────────────────────┐
              │ COMPARE (ACC.) WITH 0A H │
              └──────────────────────────┘
                        │
                      ╱IS╲        NO
                   ╱ RESULT=0 ╲ ──────────►
                      ╲  ?  ╱
                        │ YES
                 ┌──────────────────┐
                 │ STORE 00 H IN M4 │
                 └──────────────────┘
                        │
                 ┌─────────────┐
                 │ INCREMENT M3│
                 └─────────────┘
                        │
                 ┌──────────────────┐
                 │ MOVE (M3) TO ACC.│
                 └──────────────────┘
                        │
              ┌──────────────────────────┐
              │ COMPARE (ACC.) WITH 06 H │
              └──────────────────────────┘
                        │
                      ╱IS╲        NO
                   ╱ RESULT=0 ╲ ──────────►
                      ╲  ?  ╱
                        │ YES
                 ┌──────────────────┐
                 │ STORE 00 H IN M3 │
                 └──────────────────┘
                        │
                    ( RETURN )
```

Fig. 11.18 Flow chart for 'MINSEC'

## 9. ENABLE ALL THE INTERRUPTS:

To enable all the interrupts, the bit pattern in Acc. will be

| 0 | 0 | 0 | 0 | 1 | 0 | 0 | 0 | = | 08 H |
|---|---|---|---|---|---|---|---|---|------|

### THE SOFTWARE :

| MEM. LOC. | MNEMONICS | OPCODE | | COMMENTS |
|-----------|-----------|--------|----|----------|
| 4400 | EI | FB | | ENABLE ALL INTERRUPTS |
| 4401 | MVI A 08 | 3E | 08 | STORE BIT PATTERN FOR ENABLE RST 7.5, 6.5 AND 5.5 IN ACC. |
| 4403 | SIM | 30 | | SET INTERRUPT MASK |

## 10. ENABLE RST 6.5 AND DISABLE RST 7.5 AND 5.5

The bit pattern in Acc. to enable RST 6.5 and disable 7.5 and 5.5 is as follows :

| 0 | 0 | 0 | 1 | 1 | 1 | 0 | 1 | = | 1D H |
|---|---|---|---|---|---|---|---|---|------|

### THE SOFTWARE :

| MEM. LOC. | MNEMONICS | OPCODE | | COMMENTS |
|-----------|-----------|--------|----|----------|
| 4500 | EI | FB | | ENABLE INTERRUPTS |
| 4501 | MVI A 1D | 3E | 1D | STORE BIT PATTERN TO ENABLE RST 6.5 AND DISABLE RST 7.5 AND 5.5 |
| 4503 | SIM | 30 | | SET INTERRUPT MASK |

## 11. THE MICROPROCESSOR NORMALLY COUNTS 00 H TO FF H AT A REGULER INTERVAL OF TIME AND RECEIVING RST 7.5 INTERRUPT, IT OUTPUTS SIGNAL THROUGH PB2 AND PB3 FOR ANOTHER INTERVAL AND AGAIN PERFORMS THE NORMAL COUNTING. DEVELOP THE SOFTWARE.

### MAIN PROGRAM

| LABEL | MEM. LOC. | OPCODE | | | MNEMONICS | | | COMMENTS |
|-------|-----------|--------|----|----|-----------|-----|------|----------|
| | 4500 | 31 | FF | 47 | LXI | SP | 47FF | INITIALISE STACK POINTER |
| | 4503 | FB | | | EI | | | ENABLE INTERRUPT |
| | 4504 | 3E | 08 | | MVI | A | 08 | STORE BIT PATTERN FOR INTERRUPT ENABLE. |
| | 4506 | 30 | | | SIM | | | SET INTERRUPT MASK |
| LOOP1 | 4507 | 16 | FF | | MVI | D | FF | STORE FF H IN REG. D |
| | 4509 | 0E | 00 | | MVI | C | 00 | STORE 00 H IN REG. C |
| LOOP2 | 450B | CD | 00 | 41 | CALL DLY | | | CALL SUBROUTINE 'DLY' |
| | 450E | 0C | | | INR | C | | INCREMENT (REG. C) |
| | 450F | 15 | | | DCR | D | | DECREMENT (REG. D) |
| | 4510 | C2 | 0B | 45 | JNZ | LOOP2 | | JUMP ON NO ZERO TO LOOP2 |
| | 4513 | C3 | 07 | 45 | JMP LOOP1 | | | OTHERWISE, JUMP TO LOOP1 |

When RST 7.5 line attains high state, the program counter jumps to 003C H of EPROM location. Monitor transfers the program from 003C to 407F H. By JMP statement, the program is transferred to the memory location for interrupt service routine. The program is shown in the following page.

| LABEL | MEM. LOC. | OPCODE | | | MNEMONICS | | | COMMENTS |
|-------|-----------|--------|---|---|-----------|---|---|----------|
| | 003C | C3 | 7F | 40 | JMP | 407F H | | JUMP TO MEM. LOC. 407F H |
| | 407F | C3 | 00 | 46 | JMP | 4600 H | | JUMP TO MEM. LOC. 4600 H |
| INTERRUPT SERVICE ROUTINE | | | | | | | | |
| | 4600 | F5 | | | PUSH | PSW | | PUSH FLAG AND ACC. |
| | 4601 | C5 | | | PUSH | B | | PUSH REG. B AND C |
| | 4602 | D5 | | | PUSH | D | | PUSH REG. D AND E |
| | 4603 | 3E | 80 | | MVI | A | 80 | INITIALISE ALL PORTS AS OUTPUT PORTS |
| | 4605 | D3 | 0B | | OUT | CWR | | INITIALISE CONTROL WORD |
| | 4607 | 3E | 0C | | MVI | A | 0C | STORE 0C IN ACC. |
| | 4609 | D3 | 09 | | OUT | P$_B$ | | OUTPUT THROUGH PB2 AND PB3 |
| | 460B | CD | 11 | 41 | CALL | DLYOUT | | CALL 'DLYOUT' |
| | 460E | D1 | | | POP | D | | POP REG. D AND E |
| | 460F | C1 | | | POP | B | | POP REG. B AND C |
| | 4610 | F1 | | | POP | PSW | | POP FLAG AND ACC |
| | 4611 | FB | | | EI | | | ENABLE INTERRUPT |
| | 4612 | C9 | | | RET | | | RETURN |
| DLY | 4100 | D5 | | | PUSH | D | | PUSH REG. D AND E |
| | 4101 | 16 | AA | | MVI | D | AA H | STORE AA H IN REG. D |
| REPT2 | 4103 | 1E | BB | | MVI | E | BB H | STORE BB H IN REG. E |
| REPT1 | 4105 | 00 | | | NOP | | | NO OPERATION |
| | 4106 | 00 | | | NOP | | | NO OPERATION |
| | 4107 | 1D | | | DCR | E | | DECREMENT (REG. E) |
| | 4108 | C2 | 05 | 41 | JNZ | REPT1 | | JUMP ON NO ZERO TO REPT1 |
| | 410B | 15 | | | DCR | D | | OTHERWISE, DECREMENT (REG. D) |
| | 410C | C2 | 03 | 41 | JNZ | REPT2 | | JUMP ON NO ZERO TO REPT2 |
| | 410F | D1 | | | POP | D | | OTHERWISE, POP REG. D AND E |
| | 4110 | C9 | | | RET | | | RETURN |
| DLYOUT | 4111 | D5 | | | PUSH | D | | PUSH REG. D AND E |
| | 4112 | 16 | 88 | | MVI | D | 88 H | STORE 88 H IN REG. D |
| REPT4 | 4114 | 1E | 77 | | MVI | E | 77 H | STORE 77 H IN REG. E |
| REPT3 | 4116 | 00 | | | NOP | | | NO OPERATION |
| | 4117 | 00 | | | NOP | | | NO OPERATION |
| | 4118 | 1D | | | DCR | E | | DECREMENT (REG. E) |
| | 4119 | C2 | 16 | 41 | JNZ | REPT3 | | JUMP ON NO ZERO TO REPT3 |
| | 411C | 15 | | | DCR | D | | OTHERWISE, DECREMENT (REG. D) |
| | 411D | C2 | 14 | 41 | JNZ | REPT4 | | JUMP ON NO ZERO TO REPT4 |
| | 4120 | D1 | | | POP | D | | OTHERWISE, POP REG. D AND E |
| | 4121 | C9 | | | RET | | | RETURN |

## 12 DEVELOP A SOFTWARE FOR CONTINUOUS MONITORING AND DISPLAY OF ADC OUTPUT SIGNAL BASED ON 0809.

| LABEL | MEM.LOC. | OPCODE | | | MNEMONICS | | | COMMENTS |
|-------|----------|--------|---|---|-----------|---|---|----------|
| MAIN PROGRAM | | | | | | | | |
| | 41B9 | 31 | FF | 47 | LXI | SP | 47FF | INITIALISE STACK POINTER AT MEM. LOC. 47FF H |
| | 41BC | CD | 80 | 41 | CALL | ADCTRIG | | CALL SUBROUTINE 'ADCTRIG |
| | 41BF | C3 | BC | 41 | JMP | START | | JUMP TO START |
| SUBROUTINE 'ADCTRIG' | | | | | | | | |
| | 4180 | 3E | 90 | | MVI | A | 90H | ASSIGN PORT-A AS INPUT AND PORTS B AND C AS OUTPUT PORTS |
| | 4182 | D3 | 0F | | OUT | 0F | | SET CONTROL WORD FOR CHIP SELECT |

| LABEL | MEM.LOC. | OPCODE | | | MNEMONICS | | | COMMENTS |
|---|---|---|---|---|---|---|---|---|
| | 4184 | 3E | 00 | | MVI | A | 00 | KEEP ALL PINS LOW |
| | 4186 | D3 | 0D | | OUT | 0D | | OUTPUT THROUGH PORT-B |
| | 4188 | F6 | 08 | | ORI | 08 | | OR 08 H WITH (ACC. ) |
| | 418A | D3 | 0D | | OUT | 0D | | MAKE START OF CONVERSION SIGNAL HIGH THROUGH PB3 |
| | 418C | E6 | 07 | | ANI | 07 H | | AND 07 H WITH (ACC. ) |
| | 418E | D3 | 0D | | OUT | 0D H | | KEEP SOC LINE LOW |
| | 4190 | 3E | 30 | | MVI | A | 30 H | LOAD 30 H IN ACC ⎫ WAIT FOR END |
| LOOP1 | 4192 | 3D | | | DCR | A | | DECREMENT (ACC.) ⎬ OF CONVERSION |
| | 4193 | C2 | 92 | 41 | JNZ | LOOP1 | | JUMP ON NO ZERO TO LOOP1 |
| | 4196 | DB | 0C | | IN | 0C | | OTHERWISE, INPUT THROUGH PORT-A WHEN END OF CONVERSION IS OVER |
| SPLIT | 4198 | 21 | 00 | 47 | LXI | H | 4700 H | INITIALISE MEM. LOC. 4700 H |
| | 419B | 00 | | | NOP | | | NO OPERATION |
| | 419C | 77 | | | MOV | M, A | | MOVE (ACC.) TO MEM. LOC. |
| | 419D | 4F | | | MOV | C, A | | MOVE (ACC.) TO REG. C |
| | 419E | E6 | F0 | | ANI | F0 H | | ANI F0 H WITH (ACC.) |
| | 41A0 | 0F | | | RRC | | | ROTATE (ACC.) RIGHT LSB TO CY |
| | 41A1 | 0F | | | RRC | | | ROTATE (ACC.) RIGHT. LSB TO CY |
| | 41A2 | 0F | | | RRC | | | ROTATE (ACC.) RIGHT. LSB TO CY |
| | 41A3 | 0F | | | RRC | | | ROTATE (ACC.) RIGHT. LSB TO CY |
| | 41A4 | 21 | 00 | 45 | LXI | H | 4500 H | INITIALISE MEM. LOC. 4500 H |
| | 41A7 | 77 | | | MOV | M, A | | MOVE (ACC.) TO MEMORY |
| | 41A8 | 79 | | | MOV | A, C | | MOVE (REG. C) TO ACC. |
| | 41A9 | E6 | 0F | | ANI | 0F H | | AND 0F H WITH (ACC.) |
| | 41AB | 23 | | | INX | H | | INCREMENT (HL) |
| | 41AC | 77 | | | MOV | M, A | | MOVE (ACC.) TO MEMORY |
| | 41AD | 3E | 02 | | MVI | A | 02 H | SELECT DATA FIELD FOR DISPLAY |
| | 41AF | 06 | 00 | | MVI | B | 00 | DELETE DOT |
| | 41B1 | 21 | 00 | 45 | LXI | H | 4500 H | INITIALISE MEM. LOC. 4500 H |
| | 41B4 | CD | 83 | 02 | CALL | RDISP | | CALL SUBROUTINE 'RDISP' |
| | 41B7 | C9 | | | RET | | | RETURN TO MAIN PROGRAM |

## 13. DEVELOP A SOFTWARE FOR GENERATION OF SINUSOIDAL WAVEFORM THROUGH 8085 CPU

| LABEL | MEM. LOC. | OPCODE | | | MNEMONICS | | | COMMENTS |
|---|---|---|---|---|---|---|---|---|
| | 41FD | 31 | FF | 47 | LXI | SP | 47FFH | INITIALISE STACK POINTER AT MEM. LOC. 47FF H |
| START | 4200 | 3E | 80 | | MVI | A | 80H | INITIALISE ALL THE PORTS AS OUTPUT PORTS |
| | 4202 | D3 | 0B | | OUT | 0B | | |
| | 4204 | 06 | 23 | | MVI | B | 23 H | LOAD 23 H IN REG. B |
| | 4206 | 21 | 00 | 41 | LXI | H | 4100 H | INITIALISE MEM. LOC. 4100 H |
| NEXT | 4209 | 7E | | | MOV | A, M | | TRANSFER (MEMORY) TO ACC. |
| | 410A | D3 | 08 | | OUT | 08 | | OUTPUT THROUGH PORT-A |
| | 420C | CD | 50 | 41 | CALL | SDLY | | CALL SUBROUTINE 'SDLY' |
| | 420F | 3E | 00 | | MVI | A | 00 | LOAD 00 IN ACC. |
| | 4211 | D3 | 08 | | OUT | 08 | | OUTPUT THROUGH PORT A |
| | 4213 | CD | 5D | 41 | CALL | DLY | | CALL SUBROUTINE 'DLY' |
| | 4116 | 05 | | | DCR | B | | DECREMENT (REG. B) |
| | 4217 | 23 | | | INX | H | | INCREMENT (HL) |
| | 4218 | C2 | 09 | 42 | JNZ | NEXT | | JUMP ON NO ZERO TO NEXT |
| | 421B | C3 | 00 | 42 | JMP | START | | OTHERWISE, JUMP TO START |

| LABEL | MEM. LOC. | OPCODE | | | MNEMONICS | | COMMENTS |
|-------|-----------|--------|---|---|-----------|---|----------|
| SUBROUTINE: | | | | | | | |
| SDLY | 4150 | D5 | | | PUSH | D | STORE (REG. D AND E) IN STACK |
| | 4151 | 16 | 20 | | MVI | D 20 H | LOAD 20 H IN REG. D |
| NEXT1 | 4153 | 52 | | | MOV | D, D | TRANSFER DATA FROM REG. D TO REG. D |
| | 4154 | 5B | | | MOV | E, E | TRANSFER DATA FROM REG. E TO REG. E |
| | 4155 | 00 | | | NOP | | NO OPERATION |
| | 4156 | 00 | | | NOP | | NO OPERATION |
| | 4157 | 15 | | | DCR | D | DECREMENT (REG. D) |
| | 4158 | C2 | 53 | 41 | JNZ | NEXT1 | JUMP ON NO ZERO TO NEXT1 |
| | 415B | D1 | | | POP | D | OTHERWISE, LOAD DATA FROM STACK TO REG. D AND E |
| | 415C | C9 | | | RET | | RETURN |
| DLY | 415D | D5 | | | PUSH | D | STORE (REG. D AND E) IN STACK |
| | 415E | 16 | 50 | | MVI | D 50 H | LOAD 50 H IN REG. D |
| NEXT2 | 4160 | 52 | | | MOV | D, D | TRANSFER DATA FROM REG. D TO REG. D |
| | 4161 | 5B | | | MOV | E, E | TRANSFER DATA FROM REG. E TO REG. E |
| | 4162 | 00 | | | NOP | | NO OPERATION |
| | 4163 | 00 | | | NOP | | NO OPERATION |
| | 4164 | 15 | | | DCR | D | DECREMENT (REG. D) |
| | 4165 | C2 | 60 | 41 | JNZ | NEXT2 | JUMP ON NO ZERO TO NEXT2 |
| | 4168 | D1 | | | POP | D | OTHERWISE, LOAD DATA FROM STACK TO REG. D AND E |
| | 4169 | C9 | | | RET | | RETURN |

**Data Table**

| MEM. LOC. | | | INPUT | | DATA | | | | |
|-----------|---|---|-------|---|------|---|---|---|---|
| 4100 | 64 | 75 | 86 | 96 | A4 | B6 | BA | C2 | C6 |
| 4109 | C8 | C6 | C2 | BA | B6 | A4 | 96 | 86 | 75 |
| 4112 | 64 | 53 | 42 | 32 | 24 | 17 | 0D | 06 | 01 |
| 411B | 00 | 01 | 06 | 0D | 17 | 24 | 32 | 42 | 53 |

OUTPUT: SINUSOID ON THE SCREEN OF OSCILLOSCOPE THROUGH DAC.

## 14. DEVELOP A SOFTWARE FOR OBTAINING FIRST TWENTY FIVE PRIME NUMBERS IN DECIMAL VALUES

A PRIME NUMBER is a number which is divisible by 1 and by that number only. The first twenty five prime numbers are 02, 03, 05, 07, 11, 13, 17, 19, 23, 29, 31, 37, 41, 43, 47, 53, 59, 61, 67, 71, 73, 79, 83, 89, 97. This series may be obtained by computing 3N - 2 and 3N + 2 assuming N = 03 and successive odd numbers leaving all numbers divisible by 05 and 07 and considering the numbers 02, 03, 05 and 07 separately. The flow chart has been shown followed by software listing.

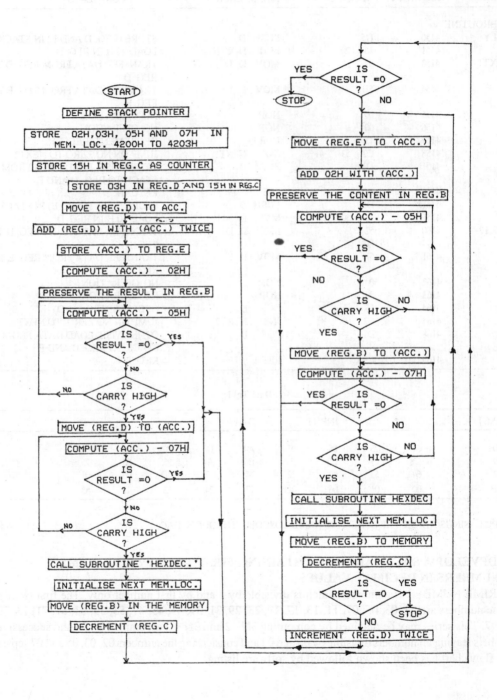

## Software Listing
## Main Program

| MEM. LOC. | LABEL | OPCODE | MNEMONICS | COMMENTS |
|-----------|-------|--------|-----------|----------|
| 4080 | ADSFA | 31 FF 47 | LXI SP 47FFH | DEFINE SP AT MEM.LOC 47FFH |
| 4083 | | 21 00 42 | LXI H 4200 | INITIALISE MEM.LOC. 4200H |
| 4086 | | 36 02 | MVI M 02 | STORE 02H IN THE MEMORY |
| 4088 | | 23 | INX H | INITIALISE NEXT MEM.LOC. |
| 4089 | | 36 03 | MIV M 03 | STORE 03H IN THE MEMORY |
| 408B | | 23 | INX H | INITIALISE NEXT MEM.LOC. |
| 408C | | 36 05 | MVI M 05 | STORE 05H IN THE MEMORY |
| 408E | | 23 | INX H | INITIALISE NEXT MEM.LOC. |
| 408F | | 36 07 | MVI M 07 | STORE 07H IN THE MEMORY |
| 4091 | | 0E 15 | MVI C 15H | STORE 15H IN REG.C |
| 4093 | | 16 03 | MVI D 03H | STORE 03H IN REG.D |
| 4095 | LOOP | 7A | MOV A,D | MOVE (REG.D) TO ACC. |
| 4096 | | 82 | ADD D | ADD (REG.D) WITH (ACC.) |
| 4097 | | 82 | ADD D | ADD (REG.D) WITH (ACC.) |
| 4098 | | 5F | MOV E,A | MOVE (ACC.) TO REG.E |
| 4099 | | D6 02 | SUI 02H | SUBTRACT 02H FROM ACC. |
| 409B | | 47 | MOV B, A | MOVE (ACC.) TO REG.B |
| 409C | REPT1 | D6 05 | SUI 05H | SUBTRACT 05H FROM ACC. |
| 409E | | CA B6 40 | JZ LEAVE | JUMP ON ZERO TO 'LEAVE' |
| 40A1 | | D2 9C 40 | JNC REPT1 | JUMP ON NO CARRY TO 'REPT1' |
| 40A4 | | 78 | MOV A,D | MOVE (REG.D) TO ACC. |
| 40A5 | REPT2 | D6 07 | SUI 07 | SUBTRACT 07H FROM ACC. |
| 40A7 | | CA B6 40 | JZ LEAVE | JUMP ON ZERO TO 'LEAVE' |
| 40AA | | D2 A5 40 | JNC REPT2 | JUMP ON NO CARRY TO 'REPT2' |
| 40AD | | CD DA 40 | CALL HEXDEC | CALL SUBROUTINE "HEXDEC" |
| 40B0 | | 23 | INX H | INITIALISE NEXT MEM.LOC. |
| 40B1 | | 70 | MOV M,B | MOVE (REG. B) TO MEMORY |
| 40B2 | | 0D | DCR C | DECREMENT (REG.C) |
| 40B3 | | CA D9 40 | JZ STOP | JUMP ON ZERO TO 'STOP' |
| 40B6 | LEAVE | 7B | MOV A,E | MOV (REG.E) TO ACC. |
| 40B7 | | C6 02 | ADI 02H | ADD 02H WITH (ACC.) |
| 40B9 | | 47 | MOV B,A | MOVE (ACC.) TO REG.B |
| 40BA | REPT3 | D6 05 | SUI 05H | SUBTRACT 05H FROM ACC. |
| 40BC | | CA D4 40 | JZ REJECT | JUMP ON ZERO TO 'REJECT' |
| 40BF | | D2 BA 40 | JNC REPT3 | JUMP ON NO CARRY TO 'REPT3' |
| 40C2 | | 78 | MOV A,B | MOVE (REG.B) TO ACC. |
| 40C3 | REPT4 | D6 07 | SUI 07 | SUBTRACT 07H FROM ACC. |
| 40C5 | | CA D4 40 | JZ REJECT | JUMP ON ZERO TO 'REJECT' |
| 40C8 | | D2 C3 40 | JNC REPT4 | JUMP ON NO CARRY TO 'REPT4' |
| 40CB | | CD DA 40 | CALL HEXDEC | CALL SUBROUTINE 'HEXDEC' |
| 40CE | | 23 | INX H | INITIALISE NEXT MEM.LOC. |
| 40CF | | 70 | MOV M,B | MOVE (REG.B) TO MEMORY |
| 40D0 | | 0D | DCR C | DECREMENT (REG.C) |
| 40D1 | | CA D9 40 | JZ STOP | JUMP ON ZERO TO 'STOP' |
| 40D4 | REJECT | 14 | INR D | INCREMENT (REG.D) |
| 40D5 | | 14 | INR D | INCREMENT (REG.D) |
| 40D6 | | C3 95 40 | JMP LOOP | JUMP TO 'LOOP' |
| 40D9 | STOP | 76 | HLT | HALT |

**Subroutine 'Hexdec'**

| MEM. LOC. | LABEL | OPCODE | MNEMONICS | COMMENTS |
|-----------|-------|--------|-----------|----------|
| 40DA | | C5 | PUSH B | SAVE (BC) IN THE STACK |
| 40DB | | D5 | PUSH D | SAVE (DE) IN THE STACK |
| 40DC | | E5 | PUSH H | SAVE (HL) IN THE STACK |
| 40DD | | 0E 10 | MVI C 10H | STORE 10H IN REG.C |
| 40DF | | 11 00 00 | LXI D 0000H | CLEAR (DE) |
| 40E2 | | 68 | MOV L, B | MOVE (REG.B) TO REG.L |
| 40E3 | | 26 00 | MVI H 00 | CLEAR REG.H |
| 40E5 | NEXT | AF | XRA A | CLEAR (ACC.) AND FLAG |
| 40E6 | | 29 | DAD H | ADD (HL) WITH (HL) |
| 40E7 | | 7B | MOV A, E | MOVE (REG.E) TO ACC. |
| 40E8 | | 8F | ADC A | ADD (ACC.) AND CY WITH (ACC.) |
| 40E9 | | 27 | DAA | DECIMAL ADJUST OF (ACC.) |
| 40EA | | 5F | MOV E, A | MOVE (ACC.) TO REG.E |
| 40EB | | 7A | MOV A, D | MOVE (REG.D) TO ACC. |
| 40EC | | 8F | ADC A | ADD (ACC.) AND CY WITH (ACC.) |
| 40ED | | 27 | DAA | DECIMAL ADJUST OF (ACC.) |
| 40EE | | 57 | MOV D, A | MOVE (ACC.) TO REG.D |
| 40EF | | 0D | DCR C | DECREMENT (REG.C) |
| 40F0 | | C2 E5 40 | JNZ NEXT | JUMP ON NO ZERO TO 'NEXT' |
| 40F3 | | EB | XCHG | EXCHANGE (DE) WITH (HL) |
| 40F4 | | 7D | MOV A, L | MOVE (REG.L) TO ACC. |
| 40F5 | | 32 7F 40 | STA 407FH | STORE (ACC.) AT MEM. LOC. 407FH |
| 40F8 | | E1 | POP H | RETRIVE (HL) |
| 40F9 | | D1 | POP D | RETRIVE (DE) |
| 40FA | | C1 | POP B | RETRIVE (BC) |
| 40FB | | 3A 7F 40 | LDA 40 7F | LOAD (407FH) TO ACC. |
| 40FE | | 47 | MOV B, A | MOVE (ACC.) TO REG.B |
| 40FF | | C9 | RET | RETURN |

**Output**

| MEM. LOC. | DATA | | | | |
|-----------|------|------|------|------|------|
| 4200 | 02 | 03 | 05 | 07 | 11 |
| 4205 | 13 | 17 | 19 | 23 | 29 |
| 420A | 31 | 37 | 41 | 43 | 47 |
| 420F | 53 | 59 | 61 | 67 | 71 |
| 4214 | 73 | 79 | 83 | 89 | 97 |

## 11.9 USE OF TIMER / COUNTER IN DIFFERENT MODES

It has been pointed out in Section 9.1 that the INTEL 8253 programmable timer operates in five different modes. Different modes of operation have been discussed in this section with software examples.

### 11.9.1 Mode 0 : Interrupt on terminal count

In this mode of operation, counting starts (i.e. counter starts decrementing) if GATE signal is high. At terminal count (i.e.when the content of the counter becomes zero), the OUT pin changes its state from low to high. Since the OUT pin is low initially and throughout the counting period, it can be used to interrupt the microprocessor after a precise time delay. In doing this, the OUT pin is to be connected to the RST pin of the microprocessor.

Example 1 : Using mode - 0 and counter - 0, generate a train of square wave through PC0 of 8255, after making a time delay corresponding to the count ABBA H,

| MEM. LOC. | LABEL | MNEMONICS | OPCODE | COMMENTS |
|-----------|-------|-----------|--------|----------|
| 4100 | START | MVI A 30 | 3E 30 | PROVIDE ACC. BIT PATTERN (DESCRIBED BELOW) |
| 4102 | | OUT 13 | D3 13 | CWR OF TIMER/COUNTER |
| 4104 | | MVI A BA | 3E BA | LOAD LOWER BIT IN ACC. |
| 4106 | | OUT 10 | D3 10 | CWR OF COUNTER - 0 |
| 4108 | | MVI A AB | 3E AB | LOAD HIGHER BIT IN ACC. |
| 410A | | OUT 10 | D3 10 | CWR OF COUNTER - 0 |
| 410C | | MVI A 90 | 3E 90 | INITIALISE PORT-A AS INPUT PORT AND PORTS B AND C AS OUTPUT PORTS |
| 410E | | OUT 0B | D3 0B | SELECT I/O CHIP WITH CWR 0BH |
| 4110 | AKM | IN PA | DB 08 | INPUT THROUGH PORT-A |
| 4112 | | ANI 01 | E6 01 | AND 01H WITH (ACC.) |
| 4114 | | JZ AKM | CA 10 41 | IF RESULT BE ZERO, JUMP TO AKM |
| 4117 | REPT | MVI A 01 | 3E 01 | LOAD 01H IN ACC. |
| 4119 | | OUT PC | D3 0A | OUTPUT THROUGH PORT-C |
| 411B | | CALL DLY | CD 28 41 | CALL DLY SUBROUTINE |
| 411E | | MVI A 00 | 3E 00 | CLEAR ACC. |
| 4120 | | OUT PC | D3 0A | OUTPUT THROUGH PORT-C |
| 4122 | | CALL DLY | CD 28 41 | CALL DLY SUBROUTINE |
| 4125 | | JMP REPT | C3 17 41 | JUMP TO REPT |
| 4128 | DLY | MVI B 80 | 06 80 | LOAD 08 H IN REG.B |
| 412A | DLY1 | NOP | 00 | NO OPERATION |
| 412B | | NOP | 00 | NO OPERATION |
| 412C | | NOP | 00 | NO OPERATION |
| 412D | | DCR B | 05 | DECREMENT REG.B |
| 412E | | JNZ DLY1 | C2 2A 41 | IF RESULT BE ZERO, JUMP TO DLY1 |
| 4131 | | RET | C9 | OTHERWISE RETURN |

Note: Connect OUT pin of 8253 with PA0 of 8255 and observe the waveform on CRO generated by pin PC0 of 8255.

Accumulator bit pattern and its significance :

| D7 | D6 | D5 | D4 | D3 | D2 | D1 | D0 |
|----|----|----|----|----|----|----|----|
| 0 | 0 | 1 | 1 | 0 | 0 | 0 | 0 |

: : : : : : : 0 : for binary count

: : : : : : :

: : : : 0 0 0 : for mode - 0 operation

: : : : : :

: : 1 1 : to load both LSB and MSB

0 0 : for counter 0

### 11.9.2 Mode 1 : Programmable one shot

In this mode of operation, counter starts decrementing at the low to high transition instant of the GATE signal. This GATE signal is known as the firing signal. The OUT signal which is initially high, remains low during counting period only. The width of the out pulse can be varied by varying the count number and this mode of operation is known as programmable one shot. It is retriggerable i.e. if the GATE pules is made low to high again, the counter is reloaded automatically and starts counting. Hence a train of pulses can be generated through OUT pin of 8253.

Example 2 : Using mode – 1 and counter – 0, develop a program to get low and high transmission of OUT – 0 pin of 8253 following a square generation by PC0 of 8255.

| MEM. LOC. | LABEL | MNEMONICS | OP-CODE | COMMENTS |
|---|---|---|---|---|
| 4100 | START | MVI A 12 | 3E 12 | PROVIDE ACC. BIT PATTERN (DESCRIBED BELLOW) |
| 4102 | | OUT 13 | D3 13 | CWR OF TIMER/COUNTER |
| 4104 | | MVI A 0A | 3E 0A | LOAD 0A IN ACC. |
| 4106 | | OUT 10 | D3 10 | CWR OF TIMER - 0 |
| 4108 | | MVI A 90 | 3E 90 | ASSIGN PORT-A AS INPUT PORT AND PORTS B AND C AS OUTPUT PORTS |
| 410A | | OUT OF | D3 0F | SELECT I/0 CHIP WITH CWR 0F H |
| 410C | LOOP | MVI A 01 | 3E 01 | LOAD 01H IN ACC. |
| 410E | | OUT 0D | D3 0D | OUTPUT THROUGH PORT-C |
| 4110 | | CALL SDLY | CD 00 42 | CALL SDLY SUBROUTINE FOR SMALL DELAY |
| 4113 | | MVI A 00 | 3E 00 | CLEAR ACC. |
| 4115 | | OUT 0D | D3 0D | OUTPUT THROUGH PORT - C |
| 4117 | | JMP LOOP | C3 0C 41 | JUMP TO LOOP |

**NOTE :** Connect PC0 of 8255 (CWR 0F H) with GATE pin of 8253 and observe the waveform on CRO. Now connect channel-1 of CRO with PC0 and channel-2 with OUT-0. Observe after high state transmission of PC-0, that OUT-0 pin of 8253 goes to low state for 10 clock periods and then it goes to high state and so on.

Accumulator bit pattern and its significance

| D7 | D6 | D5 | D4 | D3 | D2 | D1 | D0 |
|---|---|---|---|---|---|---|---|
| 0 | 0 | 0 | 1 | 0 | 0 | 1 | 0 |

: : : : : : :   0 : for binary count
: : : : : : : 
: : : : 0   0   1 : for mode - 1 operation
: : : : 
: : 0   1 : to load LSB only
0   0 : for counter 0

### 11.9.3 Mode 2 : Rate generator

In mode-2 operation, if GATE is made high throughout the operation, the OUT pin remains high throughout the (N-1) clock period and in last clock period, OUT pin goes to low state and repeats the same operation. Example 3 : In mode-2 operation, load counter–0 with the hexadecimal number 0A and observe the nature of the signal through OUT pin of 8253.

| MEM. LOC. | LABEL | MNEMONICS | OPCODE | COMMENTS |
|-----------|-------|-----------|--------|----------|
| 4100 | START | MVI A 14 | 3E 14 | PROVIDE ACC. BIT PATTERN (DESCRIBED BELLOW) |
| 4102 | | OUT 13 | D3 13 | CWR OF TIMER/COUNTER |
| 4104 | | MVI A OA | 3E 0A | LOAD LSB OF THE COUNT IN ACC. |
| 4106 | | OUT 10 | D3 10 | CWR OF TIMER–0 |
| 4108 | | HLT | 76 | HALT |

Accumulator bit pattern and its significance

| D7 | D6 | D5 | D4 | D3 | D2 | D1 | D0 |
|----|----|----|----|----|----|----|----|
| 0 | 0 | 0 | 1 | 0 | 1 | 0 | 0 |

```
:    :    :    :    :    :    :   0 : for binary count
:    :    :    :    :    :    :
:    :    :    :    0    1    0 : for mode - 2 operation
:    :    :    :
:    :    0    1 : to load LSB only
0    0 : for counter 0
```

### 11.9.4 Mode 3 : Square wave genetator

In this mode of operation, for high state of GATE pin, OUT pin of 8253 remains high for first (N/2) clock periods and goes to low state for the next (N/2) clock periods when the counter is loaded by an even number N. For odd 'N' the high and low state periods are changed into (N+1) / 2 and (N–1) / 2 clock periods respectively. In this way, the OUT pin generates a train of square wave with equal ON and OFF periods.

Example 4 : Generate a train of square wave by using counter - 0 in mode - 3 operation.

| MEM. LOC. | LABEL | MNEMONICS | OPCODE | COMMENTS |
|-----------|-------|-----------|--------|----------|
| 4100 | START | MVI A 16 | 3E 16 | PROVIDE ACC. BIT PATTERN (DESCRIBED BELOW) |
| 4102 | | OUT 13 | D3 13 | CWR OF TIMER/COUNTER |
| 4104 | | MVI A 40 | 3E 40 | LOAD LSB OF COUNT IN ACC. |
| 4106 | | OUT 10 | D3 10 | CWR OF TIMER–0 |
| 4108 | | HLT | 76 | HALT |

**Note :** Connect CLK (clock) pin with channel – 1 and OUT – 0 of 8253 with channel – 2 of CRO and observe the waveform. In channel – 2, a train of square wave with 18 clock period high and 18 clock period low will be found.

Accumulator bit pattern and its significance :

| D7 | D6 | D5 | D4 | D3 | D2 | D1 | D0 |
|----|----|----|----|----|----|----|----|
| 0  | 0  | 0  | 1  | 0  | 1  | 1  | 0  |

```
    :     :     :     :     :     :     :     0 : for binary count
    :     :     :     :     :     :     :
    :     :     :     :     0     1     1 : for made - 3 operation
    :     :     :     :
    :     :     0     1 : to load LSB only
    0     0 : for counter 0
```

### 11.9.5 Mode 4 : Software triggered storbe

In this mode of operation, GATE is to be kept continuously high. After loading the counter with a number 'N', the OUT pin goes from high state to low state for one clock period after terminal count.

Example 5 : Use counter - 0 and mode - 4 operation of 8253.

| MEM. LOC. | LABEL | MNEMONICS | OPCODE | COMMENTS |
|-----------|-------|-----------|--------|----------|
| 4100      | START | MVI A 18  | 3E 18  | PROVIDE ACC. BIT PATTERN (DESCRIBED BELOW) |
| 4102      |       | OUT 13    | D3 13  | CWR OF TIMER/COUNTER |
| 4104      | LOOP  | MVI A 10  | 3E 10  | LOAD LSB OF COUN IN ACC. |
| 4106      |       | OUT 10    | D3 10  | CWR OF TIMER-0 |
| 4108      |       | JMP LOOP  | C3 04 41 | JUMP TO LOOP |

**Note :** Connect OUT – 0 pin of 8253 with channel – 1 of CRO, observe that, this pin goes to one clock period after every 16 clock periods.

Accumulator bit pattern and its significance :

| D7 | D6 | D5 | D4 | D3 | D2 | D1 | D0 |
|----|----|----|----|----|----|----|----|
| 0  | 0  | 0  | 1  | 1  | 0  | 0  | 0  |

```
    :     :     :     :     :     :     :     0 : for binary count
    :     :     :     :     :     :     :
    :     :     :     :     1     0·    0 : for made - 4 operation
    :     :     :     :
    :     :     0     1 : to load LSB only
    0     0 : for counter 0
```

### 11.9.6 Mode 5 : Hardware triggered strobe.

In mode - 5 operation, the counter is to be loaded by a number 'N' and after making the GATE pin high, the counter starts decrementing and goes to low state for one clock period after terminal count which was in high state initially. However, after low state with one clock period, the counter is reloaded and goes to high state immediately. The same operation for transition from high state to low state is followed by tigger signal.

Example 6 : Use counter - 0 and mode - 5 operation of 8253.

| MEM. LOC. | MNEMONIC | OPCODE | DESCRIPTION |
|---|---|---|---|
| 4100 | MVI A 1A | 3E 1A | PROVIDE ACC. BIT PATTERN (DESCRIBED BELOW) |
| 4102 | OUT 13 | D3 13 | CWR OF TIMER / COUNTER |
| 4104 | MVI A 10 | 3E 10 | LOAD LSB OF COUNTER IN ACC. |
| 4106 | OUT 10 | D3 10 | CWR OF TIMER-0 |
| 4108 | HLT | 76 | HALT |

**Note :** Connect ZCD output (high and low throughout the positive and negative half cycles of input sine wave respectively) with GATE pin of 8253. Connect pin OUT – 0 of 8253 with channel – 1 and ZCD output with channel – 2 of CRO. Observe the waveform of OUT – 0 as describes above.

Accumulator bit pattern and its significance :

| D7 | D6 | D5 | D4 | D3 | D2 | D1 | D0 |
|---|---|---|---|---|---|---|---|
| 0 | 0 | 0 | 1 | 1 | 0 | 1 | 0 |

  :    :    :    :    :    :    :    0 :  for binary count

  :    :    :    :    1    0    1 : for made - 5 operation

  :    :    0    1 : to load LSB only

0    0 : for counter 0

# 12. Microprocessors: An overview

There are a number of manufacturers developing microcomputers, producing a large variety of them, each being different in specific aspects and features. In order to have a comprehensive idea of the subject, it is necessary to be familiar with the popularly used microcomputers and hence with microprocessors.

It may be remembered that a microprocessor of any type or make invariably possesses three basic sets of circuitries: (i) ALU, (ii) some registers and (iii) a control unit. But the specialities of these units are quite different in different types and make. Besides, one chip may include a very special feature which may be absent in the other developed by the other manufacturer.

One may use a particular microprocessor for a specific job which may also be possible using another microprocessor of different kind but often it is seen that one specific microprocessor is helpful and advantageous in some specific usages. Of course there is a large domain of applications where it becomes advantageous to use a particular type of microprocessor while other types may not be convenient. This situation frequently arises specially when very wide memory spaces are necessary and very high speed of operation is required.

## 12.1 TYPES OF MICROPROCESSORS

Microprocessors may be classified from different points of views considering bit-length, memory handling capacity, interfacing, different aspects of software and hardware facility, speed of execution etc. In accordance with the internal and external features of hardware, software and applications, a very broad classification of microprocessors may be made as follows:

(i)   General Purpose Microprocessors
(ii)  Single Chip Microcomputers
(iii) Super Processors
(iv)  Bit-Slice Processors

The general purpose microprocessors consist of 8-bit CPU with a clock frequency typically between 1 MHz to 10 MHz. Sometimes they are associated with a clock generator within the chip. Intel 8085, Z-80A, MC6800, MC6809, 6502 etc. are the general purpose microprocessors. They are highly versatile and powerful and may be used conveniently with moderate size of memory and speed.

The single-chip microcomputers include an 8-bit CPU, an EPROM (1KB to 4KB), a RAM (64 bytes to 256 bytes), a clock generator, one or more timers, a few interrupts, one USART, a few I/O ports etc. in a single chip. These are highly advantageous in dedicated use. Intelligent instruments, microcontrollers, toys etc. are generally developed using these chips along with a very simple and inexpensive extra interfacing circuits. Intel 8748, 8751, Motorola MC 6801, Zilog Z-8 etc. are examples of popular single-chip microcomputers.

Super-processors include 16-bit CPUs with advanced hardware features. These are highly speedy and capable of handliung a very large memory space. Instruction fetch, decoding, and execution - all are performed in parallel. Almost all features of the CPU used in main frame computer are also included. Intel 8086, 8088, 80186, 80188, 80286, Zilog Z-8000, Motorola MC68000 family, Texas Instruments TMS 9900 family etc. are 16-bit super processors while Intel 80386, Intel 80486, Zilog Z-80000, Motorola 68020, MC 68030, MC 6040, National Semiconductor's NS 32032, NS 32332 etc. are the popular 32-bit super processors.

Bit-slice processsors are 'slices' of a CPU and some slices, if cascaded, may construct a CPU of 8-bit length. A slice is generally of 4-bit, 8-bit and sometimes may be of 32-bit also. In fact these are cascadable units of ALU and control section of a CPU. A bit-slice processor along with a bit-slice sequencer, a control memory, an instruction register and a program counter may construct a complete CPU. The instruction decoding, necessary control signal generation in execution etc. are performed by microprogramming and hence the designer can create the desired instruction for the CPU. The processors are very fast in action. Motorola's 10800 family, Advance Micro Device's 2900 family etc. are popular bit-slice processors. Advance Micro Devices INC 29332, Taxas Instrument Inc 74AS8832, Integrated Device Technology Inc IDT 49C404 etc. are examples of 32-bit slice processors.

## 12.2 VARIETY OF MICROPROCESSOR

Different manufacturers produce variety of microprocessors of which two microprocessors of the same type and of the same make may differ widely, These differences may be in hardware implementation, software execution or in applications.

From the view point of interface techniques, microprocessors may be of two varieties, viz., i) Memory-oriented, and ii) I/O oriented. The memory oriented microprocessors treat all the interfaces as the memory locations and there is no physical significance of I/O Ports in them and hence they do not have instructions like IN and OUT etc. The MC6800, MC6802, MC6809, 6502, 8031, 8751 etc. are memory-oriented microprocessors where I/O Ports are all memory mapped. But microprocessors like Intel 8085, Z-80, 8748 etc. are I/O oriented having distinct significance for I/O Ports along with the instructions like IN and OUT.

When a microprocessor deals with a double byte number, sometimes it is found that the lower byte comes first. These processors may be called 'byte-reversed' microprocessors. Intel 8085, Z-80, 6502 etc. are of this kind. The 'byte-direct' microprocessors deal with a double-byte number in a sequence. Intel 8751, 6809 etc. are examples of 'byte-direct' microprocessors.

A microprocessor may further be divided into two varieties: (i) Register-based, and (ii) Memory-based. A register-based microprocessor has several general purpose registers which may be directly used as one of the operands of arithmetic or logic operations as well as the temporary locations for intermediate results. Intel 8085, Z-80, 6809 etc. are all register-based.

A memory-based microprocessor does not posses any general purpose register. They normally use a section of the RAM space as several banks of general-purpose registers and generally these bank registers are switchable by the program. This context-switching facility can be achieved in 8751, 6502, TMS 9900 family etc. which are memory-based processors.

Some microprocessors use the entire memory space at random and the instruction or code, data, stack etc. are stored anywhere within the entire memory space. These types of microprocessors are called 'Linear memory' type. 8085, 6809, 6502, etc. are examples of this type. But there are microprocessors like 8086, or 8751 in which the memory is segmented and individual segments are supposed to contain data, stack, code etc. These are known as 'Segmented memory type' processors. Out of many varieties of microprocessor systems, some are discussed in the following few articles.

## 12.3 SPECIAL FEATURES

High performance microprocessors employ a lot of interesting hardware techniques which enormously increase the versatility and drastically reduce the time of execution. 'Pipelining' hardware is one such techniques. In this technique fetching, decoding and execution are carried on simultaneously by independent units. At each clock cycle, fetching-decoding-execution are performed in parallel. For this purpose, the instruction register (a single register) is replaced by an instruction-queue (a bank of registers). Moreover, the execution unit with pipelining hardware achieves greater speed of execution. Microprocessor, 8085 does not possess pipelining hardware and it performs fetching, decoding and execution in sequential manner. But Intel 8086 and its family of processors use pipelining technique demanding very high speed of execution.

Sometimes, powerful instructions are included to increase the strength and versatility of the microprocessor. In fact, a microprocessor capable of performing only AND and invert operations may be used to perform all numerical computations at the cost of time consumption to perform a simple computation. For this, almost all microprocessors include AND, OR, NOT, XOR along with ADD, SUB and 'ROTATE' and 'SHIFT' instructions. But the microprocessors of high performances often include multiplication and division instructions. String and bit manipulating instructions are also available. Moreover, a number of elementary instructions are compounded into one instruction. One of such instructions used in 8751 is CJNE A # n, m signifying 'compare accumulator with n and if not equal, jump to m-numbered address ahead'. Further, an advanced microprocessor uses increased number of addressing modes. 6502 is much simpler in hardware implementation than 8085 and possesses a large number of addressing modes which make it far more versatile and powerful than 8085.

There are many other techniques which a powerful microprocessor may contain. Addition of some extra units like timer, USART, RAM etc., enhances the power of such microprocessors.

## 12.4 INSTRUCTION SET

Different microprocessors possess completely different types of instructions which are nearly similar. But sometimes, these may differ greatly in nature and applications, As discussed earlier, instructions of a microprocessor may be divided into five types in general:
 (i)   Data Transfer Instructions
 (ii)  Data manipulation Instructions
 (iii) Program-Control Instructions
 (iv)  Execution-Control Instructions
 (v)   Compounded Instructions

Data transfer instruction includes different 'MOVE' instructions. It is used to copy the contents of registers or memory locations. The instruction 'MOV Rm, Rn' means that the contents of register Rn is to be copied in the register Rm. Note that data-flow takes place from right to left, but in some microprocessors, this instruction may mean a left to right ward data-flow ie, Rm is to be copied by the register Rn. There may be 'EXCHANGE' instructions like 'XCHG Rm, Rn meaning that registers Rm and Rn are to exchange their contents. An immediate type of data transfer instruction may be "MVI B, n" or "MOV Rm, n" meaning that the data 'n' is to be loaded in register B or Rm.

Arithmetic and Logic instructions, string-manipulating instructions, bit manipulating instructions etc. are categorised as the Data-Manipulating Instructions. Arithmetic-Logic instructions include different arithmetic and logic operations like AND, OR, XOR, ADD, SUB etc. along with Rotate/Shift and Increment/Decrement instructions. There are some special instructions like 'SWAP A' meaning that the digits in Accumulator are to be interchanged in position. Also, there may be some instruction like "XCHD Rm, Rn" meaning that only the lower digits of registers Rm and Rn are to be exchanged. Some microprocessors possess Multiplication/Division instructions and ASCII-adjust/Decimal adjust instructions for different arithmetic operations. String manipulating instructions include storing, loading or comparing of a string. Bit-manipulating instructions give the user the scope to transfer bits or to perform an arithmetic / logic operation on bits directly.

Program-control instructions are different JUMP, CALL / RETURN and RESTART instructions. They may be (i) conditional and (ii) unconditional. These instructions may also be classified into (a) direct, (b) indirect, (c) immediate, (d) implied and (e) relative according to different addressing modes. Internal and external software and hardware interrupts may also be categorised into the Program Controlled instructions.

There are instructions like NOP, HLT or initialisation of different control registers for different internal units like interrupts, timers, counters, USART etc. They are usually grouped into Execution -Control or Machine -Control instructions. Some microprocessors may possess a number of special instructions like 'SCAPE' or 'SYNC' etc.

Further, there exist some instructions in which a number of different instructions are compounded into one. These are the compounded instructions. The string-manipulating instructions are one of the best examples of compounded instructions. Consider an instruction "DJNZ" Rn, d" which signifies 'decrement register Rn and jump to the address "d" unit forward from the next address if the register Rn is not zero'. This instruction is evidently a combination of "DEC Rn" (decrement the register Rn) and "JNZ d" (Jump to 'd' unit apart if the result is not equal to zero). These types of instructions increase the strength, compactness and speed of the program.

## 12.5 ADDRESSING MODES

In order to store DATA to or load DATA from, or perform an operation on the contents of a register of memory location, it becomes necessary to address the particular register or memory location. This may be done in different ways using different modes of addressing. The more the number of addressing modes of a microprocessor, the more is the strength of the microprocessor in applications. Of the two instructions "MOV m, A" and "MOV (Rm), A", using the first instruction, the content of the accumulator is transferred to the memory location whose address is 'm' while through the second instruction, the content of the accumulator is transferred to the memory location whose address is contained in the register Rm. In the later case, the memory locations are addressed quite differently although the results of the two instructions are identical.

The addressing modes can be classified in two main groups viz. Elementary Addressing Modes and Mixed Addressing Modes. Different Elementary Addressing modes are : i) Direct ii) Indirect iii) Implied iv) Immediate and vi) Relative.

Through direct addressing mode, the location (any register or memory location) is addressed directly as in the instruction "STA 2000" or "LDA 2000". In these instructions, the location 2000 is directly addressed. These two instructions are used in 8085 CPU. If register BC is loaded with 2000, the instructions "STAX B" or "LDAX B" will address the location 2000 indirectly.

In implied mode of addressing, the addressed location is inherently included within the instruction. The MOV instruction of 8085 is the best examples of implied addressing. In instruction "MOV A, B " ( opcode being 78 for Intel 8085), the addressed locations A and Reg. B are inherent within the opcode 78. But in Intel 8751, the instruction "MOV A, B" (opcode being 85 E0 F0), the addressed locations i.e., registers A and B with addresses E0 and F0, are directly addressed.

A Data is immediately followed by the instruction in the immediate addressing modes. In this mode, 'assignment' of a location is made. Sometimes the symbol "#" is used to indicate the immediate mode. In instruction "MOV A, # m", the register A is assigned to a value "m". The indications for various modes of addressing may be completely different in different mnemonics.

The index-register contains the address of the addressed location in the indexed addressing mode. The indexed location may be treated as a general purpose register. The memory based instructions of 8085 are of the indexed addressing mode. Sometimes a number of indexed registers are available for this purpose. It may be appeared that the indirectly addressed location is very similar to an indexed location, but it may be remembered that an indirectly addressed location can not be used as a general purpose register.

In relative addressing mode, the actual address of the addressed location, whether indirect or indexed, is displaced by 2's complemented number form one in the indexed-register. Consider an instruction:

$$\text{"MOVC A, @ A + PC"}$$

of 8751. It means that the content of the location whose address is stored in PC added with the content in Accumulator is to go to the Accumulator. An instruction of Z-80 like "LD (IX + d), B" indicates that the content of the register B is to go to the location whose address is the sum of the content of register index IX and the value `d'. Another instruction "JZ d" indicates a jump on zero to an address `d' locations apart from the next location.

Frequently more than one modes are indexed in one instruction called the mixed mode of addressing. Powerful instructions of mixed mode type are complicated in nature. In fact a large number of mixed modes are possible. Some of these are : relative indexed, relative indirect, implied indexed relative indirect, indirect implied relative indexed etc. Powerful microprocessors have several numbers of powerful mixed mode addressing capabilities.

## 12.6 WRITING PROGRAMS

Frequently problems are faced to translate a program in the mnemonics of one microprocessor from the same written in a different set of mnemonics of another microprocessor since equivalent or directly replacable instructions may not always be available. This problem may be solved by presenting the program first in flow-diagram and then writing the program in some specific mnemonics. The programs in flow diagram is quite general in nature having the difficulty that every minute step cannot be written without using mnemonics.

An alternative solution to this problem is to use first the algorithmic codes. These codes should be of simple nature and any program developed with this codes may easily be converted into any mnemonics. Though these codes are not universal and different authors may describe them differently, the following codes may be used with convenience:

(1) Data transfer is indicated by an arrow mark like $\longrightarrow$ or $\longleftarrow$

EXAMPLES:

| | | |
|---|---|---|
| MOV to A from B | : | $A \longleftarrow B$ or $B \longrightarrow A$ |
| OUTPUT A through P1 | : | $A \longrightarrow P1$ |
| INPUT through P2 to A | : | $A \longleftarrow P2$ |
| PUSH A | : | $A \longrightarrow S$ |
| POP B | : | $B \longleftarrow S$ |
| XCHG A, B | : | $A \rightleftharpoons B$ |

where S signifies the stack which may also be indicated by Ms.

(2) The arithemtic / logic operations may be represented as:

| | | |
|---|---|---|
| ADD | : | + |
| SUB | : | - |
| MULTIPLY | : | x |
| DIVIDE | : | / |
| Borrow/Carry | : | ⓒ |
| Residue/remainder | : | ⓡ |
| AND | : | • |
| OR | : | ⊕ |
| XOR | : | ⊖ |
| Compliment | : | a bar over the operand. |

EXAMPLES:

$$A \longleftarrow A + B$$
$$B \longleftarrow \overline{B} \oplus C$$
$$B \longleftarrow B + 1$$
$$C \longleftarrow C + B + ⓒ$$

| | | |
|---|---|---|
| (3) Jump | : | $\Longrightarrow$ |
| Call | : | $\Longleftarrow\!\!\rightarrow$ or $\rightleftharpoons$ |
| Return | : | $\Longleftarrow$ |

Conditions of these operations may be written over the respective symbols.

EXAMPLES:

| | | |
|---|---|---|
| JUMP P1 | : | $\Longrightarrow P1$ |
| JNZ P2 | : | $\overset{NZ}{\Longrightarrow} P1$ |
| CALL P2 | : | $\rightleftharpoons P2$ |

(4) Execution-Control instructions of any microprocessor may be used.

(5) Addressing modes may be indicated as follows:

| | | |
|---|---|---|
| indirect | : | [ ] |
| indexed | : | ( ) |
| immediate | : | # or ⓐ |
| relative | : | + ± |

EXAMPLES:

Move to R1 indirectly the immediate data 'd':

$$[R1] \leftarrow \# d$$

Move to location indexed by R2 from R3 indirectly:

$$(R2) \leftarrow [R3]$$

Move to indexed location by R3 relative to 'd' from the indirect R3:

$$(R2+d) \leftarrow [R3]$$

etc. Using the codes, a delay sub-program may be developed as under where register R1 is pushed to the stack and loaded by a number 'n'. Then, it is decremented and checked for zero. If the result is not zero, the content of the register R1 is again decremented and checked for zero in a loop. The program is as follows :

$$R1 \longrightarrow S$$
$$R1 \leftarrow \# n$$
P :   $R1 \leftarrow R1 - 1$

$$\frac{NZ}{=======} \Longrightarrow P$$

$$R1 \leftarrow S$$
$$\underset{\longleftarrow ====}{}$$

This program may easily be translated directly in the mnemonics of any microprocessor.

## 12.7 GENERAL PURPOSE MICROPROCESSORS

### 12.7.1 Zilog Z-80

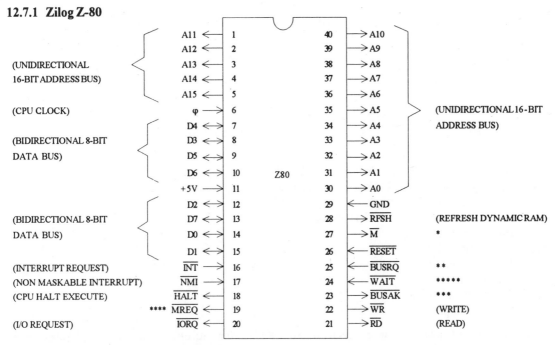

* (OUT PIN, FETCH OPERATION WHEN LOW)
** (REQUEST FOR BUS CONTROL FROM EXTERNAL DEVICE, LIKE HOLD IN 8085)
*** (BUS ACKNOWLEDGE, LIKE HLDA IN 8085)
**** (MEMORY REQUEST WHEN LOW)
***** (WAIT STATUS REQUEST SIMILAR TO READY IN 8085)

Fig. 12.1. Pin configuration and description of Z80-CPU

Zilog Inc. introduced this high performance microprocessor chip in a 40-pin package and Radio-Shack TRS-80 house computers use Z-80 as the CPU. It is a byte reversed, I/O oriented, register-based, linear memory-type 8-bit general purpose microprocessor. Z-80 operates at upto 2.5 MHz clock frequency whereas Z-80A operates at upto 4 MHz.

It has 8-bit data bus, 16-bit address bus and the control bus includes $\overline{M1}$, $\overline{MREQ}$ (memory request), $\overline{IORQ}$ (I/O request), $\overline{RD}$, $\overline{WR}$, $\overline{HALT}$, $\overline{WAIT}$, $\overline{BUSRQ}$ (bus request), $\overline{BUSAK}$ (bus acknowledge), $\overline{RFSH}$ (refresh) etc. along with two interrupts, $\overline{INT}$ and $\overline{NMI}$ (non-maskable interrupts). INT, NMI, WAIT, BUSRQ, BUSAK have identical functions to INT, TRAP, READY, HOLD and HOLDA respectively of 8085 CPU. In fact Z-80 may be considered as an enhancement of Intel 8085. $\overline{RFSH}$ is used to refresh the dynamic RAM directly. The pin configuration of z-80 has been shown in Fig. 12.1.

Besides main Register Set, Z-80 has another alternative Register set and in each register set, apart from the Accumulator and flags, there are general purpose registers B.C.D.E. H and L. There are special purpose registers like INTERRUPT VECTOR REGISTER (I) and MEMORY REFRESH REGISTER (R) each of 8-bit length and two 16-bit Registers (IX) and (IY) apart from STACK POINTER (SP) and PROGRAM COUNTER (PC). The Refresh register functions automatically. The Register configuration of Z-80 CPU is shown in Table 12.1.

**Table 12.1. Register Configuration of Z-80**

GENERAL PURPOSE REGISTER

| MAIN REGISTER SET | | ALTERNATE REGISTER SET | |
|---|---|---|---|
| ACCUMULATOR A | FLAGS F | ACCUMULATOR A | FLAGS F' |
| B | C | B' | C' |
| D | E | D' | E' |
| H | L | H' | L' |

SPECIAL PURPOSE REGISTERS

| INTERRUPT VECTOR (I) | MEMORY REFRESH (R) |
|---|---|
| INDEX REGISTER (IX) | |
| INDEX REGISTER (IY) | |
| STACK POINTER (SP) | |
| PROGRAM COUNTER (PC) | |

Compared to 80 instructions in 8085A CUP, Z-80 has 158 different instructions divided into eleven groups:

   (i)   8-bit Load Group (LD)
  (ii)   16-bit Load Group (LD) including PUSH and POP
 (iii)   Exchange group EX and EXX between main register and alternate registers.
 (iv)   8-bit Arithmetic and Logic groups
   (v)   General purpose Arithmetic and CPU control groups
 (vi)   16-bit Arithmetic group
(vii)   Rotate and shift group
(viii)  Bit mainpulation group
 (ix)   Jump group
   (x)   Call and Return group
 (xi)   Input and output group

Out of 158 instructions, 78 are common to these of 8085 A, but with different mnemonics (the uncommon instructions being SIM and RIM). All the elementary addressing modes are available along with a lot of mixed modes. There are a large number of compound instructions. Through 8-bit load group (LD), data can be transferred from ACC. to Registers and Memory; Register and Memory to ACC; Indexed Registers to ACC. and Registers and Vice-Versa. Data can be directly inserted to ACC; Registers, Memories and indexed registers.

In 16-bit load group (LD), instructions exist for 16-bit data loading to register pairs BC, DE, HL, AF; Indexed Registers and Memories. Apart from the standard PUSH and POP instructions, new instructions have been added for PUSH and POP operations for the contents of indexed Registers IX and IY.

In Exchange Group, exchange of data between (DE) and (HL) is present. New instructions for exchange of data between AF of main register set and that of alternate register set (EX, AF, AF′) and also between register pairs of two register sets are available. It is possible through instructions to exchange the content of (SP) with those of HL, IX and IY. Other new instructions available with Z-80 CPU include LDI, LDIR, LDD, LDDR, CPI, CPIR, CPO and CPOR.

Similar to INTEL 8085 A, there are 8-bit Arithmetic and Logic instructions like ADD, ADC, SUB, SBC, AND, XOR, OR, CP (compare), INC (increment) and DEC (decrement) with Z-80. Similar types of instructions with Indexed registers are also available.

In general purpose Arithmetic group, instructions for Decimal Adjust ACC (DAA), complement ACC (CPL), Negative ACC (NEG) for finding 2's complement, complement carry flag (CCF) and set carry flag (SCF) are present. NOP, HALT, DISABLE, and ENABLE Interrupt (DI and EI) are present in CPU control group.

16-bit addition and subtraction with and without carry (ADD, ADC, SBC), summation of the contents of Indexed Register and general purpose Register-Pairs of main Register set, increment and decrement of contents of register pairs, Indexed register pairs and stack pointer are the 16-bit Arithmetic operations to be performed with 16-bit Arithmetic group.

In rotate and shift group, apart from RLC, RRC, RAL and RAR which are common to 8085 A, there exist new instructions like SLA (shift left Arithmetic) SRA (shift right Arithmetic), SRL (shift right logical), RLD (rotate digit left) and RRD (rorate digit right). Except the last two instructions valid only for the contents of HL pair, all other instructions in this group can be applied with the contents of all general purpose registers of the main register set, HL pair and Indexed registers.

Instructions JMP, JC, JNC, JZ, JNZ, JP, JM, JPO, JPE are the unconditional and conditional jump instructions common in both 8085 A and Z-80 CPU. But JP (HL), JP (IX), JP (IY) and DJNZ (Decrement B, jump if B ≠ 0) are the additional instructions of this group available with Z-80 only.

In call and return group, CALL (CD), CC (CALL IF CY HIGH), CNC (CALL IF CY LOW), CZ (CALL IF RESULT = 0), CNZ (CALL IF RESULT ≠ 0), CP (CALL IF MSB OF RESULT = 0), CM (CALL IF MSB OF RESULT = 1), CPO (CALL IF RESULT HAS ODD NUMBER OF 1's), CPE (CALL IF RESULT HAS ODD NUMBER OF 1'S), RET, RC (RETURN IF CY = 1), RNC (RETURN IF CY = 0), RZ (RETURN IF Z = 1), RNZ (RETURN IF Z = 0), RP (RETURN IF S = 0), RM (RETURN IF S = 1), RPO (RETURN IF P = 0), RPE (RETURN IF P = 1) instructions are common with INTEL 8085 A. Additional instructions in Z-80 are RETI (RETURN FROM INTERRUPT), RENT (RETURN FROM NONMASKABLE INTERRUPT). All instructions in Restart group (RST) are common to both the CPUs.

In Input and output group, besides input in ACC (DB) and output through ACC (D3), Input-output of data through different registers are possible. Moreover, there exist instructions like INI (Input and Inc HL, Dec B), INTR (Input, Inc. HL, DEC B, repeat if B ≠ 1), IND (Input and DEC. HL, DEC B), INDR (Input, DEC HL, DEC B, Repeat if B ≠ 1), OUT 1 (output, Inc HL, Dec B), OTIR (output, Inc HL, DEC B, repeat if B ≠ 0), OUT D (Output, DEC HL, DEC B) and OTDR (Output, DEC HL, DEC B, Repeat if B ≠ 0). Z-80 instruction sets common to 8085/8085A instructions and also those which are available only in Z-80 have been presented in Appendix 2.

## 12.7.2 SOFTWARE EXAMPLES WITH Z-80 BASED MICROPROCESSOR

(1) Develop a software to clear the contents of the memory address 187A H - 1889 H.

| LABEL | MEM. LOC. | MNEMONICS | OPCODE | | | DESCRIPTION |
|-------|-----------|-----------|--------|---|---|-------------|
| START | 1800 | LD C, 20H | 0E | 20 | | SET LOOP COUNTER 20H IN REG. C. |
| | 1802 | LD HL, 187A | 21 | 7A | 18 | INITIALIZE STARTING ADDRESS OF MEM. LOC. TO BE CLEARED |
| | 1805 | XOR A | AF | | | CLEAR ACC |
| LOOP | 1806 | LD (HL), A | 77 | | | LOAD 00H TO THE MEMORY |
| | 1807 | INC HL | 34 | | | INCREMENT HL BY 1 |
| | 1808 | DEC C | 0D | | | DECREMENT REG. C BY 1 |
| | 1809 | JRNZ LOOP | C2 | 06 | 18 | IF C ≠ 0, JUMP TO LOOP |
| | 180C | RST 56 | FF | | | RETURN TO MONITOR PROGRAM AT MEM. LOC. 0038 H |

(2) Add 16 bit data stored in mem. locs 1900 H and 1901H to the 16-bit data stored in register pair DE. Put the results in Register pair DE.

| MEM. LOC. | MNEMONICS | OPCODE | | | DESCRIPTION |
|-----------|-----------|--------|---|---|-------------|
| 1800 | LDA, (1900 H) | 7E | 00 | 19 | LOAD THE CONTENT OF 1900 H TO ACC |
| 1803 | ADD A, E | 83 | | | ADD (ACC) AND (REG. E) |
| 1804 | LDE, A | 5F | | | LOAD (ACC) TO REG. E |
| 1805 | LDA, (1901 H) | 7E | 01 | 19 | LOAD THE CONTENT OF 1901 H TO ACC |
| 1808 | ADC A, D | 82 | | | ADD THE CONTENT OF REG. D AND CY TO THE CONTENT OF ACC. KEEP THE RESULT IN ACC. |
| 1809 | LD D, A | 57 | | | LOAD (ACC.) TO REG. D. |
| 180A | RST 56 | FF | | | RETURN TO MONITOR PROGRAM AT MEM. LOC. 0038 H. |

(3) Read the following program and state the status of Flag after each mathematical operation along with the result.

| MEM. LOC. | MNEMONICS | OPCODE | | DESCRIPTION |
|-----------|-----------|--------|---|-------------|
| 1800 | XOR A | AF | | CLEAR ACC |
| 1801 | LDA, 5F H | 3E | 5F | LOAD 5F H IN ACC. |
| 1803 | ADD A, BE H | C6 | BD | ADD (ACC.) TO BD H |
| 1805 | ADD A, 43 H | C6 | 43 | ADD (ACC) TO 43 H |
| 1807 | SUB A, 23 H | D6 | 23 | SUBTRACT 23H FROM ACC |
| 1809 | SUB A, A3 H | D6 | A3 | SUBTRACT A3H FROM ACC |
| 180B | SUB A, 25 H | D6 | 25 | SUBTRACT 25 H FROM ACC |
| 180D | XOR A | AF | | CLEAR ACC |
| 180E | LDA, 5F H | 3E | 5F | ADD (ACC), CY AND 5F H |
| 1810 | ADC A, BD H | CE | BD | ADD (ACC), CY AND BD H |
| 1812 | ADC A, 43 H | CE | 43 | ADD (ACC), CY AND 43 H |
| 1814 | SBC A, 23 H | DE | 23 | SUBTRACT CY AND 23 H FROM (ACC) |
| 1816 | SBC A, A3 H | DE | A3 | SUBTRACT CY AND A3 H FROM (ACC) |
| 1818 | SBC A, 25 H | DE | 25 | SUBTRACT CY AND 25 H FROM (ACC) |
| 181A | RST 56 | FF | | RETURN TO MONITOR PROGRAM AT MEM. LOC. 0038H |

(4) Delay Subroutine.

| LABEL | MEM. LOC. | MNEMONICS | OPCODE | | | DESCRIPTION |
|-------|-----------|-----------|--------|---|---|-------------|
| DLY | 1800 | PUSH B | C5 | | | PRESERVE (BC) IN STACK |
| | 1801 | LDB, n | 06 | n | | STORE COUNTER 'n' IN REG.B |
| LOOP | 1803 | DJNZ 0318 | 10 | 03 | 18 | DECREMENT B, JUMP ON NO ZERO TO LOOP |
| | 1806 | POP B | C1 | | | POP CONTENT OF BC |
| | 1807 | RET | C9 | | | RETURN |

(5) Arrange the given N-numbers stored in a block of memory locations in ascending order (the same example given in chapter 11)

| MEM. LOC. | LABEL | MNEMONICS | | OPCODE | | | DESCRIPTION |
|-----------|-------|-----------|------|--------|----|----|-------------|
| 4300 | START | LD B | 10 H | 06 | 10 | | Load 10 H (No. of DATA) IN REG. B |
| 4302 | | LD (HL) | 4100 H | 21 | 00 | 41 | LOAD STARTING ADDRESS IN HL PAIR |
| 4305 | | LDA, | (HL) | 7E | | | LOAD (HL) IN ACC |
| 4306 | | LD D, | A | 57 | | | LOAD (D) WITH THE CONTENT OF ACC |
| 4307 | | INC | (HL) | 23 | | | INCREMENT HL PAIR |
| 4308 | | SUB | (HL) | 96 | | | SUBTRACT MEMORY CONTENT FROM (ACC) |
| 4309 | | JNC | NEXT2 | D2 | 16 | 43 | JUMP ON NO CARRY TO 'NEXT2' |
| 430C | | SCF | | 37 | | | SET CY |
| 430D | | CCF | | 3F | | | COMPLEMENT CY |
| 430E | | DEC | B | 05 | | | DECREMENT (REG. B) |
| 430F | | J2 | NEXT1 | CA | 15 | 43 | JUMP ON ZERO TO 'NEXT 1' |
| 4312 | | JP | NEXT2 | C3 | 05 | 43 | OTHERWISE, JUMP TO 'NEXT2' |
| 4315 | NEXT 1 | HLT | | 76 | | | HALT |
| 4316 | NEXT 2 | LD C, | HL | 4E | | | LOAD (HL), TO REG. C |
| 4317 | | LD | (HL), D | 72 | | | LOAD (REG. D) TO (HL) |
| 4318 | | DEC | (HL) | 2B | | | DECREMENT HL PAIR |
| 4319 | | LD | (HL), C | 71 | | | LOAD (C) TO (HL) |
| 431A | | JP | START | C3 | 00 | 43 | JUMP START |

| INPUT : MEM. LOC. | DATA | OUTPUT : MEM. LOC. | DATA |
|-------------------|------|--------------------|------|
| 4100 | FF | 4100 | 01 |
| 4101 | 23 | 4101 | 05 |
| 4102 | 95 | 4102 | 08 |
| 4103 | C2 | 4103 | 10 |
| 4104 | 86 | 4104 | 23 |
| 4105 | 01 | 4105 | 35 |
| 4106 | 35 | 4106 | 86 |
| 4107 | 05 | 4107 | 95 |
| 4108 | 08 | 4108 | C2 |
| 4109 | 10 | 4109 | FF |

## 12.8 MOTOROLA MC 6809

MOTOROLA MC 6809 is one of the high performance microprocessors. It is an important member of Motorola 6800 family. It may be considered as a semi 16-bit processor and it includes an on chip clock. MC 6809 is a byte forward, memory oriented, memory based, linear memory-type, 8-bit General purpose microprocessor. Mc 6809 contains 8-bit data bus, 16-bit address bus along with the control bus containing R/W̄ (Read and Write), MRDY (memory ready), D̄M̄A̅/BREQ (DMA / Bus Request), BA (Bus Avialable), BS (Bus State), H̄A̅L̅T, RESET, NMI, FIRQ (First Interrupt Request), IRQ (Interrupt Request) etc. An external crystal is needed for the on-chip clock of frequency up to 4 MHz.

MC 6809 possesses two 8-bit accumulators A and B, two 16-bit index registers X and Y, two 16-bit stack pointers- User's stack pointer U and stack pointer S, one 16-bit program counter PC, an 8-bit Direct Page Register DP and one 8-bit condition Code Register CCR. Accumulators A and B and a 16-bit D register are also available to perform 16-bit operations.

Like 6801 and 6802, 6809 also incorporates all the instructions of 6800, but with increased number of addressing modes. The instruction set of 6809 comprises only of 59 mnemonics, but with a lot of addressing modes, more than 1460 instructions are available. The same delay-program may be translated as :

```
DLY    :    PUSHS A
            LDA # n
LOOP   :    DEC A
            BNE LOOP
            PULLS A
            RET
```

## 12.9 MOS TECH 6502

MOS Tech Inc. 6502 is also a high performance microprocessor. It is exceptionally simple in architecture but highly powerful in performance, so that it is popularly used in many home computers like APPLE, PET, BBC Micro, UK 101 etc. 6500 family is assumed to be conceptually similar to MC 6800 family, though not compatible anyway. Now, there are alternate sources of this chips such as Synertek Inc. and Rockwell International. 6502 is a byte-reversed, memory-oriented, memory-based, segmented memory type 8-bit general purpose microprocessor. 6502 uses 1 MHz clock frequency whereas 6502A and 6502B uses 2MHz and 3 MHz respectively. 6502 possesses 8-bit data bus, 16-bit address bus and a control bus including R/$\overline{W}$, RDY (Ready), SYNC, IRQ, NMI, RES (Reset), and SO (Set Overflow) facilities.

6502 has one 8-bit accumulator A, two 8-bit index registers X and Y, 8-bit Stack Pointer S, one 8-bit flag (PSW) register P and one 16-bit program-Counter PC. Page 01 is reserved for the stack while Page 00 is assumed to be used as general purpose registers.

This CPU has only 56 simple instructions but 13 addressing modes make it a highly versatile and poweful general purpose microprocessor. It is highly efficient (due to increased number of addressing modes) for developing shorter compilers for high level languages which home computers generally use. The delay program may be translated for this version as

```
DLY    :    PH A
            LD A # n
LOOP   :    SBC # 01
            BNE LOOP
            PLA
            RTS
```

## 12.10  BIT SLICE PROCESSORS

Bit Slice Processors are indeed a vertical slice of a CPU and several bit-slice processors, if cascaded, form a CPU of any size. A bit slice processor generally incorporates an ALU, and some registers with simple multiplex circuitry. The ALU is restricted to 2, 4, 8, 16 or 32 bits. Usually bit-slice employs bi-polar Schottky technology to achieve high speed of operation. There are a large number of manufacturers producing these chips. Motorola 10800 ECL series and the Advance Micro Devices 2900 Schottky TTL series are popular ones. 29332 of Advance Micro Devices Inc. 74A 68832 of Taxas Instruments Inc. IDT 49C404 of Integrated Device Technology Inc. etc. are some popular 32-bit slice processors.

Since bit-slices are controlled by micro-instructions, any desired set of machine instructions may be generated which is a remarkable advantage over the other types of microprocessors. Moreover, a dedicated system may be designed to be driven by micro-instructions which may result in very high speed of performance which can not be achieved by other types of microprocessors. With bit slice processors, a CPU of any bit-length may be constructed whereas the other types of microprocesssors are of 8,16 and 32-bits only. The nonconventional bit-length of CPU like 10, 12 or 14 etc. and of any size of larger length may only be achieved by bit-slices. There are situations where a complete CPU is neither necessary nor efficient and only a section of a CPU is required. In this situation, the bit slices are the only solutions. However, bit slices have some inherent disadvantages. The system design by bit slices requires very high skill for efficient performances and an inefficient design may loose all the advantages of the bit slices resulting in a very high cost inefficient system. A bit slice system necessarily requires much greater number of chips than any system designed by other types of microprocessors. Besides, the bit slice systems are relatively costlier.

Advanced micro device, 2901 is another popular member of 2900 family. It consits of a 4-bit ALU and an array of sixteen 4-bit registers along with a 4-bit Q-register and necessary multiplexers, shifters, buffers and latches. The ALU can perform eight different operations like Addition, Subtraction, OR, AND, XOR, XNOR. The two inputs of the ALU can be selected from five possible paths in eight combinations. Cascading provisions are also available. The output of the ALU can be routed to the register array or Q register or data bus. Before the data is written in register array or in Q register, it can be shifted left or right. The slice processors are controlled by the microinstructions.

Usually to construct a bit slice system, the following components are required:
- (i) A set of bit slice processors,
- (ii) A set of bit slice sequencers,
- (iii) Mapping ROM (or EPROM)
- (iv) Control ROM (or EPROM)
- (v) An instruction register
- (vi) A program counter
- (vii) A clock circuit
- (viii) Decoders, Multiplexers, Pipeline registers

Fig. 12.2 represents a 12-bit CPU developed by bit slice processors in which the program counter sends the address to the address bus and an instruction is fetched to the instruction register from the program memory. Mapping EPROM is addressed by this instructions to output the starting address of the sequencer 2909. The output of the sequencer addresses the control memory which directly outputs the control signals as required by the instruction to be executed. In the control memory, these necessary signal-codes called the micro-instructions are stored. The process is then repeated after the program counter is incremented by the ALU driven by the control signals of the control memory. All the units, i.e. the ALU, PC, IR, mapping memory, sequencers etc. are driven by the control signals of the control memory.

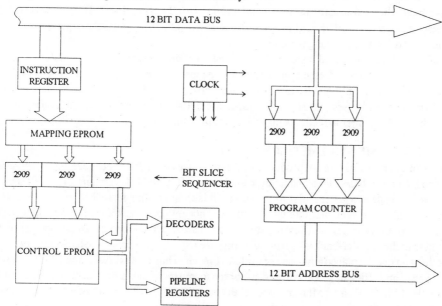

Fig. 12.2 A 12-bit slice system (CPU)

## 12.11  ZILOG Z-8000 FAMILY

Z-8000 is a high performance super processor produced by Zilog in 4, 6 and 10 MHz clock rate. It is pipelined, I/O oriented, register-based, segmented-memory type 16-bit super processor. Z-8000 CPU is offered in two versions, a 48-pin package segented CPU Z-8001 and a 40 pin package non-segmented (Linear) CPU. The main difference between the two is that in addressing range, Z-8001 can directly address 8 MB memory whereas Z-8002 can only 64 KB. There are two operating modes-system and normal. However, the distinction between code, data, and stack spaces within each mode allows memory extension up to 48 MB for Z-8001 and 384 KB for Z-8002. It is interesting to note that Z-8000 employs 16-lines as 16-bit data and address buses in common.

Z-8000 incorporates sixteen 16-bit registers, R0 to R15 in which R0 to R7 may be used as sixteen 8-bit registers, RHO and RLO, RH1 and RL1, RH2 and RL2 and so on. All the sixteen registers R0 to R15 may be grouped into pairs to form 32-bit registers and into quadruples to form 64-bit registers. All the registers are general purpose registers and may be used as accumulators.All but one may be used as index register. R14, R15 and only R15 for Z-8002 are used as stack pointers. There is a secondary set of R14 and R15 and in a mode, one of these two sets of stack pointers works. Z-8000 possesses two sets of 16-bit registers which form Program Status Area Pointer and Program Status Registers which include program Counter, Flag and Control word, and reserved word.

Z-8000 has eight modes of addressing and it deals with the data type bit, digit, byte, word, long word, byte string and word string. It has 110 instructions but a combination of data type and addressing modes results in a set of 414 powerful instruction. 32 - bit operations are also possible in it. Z-8000 supports multiprocessing, multiprogramming etc.

## 12.12  MOTOROLA MC 68000 FAMILY

Motorola intruduced MC 68000, a high performance 16-bit processor in a 68-pin package to be operated with 4, 6 and 8 MHz clock frequencies. It is a pipelined, byte-forward, memory-oriented, register-based 16-bit super processor. It contains 16-bit data bus and 23 address lines and may address over sixteen megabytes of memory.

MC 68000 has a 16-bit Status Register, 32-bit Program Counter, two 32-bit Stack Pointers, seven 32-bit address registers and eight 32-bit data registers. Data registers are used for data operations whereas the Address Registers are assumed to be used as software stack pointers and base address registers. Data Registers, Address Registers and Stack pointers may all be used as index registers. MC 68000 supports the data type bit, digits (4-bit), bytes (8-bit), word (16-bit) and long word (32-bit).

MC 68000 includes 56 powerful instruction types and 14 addressing modes are available. Combining instruction types, data types and addressing modes, over 1000 instructions are provided. These instructions include signed and unsigned multiply, divide, 'quick' arithmetic operations, BCD arithmetic, expanded operations and operations on memory addresses, status word etc. Special emphasis is given to the instruction set to support the structured high level languages to facilitate powerful programming.

## 12.13  TEXAS INSTRUMENTS TMS 9900 FAMILY

TMS 9900 family of microprocessors are produced by Texas Instruments Inc. These are highly versatile and powerful pipelined, memory-based 16-bit super processors in HMOS and $I^2$ L versions. The CPUs contains a program counter, workspace register and status register. It is an interesting feature to be noted that most of the members of the family possess neither internal accumulator nor any data register. A 256-byte space of RAM is used as 16-bit general purpose register. These registers are also used as accumulators and data/address registers. The starting address of this register-bank is kept in the workspace register. Moreover, the banks may be switched on with one another and may be placed anywhere of the RAM space. Thus context switching facility is provided which improves speed and efficiency. However, some of the members of the family include an internal RAM space. For example, TMS 9995, a 12 MHz, member of this family contains 256 bytes of on-board RAM. The architecture of TMS 9900 family is simple but the performance is highly versatile.

## 12.14  32-BIT PROCESSORS

Motorola introduced MC 68000 family in 32-bit internal architecture having capability of 32-bit operations. MC 68000, MC 68008, MC 68010, MC 68012 etc., though 16-bit processors, have capability to be operated as 32-bit processors. But the first full fledged 32-bit super processor of this family is MC 68020 and finally Motorola presented its improved version MC 68030 in 128-pin package to be operated with 20 MHz to 30 MHz clock. It is highly pipelined, memory-oriented, register-based, segmented memory-type, byte-forward 32-bit super processor.

MC 68030 contains sixteen 32-bit general purpose data and address registers, two 32-bit supervisor stack pointers and a 32-bit program counter. It includes 3-stage pipeline and dynamic bus-sizing mechanism, a 256-byte data-cache, instruction-cache, address translation-cache, a paged memory management unit. It executes more than one instructions at a time and an MC 68030 system is capable of delivering 4 MIPS (Mega-Instructions per second) to 8 MIPS. It supports high level languages, virtual memory and highly flexible coprocessor interfaces. A 68-pin floating point coprocessor MC 68882 may boost the performance of MC 68030 up to four times.

Its large number of instruction types with numerious data types in 18 addressing modes shape out MC68030 a very high performance superprocessor which may compete even the CPU of a mainframe computer. It is object code compatible to MC 68020, MC 68012, MC 68010, MC 68008, MC 68000 etc. of entire 68000 family.

## 12.15  ZILOG Z-80000

Z-8000 is a logical extension of Z-8000 to a high capability and mainframe performance. It is a highly pipelined, I/O oriented, Register-based, segemented memory type 32-bit super processor. It includes 32-bit address bus which directly addresses 4 GB of memory. It supports virtual memory management and floating point operations with a 25 MHz clock and it performs 12.5 MIPS.

Z-80000 contains 64-bytes of storage. First 16 bytes can be used as accumulators for word data, 32-bit registers as long word accumulators along with quad word registeras as acumulators for multiplication, division and extend sign operations. All these registers have the indexing capabilities. Two registers are dedicated to the Stack Pointer and Frame Pointer. Program Counter, Flag and Command Word registers form the program status registes. It also includes on-chip cache memory, memory management unit and extended processing architecture.

Z-80000 has two modes of operations-system and normal, supported by seperate Stack Pointers. User programs operate in normal mode whereas sensitive operating system function are performed in system mode. It has a six-stage pipe line and several instructions are simultaneously executed. It has a large number of instruction types with numerous date types in nine addressing modes. The instruction set supports high level language and operating systems.

# 13. INTEL 8086

## 13.1 INTEL 8086: iAPX 86 FAMILY

Intel corporation of USA produced its first sixteen bit microprocessor, the 8086 in 1979 though it is not the first one of this kind. The drawbacks inherent in TMS 9900 have been successfully overcome in Intel 8086 processor. Though initially zilog Z 8000 and Motorola MC 68000 have better performance than 8086, improved versions of 8086 family, viz. 80186 and 80286 proved to show improved performance. Further developments in this family are 8088 and 80188 which are compatible to 8086 and 80186 in features and codes with the facility of a modified Bus Interface Unit (BIU) capable of interfacing 8 bit memories and peripherals. These chips are also known as iAPX 86, iAPX 186, iAPX 286 etc.

## 13.2 ARCHITECTURE AND ORGANISATION OF 8086

Intel 8086 is a pipelined, segmented-memory based, I/O-oriented, reverse byte 16-bit super processor. It is the logical extension of the 8085 and it possesses a 16-bit data bus multiplexed with lower side of the 20-bit address bus and hence it can address up to 1M bytes of memory. The 8086 is housed in a 40 pin DIL package and works with even 10 MHz clock frequency. However, it does not incorporate the clock circuitry within the chip and always uses an external one. The improved versions (like INTEL 80186) possess the clock generator, interrupt controller, DMA controller, timer, memory decoder etc. Intel 8086 is divided into two independent functional parts, the Bus Interface Unit (BIU) and the Execution Unit (EU). The BIU deals with the transfer of data and addresses on the busses for the EU. The BIU fetches as many as six bytes of instructions from the memory and holds them in the QUEUE registers. The fetching, decoding and execution run in parallel simultaneously.

CPU has a separate Bus Interface Unit (BIU), the job assigned to the unit being to fetch instructions from memory and pass data to and from the execution hardware and the outside world. The execution unit, EU comprises of a control unit, an arithmetic-logic unit, 16-bit flag register and eight 16-bit general purpose and index registers. The BIU and EU, the two independently operating functional units are able to overlap instruction fetch with execution in general. As a result, the time normally required to fetch instruction disappears, because the EU executes instruction that has already been fetched by the BIU. A comparison between the traditional microprocessor and 8086/8088 families may be made as in fig. 13.1.

The functional block diagram of Intel 8086 has been shown in Fig. 13.2.

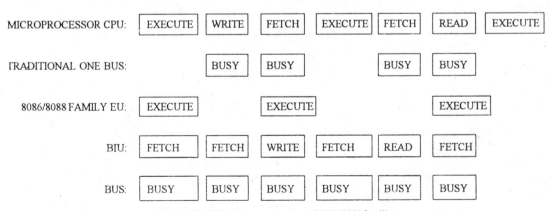

Fig. 13.1 Traditional microprocessor and 8086/8088 families

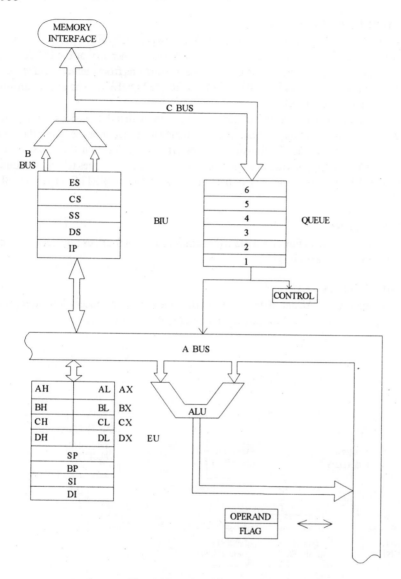

Fig. 13.2 Functional block diagram of INTEL 8086

## 13.3 EXECUTION UNIT (EU)

Execution unit is one of the functional units of 8086 and it operates independently. It consists of a 16-bit ALU together with several 16-bit registers suitable for handling 16-bit data. The function of ALU is to maintain the status flags and control flags of the CPU. It is also controls the function of General Registers and handles the instruction operands. It may be noted that EU keeps no relation with the system bus and the outside world. During operation, EU executes in conjunction with the bus interface unit. It receives instruction from a queue maintained by BIU and executes instruction already received by the BIU. During operation, BIU after receiving request of EU, fetches the stored data to EU. As a result, time required to receive instruction is reduced to a minimum.

### 13.4  BUS INTERFACE UNIT (BIU)

BIU is another functional unit of 8086 operating independently. When requested by EU, it performs bus operation for the EU. The operation includes the data transfer between CPU and the memory or the I/O device. When EU remains busy in executing its instructions, BIU receives more instructions from memory and stores them in the internal RAM array commonly known as INSTRUCTION STREAM QUEUE. The queue can store up to six instruction bytes and delivers them to EU whenever necessary.

Generally the queue contains at least one byte of instruction stream so that the EU does not require to wait for fetching the same. During serial execution procedure, the instruction in the queue of the BIU is the next logical instruction. When EU executes an instruction for transferring control to another location, the BIU starts receiving further instruction for new address, supplies the same immediately to EU and continues to store the queue from the new location. When the EU requests a memory or performs I/O READ or WRITE operation, BIU stops fetching instruction.

### 13.5  REGISTER STRUCTURE

Each of the 8086/8088 and 80186/80188 families contain the same basic set of fourteen registers of 16-bit width which are divided into following three groups :

#### 13.5.1  GENERAL REGISTERS

General Registers are analogous to the Accumulator (ACC) of the first and second generation microprocessors. They are grouped into (1) Data Register, (2) Index Register and (3) Pointer Register.

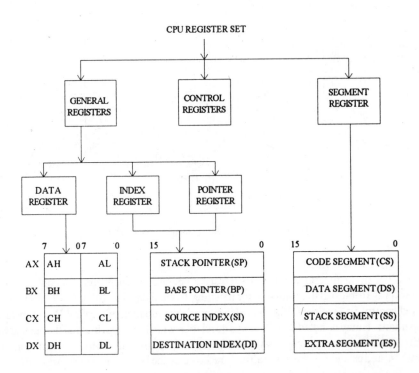

Fig. 13.3. CPU register set

The unique feature of Data Registers is that their upper and lower halves can separately be addressed. In other words, each Data register can be used as a 16-bit register or as two 8-bit registers with the provision to interchange the modes of operation. In 16-bit form, the Data Registers are composed of AX, BX, CX and DX registers as shown in fig. 13.3. In 8-bit operation each of the above mentioned registers can be divided into two registers of 8-bit length. For example, 16-bit AX Register can be divided into AH and AL registers where AH and AL are high byte and low byte of AX registers. These registers find extensive use in arithmetic and logical operations. Some registers may be assigned to perform additional special operations as described in the following table :

**Table 13.1**

| REGISTERS | OPERATIONS |
|-----------|------------|
| AX | WORD MULTIPLICATION AND DIVISION, WORD I/O |
| AL | BYTE MULTIPLICATION AND DIVISION, BYTE I/O, TRANSLATION, DECIMAL ARITHMETIC OPERATION |
| AH | BYTE MULTIPLICATION AND DIVISION |
| BP | ENTER, LEAVE (FOR 80186, 80188 ONLY) |
| BX | TRANSLATION |
| CX | STRING OPERATION |
| CL | VARIABLE SHIFT AND ROTATE |
| DX | WORD MULTIPLICATION AND DIVISION, INDIRECT I/O |
| SP | STACK OPERATION |
| SI | STRING OPERATION |
| DI | STRING OPERATION |

For example, CX Registers are frequently used to obtain a count value during repetitive instructions whereas BX is used as a base register in some of the more powerful addressing modes. Thus the register permits a very compact instruction encoding.

### 13.5.2 POINTER REGISTER AND INDEX REGISTER

The pointer and index registers consist of 16-bit registers, viz. (i) Stack Pointer (SP), (ii) Base Pointer (BP), (iii) Source Index (SI) and (iv) Destination Index (DI) registers which can be used in most mathematical and logical operations. Both of BP and SP registers point to the stack, a linear array in the memory used for subroutine parameters, subroutine return address or other data temporarily saved during execution of a program. It may be noted here that, 8086/80186 and 8088/80188 families have an additional pointer into the stack, called the Base Pointer (BP) Register, besides the stack pointer which is similar in function to first and second generation microprocessors. The SP is used for pointing to subroutine and interrupt return address whereas BP can contain an old stack pointer value or mark a zone in the subroutine stack independently.

Two index registers source index (SI) and destination index (DI) each being 16-bit wide can be used by string manipulation instruction in developing more powerful data structure and addressing modes. Both registers have auto incrementing and auto decrementing capabilities. It may be mentioned here that, the point register refers to the current stack segment while the index register refers to the current data segment.

### 13.5.3 SEGMENT REGISTERS

The segment registers are 16-bit registers and they specify four memory segments. They are (i) Code segment (CS) (ii) Data segment (DS) (iii) Stack segment (SS) and (iv) Extra segment (ES). All instructions which are offset by instruction pointer register (IP) are fetched from the code segment. The pointer register preserves the offset address of the data segment or stack segment and the operands are fetched accordingly.

### 13.5.4 CONTROL REGISTERS

It consist of two special purpose registers: (1) Instruction Pointer (IP) and (2) The status word or Flag register.

Apart from the normal working as a program counter, IP points to the next instruction to be fetched by the BIU and not to the next instruction to be executed as has been made by the traditional Program counter.

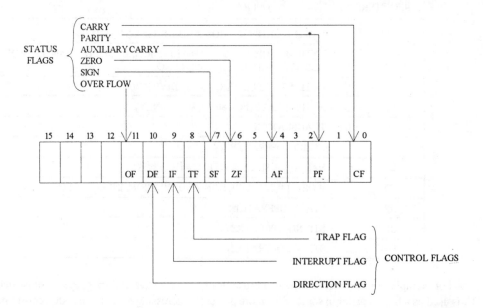

Fig. 13.4. The status word register

The status word or flag is a 16-bit register having nine flags in all. Out of them, six are status flags corresponding to the bit positions 0, 2, 4, 6, 7 and 11 and three are control flags corresponding to bit positions 8, 9 and 10. Status flags are affected out of different arithmetical and logical operations and control flags control specific operations of the CPU in a given operating mode. The six status flags are Carry (C), Parity (P), Auxiliary Carry (AC), Zero (Z), Sign (S) and Over flow (O), while the three control flags are Trap (T), Interrupt (I) and Direction (D) as shown in fig 13.4. When the status flags are affected out of arithmetic or logical operations, the program is shifted to alter its execution utilising suitable group of instructions available. A brief description of the functions of different flags together with the instructions related to flags have been shown in table 13.2.

The carry flag may be set during addition, subtraction of multi byte numbers and rotate instructions. There may be a carry out of the high order bit of the result during addition and a borrow into the high order bit during subtraction. Rotate instruction may also transfer a bit into the carry flag from memory or register.

Parity flag is set when the result has even parity. Data transmission error may be checked by testing only the low order 8-bits using this flag.

If carry occurs out of the low order 4-bits (low nibble) of a byte into the higher order 4-bits (high nibble) or borrow occurs from the higher nibble of an 8-bit number, the auxiliary carry flag (AF) is set. This flag is used

Table 13.2. Flag Status Word

| BIT POSITION | NAME | FUNCTION |
|---|---|---|
| 0 | CF (CARRY FLAG) | Set on high order bit carry or borrow, otherwise cleared. |
| 2 | PF (PARITY FLAG) | Set if low order 8 bits of result contains an even number of 1 bits, otherwise cleared. |
| 4 | AF (AUXILIARY FLAG) | Set on carry from or borrow to the low order four bits of AL; otherwise cleared. |
| 6 | ZF (ZERO FLAG) | Set if result is zero ; otherwise cleared. |
| 7 | SF (SIGN FLAG) | Set equal to high order bit of result (0 if positive ; 1 if negative). |
| 8 | TF (TRAP FLAG) | Single Step flag - Once set, a single step interrupt occurs after the next instruction executes. TF is cleared by the Single step interrupt. |
| 9 | IF (INTERRUPT FLAG) | When Set, maskable interrupt will cause the CPU to transfer control to an interrupt vector specified area. |
| 10 | DF (DIRECTION FLAG) | Causes string instruction to auto decrement when set, clearing DF causes auto increment. |
| 11 | OF (OVER FLOW FLAG) | Set under signed arithmetic over flow condition. |

by decimal arithmetic instruction also.

If zero flag (ZF) is set, the result of arithmetic and logic operation is zero.

If due to an arithmetic or logical operation, the higher order bit of the result is 1, the Sign flag (SF) is set. Further since binary numbers are represented by standard two's complement notation, SF indicates the sign (0 = positive, 1 = negative) of the result.

Due to an arithmetic overflow, the over flow flag (OF) is set. An optional interrupt on overflow instruction is available generating an interrupt in this situation.

In order to alter processor's operation through programs, three control flags (DF, IF and TF) may be used. The direction flag (DF) controls the direction of the string operations. When DF is set, string instructions are auto decremented and when reset, auto increment starts through string instructions. The interrupt flag (IF) enables or disables external interrupts when set and disables these interrupts when it is reset, but it has no effect on non-maskable interrupts generated internally or externally. The trap flag (TF) puts the processor into a single mode for debugging when set and in this mode, the CPU automatically generates an internal interrupt after each instruction allowing program to be inspected as it executes instructions one by one.

## 13.6 MEMORY ADDRESSING

The memory of 8086 is organised in set of segments. Each segment consists of up to 64 KB locations and these are stored from byte 00000H to FFFFFH. A pointer known as a 'two component address' consists of a 16 bit segment base and a 16-bit offset. The segment base specifies the beginning address of the segment in memory whereas the offset specifies the address relative to the beginning of the segment. This pointer is used to address the memory. One of the four internal segment registers viz. CS, DS, SS, ES contains the base values. With this form of addressing, one million bytes of memory may be addressed (Fig. 13.5).

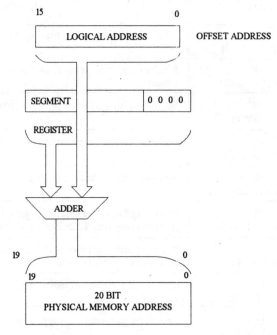

Fig. 13.5. Memory addressing

### 13.6.1  PHYSICAL ADDRESS GENERATION

In 8086, two kinds of addresses are used to identify the memory locations. These are physical address and logical address. A physical address is 20 bit wide identifying each byte location uniquely in the memory space whereas a logical address consists of segment base value and an offset value. The range of physical address is generally from 00000H to FFFFFH which are used during exchanges between CPU and memory components. In logical address, the segment base value identifies the first byte (for a given memory location) of the containing segment and the offset value indicates the distance in byte of the target location from the beginning of the segment. Segment base and offset values are unsigned 16-bit quantities. The lowest address of the segment has an offset of zero. The same physical location can be mapped into different logical address as shown in fig. 13.6. During memory access to fetch an instruction or to receive or store a data, BIU generates a physical address from a logical address. This job is performed by shifting the segement base value through four bit position and adding offset (fig. 13.7). The BIU obtains the logical address of a memory location from different sources with reference to the type of reference (Table 13.3).

Logical address rather than physical one is used in developing programs. It is interesting to note that, the physical memory location containing the code is not at all necessary in developing code using logical address.

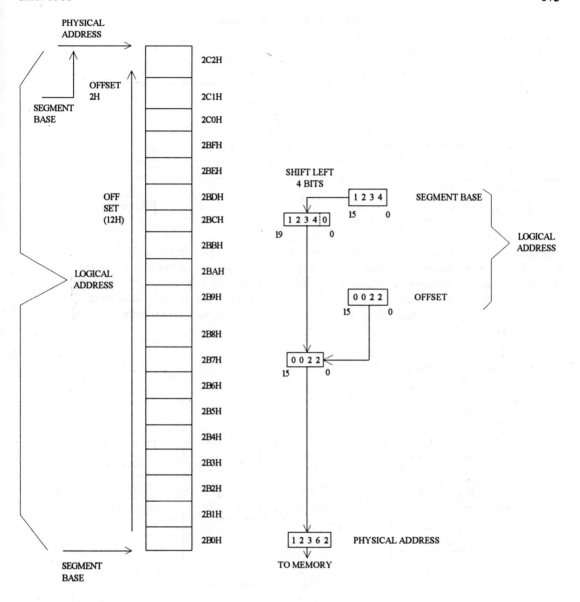

Fig. 13.6. Logical and physical address          Fig. 13.7. Physical address generation

## 13.7 DYNAMICALLY RELOCATABLE CODE

The segmented memory structure of 8086 / 80186 along with 8088 / 80286 facilitates the writing of programs which are dynamically relocatable i.e. which are position independent. Through dynamic relocation, available memory is effectively used by a multi tasking system. Generally inactive programs are developed in the disk and the space required for this purpose is allowable to other programs. When the program stored in the disk is required, they can be transferred into any available memory location. Further for a large program requiring continuous bulk memory space and if memory space is available only in non adjacent fragments, other program

**Table 13.3. Logic Address Source**

| TYPE OF MEMORY REFERENCE | DEFAULT SEGMENT BASE | ALTERNATE SEGMENT BASE | OFFSET |
|---|---|---|---|
| Instruction Fetch | CS | NONE | IP |
| Stack Operation | SS | NONE | SP |
| Variable | DS | CS, ES, SS | Effective Address |
| String source | DS | CS, ES, SS | SI |
| String destination | ES | NONE | DI |
| BP used as Base Register | SS | CS, DS, ES | Effective address |
| BU used as Base Register | DS | CS, ES, SS | Effective address |

segments may be compacted to make a continuous space. The process is shown in fig.13.8.

In order to be dynamically relocatable, a program should neither load nor alter its segments registers. Further, a program should never be transferred directly to a location outside the current code segment. In other words, all offsets in the program should always be relative to fixed values contained in segment register. This facilitates the movement of program anywhere in memory till the segment registers are updated properly in relation to the need base address.

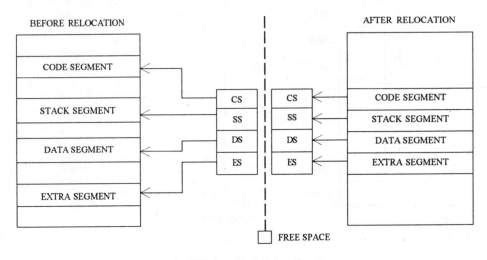

Fig. 13.8 Dynamic Code Location

## 13.8 DEDICATED AND RESERVED MEMORY LOCATION

Some areas of memory space are kept reserved and dedicated. These are stored with program or data for essential functioning of the processor. Generally, these areas occupy extreme low or high memory space. Manufacturers' utility programs are stored in the locations. Usually, 128 bytes of memory locations ranging from 00000H to 0007FH and 16-bytes of memory space ranging from FFFF0H to FFFFFH are reserved for this purpose and for interrupt and system reset processing. A programmer should never use these memory space for any other purpose.

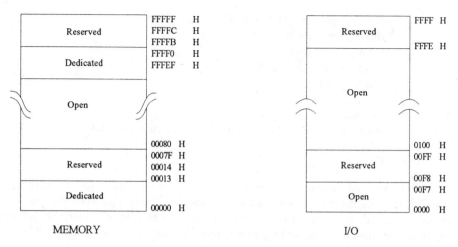

Fig. 13.9. Reserved and dedicated memory and I/O location

## 13.9  PIN CONFIGURATION OF INTEL 8086

Intel 8086 is a 40 Pin IC package operated from + 5 V DC supply. It is a 16-bit HMOS microprocessor having

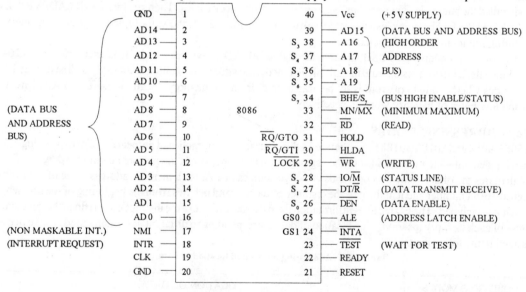

Fig. 13.10. Pin configuration of INTEL 8086

20-line address bus capable of addressing $2^{20}$ bytes or 1 Mega bytes of memory address. It uses 16-bit data word divided into a low-order byte and a high order byte. In fig. 13.10, AD0 - AD 15 are 16 low-order address bus line of which, AD0 - AD7 are used to transmit eight most significant bits. AD lines are used to transmit memory address and data. In former case, AD lines are represented by A and in the later case by D. Thus, AD0-AD15 bi-directional Address/Data bus when transmits memory address only, they can be represented by AD0-AD15 and when transmits data only, they can be represented by D0-D15..Other Pin configurations are:

A 16-A19          :     High order address bus.

A 16/S3, A17/S4   :     A16 and A 17 multiplexed with status signals S3 and S4

A18/S5            :     A18 multiplexed with intrrupt status signal S5

| A19/S6 | : | A19 multiplexed with the status signal S6 |
|--------|---|-------------------------------------------|
| BHE/S7 | : | Bus high enable/status |
| RD | : | Read (Active when low). |
| READY | : | Ready (Active when high) |
| NTR | : | Clock 5, 8 or 10 MHz |
| INTER | : | Interrupt Request |
| NMI | : | Non maskable interrupt request |
| TEST | : | Wait for Test control ( wait when high, execute when low) |
| Vcc | : | + 5V DC |
| GND | : | Ground |

Intel 8086 CPU may be operated in two different modes, viz. minimum mode and the maximum mode. Employing one CPU only, the minimum mode is achieved where the CPU supplies control signal by memory and input/output devices. In the maximum mode of operation, Intel 8288 bus controller used with 8086 supplies control signal. In the minimum mode, MN/$\overline{MX}$ pin becomes high whereas in maximum mode of operation, it becomes low.

In Intel 8086, the concept of Bus Cycle is different from the conventional one. The EU executes instruction in certain clock periods without consistituting any form of machine cycles. The BIU fetches instructions and operands from the memory. Any external access either to memory or I/O device requires a group of four clock periods called the bus cycle. Thus one bus cycle consists of four clock cycles. There are memory READ/WRITE and I/O READ/WRITE bus cycles associated with the system. Fig. 13.11, shows the timing diagram for memory read during minimum mode of operation.

Out of 20-bit address, 16 LSB, are sent through AD0- AD 15 whereas 4 MSBs are sent through A16-A 19. Since the address lines operate in multiplexed mode, the address remaining in the address line during T1 only decides whether a byte or word is to be transferred from / to memory location. $\overline{BHE}$ and A0 identify high and low bytes of memory words respectively.

## 13.10  ADDRESSING MODES
The 8086/8088 and 80186/80188 CPU operate 24 different addressing modes. The location of data is the logical address in general which when added to the segment register value, yields the physical memory address. The EU calculates the offset, known as operands effective address or EA, for a memory address. The offset is an unsigned 16-bit number and it indicates the distance of the operand in bytes from the beginning of the segment in which it is included. The EU receives information from the second byte of the instruction and finds the effective address of each memory location. The location of data corresponding to different addressing modes have been presented in the following table.

**Table 13.4.  Addressing modes and location of data**

| ADDRESSING MODES | LOCATION OF DATA |
|------------------|------------------|
| Immediate | Within instruction |
| Register | In register |
| Direct | At memory location indicated by the address followed by instruction. |
| Register indirect | At memory location indicated by the address contained in register |
| Indexed or Based | At memory location obtained by sum of the contents of index register or base register and immediate data followed by the instruction. |
| Based and Indexed with displacement | At memory location obtained by the sum of the contents of base register and index register and immediate data followed by the instruction. |

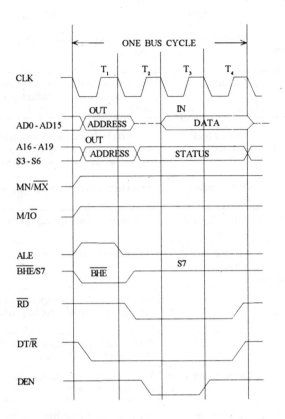

Fig. 13.11. Timing diagram of INTEL 8086 for memory read in minimum mode

## 13.11 INSTRUCTION SET

Out of the 100 instructions in the assembly language, some new instructions used by 8086 CPU are multiplication and division of signed and unsigned binary numbers and unpacked decimal numbers ; move, scan and compare operations for strings upto a length of 64 KB (Kilo-byte); nondestructive bit testing, byte translation from one code to another, additional software generated interrupt etc. The instructions can be subdivided into following groups:

1. Data transfer group
2. Arithmetic group
3. Bit Manipulation group
4. String Manipulation group
5. Control transfer
6. Process Control

By data transfer instruction, single byte, words and double byte may be transferred between memory and registers and also between AL or AX register and I/O ports. In Table 13.5 these instructions have been explained.

**Table 13.5. Data transfer Instructions**

| INSTRUCTION | MNEMONICS | ACTION | REMARKS |
|---|---|---|---|
| General Purpose | MOV (Move destination, source) | Move byte or word | Transfers byte/word from source operand to the destination operand |
| | PUSH | Transfer word | Decrements stack pointer by two and then transfers a word from the source operand to the top of the stack indicated by SP. |
| | POP (Pop destination) | Transfer back from stack | Transfers back to the word from the top of the stack indicated by SP to the destination operand and incrementing SP by two, it initialises the new top position of SP. |
| | PUSHA | Push all registers to stack | Stores contents of all General Purpose Registers in stack. |
| | POPA | Pop all registers from stack | Restores contents from stack to all General Purpose Registers. |
| | XCHG (XCHG, destination, source) | Exchange byte or words | Exchanges byte or words between destination and source. |
| | XLAT (XLAT Translate Table) | Transfer byte | Replaces a byte in AL-Register with a byte from a 256 byte, user coded translation table. Reg. BX indicates the beginning of the Table. |
| INPUT/OUTPUT | IN (In ACC, Port) | Input byte or word | Transfers a byte from input Port to AL Register and a word from Input port to AX register. |
| | OUT (out port, ACC) | Output byte or word | Transfers a byte from AL Register and a word from AX register to output port. |
| ADDRESS OBJECT TRANSFER (used to manipulate address of variables rather than the contents) | LEA (LEA, destination, source) | Load effective address | Transfers the offset of the source operand to the destination operand, source and the destination operands being the memory and a 16- bit Register respectively. The instruction does not affect flags. |
| | LDS (LDS, destination, source) | Load pointer using DS | Transfers from a memory operand, a 32- bit pointer variable, to destination operand and register DS. |
| | LES (LES destination, source) | Load pointer using ES | Transfers from a memory operand, a 32- bit pointer variable, to destination operend and register ES. |
| FLAG TRANSFER | LAHF (Load register AH from flag) | Load AH register from flag | Copies 8080/8085 Flags (Viz. Sign, Zero, Auxiliary carry, parity and carry) into bits 7,6,4,2 and 0 respectively of AH-register without affecting the flags. |
| | SAHP (Store Reg. AH into flag) | Store AH register from flag | Transfers bits 7,6,4,2 and 0 from AH- Register into Sine, Zero, Auxiliary Carry, Parity and Carry flags respectively. |
| | PUSHP | Push flag to stack | Decrementing SP by two, transfers the contents of flags into the stack without affecting the flag. |
| | POPF | Pop flag from stack | Transfers respective bits from stack into flags. |

## 13.12 ARITHMETIC INSTRUCTION
Arithmetic operations may be performed with following four types of numbers:

(i) *Unsigned binary ( 8- or 16-bit)*: All bits are considered. In case of 8-bit numbers, the range varies from 0 to 255 and for 16-bit number, this range becomes 0 to 65, 535. Different operations possible are addition, subtraction, multiplication and division.

(ii) *Signed binary integers (8- or 16-bit)* : For such numbers, the high order MSB is recognised as the sign of the number (0 : positive, 1 : negative). Hence the range of 8-bit and 16-bit integers are from 0 to 128 and from 0 to 32768 respectively, negative numbers being represented by two's complement form. If may be noted that the zero has a positive sign. For such numbers, addition and subtraction operations are similar to those of unsigned binary instructions whereas multiplication and division instructions are performed with signed binary instruction. In order to detect over flow into the sign bit in case of operation with unsigned numbers, 'conditional jump' and 'interrupt on over flow' instructions are available.

(iii) *Unsigned packed decimal numbers* : These numbers are stored as unsigned byte quantities. In each half of the byte, there is one decimal digit. In each nibble, Hexadecimal values 0-9 are valid and the range of a packed decimal number is 0-99.

(iv) *Unsigned unpacked decimal numbers* : These numbers are stored as unsigned byte quantities, the magnitude being determined from the low order half byte. In this case also Hex. values 0-9 are valid and interrupted as decimal numbers. There is no restriction in addition and subtraction though for multiplication and division, higher half byte must be zero.

Between unpacked decimal numbers and ASCII characters (0-9), there are practically no difference. But the high order half byte of an ASCII character is always 3H whereas this byte in an unpacked decimal number must be 0 Hex in case of multiplication and division. For different types of numbers, relation with Hex values are shown in Table 13.6. Different arithmetic instructions are shown in Table 13.7.

### Table 13.6. Different Types of Numbers and Hex Values

| HEX | BIT PATTERN | UNSIGNED BINARY | SIGNED BINARY | UNPACKED DECIMAL | PACKED DECIMAL |
|-----|-------------|-----------------|---------------|------------------|----------------|
| 05 | 0000 0101 | 5 | + 5 | 5 | 5 |
| 96 | 1001 0110 | 140 | - 106 | invalid | 96 |
| B9 | 1011 1001 | 185 | - 71 | invalid | invalid |

**Table 13.7. Arithmetic Instructions**

| MATHEMATICAL OPERATION | MNEMONICS | DESCRIPTION |
|---|---|---|
| ADDITION | ADD | Add byte or word |
| | ADC | Add byte or word with carry |
| | INC | Increment byte or word by 1 |
| | AAA | ASCII adjustment for addition |
| | DAA | Decimal adjustment for addition |
| SUBTRACTION | SUB | Subtract byte or word |
| | SBB | Subtract byte or word with borrow |
| | DEC | Decrement byte or word by 1 |
| | NEL | Negative byte or word |
| | CMP | Compare byte or word |
| | AAS | ASCII adjust for subtraction |
| | DAS | Decimal adjust for subtraction |
| MULTIPLICATION | MUL | Multiply byte or word unsigned |
| | IMWL | Integer multiply byte or word |
| | AAM | ASCII adjust for multiplication |
| DIVISION | DIV | Divide byte or word unsigned |
| | IDIV | Integer divided byte or word |
| | AAD | ASCII adjust for division |
| | CBW | Convert byte or word |
| | CWD | Convert word or double word |

## 13.13  BIT MANIPULATION INSTRUCTION

Several bit manipulation instructions within bytes and word are available for the processors. These are NOT, AND, OR, XOR and TEST byte or word, SHL/SAL (Shift logical /arithmetic left byte or word), SHR (shift logical right byte or word), SAR (shift arithmetic right byte or word), ROL (Rotate left byte or word), ROR (rotate right byte or word), RCL (rotate through carry left byte or word) and RCR (rotate through carry right byte or word).

STRING INSTRUCTION : Different string instructions have been shown in Table 13.8.

**Table 13.8. String instructions**

| INSTRUCTION | REMARKS |
|---|---|
| SI | Index (offset) for source string |
| DI | Index (offset) for destination string |
| DX | Port address |
| CX | Repetition counter |
| AL/AX | Scan value, destination for LODS, source for STOS |
| DF | 0 = auto increment SI, DI<br>1 = auto decrement SI, DI |
| ZF | Scan/compare terminator |

Five mnemonics for three forms of the prefix byte controlling repetition of a subsequent string instruction are also available for 8086/8088 CPU. These are REP (repeat), REPE (Repeat while equal), REPZ (repeat while zero), REPNE (repeat while not equal) and REPNZ (repeat while not equal to zero). These instructions are used with some other instructions as mentioned in Table 13.9.

**Table 13.9. Repetition of String Instruction**

| INSTRUCTIONS | TO BE USED WITH |
|---|---|
| REP<br>[Repeat while end-of-string (CX not 0)] | MOVS (move string), STOS (store tring)<br>OUTS (Out string), INS (IN String) |
| REPE, REPZ<br>[remains ZF tested by instructions] | CMPS (Compare String), SCAS (Scan String) |
| REPNE, REPNZ<br>[Zero flag must be cleared or<br>repetition to be terminated] | Same as REPE, REPZ |

Different String manipulation instructions are shown in Table 13.10.

**Table 13.10 String Manipulation Instructions**

| Mnemonics | Objective |
|---|---|
| MOVS<br>(MOVE DESTINATION STRING, SOURCE STRING) | Transfers a byte or a word from source string ( addressed by SI) to the destination string (addressed by DI), update SI and DI to indicate next string element. This instruction performs a block transfer from a memory to memory when used with REP Instruction. |
| MOVS B/MOVS W<br>(MOVE BYTE/WORD STRING) | Alternate mnemonics for MOVS. These instructions (coded without operands) are used when the assembler can not ascribe a string. |
| CMPS<br>(COMPARE DESTINATION STRING, SOURCE STRING) | Subtracts destination byte or word (addressed by DI) from the source byte or word (addressed by SI) affecting flags. |
| SCAS<br>(SCAN DESTINATION STRING) | Subtracts the destination string element (byte or word) addressed by DI from the contents of AL (byte string) or AX (word string) and updates the flag without affecting ACE and destination string. |
| LODS<br>(LOAD SOURCE STRING) | Transfers byte or word string element addressed by SI to register AL or AX updating SI to indicate the next element in the string. |
| STOS<br>(STORE DESTINATION STRING) | Transfers a byte or word from register AL or AX to the string element addressed by DI updating, DI to indicate next location in the string. |

Control transfer instructions are divided into Unconditional transfer, Conditional transfer, Iteration control and Interrupts. Different unconditional transfer instructions are (CALL, RET and JMP). Iteration control instructions are LOOP, LOOPE (Looping equal), LOOP Z (looping zero), LOOPNE (Looping not equal), LOOPNZ (looping not zero), JCXZ ( Jumping register CX - 0) while the interrupt instructions are INT (interrupt) INTO (interrupt if over flow) and IRET (interrupt return). Different conditional transfer instructions are tabulated in Table 13.11:

## Table 13.11. Conditional Transfer Instructions

| MNEMONICS | CONDITION TESTED | OBJECTIVE |
|---|---|---|
| JA/JNB E | (CF or ZF) = 0 | Jump if above/not below nor equal |
| JAE/JNB | CF = 0 | Jump if above or equal / not below |
| JB/JNAE | (CF) = 1 | Jump if below / not above nor equal |
| JBE/JNA | (CF or ZF) = 1 | Jump if below or equal / not above |
| JC | CF = 1 | Jump if carry |
| JE/JZ | ZF = 1 | Jump if equal / zero |
| Ja/JNLE | (SF XOR OF) OR ZF = 0 | Jump if greater / not less nor equal |
| JaE/JNL | (SF XOR OF) = 0 | Jump if greater or equal / not less |
| JL/JNGE | (SF XOR OF) = 1 | Jump if less / not greater nor equal |
| JLE/JNG | (SF XOR OF) OR ZF = 1 | Jump if less or equal / not greater |
| JNC | CF = 0 | Jump if not carry |
| JNE/JNZ | ZF = 0 | Jump if not equal / not zero |
| JNO | OF = 0 | Jump if not overflow |
| JNP/JPO | PF = 0 | Jump if not parity / parity odd |
| JNS | SF = 0 | Jump if not sign |
| JO | OF = 1 | Jump if overflow |
| JP/JPE | PF = 1 | Jump if parity / parity even |
| JS | SF = 1 | Jump if sign |

## 13.14   PROCESSOR CONTROL INSTRUCTION

For flag operation, different instructions are STC (Set CY flag), CLC (clear CY flag), CMC (complement CY flag), STD (Set direction flag), CLD (Clear direction flag), STI (set interrupt flag) and CLI (clear interrupt flag). Some more instructions are also available for external synchronisation. These are HLT (halt until interrupt), WAIT (wait for TEST pin active), ESC (Escape to external processor) and LOCK (lock bus during next instruction). NOP (no operation) instruction is also available in this processor.

## 13.15   PROGRAM EXAMPLES

For simplicity, it is better to assign all the segment registers by zeroes. This will lead into a linear-memory type performance within the first 64 K locations of memory. Keeping this idea in mind, consider the following problem:

There are 16 locations from 00F00 to 00F0F and the contents of these locations are to be stored in memory locations from 00FF0 to 00FFF. The program may be as follows:

```
MOV   CX,   0010      : Move to CX the data 16.
MOV   SI,   0F00
MOV   DI,   0FF0
CLD                   : Clear direction flag to auto increment SI and DI.
MOVS W                : move string word.
```

If one requires to add the bytes of data stored from 00F00 to 00F0F and to store the result in location 00D00, the program may be:

```
    MOV CX, 0010
    MOV SI, 0F00
    MOV AX, 00 00
P : ADD AL, (SI) : add byte data from the location pointed by SI, to the AL.
    ADC AH,  00
    INC  SI
    LOOP  P
    MOV  0D 00, AX
    HLT
```

In order to find the average of the bytes stored in the locations from 00F00 to 00F0F, the previous program may easily be modified as follows:

```
    MOV  CX, 0010
    MOV  SI, 0F, 00
    PUSH CX
    MOV  AX, 00 00
P : ADD  AL, (SI)
    ADC  AH, 00
    INC  SI
    LOOP P
    POP  CX
    DIV CL
    MOV 0D 00, AL : Store quotient (average) in 0D00
    MOV 0D01, AH  : Store the remainder (in division for average) in 0D01
    HLT
```

### 13.16 INTEL 8088

INTEL 8088 is an 8-bit HMOS microprocessor equivalent to 8086 in most internal functions. It has 8-bit Data Bus interfaced with 5 MHz clock frequency having 16-bit internal architecture with the capability of handling 1 MB of memory. It handles 8-bit at a time and requires two consecutive bus cycles in 16-bit operation. This processor has identical register structure with 8086 and there is practically no difference in software execution except the execution time between the two processors. The processor is a full-fledged 8-bit processor having the similarity in hardware and peripherals of 8080/8085 and a 16-bit processor having software compatability with 8086.

### 13.16.1 DIFFERENT MODES OF OPERATION OF 8088

The 8088 CPU can operate in two modes—Minimum mode and Maximum mode. In minimum mode of operation, 8088 generates all the control signals directly for all memory and peripheral devices. The 8088 CPU has a pin signal MN/$\overline{\text{MX}}$. When the signal is high, the processor operates in minimum mode and in this mode of operation, any extra processor can not be connected with it. When MN/$\overline{\text{MX}}$ signal is low, the processor operates in maximum mode. In this mode, 8088 operates with 8288 bus controller. The control decisions are taken depending on the bus status signals S0, S1 and S2 generated from the processor which are inputs to the bus controller. In this mode, there are provisions for multiprocessor connections, hardware lock and queue status.

The pin configuration of INTEL 8088 in both maximum and minimum modes of operation has been shown in fig. 13.12.

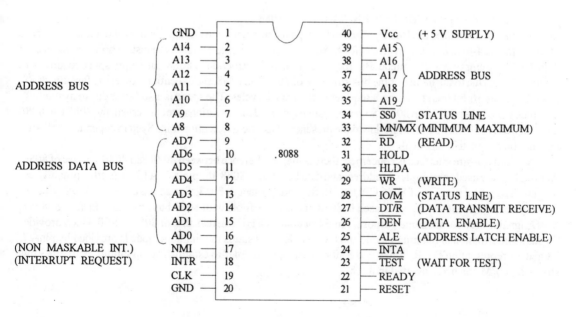

Fig. 13.12. (a) Pin configuration of 8088 for minimum mode.

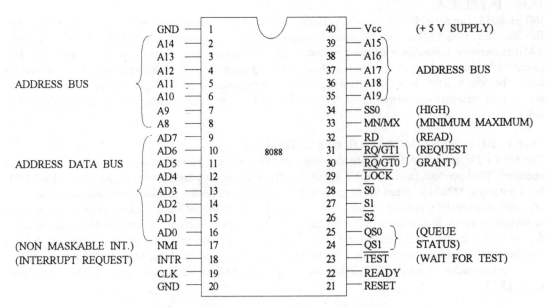

Fig. 13.12. (b) Pin configuration of 8088 for maximum mode.

## 13.16.2   COMPARISON BETWEEN 8086 AND 8088

In both of 8086 and 8088, the Bus interface unit keeps the instruction in advance in instruction queue. In case of 8086, this is 4-byte in length whereas for 8088, it is 6-byte. In case of 8086, the instruction is prefetched if there be 2-byte empty space in queue. But for prefetching the instruction in 8088, the empty space requirement is only 1-byte. Due to the nature of the bus structure of 8086 and 8088, the execution process is faster in 8088. Since 8086 has 16-bit bus structure, it requires extra 4 clock cycles. The speed is also faster due to availability of sophisticated instructions in 8088. So far as system independent operations are concerned, the 8088 and 8086 are completely software compatible due to the presence of identical execution unit. System dependent software may not be completely identical.

So far hardware interface is concerned, there is major difference between 8088 and 8086. In case of 8086, AD0 - AD15 are used as multiplexed address and data bus. But in 8088, the pin A8 - A15 are used only as address outputs. The signal pin - 34 of 8086 CPU i.e. $\overline{BHE}$ is not present in 8088. For accessing either I/O devices or memory devices, the IO/$\overline{M}$ signal is used in 8088 and is compatible with 8085 bus structure. In case of 8086, $M/\overline{IO}$ signal is used for the same purpose. Pin-34 of 8086 is $\overline{BHE}$ whereas that of 8088 is SS0 which provides S0 status information in minimum mode and the complete bus status in minimum mode is provided by pin-27, 28 and 34 representing DT/$\overline{R}$, IO/$\overline{M}$ and $\overline{SS0}$ respectively. In order to establish compatibility with 8085 bus structure, IO/$\overline{M}$ has been inverted in 8088.

# 14. Microprocessor Applications and Development of On-Line Real-Time Systems

## 14.1 INTRODUCTION

With the advent of Microprocessor, it has now become quite easy to add intelligence and computer power to any instrument, machine, process or system. The level of intelligence and computational power that can be added to a microprocessor based system depend on the memory capacity, software support and the interfacing arrangements actually provided. The total activities of any microprocessor based on-line real-time system can be divided into two separate parts, viz. (i) the activities taking place in the microprocessor world and (ii) that in the real-world as shown in Fig. 14.1. Interchange between these two worlds of activities is made possible by employing suitable interfacing arrangements.

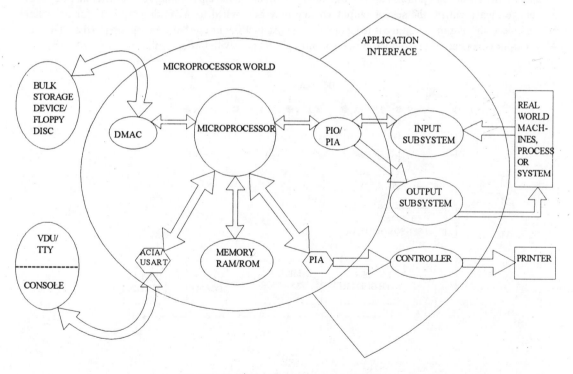

Fig. 14.1 Real World And Microprocessor World

The designer of a microprocessor based system will have to solve two problems: (1) Interfacing problems associated with the interfacing hardware and (2) the Software problem associated with the application requirements. Application of microprocessors can be made to develop any system for either OFF-line use or ON-line real-time use. For OFF-line use, inputs are nothing but man-prepared data and the outputs are meant for human interpretation whereas for ON-line real time use, the inputs will come directly from the system being controlled and outputs will be fed directly to the controlling elements. Thus interfacing hardware requirements may vary widely between the system meant for OFF-line and ON-line uses, but the software support or programming requirements may remain identical. In the following few articles, some Microprocessor based system developments have been presented to illustrate the role of microprocessor in the area of monitoring, control and protection of systems. In all the developments, the stack pointer has been assumed to be initialised through program stored in the EPROM at the memory location 47FF H and the stack pointer is initialised automatically under set condition of the microprocessor. If such facilities are not available with the kit, SP is to be initialised first.

## 14.2  VOLTAGE MEASUREMENT

### 14.2.1  System Hardware

The schematic diagram for multirange voltage measurement has been shown in Fig. 14.2. In order to develop a microprocessor based system, it is necessary to design a suitable sensor to generate a voltage signal compatible to the microprocessor. For the present system, only a potentiometric arrangement is sufficient to develop the necessary signal. The sensor consists of a multiterminal two or more staged potentiometer providing input terminals for 250 mv, 2.5 V, 25 V, 250 V and 2.5 KV supply whereas the output terminal is kept fixed so that the maximum output voltage is 500 mv corresponding to the maximum input voltage of the different ranges. For dc voltage measurement, the sensor output voltage may be applied to ADC directly but for ac voltage measurement, the output ac voltage is to be rectified using a rectifier bridge before supplying to the ADC. The ADC output is connected to the microprocessor through I/O port with buffer as shown in Fig. 14.2 (b).

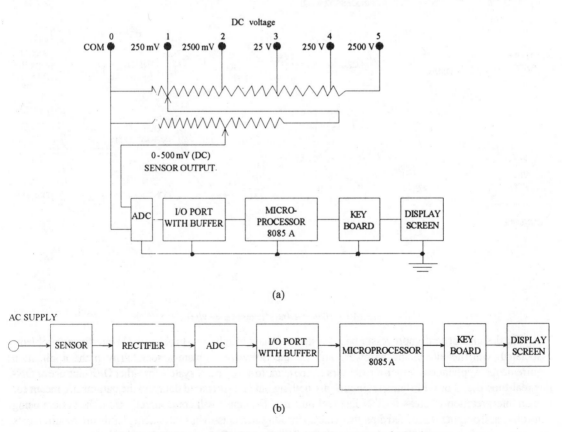

(a)

(b)

Fig. 14.2. (a) Measurement of DC voltage and (b) Measurement of AC voltage

## 14.2.2  SYSTEM SOFTWARE AND OPERATIONS

The system software for the measurement of voltages consists of the main program, Look-up table to note the analog voltage, multiplication software for counting the multiplication factor of the attenuator, the hex to digital conversion of the measured voltage, and the character display of the voltmeter range to be measured. The detail of the software is based on the flow chart shown in Fig. 14.3. The development of the Look-up Table is the most important part since the accuracy of the measuring device depends on the accuracy of the Look-up Table. The ADC is initially calibrated with known applied analog voltages to get the corresponding display on the microprocessor display screen in hex value ranging from 0000 H to 00FF H. Readings of the hex value of the applied analog voltages and microprocessor digital inputs arranged alternately in a table, may be called a look up table or search table, are stored in the EPROM. Thus the first and most important task is to monitor the voltage from ADC and then going through the software for search routine to note the corresponding analog voltage in hex form. It may be noted that the maximum output voltage of the sensor should be such that the corresponding digital signal may not exceed 00FF H in order to avoid the complication of the Table searching. The next task of the microprocessor is to multiply the noted voltage with the attenuating factor of the attenuator to change the range of this voltmeter. This is done simply by the multiplication subroutine. In order to change the range of the voltmeter from millivolt to Kilo-volt, it is sufficient to write a program for a further multiplication by decimal numbers 10, 100, 1000, and so on.

The ultimate task is to convert measured value of analog voltage from hex form to decimal form. This functional routine makes use of the monitor program of the microprocessor system available in all microprocessor kit or the subroutine 'Hex-Dec' may be developed by the programmer. A character display is also made to indicate the range either of millivolt, Volt or Kilo-volt, whichever is required for measurement.

Stepwise procedure for the microprocessor based multirange voltage measurement may be summarised as under:

(A)  For 250 mV range
   1.  The voltage to be measured is applied across terminal 1 and common of the sensor.
   2.  Microprocessor receives the input signal  to be measured through ADC.
   3.  It picks up the measured voltage on passing through the Look-up table.
   4.  The voltage in hex form to the corresponding decimal value is then converted.
   5.  The required voltage is ultimately displayed on the display screen along with the desired character (mV)

(B)  For 2500 mV range
   1.  The voltage to be  measured is applied across terminal 2 and common of the sensor.
   2.  Steps (1) and (2) of (A) are followed.
   3.  The measured voltage obtained from the Look-up table is multiplied with 0A H (10 Dec.)
   4.  Steps (3) and (4) of (A) are then followed.

(C)  For 25000 mV or 25 V range:
   1.  The voltage to measured is applied across terminal 3 and common of the sensor.
   2.  Steps (2) to (4) are followed execpting that the multiplication factor is 64 H instead of 0A H.

Similar process should be followed for the voltage range of 250 V and 2.50 KV.

### 14.2.3 SOFTWARE LISTING
Main program for voltage measurement (range 0-250 mV)

| Label | Mem. Loc. | Mnemonics | Opcode | | | Description |
|-------|-----------|-----------|--------|---|---|-------------|
|       | 4400 | LXI  SP  47FF H | 31 | FF | 47 | SP ——→47FF H |
| AGAIN | 4403 | CALL INDATA | CD | 38 | 45 | CALL INDATA |
|       | 4406 | MVI  B  00 | 06 | 00 |  | 00 H——→REG. B |
|       | 4408 | MOV C,A | 4F |  |  | (ACC.) ——→ REG. C |
|       | 4409 | CALL HEXDEC | CD | 7E | 11 | CALL HEXDEC |
|       | 440C | LXI  H  4100H | 21 | 00 | 41 | (HL)←—— 4100 H |
|       | 440F | MVI  M  16 H | 36 | 16 |  | 16 H ——→ 4100 H |
|       | 4411 | INX  H | 23 |  |  | HL——→HL + 1 |
|       | 4412 | MVI  M  19 H | 36 | 19 |  | 19 H ——→ 4101 H |
|       | 4414 | CALL DISP | CD | 83 | 02 | CALL DISP * |
|       | 4417 | CALL DLY | CD | 6C | 45 | CALL DLY |
|       | 441A | JMP  AGAIN | C3 | 03 | 44 | JMP AGAIN |

* DISP subroutine has been assumed to be stored in the EPROM starting from the Mem. Loc. 0283 H.

Main Program for Voltmeter (range 0-2500 mv)

| Label | Mem. Loc. | Mnemonics | Opcode | | | Description |
|-------|-----------|-----------|--------|---|---|-------------|
|       | 441D | LXI  SP  47FF H | 31 | FF | 47 | SP ——→ 47FF H |
| AGAIN | 4420 | CALL INDATA | CD | 38 | 45 | CALL INDATA |
|       | 4423 | CALL MULTI | CD | 5B | 45 | CALL MULTI |
|       | 4426 | CALL HEXDEC | CD | 7E | 11 | CALL HEXDEC |
|       | 4429 | LXI  H  4100H | 21 | 00 | 41 | (HL) ←—— 4100 H |
|       | 442C | MVI  M  16 H | 36 | 16 |  | 16 H ——→ 4100 H |
|       | 442E | INX  H | 23 |  |  | HL ——→ HL+1 |
|       | 442F | MVI  M  19 H | 36 | 19 |  | 19 H ——→4101 H |
|       | 4431 | CALL DISP | CD | 83 | 02 | CALL DISP |
|       | 4434 | CALL DLY | CD | 6C | 45 | CALL DLY |
|       | 4437 | JMP  AGAIN | C3 | 20 | 44 | JMP AGAIN |

Subroutine

| Label | Mem. Loc. | Mnemonics | Opcode | | | Description |
|-------|-----------|-----------|--------|---|---|-------------|
| INDATA | 4538 | MVI  A  9B | 3E | 9B |  | THIS SUBROUTINE RECEIVES INSTANTA- |
|        | 453A | OUT  0F | D3 | 0F |  | NEOUS DIGITAL SIGNAL FROM THE SENSOR |
|        | 453C | IN  0C | DB | 0C |  | THROUGH ADC, PRESERVES THE SAME IN |
|        | 453E | LXI  H  4080H | 21 | 40 | 80 | MEM. LOC. 4080 H, STORES THE SIZE (NO. OF |
|        | 4541 | MOV  M,A | 77 |  |  | INDEPENDENT VARIABLES IN THE LOOKUP |
|        | 4542 | MVI  B  70 H | 06 | 70 |  | TABLE IN REG. B) AND CALLS THE SUBROU- |
|        | 4544 | CALL BLOCKSEARCH | CD | 48 | 45 | TINE BLOCKSEARCH |
|        | 4547 | RET | C9 |  |  |  |
| BLOCKSEARCH |  |  |  |  |  |  |
|        | 4548 | MOV  C,M | 4E |  |  | THIS SUBROUTINE STORES THE INSTANTA- |
|        | 4549 | LXI  H  11B8H | 21 | B8 | 11 | NEOUS DIGITAL SIGNAL FROM 4080 H TO |
| UP     | 454C | MOV  E,M | 5E |  |  | REG. C, INITIALISES THE STARTING ADDRESS |
|        | 454D | MOV  A,E | 7B |  |  | OF THE LOOKUP TABLE AND COMPARES |
|        | 454E | CMP  C | BC |  |  | THE CONTENT WITH THE INSTANTANEOUS |
|        | 454F | JZ  DOWN | CA | 58 | 45 | SIGNAL. MATCHING BEING OBTAINED, THE |
|        | 4552 | DCR  B | 05 |  |  | CORRESPONDING DEPENDENT VARIABLE IS |
|        | 4553 | INX  H | 23 |  |  | TRANSFERRED TO ACC. OTHERWISE, NEXT |

| Label | Mem. Loc. | Mnemonics | | | Opcode | | | Description |
|---|---|---|---|---|---|---|---|---|
| | 4554 | INX | H | | 23 | | | INDEPENDENT VARIABLE IS COMPARED |
| | 4555 | JNZ | UP | | C2 | 4C | 45 | WITH THE INSTANTANEOUS SIGNAL AND |
| DOWN | 4558 | INX | H | | 23 | | | THE PROCEDURE IS CONTINUED TILL THE |
| | 4559 | MOV | A,M | | 7E | | | MATCHING IS NOT OBTAINED. |
| | 455A | RET | | | C9 | | | |
| MULTI | 455B | MOV | C,A | | 4F | | | THIS SUBROUTINE MULTIPLIES THE DEPEN- |
| | 455C | MVI | B | 00 | 06 | 00 | | DENT VARIABLES WITH 0A H AND KEEPS |
| | 455E | MVI | L | 00 | 2E | 00 | | THE RESULT IN REG. PAIR BC |
| | 4560 | MVI | H | 00 | 26 | 00 | | |
| | 4562 | MVI | D | 0A | 16 | 0A | | |
| LOOP | 4564 | DAD | B | | 09 | | | |
| | 4565 | DCR | D | | 15 | | | |
| | 4566 | JNZ | LOOP | | C2 | 64 | 45 | |
| | 4569 | MOV | B,H | | 44 | | | |
| | 456A | MOV | C,L | | 4D | | | |
| | 456B | RET | | | C9 | | | |
| DLY | 456C | PUSH | D | | C5 | | | THIS IS A SIMPLE DELAY SUBPROGRAM AND |
| | 456D | MVI | D | 0A | 16 | 0A | | THE TIME DELAY DEPENDS ON THE DATA |
| J2 | 456F | MVI | E | 05 | 1E | 05 | | STORED IN REG. D AND IN REG. E. |
| J1 | 4571 | NOP | | | 00 | | | |
| | 4572 | NOP | | | 00 | | | |
| | 4573 | DCR | E | | 1D | | | |
| | 4574 | JNZ | J1 | | C2 | 71 | 45 | |
| | 4577 | DCR | D | | 15 | | | |
| | 4578 | JNZ | J2 | | C2 | 6F | 45 | |
| | 457B | POP | D | | D1 | | | |
| | 457C | RET | | | C9 | | | |
| HEXDEC | 117E | LXI | H | 0000H | 21 | 00 | 00 | THIS SUBPROGRAM STORED IN EPROM CON- |
| | 1181 | XRA | A | | AF | | | VERTS THE HEX VALUE TO EQUIVALENT |
| | 1182 | STA | 405F H | | 32 | 5F | 40 | DECIMAL FORM. |
| | 1185 | INX | B | | 03 | | | |
| | 1186 | DCX | B | | 0B | | | |
| | 1187 | MOV | A,C | | 79 | | | |
| | 1188 | ORA | B | | B0 | | | |
| | 1189 | JZ | 11A6 H | | CA | A6 | 11 | |
| | 118C | XRA | A | | AF | | | |
| | 118D | INR | L | | 2C | | | |
| | 118E | MOV | A,L | | 7D | | | |
| | 118F | DAA | | | 27 | | | |
| | 1190 | MOV | L,A | | 6F | | | |
| | 1191 | JNZ | 1186 H | | C2 | 86 | 11 | |
| | 1194 | XRA | A | | AF | | | |
| | 1195 | INR | H | | 24 | | | |
| | 1196 | MOV | A,H | | 7C | | | |
| | 1197 | DAA | | | 27 | | | |
| | 1198 | MOV | H,A | | 67 | | | |
| | 1199 | JNZ | 1186 H | | C2 | 86 | 11 | |
| | 119C | LDA | 405F H | | 3A | 5F | 40 | |
| | 119F | INR | A | | 3C | | | |
| | 11A0 | STA | 405F H | | 32 | 5F | 40 | |
| | 11A3 | JMP | 1186 H | | C3 | 86 | 11 | |
| | 11A6 | SHLD | 404F H | | 22 | 4F | 40 | |
| | 11A9 | CALL | MODI | | CD | 37 | 02 | |
| | 11AC | LDA | 405F H | | 3A | 5F | 40 | |
| | 11AF | MOV | D,A | | 57 | | | |
| | 11B0 | CALL | SPLIT | | CD | 35 | 03 | |
| | 11B3 | XRA | A | | AF | | | |
| | 11B4 | RET | | | C9 | | | |

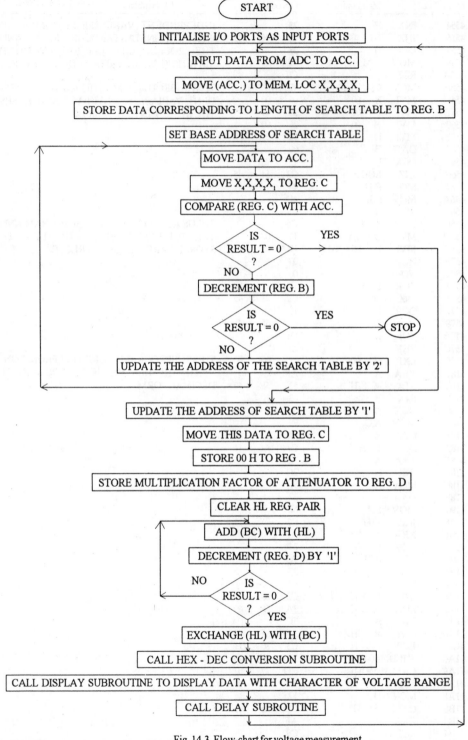

Fig. 14.3. Flow-chart for voltage measurement

**Lookup Table (Mem. Loc. 11B8 to 1299 H)**

| Mem. Loc. | Digital Input | Hex value of analog input | Corresponding analog value (mV) |
|---|---|---|---|
| 11B8 | 00 | 00 | 000 |
| 11BA | 01 | 02 | 002 |
| 11BC | 02 | 05 | 005 |
| 11BE | 03 | 07 | 007 |
| 11C0 | 04 | 09 | 009 |
| 11C2 | 05 | 0C | 012 |
| 11C4 | 06 | 0E | 014 |
| .... | ... | ..... | ......... |
| .... | .... | ..... | ......... |
| 1298 | 70 | FE | 254 |

## 14.3  CURRENT MEASUREMENT

### 14.3.1  System Hardware

With a minor change in hardware and software, the voltage monitoring scheme may be changed to monitor current. For multirange current measurement, the sensor may consists of a very low resistance having high current carrying capacity so that the total voltage drop across the resistance is negligibly small in comparison to the supply voltage. The schematic diagram of the Hardware is shown in Fig. 14.4.

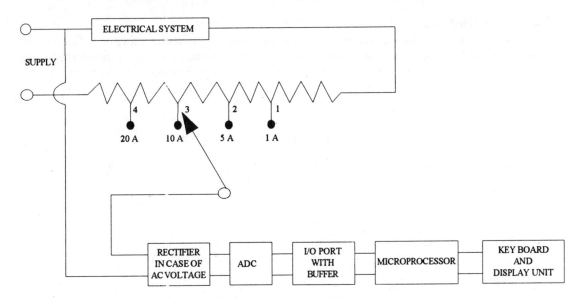

Fig. 14.4. Current measuring hardware

Terminals of the sensor is to be so designed that for different ranges of current, the maximum digital output from ADC should never exceed FF H in order to eliminate the complication of table searching. The instantaneous digital signal corresponding to the current to be measured is introduced to the microprocessor.

The resistance sensor may be replaced by a current transformer or a core balanced transformer connected with a burden in case of alternating current measurement where the signal is obtained as the voltage drop across the burden.

### 14.3.2 System Software

It is exactly the same as that of voltage measurement scheme with a change of Look-up table. To form the look-up table, the sensor is initially calibrated for the current range of 0-1A. The current is gradually controlled from zero to a maximum of 1A and the corresponding digital signal is measured through the microprocessor. Thus for every possible digital signal, the analog current flowing through the actual electrical circuit or system is determined to obtain the calibration curve of the analog current against the digital input to the microprocessor. These characteristics are stored in certain EPROM area as a look-up table with digital signals as independent and analog currents (converted to HEX form) as dependent variables. In the look up table, each digital signal and its corresponding analog current are placed in two successive locations.

The software is so developed that the microprocessor, after initialisation, receives the instantaneous signal and compares the same with the independent variables from the look up table till it is matched and then picks up the current value from the next memory location. Then depending on the range of current, it multiplies the result with a proper multiplying factor (05, 0A or 14 Hex for 5A, 10A or 20A respectively), calls the 'HEX-DEC' conversion subroutine and 'DISPLAY' subroutine to display the measured analog current in decimal form on the display screen.

## 14.4 FREQUENCY MEASUREMENT

The measuring system is simply based on a zero-crossing detecting system having the capability of establishing interrupts in microprocessor at every zero level crossing of the waveform. The task of the microprocessor is only to count the interrupts through its software within the specified time interval, displaying the frequency after calculating the same through the Arithmetic and Logical Unit.

### 14.4.1 System Hardware

The frequency of an alternating waveform can be measured by counting the cycles in a second. This counting is possible through the microprocessor, if appropriate signals, conceivable by microprocessor corresponding to each complete waveform produced by an appropriate hardware, may be supplied to the microprocessor.

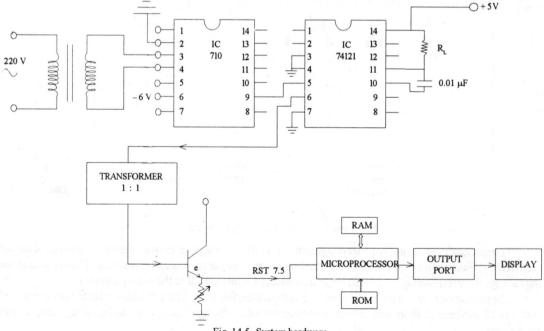

Fig. 14.5. System hardware

Sinusoidal and many other ac waveforms cross zero level twice in a complete wave and the zero crossing may be identified by proper chips producing delta functions with finite length having finite height as the signals compatible with the microprocessor. Microprocessor through RST 7.5 accepts the edge sensitive interrupts and counts the total number of interrupts in one second or a specified time interval. A zero-crossing sensor circuit for sine wave has been made using the comparator chip (IC 710) and a multivibrator chip (IC 74121) as shown in Fig. 14.5.

The comparator chip produces a square having the same frequency as that of its input waveform. The square wave is supplied to the multivibrator chip for the production of the interrupts at every level transitions of the square wave (or in other words at every zero-crossing of the sine wave). These interrupts are then fed to the microprocessor through the edge sensitive interrupt line (RST 7.5) of the microprocessor via. a buffer consisting of a transistor (SL 100). The microprocessor has then only to perform simply the counting of these interrupts for one second or within a specified time interval by executing the software program.

### 14.4.2 SYSTEM SOFTWARE

As stated earlier, the microprocessor receives the interrupt signals through the hardware and counts the same through the software for a specified time and then displays the frequency in the display screen after performing the mathematical and logical operations in its ALU. Number of interrupts per second of a sinusoidal waveform having frequency 'n' becomes equal to '2n +1'. In order to increase the accuracy of the measurements, the software is so developed that after counting the interrupts for five seconds, the microprocessor reduces the total count by one and divides the same by 10 (0A H) to obtain the frequency since total number of interrupts received in 5 seconds is '10n + 1'. After five seconds, the microprocessor is made disabled to receive the interrupts and it starts to calculate the frequency and displays on the display screen to present the frequency of the waveform. Flow Charts for the main program and interrupt service routine have been presented in Fig. 14.6 and 14.7 respectively. An accurate delay program has also been developed to consume sufficient crystal clock cycles to produce a time delay of exactly 5 seconds.

### 14.4.3 SOFTWARE LISTING

**Main Program**

| Label | Mem. Loc. | Mnemonics | | | Opcode | | | Description |
|---|---|---|---|---|---|---|---|---|
| START | 4200 | LXI | SP | 47FF H | 31 | FF | 47 | INITIALISE STACK POINTER |
| LOOP | 4203 | LXI | H | 4100 H | 21 | 00 | 41 | INITIALISE MEM. LOC. 4100 H |
| | 4206 | MVI | M | 15 | 36 | 15 | | LOAD 15 H IN MEM. LOC. 4100 H |
| | 4208 | INX | H | | 23 | | | INCREMENT MEM. LOC. |
| | 4209 | MVI | M | 00 | 36 | 00 | | LOAD 00 H IN MEMORY |
| | 420B | INX | H | | 23 | | | INCREMENT MEM. LOC. |
| | 420C | MVI | M | 00 | 36 | 00 | | LOAD 00 H IN MEMORY |
| | 420E | INX | H | | 23 | | | INCREMENT MEM. LOC. |
| | 420F | MVI | M | 00 | 36 | 00 | | LOAD 00 H IN MEMORY |
| | 4211 | INX | H | | 23 | | | INCREMENT MEM. LOC. |
| | 4212 | MVI | M | 00 | 36 | 00 | | LOAD 00 H IN MEMORY |
| | 4214 | INX | H | | 23 | | | INCREMENT MEM. LOC. |
| | 4215 | MVI | M | 15 | 36 | 15 | | LOAD 15 H IN MEMORY |
| | 4217 | MVI | A | 80 H | 3E | 80 | | INITIALISE ALL PORTS AS OUTPUT PORT |
| | 4219 | OUT | 0B | | D3 | 0B | | CHIP SELECT CONTROL WORD |
| | 421B | EI | | | FB | | | ENABLE INTERRUPT |
| | 421C | MVI | A | 0B | 3E | 0B | | BIT PATTERN TO ENABLE RST 7.5 AND TO DISABLE RST 6.5 AND 5.5. |
| | 421E | SIM | | | 30 | | | SET INTERRUPT MASK |
| | 421F | NOP | | | 00 | | | NO OPERATION |

| Label | Mem. Loc. | Mnemonics | Opcode | | | Description |
|---|---|---|---|---|---|---|
| | 4220 | MVI C 08 | 0E | 08 | | LOAD 08 H IN REG. C |
| LOOP1 | 4222 | CALL SDLY | CD | 00 | 43 | CALL SUBPROGRAM 'SDLY' |
| | 4225 | DCR C | 0D | | | DECREMENT (REG. C) |
| | 4226 | JNZ LOOP1 | C2 | 22 | 42 | JUMP TO LOOP1, IF RESULT IS NOT ZERO |
| | 4229 | DI | F3 | | | DISABLE INTERRUPT |
| | 422A | LXI H 4104H | 21 | 04 | 41 | INITIALISE MEM. LOC. 4104 H |
| | 422D | MOV A,M | 7E | | | MOVE DATA FROM ACC. TO MEM. |
| | 422E | CPI 00 | FE | 00 | | COMPARE 00 H WITH (ACC.) |
| | 4230 | JZ LOOP2 | CA | 34 | 42 | JUMP TO LOOP2, IF RESULT IS ZERO |
| | 4233 | DCR M | 35 | | | DECREMENT (MEM.) |
| LOOP2 | 4234 | MVI A 01 H | 3E | 01 | | LOAD 01 H IN ACC. TO SELECT ADDRESS FIELD OF DISPLAY |
| | 4236 | MVI B 01 H | 06 | 01 | | LOAD 01 H IN REG. B TO DISPLAY 'DOT' |
| | 4238 | LXI H 4100H | 21 | 00 | 41 | INITIALISE MEM. LOC. 4100 H |
| | 423B | CALL DISP | CD | 83 | 02 | CALL DISPLAY SUBROUTINE |
| | 423E | CALL DLY | CD | A0 | 12 | CALL DISPLAY SUBROUTINE |
| | 4241 | MVI A 02 H | 3E | 02 | | LOAD 02 H IN ACC. TO SELECT DATA FIELD OF DISPLAY |
| | 4243 | MVI B 00 H | 06 | 00 | | LOAD 00 H IN REG. B TO AVOID DOT |
| | 4245 | LXI H 4104H | 21 | 04 | 41 | INITIALISE MEM. LOC. 4104 H |
| | 4248 | CALL 0283 | CD | 83 | 02 | CALL DISPLAY SUBROUTINE |
| | 424B | CALL DLY | CD | A0 | 12 | CALL DLY SUBROUTINE |
| | 424E | JMP LOOP | C3 | 03 | 42 | JUMP TO LOOP |

**Interrupt service subroutine (ISSR)**

| Label | Mem. Loc. | Mnemonics | Opcode | | | Description |
|---|---|---|---|---|---|---|
| ISSR | 4401 | LXI H 4104 | 21 | 04 | 41 | INITIALISE MEM. LOC. 4104 H |
| | 4404 | INR M | 34 | | | INCREMENT (MEM.) |
| | 4405 | MOV A,M | 7E | | | TRANSFER (MEMORY) TO ACC. |
| | 4406 | CPI 0A | FE | 0A | | COMPARE 0A H WITH (ACC.) |
| | 4408 | JC NEXT | DA | 2C | 44 | JUMPT TO NEXT, IF CARRY SET |
| | 440B | MVI M 00 | 36 | 00 | | LOAD 00 H IN MEM. |
| | 440D | DCX H | 2B | | | DECREMENT HL PAIR |
| | 440E | INR M | 34 | | | INCREMENT (MEM.) |
| | 440F | MOV A,M | 7E | | | TRANSFER (MEMORY) TO ACC. |
| | 4410 | CPI 0A | FE | 0A | | COMPARE 0A H WITH (ACC.) |
| | 4412 | JC NEXT | DA | 2C | 44 | JUMP TO NEXT, IF CARRY SET |
| | 4415 | MVI M 00 | 36 | 00 | | LOAD 00 H IN MEM. |
| | 4417 | DCX H | 2B | | | DECREMENT HL PAIR |
| | 4418 | INR M | 34 | | | INCREMENT (MEM.) |
| | 4419 | MOV A,M | 7E | | | TRANSFER (MEMORY) TO ACC. |
| | 441A | CPI 0A | FE | 0A | | COMPARE 0A H WITH (ACC.) |
| | 441C | JC NEXT | DA | 2C | 44 | JUMP TO NEXT, IF CARRY SET |
| | 441F | MVI M 00 | 36 | 00 | | LOAD 00 H IN MEM. |
| | 4421 | DCX H | 2B | | | DECREMENT HL PAIR. |
| | 4422 | INR M | 34 | | | INCREMENT (MEM.) |
| | 4423 | MOV A,M | 7E | | | TRANSFER (MEMORY) TO ACC. |
| | 4424 | CPI 0A | FE | 0A | | COMPARE 0A H WITH (ACC.) |
| | 4426 | JC NEXT | DA | 2C | 44 | JUMP TO NEXT, IF CARRY SET |
| | 4429 | CALL 'OVER' | CD | OVER | | CALL SUBROUTINE TO DISPLAY 'OVER' |
| NEXT | 442C | RET | C9 | | | RETURN |

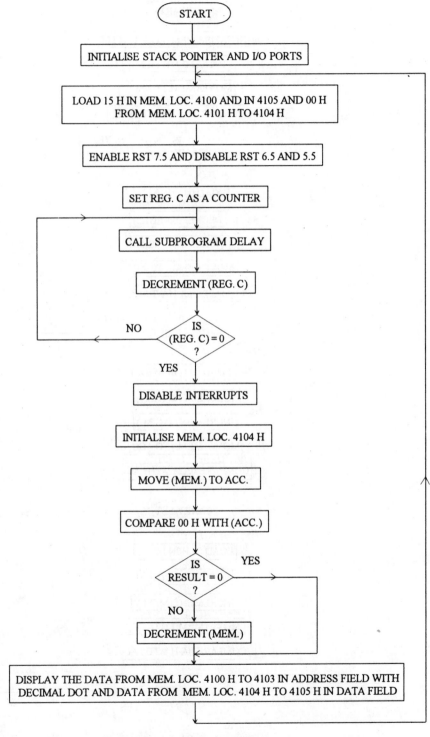

Fig. 14.6 Flow chart for main program

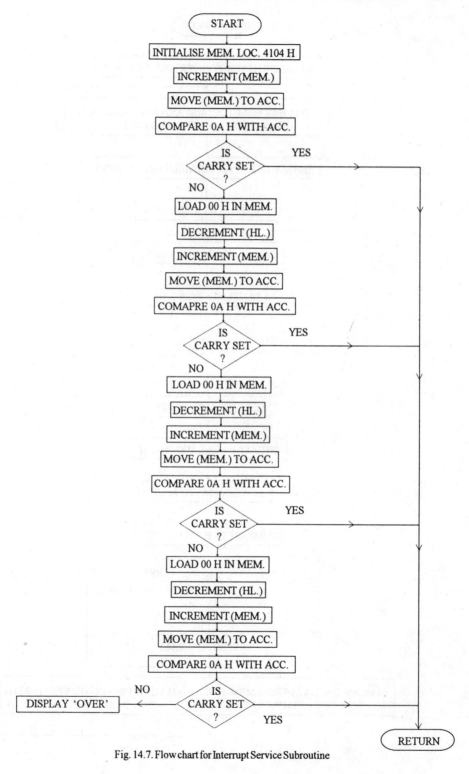

Fig. 14.7. Flow chart for Interrupt Service Subroutine

## 14.5 SPEED MEASUREMENT

As mentioned earlier, in any microprocessor based design, a system hardware necessary for inserting the reference signal compatible with the microprocessor is essential which in this particular case is a tacho-generator to be coupled with the rotating system to generate a voltage proportional to the speed. A search table, consisting of the speeds and the corresponding tacho-generated voltages converted to hex values by an ADC is developed. The system software is such that after receiving a signal through ADC from the tacho-generator, the microprocessor stores the same in some memory location. It displays the speed in decimal value on the display screen after going through the search table. Then the microprocessor receives the next instantaneous reference voltage and continues to display instantaneous speed.

### 14.5.1  System Hardware

For the measurement of any physical quantity it is desirable that the hardware should be as simple as possible. The system hardware in this case (Fig. 14.8) is simply a tacho-generator which is to be connected with the axis of the rotating system (which in the present case is a separately excited d.c. motor). The generated voltage through the tacho-generator, dependent on the number of revolutions of the rotating system, is fed to the microprocessor through a potentiometer. With the change in speed, the generator voltage will be changed feeding a new reference voltage to the microprocessor for the execution of the software.

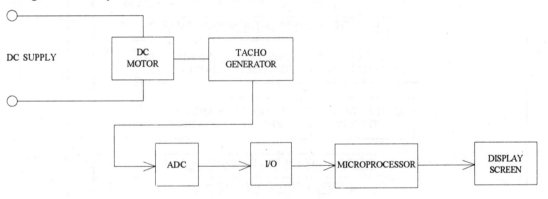

Fig. 14.8. System hardware

### 14.5.2  System Software

System software for the measurement of angular speed mainly consists of the main program, a search table and the character display of the quantities to be measured. The flow chart of the system software for the measurement of speed has been shown in Fig. 14.9.

Development of the search table is the most significant part of the measurement and the accuracy of the measurement depends on the accuracy of the characteristics stored in the search table. The calibration curve is drawn with the microprocessor digital input voltage through ADC corresponding to the reference analog voltage as abscissa and the corresponding speed as the ordinate. From the calibration curve, for every possible digital input voltage, the corresponding speed is measured accurately and stored in the memory of the microprocessor in the form of a search table taken in an order against each microprocessor input digital value. The first and the most important task is to monitor the voltage from ADC and then going through a software for search routine to note the speed. After initialisation of the I/O ports of the microprocessor, the reference voltage is brought to the accumulator of the microprocessor through ADC followed by a comparison with different digital values stored in the search table. Corresponding to one digital input voltage, two memory locations are stored with the decimal data corresponding to the speed. After block search, the data corresponding to the speed are first combined to display in the display screen together with a character display 'SP' for speed.

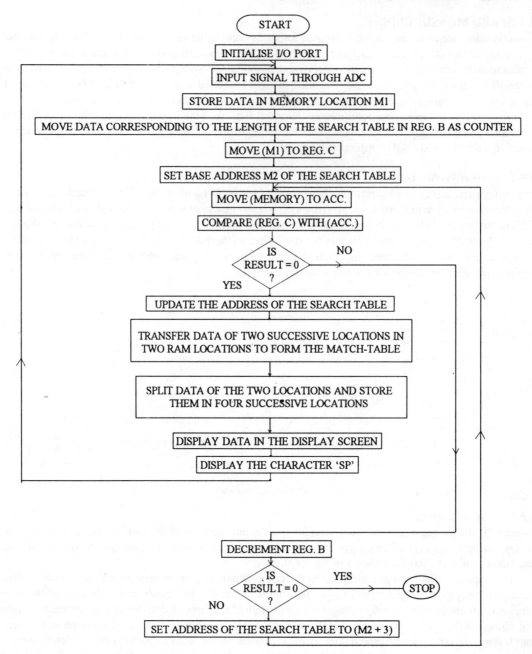

Fig. 14.9. Flow-chart for speed measurement

| Label | Mem. Loc. | Mnemonics | | | Opcode | | | Description |
|---|---|---|---|---|---|---|---|---|
| START | 41FF | MVI A 90 | | | 3E | 90 | | INITIALISE PORT A AS INPUT PORT & PORTS B & C AS OUTPUT PORTS |
| | 4201 | OUT | 0B | | D3 | 0B | | INITIALISE I/O CHIP |
| INTAKE | 4203 | IN | PORTA | | DB | 08 | | IN SIGNAL THROUGH PORT A |
| | 4205 | MVI | B | LST | 06 | LST | | STORE LENGTH OF SEARCH TABLE IN REG. B |
| | 4207 | MOV C,A | | | 4F | | | TRANSFER (ACC.) TO REG. C. |
| | 4208 | LXI H SAST | | | 21 | 00 | 43 | INITIALISE STARTING ADDRESS OF THE SEARCH TABLE |
| NEXT | 420B | MOV A,M | | | 77 | | | TRANSFER THE MEMORY CONTENT TO ACC. |
| | 420C | CMP C | | | B9 | | | COMPARE (REG. C) WITH (ACC.) |
| | 420D | JZ | DISP | | CA | 1B | 42 | JUMP ON ZERO TO 'DISP' |
| | 4210 | DCR | B | | 05 | | | OTHERWISE, DECREMENT (REG. B) |
| | 4211 | JZ | STOP | | CA | 1A | 42 | JUMP ON ZERO TO STOP |
| | 4214 | INX H | | | 23 | | | OTHERWISE, INCREMENT HL PAIR |
| | 4215 | INX H | | | 23 | | | INCREMENT HL PAIR |
| | 4216 | INX H | | | 23 | | | INCREMENT HL PAIR |
| | 4217 | JMP | NEXT | | C3 | 0B | 42 | JUMP TO "NEXT" |
| STOP | 421A | HLT | | | 76 | | | HALT |
| DISP | 421B | INX H | | | 23 | | | INCREMENT HL PAIR |
| | 421C | MOV | D,M | | 56 | | | TRANSFER MEMORY CONTENT TO REG. D. |
| | 421D | INX | H | | 23 | | | INCREMENT HL PAIR |
| | 421E | MOV | E,M | | 5E | | | TRANSFER THE MEMORY CONTENT TO REG. E |
| | 421F | LXI H 4101 H | | | 21 | 01 | 41 | INITIALISE MEM. LOC. 4101 H |
| | 4222 | MOV | M,D | | 72 | | | TRANSFER (REG. D) TO THE MEMORY |
| | 4223 | INX H | | | 23 | | | INCREMENT HL PAIR |
| | 4224 | MOV | M,E | | 73 | | | TRANSFER (REG. E) TO THE MEMORY |
| | 4225 | CALL 'DISPLAY' | | | CD | DISPLAY | | CALL 'DISPLAY' SUBROUTINE* |
| | 4228 | JMP | INTAKE | | C3 | 03 | 42 | JUMP TO 'INTAKE' |

* This subroutine may be developed or the same stored in EPROM may be used.

INPUT : LENGTH OF SEARCH TABLE IN REG. B.
SEARCH TABLE FROM MEM. LOC. 4300 H (TO BE PREPARED)
OUTPUT : DISPLAY SCREEN (SPEED).

## 14.6 TEMPERATURE MONITORING
In this section, a microprocessor based system has been developed to monitor temperature. The system hardware is discussed as under:

### 14.6.1 SYSTEM HARDWARE
The schematic block diagram of the system hardware has been shown in Fig. 14.10 (a) and the thermal sensor circuit in Fig. 14.10 (b). In the sensor circuit, two operational amplifiers A1 and A2 have been used. The operational amplifier A1 acts as a constant current source feeding the temperature sensor (Thermister or thermocouple) connected across terminals X and Y, the magnitude of constant current being $V_R/V_S$. The output voltage of the constant circuit is given by

$$V_C = V_R + V_T,$$

where $V_R$ is the voltage across the standard high stability metal film resistance $R_s$ and $V_T$ is the voltage across the temperature sensor. $V_R$ is stabilized with the help of a Zener ZD. The output voltage Vc of the constant current circuit and reference voltage Vref are fed to the differential amplifier A2 where the potentiometer $P_2$ controls the gain (Av) of the amplifier. The amplified output of the operational amplifier A2 appears across the resistance R0 which provides the signal to the microprocessor through ADC.

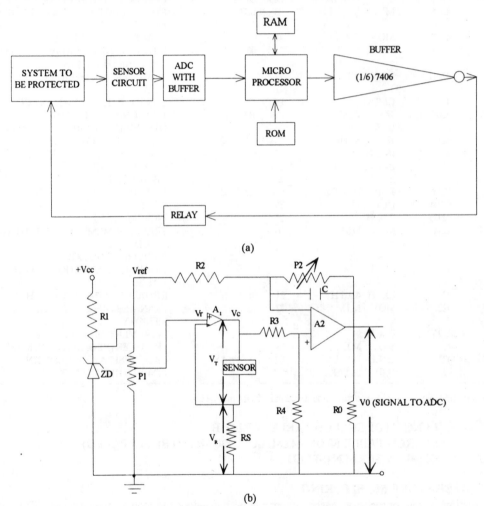

Fig. 14.10 (a) Schematic block diagram and (b) Sensor circuit

### 14.6.2  SYSTEM SOFTWARE

The flow chart of the system software has been presented in Fig. 14.11. The development of the look-up table is the most significant part of the design since the accuracy of the measurement depends on the accuracy of the characteristics stored in the look-up table. The calibration curve is drawn with the microprocessor digital input as ordinate and the corresponding temperature as abscissa. From the calibration curve, for every possible digital input value, temperatures are determined and stored in the memory in the form of a look-up table. In the look-up table, corresponding to each digital signal, two consecutive memory locations are stored with the decimal value of the temperature, most significant part being stored followed by the least significant part.

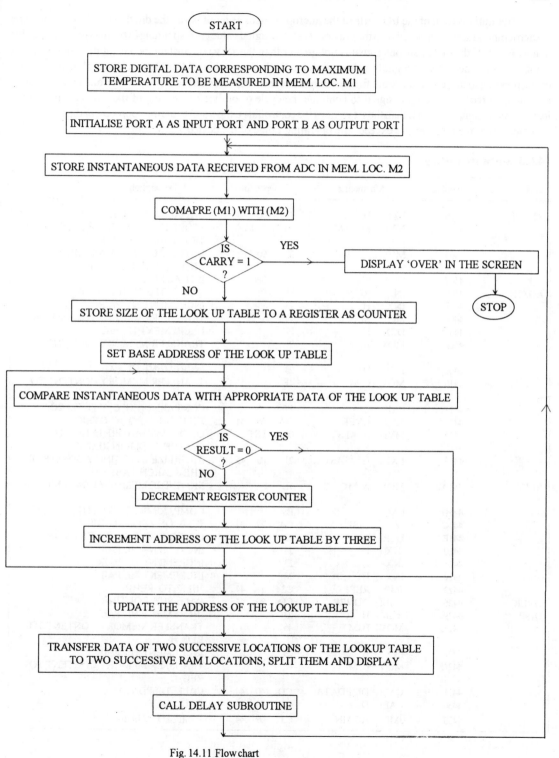

Fig. 14.11 Flow chart

After initialisation of the I/O ports of the microprocessor as input ports, the digital signal  corresponding to each temperature is compared with the previously stored digital value corresponding to the maximum allowable temperature.  If the instantaneous signal is not greater than the set value, instantaneous input digital signal is compared with the different digital   values stored in the look-up table. After the block  search is made, data corresponding to the temperature are first combined and then displayed on the display screen and and the system continues to receive new input signal to continue the cycle of on-line controlling of the temperature.  If the instantaneous signal is greater than the set value of the controlling temperature, the microprocessor displays 'over' to indicate that the temperature exceeds the operating range of the device.

## 14.6.3 Software Listing

| Label | Mem. Loc | Mnemonics | | | Opcode | | | Description |
|---|---|---|---|---|---|---|---|---|
| START | 4400 | LXI | H | M1 | 21 | 00 | 43 | INITIALIZE MEM. LOC. M1. |
| | 4403 | MVI | M | TMAX | 36 | TMAX | | STORE HEX. VALUE OF MAX. TEMPERETURE THERE. |
| | 4405 | MVI | A | 90 | 3E | 90 | | INITIALIZE PORT A AS INPUT AND B AND C AS OUTPUT PORTS |
| | 4407 | OUT | 0B | | D3 | 0B | | INITIALIZE I/O CHIP |
| AGAIN | 4409 | IN | 08 | | DB | 08 | | INPUT THROUGH PORT A |
| | 440B | INX | H | | 23 | | | INCREMENT HL PAIR |
| | 440C | MOV | M, A | | 77 | | | TRANSFER (ACC.) TO THE MEMORY |
| | 440D | DCX | H | | 2B | | | DECREMENT HL PAIR |
| | 440E | MOV | A, M | | 7E | | | TRANSFER MEMORY CONTENT TO ACC. |
| | 440F | INX | H | | 23 | | | INCREMENT HL PAIR |
| | 4410 | MOV | C, M | | 4E | | | TRANSFER MEMORY CONTENT TO REG. C |
| | 4411 | CMP | C | | B9 | | | COMPARE (REG. C) WITH (ACC.) |
| | 4412 | JC | OVER | | DA | 26 | 44 | JUMP ON ZERO TO OVER |
| | 4415 | MVI | B | LST | 06 | LST | | OTHERWISE, STORE LENGTH OF SEARCH TABLE IN REG. B. |
| | 4417 | LXI | H | SAST | 21 | 00 | 45 | INITIALIZE STARTING ADDRESS OF THE SEARCH TABLE |
| REPT | 441A | MOV | A, M | | 7E | | | MOVE THE MEMORY CONTENT TO ACC. |
| | 441B | CMP | C | | B9 | | | COMPARE (REG. C) WITH (ACC.) |
| | 441C | JZ | DISP | | CA | 29 | 44 | JUMP ON ZERO TO 'DISP' |
| | 441F | DCR | B | | 05 | | | OTHERWISE, DECREMENT REG. B. |
| | 4420 | INX | H | | 23 | | | INCREMENT HL PAIR |
| | 4421 | INX | H | | 23 | | | INCREMENT HL PAIR |
| | 4422 | INX | H | | 23 | | | INCREMENT HL PAIR |
| | 4423 | JMP | REPT | | C3 | 1A | 44 | JUMP TO 'REPT' |
| OVER | 4426 | CALL | DOVER | | CD | 80 | 44 | CALL SUB ROUTINE 'DOVER' |
| DISP | 4429 | INX | H | | 23 | | | INCREMENT HL PAIR |
| | 442A | MOV | B, M | | 46 | | | TRANSFER MEMORY CONTENT TO REG. B |
| | 442B | INX | H | | 23 | | | INCREMENT HL PAIR. |
| | 442C | MOV | C, M | | 4E | | | TRANSFER MEMORY CONTENT TO REG. C |
| | 442D | CALL | DISPDATA | | CD | 40 | 44 | CALL 'DISPDATA' |
| | 4430 | CALL | DLY | | CD | 60 | 44 | CALL 'DLY' |
| | 4433 | JMP | AGAIN | | C3 | 09 | 44 | JUMP TO 'AGAIN' |

| SUB ROUTINE | | | |
|---|---|---|---|
| DISPDATA | 4440 | : | DISPLAY OF ANALOG TEMPERATURE |
| DOVER | 4480 | : | DISPLAY 'OVER' |
| DLY | 4460 | : | DELAY |

*Input* : Search table starts from Mem. Loc 4500 H which contains the Hex. value of source signal from the sensor as independent variable followed by the 16-bit temperature (analog) as dependent variables stored in two consecutive memory locations. Length of search table (LST) is the number of independent variable in the search Table. The Hex value of the Maximum allowable temperature is to be stored in Mem. Loc. 4300 H. User may develop the subroutines necessary for the main program.

*Output* : On the screen of the display board 'OVER' will be indicated if the maximum limit of temperature is exceeded. Otherwise, the analog value of temperature is displayed.

## 14.7  OVER CURRENT PROTECTION

Many devices or instruments require protection against over current and there are conventional methods for the same. A microprocessor based system may be developed for over current protection. The advantage of the system is that the same system may provide protection against under current and also the magnitude of maximum allowable current may be adjusted. The schematic diagram of the over current protection scheme is shown in Fig. 14.12 where it is assumed that a single-phase transformer supplies the voltage to a device through an electromagnetic relay in the secondary side. A small resistance with high current carrying capacity has been connected in series with the device which acts as the sensor and the voltage drop across the resistance is supplied to the microprocessor after being rectified with a bridge circuit and converted to the digital signal by means of ADC. After receiving the signal from the sensor, the microprocessor executes a software which is so developed that the microprocessor first compares the instantaneous signal with the previously stored digital limiting value of the signal corresponding to the maximum allowable current and if the instantaneous signal is found less than the limiting one, it receives new instantaneous data and compares the same with the limiting value till the former is less than or equal to the later. When the instantaneous input signal becomes greater than the limiting value, the microprocessor generates a signal and outputs the same through an output port which passing through a buffer and an amplifier circuit, operates a relay to disconnect the supply from the system. The flow-chart for the system software is shown in Fig. 14.13.

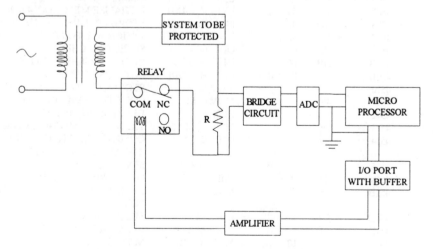

Fig. 14.12 Schematic diagram of the protective system

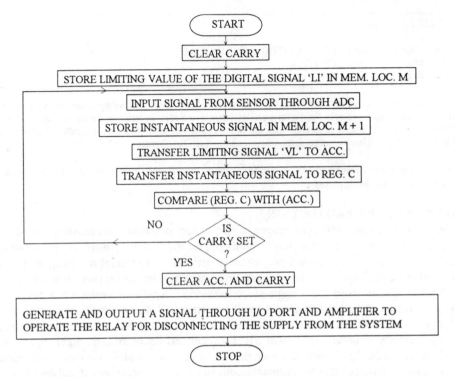

Fig. 14.13. System flow-chart

## SOFTWARE LISTING

| Label | Mem. Loc. | Opcode | | | Mnemonics | | | Description |
|---|---|---|---|---|---|---|---|---|
| START | 4500 | 37 | | | STC | | | SET CY |
| | 4501 | 3F | | | CMC | | | COMPLEMENT CY |
| | 4502 | 21 | 00 | 42 | LXI | H | 4200 | INITIALISE MEM. LOC. 4200H |
| | 4505 | 36 | 42 | | MVI | M | 42 H | STORE LIMITING VALUE OF SIGNAL (VL) |
| LOOP2 | 4507 | 3E | 9B | | MVI | A | 9B | ASSIGN ALL PORTS AS INPUT PORTS |
| | 4509 | D3 | 0F | | OUT | 0F | | SELECT I/O CHIP |
| | 450B | DB | 0C | | IN | PORT A | | INPUT THROUGH PORT A |
| | 450D | 21 | 01 | 42 | LXI | H | 4201 | INITIALISE MEM. LOC. 4201 H |
| | 4510 | 77 | | | MOV | M, A | | STORE CONTENT VI OF ACC. THERE |
| | 4511 | 4E | | | MOV | C, M | | COPY THE SAME IN REG. C |
| | 4512 | 2B | | | DCX | H | | DECREMENT HL PAIR |
| | 4513 | 7E | | | MOV | A, M | | TRANSFER LIMITING SIGNAL TO ACC. |
| | 4514 | B9 | | | CMP | C | | COMPARE LIMITING SIGNAL WITH INSTANEOUS VALUE (VI) |
| | 4515 | DA | 20 | 45 | JC | LOOP 1 | | IF VI > VL, JUMP TO LOOP 1 |
| | 4518 | C3 | 07 | 45 | JMP | LOOP 2 | | OTHERWISE, JUMP TO LOOP 2 |
| LOOP 1 | 451B | 3E | 80 | | MVI | A | 80 | INITILISE ALL PORTS AS OUTPUT PORT |
| | 451D | D3 | 0B | | OUT | 0B | | SELECT I/O CHIP |
| | 451F | AF | | | XRA | A | | CLEAR ACC. AND CY |
| | 4520 | 3E | 02 | | MVI | A | 02 | MAKE $P_{A1}$ HIGH |
| | 4522 | D3 | 09 | | OUT | PORT B | | OUTPUT THROUGH PBI |
| | 4524 | C3 | 20 | 45 | JMP | LOOP 1 | | JUMP TO LOOP 1 |

## 14.8 SPEED CONTROL OF DC SERIES MOTOR

Speed of the DC series motor varies with load and at light or no load, its speed becomes extremely high. The easiest way of controlling its speed is to control the supply voltage. The schematic block diagram of a microprocessor based speed control scheme of a DC series motor has been presented in Fig. 14.14.

In this scheme, AC voltage has been rectified through a half controlled full wave bridge circuit employing two diodes and two thyristors, the triggering signal being supplied by the microprocessor through an opto-coupler to form the first part of the hardware. The opto-coupler is a light sensitive diode being energised by means of

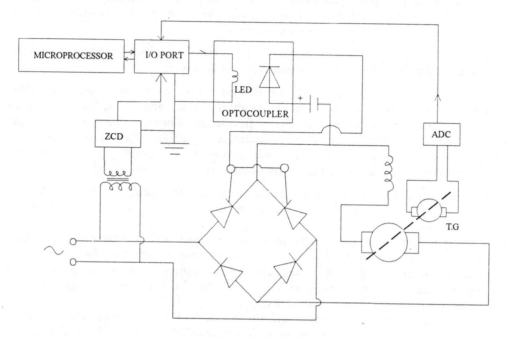

Fig. 14.14 Speed control scheme

a beam of light and the microprocessor generates a square wave through a software and supplies the same to an LED. The photo diode being excited, it outputs the voltage, the source of which being connected in series with it and providing the gate trigger pulse of the thyristor in order to deliver DC voltage to the motor and the motor starts rotating. It may be noted that the opto-coupler plays an important role of isolating the microprocessor from the DC motor. In order to control the speed, the microprocessor must receive some signal from the motor corresponding to the instantaneous speed and the sensor hardware has been developed by coupling a DC techogenerator with the rotor of the DC motor producing a DC voltage of small magnitude proportional to the speed. This sensor voltage is digitised by means of an ADC in order to provide signal to the microprocessor.

In addition to the second part of the hardware, another circuit is necessary to synchronise the microprocessor with AC signal in order to adjust the trigger angle of the thyristor and this task has been completed utilising a step down transformer associated with a zero crossing detector (ZCD) which converts the AC wave into a rectangular block of pulses being conveyed to the microprocessor through an I/O port.

### 14.8.1 SYSTEM DESCRIPTION AND SOFTWARE

Before developing the system software, the sequential steps of the system functioning have been described as:

(i) The microprocessor identifies the zero crossing at the rising edge of the AC waveform and then making a definite time delay, it generates and outputs a square wave through I/O port to the opto-coupler. It may be noted that the time delay is proportional to the trigger angle of the thyristor.

(ii) The optocoupler being energised, outputs a DC voltage signal at a trigger angle to both the thyristors though any one thyristor whose anode voltage is positive at that instant conducts and supplies DC voltage to the motor to rotate the same.

(iii) Then again, detecting the falling edge of the AC waveform, the microprocessor makes the same time delay as before and generating a square pulse again, outputs the same to energise the optocoupler. Receiving the trigger pulse, the second thyristor starts conduction and the motor gets supply voltage. These two steps are followed for a number of cycles so that the motor attains a stable speed.

(iv) The microprocessor then receives the instantaneous signal from the tachogenerator and compares the same with the set value (Vset) corresponding to the required speed of the motor.

(v) If the magnitude of the instantaneous signal is less than the set value, the microprocessor, identifying the zero crossing at the rising edge of the AC waveform, decreases the delay time by a definite smaller amount before generating the square pulse and thus the trigger angle is decreased increasing the average input voltage to the motor. Step 3 is then followed and the cyclic operation is repeated for definite number of AC cycles. It may be noted that, the same procedure is followed by increasing the delay time if the magnitude of the instantaneous signal is found greater than the set value in order to increase the trigger angle.

(vi) The reference signal from the tachogenerator being received, the microprocessor again compares the same with the set value, adjusts the time delay step by step and continues the cyclic operation till the speed of the motor is maintained.

Through this microprocessor based scheme, the motor speed can be kept at constant level from no load to full load condition. The scheme is equally applicable for the variation or fluctuation of AC supply voltage. Further, the scheme eliminates a large portion of hardware by means of software increasing the system reliability. The flow diagram of the system software is shown in Fig. 14.15. The same software with a minor change may be utilised for the soft starting of the motor eliminating starter.

In the software development, besides main program, subroutine 'SYN' for synchronising the AC waveform with the system, 'REDGE' for detecting rising edge at the zero corssing of AC wave forms, 'FEDGE' for detecting falling edge of the AC waveform, 'ADCTRIG' for trigger pulse output, 'SDLY' for small delay and 'VDLY' for variable delay have been developed. For delay, a very small delay loop has been constructed and different time delay may be obtained by a number of repetition of the same delay loop. The number of repetition has been defined as the delay number. In the software, the following set values has been used:

$\delta$start = Delay number for starting the motor at a desired speed,

$\delta$ul = Delay number corresponding to the upper limiting value of time delay

$\delta$ll = Delay number corresponding to the lower limiting value of time delay

$\delta$set = Set value of tachogenerator voltage corresponding to the desired speed of the motor

$\delta$n+ = Incremented value of the delay number

$\delta$n– = Decremented value of the delay number

NC = Number stored as counter in Reg. B

NNC = Number of new counter in Reg. B

In control philosophy, the Bang-Bang control strategy has been applied in the software development. By a minor change in the software, the proportional, proportional integral (PI) and proportional integral differential (PID) control strategies may be implemented.

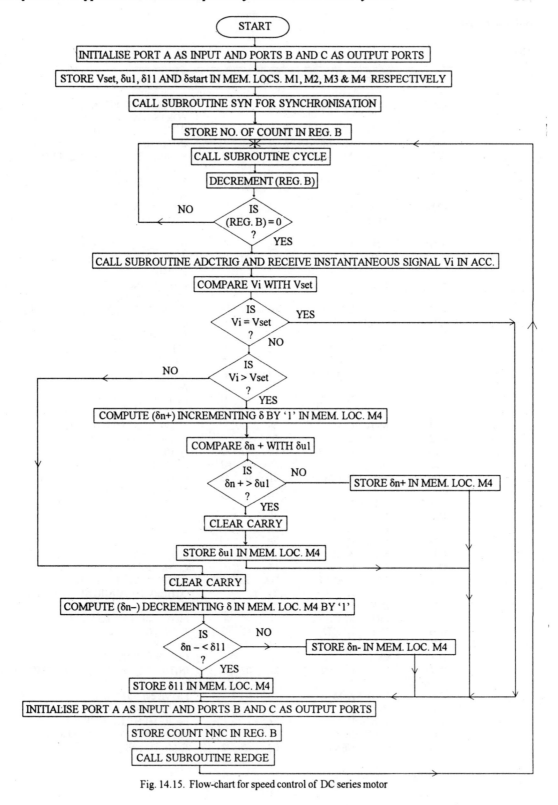

Fig. 14.15. Flow-chart for speed control of DC series motor

## Software Listing

### Main program

| Label | Mem. Loc | Mnemonics | | | Opcode | | | Description |
|---|---|---|---|---|---|---|---|---|
| START | 41FD | MVI | A | 90 | 3E | 90 | | INITIALISE PORT A AS INPUT AND PORTS B AND C AS OUTPUT PORTS |
| | 41FF | OUT | 0B | | D3 | 0B | | INITIALISE I/O CHIP |
| | 4201 | LXI | H | M1 | 21 | 00 | 43 | INITIALISE MEM. LOC. M1 |
| | 4204 | MVI | M | Vset | 36 | 6F | H | STORE SET VALUE OF SPEED THERE |
| | 4206 | INX | | | 23 | | | INCREMENT HL PAIR |
| | 4207 | MVI | M | δul | 36 | D0 | H | STORE UPPER LIMIT OF DELAY NUMBER |
| | 4209 | INX | H | | 23 | | | INCREMENT HL PAIR |
| | 420A | MVI | M | δll | 36 | 65 | H | STORE LOWER LIMIT OF DELAY NUMBER |
| | 420C | INX | H | | 23 | | | INCREMENT HL PAIR |
| | 421D | MVI | M | δstart | 36 | 97 | H | STORE δstart, THE STARTING DEALY NUMBER |
| | 420F | CALL | SYN | | CD | 00 | 41 | CALL SUBROUTINE SYN FOR SYNCHRONISATION |
| | 4212 | MVI | B | NC | 06 | FF | H | STORE NUMBER OF COUNT IN REG. B. |
| REPT | 4214 | CALL | CYCLE | | CD | 55 | 41 | CALL SUBROUTINE 'CYCLE' |
| | 4217 | DCR | B | | 05 | | | DECREMENT (REG. B) |
| | 4218 | JNZ | REPT | | C2 | 14 | 42 | IF RESULT IS NOT ZERO, JUMP TO 'REPT' |
| | 421B | CALL | ADCTRIG | | CD | 3C | 41 | OTHERWISE, CALL SUBROUTINE ADCTRIG |
| | 421E | LXI | H | M1 | 21 | 00 | 43 | INITIALISE MEM. LOC. M1 CONTAINING SET SPEED |
| | 4221 | MOV | C,M | | 4E | | | MOVE (ACC.) WITH (REG. C) |
| | 4222 | CMP | C | | B9 | | | COMPARE (ACC.) WITH (REG.C) |
| | 4223 | JZ | NEXT 2 | | CA | 62 | 42 | JUMP ON ZERO TO NEXT 2 |
| | 4226 | JC | NEXT 1 | | DA | 47 | 42 | IF CY. BE SET, JUMP TO NEXT 1 |
| | 4229 | LXI | H | M4 | 21 | 03 | 43 | OTHERWISE, INITIALISE MEM. LOC. M4 CONTAINING DELAY NUMBER |
| | 422C | INR | M | | 34 | | | INCREMENT DEALY NUMBER |
| | 422D | MOV | C,M | | 4E | | | MOVE DELAY NO. TO REG. C. |
| | 422E | DCX | H | | 2B | | | DECREMENT HL PAIR |
| | 422F | DCX | H | | 2B | | | DECREMENT HL PAIR |
| | 4230 | MOV | A,M | | 7E | | | MOVE MEMORY CONTENT TO ACC. |
| | 4231 | CMP | C | | B9 | | | COMPARE (ACC.) WITH (REG. C.) |
| | 4232 | JC | LOOP 1 | | DA | 3B | 42 | JUMP ON CALRY TO LOOP 1 |
| | 4235 | INX | H | | 23 | | | OTHERWISE, INCREMENT HL PAIR |
| | 4236 | INX | H | | 23 | | | INCREMENT HL PAIR |
| | 4237 | MOV | M,C | | 71 | | | MOVE (REG. C) TO MEM. LOC. M4 |
| | 4238 | JMP | NEXT2 | | C3 | 62 | 42 | JUMP TO NEXT2 |
| LOOP 1 | 423B | STC | | | 37 | | | SET CY. |
| | 423C | CMC | | | 3F | | | COMPLEMENT CY. |
| | 423D | LXI | H | M2 | 21 | 01 | 43 | INITIALISE MEM. LOC. CONTAINING δul |
| | 4240 | MOV | A,M | | 7E | | | MOVE δul TO MEM. |
| | 4241 | INX | H | | 23 | | | INCREMENT HL PAIR |
| | 4242 | INX | H | | 23 | | | INCREMENT HL PAIR |
| | 4243 | MOV | M,A | | 77 | | | MOVE (ACC) TO MEM. LOC. M4 |
| | 4244 | JMP | NEXT2 | | C3 | 62 | 42 | JUMP TO NEXT2 |

*(Contd.)*

| Label | Mem. Loc. | Mnemonics | | | Opcode | | | Description |
|---|---|---|---|---|---|---|---|---|
| NEXT 1 | 4247 | STC | | | 37 | | | SET CY |
| | 4248 | CMC | | | 3F | | | COMPLEMENT CY |
| | 4249 | LXI | H | M4 | 21 | 03 | 43 | INITIALISE MEM. LOC. M4 |
| | | | | | | | | CONTAINING DELAY NUMBE |
| | 424C | DCR | M | | 35 | | | DECREMENT DELAY NUMBER |
| | 424D | MOV | A, M | | 7E | | | TRANSFER DELAY NO. TO ACC |
| | 424E | MOV | D, M | | 56 | | | TRANSFER DELAY NO. TO REG. D. |
| | 424F | DCX | H | | 2B | | | DECREMENT HL PAIR |
| | 4250 | MOV | C, M | | 4E | | | MOVE δl1 TO REG. C |
| | 4251 | CMP | C | | B9 | | | COMPARE (REG. C) WITH (ACC) |
| | 4252 | JC | LOOP2 | | DA | 5A | 42 | JUMP ON CARRY TO LOOP2 |
| | 4255 | INX | H | | 23 | | | OTHERWISE, INCREMENT HL PAIR |
| | 4256 | MOV | M ,D | | 72 | | | MOVE (REG. D) TO M4 |
| | 4257 | JMP | NEXT2 | | C3 | 62 | 42 | JUMP TO NEXT2 |
| LOOP 2 | 425A | STC | | | 37 | | | SET CY. |
| | 425B | CMC | | | 3F | | | COMPLEMENT CY. |
| | 425C | LXI | H | M3 | 21 | 02 | 43 | INITIALISE HL PAIR |
| | 425F | MOV | A,M | | 7E | | | TRANSFER δl1 FROM ACC. TO M4 |
| | 4260 | INX | H | | 23 | | | INCREMENT HL PAIR |
| | 4261 | MOV | M,A | | 77 | | | TRANSFER δl1 FROM ACC. TO M4 |
| NEXT 2 | 4262 | MVI | A | 90 | 3E | 90 | | INITIALISE PORT A AS INPUT AND |
| | | | | | | | | PORTS B AND C AS OUTPUT PORT |
| | 4264 | OUT | 0B | | D3 | 0B | | INITIALISE I/O CHIP |
| | 4266 | MVI | B | NNC | 06 | 14 | | STORE NEW COUNT IN REG. B. |
| | 4268 | CALL | REDGE | | CD | 0E | 41 | CALL SUB PROGRAM 'REDGE' |
| | 426B | JMP | REPT | | C3 | 14 | 42 | JUMP TO REPT |

## Subroutines

| Label | Mem. Loc. | Mnemonics | | | Opcode | | | Description |
|---|---|---|---|---|---|---|---|---|
| SYN | 4100 | IN | PORT A | | DB | 08 | | INPUT THROUGH PA1 FROM ZCD |
| | 4102 | ANI | 01 | | E6 | 01 | | AND OPERATION BY 01H WITH (ACC.) |
| | 4104 | JZ | SYN | | CA | 00 | 41 | JUMP TO 'SYN' IF ZERO |
| LOOP 1 | 4107 | IN | PORT A | | DB | 08 | | OTHERWISE, INPUT THROUGH PA 1 |
| | | | | | | | | FROM ZCD |
| | 4109 | ANI | 01 | | E6 | 01 | | AND OPERATION BY 01H WITH (ACC) |
| | 410B | JNZ | LOOP1 | | C2 | 07 | 41 | JUMP ON NO ZERO TO LOOP1 |
| REDGE | 410E | IN | PORT A | | DB | 08 | | INPUT THROUGH PA1 |
| | 4110 | ANI | 01 | | E6 | 01 | | AND OPERATION BY 01H WITH (ACC) |
| | 4112 | JZ | REDGE | | CA | 0E | 41 | JUMP ON ZERO TO 'REDGE' |
| | 4115 | RET | | | C9 | | | RETURN |
| FEDGE | 4116 | MVI | A | 90 | 3E | 90 | | INITIALISE PORT A AS INPUT AND |
| | | | | | | | | PORTS B & C AS OUTPUT PORTS |
| | 4118 | OUT | 0B | | D3 | 0B | | SELECT I/O CHIP |
| LOOP 2 | 411A | IN | PORT A | | DB | 08 | | INPUT THROUGH PA1 FROM ZCD |
| | 411C | AN1 | 01 | | E6 | 01 | | AND OPERATION BY 01H WITH (ACC) |
| | 411E | JNZ | LOOP2 | | C2 | 1A | 41 | JUMP ON NO ZERO TO LOOP2 |
| | 4121 | RET | | | C9 | | | RETURN |
| SDLY | 4122 | PUSH | D | | D5 | | | STORE (REG. D & E) IN STACK |
| | 4123 | MVI | D | 40 | 16 | 40 | | LOAD 40 H IN REG. D. |
| LOOP 3 | 4125 | DCR | D | | 15 | | | DECREMENT (REG. D) |
| | 4126 | JNZ | LOOP3 | | C3 | 25 | 41 | JUMP ON TO ZERO TO LOOP3 |

*(Contd.)*

| Label | Mem. Loc. | Mnemonics | | | Opcode | | | Description |
|---|---|---|---|---|---|---|---|---|
| | 4129 | POP | D | | D1 | | | LOAD DATA FROM STACK TO REG. D & E |
| | 412A | RET | | | C9 | | | RETURN |
| VDLY | 412B | PUSH | D | | D5 | | | STORE (REG.D) & (REG.E) IN STACK |
| | 412C | LXI | H | M1 | 21 | 03 | 43 | INITIALISE MOM.LOC. M1 |
| | 412F | MOV | D, | M | 56 | | | MOVE DATA FROM MEM. TO REG. D. |
| LOOP 4 | 4130 | MVI | E | 05H | 1E | 05 | | STORE DATA 05H IN REG. E. |
| | 4132 | DCR | E | | 1D | | | DECREMENT (REG. E.) |
| | 4133 | JNZ | LOOP5 | | C2 | 32 | 41 | JUMP ON NO ZERO TO LOOP5 |
| | 4136 | DCR | D | | 1D | | | DECREMENT (REG.D.) |
| | 4137 | JNZ | LOOP4 | | C2 | 30 | 41 | JUMP ON NO ZERO TO LOOP5 |
| | 413A | POP | D | | D1 | | | LOAD DATA FROM STACK TO REG.D & E |
| | 413B | RET | | | C9 | | | RETURN |
| ACTRIG | 413C | MVI | A | 90 | 3E | 90 | | INITIALISE PORT A AS INPUT AND PORTS B & C AS OUTPUT PORTS |
| | 413E | OUT | 0F | | D3 | 0F | | SELECT I/O CHIP |
| | 4140 | MVI | A | 00 | 3E | 00 | | LOAD DATA 00 H IN ACC. |
| | 4142 | OUT | PORTS | | D3 | 0D | | OUTPUT THROUGH PORT B |
| | 4144 | ORI | 08 | | F6 | 08 | | OR OPERATION BY 08H WITH (ACC) |
| | 4146 | OUT | PORTB | | D3 | 0D | | OUTPUT THROUGH PORT B |
| | 4148 | ANI | 07 | | E6 | 07 | | AND OPERATION BY 07H WITH (ACC) |
| | 414A | OUT | PORTB | | D3 | 0D | | OUTPUT THROUGH PORT B |
| | 414C | MVI | A | 30 | 3E | 30 | | LOAD DATA 30 H IN ACC. |
| LOOP 6 | 414E | DCR | A | | 3D | | | DECREMENT (ACC.) |
| | 414F | JNZ | LOOP6 | | C2 | 4E | 41 | JUMP ON NO ZERO TO LOOP 6 |
| | 4152 | IN | PORTC | | DB | 0C | | INPUT THROUGH PORT A |
| | 4154 | RET | | | C9 | | | RETURN |
| CYCLE | 4155 | MVI | A | 00 | 3E | 00 | | LOAD 00 H IN ACC. |
| | 4157 | OUT | PORTB | | D3 | 09 | | OUTPUT THROUGH PORT B |
| | 4159 | CALL | VDLY | | CD | 2E | 41 | CALL ADJUSTABLE DELAY |
| | 415C | MVI | A | 01 | 3E | 01 | | LOAD 01 H IN ACC. |
| | 415E | OUT | PORTB | | D3 | 09 | | OUTPUT THROUGH PORT B |
| | 4160 | CALL | SDLY | | CD | 22 | 41 | CALL SMALL DELAY |
| | 4163 | MVI | A | 00 | 3E | 00 | | LOAD 00 H IN ACC. |
| | 4165 | OUT | PORTB | | DE | 09 | | OUTPUT THROUGH PORT B |
| | 4167 | CALL | FEDGE | | CD | 16 | 41 | DETECT FALLING EDGE |
| | 416A | MVI | A | 00 | 3E | 00 | | LOAD 00 H IN ACC. |
| | 416C | OUT | PORTB | | D3 | 09 | | OUTPUT THROUGH PORT B |
| | 416E | CALL | VDLY | | CD | 2B | 41 | CALL ADJUSTABLE DELAY |
| | 4171 | MVI | A | 01 | 3E | 01 | | LOAD 01 H IN ACC. |
| | 4173 | OUT | PORTB | | D3 | 09 | | OUTPUT THROUGH PORT B |
| | 4175 | CALL | SDLY | | CD | 22 | 41 | CALL SMALL DELAY |
| | 4178 | MVI | A | 00 | 3E | 90 | | LOAD 00 H IN ACC. |
| | 417A | OUT | PORTB | | D3 | 09 | | OUTPUT THROUGH PORT B |
| | 417C | MVI | A | 90 | 3E | 90 | | INITIALISE PORT A AS INPUT AND PORT B AND C AS OUTPUT PORTS |
| | 417E | OUT | 0B | | DE | 0B | | SELECT I/O CHIP |
| | 4180 | CALL | REDGE | | CD | 0E | 41 | DETECT RISING EDGE |
| | 4183 | RET | | | C9 | | | RETURN |

## 14.9 MONITORING OF POWER FACTOR, HORSE POWER, EFFICIENCY SLIP AND SPEED OF A THREE PHASE INDUCTION MOTOR

In this section, a technique to develop a monitoring system to monitor and display various instantaneous performance date such as power factor, horse power, efficiency, slip and speed of a three phase slip ring induction motor operating from no load to 125% of full load has been discussed. In conventional method of measurement, it is required to perform different tests to note various electromechanical meter readings in order to calculate finally the desired values. In fact the method is laborious as well as time consuming and continuous informations under operating conditions can't be readily obtained. In microprocessor based monitoring system, a reference signal developed across any one of the very small resistances connected in series with the short circuited rotor terninals is fed to the microprocessor through the Analog to Digital Converter after converting the signal to dc. Since the range of the reference voltage from no load to full load operation of the machine is narrow, for greater accuracy of the system, the reference voltage before rectification is required to be amplified using suitable amplifier circuit . For every possible microprocessor compatible digital input corresponding to the amplified reference voltage, the machine operational performances are to be calculated after proper experimentation and the results thus obtained are stored in a tabular form in the memory of the microcomputer. During on line recording, the microprocessor just receives the reference signal converted in digital form, compares the same with the values stored in a Search Table, displays the corresponding slip, power factor, speed, horse power and efficiency one after another for a preassigned period, displays END to receive the new reference voltage and continues the cyclic process.

If the input voltage to the machine falls below the rated one, the microprocessor generates an alarming signal through a proper hardware and if the load exceeds 125% of the rated value, it operates a relay to disconnect the machine from the supply.

### 14.9.1 CHOICE OF THE REFERENCE SIGNAL FROM THE INDUCTION MOTOR

An induction motor is one in which alternating voltage is supplied to the stator directly and to the rotor by induction (transformer action) from the stator. It is the most commonly used one of all rotating electrical machines. These motors are used in a wide variety of applications – from fractional single phase to 45000 horse power polyphase motors for different purposes. A typical factory will have almost all its machine tools individually driven by various sizes and classes of three phase induction motors. Even in household purposes, the larger motors used are single phase induction motors. The features that justify this popularity of induction motors are largely economic. It being mechanically very simple and extremely rugged, requires essentially no maintenance. It has sufficiently high efficiency, good capacity and reasonably good power factor. Its starting arrangement is simple and its performance characteristics can be adjusted to fit a number of different operating conditions by simply changing its design.

A three phase induction motor consists of a fixed core, called the stator, carrying a three phase winding in its slots and a rotor carrying a cage or slip ring winding which is free to rotate within the stator. When the polyphase stator windings are fed by a polyphase supply, a uniform rotaing maganetic field is set up. This rotating magnetic field induces an emf in the rotor according to the Faraday's laws of electromaganetic induction. Due to this induced emf, the current produced in the rotor circuit interacts with the rotating field to produce torque which tends to rotate the rotor in the same direction as that of the rotating flux. The motor can not drive itself at synchronous speed, and even at no load, its speed must be slightly less than the synchronous speed in order to develop sufficient torque to overcome the mechanical loss. If the rotor shaft is gradually loaded, the torque developed at no load will not be sufficient to keep the machine running at no load speed against the additional opposing torque of the load. Thus its speed slows down and the relative motion between the magnetic field and the rotor is increased so that the voltage induced in the rotor is increased and as a result more rotor current and hence greater torque are developed.

As stated earlier, the speed of the induction motor is always less than the synchronous speed and the differnce in speed between the synchronous speed and the speed of the rotor is called slip which may be expressed as a percentage or as a decimal of the synchronous speed. The slip "s" of the induction motor may be expressed in its decimal form as,

$$s = \frac{\text{Synchronous speed} - \text{Rotor speed}}{\text{Synchronous speed}}$$

On no load with the rotor short circuited, the induction motor runs at a speed very close to the synchronous speed and the rotor current is very small only to develop the torque for overcoming the friction and windage losses. As the load on the motor increases, the natural effect of the load is to slow down the motor with the increase of slip. This causes the rotor current and torque to increase till the driving torque of the motor balances the retarding torque of the load. This fact also determines the speed at which the motor will run at a definite load. Thus it is clear that the rotor current which has a direct relationship with the various performance of the induction motor, may be taken as a reference signal for studying the various performance of the induction motor running from no load to 125% of the full load condition. In the present study, the voltage across the resistance connected in series with the rotor terminal is taken as the reference signal and is fed to the microprocessor for proper comparison.

### 14.9.2 CALIBRATION CURVES

In order to draw various calibration curves, a 220 volt, 8 amps., 2 KW, 50 Hz, three phase induction motor has been selected and the following tests have been carried out :

### NO LOAD TEST

The experimental arrangement has been shown in Fig. 14.16. The induction motor is made to run at various impressed voltage (V) and the results obtained are shown in Table 14.9.1.

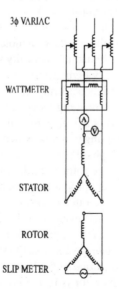

Fig. 14.16 Circuit Diagram For No Load Test

**Table 14.9.1 Data For No Load Test**
**Rated Voltage = 220 Volts.**

| APPLIED STATOR VOLTAGE IN VOLTS | NO LOAD CURRENT IN AMPS. | NO LOAD POWER IN WATTS. |
|---|---|---|
| 220 | 4.10 | 290 |
| 210 | 3.70 | 275 |
| 200 | 3.40 | 265 |
| 190 | 3.10 | 255 |
| 180 | 2.90 | 245 |
| 170 | 2.65 | 235 |
| 160 | 2.50 | 225 |
| 150 | 2.35 | 215 |
| 140 | 2.20 | 210 |
| 130 | 2.10 | 200 |
| 120 | 2.00 | 190 |
| 110 | 1.95 | 185 |
| 100 | 1.90 | 180 |
| 90 | 1.85 | 175 |
| 80 | 1.80 | 170 |

At no load, the stator of the induction motor mainly carries on the magnetising current necessary to sustain the main flux, since there is practically no armature reaction from the rotor and this is responsible for the iron and core losses, the friction and windage loss and a negligible amount of copper loss in stator winding.

As the voltage is reduced, the power and current fall because the main flux reduces simultaneously. The power curve is nearly parabolic at the voltages near normal value since the core loss is proportional to the square of the flux density and therefore of the voltage. The power versus square of the voltage curve is a straight line (shown in fig. 14.19) which gives the mechanical loss at the intersection with the power axis. Subtracting this mechanical loss from the total no load loss and correcting for the stator copper loss (which is very small), the core loss is found out.

If the stator resistance per phase at room temperature be R (dct), its value at the working temperature of 75°C is

$$R \text{ (dc 75)} = R \text{ (dct) } [1 + \alpha (75 - t)].$$

where $\alpha$ is the temperature coefficient of resistance of copper. Hence the ac resistance per phase of stator at 75°C is given by

$$R \text{ (ac 75)} = 1.6 \ R \text{ (dc 75)} = 1.6 \ R \text{ (dc t) } [1 + \alpha (75 - t) \ ].$$

## LOAD TEST

In order to draw the calibration curves representing various performance characteristics, the load test is to be performed , the circuit diagram being shown in fig. 14.18. A dc genetator loaded electrically has been used to load the motor under consideration. The motor is operated on normal voltage and frequency at loads between zero and 125% of full load, readings being taken of voltage, current, input power, slip and the rectified and magnified rotor reference voltage.

Under load condition, if P be the power input to the stator, V and I be, respectively, the line voltage and current applied to the stator, the power factor is given by

$$\cos \theta = \frac{P}{\sqrt{3} \ VI}$$

For the determination % slip, the oscillatory rotor voltage is observed and the time period for a single oscillation is computed by, T = t/20, where t represents time for 20 oscillations. Then the rotor frequency becomes f = 20/t and the percentage slip is given by, s = 40/t.

The power output from the stator or the power input to the rotor is given by

$$P_r = P - (3\,I^2\,r + P_c)$$

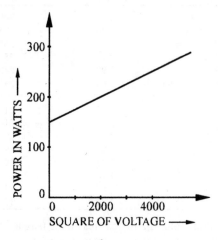

Fig. 14.17 (V$^2$–W) Characteristic

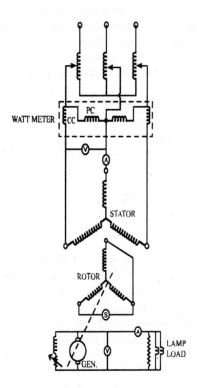

Fig. 14.18 Circuit Diagram for Load Test

where,

P = power input to the stator

I = stator line current,

r = ac resistance of the stator / phase at 75°C

$P_c$ = core loss at rated voltage and frequency

The mechanical power developed at the rotor shaft is

$$P_{mech} = P_r - \text{Rotor copper loss}$$
$$= P_r (1-s)$$

and the mechanical power output, P0, is given by

$$P_0 = P_{mech} - P_{fw}$$

where $P_{fw}$ is the friction and windage loss.

Hence the horse power output and the percentage efficiency of the machine are given by

$$HP = P_0 / 746$$

and $\% \eta = \dfrac{P_0}{P} \times 100$.

Computing all these results and having a correspondence between the reference signal and the corresponding microprocessor digital value, a family of calibration curves are drawn by plotting power factor, horsepower, percent efficiency, percent slip and speed against the microprocessor input digital values through ADC and are shown in Fig 14.19.

### 14.9.3 SYSTEM HARDWARE

To develop the present system, the complete hardware may be divided into three different parts : (1) the hardware for obtaining microprocessor reference voltage from the machine system, (2) the hardware for under voltage protection, and (3) the hardware for overload protection.

For obtaining reference voltage from the machine system, the rotor of the induction motor is shorted through a very small resistance. The voltage drop across the resistance acts as the reference signal. As stated earlier, in a three phase induction motor, a three phase ac supply is provided to the three phase star connect stator winding to produce a rotating magnetic field under the influence of which a three phase star connected short circuited rotor winding is rotated. The stator flux induces a back emf and produces induced current in the rotor winding, and the rotor rotates obeying the laws of electromagnetic induction. In each phase of the rotor, the resultant induced emf depends on the relative difference of the rotating magnetic field and the rotation of the rotor. Since the rotor terminals are shorted through very small resistors, a week alternating voltage signal is obtained across the terminals of each resistor. The magnitude of the signal increases with the reduction of the rotor speed upon application of load. But since the signal is very weak, it is properly amplified and rectified using the circuit shown in Fig 14.20.

The second part of the hardware is required for providing the under voltage protection. When the machine runs at no load with rated voltage, the microprocessor receives a signal at a particular value assigned by the particular hardware. When the applied voltage is below the rated voltage, the microprocessor receives a signal whose magnitude is less than the signal cporresponding to the rated voltage.

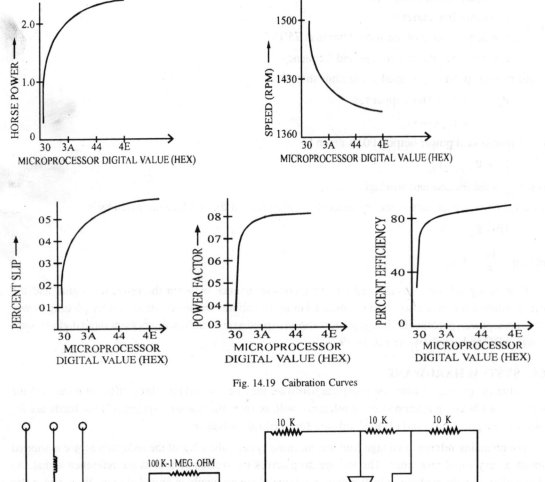

Fig. 14.19  Caibration Curves

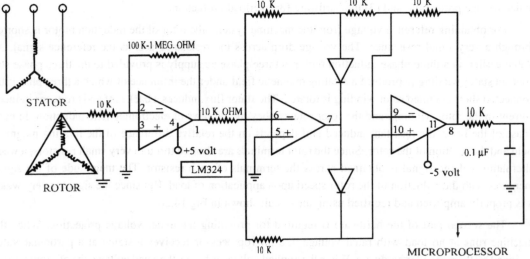

Fig. 14.20  System Hardware

In that case, the microprocessor will be allowed to generate a dc voltage (approximately equal to 5V) and send it through its output port to the hardware (Fig. 14.21) to create the alarming sound.

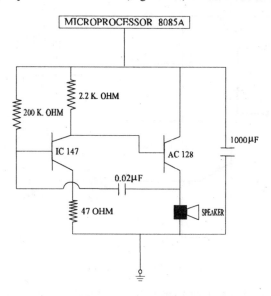

Fig. 14.21 Alarm Circuit

In the case of overloding beynod 125%, the speed of the motor drops below the speed corresponding to a load of 125% of the full load. Thus the microprocessor receives a reference voltage which is greater than voltage received at 125% of the full load condition. The microprocessor, after receiving and identifying the signal, generates and outputs a dc voltage of nearly 5 volt magnitude and actuates a relay through an optoisolator. The relay, after operating the contactor unit disconnects the machine from the supply. The schematic diagram of the overload protection is shown in fig. 14.22.

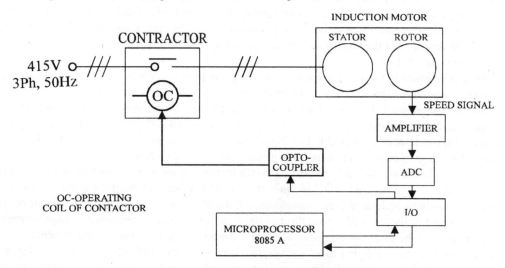

Fig. 14.22 Schematic Diagram of the over Load Protection

The MCT2E is used as an optical isolator between the microprocessor and the tripping circuit used for the protection purpose. The circuit diagram is shown in fig. 14.23.

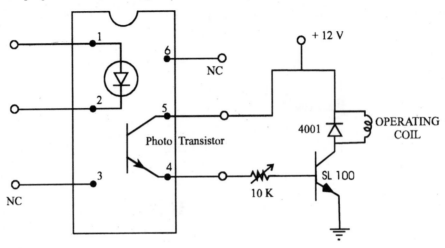

Fig. 14.23 Opto-Isolator Circuit

Receiving a signal from the microprocessor, the LED glows resulting in the photo current to flow through the photo transistor, the output of which is fed to the operating coil of the relay through a potentiometric arrangement and the SL 100. When SL 100 saturates the reverse biased diode, the current flows through the operating coil of the relay. The reversed biased diodes across the operating coil act as free wheeling diodes to protect the transistor.

### 14.9.4 SYSTEM SOFTWARE

The system software for the measurement and display of the slip (SL), power factor (PF) speed (SP) in revolution / minute, horse power (HP) and the percent efficiency (EF) of the system mainly consists of the main program, a search table to note various performances from no load to full load, sub-routines for under voltage and overload protection, and the character display of the different quantities (i.e., SL, PF, SP, HP and EF) in the data field of the display screen for a complete cycle of measurement. The flow chart of the system is shown in art. 14.9.5.

The developement of the search table is the most significant part of the measurement and the accuracy of the system depends on the accuracy of the characteristics stored in the search table.

From the calibration curves described earlier, for every possible microprocessor compatiable digital value, the different desired output quantities are calculated and stored in the memory of the microprocessor in the form of search table (shown in table 14.9.2) taken in an order. The microprocessor is initially calibrated with the voltage drop of amplified voltage drop of short circuited rotor reference voltage, applying the rated voltage to the machine under no load condition. Thus the first and the most important task of the investigation is to monitor the voltage from the ADC and then to note the machine performance corrresponding to the digital input from the search table. After initialisation of the I/O ports of the machine, the analog reference voltage is received by the microprocessor through the ADC and the digital reference voltage is brought to the accumulator and the same ins compared with the different values stored in the search table.

Corresponding to one digital input voltage, two successive memory locations each for slip, power factor and speed and three successive memory locations each for horse power and efficiency are stored with the corresponding decimal value. After the block search is made, data corresponding to the slip are first combined and displayed in the address field with a decimal dot sign at the beginning together with a character display "SL" in the data field indicating the slip. Then a specified time delay is allowed for the display of slip followed by the display of the data corresponding to the power factor with a decimal dot in the address field in the same manner together with a character display "PF" in the data field. Then again allowing a delay of desired time interval, data corresponding to the speed stored in the memory location are combined to display the same in the address field together with the character display "SP" in the data field indicating the instantaneous revolution per minute of the machine. Again allowing the specified time delay, the data corresponding to the horse power stored in the three memory location are combined and the most significant part is diplayed in the status field followed by a decimal dot, the least significant part being displayed in the address field together with the display "HP" in the data field. Ultimately after a specified delay, the data corresponding to the percent efficiency is displayed in the same manner as stated above in the status and address field. Then allowing a delay for a preassigned time interval, the microprocessor displays "END" and then taking new reference data from the system, performs the block search and continues to display the characteristics in the specified order.

The search table is bounded by the lower and the upper limits corresponding to the input rated voltage at no load and at the 125% over load conditions of the system. The digital input decreases as the input voltage decreased from the rated value and it increases with the load and crosses the upper limit when the load execeeds 125% of the rated load. In the former case, the microprocessor identifies the input signal and generates and outputs a voltage of magnitude 5 volts approximately to energise the alarm circuit.

Under the over load condition, the microprocessor after identifying the signal, generates and outputs a voltage to opperate a relay through the opto-coupler in order to disconnect the machine from the supply.

## 14.9.5 SYSTEM FLOW CHART

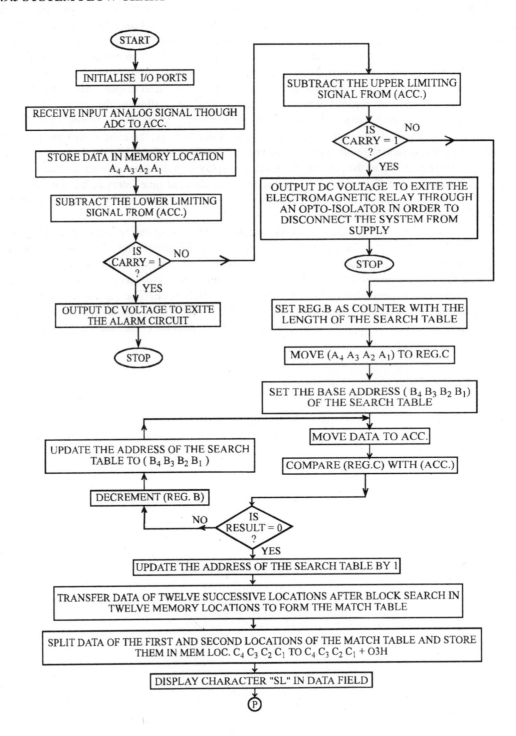

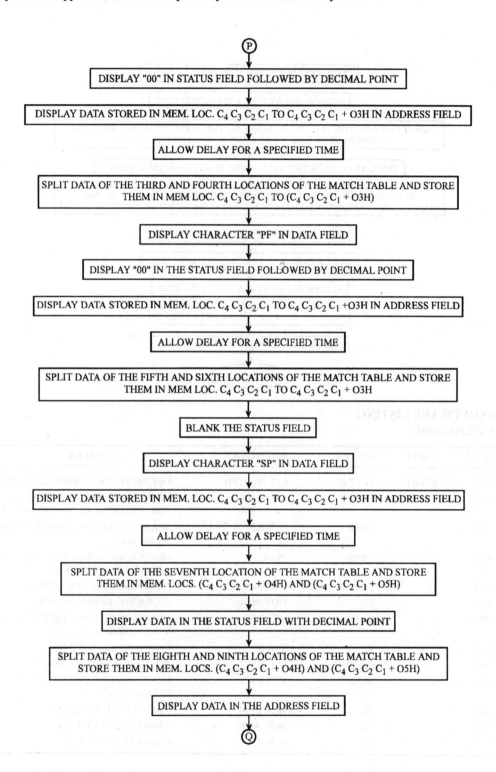

$P$

DISPLAY "00" IN STATUS FIELD FOLLOWED BY DECIMAL POINT

DISPLAY DATA STORED IN MEM. LOC. $C_4 C_3 C_2 C_1$ TO $C_4 C_3 C_2 C_1$ + 03H IN ADDRESS FIELD

ALLOW DELAY FOR A SPECIFIED TIME

SPLIT DATA OF THE THIRD AND FOURTH LOCATIONS OF THE MATCH TABLE AND STORE THEM IN MEM LOC. $C_4 C_3 C_2 C_1$ TO ($C_4 C_3 C_2 C_1$ + 03H)

DISPLAY CHARACTER "PF" IN DATA FIELD

DISPLAY "00" IN THE STATUS FIELD FOLLOWED BY DECIMAL POINT

DISPLAY DATA STORED IN MEM. LOC. $C_4 C_3 C_2 C_1$ TO $C_4 C_3 C_2 C_1$ +03H IN ADDRESS FIELD

ALLOW DELAY FOR A SPECIFIED TIME

SPLIT DATA OF THE FIFTH AND SIXTH LOCATIONS OF THE MATCH TABLE AND STORE THEM IN MEM LOC. $C_4 C_3 C_2 C_1$ TO $C_4 C_3 C_2 C_1$ + 03H

BLANK THE STATUS FIELD

DISPLAY CHARACTER "SP" IN DATA FIELD

DISPLAY DATA STORED IN MEM. LOC. $C_4 C_3 C_2 C_1$ TO $C_4 C_3 C_2 C_1$ + 03H IN ADDRESS FIELD

ALLOW DELAY FOR A SPECIFIED TIME

SPLIT DATA OF THE SEVENTH LOCATION OF THE MATCH TABLE AND STORE THEM IN MEM. LOCS. ($C_4 C_3 C_2 C_1$ + 04H) AND ($C_4 C_3 C_2 C_1$ + 05H)

DISPLAY DATA IN THE STATUS FIELD WITH DECIMAL POINT

SPLIT DATA OF THE EIGHTH AND NINTH LOCATIONS OF THE MATCH TABLE AND STORE THEM IN MEM. LOCS. ($C_4 C_3 C_2 C_1$ + 04H) AND ($C_4 C_3 C_2 C_1$ + 05H)

DISPLAY DATA IN THE ADDRESS FIELD

$Q$

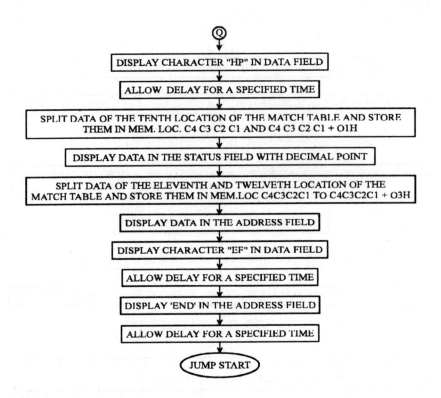

## 14.9.6 SOFTWARE LISTING
MAIN PROGRAME :

| MEM. LOC. | LABEL | OPCODE | MNEMONICS | REMARKS |
|-----------|-------|--------|-----------|---------|
| 44FD | START | 31 FF 47 | LXI SP 47FFH | DEFINE STACK AT MEM. LOC. 47FFH |
| 4500 | | 3E 90 | MVI A 90 | INITIALISE PORT A AS INPUT AND PORTS B AND C AS OUTPUT PORTS |
| 4502 | | D3 0B | OUT OB | SELECT I/O CHIP WITH CONTROL WORD 'OB' |
| 4504 | | DB 08 | IN 08 | GET INSTANTANEOUS SIGNAL V (I) IN ACC. THROUGH PORT A |
| 4506 | | 21 80 40 | LXI H 4080 | INITIALISE MEM. LOC. 4080 H |
| 4509 | | 77 | MOV M, A | STORE V(E) IN THE MEMORY |
| 450A | | 06 30 | MVI B 30 | MOVE LOWER LIMIT OF THE SIGNAL V (L) TO REG.B |
| 450C | | 90 | SUB B | COMPARE V(L) WITH V(I) |
| 450D | | DA 20 45 | JC LOW | IF V(I) < V (L), GO TO "LOW" |
| 4510 | | 06 52 | MVI B 52 | MOVE UPPER LIMIT V (U) OF THE SIGNAL TO REG.B |
| 4512 | | 4E | MOV C, M | TRANFER V(I) TO REG.C |
| 4513 | | 78 | MOV A, B | TRANSFER V(U) TO ACC. |
| 4514 | | 91 | SUB C | COMPUTE V (U) - V (I) |

| MEM. LOC. | LABEL | OPCODE | MNEMONICS | REMARKS |
|-----------|-------|--------|-----------|---------|
| 4515 | | DA 34 45 | JC HIGH | IF ·V (I) > V (U), GO TO HIGH TO DISCONNECT SYSTEM FROM SUPPLY |
| 4518 | | 06 23 | MVI B 23 | SET THE LENGTH OF THE SERCH TABLE IN REG.B AS COUNTER |
| 451A | | CD 40 45 | CALL PERFORM | CALL SUBROUTINE 'PERFORM' FOR DISPLAYING THE PERFORMANCE |
| 451D | LOOP3 | C3 00 45 | JMP START | REPEAT |

## 14.9.7 SUBROUTINE LISTING

SUBROUTINE 1. 'LOW' (THIS SUBPROGRAM OUTPUTS SIGNAL IN LOW/HIGH SEQUENCE WITH A DEFINITE DELAY TO EXICITE ALARM CIRCUIT) :

| MEM. LOC. | LABEL | OPCODE | MNEMONICS | REMARKS |
|-----------|-------|--------|-----------|---------|
| 4520 | LOW | 3E 80 | M VI A 80H | INITIALISE ALL PORTS AS OUTPUT PORTS |
| 4522 | | D3 0B | OUT 0B | SELECT I/O CHIP WITH CWR 0BH |
| 4524 | ALARM | AF | XRA A | CLEAR ACC. AND CARRY |
| 4525 | | D3 09 | OUT 09 | OUTPUT LOW THROUGH PORT-B |
| 4527 | | CD 60 45 | CALL DELAY | CALL SUBROUTINE DELAY |
| 452A | | 3E 01 | MVI A 01 | STORE 01H IN ACC. |
| 452C | | D3 09 | OUT 09 | OUTPUT THROUGH PORT-B |
| 452E | | CD 60 45 | CALL DELAY | CALL SUBROUTINE DELAY |
| 4531 | | C3 24 45 | JMP ALARM | JUMP TO ALARM FOR REPETITION |

SUBROUTINE 2. 'HIGH' (THIS PROGRAM DISCONNECTS THE MOTOR FROM SUPPLY) :

| MEM. LOC. | LABEL | OPCODE | MNEMONICS | REMARKS |
|-----------|-------|--------|-----------|---------|
| 4534 | HIGH | 3E 80 | MVI A 80 | ASSIGN ALL PORTS AS OUTPUT PORTS |
| 4536 | | D3 0B | OUT 0B | SELECT I/O CHIP WITH CWR OBH |
| 4538 | | 3E 01 | MVI A 01 | LOAD 01H IN ACC. |
| 453A | | D3 0A | OUT OA | OUTPUT THROUGH PORT-C |
| 453C | | CD 60 45 | CALL DELAY | CALL SUBROUTINE DELAY |
| 453F | | 76 | HLT | STOP |

SUBROUTINE 3. 'PERFORM' (THIS SUBROUTINE COMPARES THE INSTANTANEOUS DIGITAL SIGNAL WITH THOSE IN THE SEARCH TABLE AND AFTER OBTAINING THE MATCHING POINT, JUMPS TO THE SUBROUTINE "DP")

| MEM. LOC. | LABEL | OPCODE | MNEMONICS | REMARKS |
|-----------|-------|--------|-----------|---------|
| 4540 | PERFORM | 4E | MOV C,M | MOVE V(I) TO REG. C |
| 4541 | | 21 63 14 | LXI H 1463 H | GET STARTING ADDRESS OF SEARCH TABLE |
| 4544 | CMP | 5E | MOV E, M | TRANSFER THE MEMORY CONTENT TO REG.E |
| 4545 | | 7B | MOV· A, E | TRANSFER (REG.E) TO ACC. |
| 4546 | | B9 | CMP C | COMPARE V(I)    WITH THE CORRESPONDING SIGNAL IN THE SEARCH TABLE |

| MEM. LOC. | LABEL | OPCODE | MNEMONICS | REMARKS |
|---|---|---|---|---|
| 4547 | | CA 7A 46 | JZ DP | ON MATCHING, JUMP TO "DP" TO DISPLAY THE PERFORMANCE |
| 454A | | 05 | DCR B | DECREMENT REG.B SINCE ONE COMPARISN IS OVER |
| 454B | | 3E 0C | MVI A 0C | STORE 0C IN ACC. |
| 454D | | 85 | ADD L | ADD (REG.L) WITH (ACC.) |
| 454E | | 6F | MOV L, A | TRANSFER (ACC.) TO REG.L TO UPDATE THE LOWER HALF OF THE ADDRESS |
| 454F | | 3E 00 | MVI A 00 | CLEAR ACC. |
| 4551 | | 8C | ADC H | ADD CARRY AND (ACC.) WITH (REG.H) |
| 4552 | | 67 | MOV H, A | TRANSFER (ACC.) TO REG. H TO UPDATE THE UPPER HALF OF THE ADDRESS TO SET THE NEXT VALUE OF THE REFERENCE SIGNAL IN THE SEARCH TABLE |
| 4553 | | C3 44 45 | JMP CMP | JUMP TO 'CMP' FOR FURTHER COMPARISON |

SUBROUTINE 4. 'MTAB' (THIS SUBROUTINE COLLECTS THE DATA CORRESPONDING TO V(I) AND KEEPS THEM IN MATCH TABLE)

| MEM. LOC. | LABEL | OPCODE | MNEMONICS | REMARKS |
|---|---|---|---|---|
| 4556 | | 7E | MOV A, M | MOVE (MEMORY) TO ACC. |
| 4557 | | 32 50 42 | STA 4250 H | STORE (ACC.) TO MEM. LOC. 4250H |
| 455A | | 23 | INX H | INCREMENT NEXT MEM. LOC. |
| 455B | | 7E | MOV A, M | MOVE (MEMORY) TO ACC. |
| 455C | | 32 51 42 | STA 4251 H | STORE (ACC.) TO MEM. LOC. 4251H |
| 455F | | 23 | INX H | INCREMENT NEXT MEM. LOC. |
| 4560 | | 7E | MOV A, M | MOVE (MEMORY) TO ACC. |
| 4561 | | 32 52 42 | STA 4252 H | STORE (ACC.) TO MEM. LOC. 4252H |
| 4564 | | 23 | INX H | INCREMENT NEXT MEM. LOC. |
| 4565 | | 7E | MOV A, M | MOVE (MEMORY) TO ACC. |
| 4566 | | 32 53 42 | STA 4253 H | STORE (ACC.) TO MEM. LOC. 4253H |
| 4569 | | 23 | INX H | INCREMENT NEXT MEM. LOC. |
| 456A | | 7E | MOV A, M | MOVE (MEMORY) TO ACC. |
| 456B | | 32 54 42 | STA 4254 H | STORE (ACC.) TO MEM. LOC. 4254H |
| 456E | | 23 | INX H | INCREMENT NEXT MEM. LOC. |
| 456F | | 7E | MOV A, M | MOVE (MEMORY) TO ACC. |
| 4570 | | 32 55 42 | STA 4255 H | STORE (ACC.) TO MEM. LOC. 4255H |
| 4573 | | 23 | INX H | INCREMENT NEXT MEM. LOC. |
| 4574 | | 7E | MOV A, M | MOVE (MEMORY) TO ACC. |
| 4575 | | 32 56 42 | STA 4256 H | STORE (ACC.) TO MEM. LOC. 4256H |
| 4578 | | 23 | INX H | INCREMENT NEXT MEM. LOC. |
| 4579 | | 7E | MOV A, M | MOVE (MEMORY) TO ACC. |
| 457A | | 32 57 42 | STA 4257 H | STORE (ACC.) TO MEM. LOC. 4257H |
| 457B | | 23 | INX H | INCREMENT NEXT MEM. LOC. |

| MEM. LOC. | LABEL | OPCODE | MNEMONICS | REMARKS |
|---|---|---|---|---|
| 457E | | 7E | MOV A, M | MOVE (MEMORY) TO ACC. |
| 457F | | 32 58 42 | STA 4258 H | STORE (ACC.) TO MEM. LOC. 4258H |
| 4582 | | 23 | INX H | INCREMENT NEXT MEM. LOC. |
| 4583 | | 7E | MOV A, M | MOVE (MEMORY) TO ACC. |
| 4584 | | 32 59 42 | STA 4259 H | STORE (ACC.) TO MEM. LOC. 4259H |
| 4587 | | 23 | INX H | INCREMENT NEXT MEM. LOC. |
| 4588 | | 7E | MOV A, M | MOVE (MEMORY) TO ACC. |
| 4589 | | 32 5A 42 | STA 425A H | STORE (ACC.) TO MEM. LOC. 425AH |
| 458C | | 23 | INX H | INCREMENT NEXT MEM. LOC. |
| 458D | | 7E | MOV A, M | MOVE (MEMORY) TO ACC. |
| 458E | | 32 5B 42 | STA 425B H | STORE (ACC.) TO MEM. LOC. 425BH |
| 4591 | | C9 | RET | RETURN |

SUBROUTINE 5. 'SPLIT1' (THIS SUBROUTINE SPLITS 8-BIT DATA INTO TWO 4-BIT DATA AND KEEPS THEM IN MEM. LOC. 4102H AND 4103H RESPECTIVELY)

| MEM. LOC. | LABEL | OPCODE | MNEMONICS | REMARKS |
|---|---|---|---|---|
| 4592 | SPLIT1 | 7E | MOV A, M | MOVE (MEMORY) TO ACC. |
| 4593 | | 47 | MOV B, A | MOVE (ACC.) TO REG.B |
| 4594 | | E6 F0 | ANI F0 | AND F0H WITH (ACC.) |
| 4596 | | 07 | RLC | ROTATE (ACC.) TO LEFT, SHIFT MSB TO CARRY |
| 4597 | | 07 | RLC | ROTATE (ACC.) TO LEFT, SHIFT MSB TO CARRY |
| 4598 | | 07 | RLC | ROTATE (ACC.) TO LEFT, SHIFT MSB TO CARRY |
| 4599 | | 07 | RLC | ROTATE (ACC.) TO LEFT, SHIFT MSB TO CARRY |
| 459A | | 21 02 41 | LXI H 4102 H | INITIALISE MEM. LOC. 4102H |
| 459D | | 77 | MOV M, A | MOVE (ACC.) TO MEMORY |
| 459E | | 78 | MOV A, B | MOVE (REG.B) TO ACC. |
| 459F | | E6 0F | ANI 0F | AND 0FH WITH (ACC.) |
| 45A1 | | 23 | INX H | INITIALISE NEXT MEM. LOC. |
| 45A2 | | 77 | MOV M, A | MOVE (ACC.) TO MEMORY |
| 45A3 | | C9 | RET | RETURN |

SUBROUTINE 6. 'SPLIT2' (THIS SUBROUTINE SPLITS 8-BIT DATA INTO TWO 4-BIT DATA AND KEEPS THEM IN MEM. LOC. 4104H AND 4105H RESPECTIVELY )

| MEM. LOC. | LABEL | OPCODE | MNEMONICS | REMARKS |
|---|---|---|---|---|
| 45A4 | SPLIT2 | 7E | MOV A, M | MOVE (MEMORY) TO ACC. |
| 45A5 | | 47 | MOV B, A | MOVE (ACC.) TO REG.B |
| 45A6 | | E6 F0 | ANI F0 | AND F0H WITH (ACC.) |
| 45A8 | | 07 | RLC | ROTATE (ACC.) TO LEFT, SHIFT MSB TO CARRY |
| 45A9 | | 07 | RLC | ROTATE (ACC.) TO LEFT, SHIFT MSB TO CARRY |

| MEM. LOC. | LABEL | OPCODE | MNEMONICS | REMARKS |
|-----------|-------|--------|-----------|---------|
| 45AA | | 07 | RLC | ROTATE (ACC.) TO LEFT, SHIFT MSB TO CARRY |
| 45AB | | 07 | RLC | ROTATE (ACC.) TO LEFT, SHIFT MSB TO CARRY |
| 45AC | | 21 04 41 | LXI H 4104H | INITIALISE MEM. LOC. 4104H |
| 45AF | | 77 | MOV M, A | MOVE (ACC.) TO MEMORY |
| 45B0 | | 78 | MOV A, B | MOVE (REG.B) TO ACC. |
| 45B1 | | E6 0F | ANI 0F | AND 0FH WITH (ACC.) |
| 45B3 | | 23 | INX H | INITIALISE NEXT MEM. LOC. |
| 45B4 | | 77 | MOV M, A | MOVE (ACC.) TO MEMORY |
| 45B5 | | C9 | RET | RETURN |

SUBROUTINE 7. 'DDATAAF' (THIS SUBROUTINE DISPLAYS CONTENTS OF MEM. LOCS. 4102H TO 4105H    IN THE ADDRESS FIELD)

| MEM. LOC. | LABEL | OPCODE | MNEMONICS | REMARKS |
|-----------|-------|--------|-----------|---------|
| 45B6 | DDATAAF | 3E 01 | MVIA 01 | SELECT ADDRESS FIELD OF DISPLAY ON DISPLAY SCREEN |
| 45B8 | | 06 00 | MVIB 00 | DELETE DECIMAL POINT |
| 45BA | | 21 02 41 | LXI H 4102H | INITIALISE MEM. LOC. 4102H |
| 45BD | | CD 53 47 | CALL DISP | CALL SUBROUTINE "DISP" |
| 45C0 | | C9 | RET | RETURN |

SUBROUTINE 8. 'ZZSF' (THIS SUBROUTINE DISPLAYS 00H IN THE STATUS FIELD FOLLOWED BY A DECIMAL POINT)

| MEM. LOC. | LABEL | OPCODE | MNEMONICS | REMARKS |
|-----------|-------|--------|-----------|---------|
| 45C1 | ZZSF | 21 06 41 | LXI H 4106 H | INITIALISE MEM. LOC. 4106H |
| 45C4 | | 36 00 | MVIM 00 | STORE 00H IN THE MEMORY |
| 45C6 | | 23 | INX H | INITIALISE NEXT MEM. LOC. |
| 45C7 | | 36 00 | MVIM 00 | STORE 00H IN THE MEMORY |
| 45C9 | | 3E 00 | MVI A 00 | SELECT STATUS FIELD OF DISPLAY |
| 45CB | DDATASF | 06 01 | MVI B 01 | SELECT DECIMAL POINT. |
| 45CD | | 21 06 41 | LXI H 4106H | INITIALISE MEM.LOC. 4106H |
| 45D0 | | CD 53 47 | CALL DISP | CALL SUBROUTINE "DISP" |
| 45D3 | | C9 | RET | RETURN |

SUBROUTINE 9. 'DSL' (THIS SUBROUTINE DISPLAYS "SL" IN THE DATA FIELD)

| MEM. LOC. | LABEL | OPCODE | MNEMONICS | REMARKS |
|-----------|-------|--------|-----------|---------|
| 45D4 | DSL | 21 00 41 | LXI H 4100 H | INITIALISE MEM. LOC. 4100H |
| 45D7 | | 36 05 | MVIM 05 | SOTRE CODE FOR 'S' IN MEMORY |
| 45D9 | | 23 | INX H | INITIALISE NEXT MEM. LOC |
| 45DA | | 36 11 | MVIM 11 | STORE CODE FOR 'L' IN MEMORY |
| 45DC | | CD 40 46 | CALL DPDF | CALL SUBROUTINE "DPDF" |
| 45DF | | C9 | RET | RETURN |

## SUBROUTINE 10. 'DPF' (THIS SUBROUTINE DISPLAYS "PF" IN THE DATA FIELD)

| MEM. LOC. | LABEL | OPCODE | MNEMONICS | REMARKS |
|---|---|---|---|---|
| 45E0 | DPF | 21 00 41 | LXI H 4100H | INITIALISE MEM. LOC. 4100H |
| 45E3 |  | 36 12 | MVI M 12 | STORE CODE 'P' IN MEMORY |
| 45E5 |  | 23 | INX H | INITIALISE NEXT MEM. LOC. |
| 45E6 |  | 36 0F | MVI M 0F | STORE CODE FOR 'F' IN MEMORY |
| 45E8 |  | CD 40 46 | CALL DPDF | CALL SUBROUTINE "DPDF" |
| 45EB |  | C9 | RET | RETURN |

## SUBROUTINE 11. 'DSP' (THIS SUBROUTINE DISPLAYS "SP" IN THE DATA FIELD)

| MEM. LOC. | LABEL | OPCODE | MNEMONICS | REMARKS |
|---|---|---|---|---|
| 45EC | DSP | 21 00 41 | LXI H 4100H | INITIALISE MEM. LOC. 4100H |
| 45EF |  | 36 05 | MVI M 05 | STORE CODE FOR 'S' IN MEMORY |
| 45F1 |  | 23 | INX H | INITIALISE MEM. LOC. 4101H |
| 45F2 |  | 36 12 | MVI M 12 | STORE CODE FOR 'P' IN MEMORY |
| 45F4 |  | CD 40 46 | CALL DPDF | CALL SUBROUTINE "DPDF" |
| 45F7 |  | C9 | RET | RETURN |

## SUBROUTINE 12. 'DHP' THIS SUBROUTINE DISPLAYS "HP" IN THE DATA FIELD)

| MEM. LOC. | LABEL | OPCODE | MNEMONICS | REMARKS |
|---|---|---|---|---|
| 45F8 | DHP | 21 00 41 | LXI H 4100H | INITIALISE MEM. LOC. 4100H |
| 45FB |  | 36 10 | MVI M 10 | STORE CODE FOR 'H' IN MEMORY |
| 45FD |  | 23 | INX H | INITIALISE MEM. LOC. |
| 45FE |  | 36 12 | MVI M 12 | STORE CODE FOR 'P' IN MEMORY |
| 4600 |  | CD 40 46 | CALL DPDF | CALL SUBROUTINE "DPDF" |
| 4603 |  | C9 | RET | RETURN |

## SUBROUTINE 13. 'DEF' (THIS SUBROUTINE DISPLAYS "EF" IN THE DATA FIELD")

| MEM. LOC. | LABEL | OPCODE | MNEMONICS | REMARKS |
|---|---|---|---|---|
| 4604 | DEF | 21 00 41 | L X I H 4100H | INITIALISE MEM.LOC 4100H |
| 4607 |  | 36 0E | MVI M OE | STORE CODE FOR 'E' IN MEMORY |
| 4609 |  | 23 | INX H | INITIALISE NEXT MEM LOC. |
| 460A |  | 36 0F | MVI M 0F | STORE CODE FOR 'F' IN MEMORY |
| 460C |  | CD 40 46 | CALL SUBROUTING "DPDF" | CALL SUBROUTINE "DPDF" |
| 460F |  | C9 | RET | RETURN |

## SUBROUTINE 14. 'DEND' (THIS SUBROUTINE DISPLAYS 'END' AFTER ONE CYCLE OF DISPLAY.)

| MEM. LOC. | LABEL | OPCODE | MNEMONICS | REMARKS |
|---|---|---|---|---|
| 4610 | DEND | 21 00 41 | LXI H 4100H | INITIALISE MEM. LOC. 4100H |
| 4613 |  | 36 15 | MVI M 15 | STORE CODE FOR BLANK DISPLAY |
| 4615 |  | 23 | INX H | INITIALISE MEM. LOC. |
| 4616 |  | 36 15 | MVI M 15 | STORE CODE FOR BLANK DISPLAY |

| MEM. LOC. | LABEL | OPCODE | MNEMONICS | REMARKS |
|---|---|---|---|---|
| 4618 | | 23 | INX H | INITIALISE MEM. LOC. |
| 4619 | | 36 0E | MVI M 0E | STORE CODE FOR 'E' IN MEMORY |
| 461B | | 23 | INX H | INITIALISE MEM. LOC. |
| 461C | | 36 1E | MVI M 1E | STORE CODE FOR 'N' IN MEMORY |
| 461E | | 23 | INX H | INITIALISE MEM. LOC. |
| 461F | | 36 0D | MVI M 0D | STORE CODE FOR 'D' IN MEMORY |
| 4621 | | 23 | INX H | INITIALISE MEM. LOC. |
| 4622 | | 36 15 | MVI M 15 | STORE CODE FOR BLANK DISPLAY |
| 4624 | | 23 | INX H | INITIALISE MEM. LOC. |
| 4625 | | 36 15 | MVI M 15 | STORE CODE FOR BLANK DISPLAY |
| 4627 | | 23 | INX H | INITIALISE MEM. LOC. |
| 4628 | | 36 15 | MVI M 15 | STORE CODE FOR BLANK DISPLAY |
| 462A | | CD 40 46 | CALL DPDF | CALL SUBROUTINE 'DPDF" |
| 462D | | CD 4B 46 | CALL DPADD | CALL SUBROUTINE 'DPADD' |
| 4630 | | CD 56 46 | CALL DPSF | CALL SUBROUTINE 'DPSF' |
| 4633 | | C9 | RET | RETURN |

SUBROUTINE 15. 'BSF' (THIS SUBROUTINE MAKES THE STATUS FIELD BLANK)

| MEM. LOC. | LABEL | OPCODE | MNEMONICS | REMARKS |
|---|---|---|---|---|
| 4634 | BSF | 21 06 41 | LXI H 4106H | INITIALISE MEM.LOC. 4106H |
| 4637 | | 36 15 | MVIM 15 | STORE CODE FOR BLANK DISPALY |
| 4639 | | 23 | INXH | INITIALISE MEM.LOC. |
| 463A | | 36 15 | MVI M 15 | STORE CODE FOR BLANK DISPALY |
| 463C | | CD 56 46 | CALL DPSF | CALL SUBROUTINE 'DPSF' |
| 463F | | C9 | RET | RETURN |

16. SUBROUTINE DPDF (THIS SUBROUTINE DISPLAYS CONTENT OF 4100H AND 4101H IN DATA FIELD) :

| MEM. LOC. | LABEL | OPCODE | MNEMONICS | REMARKS |
|---|---|---|---|---|
| 4640 | DPDF | 3E 02 | MVI A 02 | SELECT DATA FIELD OF DISPLAY |
| 4642 | | 06 00 | MVI B 00 | DELETE DECIMAL POINT |
| 4644 | | 21 00 41 | LXI H 4100H | INITIALISE MEM. LOC. 4100H |
| 4647 | | CD 53 47 | CALL DISP | CALL SUBROUTINE 'DISP' |
| 464A | | C9 | RET | RETURN |

17. SUBROUTINE DPADD (THIS SUBROUTINE DISPLAYS CONTENT OF 4102H TO 4105H IN ADDRESS FIELD FOLLOWED BY A DECIMAL DOT) :

| MEM. LOC. | LABEL | OPCODE | MNEMONICS | REMARKS |
|---|---|---|---|---|
| 464B | DPADD | 3E 01 | MVI A 01 | SELECT ADDRESS FIELD OF DISPLAY |
| 464D | | 06 01 | MVI B 01 | DISPLAY DECIMAL POINT |
| 464F | | 21 02 41 | LXI H 4102H | INITIALISE MEM. LOC. 4102H |
| 4652 | | CD 53 47 | CALL DISP | CALL SUBROUTINE 'DISP' |
| 4655 | | C9 | RET | RETURN |

## 18. SUBROUTINE DPSF (THIS SUBROUTINE DISPLAYS CONTENT OF 4106H AND 4107H IN THE STATUS FIELD) :

| MEM. LOC. | LABEL | OPCODE | MNEMONICS | REMARKS |
|---|---|---|---|---|
| 4656 | DPSF | 3E 00 | MVI A 00 | SELECT STATUS FIELD OF DISPLAY |
| 4658 | | 06 00 | MVI B 00 | DELETE DECIMAL POINTS |
| 465A | | 21 06 41 | LXI H 4106H | INITIALISE MEM. LOC. 4106H |
| 465B | | CD 53 47 | CALL DISP | CALL SUBROUTINE 'DISP' |
| 4660 | | C9 | RET | RETURN |

## 19. SUBROUTINE : DELAY

| MEM. LOC. | LABEL | OPCODE | MNEMONICS | REMARKS |
|---|---|---|---|---|
| 4661 | DELAY | C5 | PUSH B | SAVE (BC) IN STACK |
| 4662 | | D5 | PUSH D | SAVE (DE) IN STACK |
| 4663 | | 21 85 40 | LXI H 4085H | INITILISE MEM. LOC. 4085H |
| 4666 | | 56 | MOV D, M | MOVE (MEMORY) TO REG.D |
| 4667 | JP1 | 21 86 40 | LXI H 4086 H | INITILISE MEM. LOC. 4086H |
| 466A | | 4E | MOV C, M | MOVE (MEMORY) TO REG.C |
| 466B | JP2 | CD 79 46 | CALL DLY | CALL SUBROUTINE 'DLY' |
| 466E | | 0D | DCR C | DECREMENT (REG.C) |
| 466F | | C2 6B 46 | JNZ JP2 | JUNP ON NO ZERO TO 'JP2' |
| 4672 | | 15 | DCR D | DECREMENT (REG.D) |
| 4673 | | C2 67 46 | JNZ JP1 | JUNP ON NO ZERO TO 'JP1' |
| 4676 | | D1 | POP D | RETRIVE (DE) |
| 4677 | | C1 | POP B | RETRIVE (BC) |
| 4678 | | C9 | RET | RETURN |
| 4679 | DLY | C5 | PUSH B | SAVE (BC) IN STACK |
| 467A | | 06 00 | MVIB 00 | STORE 00H IN REG.B |
| 467C | | 21 80 40 | LXI H 4080H | INITIALISE MEM. LOC. 4080H |
| 467F | | 23 | INX H | INITIALISE NEXT MEM.LOC |
| 4680 | | 70 | MOV M, B | MOVE (REG.B) TO MEMORY |
| 4681 | | C1 | POP B | RETRIVE (BC) |
| 4682 | | C9 | RET | RETURN |

## 20. SUBROUTINE DP THIS SUBROUTINE COLLECTS DATA FROM MATCH TABLE AND DISPLAYS DATA CORRESPONDING TO SLIP, PF, SPEED, HP AND EFFICIENCY IN CYCLIC ORDER AND DISPLAYS 'END' BEFORE RETURNING TO THE MAIN PROGRAM.

| MEM. LOC. | LABEL | OPCODE | MNEMONICS | REMARKS |
|---|---|---|---|---|
| 467A | DP | 23 | INX H | INITILISE NEXT MEM. LOC. |
| 467B | | CD 56 45 | CALL MTAB | CALL SUBROUTINE MTAB TO GET MATCH TABLE |
| 467E | | 21 50 42 | LXI H 4250 H | INITIALISE MEM. LOC 4250H TO GET UPPER PART OF SLIP |
| 4681 | | CD 92 45 | CALL SPLIT1 | CALL SUBROUTINE SPLIT1 |
| 4684 | | 21 51 42 | LXI H 4251 H | INITIALISE MEM. LOC 4251 H TO GET LOWER PART OF SLIP |
| 4687 | | CD A4 45 | CALL SPLIT2 | CALL SUBROUTINE SPLIT2 |
| 468A | | CD D4 45 | CALL DSL | CALL SUBROUTINE TO DISPLAY 'SL' IN THE DATA FIELD |

| MEM. LOC. | LABEL | OPCODE | MNEMONICS | REMARKS |
|---|---|---|---|---|
| 468D | | CD C1 45 | CALL ZZSF | CALL SUBROUTINE TO DISPLAY '00' IN THE STAUS FIELD WITH A DOT. |
| 4690 | | CD B6 46 | CALL DDATAAF | CALL SUBROUTINE TO DISPLAY 'DATA' CORRESPONDING TO SLIP IN THE ADDRESS FIELD |
| 4693 | | CD 61 45 | CALL DELAY | CALL SUBROUTINE 'DELAY' |
| 4696 | | 21 52 42 | LXI H 4252 H | INITIALISE MEM. LOC 4252 TO GET UPPER PART OF POWER FACTOR |
| 4699 | | CD 92 45 | CALL SPLIT1 | CALL SUBROUTINE SPLIT1 |
| 469C | | 21 53 42 | LXI H 4253 H | INITIALISE MEM. LOC. 4253H TO GET LOWER PART OF POWER FACTOR |
| 469F | | CD A4 45 | CALL SPLIT2 | CALL SUBROUTINE SPLIT2 |
| 46A2 | | CD E0 45 | CALL DPF | DISPLAY 'PF' IN THE DATA FIELD |
| 46A5 | | CD C1 45 | CALL ZZSF | DISPLAY '00' IN THE STATUS FIELD WITH A DOT. |
| 46A8 | | CD B6 45 | CALL DDATAAF | DISPLAY DATA FOR POWER FACTOR IN THE ADDRESS FIELD |
| 46AB | | CD 61 46 | CALL DELAY | CALL SUBROUTINE 'DELAY' |
| 46AE | | 21 54 42 | LXI H 4254 H | COLLECT DATA CORRESPONDEING TO UPPER PART OF SPEED FROM MEM.LOC. 4254 H |
| 46B1 | | CD 32 45 | CALL SPLIT1 | CALL SUBROUTINE SPLIT1 |
| 46B4 | | 21 52 42 | LXI H 4255 H | COLLECT DATA CORRESPONDING TO LOWER PART OF SPEED |
| 46B7 | | CD A4 45 | CALL SPLIT2 | CALL SUBROUTINE SPLIT2 |
| 46BA | | CD 34 46 | CALL BSF | BLANK THE STATUS FIELD |
| 46BD | | CD EC 45 | CALL DSP | DISPLAY "SP" IN THE DATA FIELD |
| 46C0 | | CD B6 45 | CALL DDATAAF | DISPLAY DATA CORRESPONDING TO SPEED IN THE ADDRESS FIELD |
| 46C3 | | CD 61 46 | CALL DELAY | CALL SUBROUTINE DELAY |
| 46C6 | | 21 56 42 | LXI H 4256 H | GET INTERGER PART OF HORSE POWER STORED IN MEM. LOC. 4256 H |
| 46C9 | | CD 92 45 | CALL SPLIT1 | CALL SUBROUTINE SPLIT1 |
| 46CC | | 21 57 42 | LXI H 4257 H | GET DATA CORRESPONDING TO UPPER DECIMAL PART OF HORSE POWER |
| 46CF | | CD A4 45 | CALL SPLIT2 | CALL SUBROUTINE SPLIT2 |
| 46D2 | | 21 02 41 | LXI H 4102 H | INITIALISE MEM. LOC. 4102H |
| 46D5 | | 7E | MOV A, M | TRANSFER (MEMORY) TO ACC. |
| 46D6 | | 23 | INX H | INITIALISE NEXT MEM. LOC. |
| 46D7 | | 46 | MOV B, M | TRANSFER MEMORY CONTENT TO REG.B |
| 46D8 | | 23 | INX H | INITIALISE NEXT MEM. LOC. |
| 46D9 | | 4E | MOV C, M | TRANSFER MEMORY CONTENT TO REG.C |
| 46DA | | 23 | INX H | INITIALISE NEXT MEM. LOC. |
| 46DB | | 56 | MOV D, M | TRANSFER MEMORY CONTENT TO REG.D |
| 46DC | | 21 06 41 | LXI H 4106 H | INTIALISE MEM.LOC. 4106H |
| 46DF | | 77 | MOV M,A | TRANSFER (ACC) TO MEMORY |
| 46E0 | | 23 | INX H | INITIALISE NEXT MEM.LOC. |

| MEM. LOC. | LABEL | OPCODE | MNEMONICS | REMARKS |
|---|---|---|---|---|
| 46E1 | | 70 | MOV M, B | TRANSFER (REG.B) TO MEMORY |
| 46E2 | | 21 02 41 | LXI H 4102H | INITIALISE MEM. LOC. 4102H |
| 46E5 | | 71 | MOV M,C | TRANSFER (REG.C) TO MEMORY |
| 46E6 | | 23 | INX H | INITIALISE NEXT MEM. LOC. |
| 46E7 | | 72 | MOV M, D | TRANSFER (REG.D) TO MEMORY |
| 46E8 | | 21 58 42 | LXI H 4258H | GET DATA CORRESPONDING TO THE LOWER DECIMAL PART OF HP. |
| 46EB | | CD A4 45 | CALL SPLIT2 | CALL SUBROUTINE SPLIT2 |
| 46EE | | CD C9 45 | CALL DDATASF | DISPLAY INTEGER PART IN THE STATUS FIELD WITH A DOT. |
| 46F1 | | CD B6 45 | CALL DDATAAF | DISPLAY DECIMAL PART IN THE ADDRESS FIELD |
| 46F4 | | CD F8 45 | CALL DHP | DISPLAY "HP" IN THE DATA FIELD |
| 46F7 | | CD 61 46 | CALL DELAY | CALL DELAY SUBROUTINE |
| 46FA | | 21 59 42 | LXI H 4259H | GET DATA CORRESPONDING TO THE INTEGER PART OF EFFICIENCY |
| 46FD | | CD 92 45 | CALL SPLIT1 | CALL SUBROUTINE SPLIT1 |
| 4700 | | 21 5A 42 | LXI H 425AH | GET DATA CORRESPONDING TO UPPER DECIMAL PART OF EFFICIENCY |
| 4703 | | CD A4 45 | CALL SPLIT2 | CALL SUBROUTINE SPLIT2 |
| 4706 | | 21 02 41 | LXI H 4102H | INITIALISE MEM LOC. 4102H |
| 4709 | | 7E | MOV A,M | TRANSFER (MEMORY) TO ACC. |
| 470A | | 23 | INX H | INITIALISE NEXT MEM. LOC. |
| 470B | | 46 | MOV B,M | TRANSFER MEMORY CONTENT TO REG. B |
| 470C | | 23 | INX H | INITIALISE NEXT MEM. LOC. |
| 470D | | 4E | MOV C,M | TRANSFER MEMORY CONTENT TO REG. D |
| 470E | | 23 | INX H | INITIALISE NEXT MEM. LOC. |
| 470F | | 56 | MOV D,M | TRANSFER MEMORY CONTENT TO REG. E |
| 4710 | | 21 06 41 | LXI H 4106 H | INITIALISE MEM. LOC. 4106H |
| 4713 | | 77 | MOV M,A | TRANSFER (ACC) TO MEMORY |
| 4714 | | 23 | INX H | INITIALISE NEXT MEM. LOC. |
| 4715 | | 70 | MOV M,B | TRANSFER (REG.B) TO MEMROY |
| 4716 | | 21 02 41 | LXI H 4102H | INITIALISE MEM. LOC. 4102H |
| 4719 | | 71 | MOV M,C | TRANSFER (REG.C) TO MEMORY |
| 471A | | 23 | INX H | INITIALISE NEXT MEM. LOC. |
| 471B | | 72 | MOV M,D | TRANSFER (REG.D) TO MEMORY |
| 471C | | 21 5B 42 | LXI H 425BH | GET DATA CORRESPONDING TO THE LOWER DECIMAL PART OF EF. |
| 471F | | CD A4 45 | CALL SPLIT2 | CALL SUBROUTINE SPLIT2 |
| 4722 | | CD C9 45 | CALL DDATASF | DISPLAY INTEGER PART OF EF IN STATUS FIELD WITH A DOT |
| 4725 | | CD B6 45 | CALL DDATAAF | DISPLAY DECIMAL PART IN THE ADDRESS FIELD |
| 4728 | | CE 04 46 | CALL DEP | DISPLAY "EF" IN THE DATA FIELD |
| 472D | | CD 61 46 | CALL DELAY | CALL DELAY SUBROUTINE |
| 472E | | CD 10 46 | CALL DEND | DISPLAY 'END' IN THE ADDRESS FIELD |
| 4731 | | CD 61 46 | CALL DELAY | CALL DELAY SUBROUTINE |
| 4734 | | C9 | RET | RETURN |

## 21. SUBROUTINE : DISP (MAIN DISPLAY SUBROUTINE)

| MEM. LOC. | LABEL | OPCODE | MNEMONICS | REMARKS |
|-----------|-------|--------|-----------|---------|
| 4753 | DISP | E5 | PUSH H | SAVE (HL) IN STACK |
| 4754 | | B7 | ORA A | CALEAR CARRY |
| 4755 | | CA 64 47 | JZ J1 | JUMP ON ZERO TO J1 |
| 4758 | | E6 02 | ANI 02 | AND 02 WITH (ACC) |
| 475A | | C2 6B 47 | JNZ J2 | JUMP ON NO ZERO TO J2 |
| 475D | | 0E 04 | MVI C 04 | MOVE IMMEDIATE 04 H TO REG.C |
| 475F | | 3E 92 | MVI A 92 | MOVE IMMEDIATE 92H TOACC |
| 4761 | | C3 6F 47 | JUMP OUT0 | JUMP TO OUT0 |
| 4764 | J1 | 0E 02 | MVI C 02 | MOVE IMMEDIATE 02H TO REG.C |
| 4766 | | 3E 90 | MVI A 90 | MOVE IMMEDIATE 90H TO ACC. |
| 4768 | | C3 6F 47 | JMP OUT0 | JUMP TO OUT0 |
| 476B | J2 | 0E 02 | MVI C 02 | MOVE IMMEDIATE 02H TO REG.C |
| 476D | | 3E 96 | MVI A 96 | MOVE IMMEDIATE 96H TO ACC. |
| 476F | OUT0 | D3 03 | OUT 03 | OUTPUT THROUGH PC |
| 4771 | OUT1 | 7E | MOV A,M | MOVE (MEMORY) TO ACC. |
| 4772 | | E5 | PUSH H | SAVE (HL) IN STACK |
| 4773 | | 21 90 47 | LXI H 4790 H | INITIALISE MEM.LOC. 4790H |
| 4776 | | 85 | ADD L | ADD (ACC.) WITH (REG.L) |
| 4777 | | 6F | MOV L,A | MOVE (ACC.) TO REG.L |
| 4778 | | 7E | MOV A,M | MOVE (MEMORY) TO ACC. |
| 4779 | | 61 | MOV H,C | MOVE (REG.C) TO REG.H |
| 477A | | 25 | DCR H | DECREMENT (REG.H) |
| 477B | | C2 84 47 | JNZ OUT2 | JUMP ON NO ZERO TO OUT 2 |
| 477E | | 05 | DCR D | DECREMENT (REG.D) |
| 477F | | C2 84 47 | JNZ OUT2 | JUMP ON NO ZERO TO OUT 2 |
| 4782 | | F6 08 | ORI 08 | OR (ACC) WITH 08H |
| 4784 | OUT2 | 2F | CMA | COMPLEMENT (ACC.) |
| 4785 | | D3 00 | OUT 00 | OUTPUT THROUGH PA |
| 4787 | | E1 | POP H | RETRIVE (HL) |
| 4788 | | 23 | INX H | INCREMENT (HL) |
| 4789 | | 0D | DCR C | DECREMENT (REG.C) |
| 478A | | C2 71 47 | JNZ OUT1 | JUMP ON NO ZERO TO OUT1 |
| 478D | | E1 | POP H | RETRIVE (HL) |
| 478E | | C9 | RET | RETURN |

| MEM. LOC. | DATA CODE | DATA TO BE LOADED | LETTER/CHARACTER |
|-----------|-----------|-------------------|------------------|
| 4790 | F3 | 00 | 0 |
| 4791 | 60 | 01 | 1 |
| 4792 | B5 | 02 | 2 |
| 4793 | F4 | 03 | 3 |
| 4794 | 66 | 04 | 4 |
| 4795 | D6 | 05 | 5 |
| 4796 | D7 | 06 | 6 |
| 4797 | 70 | 07 | 7 |
| 4798 | F7 | 08 | 8 |

| MEM. LOC. | DATA CODE | DATA TO BE LOADED | LETTER/CHARACTER |
|---|---|---|---|
| 4799 | 76 | 09 | 9 |
| 479A | 77 | 0A | A |
| 479B | C7 | 0B | B |
| 479C | 93 | 0C | C |
| 479D | E5 | 0D | D |
| 479E | 97 | 0E | E |
| 479F | 17 | 0F | F |
| 47A0 | 67 | 10 | G |
| 47A1 | 83 | 11 | L |
| 47A2 | 37 | 12 | P |
| 47A3 | 60 | 13 | I |
| 47A4 | 05 | 14 | r |
| 47A5 | 00 | 15 | BLANK |
| 47A6 | 45 | 16 | n |

**Table 14.9.2 Search Table**

| MEMORY ADDRESS | DATA CORRESPONDING TO | | | | | |
|---|---|---|---|---|---|---|
| | REF. SIGNAL | SLIP | POWER FACTOR | SPEED | HORSE POWER | EFFICIENCY |
| 1463 | 30 | | | | | |
| 1464 | | 0125 | 4000 | 1495 | 007500 | 525000 |
| 1470 | 31 | | | | | |
| 1471 | | 0170 | 3564 | 1482 | 002052 | 278400 |
| 147D | 32 | | | | | |
| 147E | | 0203 | 5750 | 1475 | 011375 | 450000 |
| 148A | 33 | | | | | |
| 148B | | 0280 | 6950 | 1452 | 014375 | 662611 |
| 1497 | 34 | | | | | |
| 1498 | | 0320 | 7602 | 1444 | 016077 | 695000 |
| 14A4 | 35 | | | | | |
| 14A5 | | 0348 | 7800 | 1439 | 017563 | 710000 |
| 14B1 | 36 | | | | | |
| 14B2 | | 0367 | 7938 | 1435 | 018564 | 719399 |
| 14BE | 37 | | | | | |
| 14BF | | 0380 | 8013 | 1431 | 019250 | 727500 |
| 14CB | 38 | | | | | |
| 14CC | | 0394 | 8075 | 1428 | 019813 | 732500 |
| 14D8 | 39 | | | | | |
| 14D9 | | 0405 | 8113 | 1425 | 020250 | 736250 |
| 14E5 | 3A | | | | | |
| 14E6 | | 0415 | 8150 | 1422 | 020688 | 740000 |
| 14F2 | 3B | | | | | |
| 14F3 | | 0425 | 8165 | 1420 | 021063 | 742500 |
| 14FF | 3C | | | | | |
| 1500 | | 0435 | 8188 | 1417 | 021500 | 743750 |
| 150C | 3D | | | | | |
| 150D | | 0443 | 8200 | 1415 | 021750 | 747507 |
| 1519 | 3E | | | | | |

| MEMORY ADDRESS | DATA CORRESPONDING TO | | | | | |
|---|---|---|---|---|---|---|
| | REF. SIGNAL | SLIP | POWER FACTOR | SPEED | HORSE POWER | EFFICIENCY |
| 151A | | 0450 | 8238 | 1412 | 022063 | 747500 |
| 1426 | 3F | | | | | |
| 1427 | | 0458 | 8250 | 1410 | 022375 | 748125 |
| 1533 | 40 | | | | | |
| 1534 | | 0465 | 8275 | 1408 | 022625 | 748750 |
| 1540 | 41 | | | | | |
| 1541 | | 0471 | 8300 | 1406 | 022875 | 749375 |
| 15AD | 42 | | | | | |
| 15AE | | 0478 | 8315 | 1405 | 023125 | 750000 |
| 155A | 43 | | | | | |
| 155B | | 0485 | 8325 | 1404 | 020375 | 750625 |
| 1567 | 44 | | | | | |
| 1568 | | 0491 | 8338 | 1402 | 023625 | 751250 |
| 1574 | 45 | | | | | |
| 1575 | | 0496 | 8350 | 1401 | 023750 | 752500 |
| 1581 | 46 | | | | | |
| 1582 | | 0503 | 8363 | 1401 | 024000 | 753125 |
| 158E | 47 | | | | | |
| 158F | | 0508 | 8375 | 1400 | 024250 | 753750 |
| 159B | 48 | | | | | |
| 159C | | 0513 | 8388 | 1400 | 024375 | 755000 |
| 15A8 | 49 | | | | | |
| 15A9 | | 0518 | 8394 | 1400 | 024625 | 755375 |
| 15B5 | 4A | | | | | |
| 15B6 | | 0520 | 8400 | 1399 | 024813 | 755400 |
| 15C2 | 4B | | | | | |
| 15C3 | | 0525 | 8405 | 1399 | 025000 | 755175 |
| 15CF | 4C | | | | | |
| 15D0 | | 0528 | 8408 | 1400 | 025125 | 755500 |
| 15DC | 4D | | | | | |
| 15DD | | 0530 | 8412 | 1400 | 025375 | 756250 |
| 15E9 | 4E | | | | | |
| 15EA | | 0534 | 8425 | 1401 | 025438 | 756750 |
| 15F6 | 4F | | | | | |
| 15F7 | | 0536 | 8438 | 1400 | 025625 | 757000 |
| 1603 | 50 | | | | | |
| 1604 | | 0538 | 8440 | 1402 | 025813 | 757250 |
| 1610 | 51 | | | | | |
| 1611 | | 0540 | 8443 | 1399 | 025938 | 757500 |
| 161D | 52 | | | | | |
| 161E | | 0544 | 8450 | 1399 | 026063 | 757750 |

# 15. Single Chip Microcomputers (Microcontroller)

Intel first produced its 8048 family of Single chip Microcomputers along with 8022, 8041, 8048, 8051, 8052 and 8094 series. Each one of these series includes a number of different versions and practically these products are various enhancements of 8048 family with a lot of modifications. At present, a large number of manufacturers are producing their own products viz. Zilog Z-8, Motorola MC 6801, MC 68701, RCA CPD 1804 etc. These are ideally suited for small systems, dedicated systems and sub-systems of a larger one. Its popularity and usages are highly increasing. Some of these are associated with high level language, A/D converters, analog outputs etc. Sometimes these are called Microcontrollers and in industries, they are extensively used.

Intel MCS-51 family is a highly versatile general purpose 8-bit system. Its enhanced architecture offers applications requiring a high degree of on-chip functionality. It is most suitable for control-oriented applications. The family includes 8031, 8051 and 8751. The 8031 has control oriented CPU with RAM and I/O. It is actually a ROM-less version of the 8051 and it fetches all instructions from external memory. The 8051 has 4K-bytes of ROM whereas the 8751 is an 8051 having EPROM instead of ROM.

## 15.1 INTEL 8031

The CPU of INTEL 8031 is very fast with larger number of powerful single cycle opcodes. Unlike other general purpose microprocessors such as 8085, Z-80, 6502, 6809 etc. where a lot of hardware is necessary, the single chip 8031 microcomputer needs very few simple interfaces to be associated with, due to its very large scale integration on a single chip. It includes a clock, interrupts, timers, UART, I/O Ports, RAM etc. This chip is ideal in control, Instrumentation, robotics and data processing applications. The internal architecture of the 8031 is shown in fig. 15.1

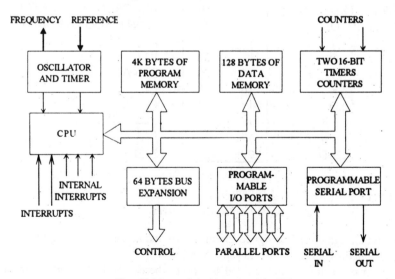

Fig. 15.1 Internal Architecture of the 8031

## 15.2 DESCRIPTION OF THE 8031 CHIP

The 8031 operates on 5V supply with power down mode for saving internal RAM contents. It possesses

128 bytes of register-memory on chip. Four banks of eight registers have special functions, and two registers have special indexing capability in each bank.

The program memory size of the 8031 is 64 KB wide, switchable in 4K banks. It also has fully addressable data memory of 64 KB. It is equipped with 12 MHz crystal having clock time 1 micro-sec instruction cycle. It has two level priority, level or edge triggerable external interrupts, two timer interrupts and one UART interrupt.

The 8031 possesses one bit-addressable 8 bit I/O port and one UART port which is high speed programmable. Two timer inputs may be gated by interrupt inputs. Two multimode- 16 bit (or 8-bit) timers/counters enhance the system performance.

The ALU has the capability of performing binary or decimal arithmetic, boolean bit processing for control logic programs, 8 bit multiplication or division in 4 micro-sec, parity computation, overflow detection etc.

## 15.3 PIN CONFIGURATION OF THE 8031 AND INTEL 51 - FAMILY
The pin configuration of an INTEL 51 FAMILY has been presented in fig. 15.2

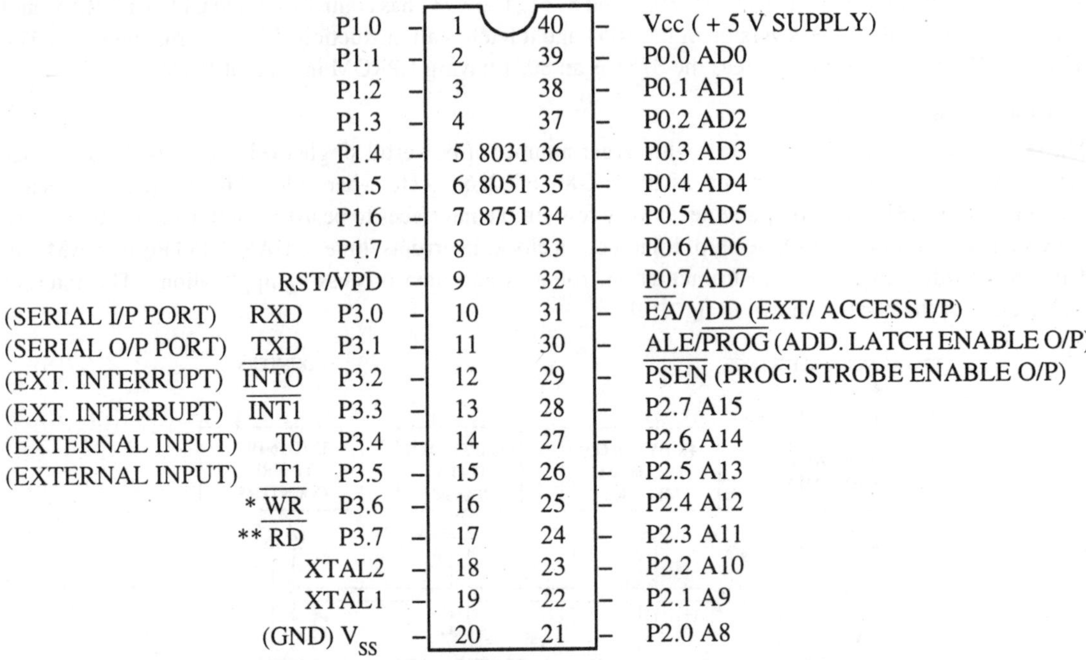

```
                           P1.0  ─| 1      40 |─  Vcc ( + 5 V SUPPLY)
                           P1.1  ─| 2      39 |─  P0.0 AD0
                           P1.2  ─| 3      38 |─  P0.1 AD1
                           P1.3  ─| 4      37 |─  P0.2 AD2
                           P1.4  ─| 5 8031 36 |─  P0.3 AD3
                           P1.5  ─| 6 8051 35 |─  P0.4 AD4
                           P1.6  ─| 7 8751 34 |─  P0.5 AD5
                           P1.7  ─| 8      33 |─  P0.6 AD6
                       RST/VPD   ─| 9      32 |─  P0.7 AD7
(SERIAL I/P PORT)  RXD  P3.0  ─| 10      31 |─  EA/VDD (EXT/ ACCESS I/P)
(SERIAL O/P PORT)  TXD  P3.1  ─| 11      30 |─  ALE/PROG (ADD. LATCH ENABLE O/P)
(EXT. INTERRUPT)  INT0  P3.2  ─| 12      29 |─  PSEN (PROG. STROBE ENABLE O/P)
(EXT. INTERRUPT)  INT1  P3.3  ─| 13      28 |─  P2.7 A15
(EXTERNAL INPUT)   T0   P3.4  ─| 14      27 |─  P2.6 A14
(EXTERNAL INPUT)   T1   P3.5  ─| 15      26 |─  P2.5 A13
                  * WR   P3.6  ─| 16      25 |─  P2.4 A12
                 ** RD   P3.7  ─| 17      24 |─  P2.3 A11
                       XTAL2   ─| 18      23 |─  P2.2 A10
                       XTAL1   ─| 19      22 |─  P2.1 A9
                    (GND) Vss  ─| 20      21 |─  P2.0 A8
```

\*   EXTERNAL DATA MEMORY WRITE STROBE

\*\* EXTERNAL DATA MEMORY READ STROBE

Fig. 15.2 Pin Configuration of INTEL 51 Family

In this configuration, Pin - Vss is assigned for circuit ground potential and a supply voltage of +5 V is to be applied to Vcc pin during operation and programming.

Port-0 is an 8-bit open drain bi-directional I/O port whereas ports 1, 2 and 3 are all 8-bit quasi bi-directional I/O ports. Further, Port-0 is the multiplexed low-order address bus when using external memory. It is used for data input and data output during programming. Port-1 is used for the low-order address byte when accessing external memory. Port-2 emits the high-order address byte when accessing external memory.

It is used for the high-order address and the control signals during programming. Port-3 contains the interrupt, timer, serial port and $\overline{RD}$ and $\overline{WR}$ pins those are used by various options. The output latch corresponding to a secondary function must be programmed to a one (1) for the function to operate. The secondary functions are assinged to the pins of Port-3 as under:

RXD/data (P3.0) - serial port's receiver data input (asynchronous) or data input/output (synchronous).

TXD/clock (P3.1) - serial port's transmitter data output (asynchronous) or clock output (synchronous).

$\overline{INT0}$ (P3.2) - Interrupt 0 input or gate control input for counter 0

$\overline{INT1}$ (P3.3) - Interrupt 1 input or gate control input for counter 1

T0 (P3.4) - Input to counter 0

T1 (P3.5) - Input to counter 1

$\overline{WR}$ (P3.6) - The write control signal which latches the data byte from port 0 into the external data memory

$\overline{RD}$ (P3.7) - The read control signal which enables external data memory to Port 0.

RST/VPD - A low to high transition on this Pin resets the 8051. If VPD is held within +5 V while Vcc drops below 5V, VPD will provide stand-by power to the RAM. When VPD is low, the RAM's current is drawn from Vcc.

$\overline{ALE}$/PROG - This pin provides ALE output used for latching the address into external memory during normal operation. It also receives the program pulse input during EPROM programing.

$\overline{PSEN}$ - It is the program store enable output which is a contorl signal that enables the external program memory to the bus during normal fetch operations.

$\overline{EA}$/VD - When this pin is held at a TTL high level, the 8051 executes instructions from the internal ROM/EPROM when the PC is less than 4096. When it is held at a TTL low level, the 8051 fetches all EPROM programming supply voltage.

XTAL1 - It is the input to the oscillator's high gain amplifier which is intended for use as a crystal or external source can be used.

XTAL2 - It is the output from the oscillator's amplifier which is required when a crystal is used.

A Simplified configuration of INTEL 51-family has been shown in Fig. 15.3.

## 15.4 ORGANISATION OF THE 8031

Intel produced the 8022 and 8048 series of single chip microcontroller earlier. 8031 family is software compatible with this series, but not at the code level. Its instruction set is designed to make the program efficient both in space and speed. An instuction cycle may take only 1 micro-sec (with 12MHz Crystal) and most instructions take only 1 or 2 micro-sec, though multiplication and division require 4 microsecs. The 8031 fetches two bytes of codes per cycle. About 110 instructions are available with direct, immediate, extended, relative, indexed and indirect addressing modes. The lengths of opcodes vary from 1 to 3 bytes.

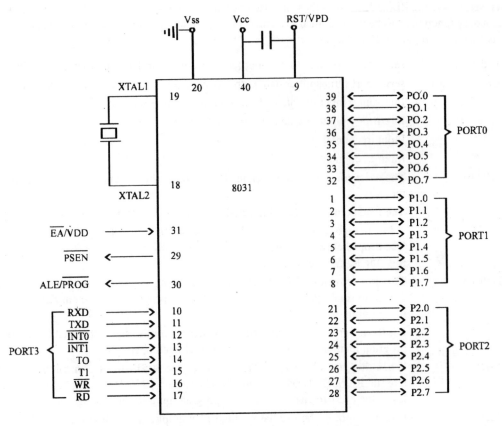

Fig 15.3 Simplified configuration of INTEL 51-Family

There are two accumulators, 'A' and 'B', each of 8 bits. The Acc. 'A' is used as a general purpose accumulator whereas Acc. B is used only in multiplication and division. The status flags are in the flag register called Programe Status Word (PSW). There is a 16 bit Program Counter (PC) to access upto 64K program or data memory. The Stack Pointer (SP) is of 8 bit length, which points at the internal RAM of 128 bytes only and fills upwards. There is a 16 bit Data Pointer (DP) comprising of two 8 bit registers DPH and DPL to access data memory. There are 8 general purpose 8 bit registers, R0, R1, R2, R3, R4, R5, R6 and R7,

This chip has 128 bytes of internal RAM which are treated as general purpose registers and RAM spaces. Address 00 to 1F may be assigned as general purpose registers. Address 20 to 2F are bit addressable, and addresses 30 to 7F are kept preserved as general purpose internal RAM space. With 8031, it is possible to connect externally, a 2K RAM along with 4K EPROM. Though 8031 is not intended to execute any programs in the RAM, using special hardware, this facility may be incorporated. Another interesting point is that unlike 8085, higher byte comes first in 8031. Mereover, this system has the bit addressing facility. To address the bits from RAM location 20 to 2F (16 bytes or 128 bits), it is required to address them by 00 to 7F. Even the ports, accumulators, registers are bit addressable. The special function Registers along with their bit addresses shown in the parenthesis are :

Accumulator 'Acc' or 'A' (EOH)
B-Register 'B' (FOH)
Program Status Word 'PSW' (DOH)
Stack Pointer 'SP' (81H)
Data Pointer 'DPTR' consisting of Data Pointer low 'DPL' (82H) and Data Pointer high 'DPH' (83H)
Timer / Counter Control Register 'TCON' (88H)
Timer / Counter Mode Register 'TMOD' (89H)
Timer / Counter 0 (low byte) 'TL0' (8AH)
Timer / Counter 0 (high byte) 'TH0' (8CH)
Timer / Counter 1 (Low byte) 'TL1' (8BH)
Timer / Counter 1 (High byte) 'TH1' (8DH)
Port 0 'P0' (80H)
Port 1 'P1' (8CH)
Port 2 'P2' (8BH)
Port 3 'P3' (8DH)
Serial Port Control Register 'SCON' (98H)
Receive Serial Buffer 'SBUF' (99 H)
Internal Enable Control Register 'IE' (A8H)
Internal Priority Register 'IP' (B8H)

Out of these Registers, TCON, SCON, IE, IP, P0, P1, P2, P3, PSW, A and B Registers are bit addressable. Table 15. 1 shows the Bit Address Maps and Table 15.2 presents RAM bit Address.

**Table 15.1**
**Hardware Register Bit Address**

| DIRECT BYTE ADDRESS | BIT ADDRESS | | | | | | | | HARDWARE REGISTER SYMBOL |
|---|---|---|---|---|---|---|---|---|---|
| | D7 | D6 | D5 | D4 | D3 | D2 | D1 | D0 | |
| 080H | 87 | 86 | 85 | 84 | 83 | 82 | 81 | 80 | P0 |
| 090H | 97 | 96 | 95 | 94 | 93 | 92 | 91 | 90 | P1 |
| 0A0H | A7 | A6 | A5 | A4 | A3 | A2 | A1 | A0 | P2 |
| 0B0H | B7 | B6 | B5 | B4 | B3 | B2 | B1 | B0 | P3 |
| 088H | 8F | 8E | 8D | 8C | 8B | 8A | 89 | 88 | TCON |
| 098H | 9F | 9E | 9D | 9C | 9B | 9A | 99 | 98 | SCON |
| 0A8H | AF | - | - | AC | AB | AA | A9 | A8 | IE |
| 0B8H | - | - | - | BC | BB | BA | B9 | B8 | IP |
| 0D0H | D7 | D6 | D5 | D4 | D3 | D2 | D1 | D0 | PSW |
| 0E0H | E7 | E6 | E5 | E4 | E3 | E2 | E1 | E0 | ACC |
| 0F0H | F7 | F6 | F5 | F4 | F3 | F2 | F1 | F0 | B |

The stack pointer 'SP' is linked with the internal RAM and hence it is of 8-bit lengh. After a reset, the monitor of this system initialises SP to 60. Since SP of the 8031 is designed to be filled up in upward direction (and not in  downward direction as in the  case of 8085 microprocessor), stack is of 32 locations only from 60 to 7F in the internal RAM. PC point at the external program memory only. The internal RAM space 00 to 1F are divided into four banks of 8 bytes and only one bank is addressable at a time in the name of registers R0 to R7. These registers are addressed by 00 to 07,08 to 0F, 10to 17 and 18 to 1F in banks 0, 1,2 and 3 respectively although these locations may be directly addressable at any time. The registers R0 and R1 have the indexing capability. They point at the internal RAM in indexing or indirect addressing

The program flags are arranged in PSW as follows:

| | D7 | D6 | D5 | D4 | D3 | D2 | D1 | D0 |
|------|----|----|----|-----|-----|----|----|---|
| PSW: | CY | AC | F0 | RS1 | RS0 | OV | -  | P |

The CY flag is used in arithmetic and logic operations while AC in decimal arithmetic. F0 is an indicator in any program which may be set or cleared by instructions to indicate something in the program as required by the user. The RS1 and RS0 select the register bank. Upon reset, the first bank (00 to 07) is selected. These two bits may be set to 00 , 01 10 and 11 to select the desired bank. In signed binary addition , if there be a carry from bit 6 to 7 , OV is set implying that the result needs correction. P indicates the parity in Acc. 'A'.

**Table 15.2**

**Bit Address Map**

| RAM BYTES | BIT ADDRESS | | | | | | | |
|-----------|----|----|----|----|----|----|----|----|
|           | D7 | D6 | D5 | D4 | D3 | D2 | D1 | D0 |
| 2FH | 7F | 7E | 7D | 7C | 7B | 7A | 79 | 78 |
| 2EH | 77 | 76 | 75 | 74 | 73 | 72 | 71 | 70 |
| 2DH | 6F | 6E | 6D | 6C | 6B | 6A | 69 | 68 |
| 2CH | 67 | 66 | 65 | 64 | 63 | 62 | 61 | 60 |
| 2BH | 5F | 5E | 5D | 5C | 5B | 5A | 59 | 58 |
| 2AH | 57 | 56 | 55 | 54 | 53 | 52 | 51 | 50 |
| 29H | 4F | 4E | 4D | 4C | 4B | 4A | 49 | 38 |
| 28H | 47 | 46 | 45 | 44 | 43 | 42 | 41 | 40 |
| 27H | 3F | 3E | 3D | 3C | 3B | 3A | 39 | 38 |
| 26H | 37 | 36 | 35 | 34 | 33 | 32 | 31 | 30 |
| 25H | 2F | 2E | 2D | 2C | 2B | 2A | 29 | 28 |
| 24H | 27 | 26 | 25 | 24 | 23 | 22 | 21 | 20 |
| 23H | 1F | 1E | 1D | 1C | 1B | 1A | 19 | 18 |
| 22H | 17 | 16 | 15 | 14 | 13 | 12 | 11 | 10 |
| 21H | 0F | 0E | 0D | 0C | 0B | 0A | 09 | 08 |
| 20H | 07 | 06 | 05 | 04 | 03 | 02 | 01 | 00 |

| 1FH | BANK 3 |
|-----|--------|
| 18H | |

| 17H | BANK 2 |
|-----|--------|
| 10H | |

| 0FH | BANK 1 |
|-----|--------|
| 08H | |

| 07H | BANK 0 |
|-----|--------|
| 00H | |

There are two timers, timer-0 and timer-1. Actually two 16 bit registers are used which increment one by one either by a tick of the timer clock or by a count pulse at pins T0 and T1. The system is associated with a 3.58 MHz clock and each tick is of 3.35 micro-sec duration. Thus a timer register may fill up to 65536 clock ticks (220ms). Each register has a high byte (TH) and a low byte (TL) and each byte may be located individually at its address. As a counter, the same could accumulate pulses at frequencies DC to 500 KHz with 16 bit precision. Each timer may be operated in four modes set by TMOD register as indicated below :

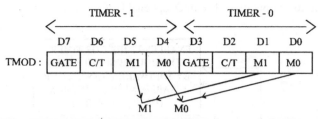

| Mode | M1 | M0 | Operation |
|------|----|----|-----------|
| 8-BIT TIMER | 0 | 0 | TL SERVES AS A 5-BIT PRE-SCALAR, TH AS AN 8 BIT COUNTER. |
| 16-BIT TIMER | 0 | 1 | 16 BIT TIMER / COUNTER |
| AUTO RE-LOAD | 1 | 0 | 8 BIT TIMER/COUNTER TH HOLDS A VALUE THAT IS RE-LOADED INTO TL, EACH TIME TL FILLS OVER FF |
| TIMER TWIN (8-BIT) | 1 | 1 | FOR TL0 8-BIT TIMER, TH0 8-BIT TIMER CONTROLLED BY TIMER-1 CONTROL BITS FOR START OR STOP, TIMER-1 STOPS, TIMER-0 ALONE WORKS. |

The Gate bit should be '0' for normal timer or counter operations and '1' for the timer or counter to work when INT0 or INT1 is high. It is necessary to set C/T bit for counter and clear for timer. Timer control register TCON has the following functions :

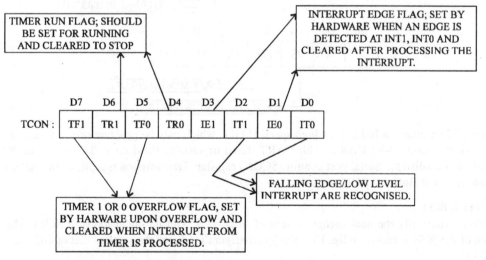

There are two external interrupts INT1 and INT0 and three internal interrupts–two from timers/counters and one from the UART. Both INT1 and INT0 require low-going inputs for interrupting. TH timer-register's serial byte is transmitted or received.

The interrupts have to be enabled to be operative. The interrupt enable register IE is as follows -

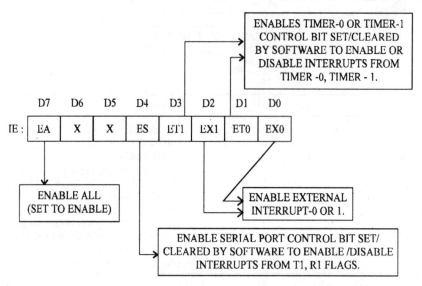

Since there is more than one interrupts, priority is given to them. It is required to set or clear five bits of the Interrupt Priority register 'IP' to make priority high or low respectively.

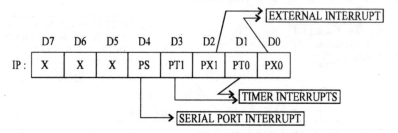

The 8031 contains a full duplex high speed UART, which may be programmed to function in four modes - shift register, 8-bit UART, 9-bit UART, fixed or variable baud rates. To use the UART, it is necessary to initialise the Serial port control (SCON) register. Transmission reception are finally carried out via Serial port Buffer (SBUF) register

## 15.5 INTEL 8051

Intel 8051 is basically the next higher version of Intel 8031 with the inclusion of a ROM. The block diagram of the 8051 is shown in fig. 15.4, the pin configuration being the same as that of 8031.

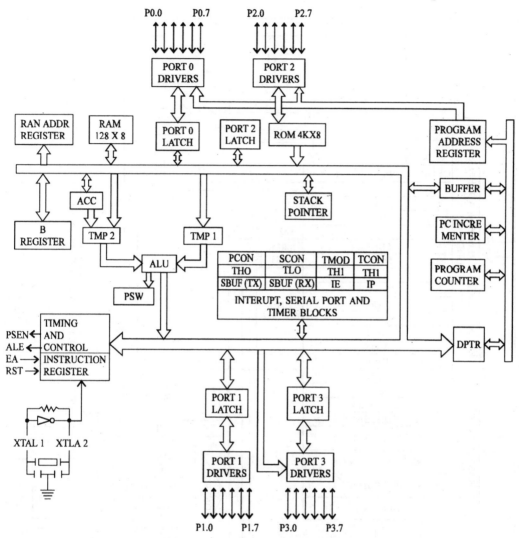

Fig. 15.4 The Block Diagram of the 8051

    The 8051 contains a non-volatile 4K x 8 ROM, a volatile 128 X 8 RAM having 64K address space for external Data Memory, 64 K address space for external program Memory and 21 special Function Registers. It is equipped with 32 I/0 lines; two 16 bit timer counter; a five volt source, two priority level, nested interrupt structure, a serial I/O port for using as either multiprocessor communication on I/O expansion or full duplex UART ; an on-chip oscillator and clock circuit. The 8051 has the facility for expansion using standard TTL compatible memories.

    The 8051 microcomputer is efficient both as a controller and as an arithmetic processor. The 8051 has extensive facilities for binary and BCD arithmetics and it is excellent in bit-handling capabilities. The instruction set of 51 family consists of 44 number of one byte, 41 number of two byte and 15 number of three-byte instructions. The 8051 family functional block diagram is shown in Fig. 15.5.

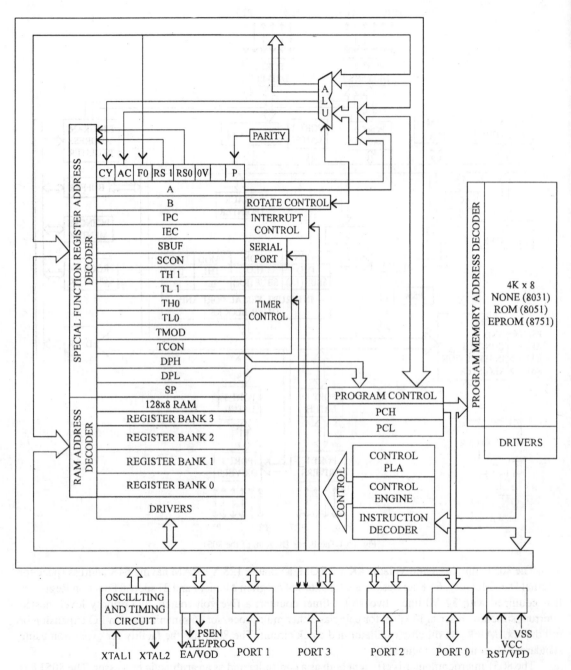

Fig. 15.5 The 8051 - Family Functional Block Diagram

## 15.6 MEMORY ORGANISATION

The 8051 maintains separate address spaces for program Memory and Data Memory as shown in Fig. 15.6.

The logical separation of program and Data Memory allows the Data Memory to be accessed by 8 bit address which can be more quickly stored and manipulated by an 8-bit CPU.

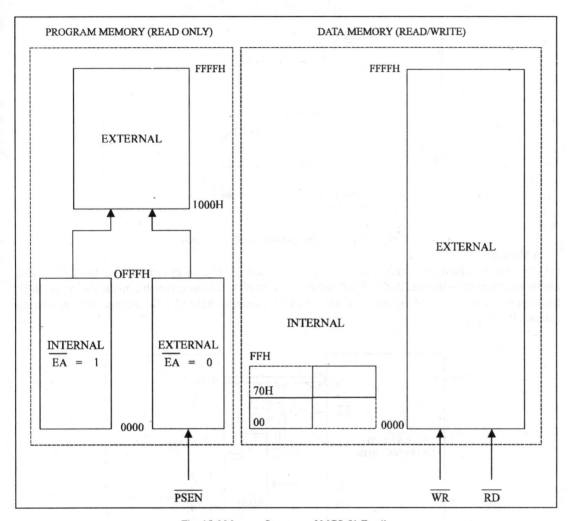

Fig. 15.6 Memory Structure of MCS-51 Family

**Program Memory**

Fig. 15.7 shows the configuration for executing from External Program Memory. If EA pin is connected to Vss, all program fetches are directed to external ROM. The read strobe to external strobe, PSEN, is used for all external program fetches. PSEN is not activated for internal program fetches.

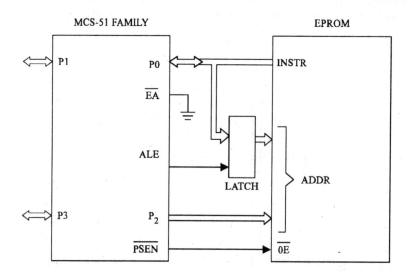

Fig. 15.7 External Program Memory Configuration

### Data Memory

Fig. 15.8 Shows a hardware configuration for accessing upto 2k byte of external RAM. The CPU in this case is executing from internal ROM. Port 0 serves as a multiplexed address/data bus to the RAM, and three lines of port 2 are being used to page the RAM. The CPU generates RD and WR signals as required during external RAM access.

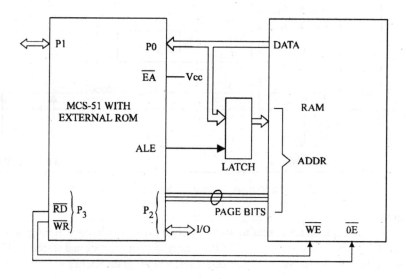

Fig 15.8 External Data Memory RAM Configuration

The Minimum length of program Memory may be extended upto 64K-bytes of which the lowest 4K bytes are included in the on-chip ROM. When the External Access Input ($\overline{EA}$) line is made high, the 8051 starts executing from internal ROM provided, the program counter exceeds 0FFFH. If $\overline{EA}$ pin is low, the 8051 executes instructions stored in external program memory. The Data Memory consists of 128 bytes of on-chip RAM together with 21 special function Registers. The external data memory may be extended upto 64K bytes.

The internal data Memory consists of 256 locations of address space and uses 8-bit address. The lower 128 addresses are used for on-chip RAM, the upper 128 bytes of the same being occupied by the special function registers.

The memory locations 00 through 1FH i.e. the lowest 32 bytes in the internal RAM are divided into 4 banks of registers, each bank consisting of 8-bytes. These banks may be assigned as 'working' Registers' of the CPU. The next higher 16 bytes of the internal RAM (locations 20H through 2FH) have individually addressable bits. These are utilised as software flags or during boolean processing. The bit addressing facility is an important feature of the 8051. Some special function registers such as A, B, PSW, Ports P0, P1, P2, P3; IP, IE; TCON and SCON have individually addressable bits.

Acc. or 'A' is the general Accumulator while B Register is also regarded as the second Accumulator used during multiplication and division. In other operations, it behaves as a Scratch register. The stack pointer having a size of 8-bits, may reside anywhere in 128 bytes of on-chip RAM. Under RESET condition, the SP is initialised to 07H. During 'PUSH' operation or a 'CALL', the SP is incremented before storing the data. Thus the SP may be made to save data from 08H upwards.

The Data pointer (DPTR), a 16-bit register, is divided into two parts-DPH (Data Pointer High) and DPL (Data Pointer Low) and its function is to hold a 16-bit address.

In 8051, there is the facility of having 32 I/O lines divided into four parallel ports P0, P1, P2 and P3. Each of these ports are equipped with a latch, an output driver and an input buffer. Port 3 is a multifunctional device having the capability of serial Input/output, External Interrupt, Timer external input, External data memory READ and WRITE strobes.

The Serial Data Buffer (SDBF) consists of two separate registers. These are utilised for serial data transfer. Special function registers IP, IE, TMOD, TCON, SCON and PSEN contain control and status bits for the interrupt system, the timers and the serial port.

## 15.7 INTEL 8751

The 8751 is a high performance single chip Microcomputer. It has a ROM-less version 8031 and a ROM-version 8051. Basically the 8751 is the EPROM version of the 8051. The 8751 possesses a powerful 8-bit CPU, 4K EPROM, 128 byte RAM, two 16-bit timers/ counters two external hardware and three internal hardware interrupts, one full duplex USART, a clock generator and four 8-bit I/O ports. It uses a 12MHz crystal and typical instruction cycle is of one micro-second. The on-chip program memory in the 8751 can be electrically programmed and can be erased by exposure to ultraviolet light.

The 8751 is a byte forward, memory-oriented, memory-based, segmented memory-type 8-bit single chip microcomputer. Its CPU incorporates two 8-bit accumulators A and B, one 16-bit Data Pointer DP, one 16-bit Programe Counter PC, one 8-bit stack pointer, one 16-bit Counter register, one 8-bit interrupt enable register IE, one 8-bit interrupt-priority register IP and one 8-bit PSW. The internal RAM contains four banks of eight general purpose 8-bit registers, of which two registers have indexing capability.

The 8751 has an elaborate set of instructions with all the addressing. There exists a lot of highly powerful compounded instructions. Multiplication and division operations are also available. The instructions are designed for efficient programming both in space and speed. The 8751 has very strong bit-manipulation capabilities. The control-registers, 16 bytes of RAM, I/O Ports etc. are bit-addressable.

## 15.8 PROGRAMMING TECHIQUE OF INTEL 51-FAMILY

The 8031 (and also the other two members 8051 or 8751) possesses a set of very powerful instructions which make the programming highly effective both in space and speed. The instruction set of Intel 51-family has been presented in Table 15.3. There are five modes of addressing -direct, indexed, immediate and relative.

**TABLE 15.3**
**INSTUCTION SET OF 51-FAMILY OF MICROCONTROLLER***
(Each instruction requires 1 cycle for execution if not stated otherwise)

1. ARITHMETIC AND LOGICAL OPERATIONS

| *Rn | R0 | R1 | R2 | R3 | R4 | R5 | R6 | R7 | COMMENTS |
|---|---|---|---|---|---|---|---|---|---|
| ADD A, Rn | 28 | 29 | 2A | 2B | 2C | 2D | 2E | 2F | ADD CONTENT OF REG. TO THAT OF 'A' |
| ADDC, A,Rn | 38 | 39 | 3A | 3B | 3C | 3D | 3E | 3F | ADD CONTENT OF REG. AND CY TO THAT OF 'A' |
| SUB B A,Rn | 98 | 99 | 9A | 9B | 9C | 9D | 9E | 9F | SUBTRACT CONTENT OF REG. FROM THAT OF 'A' WITH BORROW |
| INC Rn | 08 | 09 | 0A | 0B | 0C | 0D | 0E | 0F | INCREMENT REG. |
| DEC Rn | 18 | 19 | 1A | 1B | 1C | 1D | 1E | 1F | DECREMENT REG. |
| ANL A,Rn | 58 | 59 | 5A | 5B | 5C | 5D | 5E | 5F | AND REG. TO 'A' |
| ORL A,Rn | 48 | 49 | 4A | 4B | 4C | 4D | 4E | 4F | OR REG. TO 'A' |
| XRL A, Rn | 68 | 69 | 6A | 6B | 6C | 6D | 6E | 6F | EXCLUSIVE -OR REG. TO 'A' |

* Rn → WORKING REGISTER

| | | |
|---|---|---|
| ADD A DIRECT * | 25 | ADD DIRECT BYTE TO 'A' |
| ADDC A, DIRECT | 32 | ADD DIRECT BYTE TO 'A' WITH CY |
| SUBB A, DIRECT | 95 | SUBTRACT DIRECT BYTE FROM 'A' WITH BORROW |
| INC DIRECT | 05 | INCREMENT DIRECT BYTE |
| DEC DIRECT | 15 | DECREMENT DIRECT BYTE |
| ANL A, DIRECT | 55 | AND DIRECT BYTE TO 'A' |
| ANL DIRECT, A | 52 | AND 'A' TO DIRECT BYTE |
| ORL A, DIRECT | 45 | OR DIRECT BYTE TO 'A' |
| ORL DIRECT, A | 42 | OR 'A' TO DIRECT BYTE |
| XRL A, DIRECT | 65 | EXCLUSIVE-OR DIRECT BYTE TO 'A' |
| XRL DIRECT, A | 62 | EXCLUSIVE-OR 'A' TO DIRECT BYTE |

*DIRECT → 128 RAM LOCATIONS, INTERNAL RAM LOCATIONS AND I/O PORT, CONTROL OR STATUS REGISTER.

| *Ri | R0 | R1 | |
|---|---|---|---|
| ADD A, @ Ri | 26 | 27 | ADD INDIRECT RAM TO 'A' |
| ADDC A, @ Ri | 36 | 37 | ADD INDIRECT RAM TO 'A' WITH CY |
| SUBB A, @ Ri | 96 | 97 | ADD INDIRECT RAM FROM 'A' WITH BORROW |
| INC @ Ri | 06 | 07 | INCREMENT INDIRECT RAM |
| DEC @ Ri | 16 | 17 | DECREMENT INDIRECT RAM |
| ANL A, @ Ri | 56 | 57 | AND INDIRECT RAM TO 'A' |
| ORL A,@ Ri | 46 | 47 | OR INDIRECT RAM TO 'A' |
| XRL A, @ Ri | 66 | 67 | EXCLUSIVE-OR INDIRECT RAM TO 'A' |

*Ri → INTERNAL RAM LOCATION ADDRESSED BY REGISTER R0 OR R1

REF. * INTEL MICROCONTROLLER USER'S MANUAL, MAY 1982

| | | | |
|---|---|---|---|
| ADD A, # DATA ** | 24 | ADD IMMEDIATE DATA TO 'A' | |
| ADDC A, # DATA | 34 | ADD IMMEDIATE DATA TO 'A' WITH CY | |
| SUBB A, # DATA | 94 | SUBTRACT IMMEDIATE DATA FROM 'A' WITH BORROW | |
| ANL A, # DATA | 54 | AND IMMEDIATE | |
| ANL DIRECT, # DATA | 53 | AND IMMEDIATE DATA TO DIRECT BYTE * | |
| ORL A, # DATA | 44 | OR IMMEDIATE DATA TO 'A' | |
| ORL DIRECT, # DATA | 43 | OR IMMEDIATE DATA TO DIRECT BYTE * | |
| XRL A, # DATA | 64 | EXCLUSIVE-OR IMMEDIATE DATA TO 'A' | |
| XRL DIRECT, # DATA | 63 | EXCLUSIVE-OR IMMEDIATE DATA TO DIRECT BYTE * | |

* REQUIRES TWO CYCLES

** # DATA → 8-BIT CONSTANT INCLUDED IN INSTRUCTION

| | | |
|---|---|---|
| INC A | 04 | INCREMENT 'A' |
| DEC A | 14 | DECREMENT 'A' |
| CLR A | E4 | CLEAR 'A' |
| CPL A | F4 | COMPLEMENT 'A' |
| RL A | 23 | ROTATE 'A' LEFT |
| RLC A | 33 | ROTATE 'A' LEFT THROUGH CY FLAG |
| RR A | 03 | ROTATE 'A' RIGHT |
| RRC A | 13 | ROTATE 'A' RIGHT THROUGH CY FLAG |
| INC DPTR | A3 | INCREMENT DATA POINTER (REQUIRES 2 CYCLES) |
| DAA | D4 | DECIMAL ADJUST 'A' |
| MUL AB | A4 | MULTIPLY 'A' AND 'B' |
| DIV AB | 84 | DIVIDE 'A' BY 'B' (REQUIRES 4 CYCLES) |
| SWAP A | C4 | SWAP NIBBLES WITHIN 'A' |

## 2. DATA TRANSFER INSTRUCTIONS

| Rn | R0 | R1 | R2 | R3 | R4 | R5 | R6 | COMMENTS |
|---|---|---|---|---|---|---|---|---|
| MOV A, Rn | E8 | E9 | EA | EB | EC | ED | EF | MOVE (Rn) TO 'A' |
| MOV Rn, A | F8 | F9 | FA | FB | FC | FD | FE | MOVE (A) TO REGISTER |
| MOV Rn, DIRECT* | A8 | A9 | AA | AB | AC | AD | AF | MOVE DIRECT BYTE TO Rn |
| MOV DIRECT, Rn * | 88 | 89 | 8A | 8B | 8C | 8D | 8F | MOVE Rn TO DIRECT BYTE |
| MOV Rn, # DATA | 78 | 79 | 7A | 7B | 7C | 7D | 7F | MOVE IMMEDIATE DATA TO |
| MOVE A, DIRECT | E5 | | | | | | | MOVE DIRECT BYTE TO 'A' |
| MOV A, @ Ri | E6 | E7 | | | | | | MOVE (INDIRECT RAM) TO 'A' |
| MOV A, # DATA | 74 | | | | | | | MOVE IMMEDIATE DATA TO 'A' |
| MOV DIRECT, A | F5 | | | | | | | MOVE (A) TO DIRECT BYTE |
| MOV DIRECT1, DIRECT2* | 85 | | | | | | | MOVE DIRECT BYTE 1 TO DIRECT BYTE 2 |
| MOV, DIRECT, @ Ri* | 86 | 87 | | | | | | MOVE INDIRECT RAM TO DIRECT BYTE |
| MOV DIRECT, # DATA* | 75 | | | | | | | MOVE INDIRECT DATA TO DIRECT BYTE |
| MOV @ Ri, A | F6 | F7 | | | | | | MOVE (A) TO INDIRECT RAM |
| MOV @ Ri, DIRECT* | A6 | A7 | | | | | | MOVE DIRET BYTE TO INDIRECT RAM |
| MOV @ RI, # DATA | 76 | 77 | | | | | | MOVE IMMEDIATE DATA TO INDIRECT RAM |
| MOV DPRT, # DATA 16* | 90 | | | | | | | LOAD DPTR WITH A 16-BIT CONSTANT |
| MOVC A, @ A * DPTR* | 93 | | | | | | | MOVE CODE BYTE RELATIVE TO DPTR TO 'A' |
| MOVC A, @ A * PC | 83 | | | | | | | MOVE CODE BYTE RELATIVE TO PC TO 'A' |
| MOVX A, @ Ri* | E2 | E3 | | | | | | MOVE EXT. RAM (8-BIT ADDRESS) TO 'A' |
| MOVX A, @ A * DPTR* | E0 | | | | | | | MOVE EXT. RAM (16-BIT ADDRESS) TO 'A' |

| MOVX @ Ri, A | F2 | F3 | | | | | MOVE 'A' TO EXT. RAM (8-BIT ADDRESS) |
|---|---|---|---|---|---|---|---|
| MOVX @ DPTR, A* | F0 | | | | | | MOVE 'A' TO EXT. RAM (16-BIT ADDRESS) |
| PUSH DIRECT * | C0 | | | | | | PUSH DIRECT BYTE INTO STACK |
| POP DIRECT* | D0 | | | | | | POP DIRECT BYTE FROM STACK |
| XCH A, Rn | C8 | C9 | CA | CB | CC | CD | CF | EXCHANGE (REG. Rn) WITH (A) |
| XCH A, DIRECT | C5 | | | | | | EXCHANGE DIRET BYTE WITH 'A' |
| XCH A, @ Ri | C6 | C7 | | | | | EXCHANGE INDIRECT RAM WITH 'A' |
| XCHD A, @ Ri | D6 | D7 | | | | | EXCHANGE LOW ORDER DIGIT INDIRECT RAM WITH 'A' |

*REQUIRES TWO EXECUTION CYCLES
#DATA 16 ⟶   16-BIT CONSTANT INCLUDED AS BYTES 2 AND 3 OF INSTRUCTIONS

## 3. BOOLEAN VARIABLE MANIPULATION

| CLR C | C3 | CLEAR CARRY FLAG |
|---|---|---|
| CLR BIT ** | C2 | CLEAR DIRECT BIT |
| SETB C | D3 | SET CARRY FLAG |
| SETB BIT | D2 | SET DIRECT BIT |
| CPL C | B3 | COMPLEMENT CARRY FLAG |
| CPL BIT | B2 | COMPLEMENT DIRECT BIT |
| ANI C, BIT * | B1 | AND DIRECT BIT TO CARRY FLAG |
| ANL C,/BIT * | B0 | AND COMPLEMENT OF DIRECT BIT TO CARRY FLAG |
| ORL C, BIT * | 72 | OR DIRECT BIT TO CARRY FLAG |
| ORL C,/BIT * | A0 | OR COMPLEMENT OF DIRECT BIT OT CARRY FLAG |
| MOV C, BIT * | A2 | MOVE DIRECT BIT TO CARRY FLAG |
| MOV BIT, C * | 92 | MOVE CARRY FLAG TO DIRECT BIT |

* REQUIRES 2 EXECUTION CYCLES
** BIT ⟶   128 SOFTWARE FLAGS AND I/O PINS, CONTROL AND STATUS BIT

## 4. PROGRAM AND MACHINE CONTROL INSTRUCTIONS

| ACALL ADDR 11 * | XXX10001 | ABSOLUTE SUBROUTINE CALL |
|---|---|---|
| LCALL ADDR16 ** | 12 | LONG SUBROUTINE CALL |
| RET | 22 | RETURN FROM SUBROUTINE |
| RET1 | 32 | RETURN FROM INTERRUPT |
| AJMP ADDR11 | XXX00001 | ABSOLUTE JUMP |
| LJMP ADDR16 | 02 | LONG JUMP |
| SJMP REL *** | 80 | SHORT JUMP (RELATIVE ADDRESS) |
| JMP @ A*DPTR | 73 | JUMP INDIRECT RELATIVE TO DPTR |
| JZ REL | 60 | JUMP IF (ACC) IS ZERO |
| JNZ REL | 70 | JUMP IF (ACC) IS NOT ZERO |
| JC REL | 40 | JUMP IF CARRY FLAG IS SET |
| JNC REL | 50 | JUMP IF CARRY FLAG IS NOT SET |
| JB BIT, REL | 20 | JUMP IF DIRECT BIT IS SET |
| JNB BIT, REL | 30 | JUMP IF DIRECT BIT IS NOT SET |
| JBC BIT, REL | 10 | JUMP IF DIRECT BIT IS SET AND CLEAR BIT |
| CJNE A, DIRECT, REL | B5 | COMPARE DIRECT TO 'A' AND JUMP IF NOT EQUAL |
| CJNE A, # DATA, REL | B4 | COMPARE IMMEDIATE TO 'A' AND JUMP IF NOT EQUAL |
| CJNE RN, #DATA, REL | B8  B9  BA  BB BC BD BF | COMPARE IMMEDIATE TO (REG. Rn) AND JUMP IF NOT EQUAL |

| CJNE @Ri, # DATA, REL | B6  B7 | COMPARE IMMEDIATE TO INDIRECT AND JUMP IF NOT ZERO |
| DJNZ Rn, REL | D8  D9  DA | DECREMENT Rn AND JUMP IF NOT ZERO |
| | DB DC DD DF | |
| DJNZ DIRECT, REL | D5 | DECREMENT DIRECT AND JUMP IF NOT ZERO |
| NOP | 00 | NO OPERATION |

ALL THE INSTRUCTIONS EXCEPT 'NOP' REQUIRE 2 EXECUTION CYCLES EACH

\*       ADD R 11       $\rightarrow$   11 BIT DESTINATION ADDRESS FOR ACALL AND AJMP WITHIN THE SAME 2- KB PAGE OF PROGRAM MEMORY AS THE FIRST BYTE OF THE FOLLOWING INSTRUCTION.

\*\*      ADD R 16       $\rightarrow$   16-- BIT DESTINATION ADDRESS FOR LCALL AND LJMP, MAY BE ANYWHERE WITHIN THE 64-KB PROGRAM MEMORY ADDRESS SPACE.

\*\*\*    REL            $\rightarrow$   SIGNED (2'S COMPLEMENT ) 8-BIT OFFSET BYTE, USED BY SJMP AND ALL CONDITIONAL JUMPS, RANGE IS -128 TO +127 BYTES RELATIVE TO FIRST BYTE OF THE FOLLOWING INSTRUCTION.

EXPLANATION:

Data transfer may be done by 'MOV' instruction. A direct move instruction is as follows:

MOV A, DIRECT

MOV DIRECT, A

MOV Rn , DIRECT

MOV DIRECT, DIRECT

Here 'DIRECT' signifies any address of internal RAM, any register, accummulator etc. and 'Rn' signifies one of the registers R0 to R7. Both R0 and R1 have the indexing capability and these are used in indirect addressing as under :

MOV A,@ Rn

MOV @ Rn, DIRECT

Here Rn is R0 or R1, and the symbol '@' is used to indicate indirect addressing. By @ Rn, one of the locations of internal RAM, accumulators, general purpose or control registers is meant whose address is in Rn. However a general indexed addressing to the external RAM, external I/O ports and other external interfaces is also available. Some of these are

MOVX @ DPTR, A

MOVX A, @ DPTR.

Thus all the external interfaces are treated as external data memory and these are always accessed by data pointer (DPTR). The symbol, # is used to indicate immediate data addressing such as

MOV A, # DATA

MOV Rn, # DATA

MOV @ Rn, # DATA

MOV DIRECT, # DATA

Thus A, Rn, @ Rn or DIRECT may be loaded with 'DATA' which is an 8- bit number.

A relative addressing is

MOV C, A @A\* DPTR

where 'A' is copied by the value stored in an address obtained by DPTR added with the content in 'A'. This helps to find a code correspoding to the value in 'A' arranged from the address as in DPTR. Another one of the similar instructions is MOVC, A@ A \* PC. However this instruction for relative addressing is not intended by INTEL to be used with data memory or external RAM, but using special hardware, this instruction may be provided with data memory or external RAM.

There are three types of unconditional jumps. One is Absolute jump or AJUMP coded by XXX10001. Here XXX is the right digit of the higher byte of the address and after the instruction, the lower byte of the address is to be used. Thus it makes a jump within 4K block - 2k forward, 2K backward. There exists a general unconditional jump instruction viz. 'LJMP ADDRESS' which is referred to as ' long jump' and it makes a jump to anywhere of the program memory (and of the data memory also with the help of special hardware). There is a short jump or relative jump instruction also. That is 'SJMP REL' where 'rel' is an 8-bit 2's complimented number of address to be jumped taking the next address after the instruction as the zeroeth one. Thus 'SJMP 07' implies a jump to 8th address forward. A 'SJMP F6' implies a jump to 10th address backward. There exists many other conditional jumps, some of which compares and/or decrements registers, accummulators or internal RAM locations or checks addressable bits. Call instructions are similar to jump instructions.

Arithmetic and logical instructions are quite similar to the instructions of most of the usual microprocessors. But there exists some convenient and powerful instruction also. Excepting increment (INC) and decrement (DEC) instructions, all arithmetic and logical instructions are accumulator (A) based. Accumulator B is used in multiplication and division only. 'MULT AB' makes (A) multiplied by (B) i.e. A X B = BA. If B is empty , OV flag is set. In case of division, A is divided by B keeping the quotient in 'A' and storing the remainder in 'B'. If B is not empty, OV flag is set. In 'SWAP A' instruction, the hexadecimal digits in A are interchanged within A. With 'XCHD A' @ Rn' instruction, the LSD of A and @ Rn are interchanged. The instructions DA A, RL A etc. are exactly similar to DDA, RLC etc. used in Intel 8085. A number of bit operations are possible by Intel 51-family using special bit instructions. To manipulate a bit, the addressable bits are numbered by which they are addressed as shown in Table 15.2. Some of these types of instructions are :

SETB bit
CLR bit
ANL C, bit
MOV C, bit
JB bit, rel

By 'bit', the address of the particular bit is meant.

## 15.9 SOME PROGRAMMING EXAMPLES

1. Display 1 2 3 4 5 6 7 8 using registers only

| MEM.LOC | LABEL | OPCODES | MNEMONICS | COMMENTS |
|---------|-------|---------|-----------|----------|
| 2000 | DISPR | 78 78 | MOV R0 # 78 | LOAD 78H IN REG. R0 |
| 2002 | | 79 56 | MOV R1 # 56 | LOAD 56H IN REG. R1 |
| 2004 | | 7A 34 | MOV R2 # 34 | LOAD 34H IN REG. R2 |
| 2006 | | 7B 12 | MOV R3 # | LOAD 12H IN REG. R3 |
| 2008 | | 12 00 90 | LCALL DISP | CALL SUBROUTINE DISP |
| 200B | | 80 FE | L : SJMP L | LOOP INFINITELY |

(The Subroutines have been presented in section 15.10)

2. Develop a software to read and display the input through 00 channel of ADC or AD00 to which the 0-5V variable supply has been impressed. Output the same through DAC. Measure the DAC output with the help of a voltmeter.

| MEM.LOC | LABEL | OPCODES | MNEMONICS | COMMENTS |
|---------|-------|---------|-----------|----------|
| 2200 | P | 74 00 | MOV A, # 00 | SELECT ADC CHANNEL |
| 2202 | | 12 03 30 | LCALL ADC | READ ADC, VALUE IS IN ACC. |
| 2205 | | 12 01 30 | LCALL DAC | OUTPUT (ACC.) THROUGH DAC |

| MEM.LOC | LABEL | OPCODES | MNEMONICS | COMMENTS |
|---------|-------|---------|-----------|----------|
| 2208 | | FA | MOV R2,A | BREAK THE NUMBERS IN REGISTERS |
| 2209 | | 12 00 E0 | LCALL BRK | INTO TWO DIGITS |
| 220C | | 74 3A | MOV A, # 3A | CODE FOR BLANK |
| 220E | | F8 | MOV R0, A | MOV (A) TO R0 |
| 220F | | F9 | MOV R1, A | MOV (A) TO R1 |
| 2210 | | FC | MOV R4, A | MOV (A) TO R4 |
| 2211 | | FD | MOV R5, A | MOV (A) TO R5 |
| 2212 | | FE | MOV R6, A | MOV (A) TO R6 |
| 2213 | | FF | MOV R7, A | MOV (A) TO R7 |
| 2214 | | 12 00 B0 | LCALL DPCH | CALL SUBROUTINE 'DPCH' |
| 2217 | | 80 F7 | SJMP P | REPEAT |

3. Develop a software to sense ZCD inputs Z0 and Z1 and hence make the switches S0 and S1 ON and OFF according to following sequences.

| STATUS OF ZCD INPUTS | SWITCHES | MODE |
|----------------------|----------|------|
| Z > 0 | S1 | ON |
| Z ≤ 0 | S1 | OFF |
| Z > 0 | S0 | ON |
| Z ≤ 0 | S0 | OFF |

| MEM.LOC | LABEL | OPCODES | MNEMONICS | COMMENTS |
|---------|-------|---------|-----------|----------|
| 2300 | P | 75 20 00 | MOV 20, # 00 | MOVE IMMEDIATE DATA '00' TO RAM BYTE 20 |
| 2303 | | 12 01 50 | LCALL ZCD | RECEIVE INPUT THROUGH ZCD |
| 2306 | | F5 21 | MOV 21, A | MOVE (A) TO RAM BYTE 21 |
| 2308 | | A2 28 | MOV C, 28 | MOVE TO CY BIT FROM D0 BIT OF 21 |
| 230A | | B3 | CPL C | COMPLEMENT CARRY |
| 230B | | 92 20 | MOV 20, C | MOVE TO D0 BIT OF 20 FROM CY |
| 230D | | A2 29 | MOV C, 29 | MOVE TO CY BIT FROM D1 BIT OF 20 |
| 230F | | 95 21 | MOV 21, C | COMPLEMENT CARRY |
| 2311 | | E5 20 | MOV A, 20 | MOVE 20 BYTE TO A |
| 2313 | | 12 01 40 | LCALL SWCH | CALL SUBROUTINE TO CLEAR SWITCHES |
| 2316 | | 80 E8 | SJMP P | REPEAT |

This program shows bit manipulation capabilities of 51-family

4. Asumming that INTEL 8255 having specifications

PA = 1000, PB = 1001, PC = 1002, CWR = 1003

has been connected to the 8031, develop a software to intialise PA and PC as output ports and PB as input, store the content of PB in Mem. Loc 2771 and output contents of Mem.Loc. 2770 and 2772 through PA and PC respectively.

Note : The 8031 has no IN/OUT instructions and all the interphases are treated as memory locations. If Intel 8253 be interfaced to the 8031, for initialisation of I/O ports in zero mode, the following format may be used :

CWR :

| D7 | D6 | D5 | D4 | D3 | D2 | D1 | D0 |
|----|----|----|----|----|----|----|----|
| 1 | 0 | 0 | A | C1 | 0 | B | C2 |

↓ (A) ↓ (C1) ↓ (B) ↓ (C2)

1    1        1    1    FOR INPUT
0    0        0    0    FOR OUTPUT

| MEM.LOC | LABEL | OPCODES | MNEMONICS | COMMENTS |
|---------|-------|---------|-----------|----------|
| 2400 | | 74 82 | MOV A, # 82 | SELECT CODE FOR PA AND PC AS OUTPUT, PB AS INPUT PORT |
| 2402 | | 90 10 03 | MOV DPTR, # 1003 | PROVIDE CONTROL WORD '1003' TO DATA POINTER |
| 2405 | | F0 | MOV @DPTR, A | INITIALISE I/O PORTS |
| 2406 | | 90 10 01 | MOV DPTR, #1001 | PROVIDE ADDRESS OF PB AT DATA POINTER |
| 2409 | | ED | MOV A, @DPTR:P | INPUT THROUGH PB AND KEEP IT IN 'A' |
| 240A | | F9 | MOV R1, A | MOVE (A) TO REG. R1 |
| 240B | | 90 27 70 | MOV DPTR, #2770 | LOAD DATA POINTER WITH THE 16-BIT MEM.ADDRESS 2770 |
| 240E | | E0 | MOV A, @DPTR | MOVE THE EXTERNAL RAM ADDRESS TO 'A' |
| 240F | | F8 | MOV R0, A | MOVE (A) TO R0 |
| 2410 | | A3 | INC DPTR | INCREMENT DATA POINTER |
| 2411 | | E9 | MOV A, R1 | MOVE (R1) TO A |
| 2412 | | F0 | MOV @DPTR, A | STORE INPUT FROM PB AT MEM LOC. 2771 |
| 2413 | | A3 | INC DPTR | INCREMENT DATA POINTER |
| 2414 | | ED | MOV A @DPTR | INPUT THROUGH PB AND KEEP IT IN 'A' |
| 2415 | | FA | MOV R2, A | MOVE (A) TO REG.R2 |
| 2416 | | 90 10 00 | MOV DPTR, #10 00 | PROVIDE ADDRESS OF PA AT DATA POINTER |
| 2419 | | E8 | MOV A, R0 | MOVE (R0) TO ACC |
| 241B | | A3 | INC DPTR | INCREMENT DATA POINTER |
| 241C | | EA | MOV A, R2 | MOVE (R2) TO ACC |
| 241D | | F0 | MOV @ DPTR, A | OUTPUT THE CONTENT OF MEM LOC. 2772 THROUGH PC |
| 241E | | 80 FE | L: SJMP L | REPEAT |

5. Develope a programe to display 'RUN' under normal condition and display 'INT' for two seconds when interrupted and display 'RUN' again.
MAIN PROGRAME

| MEM.LOC | LABEL | OPCODES | MNEMONICS | COMMENTS |
|---------|-------|---------|-----------|----------|
| 2500 | | 43 A8 84 | ORL A, #84 | ENABLE INTERRUPT |
| 2503 | | D2 8A | SETB IT1 | ENABLE EDGE TRIGGERABLE INTERRUPT |
| 2505 | | 7F 3A | MOV R7, #3A | STORE CODE FOR BLANK DISPLAY IN REG.R7 |
| 2507 | | 7E 3A | MOV R6, #3A | STORE CODE FOR BLANK DISPLAY IN REG.R6 |
| 2509 | | 7D 3A | MOV R5, #3A | STORE CODE FOR BLANK DISPLAY IN REG.R5 |
| 250B | | 7C 33 | MOV R4, #33 | STORE CODE FOR 'r' DISPLAY IN REG.R4 |
| 250D | | 7B 36 | MOV R3, #36 | STORE CODE FOR 'u' DISPLAY IN REG.R3 |
| 250F | | 7A 2F | MOV R2, #2F | STORE CODE FOR 'n' DISPLAY IN REG.R2 |
| 2511 | | 79 3A | MOV R1, #3A | STORE CODE FOR BLANK DISPLAY IN REG.R1 |
| 2513 | | 78 3A | MOV R0, #3A | STORE CODE FOR BLANK DISPLAY IN REG.R0 |

| MEM.LOC | LABEL | OPCODES | MNEMONICS | COMMENTS |
|---------|-------|---------|-----------|----------|
| 2515 | | 12 00 B0 | LCALL DPCH | CALL 'DPCH' TO DISPLAY 'run' |
| 2518 | | 74 FA | MOV A, #250 (Dec) | MOVE IMMEDIATE FAH TO ACC |
| 251A | | 72 00 80 | LCALL DLY(A) | CALL SUBROUTINE 'DLY' (A) |
| 251D | | 80 E6 | SJMP P | REPEAT |

INTERRUPT SERVICE ROUTINE :

| MEM.LOC | LABEL | OPCODES | MNEMONICS | COMMENTS |
|---------|-------|---------|-----------|----------|
| 2740 | | 74 3A | MOV A, #3A | STORE CODE FOR BLANK DISPLAY IN 'A' |
| 2742 | | FF | MOVE R7, A | MOVE (A) TO REG. R7 |
| 2743 | | FE | MOVE R6, A | MOVE (A) TO REG. R6 |
| 2744 | | FD | MOVE R5, A | MOVE (A) TO REG. R5 |
| 2745 | | 7C 2C | MOV R4, #2C | MOVE CODE FOR 'I' IN REG. R4 |
| 2747 | | 7B 2F | MOV R3, #2F | MOVE CODE FOR 'n' IN REG. R4 |
| 2749 | | 7A 35 | MOV R2, #35 | MOVE CODE FOR 't' IN REG. R4 |
| 274B | | F9 | MOV R1, A | MOVE (A) TO REG. R1 |
| 274C | | F8 | MOV R0, A | MOVE (A) TO REG. R0 |
| 274D | | 12 00 B0 | LCALL DPCH | CALL SUBROUTINE 'DPCH' TO DISPLAY 'Int' |
| 2750 | | 7A 08 | MOV R2, #08 | MOVE IMMEDIATE 80H TO R2 |
| 2752 | D | 74 FA | MOV A, #250 | MOVE IMMEDIATE FAH TO 'A' |
| 2754 | | 12 00 80 | MOVE LCALL DLY (A) | CALL SUBROUTINE 'DLY (A)' |
| 2757 | | DA F9 | DJNE R2, D | DECREMENT REG. R2 AND JUMP IF NO ZERO (FOR MAKING DELAY OF 2 SECS) |
| 2759 | | C2 8B | CLR IE1 | CLEAR FOR NEXT INTERRUPT |
| 275B | | 32 | RET1 | RETURN. |

To use an interrupt, IE port is required to be initialised according to the format.

| | D7 | D6 | D5 | D4 | D3 | D2 | D1 | D0 |
|---|---|---|---|---|---|---|---|---|
| IE : | EA | X | X | ES | ET1 | EX1 | ET0 | EX0 |
| | 1 | 0 | 0 | 0 | 1 | 0 | 0 | 0 |
| BIT ADDRESS : 0A8H | AF | - | - | AC | AB | AA | A9 | A8 |

For interrupt, the D2 bit or EX1 and D7 bit or EA are required to be set i.e., IE format should be 10000100 or 84H. Again to set the falling edge triggerable interrupt circuit, TCON register is to be initialised accroding to the following TCON format:  ·

| | D7 | D6 | D5 | D4 | D3 | D2 | D1 | D0 |
|---|---|---|---|---|---|---|---|---|
| TCON : | TF1 | TR1 | TF0 | TR0 | IE1 | IT1 | IE0 | IT0 |

For interrupt, D2 bit of TCON (i.e. IT1) is to be set. The D3 bit of TCON (i.e IE1) is also to be set by the hardware when interrupted and at the end of the interrupt service routine, it is necessary to clear the same.

The program display 'run' when interrupted, displays 'Int' for two seconds and then returns to the normal program to display 'run'. Interrupt pulse is to be supplied. INT forces to execute the Interrupt service routine from Mem Loc. 2740 onwards.

## 6. Develop a program of time delay using Timer

When the CPU remains busy with executing a particular program and a precise time delay is required, the time delay by counting down the set counter by CPU may not be possible. The 8031 has two timers T0 and T1 which count at the rate of 300 per millisecs (i.e., 012CH per milliseconds).

To use them, initialisation of TMOD, TCON and IP and /or IE is necessary. To use Timer T0 in 16-bit non-gated timer mode, the TMOD format will be as under :

| | | $\longleftarrow$ TIMER 1 $\longrightarrow$ | | | $\longleftarrow$ TIMER 0 $\longrightarrow$ | | | |
|---|---|---|---|---|---|---|---|---|
| | D7 | D6 | D5 | D4 | D3 | D2 | D1 | D0 |
| TMOD : | GATE | C/T | M1 | M2 | GATE | C/T | M1 | M0 |
| | 0 | 0 | 0 | 0 | 0 | 0 | 0 | 1 |

= 01H

Further, for interruption by the timer, ET0 and EA of IE should be set. The TR0 of TCON being set, timer 0 starts counting up. When Timer 0 counts upto FFF1, the TF0 of TCON is set, the CPU is interrupted and it is forced to execute the interrupt program. The interrupt program should clear TR0 and TF0. Whenever the TR0 is set, the Timer-0 starts up counting. If a negative number be inserted in TR0, the timer counts down the number to zero. Thus in order to get a time delay of 1 milli-sec, it is necessary to insert (-300) or FED3 into Timer 0.

## TIMER SETTING PROGRAME

| MEM.LOC | LABEL | OPCODES | MNEMONICS | COMMENTS |
|---|---|---|---|---|
| 2600 | | 75 98 01 | MOV TMOD, #01 | SELECT T0 AS 16-BIT NON GATED TIMER |
| 2603 | | 75 8C FE | MOV TH0, #FE | STORE FE IN TH0 |
| 2606 | | 75 8A D3 | MOV TL0, #D3 | STORE D3 IN TL0 |
| 2609 | | 43 A8 82 | ORL IE, #82 | OR IMMEDIATE INTO DATA TO SET (-300) FOR 1 ms DELAY |
| 260C | | D2 8C | SETB TR0 | SET TR0 TO START RUNNING |
| 260D | | 80 FE | L : SJMP L | LOOP INFINITELY TO WAIT FOR INTERRUPT |

## INTERRUPT SERVICE ROUTINE

| MEM.LOC | LABEL | OPCODES | MNEMONICS | COMMENTS |
|---|---|---|---|---|
| 2700 | | C2 8C | CLR TR0 | STOP TIMER T0 |
| 2702 | | C2 8D | CLR TF0 | CLEAR INTERRUPT |
| 2704 | | 74 3A | MOV A, #3A | STORE CODE FOR BLANK DISPLAY IN 'A' |
| 2706 | | FF | MOV R7, A | MOVE (A) TO REG. R7 |
| 2707 | | FE | MOV R6, A | MOVE (A) TO REG. R6 |
| 2708 | | FD | MOV R5, A | MOVE (A) TO REG. R5 |
| 2709 | | 7C 2C | MOV R4, #2C | MOVE CODE FOR 'I' IN REG. R4 |
| 270B | | 7B 2F | MOV R3, #2F | MOVE CODE FOR 'n' IN REG. R4 |
| 270D | | 7A 35 | MOV R2, #35 | MOVE CODE FOR 't' IN REG. R4 |
| 270F | | F9 | MOV R1, A | MOVE (A) TO REG. R1 |
| 2711 | | F8 | MOV R0, A | MOVE (A) TO REG. R0 |
| 2712 | | 12 00 B0 | LCALL DPCH | CALL SUBROUTINE 'DPCH' TO DISPLAY |
| 2714 | | 7A 08 | MOV R2, #08 | MOVE IMMEDIATE 80H TO R2 |
| 2716 | D | 7A FA | MOV A, #250 | MOVE IMMEDIATE FAH TO 'A' |
| 2718 | | 12 00 80 | LCALL DLY (A) | CALL SUBROUTINE 'DLY' (A) |
| 271B | | DA F9 | DJNE R2, D | DECREMENT REG. R2 AND JUMP IF NO ZERO (FOR MAKING DELAY OF 2 SECS) |
| 271D | | C2 8B | CLR IE1 | CLEAR FOR NEXT INTERRUPT |
| 271F | | 32 | RET1 | RETURN. |

**7. DEVELOP A SOFTWARE TO MEASURE FREQUENCY OF THE RANGE 2KHz TO 100KHz.**
The program has been developed after setting C/T bit of TMOD and defining the frequency as pulse/ms.

| MEM.LOC | LABEL | OPCODES | MNEMONICS | COMMENTS |
|---------|-------|---------|-----------|----------|
| 2500 | P | 75 89 05 | MOV TMOD, # 05 | SELECT 'T0 ' AS 16-BIT NON-GATED COUNTER |
| 2503 | | 75 8C 00 | MOV TH0, #00 | CLEAR COUNTER 'TH0' |
| 2506 | | 75 8A 00 | MOV TL0, #00 | CLEAR COUNTER 'TL0' |
| 2509 | | D2 8C | SETB TR0 | SET TR0 TO START COUNTER-0 |
| 250B | | 74 01 | MOV A, #01 | STORE 01H TO 'A' |
| 250D | | 12 00 80 | LCALL DLY (A) | CALL SUBROUTINE 'DLY (A)' |
| 2510 | | C2 8C | CLR TR0 | STOP COUNTING |
| 2512 | | A8 8A | MOV R0, TL0 | MOVE THE CONTENT OF 'TL0' TO REG. R0 |
| 2514 | | A9 8C | MOV R1, TH0 | MOVE THE CONTENT OF 'TH0' TO REG. R1 |
| 2516 | | 7A 00 | MOV R2, #00 | STORE 00 TO REG. R2 |
| 2518 | | 7B 00 | MOV R3, #00 | STORE 00 TO REG. R3 |
| 251A | | 12 00 90 | LCALL DISP | CALL SUBROUTINE 'DISP' |
| 251D | | 80 IE | SJMP P | REPEAT |

## 8. DEVELOP A PROGRAM TO INTERRUPT CPU USING UART

To use UART, it is necessary to initialise SCON Register. Since Timer-1 keeps time or baud rate, TMOD is also to be initialised. In a system giving upto 9600 baud, for 1200 baud, it necessary to count upto -8 (i.e., F7H). Hence for such a system, Timer-1 may be initialised in non-gated 8-bit auto re-loaded mode and SCON in 8-bit programmable baud receiver interrupt mode. After a transmission, T1 bit of SCON (address 99) becomes high and remains low during transmission. Hence it may be sensed by polling.

| MEM.LOC | LABEL | OPCODES | MNEMONICS | COMMENTS |
|---------|-------|---------|-----------|----------|
| 2500 | | 75 98 52 | MOV SCON, #52 | INITIALISE SCON REGISTER |
| 2503 | | 75 89 25 | MOV TMOD, #25 | INITIALISE TMOD REGISTER |
| 2506 | | 75 8D F7 | MOV TH1, #8 | STORE F7H (i.e., -8) IN TH1 |
| 2509 | | D2 8E | SETB TR1 | SET TR1 TO START RUNNING |
| 250B | P | 90 24 00 | MOV DPTR, # 2400 | STORE 2400H IN DATA POINTER |
| 250E | | E0 | MOVX A,@ DPTR | MOV EXTERNAL RAM ADDRESS (16-BIT) TO 'A' |
| 250F | | A2 D0 | MOV C, BIT | MOV D0 BIT TO CY |
| 2511 | | B3 | CPL C | COMPLEMENT CY |
| 2512 | | 92 D7 | MOV A7, C | MOVE (CY) TO 'D7' BIT OF 'A' |
| 2514 | | 30 99 FD | JNB T1, CH | CHEAK WHETHER PREVIOUS TRANSMISSION IS OVER |
| 2517 | | C2 99 | CLR T1 | CLEAR FOR NEXT TRANSMISSION. |
| 2519 | | F5 99 | MOV SBUF | MOVE NEXT TRANSMISSION BYTE TO 'A' |
| 251B | | 75 A8 90 | MOV IE, #90 | INITIALISE FOR RECEIVER |
| 251E | | 80 EB | SJMP P | REPEAT |

### INTERRUPT ROUTINE FOR RECEPTION

| MEM.LOC | LABEL | OPCODES | MNEMONICS | COMMENTS |
|---------|-------|---------|-----------|----------|
| 27C0 | | E5 99 | MOV A, SBUF | GET THE RECEIVED BYTE |
| 27C2 | | A2 D0 | MOV C, P BIT | MOVE D0 BIT TO CY |
| 27C4 | | B3 | CPLC | COMPLEMENT CY |
| 27C5 | | 54 7F | ANL A, #7F | GET THE 7-BIT WORD |
| 27C7 | | 90 23 00 | MOV DPTR, #2300 | STORE 2300H IN DATA POINTER |
| 27CA | | F0 | MOV @ DPTR, A | MOVE TO EXTERNAL RAM WHOSE ADDRESS IS 2300H |
| 27CB | | 32 | RET1 | RETURN |

In this program, from the transmitter, a value stored in Mem. Loc. 2400H is transmitted and another value received by the receiver is stored in Mem.Loc. 2300H. By connecting RXD and TXD pins, the transmitted value will be seen to store in respective locations. It may be noted that, in 8-bit UART mode, 7-bit number is practically transmitted along with the parity bit in complement as the 8th bit. Interrupt of serial port forces the CPU to execute the interrupt service routine.

## 9. DEVELOP A PROGRAM FOR ROLLING DISPLAY

| MEM.LOC | LABEL | OPCODES | MNEMONICS | COMMENTS |
|---|---|---|---|---|
| 2400 | | 78 40 | MOV R0, #40 | MOVE IMMEDIATE 40H TO REG. R0 |
| 2402 | | 76 20 | MOV @ R0, #20 | MOVE IMMEDIATE 20H TO INDIRECT RAM R0 |
| 2404 | | 08 | INC R0 | INCREMENT REG. R0 |
| 2405 | | 76 34 | MOV @ R0, #34 | MOVE IMMEDIATE 34H TO REG. R0 |
| 2407 | | 08 | INC R0 | INCREMENT REG.R0 |
| 2408 | | 76 20 | MOV @ R0, #20 | MOVE IMMEDIATE 20H TO REG. R0 |
| 240A | | 08 | INC R0 | INCREMENT REG.R0 |
| 240B | | 76 3A | MOV @ R0, #3A | MOVE IMMEDIATE 3AH TO REG. R0 |
| 240D | | 08 | INC R0 | INCREMENT REG.R0 |
| 240E | | 76 36 | MOV @ R0, #36 | MOVE IMMEDIATE 36H TO REG. R0 |
| 2410 | | 08 | INC R0 | INCREMENT REG.R0 |
| 2411 | | 76 23 | MOV @ R0, #23 | MOVE IMMEDIATE 23H TO REG. R0 |
| 2413 | | 08 | INC R0 | INCREMENT REG.R0 |
| 2414 | | 76 3D | MOV @ R0, #3D | MOVE IMMEDIATE 3DH TO REG. R0 |
| 2416 | | 08 | INC R0 | INCREMENT REG.R0 |
| 2417 | | 76 03 | MOV @ R0, #03 | MOVE IMMEDIATE 03H TO REG. R0 |
| 2419 | | 08 | INC R0 | INCREMENT REG.R0 |
| 241A | | 76 01 | MOV @ R0, #01 | MOVE IMMEDIATE 01H TO REG. R0 |
| 241C | | 08 | INC R0 | INCREMENT REG.R0 |
| 241D | | 76 3A | MOV @ R0, #3A | MOVE IMMEDIATE 3AH (FOR BLANK DISPLAY) TO REG.R0 |
| 241F | | 08 | INC R0 | INCREMENT REG.R0 |
| 2420 | | 76 28 | MOV @ R0, #28 | MOVE IMMEDIATE 28H TO REG. R0 |
| 2422 | | 08 | INC R0 | INCREMENT REG.R0 |
| 2423 | | 76 30 | MOV @ R0, #30 | MOVE IMMEDIATE 30H TO REG. R0 |
| 2425 | | 08 | INC R0 | INCREMENT REG.R0 |
| 2426 | | 76 30 | MOV @ R0, #30 | MOVE IMMEDIATE 30H TO REG. R0 |
| 2428 | | 08 | INC R0 | INCREMENT REG.R0 |
| 2429 | | 76 24 | MOV @ R0, #24 | MOVE IMMEDIATE 24H TO REG. R0 |
| 242B | | 08 | INC R0 | INCREMENT REG.R0 |
| 242C | | 76 3A | MOV @ R0, #3A | MOVE IMMEDIATE 3AH TO REG. R0 |
| 242E | | 08 | INC R0 | INCREMENT REG.R0 |
| 242F | | 76 36 | MOV @ R0, #36 | MOVE IMMEDIATE 36H TO REG. R0 |
| 2431 | | 08 | INC R0 | INCREMENT REG.R0 |
| 2432 | | 76 23 | MOV @ R0, #23 | MOVE IMMEDIATE 23H TO REG. R0 |
| 2434 | | 08 | INC R0 | INCREMENT REG.R0 |
| 2435 | | 76 3A | MOV @ R0, #3A | MOVE IMMEDIATE 3AH TO REG. R0 |
| 2437 | | 08 | INC R0 | INCREMENT REG.R0 |
| 2438 | | 76 3A | MOV @ R0, #3A | MOVE IMMEDIATE 3AH TO REG. R0 |
| 243A | | AF 40 | MOV R7, 40 | MOVE 40H TO REG. R7 |
| 243C | | AE 41 | MOV R6, 41 | MOVE 41H TO REG. R6 |
| 243E | | AD 42 | MOV R5, 42 | MOVE 42H TO REG. R5 |
| 2440 | | AC 43 | MOV R4, 43 | MOVE 43H TO REG. R4 |
| 2442 | | AB 44 | MOV R3, 44 | MOVE 44H TO REG. R3 |
| 2444 | | AA 45 | MOV R2, 45 | MOVE 45H TO REG. R2 |
| 2446 | | A9 46 | MOV R1, 46 | MOVE 46H TO REG. R1 |
| 2448 | | A8 47 | MOV R0, 47 | MOVE 47H TO REG. R0 |
| 244A | | 12 00 B0 | LCALL DPCH | CALL SUBROUTINE 'DPCH' FOR DISPLAY |

| MEM.LOC | LABEL | OPCODES | MNEMONICS | COMMENTS |
|---------|-------|---------|-----------|----------|
| 244D | | 74 FA | MOV A, #FA | MOVE IMMEDIATE FAH TO 'A' |
| 244F | | 12 00 80 | LCALL DLY(A) | CALL SUBROUTINE 'DLY (A)' |
| 2452 | | 78 3F | MOV R0, #3F | MOVE IMMEDIATE 3FH TO REG. R0 |
| 2454 | | 79 40 | MOV R1, #40 | MOVE IMMEDIATE 40H TO REG. R1 |
| 2456 | | E7 | MOV A, @R1 | MOVE INDIRECT RAM (R1) TO A |
| 2457 | | F6 | MOV @ RD, A | MOVE (A) TO INDIRECT RAM R0 |
| 2458 | | 08 | INC R0 | INCREMENT REG. R0 |
| 2459 | | 09 | INC R1 | INCREMENT REG. R1 |
| 245A | | B8 52 F9 | CJNE R0, #52, L | COMPARE IMMEDIATE 52H TO REG. R0 AND JUMP IF NOT EQUAL |
| 245D | | A6 3F | MOV @ R0, 3F | MOVE DIRECT BYTE TO INDIRECT RAM R0 |
| 245F | | 02 24 00 | LJMP 24 00 | JUMP TO 2400H |

It may be noted that since the 8031 is a microcomputer chip, necessarily it has no HALT instruction. But the instruction L : SJMPL (opcode : 80FE) makes an infinite looping. In place of SJMP instructions LJMP or JMP may also be used. Both of these instructions make the program address dependent but SJMP makes the program independent of address. Further the use of internal RAM is extremely helpful in may cases. For this, locations 20 to 2E may be used which are bit-addresssable.

## 15.10 SOME USEFUL SUB-ROUTINES

1. SUB-ROUTINE 'DLY (A)' : This sub-routine makes a delay in millisec., numerically equal to the content of Acc. No register is affected in this sub-routine.

| MEM.LOC | LABEL | OPCODES | MNEMONICS | COMMENTS |
|---------|-------|---------|-----------|----------|
| 0080 | DLY (A) | F5 2F | MOV DIRECT, A | MOVE ACCUMULATOR TO DIRECT BYTE (2F) |
| 0082 | | 12 00 70 | LCALL 0070H | CALL LONG SUBROUTINE 0070H (DLY) |
| 0085 | | D5 2F FA | DJNZ DIRECT, REL | DECREMENT DIRECT AND JUNP IF NOT ZERO |
| 0088 | | 22 | RET | RETURN |
| 0070 | DLY | C0 00 | PUSH 00 | PUSH DIRECT BYTE (00) TO STACK |
| 0072 | | 78 60 | MOV R0, #60 | MOVE IMMEDIATE 60H TO REG. R0 |
| 0074 | | 00 | NOP | NO OPERATION |
| 0075 | | D8 FD | DJNZ R0, REL | DECREMENT REG.R0 AND JUMP IF NOT ZERO |
| 0077 | | D0 00 | POP 00 | POP DIRECT BYTE (00) FROM STACK |
| 0079 | | 22 | RET | RETURN |

2. DISP : This sub-routine displays the contents of R0, R1, R2 and R3 without affecting any register.

| MEM.LOC | LABEL | OPCODES | MNEMONICS | COMMENTS |
|---------|-------|---------|-----------|----------|
| 0090 | DISP | 12 02 30 | LCALL 0230 H | CALL LONG SUBROUTINE 0230H (GITA) |
| 0093 | | 88 30 | MOV DIRECT, R0 | MOVE DIRECT R0 TO DIRECT BYTE |
| 0095 | | 89 32 | MOV DIRECT , R1 | MOVE DIRECT R1 TO DIRECT BYTE |
| 0097 | | 8A 34 | MOV DIRECT , R2 | MOVE DIRECT R2 TO DIRECT BYTE |
| 0099 | | 8B 36 | MOV DIRECT , R3 | MOVE DIRECT R3 TO DIRECT BYTE |
| 009B | | 12 01 90 | LCALL 0190H | CALL LONG SUBROUTINE 0190H (SITA) |
| 009E | | 12 01 70 | LCALL 0170H | CALL LONG SUBROUTINE 0170H (RITA) |
| 00A1 | | 12 02 40 | LCALL 0240H | CALL LONG SUBROUTINE 0240H (DB) |
| 00A4 | | 22 | RET | RETURN |

| MEM.LOC | LABEL | OPCODES | MNEMONICS | COMMENTS |
|---|---|---|---|---|
| 0170 | RITA | 90 60 01 | MOV DPTR, # DATA 16) | LOAD DATA POINTER WITH 6001H (16 BIT ADDRESS) |
| 0173 | | 74 DE | MOV A, #DATA | MOVE IMMEDIATE DEH TO 'A' |
| 0175 | | F0 | MOV X @ DPTR, A | MOVE A TO EXT. RAM 6001H |
| 0176 | | 12 00 70 | LCALL ADDR. 16 | CALL LONG SUBROUTINE 'DLY' |
| 0179 | | 78 30 | MOV R0, #30 | MOVE IMMEDIATE 30H TO REG. R0 |
| 017B | | 90 60 01 | MOV DPTR, #DATA 16) | LOAD DATA POINTER WITH 6001H (16 BIT ADDRESS) |
| 017E | | E8 | MOV A, R0 | MOVE (R0) TO 'A' |
| 017F | | 24 50 | ADD A, # DATA | ADD IMMEDIATE 50H TO 'A' |
| 0181 | | F0 | MOV X, @ DPTR, A | MOVE (A) TO EXT. RAM 6001 H |
| 0182 | | 90 60 00 | MOV DPTR, # DATA 16 | LOAD DATA POINT POINTER WITH 6001H (16 BIT ADDRESS) |
| 0185 | | E6 | MOVE A, @ R0 | MOVE IMMEDIATE RAM TO 'A' |
| 0186 | | F0 | MOVX @ DPTR, A | MOVE A TO EXT. RAM 6001H |
| 0187 | | 08 | INC R0 | INCREMENT REG. R0 |
| 0188 | | B8 38 F0 | CJNE R0, #DATA, REL) | COMPARE IMMEDIATE TO REG. R0 AND JUMP IF NOT EQUAL |
| 018B | | 22 | RET | RETURN |
| 0240 | DB | E5 58 | MOV A, DIRECT | MOVE DIRECT BYTE 58H TO 'A' |
| 0242 | | 85 59 83 | MOV DIRECT1, DIRECT 2 | MOVE DIRECT BYTE 59 TO DIRECT BYTE 83 |
| 0245 | | 85 5A 82 | MOV DIRECT 1, DIRECT 2 | MOVE DIRECT BYTE 5A TO DIRECT BYTE 82 |
| 0248 | | 85 5B D0 | MOV DIRECT 1, DIRECT 2 | MOVE DIRECT BYTE 5B TO DIRECT BYTE D0 |
| 024B | | A8 5C | MOV R0; DIRECT | MOVE DIRECT BYTE 5C TO REG. R0 |
| 024D | | 22 | RET | RETURN |
| 0190 | SITA | 78 30 | MOV R0, #30 | MOVE IMMEDIATE 30H TO REG. R0 |
| 0192 | | 90 00 30 | MOV DPTR, #DATA 16 | LOAD DATA POINTER WITH 0030H (16 BIT ADDRESS) |
| 0195 | | E4 | CLR A | CLEAR ACCMULATOR |
| 0196 | | D6 | XCHD A, @R1 | EXCHANGE LOW ORDER DIGIT INDIRECT RAM WITH 'A' |
| 0197 | | 93 | MOVC A, @A*DPTR | MOVE CODE BYTE RELATIVE TO DPTR TO ACCUMULATOR |
| 0198 | | C6 | XCH A, @ R1 | EXCHANGE INDIRECT RAM WITH A |
| 0199 | | 08 | INC R0 | INCREMENT REG. R0 |
| 019A | | C4 | SWAP A | SWAP NIBBLES WITHIN (A) |
| 019B | | 93 | MOVC A, @A*DPTR | MOVE CODE BYTE RELATIVE TO DPTR TO ACCUMULATOR |
| 019C | | F6 | MOV @ R1, A | MOVE (A) TO INDIRECT RAM |
| 019D | | 08 | INC R0 | INCREMENT REG. R0 |
| 019E | | B8 38 F4 | CJNE R0, #DATA, REL | COMPARE IMMEDIATE TO REG. R0 AND JUMP IF NOT EQUAL |
| 01A1 | | 22 | RET | RETURN |
| 0230 | GITA | F5 58 | MOV DIRECT, A | MOVE 'A' TO DIRECT BYTE (58) |
| 0232 | | 85 83 59 | MOV DIRECT1, DIRECT2 | MOVE DIRECT BYTE 59 TO DIRECT BYTE 83 |
| 0235 | | 85 82 5A | MOV DIRECT1, DIRECT2 | MOVE DIRECT BYTE 5A TO DIRECT BYTE 82 |
| 0238 | | 85 D0 5B | MOV DIRECT1, DIRECT2 | MOVE DIRECT BYTE 5B TO DIRECT BYTE D0 |
| 023B | | 85 5C | MOV DIRECT, R0 | MOVE REG. R0 TO DIRECT BYTE 5C |
| 023D | | 22 | RET | RETURN |

3. SUB-ROUTINE 'DPCH' : This sub-routine displays contents of registers R0 to R7 containing character codes, no register being affected.

| MEM.LOC | LABEL | OPCODES | MNEMONICS | COMMENTS |
|---|---|---|---|---|
| 00B0 | DPCH | 12 02 10 | LCALL 0210H | CALL LONG SUBROUTINE 0210H |
| 00B3 | | 88 30 | MOV DIRECT, R0 | MOVE (REG. R0) TO DIRECT BYTE |
| 00B5 | | 89 31 | MOV DIRECT, R1 | MOVE (REG. R1) TO DIRECT BYTE |
| 00B7 | | 8A 32 | MOV DIRECT, R2 | MOVE (REG. R2) TO DIRECT BYTE |
| 00B9 | | 8B 33 | MOV DIRECT, R3 | MOVE (REG. R3) TO DIRECT BYTE |
| 00BB | | 8C 34 | MOV DIRECT, R4 | MOVE (REG. R4) TO DIRECT BYTE |
| 00BD | | 8D 35 | MOV DIRECT, R5 | MOVE (REG. R5) TO DIRECT BYTE |
| 00BF | | 8E 36 | MOV DIRECT, R6 | MOVE (REG. R6) TO DIRECT BYTE |
| 00C1 | | 8F 37 | MOV DIRECT, R7 | MOVE (REG. R7) TO DIRECT BYTE |
| 00C3 | | 78 30 | MOV Rn, # DATA | MOVE IMMEDIATE DATA TO REG. R0 |
| 00C5 | | 90 00 30 | MOV DPTR, # DATA 16 | LOAD DATA POINTER WITH 0030H |
| 00C8 | | E6 | MOV A, @ R1 | MOVE INDIRECT RAM TO 'A' |
| 00C9 | | 93 | MOVC @ A DPTR | MOVE CODE BYTE RELATIVE TO DPTR TO 'A' |
| 00CA | | F6 | MOV @ R1, A | MOVE ACC. TO INDIRECT RAM |
| 00CB | | 08 | INC R0 | INCREMENT (R0) |
| 00CC | | B8 38 F9 | CJNE R0, # DATA REL | COMPARE IMMEDIATE TO REGISTER AND JUMP IF NOT EQUAL |
| 00CF | | 12 01 70 | LCALL 0170H | CALL LONG SUBROUTINE 0170H (RITA) |
| 00D2 | | 12 02 40 | LCALL 0240H | CALL LONG SUBROUTINE 0240H (DB) |
| 00D5 | | 22 | RET | RETURN |
| 0210 | MITA | C0 00 | PUSH 00 | PUSH DIRECT BYTE (00) TO STACK |
| 0212 | | 78 2F | MOV R0, # DATA | MOVE IMMEDIATE 2FH TO REG. R0 |
| 0214 | | A6 82 | MOV @ R0, DIRECT | MOVE DIRECT BYTE 82H TO INDIRECT RAM R0 |
| 0216 | | C4 | SWAP A | SWAP NIBBLES WITHIN (A) |
| 0217 | | D6 | XCHD A @ R0 | EXCHANGE LOW ORDER DIGIT INDIRECT RAM R0 WITH (A) |
| 0218 | | C4 | SWAP A | SWAP NIBBLES WITHIN (A) |
| 0219 | | F5 82 | MOV DIRECT, A | MOVE ACCUMULATOR TO DIRECT BYTE |
| 021B | | E5 83 | MOV A, DIRECT | MOVE DIRECT BYTE 83H TO 'A' |
| 021D | | D6 | XCHD A @ R0 | EXCHANGE LOW ORDER DIGIT INDIRECT RAM R0 WITH 'A' |
| 021E | | C6 | XCH A, @ R0 | EXCHANGE DIRECT (RAM) R0 WITH A |
| 021F | | C4 | SWAP A | SWAP NIBBLES WITHIN (A) |
| 0220 | | F5 33 | MOV DIRECT, A | MOVE (ACCUMULATOR) TO DIRECT BYTE |
| 0222 | | D0 00 | POP 00 | PUSH DIRCT BYTE (00) T0 STACK |
| 0224 | | 22 | RET | RETURN. |

4. BRK : This sub-routine breaks the bytes in register R0, R2, R4 and R6 into two digits and places them respecctively into registers R0 to R7. It helps to use 'DPCH' and affects registers R0 to R7 only.

| MEM.LOC | LABEL | OPCODES | MNEMONICS | COMMENTS |
|---|---|---|---|---|
| 00E0 | BRK | C0 E0 | PUSH DIRECT | PUSH DIRECT BYTE INTO STACK |
| 00E2 | | E8 | MOV A, R1 | MOV (REG. R1) TO ACC |
| 00E3 | | 54 F0 | ANL A, # DATA | AND IMMEDIATE DATA TO ACC |
| 00E5 | | C4 | SWAP A | SWAP NIBBLES WITHIN THE ACCUMULATOR |

| MEM.LOC | LABEL | OPCODES | MNEMONICS | COMMENTS |
|---------|-------|---------|-----------|----------|
| 00E6 | | F9 | MOVE R1, A | MOVE (ACC.) TO R1 |
| 00E6 | | 53 00 0F | ANL DIRECT, # DATA | AND IMMEDIATE TO DIRECT BYTE |
| 00EA | | EA | MOV A, R2 | MOV (REG.R2) TO ACC. |
| 00EB | | 54 F0 | ANL A, # DATA | AND IMMEDIATE DATA TO ACC. |
| 00ED | | C4 | SWAP A | SWAP NIBBLES WITHIN THE ACCUMULATOR |
| 00EE | | FB | MOV R3, A | MOV (ACC.) TO R3 |
| 00EF | | 53 02 0F | ANL DIRECT, # DATA | AND IMMEDIATE DATA TO DIRECT BYTE |
| 00F2 | | EC | MOV A, R4 | MOV (REG.R4) TO ACC. |
| 00F3 | | 54 F0 | ANL A, # DATA | AND IMMEDIATE DATA TO ACC. |
| 00F5 | | C4 | SWAP A | SWAP NIBBLES WITHIN THE ACCUMULATOR |
| 00F6 | | FC | MOV R4, A | MOV (ACC.) TO R4 |
| 00F7 | | 53 0A 0F | ANL DIRECT, # DATA | AND IMMEDIATE DATA TO DIRECT BYTE |
| 00FA | | ED | MOV, R5 | MOV (REG. R5) TO ACC. |
| 00FB | | 54 F0 | ANL A, # DATA | AND IMMEDIATE DATA TO ACC. |
| 00FD | | C4 | SWAP A | SWAP NIBBLES WITHIN THE ACCUMULATOR |
| 00FE | | FF | MOV R7, A | MOVE (ACC.) TO R7 |
| 00FF | | 53 06 0F | ANL DIRECT, # DATA | AND IMMEDIATE DATA TO DIRECT BYTE |
| 0102 | | D0 E0 | POP DIRECT | POP DIRECT BYTE FROM STACK |
| 0104 | | 22 | RET | RETURN |

5.DAC : This Subroutine outputs the contents of Accumulator through DAC to deliver an equivalent analog voltage. No register is affected.

| MEM.LOC | LABEL | OPCODES | MNEMONICS | COMMENTS |
|---------|-------|---------|-----------|----------|
| 0130 | DAC | F5 5E | MOV DIRECT, A | MOVE ACCUMULATOR TO DIRECT BYTE |
| 0132 | | C0 83 | PUSH DIRECT | PUSH DIRECT BYTE INTO STACK |
| 0134 | | C0 82 | PUSH DIRECT | PUSH DIRECT BYTE INTO STACK |
| 0136 | | 90 30 01 | MOV DPTR, # DATA 16 | LOAD DATA POINTER WITH A 16 BIT CONTENT |
| 0139 | | F0 | MOV @ DPTR, A | MOVE 'A' TO EXTERNAL RAM (16 BIT ADDRESS) |
| 013A | | D0 82 | POP DIRECT | POP DIRECT BYTE INTO STACK |
| 013C | | D0 83 | POP DIRECT | POP DIRECT BYTE INTO STACK |
| 013E | | 22 | RET | RETURN |

6. SWCH : This subroutine outputs the content of 'A' through AC switches, D0 and D1 being given to S0 and S1. Si becomes ON and OFF depending on Di = 1 or 0. No register is affected in this subruline

| MEM.LOC | LABEL | OPCODES | MNEMONICS | COMMENTS |
|---|---|---|---|---|
| 0140 | SWCH | F5 5F | MOV DIRECT, A | MOVE ACCUMULATOR TO DIRECT BYTE |
| 0142 | | F5 5F | PUSH DIRECT | PUSH DIRECT BYTE INTO STACK |
| 0144 | | C0 83 | PUSH DIRECT | PUSH DIRECT BYTE INTO STACK |
| 0146 | | 90 30 02 | MOV DPTR, # DATA 16 | LOAD DATA POINTER WITH A 16-BIT CONTENT |
| 0149 | | F0 | MOVX @ DPTR, 16 | MOVE 'A' TO EXTERNAL RAM (16 BIT ADDRESS) |
| 014A | | D0 83 | POP DIRECT | POP DIRECT BYTE INTO STACK |
| 014C | | D0 82 | POP DIRECT | POP DIRECT BYTE INTO STACK |
| 014E | | 22 | RET | RETURN |

7. ZCD : This sub-routine inputs the states of the zero crossing delectro. $Z_i > 0$ when $D_i = 1$ and $Z_i < 0$ if $D_i = 0$ where D0 and Di correspond to Z0 and Zi, Acc, is affected.

| MEM.LOC | LABEL | OPCODES | MNEMONICS | COMMENTS |
|---|---|---|---|---|
| 0150 | ZCD | E5 90 | MOV A, DIRECT | MOVE DIRECT BYTE TO ACC. |
| 0152 | | 54 03 | ANL A, # DATA | AND IMMEDIATE DATA TO ACC. |
| 0154 | | 22 | RET | RETURN |

8. ADC : This sub-routine reads the analog value at the channel of ADC whose address (00-30) is in A and returns after A/D conversion with the digitised value into A. Acc is affected.

| MEM.LOC | LABEL | OPCODES | MNEMONICS | COMMENTS |
|---|---|---|---|---|
| 0330 | ADC | C0 82 | PUSH DIRECT | PUSH DIRECT BYTE INTO STACK |
| 0332 | | C0 83 | PUSH DIRECT | PUSH DIRECT BYTE INTO STACK |
| 0334 | | 90 30 02 | MOV DPTR, # DATA 16 | LOAD DATA POINTER WITH A 16-BIT CONTENT |
| 0337 | | F5 5D | MOV DIRECT, A | MOVE ACCUMULATOR TO DIRECT BYTE |
| 0339 | | 45 5F | ORL A, DIRECT | OR DIRECT BYTE OT ACC. |
| 033B | | F0 | MOVX @ DPTR, A | MOVE 'A' TO EXTERNAL RAM (16 BIT ADDRESS) |
| 033C | | 44 80 | ORL A, # DATA | OR IMMEDIATE DATA TO ACC. |
| 033E | | 00 | NOP | NO OPERATION |
| 033F | | 00 | NOP | NO OPERATION |
| 0340 | | F0 | MOVX @ DPTR, A | MOVE 'A' TO EXTERNAL RAM (16 BIT ADDRESS) |
| 0341 | | 54 7F | ANL A, # DATA | AND IMMEDIATE DATA TO ACC. |
| 0343 | | 00 | NOP | NO OPERATION |
| 0344 | | 00 | NOP | NO OPERATION |
| 0345 | | F0 | MOVX @ DPTR, A | MOVE 'A' TO EXTERNAL RAM (16 BIT ADDRESS) |
| 0346 | | 12 00 70 | LCALL ADDRESS | LONG SUBROUTINE CALL |
| 0349 | | 90 30 00 | MOV DPTR, # DATA 16 | LOAD DATA POINTER WITH A 16-BIT CONTENT |
| 034C | | E0 | MOVX A, @ DPTR | MOVE EXTERNAL RAM ADDRESS (16-BIT) TO 'A' |
| 034D | | D0 83 | POP DIRECT | POP DIRECT BYTE INTO STACK |
| 034F | | D0 82 | POP DIRECT | POP DIRECT BYTE INTO STACK |
| 0351 | | 22 | RET | RETURN |

9. BCD : This sub-routine converts the contents in DPTR into BCD, registers R0, R1, R2, R3 and DPTR being affected.

| MEM.LOC | LABEL | OPCODES | MNEMONICS | COMMENTS |
|---------|-------|---------|-----------|----------|
| 04B0 | BCD (D) | 7A 10 | MOV R2, # DATA | MOVE IMMEDIATE DATA TO REGISTER |
| 04B2 | | 79 00 | MOV R1, # DATA | MOVE IMMEDIATE DATA TO REGISTER |
| 04B4 | | 78 00 | MOV R0, # DATA | MOVE IMMEDIATE DATA TO REGISTER |
| 04B6 | | C3 | CLR C | CLEAR CARRY FLAG |
| 04B7 | | E5 82 | MOV A, DIRECT | MOVE DIRECT BYTE TO ACC. |
| 04B9 | | 25 82 | ADD A, DIRECT | ADD DIRECT BYTE TO ACC. |
| 04BB | | F5 82 | MOV DIRECT, A | MOVE ACCUMULATOR TO DIRECT BYTE |
| 04BD | | E5 83 | MOV A, DIRECT | MOVE DIRECT BYTE TO ACC. |
| 04BF | | 35 83 | ADC A, DIRECT | ADD DIRECT BYTE TO 'A' WITH (CY) |
| 04C1 | | F5 83 | MOV DIRECT, A | MOVE ACCUMULAROT TO DIRECT BYTE |
| 04C3 | | E8 | MOV A, R0 | MOV (REG.R0) TO A CC. |
| 04C4 | | 38 | ADDC A, R0 | ADD (REG.R0) TO (ACC.) WITH CY |
| 04C5 | | D4 | DAA | DECIMAL ADJUST ACC. |
| 04C6 | | F8 | MOV R0, A | MOV ACC. TO REG.R0 |
| 04C7 | | E9 | MOV A, R1 | MOV (REG.R1) TO ACC. |
| 04C8 | | 39 | ADC A R1 | ADD (REG.R1) TO ACC. WITH CY |
| 04C9 | | D4 | DAA | DECIMAL ADJUST ACC. |
| 04CA | | E9 | MOV R1, A | MOVE (ACC.) TO R1 |
| 04CB | | DA E9 | DJNZ R2, REL | DECREMENT REG. AND JUMP IF NOT ZERO |
| 04CD | | 88 82 | MOV DIRECT, R0 | MOVE (REG.R0) TO DIRECT BYTE |
| 04CF | | 89 83 | MOV DIRECT, R1 | MOVE (REG.R1) TO DIRECT BYTE |
| 04D1 | | 22 | RET | RETURN |

## 15.11 THE MOTOROLA MC 68701

MC 68701 is one of the high performance Single Chip Microcomputer by Motorola in a 40 pin package. Its ROM-versions are MC 6801, MC 6801E etc. The chip includes a clock generator, an 8-bit high performance CPU, 2K EPROM, 128 bytes of RAM, 29 parallel I/O lines and two control lines, one serial communication interface and one 16-bit programmable timer. The CPU closely resembles an MC 6800. Two interrupts IRQ and NMI are also included. MC 68701 is a byte-forward, memory-oriented, memory-based, 8-bit single chip microcomputer.

Like MC 6800 CPU, MC 68701 possesses two accumulators A and B, one 16-bit program counter, 16-bit stack pointer, 16-bit index register and 8-bit condition code register etc. Moreover MC 6800 and MC 68701 are object code compatible, though MC 68701 possesses improved execution time of key instructions and in addition to the 6800 instruction set, it incorporates a number of new enhanced instructions including 16-bit addition and subtraction and unsigned (8-bit) X (8-bit) multiplication to give 16-bit results.

MC 68701 can emulate MC 6801/03 directely. It may operate in three modes. In single-chip mode, it uses all the I/O lines as programmable I/O ports. The expanded non-multiplexed mode uses 16-I/O lines as 8-bit data and 8-bit address bus whereas in expanded multiplexed mode, it uses 8-I/O lines as 8-bit data multiplexed with lower half of 16-bit address bus along with another 8-I/O lines as upper half of the address bus.

# 16. From Intel 8086 to the Pentium Processor

## 16.1 INTRODUCTION

Powerful General Purpose Microprocessors may be devided into two groups viz.

i)      pure complex instruction set computer (CISC) processors

ii)      pure reduced instruction set computer (RISC) processors.

Examples of CISC processors are the 8086, 80186, 80286 and 80386 of Intel family, 68000 and 68040 from Motorola family though the two families are not compatible with reference to instructions, memory address and I/O address. The 80386 is the last pure CISC model of Intel family since the 80486 has the facility of RISC technology partially.

The CISC microprocessors have

i)      complex instructions including machine instructions,

ii)      microencoding of machine instructions,

iii)      extensive addressing capability of memory operations and

iv)      smaller number of useful registers.

The CPU of CISC microprocessor has four functional blocks viz.

i)      The Bus unit (BU)

ii)      The Instruction unit (IU)

iii)      The Execution unit (EU)

iv)      The Address unit (AU)

The prefetch queue inherent in the bus interface reads instructions from the memory and makes them ready for the CPU. The EU performs the data processing such as addition, subtraction, comparison etc. It includes

i)      a Control Unit (CU).

ii)      an Arithmetic and Logic Unit (ALU) and

iii)      the Registers.

The general purpose registers are used as a fast internal data memory for the CPU and perform register to register operations through EU. The EU reads data from one or more registers, sends it to the ALU for manipulation and transfers them from ALU to one or more registers. Memory to memory, register to memory and memory to register operations are also possible. There are segment registers for Memory Management, Control registers etc. other than general purpose registers.

The data, Address and Control buses constitute the bus interface which is the link to the other components. Buses carry instructions from the memory in the prefetch queue to the Instruction Unit (IU) which controls the Execution Unit (EU) and allows the ALU to follow instructions. The CPU reads data from or writes data to the memory through the data bus. The memory address is calculated with the help of the Address Unit (AU). The processor communicates with memory through bus interface and the Bus Unit (BU) during read and write operations. During read operation, the Execution Unit (EU) transfers the data to the prefetch queue, Instruction Unit (IU) reads the instructions/data from the prefetch queue, decodes it and sends the decoded instrucions to the Execution Unit (EU). The structure of a typical CISC microprocessor is shown in Fig. 16.1

**MICROPROCESSOR**

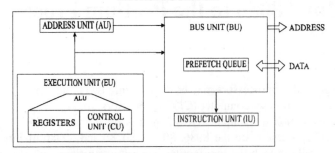

Fig 16.1 Structure of a typical CISC Microprocessor

## 16.2 THE INTEL 80186 (i186) MICROPROCESSOR

The Intel 80186 (iAPX 186) is a 68-Pin package on a ceramic flat pack. This highly integrated 16-bit microprocessor available in 8 MHz clock frequency is a higher version of the Intel iAPX 86 and compatible with the 8086 and the 8088. It has capability of addressing 1-Mbyte of memory and numerical coprocessing through the 8087 interface. The architecture is common to the iAPX 86 and iAPX 88 microprocessor families. It includes 15-20 of the most common microprocessor system components into one chip while providing twice the performance of the iAPX 86. The 80186 is object code compatible with the iAPX 86 and iAPX 88 microprocessors and adds 10 new instruction types of the existing iAPX 86 and 88 instruction set.

The iAPX 86, 88 and 186 families contain the same basic set of registers, instructions and addressing modes. Like the 8086, the 80186 has 14 registers grouped into

  i)     general registers,
  ii)    control registers and
  iii)   segments registers

which function exctly in the same way as discussed in article 13.5.

### 16.2.1 PIN CONFIGURATION OF INTEL 80186

The pin configuration of the Intel 80186 is shown in Fig. 16.2
Pin description :

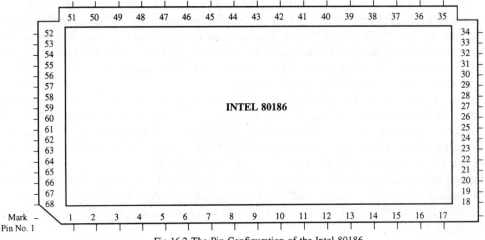

Fig 16.2 The Pin Configuration of the Intel 80186

ADDRESS BUS :

| PIN NO. | 17 | 15 | 13 | 11 | 8 | 6 | 4 | 2 |
|---------|-----|-----|------|------|------|------|------|------|
| BUS NO. | AD0 | AD1 | AD2 | AD3 | AD4 | AD5 | AD6 | AD7 |
| PIN NO. | 16 | 14 | 12 | 10 | 7 | 5 | 3 | 1 |
| BUS NO. | AD8 | AD9 | AD10 | AD11 | AD12 | AD13 | AD14 | AD15 |

Pins :

9, 43 : Vcc (+ 5V power supply)

18-19 : DRQ0, DRQ1 (DMA request by an external device; these signals are active high, level triggered and internally synchronised).

20-21 : TMRIN 0, TMRIN 1 (TIMER INPUTS)
Active high; used either as a clock or control signals.

22-23 : TMROUT 0, TMROUT 1 (TIMER OUTPUTS)
Used to provide single pulse or continuous generation.

24 : $\overline{\text{RES}}$ (SYSTEM RESET)
Immediately terminates its present activity and enters into the dormant state.

25, 27-29 : $\overline{\text{PCS}}$ 0, $\overline{\text{PCS}}$ 1, $\overline{\text{PCS}}$ 2, $\overline{\text{PCS}}$ 3 (PERIPHERAL CHIP SELECT SIGNALS) Active low.

26, 60 : Vss (GND)

30 : PCS4 (PERIPHERAL CHIP SELECT SIGNALS)
Active low, software programable.

31, 32 : $\overline{\text{PCS5}}$/A1, $\overline{\text{PCS6}}$/A2 (PERIPHERAL CHIP SELECT SIGNALS)
Software programable.

33 : $\overline{\text{LCS}}$ (LOWER MEMROY CHIP SELECT)
Active low.

34 : $\overline{\text{UCS}}$ (UPPER MEMORY CHIP SELECT)
Active low.

35-38 : $\overline{\text{MCS3}}$, $\overline{\text{MCS2}}$, $\overline{\text{MCS1}}$, $\overline{\text{MCS0}}$ (MID RANGE MEMORY CHIP SELECT)
Active low.

39 : $\overline{\text{DEN}}$ (DATA ENABLE)
Active low during memory and 1/0 access;
Active high when DT/$\overline{\text{R}}$ changes state.

40 : DT/$\overline{\text{R}}$ (DATA TRANSFER / RECEIVE)
Controls direction of data flow.

41-42 : INT3/$\overline{\text{INTA}}$1, INT2/$\overline{\text{INTA}}$0 (MASKABLE INTERRUPT REQUEST)
Configured via. software to provide active low INTR-acknowledge output signals.

44-45 : INT1, INT0 (MASKABLE INTERRUPT REQUEST)

46 : NMI (NON MASKABLE INTERRUPT)
Edge triggered input, latched internally.

47 : $\overline{\text{TEST}}$ (TEST SIGNAL)
If high, wait execution begins, instruction execution being suspended.

48 : $\overline{\text{LOCK}}$ (LOCK OUTPUT)
Provides indication that other system bus masters are not to gain control of the system bus when LOCK is active low.

Pins                :

49          :   SRDY (SYNCHRONOUS READY)
               To be synchronised externaly to the 80186.

50          :   HOLD (HOLD INPUT)

51          :   HLDA (HLDA OUTPUT)

52-54       :   $\overline{S0}$, $\overline{S1}$, $\overline{S2}$ (BUS CYCLE STATUS)
               Provides bus transaction information, floats during "HOLD"; $\overline{S2}$ may be used as a logical
               M/10 indicator and $\overline{S1}$ as a DT/$\overline{R}$ indicator.

55          :   ARDY (ASYNCHRONOUS READY)
               Active high; informs the processor that the addressed memory space or I/O device
               completes a data transfer.

56          :   CLKOUT (CLOCK OUTPUT)

57          :   RESET (RESET OUTPUT)
               Active high, synchronised with the clock.

58-59       :   X2, X1 (CRYSTAL INPUTS)

61          :   ALE/QS0 (ADDRESS LATCH ENABLE / QUEUE STATUS 0)

62          :   RD/QSMD (READ STROBE)
               Active low.

63          :   WR/QS1 (WRITE STROBE, QUEUE STATUS 1)

64          :   BHE (BUS HIGH ENABLE SIGNAL)

65-68       :   A19/S6, A18/S5, A17/S4, A16/S3 (ADDRESS BUS OUTPUTS AND BUS CYCLE
               STATUS)

## 16.2.2 INSTRUCTION SET

All instructions of the 8086 are available in the 80186. Moreover, it adds 10 new high level, iteration control
and interrupt instructions. Basically iAPX 186 offers extended instruction set over and above basic instruction
set available in iAPX 86 and 88. These are as under :

HIGH LEVEL INSTRUCTIONS :

| MNEMONICS | COMMENTS |
|-----------|----------|
| ENTER | FORMAT STACK FOR PROCEDURE ENTRY |
| LEAVE | RESTORE STACK FOR PROCEDURE EXIT |
| BOUND | DETECT VALUES OUTSIDE PRESCRIBED RANGE |

INERATION CONTROL INSTRUCTION :

| MNEMONICS | COMMENTS |
|-----------|----------|
| LOOP | LOOP |
| LOOPE/LOOPZ | LOOP IF EQUAL/ZERO |
| LOOPNE/LOOPNZ | LOOP IF NOT EQUAL/NOT ZERO |
| JCXZ | JUMP ON REGISTER CX=0 |

INTERRUPT INSTRUCTIONS :

| MNEMONICS | COMMENTS |
|-----------|----------|
| INT | INTERRUPT |
| INT0 | INTERRUPT IF OVERFLOW |
| IRET | INTERRUPT RETURN |

## 16.3 THE INTEL 80286 (i286) MICROPROCESSOR

The 8086 being the first 80 x 86 CPU, its available memory is divided into segments. The latter versons of CPUs starting from the 80186 to the pentium, the same thing being followed. The 8086 has only 20 address lines whereas i286 has 24 address lines and i386 has 32 address lines. The 8086 can address a maximum of only $2^{10}$ bytes (1Mbyte) of memory. Each of the general purpose registers in the 8086 is 16-bit and hence it can address a maximum of $2^{16}$ bytes (64Kbytes). The 8086 divides the physical address area into 64K segments with a capacity of 64 Kbytes (i.e. 65536 bytes). Thus theoretically, 64K * 64Kbytes i.e 4 Gbytes of address space is possible. But 20-bit address bus of the 8086 has the capacity of addressing 1M byte. In a segment, the position of a byte is given by an offset which are stored in the general purpose registers. The segments are controlled by the segment registers CS to ES. The CPU uses a segment and offset pair to access the memory. Byte, word etc. used are indicated by the segment register whereas the offset is indicated by the general purpose register. The 8086 can work only in real mode in which the AU shifts the segment register value left by 4-bits in order to multiply the segment value by 16 and adds the offset to get a 20-bit address.

The 80286 has a maximum physical address space of 16 Mbytes for its 24 address lines ($2^{24}$ = 16M) though in the 80386, 4 Gbytes of memory are available. The internal block diagram of Intel 80286 microprocessor is shown in Fig. 16.3.

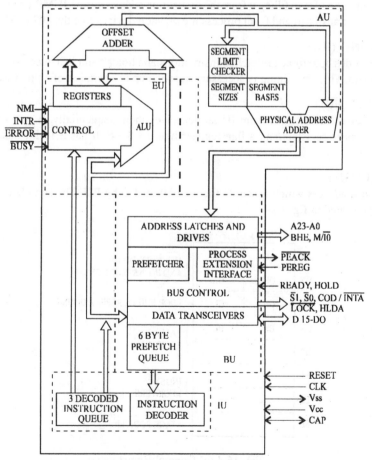

Fig. 16.3 Internal block diagram of Intel 80286 microprocessor

### 16.3.1 PROCESSING UNITS OF THE 80286

The INTEL 80286 microprocessor has been designed to develop a CPU suitable for a multi-tasking microcomputer system. IBM PC/AT uses the 80286 as CPU. The 80286 contains the following four separate processing units :

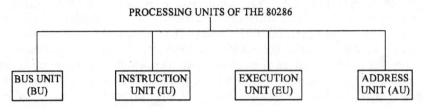

PROCESSING UNITS OF THE 80286

BUS UNIT (BU) :
The functions of the BUS UNIT are to
i)      read Memory, I/O and write.
ii)     Prefetch instruction bytes and put them in a 6-byte prefetch queue when the buses are not used for other operation.
iii)    dump the queue and start filling it from the destination address during JUMP and CALL instructions.
iv)     Control data transfer to and from processor extension devices like the 80287 Math co-processor.

INSTRUCTION UNIT (IU) :
Instruction unit decodes upto three prefetched instructions and holds them in a queue so that the Execution Unit can access them. This pipe lining is necessary to speed up to operation of a processor.

EXECUTION UNIT (EU) :
Execution unit receives instructions from IU and executes them sequentially. It contains a set of index pointer, general purpose registers and a flag register like the 8086. It has a 16-bit machine status word (MSW) register.

ADDRESS UNIT (AU) :
It computes physical address which is sent to the memory or I/O by BU. The complete register set of the 80286 has been presented in fig. 16.4.

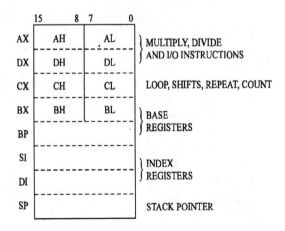

Fig. 16.4 (a) General Registers

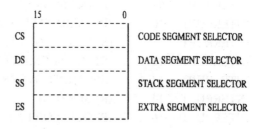

Fig. 16.4 (b) Segment Registers

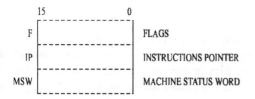

Fig. 16.4 (c) Status and Control Registers

## 16.3.2 MEMORY ADDRESS MODES OF THE 80286

The 80286 can operate in two memory address modes :
  i)    Real Address Mode,
  Mii)  Protected Virtual Address Mode (PVAM).

REAL ADDRESS MODE

The action in this mode is similar to that of the 8086. In this mode, physical memory addresses are produced directly by adding an offset to a segment base. The AU computes addresses with a segment base and an offset component. The CS (Code Segment), DS (Data Segment), SS (Stack Segment) and ES (Extra Segment) registers are used to hold the base address for the segments currently in use. The instruction pointer (IP) holds the offset of the currently addressed code byte in the code segment and the stack. The maximum physical address space in this mode is 1 Mbyte like the 8086.

In this mode, the 80286 directly executes the 8086 machine code programs with a minor modification. Due to extensive pipelining and other hardware improvements, the 80286 executes programs with much more faster rate. The instruction set of the 80286 in real address mode is a superset of the 8086 instructions having facilities of extended instruciton set of the 80186 (such as ENTER, LEAVE, BOUND), a few instructions required to switch the 80286 from real address mode to virtual address mode and its own system control instruction set. The machine cycle waveforms for the 80286 is similar to those of the 8086. The 80286 has several additional built-in interrupt types such as

| INTERRUPT | 0 | (DIVIDE ERROR EXCEPTION) |
|-----------|---|--------------------------|
| INTERRUPT | 1 | (SINGLE STEP INTERRUPT) |
| INTERRUPT | 2 | (NON MASKABLE INTERRUPT, NMI) |
| INTERRUPT | 3 | (BREAK POINT INTERRUPT) |
| INTERRUPT | 4 | (INT0 DETECTED OVERFLOW EXCEPTION) |
| INTERRUPT | 5 | (BOUND RANGE EXCEEDED EXCEPTION) |
| INTERRUPT | 6 | (INVALID OPCODE EXCEPTION) |
| INTERRUPT | 7 | (PROCESSOR EXTENSION NOT AVAILABLE EXCEPTION) |
| INTERRUPT | 8 | (INTERRUPT TABLE LIMIT TOO SMALL) |

| INTERRUPT | 9 | (PROCESSOR EXTENSION SEGMENT OVERRUN INTERRUPT) |
|-----------|-----|---|
| INTERRUPT | 10 | (INVALID TASK STATE SEGMENT) |
| INTERRUPT | 11 | (SEGMENT NOT PRESENT) |
| INTERRUPT | 12 | (STACK SEGMENT OVERRUN OR NOT PRESENT) |
| INTERRUPT | 13 | (SEGMENT OVERRUN EXCEPTION) |
| INTERRUPT | 14, 15 | (RESERVED) |
| INTERRUPT | 16 | (PROCESSOR EXTENSION ERROR INTERRUPT) |
| INTERRUPT | 17-31 | (RESERVED) |
| INTERRUPT | 32-255 | (USER DEFINED) |

When an interrupt occurs, the 80286 (like the 8086) multiplies the interrupt type number by 4 and goes to the resulting address in the interrupt vector table to get the CS and IP values for the interrupt procedure. In real address mode, the interrupt vector table is kept in the first 1 Kbyte of memory. The interrupt vector table has no-fixed physical address in memory in the virtual address mode.

## PROTECTED VIRTUAL ADDRESS MODE (PVAM)

The virtual address mode computes addresses in a different way. In this mode, the function of AU is to act as a complete memory management unit (MMU) and the 80286 uses all 24-addrss lines to access 16-Mbytes of physical memory. This mode provides protection and virtual memory capability necessary in multi tasking operating systems.

The major features of the protected virtual address mode, PVAM, of the 80286 may be listed as

- i) Memory management,
- ii) Protection,
- iii) Task switching and
- iv) Interrupt Processing.

After the 80286 is reset, it initially operates in real address mode in order to

- i) initialise peripheral devices,
- ii) load the main part of the operating system from disk memory,
- iii) load some registers,
- iv) enable interrupts and
- v) enter into the PVAM by setting the protection enable bit of the machine status word (MSW) in the 80286.

The Flag Word and Machine Status Word are shown in Fig. 16.5 The iAPX 286 possesses 6 status flags such as

- i) Carry (CF), Parity (PF), Auxiliary Carry (AF), Zero (ZF), Sign (SF) and Overflow (OF) (like Intel 8086 and 80186) flags occupying 0, 2, 4, 6, 7 and 11-th bit positions.
- ii) three control flgs viz. Trap flag (TF), Interrupt Enable flag (IF) and Direction flag (DF) occupying 8, 9, 10-th bit positions of status word and
- iii) Two special flags viz. I/O privilage level flags (IO and PL) occupying 12 and 13-th bit positions and Nested Task flag (NT) occupying 14-th bit position of status word newly introduced in the 80286.

FLAGS

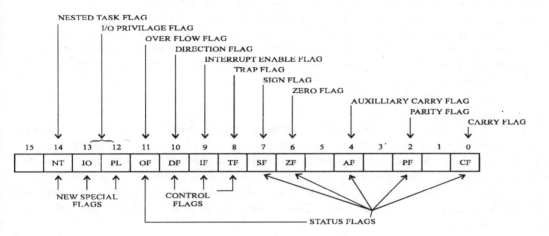

MACHINE STATUS WORD (MSW)

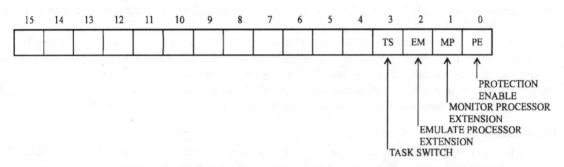

Fig. 16.5  The 80286 Flag word and Machine Status Word

It may be noted that bit 0 of MSW is the protection enasble bit. Bits 1, 2 and 3 are used to indicate the presence of a processor extension. For operating the 80286 in PVAM, an intersegment jump to the start of the main system program is necessary. It may be noted that once the PVAM is entered by executing the load machine status word (LMSW) instruction, the real address mode may be regained only by reseting the system.

Like the 8086, the basic building block of memory management in PVAM are logical segments. This segments may be referred to as "virtual segments" because all of them may or may not be present in physical memory at the same time. Unlike 8086 segments, those for the 80286 can be of any length form 1 byte to 64 Kbytes. In PVAM, all 24 address lines are active, so that 16 Mbytes of physical memory can be accessed.

### 16.3.3 DESCRIPTORS AND SELECTORS

The major building block of programs in PVAM are segments. When a program is assembled and made ready for execution in PVAM, a unique 8-byte quantity is produced for each segment. This is called a DESCRIPTOR. Each segment contains the length, starting address and access rights for that segments. Bytes 0 and 1 of a descriptor contain the length or limit of the segment in bytes. The Machine Management Unit (MMU) uses this limit value to produce an interrupt in order to access a location beyond the end of a segment. Bytes 2, 3 and 4 of the descriptor contain the 24-bit base address (out of 16Mbyte - physical address space) where the segment is or will be located. Byte 5 of a descriptor is the access byte which contains information regarding the privilege level, access and type of the segment. Bytes 6 and 7 of a descriptor have been included in the descriptor format in order to make the 80286 compatible with the 80386 microprocessor. Usually all these bytes are filled with 0's for the normal operation of the 80286.

The descriptors for an 80286 system are kept in tables in the memory called the "descriptor Table". Two different types of descriptor tables are available :

i)      the global descriptor table and
ii)     the local descriptor table.

A system may have only one global descriptor table for holding the segments' descriptors for the operating system segments and the descriptors for segments which may be necessary for performing user's tasks. The 80286 keeps the base addresses and limits for the descriptor tables currently in use in internal registers. For each task or closely related group of tasks, a local descriptor table is set up in the system.

The global descriptor table register (GDTR) contains the 24-bit base address and limit for the table containing the global address space descriptors. This register is initialised with the LGDT instruction when the system is booted.

The local descrptor table register (LDTR) in the 80286 contains the base address and limit of the local descriptor table for the task currently being executed. The LLDT instruction is used to load this register when the system is booted. The LLDT instruction can only be executed by programs executing at the highest privilege level.

Each local descriptor table is actually a named segment and it has its own unique descriptor. The descriptors for the local descriptor tables in the system are kept in the global descriptor table. When the operating system does a task switch, the new local descriptor table is read from the global descriptor table and the content is kept into the LDTR register in the 80286. As the new task executes, it uses the descriptor in the local descriptor table identified by the LDT register to access the segments it requires.

## SELECTORS

In real address mode, when a program is assembled and prepared for execution on an 8086 or on an 80286, each named segment is given a 16-bit base addres, offsets in program instruction are added to this segment base address and a physical address is produced. When a program is reassembled for execution on an 80286 in PVAM, in stead of being directly assigned a base address, each segment is assigned a 16-bit selector. The upper 13 bits of a selector contain the number of the descriptor in a descriptor table. This part of the selector is referred to as an index because the value in these bits when internally multiplied by 8, points to the descriptor for that segment in a descriptor table. The upper 13 bits will index a segments descriptor in the "global descriptor table" or in the "local descriptor table" according as the table indicator bit of the selector is 0 or 1. This is a form of indirect addressing. In a descriptor table, the selector points to a descriptor location, the descriptor of which contains actual base address and other information about the desired segments. The least significant two bits of a selector viz. the requested privilege level or RPL bits are a part of the protection mechanism.

## 16.3.4 ADDRESS TRANSLATION REGISTERS AND PHYSICAL ADDRESSES

In the real address mode of the 8086 or the 80286, the base addresses for the currently used segments are kept in the CS, DS, SS and ES registers in the processor where they may be used to produce physical addresses. For the 80286 operating in PVAM, descriptor must be transferred from descriptor table in memory to registers where they can be used for producing and checking physical addresses. "Segment address translation registers" hold the descriptors for the currently used segments.

The descriptor table registers hold the 24-bits physical starting addresses for the global and local descriptor tables. The physical address of the descriptor corresponding to the selector is produced by multiplying the 13-bit index part of a selector by 8 followed by the addition to one of these bases. When a selector is loaded into the visible part of the segment register, the 80286 automatically computes the physical address of the corresponding descriptor and loads the descriptor into the hidden part of the segment register.

### 16.3.5 PROTECTION MECHANISMS IN THE 80286
The 80286 operating in PVAM has the mechanism to protect the following from the accidental access :
- i) system software from users' program,
- ii) user-tasks from each other,
- iii) regions of memory.

For these, every attempt to access memory is checked using information in segment descriptors and the memory access is allowed if the attempt is valid. Otherwise an error interrupt is produced.

During loading a segment selector into a segment register, the 80286 checkes the following :
- i) Whether the descritor table indexed by the selector contains a valid descriptor for that selector. If it is valid, bytes corresponding to the limit, base and access rights of the descriptor are loaded into the hidden part of the segment register. Otherwise an interrupt is produced.
- ii) Whether the segment for that descriptor is present in physical memory. If not, an interrupt is produced.
- iii) Whether the segment descriptor to be loaded into the specified segment register is of the right type. It may be noted that the descriptor for a read-only data segment and code segment cannot be loaded into the SS and DS registers respectively.
- iv) Whether any attempt has been made to write to a code segment / read-only data segment.
- v) Whether an address produced by program instructions falls outside the limit defined for the segment.
- vi) Whether one task has accessed descriptors in the local descriptor table for another task when execution is switched from one task to another.

The protected mechanism has also been extended to protect system software using privilage level. Operating system is assigned the highest privilege level keeping the other system levels at lower privilege levels. The privilege level of a code or data segment is inserted as bits 5 and 6 of the access byte of the segment privilege level (DPL). The privilege level of the executing task referred to as the 'current privilege level (CPL)" is contained in the least significant bit of the selector in the CS registor. In order to access a data segment by loading its selector and descriptor tie in the DS register, the DPL from the descriptor is compared with the CPL. The access is only allowed if (DPL) is not greater than the (CPL). Otherwise an error interrupt is produced. It may be noted that a segment at a higher privilage level may be called through a special structure known as a "gate" and should never be called directly. The "gate" is a special type of descriptor and in the 80286, four types of gates viz. CALL, TRAP, INTERRUPT and TASK are available.

### 16.3.6 TASK SWITCHING AND TASK GATES
In a PVAM, each task is associated with a 22-word Task State Segment (TSS) which keeps copies of
- i) all registers and flags,
- ii) the selector for the task's LDT and
- iii) a link to the TSS of the previously executing task.

Descriptors for each TSS are kept in the global descriptor table. In the 80286, a table register (TR) holds the selector and the TSS descriptor for the currently executing task. To initialise the task registers to the TSS for the particular task, the instruction LTR (Load Task Register) may be used. During a task switch, the task register is automatically loaded with the selector and the descriptor for the new task. A task switch may be performed by any one of the three ways :

i)     a long jump or call instruction,

ii)    an IRET instruction,

iii)   an interrupt.

In real address mode, the first 1 Kbyte of memory of the 8086 or the 80286 is kept reserved as an interrupt vector table and the CS and the IP values for upto 256 interrupt types are put in this table. When operating in PVAM, the 80286 can also handle upto 256 interrrupts but in order to provide protection, it is performed with descriptors. For this purpose, an interrupt descriptor table (IDT) is set up in memory. The interrupt descriptor table can be located anywhere in the memory. The interrupt descriptor table can be located any where in the memory. The base address, access byte and limit for the interrupt descriptor table are held in a special interrupt descriptor table register in the 80286. When an interrupt occurs the following mechanisms take place :

i)     The interrupt type is first multiplied by 8 and is used as a selector to indicate the desired descriptor in the IDT (interrupt descriptor table).

ii)    It is then added to the IDT register to index a gate descriptor in the IDT.

iii)   The gate descriptor contains a selector for the segment which holds the interrupt service procedure and offset of the procedure in the segment.

The selector from the gate descriptor is loaded into the visible part of the CS registor and the segment descriptor indicated by the selector is loaded into the hidden part of the CS register, provided the access is valid.

### 16.3.7 SOME INSTRUCTIONS FOR PVAM

CTS    -   Clear task switched flag in MSW

LGDT -   Load global descriptor table register from memory

SGDT -   Store contents of the global descriptor table register in memory

LIDT  -   Load interrupt descriptor table register from memory

LLDT -   Load selector and associated descriptor into Local Descriptor Table Register (LDTR)

SLDT -   Store selector from LDTR in specified register or memory

LTR    -   Load task register with selector and descriptor for TSS

STR    -   Store selector form task register in register or memory

LMSW -  Load Machine Status Word (MSW) from register or memory

SMSW -  Store Machine Status Word (MSW) in register or memory

LAR    -   Load access right-byte of descriptor into register or memory

LSL    -   Load segment limit from descriptor into register or memory

ARPL -   Adjust requested privilege level of selector

VERR -   Determine if segment indicated by selector is readable

VEWR -   Determine if segment indicated by selector is writable.

### 16.3.8 PIN CONFIGURATION OF INTEL 80286

The intel 80286 is a 68-pin package on a ceramic flat-pack. An external 82284 clock generator is required for producing single phase clock signals which are synchronised with the RESET and READY signals by the clock genrator. The 80286 has a 16-bit data bus and a 24-bit non-multiplexed address bus for accessing 16Mbytes of physical memory. External buffers are used on both the address and data bus. Like the 8086, the memory set up of 80286 consists of an odd bank enabled when $\overline{BHU}$ is low and an even bank enabled when A0 is low. When operated in maximum mode, the 80286 like the 8086, requires the status signals $\overline{S0}$, $\overline{S1}$, and M/$\overline{IO}$ to be decoded by an external 82288 bus controller to produce the control bus READ, WRITE and INTERRUPT ACKNOWLEDGE signals. The pin configurations of the 80286 is shown in Fig. 16.6

Pin description :

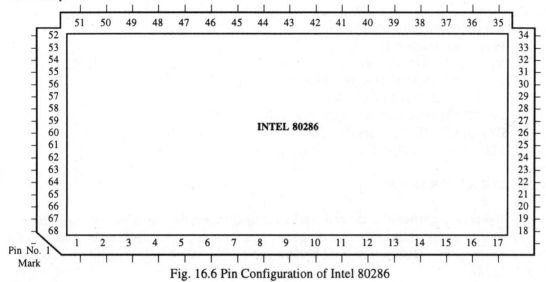

Fig. 16.6 Pin Configuration of Intel 80286

Pin description :
24-BIT ADDRESS BUS :

| PIN NO. | 34 | 33 | 32 | 28 | 27 | 26 | 25 | 24 | 23 | 22 | 21 | 20 |
|---------|-----|-----|-----|-----|-----|-----|-----|-----|-----|-----|-----|-----|
| BUS NO. | A00 | A01 | A02 | A03 | A04 | A05 | A06 | A07 | A08 | A09 | A10 | A11 |
| PIN NO. | 19 | 18 | 17 | 16 | 15 | 14 | 13 | 12 | 11 | 10 | 8 | 7 |
| BUS NO. | A12 | A13 | A14 | A15 | A16 | A17 | A18 | A19 | A20 | A21 | A22 | A23 |

16-BIT DATA BUS

| PIN NO. | 36 | 38 | 40 | 42 | 44 | 46 | 48 | 50 |
|---------|-----|-----|-----|-----|-----|-----|-----|-----|
| BUS NO. | D0 | D1 | D2 | D3 | D4 | D5 | D6 | D7 |
| PIN NO. | 37 | 39 | 41 | 49 · | 45 | 47 | 48 | 51 |
| BUS NO. | D8 | D9 | D10 | D11 | D12 | D13 | D14 | D15 |

Pins :
1    $\overline{\text{BHE}}$ (BUS HIGH ENABLE)
2-3, 55-56, 58    NC (NO CONNECTION)
4-5   $\overline{\text{S1}}$, $\overline{\text{S0}}$ (STATUS SIGNAL)
6    PEACK (PROCESSOR EXTENSION ACKNOWLEDGE)
    This output signals the processors extension when the requested operand is being transferred.
9, 35, 60  Vss

29    RESET (RESET INPUT)

If made high for a required time and then made low, the 80286 starts executing in the real address mode at address FFFFF0 H with the initialisatin of registers as follows :

    FLAG WORD - 0002 H
    MACHINE STATUS WORD - FFF0 H
    INSTRUCTION POINTER (IP) - FFF0 H
    CARRY SEGMENT REGISTER (CS) - F000 H
    DESTINATION SEGMENT REGISTER (DS) - 0000 H
    EXTRA SEGMENT REGISTER (ES) - 0000 H
    STATUS SEGMENT REGISTER (SS) - 0000 H

30, 62    Vcc

31    CLK (CLOCK SIGNAL)

52    CAP

This pin is connected to an external capacitor to filter the negative bias voltage produced from the +5 V supply by a bias genrator on the 80286. This negative bias voltage is necessary to bias the substates of the MOS devices in the 80286 in order to operate the same at maximum speed.

53    ERROR

If a co-processor finds some error during processing, it will assert the error input of the 80286. This will cause the 80286 to automatically do a type 16 H interrupt call. An interrupt service procedure can be written to make the desired response to the error condition.

54    BUSY (BUSY SIGNAL INPUT)

During wait instruction, the processor remains in wait loop untill the busy signal form the co-processor becomes high.

57    INTR (INTERRUPT INPUT PIN)

Used for connecting an 8259A priority interrupt controller to receive external hardware interrupt.

59    NMI (NON MUSKABLE INTERRUPT INPUT)

61    PEREQ (PROCESSOR EXTENSION REQUEST)

This input pin is asserted by a co-processor to inform the 80286 to perform a data transfer to or from memory for it.

63    READY (READY INPUT)

64    HOLD

Used to request the use of buses for DMA operations.

65    HLDA (HOLD ACKNOWLEDGE INPUT)

Used to inform DMA controller regarding the availability of buses.

66    COD / INTA (STATUS SIGNAL OUTPUT)

Used with M/IO to produce early control bus signal,

    0  :    for interrupt acknowledge, memory data read or write signals.
    1. :    for I/O read /write or memory instruction read machine cycles.

67    M/IO (MEMORY / IO SELECT)

68    LOCK (LOCK OUTPUT PIN)

This indicates that other system bus masters are not to gain control of the sysem bus following the current bus cycle.

## 16.4  THE INTEL 80386 32-BIT MICROPROCESSOR

The 80386 microprocessor is a logical extension of the 80286. It is a 32-bit microprocessor fully compatible with its predecessor, the 16-bit 80286. The 80286 in PVAM can address upto 8192 virtual memory segments of 64 Kbytes each and hence it has a virtual address space of 1 Gigabyte. In order to operate with maximum efficiency, a processor working with virtual memory should have an addressing capability equivalent to the size of the secondary storage. As the capacity of optical disk storage units tends to 10 Gbyte, processors with greater addressing range than the 80286 are needed. The 80386 is more highly pipelined than the 80286. Fig. 16.7 shows a block diagram of the functional processors within the 80386. Instruction fetching, instruction decoding, instruction execution and memory management are all carried out in parallel. The 80386 instruction set is a superset of that of the other members of the 8086 family.

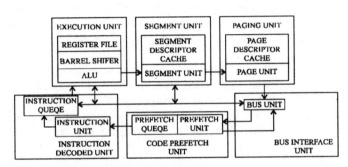

FIG. 16.7 Internal Block Diagram of Intel 80386

The general purpose registers in the i386 are of 32 bits but they can also be used as 16-bit or 8-bit registers. These are compatible with the 8086/186/286. The i386 has seven general purpose registers, six segment registers, an instruction pointer, a stack pointer and a flag register. Sevens general purpose registers are Accumulator (EAX), Base register (EBX), Count register (ECX), Data Register (EDX), Source Index register (ESI), Destination Index register (EDI) and Base pointer (EBP). All these are of 32-bit registers and they can be used for 32-bit data handling. For 16-bit data handling, all these registers may be used using two lower byte values which constitute the 16-bit registers AX, BX, CX, DX, SI, DI and BP. Each of the first four genral purpose 16-bit registers viz. AX, BX, CX and DX may be sub-divided into two single byte registers. These are AH, AL; BH, BL; CH, CL; DH, DL as shown in Table 16.1.

**Table 16.1**
**General Purpose Registers, Instruction Pointer and Stack Pointer**

| (32-BIT) | 31 | 16 | 15 | 8 | 7 | 0 | (16-BIT) |
|----------|----|----|-----|-----|-----|---|----------|
| EAX | | | AH | | AL | | AX |
| EBX | | | BH | | BL | | BX |
| ECX | | | CH | | CL | | CX |
| EDX | | | DH | | DL | | DX |
| ESI | | | | SI | | | SI |
| EDI | | | | DI | | | DI |
| EBP | | | | BP | | | BP |
| EIP | | | | IP | | | IP |
| ESP | | | | SP | | | SP |
| | | | 286 REGISTER SET | | | | |

The major functions assigned to the 32-bit accumulator (EAX) are multiplication, division, input / output, fast shifts etc. Majority of instructions including fastest executing instrucitons are available to EAX and its subdivisions AX, AH and AL. The base register EBX acts as a pointer to base address in data segment. The count register (ECX) is mainly used as a counter during programming and execution of loops. It counts value for repetitions, shifts, rotates etc. The tasks assigned to the data register (EDX) are multiplications, division and I/O operation. The base pointer (EBP) acts as thr pointer to base address in stack segment. The source index register (ESI) functions as source string and index pointer whereas the destination index register (EDI) acts as destination string and index pointer. The instruction pointer (EIP), stack pointer (ESP) and a flag register (EFLAG) all are of 32-bits.

Two lower bytes of each of these registers constitute the 16-bit index pointer (IP), stack pointer (SP) and flag (FLAG) registers. The instruction pointer (EIP) holds offset of instructions and EFLAG register is the indicator for processor's status and operation results. It is the 32-bit EIP which makes possible up to a maximum of 4Gbytes whereas the 80286 only allows programs upto 64Kbytes with the use of the 16-bit offset registers.

The use of registers in the i386 with 32-bit or 16-bit depends on the operating mode to be selected. The i386 can perform all activities which its predecessors, the 8086 and 80286 can perform. The segment registers are of 16-bit and these are designated as code segment (CS), stack segment (SS), data segment (DS) and extra segments (ES, FS, and GS). First three segment registers are used as the segment of instructions, segment of stack and standard segment of data respectively and the three extra segments can be used freely.

During a program execution, the code segment and instruction pointer constitute a register pair to indicate the next instruction in memory to the processor to follow. The processor fetches instructions from memory and executes them, the code segment sets the segment for the next instructions and the instruction pointer gives the offset for the next instruction to be read.

The 80386 has a 32-bit data bus and produces a full 32-bit non-multiplexed address bus. This 32-bit address bus allows it to address $2^{32}$, or about 4 Gigabytes of physical memory. The 80386 can be operated in one of two memory management modes viz.

i)    paged mode and
ii)   nonpaged mode.

In nonpaged mode, the MMU operates very similary to that of the 80286. Similar to the 80286 processor, virtual addresses of i386 are represented with a selector component and an offset component. The selector component is used to index a descriptor in a physical base address for the desired segment. The offset part of the virtual address is added to the base address from the descriptor to produce the actual physical address. The offset part of a virtual address can be of 16 or 32 bit so that segments can be as large as 4 Gigabytes. In nonpaged mode, name segments are swapped into physical memory as and when required.

In paged mode, the 80386 switches the paging unit in, after the segment unit is made on. The paging unit allows those memory pages which are actually required from a large system to communicate with the disk. This type of operation is often called 'Demand-Paged Virtual Memory'.

The 32-bit address produced by adding a base address form a descriptor and an offset is referred to as a 'Linear Address'. Components of this linear address are used as pointers to two levels of paging tables. This first level is the page table directory which contains the base address of all the page tables for the system, the second level being the actual page tables containig the addresses of each page in the system.

Like the 80286 operating in PVAM, descripor tables and the segment unit provide task and memory protecting in paging mode of i386. When required, the paging unit allows pages of small fixed length to be associated with the physical memory enhancing the system efficiency.

### 16.4.1 CODE SEGMENT, INSTRUCTION POINTER AND PROGRAM EXECUTION

The code segment and the instruction pointer form the basis of the processor for fetching instrucitons from memory and executing them in order to run a program.

The instruction being executed, the instruction counter is incremented by the number of bytes contained in the executed instruction. When a 2 byte instruction is executed, the instruction counter is incremented by two and the code segment instruction counter pair refers to the next instruction to be executed. The next instruction being read and executed in the same way, the processor increments the instruction counter again. These reading and the incrementing procedure are carried out by the processor independently without requiring any action from the control program or from the user. Once activated, the CPU allows to read and execute instructions continuously.

The prefetch queue and the bus interface both play an important role in instruction fetching. The instruction is first read into the prefetch queue. It is then transferred to the instruction unit (IU). When the instruction bytes are sent to the control unit (CU), the number of free bytes in the prefetching queue becomes equal to the width of the data bus of the processor. Then the bus interface reads the applicable number of bytes from the memory into the prefetching queue. The i386 has a four byte (32-bit) data bus. It independently reads four bytes when these bytes are free in the prefetch queue. When the i386 carries out an instruction without immediate memory access, the bus interface can load the prefetch queue without hindering the currently active instruction. After executing an instruction, the processor receives the next instruction for which reading from memory is necessary. Thus parallel to the execution of the currently active instruction and reloading of the prefetching queue, the IU decodes the next instruction and prepares it for the execution unit (EU) and for execution. The EU carries out the instruction in a specific number of clock cycles. Simple instructions require two clock cycles whereas complicated instructions such as a task switch via, a protected mode need more than 300 cycles.

There is a uniform instruction flow from the memory to the processor. A program is executed sequentially. In order to increase capabilities of the computer, it is necessary to perform as many independent steps as possible, in parallel. The Pentium can use three independent pipelines for parallel processing.

The uniform flow of instructions can be interrupted and redirected by conditional and unconditional jumps and branchings. In order to carry out a jump or a branching, only the value of the instruction pointer and, if necessary, the code segment need to be changed.

The code segment can be changed, but the instruction pointer can not be changed. There is no direct loading instruction for the EIP. The value in the instruction pointer can only be changed with a conditional or unconditional jump to another program.

## 16.4.2 STACK SEGMENT AND STACK POINTER

Every program is normally assigned a stack segment in order to store the content of a register or a memory operand with the help of the PUSH instruction. The PUSH instruction transfers the contents of the flags, and the PUSHA instruction is used to move the contents of all of the general purpose registers to the stack. It is also possible to use the instructions POP, POPF and POPA to transfer the necessary data from the stack and to write the memory operand or the flag to a register. If data is stored on the stack, the value of ESP is reduced by four. When the i386 operates in 16-bit mode like the 8086 and 80286, only 2bytes are written to the stack and the value of ESP is only reduced by two with every PUSH. After the word has been stored, the stack pointer indicates the last stored word in the stack. By a PUSH insruction, the value of the stack pointer EPS is increased and the register or memory content is stored in the stack.

The probable cases of program crash are called 'stack overflow'. This is caused if an attempt is made to write additional data to the stack using a new PUSH instruction when its capacity is exceeded. In real mode, it is easily identified by examining the content of ESP. When the stack is full, the content of ESP becomes zero and a new PUSH instruction makes the stack-overflow. Thus it is necessary to test the content of ESP before every PUSH instruction. This disadvantage is overcome in the protected mode where the i386 can identifiy such failure automatically. The 80386 uses the stack mainly as a temporary storage for return address or register contents. By means of PUSH EAX instruction, the accumulator content is saved on the stack. Simultaneously the stack pointer is decremented by four and stack moves towards lower addresses.

The stack may further be used as an intermediate storage space for the use of data that can not easily be accessed without PUSH and POP instrucions. The trap flag is such an example. The stack is mainly used for storing parameters and procedures of subroutines. Parameters for procedures containing one or more PUSH instructions of the current program are also stored there. The applicable procedure can then use these parameters with one or more POP instructions as necessary or with the help of addressing through the base ponter (BP). In the i386, stack frames are created using the instruction pair ENTER and LEAVE and local variables stored using the applicable procedure. The stack is reset to its previous condition with a RETURN instruction before the current program is executed. In this way, the stored parameters and the temporary local variables are deleted. The PUSH SP instruction is used to write the stack register to the stack. The i386 first writes ESP to the stack, and then the ESP is reduced by two or four. It may be noted that the 8086/8088 first reduces SP by two and then copies SP to the stack.

### 16.4.3 DATA SEGMENT AND MEMORY ADDRESSING

The data segment (DS) register has a special use when an instruction reads data from or writes data to the memory. The offset of the memory operand is usually contained in a general purpose register and the DS-offset pair identifies the applicable value. The data segment register (DS) is normally used as an 'Offset Associated Segment Register'. When it is necessary to read or write a value into another segment, the segment register DS must be loaded with the value of the new segment so that data register DS is replaced with an extra segment register ES to GS. The logically different steps of a program are separated using different segments for code, stack and data. The protected mode utilises this technique to prevent program failures.

### 16.4.4 RISC MECHANISM AND HARDWARE INSTRUCTIONS

The term RISC stands for reduced instruction set computer. A microprocessor can operate faster if an instruction set is developed with only simple logical and arithmetic instructions. Fewer number of instrucions mean a simpler and faster instruction decoder and the instruction sequences can be written most efficiently to perform the desired operation. The RICS mechanism has been developed reducing highly complex CISC instruction set. The simple structure due to the reduced instruction set minimises the number of electronic components of a typical RISC processor and the developement time has become much more reduced compared to that of CISC CPUs.

The RISC CPU has a complex hardware multiplier which multiplies the two numbers in a multiplier registers and stores the product in the results register. In a CISC CPU, a simple added circuitry is driven by the micro-coded Control Unit (CU) so that the multiplicand is successively shifted to the left by a shifter and the increased value is repeatedly added to the multiplicand until the result register contains the final result. The most important characteristic of the RISC processor is inherent in this hardwared instructions or hardwared control unit (CU). In a RISC processor, the execution unit (EU) in the CU is not controlled with the help of extensive micro-codes. Instead, the whole operation is achieved in the form of hardwared logic enhancing the speed of instruction. The CU and EU for RISC may be larger and more efficient compared to those of CISC processor since smaller number of instruction are to be implemented in RISC without increasing the size of the chip.

The procedure for multiplication in a CISC processor is to move the multiplicand successively by 'one' position to the left and to add up the sub-total, if the corresponding position in the multiplicator is a '1'. With a '0', the multiplicand is simply moved a further position to the left. For this, the CISC CPU only requires a full adder whereby in each case, the CU under the control of the microcodes for the multiplication function in the adder, only repeats the movement of the multiplicand one position further and adds the sub-total of the previous addition. With a 32-bit multiplication instruction, the operation is completed after a maximum of 32 runs.

A multiplication is executed completely differently in a powerful RISC CPU. In place of an adder, the RISC CPU has a hardwared multiplication unit. The multiplication is dependent on the multiplication unit. The multiplication unit is dependent on the multiplicand and multiplicator values. It executes a multiplication in a fixed number of clock cycles. Thus the process is completed more quickly due to its increased performance. Since the time to deliver the result by the EU is known to the CU at the time of release of the multiplication instruction, the components of the RISC CPU can be dynamically synchronised more efficiently with one another. This is urgent for enhancing efficiency of the instruction pipeline which is another characteristic element of the RISC processors.

## 16.4.5 NON DESTRUCTIVE OPERATION

The majority of CISC processors has a reduced register set. The RISC processors have enough registers in the form of a register file. They are generally non-destructive and after the execution of an instruction, the operands remain unchanged and available, the instruction result being stored in another register. The i386 adopts a destructive method for all two-operand instructions if both operands are not readily available as operands in the instructions flow, but available as register and/or memory contents. The i386 32-bit processor can multiply two 32-bit numbers, the result extending to 64-bit. The most significant double word is stored in the EDX register so that this register value can also be destroyed.

On the other hand, RISC processors operate in a non-destructive manner preserving the source operands after the execution of the instruction. Hence the operand values can be used for further calculations without loading them again. Thus the RISC may be interpreted as RE-USABLE INFORMATION STORAGE COMPUTER". Under normal operating condition, RISC processors work with three operands - tow source operands and a destiantion operand.

## 16.4.6 INSTRUCTION PIPELINING

The execution structure of an instruction remains the same for the majority of machine coded instructions and follows the steps as under :

i)      instruction fetching to read the instruction from the memory
ii)     instruction decoding
iii)    operand fetching where necessary
iv)     execution of the instruction
v)      writing the results

In a CISC processor, this instruction step is preformed by the bus interface and the prefetcher. The decoding unit executes the decoding of the instructions prior to the instruction execution and thus the decoded microcode is available in the microcode queue. The remaining three steps are executed by microcode in the EU under the control of CU. Normally a single clock cycle is not sufficient to perform all these steps provided the clock frequency is not very low. Instruction pipelining has been implemented in order to obtain single cycle machine instructions for executing machine code instruction within one processor-clock cycle. These instructions help to complete one instructin in one clock cycle making clocks per instruction CPI = 1. Generally an instruction is not executed within a cycle but an instruction pipelinign in which each instruction to be executed is devided into a set of substeps and the processor executes every substep in a single stage of pipelining. Processor clock cycle (PCLK) is necessary per instruction phase. The processor sarts the execution of the current instruction as soon as the previous instruction enters the decoding phase.

RISC characterstics have been combined with CISC characteristics to develop the Complexity Reduced Instruction Set Processor (CRISP). Many scientific and graphical applications including the operations related to the artificial intelligence require a maximum rate of performance which can not be solved by a single processor. Modern RISC CPUs are designed for multi-processor operation to meet the demand of the modern technology.

## 16.5  THE INTEL 80486 PROCESSOR

In order to execute frequently used instructions in the shortest time, certain (i486) RISC concepts have been introduced in high performance CISCs which affects the partial hardwaring of the units. This facilitates extensions to the pipelined processing of the instructions and the integration of on-chip caches. An example of this type of device is the i486 from Intel.

The i486 represents a hybrid between CISC and RISC processors in which frequently used instructions are hardwared in RISC fashion enhancing their execution speed. Complex and less commonly used instructions are available in it in micro-encoded form. A sequence of simple instructions can be operated more quickly compared to complex instructions producing the same effect. The instructions are executed in a five stage pipeline.

The 80486 microprocessor is a highly integrated device containing more than 1200000 transistors. This powerful integrated circuit is a combination of

i)      A Memory Management Unit (MMU).

ii)     A complete numeric coprocessor compatible with the 80387,

iii)    A high speed cache memory containing 8K-byte of space and

iv)     A full 32-bit microprocessor upward compatible with the 80386 microprocessor.

The 80486 is available as 25MHz, 33MHz and 50MHz versions. The 80486 may be obtained as 80486DX and 80486SX. The only difference between these devices is that the 80486SX does not contain the numeric coprocessor which reduces its price.

**DIFFERENT VERSIONS OF THE 80486**

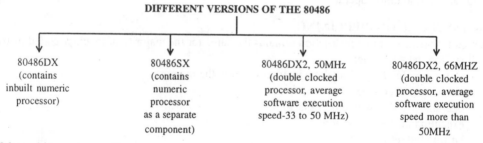

| 80486DX (contains inbuilt numeric processor) | 80486SX (contains numeric processor as a separate component) | 80486DX2, 50MHz (double clocked processor, average software execution speed-33 to 50 MHz) | 80486DX2, 66MHZ (double clocked processor, average software execution speed more than 50MHz) |

The i486 combines on one chip

i)      an improved i386 CPU,

ii)     an improved coprocessor,

iii)    a cache controller,

iv)     8K bytes of cache memory.

The i486 can be obtained with 25-50MHz clock frequencies or even 100MHz with internal clock tripling (the i486 DX4). Using the 32-bit data bus, it is possible to transfer data at a rate of upto 160Mbytes per second in burst mode. Due to hardware and instruction pipelining, the i486 is approximately 3 times faster than an i386, the frequency remaining the same. More than a million transistors are incorporated in a thump sized i486 chip. The i486 is fully compatible with the i386/i387 combination. It uses the same instructions and types of data; the same real, protected and virtual 8086 modes and performs memroy segmentation and demand paging in the same way. As the coprocessor is on the same chip as the CPU, data transfer between them is quicker. The i486 shows its main strengths in applications involving intensive calculations such as CAD or computer graphics.

### 16.5.1 BASIC 80486 ARCHITECTURE

The architecture of the 80486DX is almost identical to the 80386 combined with the 80387 math coprocessor and an internal 8k-bytes cache, whereas the 80486SX is almost identical to an 80386 with an internal 8k-byte cache. The most remarkable difference between the 80386 and the 80486 is that almost half of the 80386 instructions consume 2 clock periods for execution whereas 1 clock period is required to execute similar instructions in the 80486.

Like the 80386, the 80486 contains eight general-purpose 32-bit registers: EAX, EBX, ECX, EDX, EBP, EDI, ESI and ESP. These registers may be used as 8-, 16-, or 32-bit data registers or to address a location in the memory system. The 16-bit registers are the same set as found in the 80286. These are assigned as AX, BX, CX, DX, BP, DI, SI and SP. The 8-bit registers are AH, AL; BH, BL; CH, CL; DH and DL.

In addition to the general-purpose registers, the 80486 also contains the same segment registers as the 80386 which are CS, DS, ES, SS, FS and GS. Each of them are 16-bit wide like all earlier versions of the family.

The IP (instruction pointer) addresses the program located within the 1M-byte of memory in combination with CS whereas EIP (extended instruction pointer) addresses a program at any location within 4G- byte memory system. In protected mode operation, the segment registers hold selectors like the 80286 and 80386 microprocessors.

Similar to the 80386, the 80486 also contains the global, local and interrupt descriptor table registers and memory-management unit. The function of the MMU and its paging unit is exactly the same as the 80386.

The extended flag register (EFLAGS) is illustrated in Fig. 16.8. A brief description of the flag register is as under :

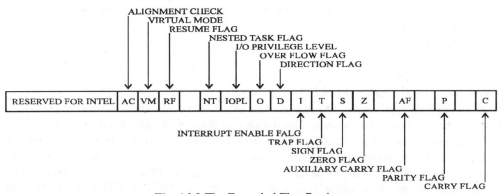

Fig. 16.8 The Extended Flag Register

1.  AC (Alignment Check) : This flag is new to the 80486 Microprocessor. This provides an indication that the microprocessor has assessed a word at an odd address or a double word stored at a non-double-word boundary.

2.  VM (Virtual Mode) : This bit is set when the 80486 is operated in the protected mode.

3.  RF (Resume) : This 'resume' bit is used in conjunction with the debug registers.

4.  NT (Nested Task) : When set, it gives an indication that the 80486 is performing a task, nested within another task.

5.  IOPL (I/O Privilege Level) : This indicates the current maximum privilege level assigned to the I/O system.

6.   OF (Overflow) : This flag is set when the result of a signed arithmetic operation has overflown the capacity of the destination. It is also used with the multiply instruction.

7.   DF (Direction) : The direction flag is set (i.e., DF=1) during auto-decrement operation for the string instructions. For auto-increment of the same, DF remains at reset (i.e, DF=0) condition.

8.   IE (Interrupt Enable) : This bit when set, enables the INTR pin.

9.   TF (Trap) : It is set to enable debugging as described by the debug registers.

10.  SF (Sign) : This indicates that the sign of the result is set or cleared.

11.  ZF (Zero) : Zero flag becomes set (i.e., ZF=1) when the result of an arithmetic or logic operation is zero. It becomes reset (i.e., ZF=0) when the result is non-zero.

12.  AF (Auxiliary) : This is used with the DAA and DAS instructions to adjust the result of a BCD addition or subtraction.

13.  PF (Parity) : This parity flag indicates the parity of the result of an arithmetic or logic operation. If the parity is odd, this flag is reset (i.e., PF=0) and if the parity is even, this bit is set (i.e., PF=1).

14.  CF (Carry) : When a carry occurs after an addition or a borrow after a subtraction, this flag is set.

### 16.5.2  THE INTERNAL STRUCTURE OF THE i486

The Internal structure of the i486 is much more complicated in comparison to the i386. For the i386 processor family, three separate units are necessary. These are

 i)      the i386 CPU,
 ii)     the i387 coprocessor and
 iii)    the 82395 cache controller.

The i486 whose internal structure is shown in Fig. 16.9, combines on a single chip
 i)      an improved CPU core,
 ii)     a more powerful i387,
 iii)    a cache controller and
 iv)     an 8-Kbyte cache,
the prefetch queue being enlarged to 32 bytes.

Like all other microprocessors, the bus interface of the i486 communicates with the out side world. The bus interface receives or sends data through the data bus D31-D0. It addresses memory and I/O address space with the help of the address bus A31-A2 and the byte enable signals BE3-BE0. It sends information about the condition of the i486 and receives instructions from external devices through the control bus. The on-chip cache is directly connected to the bus interface. This integrated 8-Kbyte cache memory is used as either a data cache or as a code cache. It may be noted that powerful RISC CPUs and the Pentium use separate data and code caches for the independent buffering of instructions and program data. The i486 cache buffers the data and with the help of instructions, these are sent to the registers, ALU, floating point unit or prefetcher as applicable. Two clock cycles are necessary in a bus cycle when it is required to access an external cache memory whereas only one clock cycle is necessary when internal cache is used.

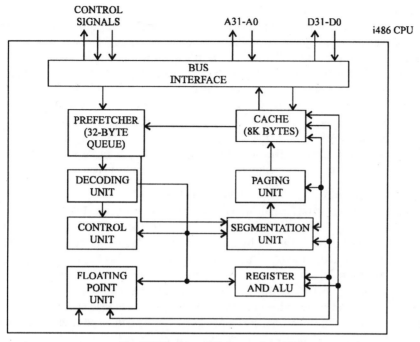

Fig. 16.9 The Internal Structure of the i486

Data or instructions those are not buffered in the cache, must be read form memory, register or prefetcher directly. In i486, the data bytes are moved to the registers or floating point unit and the instruction bytes are sent to the prefetch queue which in the i486 consists of 32-bits. The decoder unit decodes all instructions in the prefetch queue and passes them to the control unit (CU) that controls the

i)    registers
ii)   ALU
iii)  segmentation unit
iv)   floating point unit

The decoder and the execution unit (EU) are parts of five stage i486 pipeline. Many instructions pass through the partially hardwared control unit of the i486 without the help of microprogram and operands in the instruction flow and sends them to the ALU or addressing unit (AU), which consists of the paging unit and the segmentation unit as applicable.

The two 32-bit data buses together form the internal 64-bit data bus for the transfer of data between the CPU and the floating point unit, corresponding to the i386. Unlike the i386/i387 combination, no I/O bus cycles are necessary for the transfer of opcodes and data between the CPU and the coprocessor, In addition, the 64-bit data transfer occurs in i486 internally compared to the 32-bit data of the i386 / i387. This enables the i486 to process ESC instructions considerably quicker than the i386 / i387 combination.

For the generation of addresses, like other members of 80i86 family, the i486 uses a segment and an offset register. In the segment unit, the contents of both registers are combined to form the linear address. In protected mode, the segmentation unit executes an access check at the same time in order to ensure the protection of the separate tasks and the system. When paging is active, the linear address determined in the segmentation unit is covered to a physical address in the paging unit. Without paging, the linear address is also the physical address. The bus interface sends the physical address and if necessary, it sends the data to be wirtten or reads the addressed data.

The bus interface of the i486 contains 4 write buffers for the acceleration of write access to external memory. If the i486 bus is not immediately available due to the execution of a cache line fill, the data is first written to the wirte buffer. The internal buffers can be filled at a rate of one write operation for each PCL. The data is written to the 4 buffers in the order in which the data are supplied from the i486 to the data bus. When the cache line is full, the processor becomes available again and the bus interface loads the data in the write buffers into the bus independently. When the i486 bus is free during a write operation, the write buffers are bypassed and the data to be written is transferred immediately to the bus.

In order to increase the efficiency of the processor still further, the i486 can transpose the sequence of read and write operations on the bus. The i486 first carries out the read access and then the write access since the read access does not affect a memory position which must be updated first by the write access.

### 16.5.3 THE 80486 MEMORY AND MEMORY MANAGEMENT

The memory system for the 80486 is identical to the 80386 microprocessor. The 80486 contains 4G-bytes of memory locations starting from 00000000 H to FFFFFFFF H. The major change to the memory system is internal to the 80486 in the form of an 8K-byte cache memory which enhances the speed of execution of instructions and that of data acquisition. Another addition is the parity checker/generator parity during each write cycle. Parity is generated as even parity and a parity bit is provided for each byte of memory. The parity check bits appear on pins DP0-DP3, which are also parity inputs as well as outputs. These are stored in memory during each write cycle and read from memory during each read cycle.

During a read operation, the microprocessor checks parity and if there be an error, it generates a parity check error, on the PCHK pin. A parity error causes no change in processing unless the user applies the PCHK signal to an interrupt input. Interrupts are often used to signal a parity error in DOS-based computer systems. The organization of the 80486 memory system is the same as that for the 80386, except for the parity bit storage.

The cache memory system caches or stores both the data used by a program and also the instructions of the program. The cache is organized as a four-way set associative cache with each location (line) containing 16 bytes or four double words of data. The cache operates as a wirte-through cache. The cache only changes if a miss occurs. In many cases, much of the active portion of a program is found completely inside the cache memory. Many of the instructions that are commonly used in a program may be executed at the rate of 1 clock cycle due to this reason.

Control register CR0 (Fig. 16.10) is used to control the cache with two new control bits not present in the 80386 microprocessor. The CD (cache disable) and NW (noncache write-through) bits are new to the 80486 and these are used to control the 8k-byte cache. If the CD bit is set, all cache operations are inhibited or checked. Normally, this bit remains cleared and it is set for debugging software. The NW bit is used to inhibit cache write-through operation. As with CD, cache write-through is only inhibited for testing. For normal program operation, both CD and NW remain at reset condition.

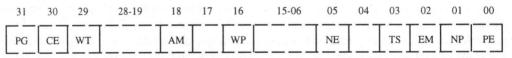

Fig. 16.10 Control register zero (CR0) for the 80486 microprocessor

The cache is new to the 80486 microprocessor and the cache is filled using burst cycles not present on the 80386. When a bus line is filled, the 80486 requires four 32-bit numbers from the memory system to fill a line in the cache. Filling is accomplished with burst cycle. The burst cycle is a special memory where four 32-bit numbers are fetched from the memory system in 5 clock periods.

The memory-management system of the of 80486 is similar to the 80386. This includes a paging unit to allow any 4k-byte block of physical memory to be assigned to any 4k-byte block of linear memory. The descriptor types are exactly the same as that for the 80386 microprocessor. The only difference between the 80386 memory-management system and the 80486 memory-management system is 'paging'. Unlike the 80386, the 80486 paging system can disable a section of translated memory pages. The page write-through (PWT) and page cache disable (PCD) control caching are the two control bit pins in the 80486.

The PWT controls the functioning of the cache for a write operation of the external cache memroy. It does not control writing to the internal cache. The logic level of this bit is found on the PWT pin of the 80486 microprocessor. Externally it can be used to dictate the write-through policy of the external cache. The PCD bit controls the on-chip cache. When the PCD bit is reset (i.e. PCD=0), the on-chip cache is enabled for the current page of memory. When PCD bit is set (i.e. PCD=1), it disables the on-chip cache.

## 16.5.4 THE i486 PIPELINE AND THE CACHE REGISTER

The different CPU units of the i486 can operate in parallel. In this process when an instruction is executed, the next instruction can be decoded and the next instruction can be fetched. Instruction pipelining is performed with the parallel operation of the prefetcher, decoder and EU and a register write stage. It may be mentioned here that a 'true' RISC pipeline (a pipeline with closely joined stages) is first realised in the Pentium. The i486 pipeline consists of

i) one prefetch stage
ii) two decoding stages
iii) one execution stage
iv) one write back stage

During the prefetch stage, the system reads 16-byte instruction blocks from memory in the prefetch queue and on-chip cache simultaneously in the burst mode. The prefetch queue may contain 32-bytes which is just double compared to that in the i386. The decoding unit forms the second and third stages in the i486 pipeline. It converts simple machine instructions directly into control instructions for the CU and more complex machine instruction into microcode jump addresses. The microcode being transferred to the CU, controls the execution of the instruction. Thus the first decoding stage can access memory producing a considerable effect on the performance of the pipeline. The first stage corresponds to the decoding and the second stage coresponds to the operand fetching in the true RISC pipeline model. On the other hand, a two stage decoding is necessary due to the complex CISC instructions of the i486. When memory operands are needed to be loaded, the first decoding stage sends out memory access. If the operand is located in the on-chip cache, it can be read form the on chip cache in one clock cycle and during this time the instruction is processed in the second decoding stage. Memory operand is therefore available during the execution phase of the instruction without obstructing the pipeline producing a considerable improvement.

During the execution stage, the CU interprets the control signals or the microcode jump address and controls the ALU, floating point unit or other logic elements of the i486 in order to carry out the instruction requiring one or more clock cycles, depending on the instruction. This characteristic differs widely from RISC methodology because in RISC, every pipeline step should be executed in one single processor clock cycle. The execution of the next instruction which is already decoded, is delayed till the execution of the current instruction is complete. In the last pipeline stage, the result of the instruction is written into the target register or a temporary register.

The 80486 has three cache test registers and these are

i) Cache data register (TR3)
ii) Cache status test register (TR4)
iii) Cache control test register (TR5)

These are not defined for the 80386 microprocessor.

The uses of the cache data register (TR3) are to access

i)     the cache fill buffer for a write test operation and

ii)    the cache read buffer for a cache read test operation.

The contents of the Cache Control Test Register (TR5) determine which internal cache line is written or read through TR3. The cache status register (TR4) holds the necessary information before a cache write operation.

The 80486 uses TR3, TR4 and TR5 to completely test the internal cache. Its outcome is passed to the register EAX. The microprocessor, coprocessor and cache have passed the self-test if the content of EAX is a zero. The value of EAX can be tested after a reset to determine if an error is detected.

### 16.5.5  THE 80486 INSTRUCTION SET

The instruction set of the 80486 is almost identical to that of the 80386 including some additional instructions. Overall speed improvement is about 50 percent in the 80486 compared to the 80386 microprocessor. TABLE 16-2 shows the new instructions to the 80486 microprocessor.

**TABLE 16.2 New Instructions for the 80486 Microprocessor**

| Instruction | Function | Example |
|---|---|---|
| BSWAP (Bites to be swapped) | Allows bytes to be swapped in any 32-bit extended register. It exchanges the rightmost byte with the leftmost byte and also exchanges the two middle bytes. | If EAX =39402786 H, the BSWAP EAX instruction puts 86274093 H in EAX. |
| CMPXCHG (compare and exchange) | Compares the destination operand to the contents of the accumulator, (EAX, AM, or AL) affecting flag. If the destination operand is equal to the accumulator, the source operand is copied to the destination operand. If the destination operand is not equal to the accumulator, the destination operand is copied to the accumulator. | CMPXCHG CX, DX copies DX into CX if DX=AX; otherwise copies CX into AX if DX ≠ AX, flag being affeced. CMPXCHG CL, DATA copies the contents of memory location into CL if Cl=AL; otherwise copies CL into AL if CL ≠ AL. |
| INVD (Invalidate data cache) | The INVD instruction empties the contents of the current data cache without writing changes to the memory system. | |
| INVLPG (Invalidates a TLB entry) | The INVLPG instruction invalidates an entry in the translation look aside buffer (TLB) used by the demand-paging system in a virtual memory system. The instruction calculates the address of the operand and removes it from the TLB if the entry has been mapped into the TLB. | |
| WBINVD (Write before invalidated data cache | The WBINVD instruction is like the INVD instruction except that, the contents of any dirty location in the data cache is first written to memory before the cache is flushed. | |
| XADD (Exchange and add) | Exchanges and adds data in two registers or between memory and a register. | XADD EAX, EBX instruction adds EBX to EAX and stores the sum in EAX, just as an add instruction. |

## 16.5.6 PIN CONFIGURATION OF THE INTEL 80486 MICROPROCESSOR

| Pin No. Mark | A | B | C | D | E | F | G | H | I | J | K | L | M | N | O | P | Q | R | S |
|---|---|---|---|---|---|---|---|---|---|---|---|---|---|---|---|---|---|---|---|
| 1 | 1A | 1B | 1C | 1D | 1E | 1F | 1G | 1H | 1I | 1J | 1K | 1L | 1M | 1N | 1O | 1P | 1Q | 1R | 1S |
| 2 | 2A | 2B | 2C | 2D | 2E | 2F | 2G | 2H | 2I | 2J | 2K | 2L | 2M | 2N | 2O | 2P | 2Q | 2R | 2S |
| 3 | 3A | 3B | 3C | 3D | 3E | 3F | 3G | 3H | 3I | 3J | 3K | 3L | 3M | 3N | 3O | 3P | 3Q | 3R | 3S |
| 4 | 4A | 4B | 4C | | | | | | | | | | | | | | 4Q | 4R | 4S |
| 5 | 5A | 5B | 5C | | | | | | | | | | | | | | 5Q | 5R | 5S |
| 6 | 6A | 6B | 6C | | | | | | | | | | | | | | 6Q | 6R | 6S |
| 7 | 7A | 7B | 7C | | | | | | | | | | | | | | 7Q | 7R | 7S |
| 8 | 8A | 8B | 8C | | | | | | | | | | | | | | 8Q | 8R | 8S |
| 9 | 9A | 9B | 9C | | | | | | 80486 | | | | | | | | 9Q | 9R | 9S |
| 10 | 10A | 10B | 10C | | | | | | | | | | | | | | 10Q | 10R | 10S |
| 11 | 11A | 11B | 11C | | | | | | | | | | | | | | 11Q | 11R | 11S |
| 12 | 12A | 12B | 12C | | | | | | | | | | | | | | 12Q | 12R | 12S |
| 13 | 13A | 13B | 13C | | | | | | | | | | | | | | 13Q | 13R | 13S |
| 14 | 14A | 14B | 14C | | | | | | | | | | | | | | 14Q | 14R | 14S |
| 15 | 15A | 15B | 15C | 15D | 15E | 15F | 15G | 15H | 15I | 15J | 15K | 15L | 15M | 15N | 15O | 15P | 15Q | 15R | 15S |
| 16 | 16A | 16B | 16C | 16D | 16E | 16F | 16G | 16H | 16I | 16J | 16K | 16L | 16M | 16N | 16O | 16P | 16Q | 16R | 16S |
| 17 | 17A | 17B | 17C | 17D | 17E | 17F | 17G | 17H | 17I | 17J | 17K | 17L | 17M | 17N | 17O | 17P | 17Q | 17R | 17S |

Fig. 16.11 The Intel 80486 Pin Layout

## PIN DESCRIPTION :
### 32-BIT DATA BUS -
(Transfers data between the microprocessor and its memory and I/O system;
D7 - D0 are used to accept the interrupt vector type number during an interrupt acknowledge cycle)

| PIN NO. | 1P | 2N | 1N | 2H | 3M | 2J | 2L | 3L | 2F | 1D | 3E | 1C | 3G | 2D | 3K | 3F | 3J | 3D |
|---|---|---|---|---|---|---|---|---|---|---|---|---|---|---|---|---|---|---|
| BUS NO. | D0 | D1 | D2 | D3 | D4 | D5 | D6 | D7 | D8 | D9 | D10 | D11 | D12 | D13 | D14 | D15 | D16 | D17 |

| PIN NO. | 2C | 1B | 1A | 2B | 2A | 4A | 6A | 6B | 7C | 6C | 8C | 8A | 9C | 8B |
|---|---|---|---|---|---|---|---|---|---|---|---|---|---|---|
| BUS NO. | D18 | D19 | D20 | D21 | D22 | D23 | D24 | D25 | D26 | D27 | D28 | D29 | D30 | D31 |

## ADDRESS BUS
(Provides the memory address and I/O during normal operation and during a cache line invalidation, A31-A4 are used to drive the microprocessor).

| PIN NO. | 14Q | 15R | 16S | 12Q | 15S | 13Q | 13R | 11Q | 13S | 12R | 7S | 10Q | 5S | 7R | 9Q | 3Q |
|---|---|---|---|---|---|---|---|---|---|---|---|---|---|---|---|---|
| BUS NO. | A2 | A3 | A4 | A5 | A6 | A7 | A8 | A9 | A10 | A11 | A12 | A13 | A14 | A15 | A16 | A17 |

| PIN NO. | 5R | 4Q | 8Q | 5Q | 7Q | 3S | 6Q | 2R | 2S | 1S | 1R | 2P | 3P | 1Q |
|---|---|---|---|---|---|---|---|---|---|---|---|---|---|---|
| BUS NO. | A18 | A19 | A20 | A21 | A22 | A23 | A24 | A25 | A26 | A27 | A28 | A29 | A30 | A31 |

## NO CONNECTION (NC) :
3A 10A 12A 13A 14A 10B 12B 13B 14B 16B 10C 11C 12C 13C 15G 17R 4S

Vss - 7A 9A 11A 3B 4B 5B 1E 17E 1G 17G 1H 17H 1K 17K 1L 17L 1M 17M
17P 2Q 4R 6S 8S 9S 10S 11S 12S 14S

Vcc - 7B 9B 11B 4C 5C 2E 16E 2G 16H 1J 2K 16K 16L 2M 16M 16P 3R 6R
8R 9R 10R 11R 14R

PIN NO. :

3B   -   CLK (CLOCK INPUT) :

      Provides the 80486 with its basic timing signal.

5A, 3H, 1F, 3N — DP3, DP2, DP1, DP0 (DATA PARITY I/O) :

      Provide even parity for a write operation / check parity for a read operation.

14C  -   $\overline{\text{FERR}}$ (FLOATING POINT ERROR OUTPUT) :

      Indicates that the floting-point coprocessor has detected an error condition. Used to maintain error compatibility with DOS software.

15A  -   $\overline{\text{IGNEE}}$ (IGNORE NUMRIC ERROR INPUT) :

      Causes the coprocessor to continue processing data ignoring floating errors.

15B  -   NMI (NON-MASKABLE INTERRUPT INPUT)

15C  -   $\overline{\text{FLUSH}}$ (CACHE FLUSH INPUT) :

      Forces the microprocessor to erase the contents of its 8-K byte internal cache.

15D  -   $\overline{\text{A20M}}$ (ADDRESS BIT 20 MASK) :

      Used to cause the 80486 to wrap its address around from lacation 000FFFFFH TO 00000000 H like the 8086.

15E  -   HOLD (HOLD INPUT)

15F  -   $\overline{\text{KEN}}$ (CACHE ENABLE INPUT) :

      Causes the current bus to store in the internal cache.

15H  -   $\overline{\text{BRDY}}$ (BURST READY INPUT) :

      Used to signal the microprocessor that a burst cycle is complete.

15L  -   PWT (PAGE $\overline{\text{WRITE THROUGH}}$ OUTPUT)

15M  -   D/$\overline{\text{C}}$ (DATA / CONTROL)

      Indicates whether the current operation is a data transfer or a control cycle. Bus cycle identification follows the table as under :

| M/IO | D/C | W/R | BUS CYCLE TYPE |
|------|-----|-----|----------------|
| 0 | 0 | 0 | INTERRUPT ACKNOWLEDGE |
| 0 | 0 | 1 | HALT/SPECIAL |
| 0 | 1 | 0 | I/O READ |
| 0 | 1 | 1 | I/O WRITE |
| 1 | 0 | 0 | CODE CYCLE |
| 1 | 0 | 1 | RESERVED |
| 1 | 1 | 0 | MEMORY READ |
| 1 | 1 | 1 | MEMORY WRITE |

15N  -   $\overline{\text{LOCK}}$ (LOCK OUTPUT)

150  -   HLDA (HOLD ACKNOWLEDGE OUTPUT)

15Q  -   $\overline{\text{BREQ}}$ (BUS REQUEST) :

      Indicates that the 80486 has generated an internal bus request.

16A  -   INTR (INTERRUPT REQUEST INPUT)

16C  -   RESET (RESET INPUT)

16D  -   $\overline{\text{BS8}}$ (BUS SIZE 8 INPUT)

      Causes the 80486 to transfer itself with an 8-bit data bus to access bytewide memory and I/O components.

16F  -   $\overline{\text{RDY}}$ (READY INPUT) :

      Indicates that a nonburst bus cycle is complete.

16N  -   M/$\overline{\text{IO}}$ (MEMORY / $\overline{\text{IO}}$)

      Defines whether the address bus contains a memory address or an I/O port number.

16Q - $\overline{\text{PLOCK}}$ (PSEUDO - LOCK OUTPUT) :
Indicates that the current operation requires more than one bus cycle to perform :

16R - $\overline{\text{BLAST}}$ (BURST LAST OUTPUT)
Shows that the burst bus cycle is complete on the next activation of the BRDY signal.

17A - AHOLD (ADDRESS HOLD INPUT)

17B - $\overline{\text{EADS}}$ (EXTERNAL ADDRESS STORE INPUT) :
Used with AHOLD to signal that an external address is used to perform a cache invalidation cycle.

17C - $\overline{\text{BS16}}$ (BUS SIZE 16 INPUT) :
Causes the 80486 to structure itself with a 16-bit data bus to access bytewide memory and I/O components.

17D - $\overline{\text{BOFF}}$ (BACKOFF INPUT) :
Causes the microprocessor to place its buses at their high impedance state during the next clock cycle. The microprocessor remains in bus hold state untill the $\overline{\text{BOFF}}$ pin is placed at a logical 1 level.

17F, 15J, 16J, 15K, — $\overline{\text{BE3}}$, $\overline{\text{BE2}}$, $\overline{\text{BE1}}$, $\overline{\text{BE0}}$ (BYTE ENABLE OUTPUTS) :
Selects a bank of the memory system when the information is transferred between the microprocessor and its memory and I/O space. The $\overline{\text{BE3}}$, $\overline{\text{BE2}}$, $\overline{\text{BE1}}$ and $\overline{\text{BE0}}$ signals enable D31-D24; D23-D16; D15-D8 and D7-D0 respectively.

17J - PCD (PAGE CACHE DISABLE OUTPUT)

17N - $\overline{\text{W/R}}$ (WRITE / READ)

17Q - $\overline{\text{PCHK}}$ ( PARITY CHECK OUTPUT) :
Indicates that a parity error has been detected during a read operation on the DP3-DP0 pins.

17S - ADS (ADDRESS DATA STROBE) :
If 0, gives indication of a valid memory adderss in address bus.

## 16.6 THE PENTIUM PROCESSOR

The pentium processor, the single chip Supercomputer, first appeared in March 1993, This modern RISC technology based super scalar Pentium Processor P5 introduced by Intel Corporation has great advantage over its predecessors - the 8086 to i486 DX2.

Like the i386 and the i486 processors, the Pentium Processor is a 32-bit Processor having a 64-bit data bus and 32-bit address bus. The data bus does not serve the 32-bit Processor directly but serves the on-chip caches. The internal data paths of Pentium vary from 128 to 256 bit enhancing the speed of data and code transfer. All internal and external buses are connected through the caches. The i486 has only one unified cache of 8 Kbyte capacity, the cache line size being 16 bytes. But the Pentium Processor Possesses two separate and independent on-chip caches of 8 Kbyte capacity for code and data and these are directly connected to the bus interface. The cache line size in the i486 is 16 bytes whereas that in pentium is 32-bytes. Each cache of the Pentium is connected to its own Translation Look Aside Buffers (TLB). This reduces remarkable time of conversion of the linear code or data addresses into physical address mode by paging unit (PU) of the Machine Management Unit (MMU). In addition to the standard 4-byte pages, 4-Mbyte pages are also provided to support the larger systems. The caches use physical address and the data cache can work with both write-through and write-back strategies as necessary.

The Control Unit (CU) forms the heart of the pentium. It controls the five-step integer pipelines U and V and the eight-step floating point pipeline. The Pentium can carry out all sorts of commands in the U pipeline and a command indicated in the V pipeline simultaeously. Thus the Pentium can execute two integer commands in one single clock cycle. The first four steps of the floating point pipe line overlap with those of the U pipe line, so that the integer and the floating point pipelines can only work in parallel under certain conditions. Here, the term integer refers to all commands such as addition, comparison, move and jump etc. not containing floating point operations. The Pentium floating point unit executes floating point commands with a speed about ten times faster than the i486 DX having the same clock speed. This is achieved through the following :

  i)  intergration of a hardware multiplier and divider

  ii)  implementation of quicker algorithms for the microcoded floating point commands

  Two independent 32-byte prefetch buffers supply codes to the two pipelines. The Pentium consits of a CPU and a Branch Trace Buffer (BTB). It stores the target address of the branches and also statistical informations concerning the frequency of the current branch known as 'Taken Branch'. For handling the brances, the branch prediction logic is applied to the Pentium. This is much more advantageous with reference to the i486.

  The Pentium supports all commands of the microcoded i386 and i387 processors. The Pentium contains microcode in a support unit for executing these complex functions. The support unit controls the pipelines with the help of the microcode in order to carry out complex functions. It may be noted that all ALU functions are performed by the hardware logic in accordance with the RISC principle.

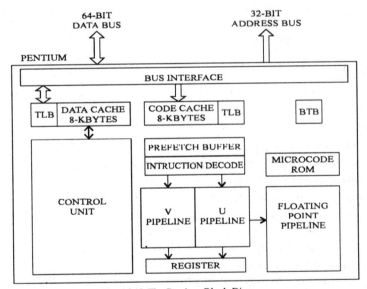

Fig. 16.12 The Pentium Block Diagram.

## 16.6.1 THE PENTIUM REGISTERS

The Pentium includes

  i)  General purpose register

  ii)  Segment register

  iii)  Status register

  iv)  Control register

  v)  Registers of the floating point unit

  All registers other than the control register CR4 and the test register TR12, are already implemented in the i386 and i486. The control register CR4, the test register TR12 and a new pair of bits have been introduced to the registers of the pentium for the first time.

Like i486, the pentium has seven (32-bit wide) general purpose registers EBP and six ( 16- bit wide) segment registers CS to GS. The instuction pointer (EIP), stack pointer (ESP) and a flag register (EFLAG) are all 32-bit wide. The size of the general purpose register in the pentium is 32-bit. This with an offset of 32-bit enhances the size of pentium registers. It is also possible to address only the two least significant bytes with the help of 32-bits registers. The 16-bit registers are identified as AX to DX ( general purpose registers), IP (instrudction pointer), SP (stack pointer) and flag. The least significant word of each of the four general purpose registers AX to DX can be divided further into two 8- bit register bytes. The pentium can work with single data bytes also. The pentium is compatible with the 16-bit 8086 and 80286 CPUs since the 32-bit accumulator EAX has been divided to the 16-bit AX and then further into 8-bit AH and AL. The full 32-bit registers are identified by the i386 and i486.

## ACCUMULATOR (EAX)

The accumulator (EAX) is generally engaged as a temporary storage area for holding data and operands. The base register (EBX) is used to store a value temporarily. It also serves as a pointer to the start of a data object by indirect addressing. The count register (ECX) is utilised to determine the number of repetitions of loops, string instructions (REP) or shifting and rotation ( SHL, ROL) etc. At the end of each loop, the value in ECX is reduced by one.

## DATA REGISTER (EDX)

In normal functioning, the data register is used for storing data temporarily. Occasionally, EDX contents I/O address of the respective ports.

## BASE POINTER (EBP)

The base pointer can also be utilised to store data temporarily. Unlike other registers, this register is assigned to the SS segment register. Normally, the SS-EBP register pair is used for memory access .

## SOURCE INDEX (EDI)

Besides the use as a temporary data storage unit, the source index can also act as a pointer during string operations, In string instructions, the ESI indicates single bytes, words or double words contained in the output string. The ESI is automatically incremented or reduced when a string instruction is repeated using the REP prefix.

## DESTINATION INDEX (EDI)

The destination index can also be used as a temporary data storage unit or as a pointer at the end of an operation. In string instructions, the EDI indicates bytes, words or double words in the string. Like the ESI, the EDI also is automatically incremented or decremented when instructions with the REP prefix are used

## CODE SEGMENT (CS)

The code segment develops a data block for holding the instruction and the addressed data.

## DATA SEGMENT (DS)

The data segment usually contains the data for the active task. Many instructions use this data segment only to address data in the memory with an offset. The pentium can only change this setting using another extra segment .

## STACK SEGMENT (SS)

The data contained in the stack segment can be addressed with stack instructions such as PUSH, POP, PUSHALL etc. Stack instructions use the value of SS to store data on the stack or read data from the stack.

EXTRA SEGMENTS (ES, FS and GS)
The extra segments and their registers are used mainly for string instrutions. These segments may also be used to address data not contained in the standard data segment (DS).

### 16.6.2 THE FLAG REGISTER OF THE PENTIUM

The EFLAGS (shown in fig. 16. 13 ) indicate processor's current status and control the identification of maskable interrupts and other reactions of the Pentium. The CARRY (C), PARITY (P), AUXILIARY CARRY (AC), ZERO (Z), SIGN (S) , TRAP (T), INTERRUPT ENABLE (IE), DIRECTION (D) and OVER FLOW (O) flags are common to the 8086. The I/O protection level (IOPL) flag and nested task (NT) flag are common to the 80286. The virtual 8086 mode (VM) and resume (R) are similar to the i386 whereas the alignment check (AC) is similar to the i486. The new flags introduced in the pentium processor are.

   i)     Virtual Interrupt (VI)
   ii)    Virtual Interrupt Pending (VIP)
   iii)   Identification (ID)

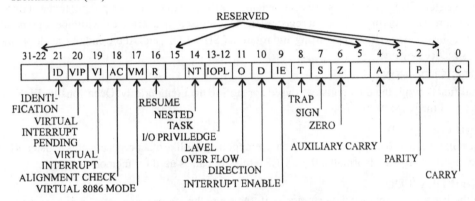

Fig. 16.13 The Flag Register of the Pentium

   The VI flag is a vertual version of IE used for sending interrupts in virtual 8086 mode. The VIP flag works together with the VI flag in order to have its own virtual version of the IE flag corresponding to each task in virtual 8086 mode. The ID flag indicates whether the processor supports the CPUID instruction for its identification.

### 16.6.3 CONTROL REGISTERS OF THE PENTIUM

The pentium contains five separate control registers CR0 to CR4 and four memory management registers for the protected mode and eight debug registers. The control and debug registers are all of 32-bit

### CONTROL REGISTER CR0

Similar to the 80286 to 80486, the control register CR0 contains eleven entries. The 80286 uses the Machine status word (MSW) for supporting the 16-bit protected mode . In pentium, the same MSW is located in the control register CR0 as shown in Fig, 16.14.

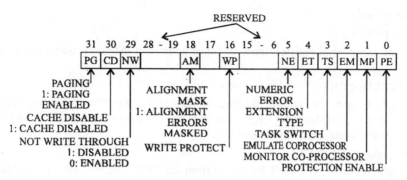

Fig. 16.14 Structure of Control Register CR0

## PROTECTION ENABLE (PE)
The pentium enters into the protected mode when PE bit is set.

## MONITOR CO-PROCESSOR (MP)
Like the 80286, the pentium possesses Monitor Co- processor. If the MP bit is set, a WAIT instruction can issue the "no co-processor available" exception leading to an interrupt 7. The Monitor co-processor is used for synchronization between the CPU and the Floating Point Unit before the pentium.

## EMULATE CO-PROCESSOR (EM)
When MP bit is set and the no co-processor available exception is issued, the coprocessor starts emulating floating- point instruction.

## TASK SWITCH (TS)
Like the 80286, when this bit is set, a task switch has occurred and in the protected mode, the pentium has run into a task gate at least once..

## EXTENSION TYPE (ET)
Like the i486, in the pentium the ET bit always equals 1 indicating that i387 coprocessor instructions are supported.

## NUMRIC ERROR (NE)
Like the i486, the NE bit controls the behaviour of the pentium when a non masked numerical exception occurs. If NE bit is set, the pentium issues an Interrupt-16.

## WRITE PROTECT (WP)
Like the i486, read-only pages can be protected from being over written by a supervisor of the pentium with the help of WP bit.

## ALIGNMENT MASK (AM)
This bit is also available in i486. Using the AM bit, AC bit in the EFLAG register can generate an alignment exception through Interrupt-17.

## NOT WRITE-THROUGH (NW)
This bit is also available in i486. With the help of the NW bit, write operations can be controlled for the activated on-chip data cache.

## CACHE DISABLE (CD)
This bit is also available in i486. The CD bit controls the operating mode of the two on-chip caches.

## PAGING ENABLE (PG)
This bit is also available in i386. By setting or resetting the PG bit, it is possible to enable or disable the PU

in the MMU of the pentium.

## CONTROL REGISTER CR2

After a page fault, this control register stores the linear address of the instruction responsible for the page fault.

## CONTROL REGISTER CR3

With an active paging unit, the Pentium like the i486, stores the twenty most significant bits of the page directory address in the control register CR3. All control bits other than 3 and 4 of this register are reserved. These two bits are PWT and PCD bits respectively.

## PAGE WRITE-THROUGH (PWT)

Like i486, if paging is active, the PWT bit is sent from the PWT output of the Pentium for those cycles which require on paging.

## PAGE CACHE DISABLE (PCD)

The PCD bit is similar to the PWT bit.

## CONTROL REGISTER (CR4)

In the Pentium, the control register CR4 has been newly implemented. It supports the extensions for the virtual 8086 mode and other different properties. The structure of the control register CR4 has been presented in Fig. 16.15.

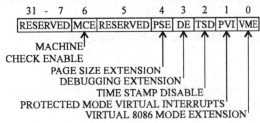

Fig. 16.15 The Structure of the Control Register CR4.

## VIRTUAL 8086 MODE EXTENSION (VME)

The VME bit when set, enables the support of virtual Interrupt flags in the virtual 8086 mode.

## PROTECTED MODE VIRTUAL INTERRUPTS (PVI)

In protected mode, the PVI bit of the Pentium serves the same purpose as the VME bit in the virtual 8086 mode.

## TIME STAMP DISABLE (TSD)

The RDTSC instruction reads the value of the time stamp counter. By setting the TSD bit, it becomes a so called previleged instruction. The DE, PSE and MCE bits refer to Debugging Extension, Page Size Extension and Machine Cache Enable when set.

### 16.6.4 THE DEBUG REGISTERS

A Pentium in protected mode usually operates in a multitasking environment. In this mode, other tasks are also active besides the debugger. The Pentium provides powerful hardware support for the debugger. In it, there are eight debug registers (DR0 to DR7) each of 32-bits. These are identical to the debug registers in the i386/i486 and support debuggers at the hardware level in both protected and virtual 8086 modes. In general, the contents of debug registers are as followes :

DR0 to DR3    -    Linear addresses of four break points

DR4 and DR5    -    reserved for future use,

DR6 and DR7 - Entries required to control the behaviour of the pentium at a breakpoint.

DE6 and DR7 - These acts as the debug control and status registers.

## 16.6.5 THE MEMORY MANAGEMENT, TEST AND MODEL SPECIFIC REGISTERS

The Pentium possesses four memory Management registers as shown in Fig. 16.16. Besides the control and debug registers, these registers operate as memory managers and divide the memory into segments during protected mode.

| | 15                    0 | 31                         0 | 19                0 |
|------|------------------|--------------------|--------------|
| TR | TSS   selector | TSS   base   address | TSS limit |
| LDRT | LDT   selector | LDT   base   address | LDT limit |
| IDTR | | IDT   base   address | IDT limit |
| GDTR | | GDT   base   address | GDT limit |

Fig. 16.16 The Pentium Memory Management Registers

As a part of the model specific register, test registers TR6 and TR7 are implemented in the Pentium for checking the TLB.

The model-specific registers of the Pentium consist of the following registers and counters :

i) Machine check address register
ii) Machine check type register
iii) Test registers TR1 to TR12
iv) Time stamp counter,
v) Control/event select register
vi) Two counters 0 and 1

Two new instructions viz. RDMSR (read model-specific register) and WRMSR (write model-specific register) have been implemented in order to access these registers.

## 16.6.6 REGISTERS OF THE FLOATING-POINT UNIT

The floating point unit of the Pentium has a register stack containing eight numbers of 80-bit registers (R1 to R8) along with several control and status registers.

The eight data registers correspond to the temporary real format. Each of them has been divided into three sections : sign S, 15-bit exponent and 64-bit mantissa. They are organized as a stack and not as individual registers. The 3-bit field (TOP) in the status word (Fig 16.17) shows the current 'TOP' registers. TOP has similar qualities and tasks to those of the stack pointer ESP. These can reduce TOP by 1 and place a value in its respective register or increase TOP by 1 and take off the applicable stack register. In doing these, floating-point instructions such as FLP (floating load and push) and FSTP (floating store and pop) are used. These instructions are similar to the integer instuctions PUSH and POP respectively. The stack increases downwards to register samller numbers. Most instructions implicitly address the top register in the stack.

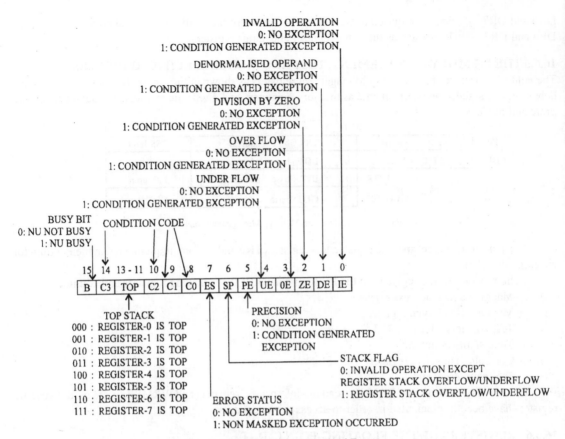

Fig. 16.17 Floating-Point Status Word Format

The status word contains information. The Pentium uses the instructions FSTSW/FNSTSW to write the status word to memory. It uses the instruction FSTSW AX to write the same in the AX register. The Pentium has the capability to examine the status word.

The Busy bit (B) is only partly available due to compatibility with the 8087 and is always equal to the ES bit. The Pentium Error Status (ES) is indicated by the ES bit. An unmasked exception occurs if ES is set. Bit SP differentiates between invalid operations caused by register stack underflow or overflow and invalid operations. The bit 1 differentiates between an overflow (C1=1) and an underflow (C1=0) provided SP is set and an underflow or overflow of the stack register has occurred. The condition code C3-C0 are similar to the EFLAGS. The Pentium is capable of operating with two floating-point zeros. The three TOP bits are used to form the stack pointer for the registers R7 to R0.

### 16.6.7 THE INTEGER PIPELINES U AND V

Like the i486, the pentium uses RISC concepts to strengthen the computation capability using instruction pipelining. The i486 contains only one instruction pipeline but the Pentium can use two integer pipelines, known as the U pipeline and the V pipeline. They can be operated in parallel following paired instructions.

Each of the two Pentium pipelines contains five stages for instruction fetch (IF). The main pipeline U can carry out all instructions of the 8086 family including complex instructions in microcode format. The V pipeline is used only for simple integer instructions and the floating-point unit instructions.

Instruction pairing follows some rules under certain limitations. Since the instructions of the Pentium are completely hardwared, inputs of microcode from the microcode ROM are not necessary. Both the instructions of a pair must be simple. It may be noted that unconditional jumps, conditional jumps and function calls can only be paired if they are loaded into the V pipeline as the second instruction. Instructions concerning the shifting and rotations by one position should be loaded into the U pipeline as the first instruction in an instruction pair. Care must be taken that instructions in an Instruction pair should be independent on register.

Further, instructions with a prefix can only be loaded in the U pipeline. It may also be noted that the exception of the prefix decoding stage sends the prefixes through the U pipeline at a rate of one prefix per clock cycle. The 0-th prefix indcates the 2-byte opcode.

## 16.6.8 THE FLOATING-POINT PIPELINE

The Pentium contains a floating-point unit in addition to the two integer pipelines. It executes floating-point instructions in a pipelined way.

Unlike the U and V pipelines, the floating-point pipeline contains eight stages viz. IF, D1, D2, EX, WB/X1, WF and ER. The first five stages are shared with U pipeline. The pairing rules prevent the parallel execution of integer and floating-point instructions.

The floating-point unit of the Pentium is completely compatible with the X87 coprocessor and the on-chip coprocessor of the i486DX though there is a number of internal differences. The floating-point unit of the i486DX has been implemented as an on-chip coprocessor but the floating-point unit of the Pentium is an integral part of the CPU. The Pentium possesses the hardware multiplier and divider with the help of which the calculation performance is enhanced. The rate of execution of the floating point instructions in the Pentium is two to five times faster than the i486DX2.

The first stage IF, reads in the instruction and then passes it to the first decoding stage D1. The second decoding stage D3 produces the operand addresses. In the EX stage, the data cache and the register operand are read. For the U pipeline, X1 represents the register write state WB, which updates the register content and the status register.

In addition to this, the X1 stage has the task of identifying those instructions which do not cause an overflow, underflow or exception through an inaccuracy. The X1 stage also examines the operand values and the opcode of the instruciton. If the current instruction is found to be safe, the subsequent floating-point instruction leaves the EX stage and enters the X1 stage, as soon as the previous instruction has proceeded to the second execution stage X2. If the current instruction is not safe, the subsequent instruction in the EX stage is held up until the current instruction has left the first ER stage without producing an error. In this way, unsafe instructions are prevented from interference produced by subsequent instructions.

The floating-point pipeline also contains two register bypasses for the acceleration of those instructions which require the results of previously executed instructions as operands. The first bypass connects the output of the X1 stage with the input of the EX stage. The second bypass connects the output of the WF stage directly to the input of the EX stage. With this, the result of an instruction is available for the next instruction without the delay of the write operation. The bypasess do not stop the operation of the X1 and WF stages. These supply result to the instructions that follow, in parallel to executing the write operation to the applicable register. This produces a gain of one clock.

## 16.6.9 PIN CONFIGURATION OF THE PENTIUM

The Pin configuration of Pentium P5 processor has been shown in Fig. 16.18.

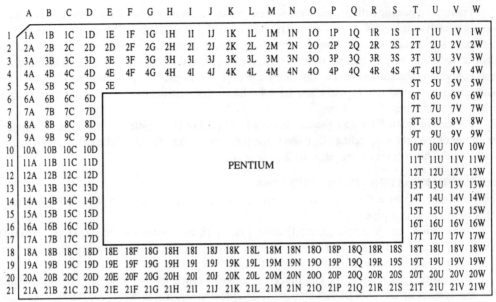

Fig. 16.18 Pin configuration of Pentium

The description of 289 pins of the pentium is as under :

DATA BUS

( 64 pin bi-directional Data Bus; used for input and output of data. Data size is double that of i386.)

| BUS NO. | D0 | D1 | D2 | D3 | D4 | D5 | D6 | D7 | D8 | D9 | D10 | D11 | D12 | D13 | D14 | D15 |
|---|---|---|---|---|---|---|---|---|---|---|---|---|---|---|---|---|
| PIN NO. | 19L | 19K | 19J | 18J | 21H | 19H | 18H | 19G | 18G | 4G | 3G | 20F | 19F | 18F | 4F | 3F |
| BUS NO. | D16 | D17 | D18 | D19 | D20 | D21 | D22 | D23 | D24 | D25 | D26 | D27 | D28 | D29 | D30 | D31 |
| PIN NO. | 20E | 18E | 5E | 4E | 3E | 21D | 20D | 19D | 17D | 16D | 15D | 14D | 13D | 12D | 10D | 19D |
| BUS NO. | D32 | D33 | D34 | D35 | D36 | D37 | D38 | D39 | D40 | D41 | D42 | D43 | D44 | D45 | D46 | D47 |
| PIN NO. | 7D | 6D | 5D | 4D | 3D | 21C | 20C | 19C | 18C | 17C | 16C | 15C | 14C | 13C | 12C | 11C |
| BUS NO. | D48 | D49 | D50 | D51 | D52 | D53 | D54 | D55 | D56 | D57 | D58 | D59 | D60 | D61 | D62 | D63 |
| PIN NO. | 10C | 9C | 8C | 7C | 6C | 4C | 21B | 20B | 19B | 10B | 9B | 4B | 20B | 21B | 20A | 10A |

ADDRESS BUS

( Represents the 29 most significant address lines of the pentium. It may be noted the three least significant address bits A0 to A2 are coded by the eight bit enable signals BE0-BE7.)

| BUS NO.<br>PIN NO. | A0 | A1 | A2 | A3 | A4 | A5 | A6 | A7 | A8 | A9 | A10 | A11 | A12 | A13 | A14 | A15 |
|---|---|---|---|---|---|---|---|---|---|---|---|---|---|---|---|---|
|  |  |  |  | 17T | 19W | 18U | 17U | 16T | 16U | 15T | 15U | 14T | 12U | 13T | 13U | 12T |
| BUSNO.<br>PIN NO. | A16 | A17 | A18 | A19 | A20 | A21 | A22 | A23 | A24 | A25 | A26 | A27 | A28 | A29 | A30 | A31 |
|  | 12U | 11T | 11U | 10T | 10U | 21U | 9V | 20U | 8U | 19U | 9T | 21V | 6V | 20V | 5W | 19V |

FREE PINS

PIN NO.　　3L　4N　19Q　19R　18T

GND:

| PIN NO. | 5B | 6B | 7B | 8B | 11B | 12B | 13B | 14B | 15B | 16B | 17B | 18B | 2E | 2F | 2G | 20G |
|---|---|---|---|---|---|---|---|---|---|---|---|---|---|---|---|---|
|  | 2H | 20H | 1J | 20J | 1K | 20K | 1L | 20L | 1M | 20M | 2N | 20N | 2P | 20P | 2Q | 20Q |
|  | 2R | 20R | 2S | 2T | 7V | 8V | 9V | 10V | 11V | 12V | 13V | 14V | 15V | 16V | 17V | 18V |

Vcc:

| PIN NO. | 4A | 5A | 6A | 7A | 8A | 11A | 12A | 13A | 14A | 15A | 16A | 17A | 18A | 1C | 1D | 1E |
|---------|-----|-----|-----|-----|-----|-----|-----|-----|-----|-----|-----|-----|-----|-----|-----|-----|
|         | 1F | 21F | 1G | 21G | 1H | 21J | 21K | 21L | 21M | 1N | 21N | 1P | 21P | 1Q | 18Q | 21Q |
|         | 1R | 21R | 1S | 1T | 1U | 6W | 7W | 8W | 9W | 10W | 11W | 12W | 13W | 14W | 15W | 16W |
|         | 17W | 18W | | | | | | | | | | | | | | |

OTHER PINS

PIN NO.

IA - INV (INVALIDATION REQUEST)

Invalidation input request leads to the invalidation of the applicable cache line, if hit occurs. If no hit occurs, INV has no effect.

1B - IV (INSTRUCTION IN THE V PIPELINE)

It sends out signal with a high level from this instruction/ V pipeline pin.

2B 3B 2D - BP3-BP2, PM1/BP1-PM0/BP0 (O) (BREAKOUT PINS)

1: indicates the occurrence of a breakpoint for the corresponding register. Through the two bits BP1 and BP0 in the debug mode control register DR4, PM1/BP1 or PM0/BP0 may be set to act as a breakpoint pin.

2C - IERR (INTERNAL ERROR OUTPUT SIGNAL)

0: Indicates an internal error in the Pentium. The Pentium, working as a controller, then goes into a shutdown condition.

2J - IU (INSTRUCTION IN THE U PIPELINE)

It sends out a signal with a high level from this instruction U pipeline pin.

2L - AHOLD (ADDRESS HOLD INPUT PIN)

0: A different bus controller can access the address bus of the Pentium in order to perform an enquiry cycle for the Pentium;

1: the Pentium does not use its address bus A31-A3, BT3-BT0 and AP; all other signals remaining active.

2M - WB/WT (WRITE-BACK/WRITE-THROUGH PIN)

Write-back write-through pin defines the corresponding cache line as write-back, or otherwise write-through, during a memory access.

2U - FLUSH (CACHE FLUSH INPUT PIN)

0: The Pentium writes back to memory all changed cache lines of the on-chip data cache and invalidates both on chip date and cache. 1 : Forces the Pentium to execute a cache flush.

2V - BREQ (BUS REQUEST OUTPUT SIGNAL)

Bus request signal indicates the request of the programmer of the internal bus.

2W - HIT (HIT OUTPUT SIGNAL)

HIT signal indicates the result of an inquiry cycle.

3A - EWBE (EXTERNAL WRITE BUFFER EMPTY PIN)

0: This input informs the Pentium that the external system is ready to take write data from the Pentium. At a high level, the system must first execute an additional write cycle before the Pentium can proceed with transferring data.

3H - FERR (AN OUTPUT PIN)

Sends out an active signal with a low level if a non-masked exception occurs in floating-point unit of the Pentium.

3J - KEN (CACHE ENABLE INPUT)

Used for determination by the pentium whether the addressed address area can be transferred to the cache.

3K - NA (NEXT ADDRESS INPUT SIGNAL)
Used for the implementation and control of address pipelining.

3L - AP (I/O) (ADDRESS PARITY PIN FOR PARITY FORMATION FOR THE ADDRESS BUS)
The Pentium sends out the AP parity bit in order to achieve parity.

3M - EADS (EXTERNAL ADDRESS PIN)
External address Input pin indicates to the Pentium that an external bus controller has sent a valid address to its addrss pins during inquiry cycles.

3P - AP (I/O) (PIN FOR PARITY INFORMATION FOR ADDRESS BUS)
In order to achieve parity, the Pentium sends out the AP parity bit

3Q - HLDA (BUS HOLD ACKNOWLEDGE)
Used for controlling the transfer of the control of the local bus between the different local bus controllers.

3R - PCHK (PARITY CHECK OUTPUT PIN)
Parity check pin indicates whether the transferred data bits D86 - D0 and the parity bits DP7-DP0 are consistent.

3S - PWT (PAGE WRITE THROUGH)
Indicates the values of the PWT bit in the CR3 control register.

3T - BUSCHK (BUS CHECK PIN)
Bus check Input pin informs the Pentium about an incomplete bus cycle data read, data write or other access,. If BUSCHK is low, the Pentium stroes the address and values in the machine check register according to the control signals.

3U - PRDY (PROBE READY OUTPUT PIN)
Probe ready pin indicates that the Pentium has stopped normal operation and has gone into probe as a reaction to a low level R/S signal.

3V - LOCK (LOCK OUT SIGNAL)
0: The Pentium does not pass control of the local bus to another bus controller which requests controller using HOLD.

3W - APCHK (ADDRESS PARITY CHECK OUTPUT PIN)
It indicates whether the transferred address bits A31-A3 and the address parity bit AP are consistent; 0: address parity error has occurred.

4J - CACHE (CACHE SIGNAL)
CACHE output signal indicates that the current memory cycle sent by the Pentium is internally cacheable. At a low level, the Pentium extends read cycle to a cache fill in burst mode. An inactive CACHE signal always leads to a single transfer without internal cacheing of the transferred data or bytes. CACHE signal when low, results in a burst mode and the transfer of 32 bytes of code or data.

4K - BOFF (BACK OFF INPUT PIIN)
0: The Pentium disables its bus at the next clock cycle,
1: the Pentium restarts the interrupted bus cycle again from the beginning.

4L - BRDY (BURST READY INPUT SIGNAL
0: indicates whether the addressed pripheral system, the main memory, or an I/O device has already completed the requested access.
1: requires more time (BRDY=high). BRDY signal inserts one or more WAIT states required for the slower peripheral devices.

4M - HITM (HIT MODIFIED LINE OUTPUT SIGNAL)
HIT modified line signal indicates the result of an inquiry cycle. The Pentium activates the HITM signal at a low level. If a miss, or a hit to an unchanged line occurs, the pin sends out a signal with

a high level.

4P - $\overline{ADS}$ (ADDRESS STATUS SIGNAL)

At low level, this output pin gives indication that the Pentium has started a new bus cycle.

4R - SCYC (SPLIT CYCLE)

The Pentium outputs an active split cycle signal at the SCYC pin, in order to indicate that more than two locked bus cycles are to follow.

4T - TCK (TEST CLOCK INPUT PIN)

4U 6U 7U 4Q 4S 6T 1V 1W - $\overline{BE7}$-$\overline{BE0}$ (BYTE ENABLE PIN)

These output pins give indication regarding the particular byte group out of 64-bit data which actually transfers data in the current bus cycle. BE0 corresponds to the least significant data byte D7-D0 and BE7 corresponds to the most significant data byte D63-D56.

4V 2A 3N- $D/\overline{C}$, $M/\overline{IO}$, $W/\overline{R}$, (DATA CONTROL, MEMORY/ IO AND READ/ WRITE OUTPUT PINS)

DATA CONTROL - 1: DATA CYCLE;  0:  INSTRUMENTATION CYCLE

MEMORY/ IO     - 1: MEMORY;       0:  I/O CYCLE

READ/ WRITE    - 1: WRITE CYCLE;  0:  READ CYCLE

| $D/\overline{C}$ | $M/\overline{IO}$ | $W/\overline{R}$ | | |
|---|---|---|---|---|
| (0 | 0 | 0) | : | Interrupt acknowledge sequence |
| (0 | 0 | 1) | : | Special cycle |
| (0 | 1 | 0) | : | Reading from an I/O port |
| (0 | 1 | 1) | : | Writing to an I/O port |
| (1 | 0 | 0) | : | Instruction fetching |
| (1 | 0 | 1) | : | Invalid |
| (1 | 1 | 0) | : | Reading of data from memory |
| (1 | 1 | 1) | : | Writing of data to memory |

4W, 3S - PCD, PWT (PAGE CACHE OUTPUT DISABLE, PAGE WRITE-THROUGH OUTPUT SIGNAL)

Page cache disable indicates the value of the PCD bit in the CR3 control register, the page table entry or the page directory entry for the current page. The Pentium delivers external cacheing information on a page basis. Page write-through signal indicates the value of the page write-through bit PWT in the CR3 control register, the page table entry or the page directory entry for the current page. The Pentium delivers external write-back or write through information on a page basis.

5T - $\overline{SMIACT}$ (SYSTEM MANAGEMENT INTERRUPT ACTIVE PIN)

System management interrupt active pin indicates to the system that the Pentium is currently running in system management mode and only accesses the SMRAM.

5U - $\overline{A20M}$ (ADDRESS 20 MASK PIN)

When this input pin is low, the Pentium internally masks the address bit A20 before every memory access.

5V - HOLD (BUS HOLD REQUEST INPUT)

7T 8T 20W 21W - BT3-BT0 (BRANCH TRACE OUTPUT SIGNALS)

BT2-BT0 gives the bits A2-A0 the linear branch address during a branch trace message cycle; BT3 defines the standard operand size. If BT3 is active high, the standard operand size is 32-bits, otherwise it is 16-bit.

9A 19A 5C 8D 18D 19E 21E 4H - DP7-DP0 (I/O) (DATA PARITY BITS)

It sends out the parity DP7-DP0 for every byte of the data bus D63-D0 during every write cycle. When reading data, the system must send signals to the pins DP7-DP8 that will give an even parity. Systems that do not support this parity function, usually fix DP7-DP0 at Vcc or GND. The signals sent to the pins during a read operation do no influence the program execution.

18K - CLK (CLOCK SIGNAL)

The internal processor input signal.

18L - RESET (RESET IN)

1: the Pentium completely stops its current activities and carries out an internal processor reset.

18M - $\overline{PEN}$ (PARTLY ENABLE INPUT PIN)

Parity enable pin defines whether the Pentium should send out a machine check exception corresponding to interrupt -18 if a data parity error occus during a read cycle.

18N - INTR (INTERRUPT REQUEST INPUT)

1: indicates that an interrupt request from a hardware unit exists.

18P - $\overline{SMI}$ (SYSTEM MANAGEMENT INTERRUPT)

The Pentium branches to the SMM (system management mode) handler, in order to carry out the necessary functions. An RSM (resume from system management mode) instruction reloads the register values from the system management ROM into the Pentium and enables the processor to resume the interrupted program.

18R - $R/\overline{S}$ (RESUME / STOP PIN)

0: Interrupts the currently running program executions.

1: Pentium restarts the instruction execution.

18S - $\overline{TEST}$ (TEST RESET INPUT PIN)

19N - NMI (NON MASKABLE INTERRUPT)

19M - $\overline{FRCMC}$ (FUNCTIONAL REDUNDANCY CHECKING MASTER/CHECKER INPUT)

Functional redundancy checking master/checker input indicates to the Pentium during a reset whether it should operate as a master or a checker.

1: The Pentium controls the bus according to usual bus protocol.

0: The Pentium determines the signal level at all output pins and compares them within internal values.

19P - TMS (TEST MODE SELECT INPUT PIN)

19T - IBT (INSTRUCTION BRANCH TAKEN OUTPUT PIN)

Instruction branch taken pin outputs a signal with a high level if the Pentium executes a branch internally.

*20S - $\overline{IGNNE}$ (IGNORE NUMERIC ERROR INPUT PIN)

0: The pentium ignores numerical errors and continues to execute floating point instructions.

20T - INIT (INITIALIZATION PIN FOR A MINIMUM OF TWO CLK CLOCK CYCLES)

Similar to a reset, the initialization pin for a minimum of two CLK clock cycles, sets the Pentium into a defined initial start condition.

21S - TDO (TEST DATA OUTPUT PIN)

21T - TDI (TEST DATE INPUT PIN)

*Courtesy : Intel Corporation, USA.

# 17. Introduction to Embedded System

## 17.1 INTRODUCTION

An embedded system is a large or small computer system which is a piece of equipment or another computer system. It performs some task useful to the product, equipment or system. It is a computer system and it is programmed to perform a particular task. This task may be very simple or very complex but it is not a relevant distinction. It is known that all computers are programmed to perform tasks. However an embedded system is programmed to perform its task from the time when it is powered up and continues to act till it is shut down. Its programming is permanently stored and it cannot be changed till the original programmer so desires.

Just like a logic gate or other electronic component, an embedded systems has a single task to perform. Again, the task may be extremely complex or extremely simple, but in either case the task is performed by a computer system having an appropriate program. An embedded system is a component of a larger system of some kind. Embedded systems may also be nested within other embedded systems.

As an example of nested embedded system, a walking robot may be considered. Each motor on each joint of each leg may be controlled by its own embedded system which implements some form of motor control strategy such as pulse width modulation or stepper motor control as appropriate, and acquires sensory input. In a multi-legged robot, these low-level embedded systems may also be controlled by a higher-level embedded system. Higher level embedded system issues commands for each leg to implement the desired robot motion. Thus, these two levels of embedded system implement a motion control platform, where other commands are sent by higher-level system which performs robot path planning and computes the overall motion for the robot. This system may not be considered as the top of the embedded system hierarchy; it is entirely possible that a still-higher level system controls the path planner. In this example, we see a hierarchy of four levels of nested embedded system.

Embedded systems are appearing in a tremendous variety of sizes and activities. An embedded system may be as small as a single 8-pin integrated circuit which performs the functions of a few logic gates, or may be as large as a system with 256 megabytes of memory, a small disc (20 gigabytes or so), a Pentium processor and a host of intelligent peripherals. The range of physical and computing sizes is large.

## 17.2 FEATURES OF EMBEDDED SYSTEM

- these perform a very well-defined task for the product, equipment or system in which these are found;
- these do not permit user interaction with their operation except where such interaction may be the task of the embedded system, and
- these are considered to be a component of much larger product, equipment or system.

## 17.3 SOME EXAMPLES OF EMBEDDED SYSTEM

- keyboard and other controllers for computers, CD players and consumer electronics,
- timing and control electronics in microwave ovens, coffee makers,
- controllers for vacuum cleaners and washing machines for sensing dirt loads,
- control of the dashboard, ignition, fuel injection, suspension stiffness and environmental temperature and noise in automobiles,

- parking meter controllers,
- elevator, environmental and security systems in buildings,
- internal operation of medical instrumentation such as infusion pumps, pulse oximeters, etc
- disc controllers for computer systems,
- control of data communications routers for wide-band communications, and many more.

The embedded systems have more similarity than dissimilarity. These differ in scale keeping the same concept.

## 17.4 CHARACTERISTICS OF AN EMBEDDED SYSTEM:

Embedded computer systems constitute the widest possible use of computer systems; it includes all computers other than those specifically intended as general-purpose computers. Examples of embedded systems range from a portable music player, to real-time control of systems like the space shuttle. These are characterized by providing a function, or functions, that is not itself a computer.

The majority of commercial embedded systems are designed to perform selected functions at a low cost. Many, but not all embedded systems, have real-time system constraints that must be met. In some cases, these systems act very fast but in some other case these systems act at a comparatively low speed. These systems meet their real-time constraints with a combination of special purpose hardware and software tailored to the system requirements.

It is difficult to characterize embedded systems by speed, or by cost requirements, but for high volume systems, cost will often dominate much of the system design. Fortunately, most systems have limited real-time requirements which can usually be met with a combination of custom hardware and a limited amount of high performance software. Consider for instance a digital set-top box. Such a system has to process tens of megabits of continuous-data per second, but majority of work is done by custom hardware which analyzes, directs, and decodes the multi-channel digital stream down into a single video output. The embedded CPU is used to determine data paths, handle interrupts, generate and display graphics, etc. Therefore, often many parts of an embedded system will require low performance compared to primary mission of the system. This allows architecture of an embedded system to be intentionally simplified to lower costs compared to a general-purpose computer accomplishing the same task, by using a CPU that is good enough for these secondary functions.

For embedded systems having no high volume, personal computers can often be used either by limiting the programs or by replacing the operating system with a real-time operating system. In this case special purpose hardware may be replaced by one or more high performance CPUs. Still, some embedded system may require both high performance CPUs, special hardware, and large memories to complete a required task.

The software written for many embedded systems, especially those without a disk drive is sometimes called firmware, the name for software that is embedded in hardware devices, like one or more ROM / Flash memory IC chips, etc

Programs on an embedded system often run with real-time constraints with limited hardware resources; having no disk drive, operating system, keyboard or screen. The software may not have anything remotely like a file system, or if one is present, a flash drive may replace rotating media. If a user interface is present, it may be a small keypad and liquid crystal display.

Embedded systems reside in machines. These are expected to run continuously for years without errors. Therefore the software or Firmware is usually developed and tested more carefully than Software for Personal computers. Many embedded systems avoid mechanical moving parts such as Disk drives, switches or buttons because these are unreliable compared to solid-state parts such as Flash memory.

In addition, the embedded system may be outside the reach of humans in such a way that the embedded system must be able to restart itself even if catastrophic data corruption has taken place. This is usually accomplished with a standard electronic part called a watchdog timer that resets the computer unless the software periodically resets the timer.

## 17.5 8/16 BITS MICROPROCESSOR/MICROCONTROLLER

Earlier 8 and 16 bit processors were universal computing machine found in all smart products, but today these are used in the kingdom of deeply embedded applications, having a lot of I/O. Peripherals are important, as evidenced by the large number of variants for some devices. Some 200 different 8051s may be used practically utilizing any number of I/O devices.

Today many devices offer sophisticated special-purpose functions like LCD drivers and fast A/D converters.

Microcontrollers are finally moving from OTP (One Time Programmable – an EPROM with no erasure window) to Flash. Though Flash remains a more expensive technology, but its use in the circuit board reduces manufacturing costs. Updating code without disassembling a product is a powerful argument for Flash.

As an example, an embedded system for controlling reactive power using Intel 8051 based Microcontroller has been developed and presented. The Signal receiving circuit (SR), Zero Crossing Detector (ZCD), Firing Angle Controller Module, Opto-Isolator Circuitry and Signal Transmitting Circuitry are all embedded within the Microcontroller.

## 17.6 STATIC VAR CONTROLLER

### ENERGY CRISIS IS NOW AN ACUTE GLOBAL CRISIS

Conventional sources of energy:

      Coal (Thermal Energy)

      Water (Hydel Energy)

      Nuclear Energy

Non-Conventional sources of energy:

      Sun – Solar energy

      Wind – Wind energy

      Tide – Tidal Energy

These are not economical at present to produce.

Major conventional source of energy is Coal.

Coal reserve will be used up to third decade of the 21st century if utilization rate is not controlled.

Hence slogan of the day should be **"Save energy, Save our World"**.

## 17.7 MAJOR CAUSES OF ENERGY LOSS

1. Socio-economic reason: Power theft, hooking can be controlled by public awareness, discipline and severe punishment.

2. Power loss due to reactive load.

   Total global loss of energy is 40% of generation. More reactive load means inferior power factor. Inferior Power factor means reduced active power. Due to inferior Power factor of industrial load, cost of depreciation increases and industry has to pay for the loss of energy regularly

## 17.8  INTRODUCTION TO SVC

- Metropolis and suburban areas are subjected to frequent reactive power disturbances, resulting voltage fluctuation. This also causes low power factor operation.
- It is necessary to maintain constancy of voltage within specified limits.
- : This can be efficiently managed by using static VAR Compensator (SVC) by injecting reactive power into the system during rapid fluctuation of load
- SVC can be used at the receiving end to avoid transmission of reactive power through the transmission line.

## 17.9  WHY STATIC VAR COMPENSATOR (SVC)

- High potentiality to supply very good amount of reactive power.
- Characterized by fast response, high efficient, low operating cost and enough flexibility. Response time of SVC is in the range of two /three cycles.
- Most suitable where fast reactive power control is required.
- SVC with higher rating can be used efficiently for transmission system where large industrial loads are connected.
- Its performances is very good in order to improve voltage regulation, dynamic response, voltage and current unbalance and voltage flickering.
- Static device and hence free from mechanical hazards.

## 17.10  TYPES OF SVC

**Two types of SVC**
- FC-TCR {Fixed Capacitor/Thirstier Controlled Reactor.}
- TSC-TCR {Thyristor Switched Capacitor/Thyristor Controlled Reactor}
- Both the types work on the same philosophy and provide identical response.
- Originally FC-TCR scheme had been developed for the industrial application.
- TSC-TCR scheme is progressively used in power transmission only.
- Choice of SVC depends on requirement of power and system disturbances.

## 17.11  WHY 8051 CPU BASED MICROCONTROLLER USED

- Interfacing is simple, Programming is not very difficult.
- Assembly level programming is required which is not very difficult to develop software.
- Modification in programming can easily be done.
- Speed of operation is very much compatible with the power system operation.
- System is simple and reliable. All peripherals are integrated in a single chip.
- Digital and intelligent system.
- During operation, set value (s) and parameter (s) if any can be altered through keyboard.

- Control, protection and monitoring can be done efficiently and at a time.
- Low cost and portable.

## 17.12 MODELING

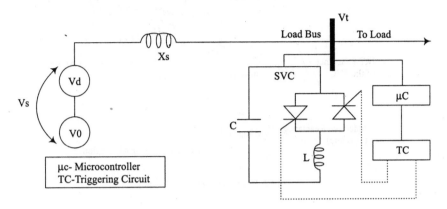

Fig. 17.1 Theoritical Model of the Developed Scheme

In this Scheme
- Xs represents series equivalent reactance of power supply
- Power System has been considered as a resultant voltage source(Vs) which consists of a fixed system voltage (V0) and a voltage disturbance (Vd).
- The reactive current may be capacitive or inductive which produces voltage drop across source reactance.
- The drop increases or decreases terminal voltage (Vt) depending on wheather the current injection is capacitive or inductive.
- Compensator operates as a terminal voltage regulator.
- Microcontroller senses the load bus voltage, determines firing angle to be modified, if any and generates a set of six triggering pulses with 60 degree interval after following a delay for triggering thyristors.
- Change of reactance causes changes in terminal voltage.

## 17.13 LOAD BUS VOLTAGE CONTROL PHILOSOPHY
- Here FC-TCR scheme has been discussed.
- Fixed capacitor supplies fixed VAR: QCOMP(C).
- Thyristor controlled reactor provides variable inductive VAR output : QCOMP(L).
- Qnet : Net reactive power which depends on triggering angle.
- Qnet : supplies reactive power demand at load bus.
- Balance reactive power condition ensures operation of system at nominal voltage.

In Load Bus Voltage Control Philosophy, FC-TCR scheme has been discussed.

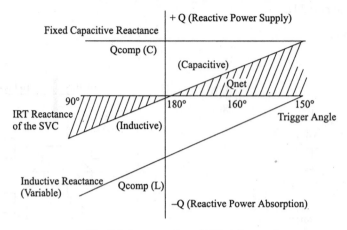

Fig. 17.2  Reactance Control Philosophy

## 17.14  SYSTEM HARDWARE

The block diagram of the developed Scheme has been shown in Fig. 17.3

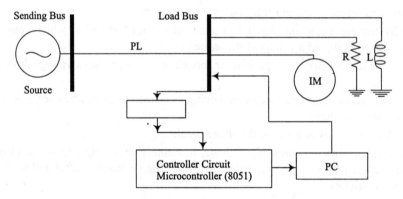

Fig. 17.3  Schematic Block Diagram of the proposed Scheme

- Source is a DC motor – AC generator set at the sending end.
- Transmission – distribution system is simulated equivalent to pi-configuration of 600 km single circuit 400 kv two bus line model.
- FC- TCR type SVC is at receiving end.
- Load consists of Induction motor and Static impedance loads.
- VAR Compensator consists of a) Power Circuit Modulate (PC) b) Firing Angle controller Modulate (FAC), c) signal Reciever circuitry d) signal transmitting circuitry.

## 17.15 POWER CIRCUIT

- The power circuit module shown in Fig. 17.4 consists of conventional Static VAR compensator (SVC) which is the combination of i) Anti-parallel thyristors in series with an inductor and ii) A capacitor bank.
- The three phase SVC are connected in star.
- Power circuit is connected at load end.

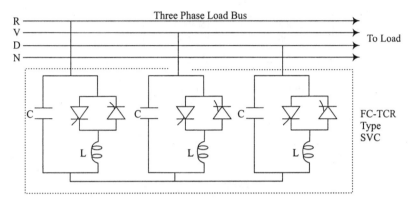

Fig. 17.4 Power Circuit Module

## SIGNAL RECIEVER (SR)

Microcontroller receives signal proportional to system voltage through ADC after proper scale down and rectification.

## 17.16 FIRING ANGLE CONTROLLER MODULE

- Microcontroller receives signal from Zero Crossing Detector (ZCD).
- After receiving signal from ZCD, it detects zero crossing instant of sinusoidal waveform, and transmits a set of six triggering pulses to trigger Thyristors.

## 17.17 SIGNAL TRANSMITTING CIRCUITRY

Here Microcontroller transmits triggering pulses to the gate of the thyristor through Opto-isolator circuitries.

## 17.18 SYSTEM SOFTWARE

System software is the most vital part of the developed scheme.

The necessary steps are:

- Initialise Stack Pointer and I/O ports.
- Store delay number (may be treated as firing angle) corresponding to operating firing angle, lower limit of firing angle and upper value of firing angle.
- Receive signal from ZCD and detect Zero crossing instant at the rising edge of the R-phase.
- Receive voltage signal through I/O port from ADC.
- Compare the instantaneous signal with the set value of voltage.

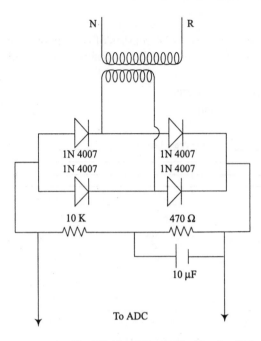

Fig. 17.5  Signal Transmitting Circuitry (VT)

- For higher value of instantaneous voltage, microcontroller reduces the Delay number (i.e., reduces the triggering angle) and emits a set of six triggering pulses for a number of cycles to stabilize the system.
- For lower value of instantaneous voltage, microcontroller increases the Delay nunber (i.e, increases the triggering angle) and emits a set of six triggering pulses for a number of cycles to stabilizes the system.
- In the case when there is no deviation of instantaneous voltage from the set value, microprocessor emits a set of six triggering pulses with previous delay number for a number of cycles.
- During increment and decrement of Delay number, microcontroller always compares the new Delay number with Upper and Lower limits of the Delay Number respectively.
- If the new Delay number is found less than the Lower value of delay number or greater than the Upper value of the delay number, the microcontroller blocks the Delay nunber at the lower or upper limiting value respectively and follows the same cyclic operation.
- This is necessary to avoid the mis-firing due to local sort circuit arising due to the transient.

The purpose of the SVC is to operate the system at a power factor ranging from 85% to 95%. When the power factor drops below 85%, the terminal voltage drops and then trigger angle is decreased. But when *Pf* goes above 95%, the trigger angle is increased.

## 17.19 GENERATION OF A SET OF SIX TRIGGERING PULSES

Here an intelligent strategy has been developed to generate a set of six triggering pulses during a small fluctuation of supply frequency.

This strategy has been incorporated in developing software which has been described as under:

- The total triggering angle has been divided into three zones viz. 0 to 60, 60 to 120 and 120 to 180 degree.
- After computation of Delay number, microcontroller detects the zone for triggering.
- For the first zone microcontroller only detects the zero crossing instant of R-phase and after a time delay corresponding to the new delay number, emits a set of six triggering pulses with 60 degree interval. In this case the triggering sequence is : TH1, TH6, TH3, TH2, TH5, TH4.
- For the second zone, microcontroller sutracts delay number corresponding to 60° from the computed delay number. The microcontroller detects the zero crossing instant of R-phase and after a time delay corresponding to new delay number emits a set of six triggering pulses with 60° internal. In this case, the sequence is: TH4, TH1, TH6, TH3, TH2, TH5.
- For the third zone, microcontroller substracts delay number corresponding to 120 degree from the computed delay number. The microcontroller detects the zero crossing instant of R-phase and after a time delay corresponding to new delay number, emits a set of six triggering pulses with 60 degree interval. In this case the triggering sequence is : TH5, TH4, TH1, TH6, Th3, TH2.

## THE PHILOSOPHY HAS BEEN PRESENTED IN THE FOLLOWING TABLE:

| Triggering angle (A) in degree | Phase | Firing sequence | Firing instant in degree | Conduction period in respect to R-phase |
|---|---|---|---|---|
| 0° to 60° | R | THI | A | A to180° |
| | B | TH6 | A + 60° | A + 60° to 240° |
| | Y | TH3 | A + 120° | A + 120° to 300° |
| | R | TH2 | A + 180° | A + 180° to 360° |
| | B | TH5 | A + 240° | A + 240° to 60° |
| | Y | TH4 | A + 300° | A + 300° to 120° |
| 60° to 120° | Y | TH4 | A – 60° | A-60° to 120° |
| | R | TH1 | A | A to 180° |
| | B | Th6 | A + 60° | A + 60° to 240° |
| | Y | TH3 | A +120° | A +120° to 300° |
| | R | TH2 | A +180° | A +180° to 360° |
| | B | TH5 | A +240° | A +240° to 360° |
| 120° to180° | B | TH5 | A – 120° | A-120° to 60° |
| | Y | TH4 | A – 60° | A-60° to 120° |
| | R | TH1 | A | A to 180° |
| | B | TH6 | A + 60° | A + 120° to 300° |
| | Y | TH3 | A +180° | A +180° to 360° |
| | R | TH2 | A +180° | |

## 17.20 LIMITATION

- The system is unable to compensate reactive power during large voltage disturbance.
- This is built for symmetrical operation.

# Appendices

# 1. 8085/8085A Instruction Set

**Table 1.1 Move Instructions (Data Movement from Reg. to Reg./Acc. to Reg./Reg. to Acc./Acc. to Memory/Memory to Acc./ Reg. to Memory/Memory to Reg.)**

| MOV | B | C | D | E | H | L | M | A |
|-----|-----|-----|-----|-----|-----|-----|-----|-----|
| B, | 40 | 41 | 42 | 43 | 44 | 45 | 46 | 47 |
| C, | 48 | 49 | 4A | 4B | 4C | 4D | 4E | 4F |
| D, | 50 | 51 | 52 | 53 | 54 | 55 | 56 | 57 |
| E, | 58 | 59 | 5A | 5B | 5C | 5D | 5E | 5F |
| H, | 60 | 61 | 62 | 63 | 64 | 65 | 66 | 67 |
| L, | 68 | 69 | 6A | 6B | 6C | 6D | 6E | 6F |
| M, | 70 | 71 | 72 | 73 | 74 | 75 | 76 | 77 |
| A, | 78 | 79 | 7A | 7B | 7C | 7D | 7E | 7F |

**Table 1.2**

| Instruction | Mnemonics | A | B | C | D | E | H | L | M | SP | Comments |
|-------------|-----------|-----|-----|-----|-----|-----|-----|-----|-----|-----|----------|
| Data movement | MVI | 3E | 06 | 0E | 16 | 1E | 26 | 2E | 36 | - | MOVE DATA (FOLLOWED BY INSTRUCTION) TO ACC./REG./MEMORY. |
| | LXI | | 01 | | 11 | | 21 | | | 31 | MOVE MSB & LSB OF DATA FOLLOWED TO REG. PAIR BC/DE/HL/SP. |
| Increment/ Decrement | INR<br>DCR | 3C<br>3D | 04<br>05 | 0C<br>0D | 14<br>15 | 1C<br>1D | 24<br>25 | 2C<br>2D | 34<br>35 | -<br>- | INCREMENT/DECREMENT REGISTER |
| | INX<br>DCX | | 03<br>0B | | 13<br>1B | | 23<br>2B | | | 33<br>3B | INCREMENT/DECREMENT REGISTER PAIR AND SP |
| Add/Subtract | ADD<br>SUB | 87<br>97 | 80<br>90 | 81<br>91 | 82<br>92 | 83<br>93 | 84<br>94 | 85<br>95 | 86<br>96 | | ADD/SUBTRACT CONTENT OF ACC/REG./ MEM. TO/FROM THE CONTENT OF ACC., PUT THE RESULT IN ACC. |
| Add/Subtract | ADC<br>SBB<br>DAD | 8F<br>9F | 88<br>98<br>09 | 89<br>99 | 8A<br>9A<br>19 | 8B<br>9B | 8C<br>9C<br>29 | 8D<br>9D | 8E<br>9E | 39 | ADD/SUBTRACT CARRY & CONTENT OF ACC./REG./ MEM. TO/ FROM THE CONTENT OF ACC., PUT THE RESULT IN ACC. |
| Compare | CMP | BF<br>* | B8 | 89 | BA | BB | BC | BD | BE | - | SUBTRACT CONTENT OF REG./ACC/MEM. FROM ACC., DON'T PUT RESULT IN ACC. (* SET Z-FLAG TO ZERO) |
| AND/OR/ EX-OR | *ANA<br>** XRA<br>*ORA | A7<br>AF<br>B7 | A0<br>A8<br>B0 | A1<br>A9<br>B1 | A2<br>AA<br>B2 | A3<br>AB<br>B3 | A4<br>AC<br>B4 | A5<br>AD<br>B5 | A6<br>AE<br>B6 | - | AND/OR/EX-OR WITH THE CONTENT OF ACC., PUT RESULT IN HL/SP RESPECTIVELY. (*CLEAR CARRY. ** CLEAR CY. & ACC.) |

**Table 1.3**

| Instruction | Mnemonics | Opcode | Comments |
|---|---|---|---|
| Data | LDA  4250 | 3A 50  42 | LOAD DATA TO ACC. FROM MEM. LOC. 4250 H |
| Movement | STA  4250 | 32 50  42 | STORE DATA FROM ACC. TO MEM. LOC. 4250 H |
| | LHLD 4250 | 2A 50  42 | LOAD DATA TO H AND L FROM MEM. LOC. 4251 H AND 4250 H RESPECTIVELY |
| | SHLD 4250 | 22 50  42 | STORE DATA TO MEM. LOC. 4251 H AND 4250 H FROM H AND L RESPECTIVELY |
| | LDAX B | 0A | LOAD DATA TO ACC. FROM MEM. LOC. WHOSE ADDRESS IS CONTENT IN REG. PAIR BC. |
| | LDAX D | 1A | LOAD DATA TO ACC. FROM MEM. LOC. WHOSE ADDRESS IS CONTENT IN REG. PAIR DE. |
| | STAX B | 02 | STORE DATA FROM ACC. TO MEM. LOC. WHOSE ADDRESS IS CONTENT IN REG. PAIR BC. |
| | STAX D | 12 | STORE DATA FROMACC. TO MEM. LOC. WHOSE ADDRESS IS CONTENTIN REG. PAIR DE. |
| | XCHG | EB | EXCHANGE DATA IN D WITH H AND DATA IN E WITH L |
| | SPHL | F9 | MOVE DATA FROM HL TO SP |
| | XTHL | E3 | EXCHANGE DATA IN H WITH LOC. (SP+1) AND IN L WITH LOC. (SP) |
| | PUSH B | C5 | MOVE DATA FROM B TO LOC. (SP-1) AND DATA FROM C TO LOC. (SP-2) |
| | PUSH D | D5 | MOVE DATA FROM D TO LOC. (SP-1) AND DATA FROM E TO LOC. (SP-2) |
| | PUSH H | E5 | MOVE DATA FROM H TO LOC. (SP-1) AND DATA FROM L TO LOC. (SP-2) |
| | PUSH PSW | F5 | MOVE DATA FROM A TO LOC. (SP-1) AND DATA FROM FLAG TO LOC. (SP-2) |
| | POP   PSW | F1 | MOVE DATA FROM LOC. (SP) TO FLAG AND DATA FROM LOC. (SP+1) TO A |
| | POP   H | E1 | MOVE DATA FROM LOC. (SP) TO L AND DATA FROM LOC. (SP+1) TO  H |
| | POP   D | D1 | MOVE DATA FROM LOC. (SP) TO E AND DATA FROM LOC. (SP+1) TO D |
| | POP   B | C1 | MOVE DATA FROM LOC. (SP) TO C AND DATA FROM LOC. (SP+1) TO B |

\*  Memory location has been assumed to be 4250 H

**Table 1.4**

| Instruction | Mnemonics | Opcode | Comments |
|---|---|---|---|
| Jump/ | JMP  4250 H | C3 50  42 | JUMP (UNCONDITIONALLY) TO LOCATION 4250 H |
| Conditional | JC    4250 H | DA 50  42 | IF CARRY  =   1, JUMP TO LOCATION 4250 H |
| jump | JNC  4250 H | D2 50  42 | IF CARRY  =   0, JUMP TO LOCATION 4250 H |
| instructions | JZ    4250 H | CA 50  42 | IF RESULT =   0, JUMP TO LOCATION 4250 H |
| | JNZ  4250 H | C2 50  42 | IF RESULT =   0, JUMP TO LOCATION 4250 H |
| | JP    4250 H | F2 50  42 | IF MSB OF RESULT BE ZERO, JUMP TO LOCATION 4250 H |
| | JM    4250 H | FA 50  42 | IF MSB OF RESULT BE 1, JUMP TO LOCATION 4250 H |
| | JPO  4250 H | E2 50  42 | IF THE RESULT BE ODD, JUMP TO LOCATION 4250 H |
| | JPE  4250 H | EA 50  42 | IF THE RESULT BE EVEN, JUMP TO LOCATION 4250 H |
| | PCHL 4250 H | E9 50  42 | JUMP TO MEMORY LOCATION WHOSE ADDRESSES IS CONTENT IN HL PAIR. |

\*  Memory location has been assumed to be 4250H

## Table 1.5

| Instructions | Mnemonics | Opcode | Comments |
|---|---|---|---|
| Call/ Conditional Call/Return/ Conditional Return | CALL 4250 H | CD 50 42 | MOVE PC TO LOC. (SP-1) AND LOC. (SP-2) AND JUMP TO LOC. 4250 H WHERE LOC. (SP-N) MEANS MEM. LOC. WHOSE ADDRESS IS THE CONTENT OF SP REDUCED BY N ( N = 1,2) |
| | RET | C9 | MOVE LOC. (SP+1) AND LOC. (SP) TO PC |
| | CC 4250 H | DC 50 42 | IF CARRY = 1, CALL SUBROUTINE AT 4250 H |
| | RC | D8 | IF CARRY = 1, RETURN |
| | CNC 4250 H | D4 50 42 | IF CARRY = 0, CALL SUBROUTINE AT 4250 H |
| | RNC | D0 | IF CARRY = 0, RETURN |
| | CZ 4250 H | CC 50 42 | IF RESULT = 0, CALL SUBROUTINE AT 4250 H |
| | RZ | C8 | IF RESULT = 0, RETURN |
| | CNZ 4250 H | C4 50 42 | IF RESULT $\neq$ 0, CALL SUBROUTINE AT 4250 H |
| | RNZ | C0 | IF RESULT $\neq$ 0, RETURN |
| | CP 4250 H | F2 50 42 | IF MSB OF RESULT = 0, CALL SUBROUTINE AT 4250 H |
| | RP | F0 | IF MSB OF RESULT = 0, RETURN |
| | CM 4250 H | FC 50 42 | IF MSB OF RESULT = 1, CALL SUBROUTINE AT 4250 H |
| | RM | F8 | IF MSB OF RESULT = 1, RETURN |
| | CPO 4250 H | E4 50 42 | IF THE RESULT HAS ODD NO. OF 1'S, CALL SUBROUTINE AT 4250 H |
| | RPO | E0 | IF THE RESULT HAS ODD NO. OF 1'S, RETURN |
| | CPE 4250 H | EC 50 42 | IF RESULT HAS EVEN NO. OF 1'S, CALL SUBROUTINE AT 4250 H |
| | RPE | E8 | IF RESULT HAS EVEN NO. OF 1'S, RETURN. |

*Memory Location has been Assumed to be 4250 H

## Table 1.6

| Instruction | Mnemonics | Opcode | Comments |
|---|---|---|---|
| Add/Subtract AND/OR/ EX-OR compare immediate. | ADI | C6 | ADD DATA FOLLOWED BY INSTRUCTION TO ACC, PUT RESULT IN ACC. |
| | ACI | C5 | ADD CARRY AND DATA FOLLOWED BY INSTRUCTION TO ACC., PUT RESULT IN ACC. |
| | SUI | D6 | SUBTRACT DATA FOLLOWED BY INSTRUCTION FROM ACC., PUT RESULT IN ACC. |
| | SBI | DE | SUBTRACT CARRY AND DATA FOLLOWED BY INSTRUCTION FROM ACC., PUT RESULT IN ACC |
| | ANI | E6 | AND DATA FOLLOWED BY INSTRUCTION WITH ACC., PUT RESULT IN ACC. |
| | ORI | F6 | OR DATA FOLLOWED BY INSTRUCTION WITH ACC., PUT RESULT IN ACC. |
| | XRI | EE | EX-OR DATA FOLLOWED BY INSTRUCTION WITH ACC., PUT RESULT IN ACC. |
| | CPI | FE | SUBTRACT DATA FOLLOWED BY INSTRUCTION FROM ACC., PUT RESULT IN ACC. |

## Table 1.7

| Instruction | Mnemonics | Opcode | Comments |
|---|---|---|---|
| Rotate and Shift | RAL | 17 | ROTATE CARRY AND CONTENT OF ACC. TO LEFT |
| | RAR | 1F | ROTATE CARRY AND CONTENT OF ACC. TO RIGHT |
| | RLC | 07 | ROTATE ACC. LEFT AND MSB TO CARRY |
| | RRC | 0F | ROTATE ACC. RIGHT AND LSB TO CARRY |

**Table 1.8**

| Instruction | Mnemonics | Opcode | Comments |
|---|---|---|---|
| Set/Complement/ | STC | 37 | SET CARRY |
| Decimal/Adjust | CMC | 3F | COMPLEMENT CARRY |
| Interrupt Halt/ | CMA | 2F | COMPLEMENT ACC. |
| Interrupt Mask and | DAA | 27 | ADJUST ACC. TO FORM TWO DECIMAL DIGITS (USE AFTER |
| No Operation |  |  | ADD INSTRUCTION) |
|  | SIM | 30 | MOVE MSB OF ACC. TO SOD LINE IF NEXT LOWER BIT OF |
|  |  |  | ACC. IS '1', ALSO SET INTERRUPT MASK ACCORDING TO ACC. |
|  | RIM | 20 | MOVE SID BIT TO MSB POSITION IN ACC., READ INTERRUPT |
|  |  |  | MASK IN ACC. |
|  | HLT | 76 | HALT UNTIL INTERRUPT |
|  | EI | FB | ENABLE INTERRUPT |
|  | DI | F3 | DISBLE INTERRUPT |
|  | IN | DB | INPUT SIGNAL |
|  | OUT | D3 | OUTPUT SIGNAL |
|  | NOP | 00 | NO OPERATION |

**Table 1.9**

| Instruction | Mnemonics | Opcode | Comments |
|---|---|---|---|
| Restart | RST 0 | C7 | MOVE PC TO LOC. (SP-1) AND LOC. (SP-2)* AND JUMP TO MEM. LOC. 0000 H |
| Instruction | RST 1 | CF | MOVE PC TO LOC. (SP-1) AND LOC. (SP-2)* AND JUMP TO MEM.LOC. 0008 H |
|  | RST 2 | D7 | MOVE PC TO LOC. (SP-1) AND LOC. (SP-2)* AND JUMP TO MEM. LOC. 0010 H |
|  | RST 3 | DF | MOVE PC TO LOC. (SP-1) AND LOC. (SP-2)* AND JUMP TO MEM. LOC. 0018 H |
|  | RST 4 | E7 | MOVE PC TO LOC. (SP-1) AND LOC. (SP-2)* AND JUMP TO MEM. LOC. 0020 H |
|  | RST 5 | EF | MOVE PC TO LOC. (SP-1) AND LOC. (SP-2)* AND JUMP TO MEM. LOC. 0028 H |
|  | RST 6 | F7 | MOVE PC TO LOC. (SP-1) AND LOC. (SP-2)* AND JUMP TO MEM. LOC. 0030 H |
|  | RST 7 | FF | MOVE PC TO LOC. (SP-1) AND LOC. (SP-2)* AND JUMP TO MEM. LOC. 0038 H |

* LOC. (SP-1) => Mem. Loc. whose address is content of SP reduced by '1'.

**Table 1.10**

| Type of Instruction | Mnemonics | Clock Period | Flag Affected |
|---|---|---|---|
| DATA MOVEMENT | MOV X,Y | 4:X,Y ≠ M ; 7 : X OR Y = M | NONE |
| DATA MOVEMENT | MVI R | 7: R=B,C,D,E,H,L,A ; 10: R = M | NONE |
| DATA MOVEMENT | LDA / STA | 13 | NONE |
| DATA MOVEMENT | LDAX / STAX | 7 | NONE |
| DATA MOVEMENT | LHLD / SHLD / STHL | 16 | NONE |
| DATA MOVEMENT | XCHG | 4 | NONE |
| DATA MOVEMENT | SPHL | 6 | NONE |
| DATAMOVEMENT | LXI | 10 | NONE |
| DATAMOVEMENT | PUSH | 12 | NONE |
| DATAMOVEMENT | POP | 10 | NONE |
| INPUT/OUTPUT | IN / OUT | 10 | NONE |
| INCREMENT/DECREMENT | INR / DCR | 4:R=B,C,D,E,H,L,A; 10:R = M | ALL BUTCARRY |
|  | INX / DCX | 6 | NONE |
| ROTATE/ SHIFT | RAL / RAR / RLC / RRC | 4 | CARRY |
| SET/COMPLEMENT | STC / CMC | 4 | CARRY |
|  | CMA | 4 | NONE |
| DECIMAL ADJUST | DAA | 4 | ALL |
| ADD/SUBTRACT/ | ADD R/ADC/SUB R/ SBB R | 4 :R=B,C,D,E,H,L,A ; 7: R=M | ALL |
|  | DAD | 10 | CARRY |
|  | ADI/ACI/SUI/SBI/CPI | 7 | ALL |
| COMPARE | CMP R | 4: R=B,C,D,E,H,L,A ; 7: R=M | ALL |
| AND/OR/X-OR | ANA R/ORA R/ ANI/ORI/ | 4; R=B,C,D,E,H,L,A | ALL |
|  | XRA R/ XRI | 7; R=M | ALL |
| JUMP/CALL/RESTART | JMP | 10 | NONE |
|  | PCHL | 6 | NONE |
|  | CALL | 18 | NONE |
|  | RET | 10 | NONE |
|  | RST 0 -7 | 12 | NONE |
| CONDITIONAL JUMP/ | JC/JNC/JZ/JNZ/JP/JM/JPO/JPE | 10 (IF TRUE) | NONE |
| CALL/RESTART |  | 7; (IF NOT TRUE) | NONE |
|  | CC/CNC/CZ/CNZ/CP/CM/CPO/CPE | 10 (IF TRUE) | NONE |
|  |  | 9 (IF NOT TRUE) | NONE |
|  | RC/RNC/RZ/RNZ/RP/RM/RPO/ | 10 (IF TRUE) | NONE |
|  |  | 6 (IF NOT TRUE) | NONE |
| INTERRUPT MASK, | EI/DI/SIM/RIM | 4 | NONE |
| SERIAL I/O |  |  |  |
| HALT | HLT | 5 | NONE |
| NO OPERATION | NOP | 4 | NONE |

# 2. Z-80 Instruction Set

**Table 2.1  Load Instruction (Data Movement from Reg. to Reg./Acc. to Reg./Reg. to Acc./Acc. to Memory/Memory to Acc./Reg. to Memory/Memory to Reg.)**

| LD (MOV IN 8085) | B | C | D | E | H | L | (HL) M | A |
|---|---|---|---|---|---|---|---|---|
| B, | 40 | 41 | 42 | 43 | 44 | 45 | 46 | 47 |
| C, | 48 | 49 | 4A | 4B | 4C | 4D | 4E | 4F |
| D, | 50 | 51 | 52 | 53 | 54 | 55 | 56 | 57 |
| E, | 58 | 59 | 5A | 5B | 5C | 5D | 5E | 5F |
| H, | 60 | 61 | 62 | 63 | 64 | 65 | 66 | 67 |
| L, | 68 | 69 | 6A | 6B | 6C | 6D | 6E | 6F |
| M, | 70 | 71 | 72 | 73 | 74 | 75 | 76 | 77 |
| A, | 78 | 79 | 7A | 7B | 7C | 7D | 7E | 7F |

**Table 2.2  Data Movement Instructions- Increment/Decrement; Add/Subtract;  Compare; AND/OR/EX-OR**

| Mnemonics in 8085 | Z-80 | A | B | C | D | E | H | L | HL | SP | Comments |
|---|---|---|---|---|---|---|---|---|---|---|---|
| MVI | LD | 3E | 06 | 0E | 16 | 1E | 26 | 2E | 36 | - | MOVE DATA (FOLLOWED BY INSTRUCTION) TO ACC./REG./MEM. |
| LXI B | LD(BC),M | | 01 | | | | | | | | MOVE MSB & LSB OF DATA (M) FOLLOWED TO REG. PAIR BC/DE/ HL/SP RESPECTIVELY. |
| LXI D | LD(DE),M | | | | 11 | | | | | | |
| LXI H | LD(HL),M | | | | | | 21 | | | | |
| LXI SP | LD(SP),M | | | | | | | | | 31 | |
| INR | INC | 3C | 04 | 0C | 14 | 1C | 24 | 2C | 34 | - | INCREMENT REGISTER |
| DCR | DEC | 3D | 05 | 0D | 15 | 1D | 25 | 2D | 35 | - | DECREMENT REGISTER |
| INX B | INC (BC) | | 03 | | | | | | | | INCREMENT REGISTER PAIR / SP. |
| INX D | INC (DE) | | | | 13 | | | | | | |
| INX H | INC (HL) | | | | | | 23 | | | | |
| INX SP | INC SP | | | | | | | | | 33 | |
| DCX B | DEC (BC) | | 0B | | | | | | | | DECREMENT REGISTER PAIR / SP. |
| DEX D | DEC (DE) | | | | 1B | | | | | | |
| DEX H | DEC (HL) | | | | | | 2B | | | | |
| DEX SP | DEC SP | | | | | | | | | 3B | |
| ADD | ADD A | 87 | 80 | 81 | 82 | 83 | 84 | 85 | 86 | | ADD/SUBTRACT CONTENT OF ACC. REG./MEM. TO / FROM THE CONTENT OF ACC, PUT RESULT IN ACC. |
| SUB | SUB | 97 | 90 | 91 | 92 | 93 | 94 | 95 | 96 | | |
| ADC | ADC A | 8F | 88 | 89 | 8A | 8B | 8C | 8D | 8E | | ADD/SUBTRACT CARRY & CONTENT OF ACC./REG./MEMORY TO/FROM THE CONTENT OF ACC. |
| SBB | SBC A | 9F | 98 | 99 | 9A | 9B | 9C | 9D | 9E | | |

| Mnemonics | in | A | B | C | D | E | H | L | HL | SP | Comments |
|---|---|---|---|---|---|---|---|---|---|---|---|
| DAD B | ADD HL,BC | | 09 | | | | | | | | ADD CONTENT OF BC/DE/HL TO THE CONTENT OF HL PAIR, PUT THE RESULT IN HL. |
| DAD D | ADD HL,DE | | | | 19 | | | | | | |
| DAD H | ADD HL,HL | | | | | | 29 | | | | |
| DAD SP | ADD HL,SP | | | | | | | | | 39 | |
| CMP | CP | BF | B8 * | B9 | BA | BB | BC | BD | BE | - | SUBTRACT CONTENT OF REG/ACC/ MEM. FROM ACC. DON'T PUT RESULT IN ACC.(* SET Z-FLAG TO ZERO) |
| ANA * | AND | A7 | A0 | A1 | A2 | A3 | A4 | A5 | A6 | - | AND/OR/EX-OR WITH THE CONTENT OF ACC., PUT RESULT IN HL/SP RESPECTIVELY.(* CLEAR CARRY, **CLEAR CARRY & ACC.) |
| XRA ** | XOR | AF | A8 | A9 | AA | AB | AC | AD | AE | | |
| ORA * | OR | B7 | B0 | B1 | B2 | B3 | B4 | B5 | B6 | | |

**Table 2.3 Data Movement Instruction**

| Mnemonics | | | | |
|---|---|---|---|---|
| 8085 | Z-80 | Opcode | Comments | |
| MOV A,M | LDA M | 3A M | LOAD DATA TO ACC. FROM MEM. LOC. M | |
| STA | LDM, A | 32 M | STORE DATA FROM ACC. TO MEM.LOC.M | |
| LHLD | DHL M | 2A M | LOAD DATA TO H AND L FROM MEM. LOC.(M+1) AND M RESPECTIVELY | |
| SHLD | LD(M), HL | 22 M | STORE DATA TO MEM. LOC.(M+1) AND M FROM H AND L RESPECTIVELY | |
| LDAX B | LDA, (BC) | 0A | LOAD DATA TO ACC. FROM MEM. LOC. WHOSE ADDRESS IS CONTAINED IN REG. PAIR BC | |
| LDAX D | LDA,(DE) | 1A | LOAD DATA TO ACC. FROM MEM. LOC. WHOSE ADDRESS IS CONTAINED IN REG. PAIR DE. | |
| STAX B | LD(BC),A | 02 | STORE DATA FROM ACC. TO MEM.LOC. WHOSE ADDRESS IS CONTAINED IN REG. PAIR BC | |
| STAX D | LD(DE), A | 12 | STORE DATA FROM ACC. TO MEM.LOC. WHOSE ADDRESS IS CONTAINED IN REG. PAIR DE | |
| XCHG | EX DE,HL | EB | EXCHANGE DATA IN D WITH H AND DATA IN E WITH L | |
| SPHL | LD SP, HL | F9 | MOVE DATA FROM HL TO SP | |
| XTHL | EX(SP),HL | E3 | EXCHANGE DATA IN H WITH LOC. (SP+1) AND IN L WITH LOC. (SP) | |
| PUSH B | PUSH BC | C5 | MOVE DATA FROM B TO LOC. (SP-1) AND DATA FROM C TO LOC. (SP-2) | |
| PUSH D | PUSH DE | D5 | MOVE DATA FROM D TO LOC. (SP-1) AND DATA FROM E TO LOC.(SP-2) | |
| PUSH H | PUSH HL | E5 | MOVE DATA FROM H TO LOC.(SP-1) AND DATA FROM L TO LOC.(SP-2) | |
| PUSH PSW | PUSH AF | F5 | MOVE DATE FROM A TO LOC.(SP-1) AND DATA FROM FLAG TO LOC. (SP-2) | |
| POP PSW | POP AF | F1 | MOVE DATA FROM LOC.(SP) TO FLAG AND DATA FROM LOC.(SP+1) TO A | |
| POP H | POP HL | E1 | MOVE DATA FROM LOC.(SP) TO L AND DATA FROM LOC. (SP+1) TO H | |
| POP D | POP DE | D1 | MOVE DATA FROM LO.(SP) TO E AND DATA FROM LOC. (SP+1) TO D | |
| POP B | POP BC | C1 | MOVE DATA FROM LOC.(SP) TO C AND DATA FROM LOC.(SP+1) TO B | |

**Table 2.4 Jump/Conditional jump instructions**

| Mnemonics | | Opcode | Comments |
|---|---|---|---|
| 8085 | Z-80 | | |
| JMP | JPM | C3  M | JUMP (UNCONDITIONALLY) TO LOCATION M |
| JC | JC  M | DA M | IF CARRY = 1, JUMP TO LOCATION M |
| JNC | JNC M | D2 M | IF CARRY = 0, JUMP TO LOCATION M |
| JZ | JZ  M | CA M | IF RESULT = 0, JUMP TO LOCATION M |
| JNZ | JNZ M | C2 M | IF RESUTL = 0, JUMP TO LOCATION M |
| JP | JPP  M | F2  M | IF MSB OF RESULT IS ZERO, JUMP TO LOCATION M |
| JM | JPMM | FA M | IF MSB OF RESULT IS 1, JUMP TO LOCATION M |
| JPO | JPO M | E2  M | IF THE RESULT IS ODD, JUMP TO LOCATION M |
| JPE | JPE  M | EA M | IF THE RESULT IS EVEN, JUMP TO LOCATION M |
| PCHL | JP (HL) M | E9  M | JUMP TO MEMORY LOCATION WHOSE ADDRESS IS CONTAINED IN HL PAIR. |

**Table 2.5 Call/Conditional call/ Return/ Conditional return instructions**

| Mnemonics | | Opcode | Comments |
|---|---|---|---|
| 8085 | Z-80 | | |
| CALL | CALL  M | CD  M | MOVE PC TO LOC.(SP-1) AND LOC. (SP-2) AND JUMP TO LOC. M WHERE LOC.(SP-N) MEANS MEM. LOC. WHOSE ADDRESS IS THE CONTENT OF SP REDUCED BY N |
| RET | RET | C9 | MOVE LOC. (SP+1) AND LOC. (SP) TO PC |
| CC  M | CALL  CC  M | DC  M | IF CARRY = 1, CALL SUBROUTINE M |
| RC  M | RET  C | D8 | IF CARRY = 1, RETURN |
| CNC  M | CALL  CNC  M | D4  M | IF CARRY = 0, CALL SUBROUTINE M |
| RNC | RET  NC | D0 | IF CARRY = 0, RETURN |
| CZ  M | CALL  Z  M | CC  M | IF RESULT = 0, CALL SUBROUTINE M |
| RZ | RET  Z | C8 | IF RESULT = 0, RETURN |
| CNZ  M | CALL  NZ  M | C4  M | IF RESULT $\neq$ 0, CALL SUBROUTINE M |
| RNZ | RET  NZ | C0 | IF RESULT $\neq$ 0, RETURN |
| CP  M | CALL  P  M | F2  M | IF MSB OF RESULT = 0, CALL SUBROUTINE M |
| RP | RET  P | F0 | IF MSB OF RESULT = 0, RETURN |
| CM  M | CALL  M  M | FC  M | IF MSB OF RESULT = 1, CALL SUBROUTINE M |
| RM | RET  M | F8 | IF MSB OF RESULT = 1, RETURN |
| CPO  M | CALL  PO  M | E4  M | IF THE RESULT HAS ODD NO. OF 1'S CALL SUBROUTINE M |
| RPO | RET  PO | E0 | IF THE RESULT HAS ODD NO. OF 1'S, RETURN |
| CPE  M | CALL  PE  M | EC  M | IF RESULT HAS EVEN NO. OF 1'S, CALL SUBROUTINE M |
| RPE | RET  PE | E8 | IF RESULT HAS EVEN NO. OF 1'S, RETURN. |

**Table 2.6 Add/Subtract/and/or/Ex-or/Compare immediate instructions**

| Mnemonics | | Opcode | Comments |
|---|---|---|---|
| 8085 | Z 80 | | |
| ADI | ADD A, n | C6 | ADD DATA (n) FOLLOWED BY INSTRUCTION TO ACC. , PUT RESULT IN ACC. |
| ACI | ADC, n | CE | ADD CARRY AND DATA (n) FOLLOWED BY INSTRUCTION TO ACC., PUT RESULT IN ACC. |
| SUI | SUB A, n | D6 | SUBTRACT DATA (n) FOLLOWED BY INSTRUCTION FROM ACC., PUT RESULT IN ACC. |
| SBI | SBC A, n | DE | SUBTRACT CARRY AND DATA (n) FOLLOWED BY INSTRUCTION FROM ACC.PUT RESULT IN ACC. |
| ANI | AND, n | E6 | AND DATA (n) FOLLOWED BY INSTRUCTION WITH ACC., PUT RESULT IN ACC. |
| ORI | OR, n | F6 | OR DATA (n) FOLLOWED BY INSTRUCTION WITH ACC., PUT RESULT IN ACC. |
| XRI | XOR, n | EE | EX-OR DATA (n) FOLLOWED BY INSTRUCTION WITH ACC., PUT RESULT IN ACC. |
| CPI | CP, n | FE | SUBTRACT DATA (n) FOLLOWED BY INSTRUCTION FROM ACC., DON'T PUT RESULT IN ACC. |

**Table 2.7 Rotate and shift instructions**

| Mnemonics | | Opcode | | Comments |
|---|---|---|---|---|
| 8085 | Z 80 | 8085 | Z 80 | |
| RAL | RLA | 17 | CB17 | ROTATE CARRY AND ACC. TO LEFT |
| RAR | RRA | 1F | CB1F | ROTATE CARRY AND ACC.TO RIGHT |
| RLC | RLC A | 07 | CB07 | ROTATE ACC. LEFT AND MSB TO CARRY |
| RRC | RRC A | 04 | CB0F | ROTATE ACC. RIGHT AND LSB TO CARRY |

**Table 2.8 Set/Complement /Decimal adjust/Interrupt halt/Interrupt mask-serial I/O and no operation instuctions**

| Mnemonics | | Opcode | Comments |
|---|---|---|---|
| 8085 | Z 80 | | |
| STC | SCF | 37 | SET CARRY TO 1 |
| CMC | CCF | 3F | COMPLEMENT CARRY |
| CMA | CPL | 2F | COMPLEMENT ACC. |
| DAA | DAA | 27 | ADJUST ACC. TO FROM TWO DECIMAL DIGITS (USE AFTER ADD INSTRUCTION) |
| SIM | SIM | 30 | MOVE MSB TO ACC. TO SOD LINE IF NEXT LOWER BIT OF ACC. IS '1', ALSO SET INTERRUPT MASK ACCORDING TO ACC. |
| RIM | RIM | 20 | MOVE SID BIT TO MSB POSITION IN ACC., ALSO READ INTERRUPT MASK IN ACC. |
| HLT | HLT | 76 | HALT UNTIL INTERRUPT |
| EI | EI | FB | ENABLE INTERRUPT |
| DI | DI | F3 | DISBLE INTERRUPT |
| IN | IN | DB | IN SIGNAL |
| OUT | OUT | D3 | OUTPUT SIGNAL |
| NOP | NOP | 00 | NO OPERATION |

Table 2.9 Restart Instructions

| Mnemonics 8085 | Z 80 | Opcode | Comments |
|---|---|---|---|
| (0) | RST 0 | C7 | MOVE PC TO LOC. (SP-1) AND LOC. (SP-2) * AND JUMP TO MEM. LOC. 0000 H |
| (1) | RST 8 | CF | MOVE PC TO LOC. (SP-1) AND LOC. (SP-2) * AND JUMP TO MEM. LOC. 0008 H |
| (2) | RST 16 | D7 | MOVE PC TO LOC. (SP-1) AND LOC. (SP-2) * AND JUMP TO MEM. LOC. 0010 H |
| (3) | RST 24 | DF | MOVE PC TO LOC. (SP-1) AND LOC. (SP-2) * AND JUMP TO MEM. LOC. 0018 H |
| (4) | RST 32 | E7 | MOVE PC TO LOC. (SP-1) AND LOC. (SP-2) * AND JUMP TO MEM. LOC. 0020 H |
| (5) | RST 40 | EF | MOVE PC TO LOC. (SP-1) AND LOC. (SP-2) * AND JUMP TO MEM. LOC. 0028 H |
| (6) | RST 46 | F7 | MOVE PC TO LOC. (SP-1) AND LOC. (SP-2) * AND JUMP TO MEM. LOC. 0030 H |
| (7) | RST 56 | FF | MOVE PC TO LOC. (SP-1) AND LOC. (SP-2) * AND JUMP TO MEM. LOC. 0038 H |

* Loc. (SP-1) => Mem. Loc. whose address is content of SP reduced by '1'.

**(B) Z-80 Instruction set (Not common to 8085/8085A instuction set)**

Table 2.10 LD group

| Mnemonics | | | Opcode | | | Symbolic Description |
|---|---|---|---|---|---|---|
| LD | B, | (IX+d) | DD | 46 | d | LD r, (IX+d), r ←— (IX+d) |
| | C, | (IX+d) | DD | 4E | d | r: B,C,D,E,H,L,A; (HL) |
| | D, | (IX+d) | DD | 56 | d | |
| | E, | (IX+d) | DD | 5E | d | |
| | H, | (IX+d) | DD | 66 | d | |
| | L, | (IX+d) | DD | 6E | d | |
| | (HL), | (IX+d) | DD | 76 | d | |
| | A, | (IX+d) | DD | 7E | d | |
| LD | B, | (IY +d) | FD | 46 | d | LD r, (IY+d), r ←— (IY+d) |
| | C, | (IY +d) | FD | 4E | d | r: B,C,D,E,H,L,(HL),A |
| | D, | (IY +d) | FD | 56 | d | |
| | E, | (IY +d) | FD | 5E | d | |
| | H, | (IY +d) | FD | 66 | d | |
| | L, | (IY +d) | FD | 6E | d | |
| | (HL), | (IY +d) | FD | 76 | d | |
| | A, | (IY +d) | FD | 75 | d | |
| LDI,A | | | ED | 47 | | I ←— A |
| LDR,A | | | ED | 4F | | R ←— A |
| LDA,I | | | ED | 57 | | A ←— I |
| LDA,R | | | ED | 5F | | A ←— R |
| LD(IX+d), DATA | | | DD, 36 d,DATA | | | (IX+d) ←— DATA |
| LD(IY +d),DATA | | | FD, 36 d,DATA | | | (IY +d) ←— DATA |
| LD | (IX+d), B | | DD | 70 | d | LD (IX+d),r (IX+d) ←— r |
| | (IX+d), C | | DD | 71 | d | r:B,C,D,E,H,L,A. |
| | (IX+d), D | | DD | 72 | d | |
| | (IX+d), E | | DD | 73 | d | |
| | (IX+d), H | | DD | 74 | d | |
| | (IX+d), L | | DD | 75 | d | |
| | (IX+d), A | | DD | 77 | d | |
| LD | (IY+d), B | | FD | 70 | d | LD (IY+d), r —→(IY+d) |
| | (IY+d), C | | FD | 71 | d | r: B,C,D,E,H,L,A |
| | (IY+d), D | | FD | 72 | d | |

| Mnemonics | | Opcode | | | Symbolic Description |
|---|---|---|---|---|---|
| LD | (IY+d), E | FD | 73 | d | |
| | (IY+d), H | FD | 74 | d | |
| | (IY+d), L | FD | 75 | d | |
| | (IY+d), A | FD | 77 | d | |
| LD | IX, 16 BIT DATA | DD | 21 | DATA | IX ⟵ 16-BIT DATA |
| | IY, 16 BIT DATA | FD | 21 | DATA | IY ⟵ 16-BIT DATA |
| | SP, IX | DD | F9 | | SP ⟵ IX |
| | SP, IY | FD | F9 | | SP ⟵ IY |
| | BC, (MEMORY) | ED | 48 | M | BC ⟵ (M) |
| | DE, (MEMORY) | ED | 58 | M | DE ⟵ (M) |
| LD | IX, (MEMORY) | DD | 2A | M | IX ⟵ (M+1), IX ⟵ M |
| | IY, (MEMORY) | FD | 2A | M | IY ⟵ (M+1), IY ⟵ M |
| | SP, (MEMORY) | ED | 78 | M | SP ⟵ (M+1), SP ⟵ M |
| LD | (M), BC | ED | 43 | M | (M+1) ⟵ B, M ⟵ C |
| | (M), DE | ED | 53 | M | (M+1) ⟵ D, M ⟵ E |
| | (M), SP | ED | 73 | M | (M+1) ⟵ SP, M ⟵ SP |
| | (M), IX | DD | 22 | M | (M+1) ⟵ IX, M ⟵ IX |
| | (M), IY | FD | 22 | M | (M+1) ⟵ IY, M ⟵ IY |
| PUSH IX | | DD | E5 | | (SP-2) ⟵ IX, (SP-1) ⟵ IX |
| PUSH IY | | FD | E5 | | (SP-2) ⟵ IY, (SP-1) ⟵ IY |
| POP IX | | DD | E1 | | IX ⟵ (SP+1), IX ⟵ (SP) |
| POP IY | | FD | E1 | | IY ⟵ (SP+1), IY ⟵ (SP) |
| RET I | | ED | 40 | | RETURN FROM INTERRUPT |
| RETN | | ED | 45 | | RETURN FROM NON MASKABLE INTERRUPT |
| EX AF, AF | | 08 | | | (REGISTER BANK AND AUXILIARY BANK EXCHANGE) |
| EXX | | 09 | | | BC == BC', DE == DE', HL == HL' |
| EX (SP), IX | | DD | E3 | | UPPER HALF OF IX ⟵ (SP+1), LOWER HALF OF IX ⟵ (SP) |
| EX (SP), IY | | FD | E3 | | UPPER HALF OF IY ⟵ (SP+1), LOWER HALF OF IY ⟵ (SP) |
| LDI | | ED | A0 | | DE ⟵ (HL), DE ⟵ DE+1, HL ⟵ HL+1, BC ⟵ BC -1 |
| | | | | | LOAD (HL) INTO DE, INCREMENT THE POINTERS AND |
| | | | | | DECREMENT THE BYTE COUNTER (BC) i.e. LOAD |
| | | | | | (DE) ⟵ HL, JNC HL AND DE, DEC (BC) HERE HL |
| | | | | | POINTS TO SOURCE, DE POINTS TO DESTINATION, BC |
| | | | | | IS A BYTE COUNTER |
| LDIR | | ED | B0 | | DE ⟵ (1+L), DE ⟵ DE+1, HL ⟵ HL+1 |
| | | | | | BC ⟵ BC-1 REPEAT UNTIL (BC)=0 |
| | | | | | DE ⟵ (HL), INC HL AND DE, DEC (BC) |
| LDD | | ED | A8 | | REPEAT UNTIL (BC)=0 |
| | | | | | DE ⟵ (HL), DE ⟵ DE-1, HL ⟵ HL-1, BC ⟵ BC-1 |
| | | | | | DE ⟵ (HL), DEC HL AND DE, DEC BC |
| LDDR | | ED | B8 | | DE ⟵ (HL), DE ⟵ DE-1, HL ⟵ HL-1, |
| | | | | | BE ⟵ BC-1 REPEAT UNTIL (BC)=0 |
| | | | | | DE ⟵ (HL), DEC HL, DE AND BC, REPEAT UNTIL (BC)=0 |
| CPI | | ED | A1 | | A ⟵ (HL), HL ⟵ HL+1, BC ⟵ BC-1 |
| | | | | | INC HL, DEC BC |
| PIR | | ED | B1 | | A ⟵ (HL), HL ⟵ HL+1, BC ⟵ BC+1 |
| | | | | | REPEAT UNTIL A=(HL) OR BC =0 |
| | | | | | INC HL, DEC BC, REPEAT UNTIL BC=0 OR A=(HL) |
| CPD | | ED | A9 | | A ⟵ HL, HL ⟵ HL+1, BC ⟵ BC-1 |
| | | | | | DEC HL AND BC |
| CPDR | | ED | B9 | | A ⟵ HL, HL ⟵ HL-1, BC ⟵ BC-1, |
| | | | | | REPEAT UNTIL A=(HL), BC=0 |
| | | | | | DEC HL AND BC, REPEAT UNTIL BC=0 OR A=(HL) |

**Table 2.11 A  8-Bit Arithmetic and Logic instructions**

| Mnemonics Code | Opcode | Symbolic Meaning |
|---|---|---|
| ADD A, (IX+d) | DD 86 d | A ⟵ A+(IX+d) |
| ADD A, (IY+d) | FD 86 d | A ⟵ A + (IY+d) |
| ADC A, (IX+d) | DD 8E d | A ⟵ A+(IX+d)+CY |
| ADC A, (IY+d) | FD 8E d | A ⟵ A+(IY+d)+CY |
| SUB (IX+d) | DD 96 d | A ⟵ A–(IX+d) |
| SUB (IY+d) | FD 96 d | A ⟵ A–(IY+d) |
| SBC A, (IX+d) | DD 9E d | A ⟵ A–(IX+d)–CY |
| SBC A, (IY+d) | FD 9E d | A ⟵ A–(IY+d)–CY |
| AND (IX+d) | DD A6 d | A ⟵ A · (IX+d) |
| AND (IY+d) | FD A6 d | A ⟵ A · (IY+d) |
| XOR (IX+d) | DD AE d | A ⟵ A ⊖ (IX+d) |
| XOR (IY+d) | FD AE d | A ⟵ A ⊖ (IY+d) |
| OR (IX+d) | DD 86 d | A ⟵ A ⊕(IX+d) |
| OR (IY+d) | FD 86 d | A ⟵ A ⊕(IY+d) |
| CP (IX+d) | DD BE d | |
| CP (IY+d) | FD BE d | |
| INC (IX+d) | DD 34 d | |
| INC (IY+d) | FD 34 d | |
| DEC (IX+d) | DD 35 d | |
| DEC (IY+d) | FD 35 d | |
| IM 0 | ED 46 | SET INTERRUPT MODE 0  (8080 A MODE) |
| IM 1 | ED 56 | SET INTERRUPT MODE 1  (RESTART TO 0038 H) |
| IM 2 | ED 5E | SET INTERRUPT MODE 2 (AND 8-BITS FROM INTERRUPTING DEVICE AS A POINTER) |
| NEG | ED 44 | 2'S COMPONENT OF ACC. CONTENT |

**Table 2.11 B  16 - Bit Arithmetic and Logic Instructions**

| Mnemonics Code | Opcode | Symbolic Meaning |
|---|---|---|
| ADC HL, BC | ED 4A | HL ⟵ HL + (BC) + CY |
| ADC HL, DE | ED 5A | HL ⟵ HL + (DE) + CY |
| ADC HL, HL | ED 6A | HL ⟵ HL + (HL) + CY |
| ADC HL, SP | ED 7A | HL ⟵ HL + (SP) + CY |
| SBC HL, BC | ED 42 | HL ⟵ HL – (BC) – CY |
| SBC HL, DE | ED 52 | HL ⟵ HL – (DE) – CY |
| SBC HL, HL | ED C2 | HL ⟵ HL – (HL) – CY |
| SBC HL, SP | ED 72 | HL ⟵ HL – (SP) – CY |
| ADD IX, BC | BD 09 | IX ⟵ IX + BC |
| ADD IX, DE | BD 19 | IX ⟵ IX + DE |
| ADD IX, SP | BD 39 | IX ⟵ IX + SP |
| ADD IX, IX | BD 29 | IX ⟵ IX + IX |
| ADD IY, BC | FD 09 | IY ⟵ IY + BC |
| ADD IY, DE | FD 19 | IY ⟵ IY + DE |
| ADD IY, SP | FD 39 | IY ⟵ IY + SP |
| ADD IY, IY | FD 29 | IY ⟵ IY + IY |
| INX IX | DD 23 | IX ⟵ IX + 1 |
| INX IY | FD 23 | IY ⟵ IY + 1 |
| DEC IX | DD 2B | IX ⟵ IX – 1 |
| DEC IY | FD 2B | IY ⟵ IY – 1 |

### Table 2.12 Bit Manipulation instruction

| | BIT | Register Addressing | | | | | | | Reg. Indir. | Indexed | |
| | | A | B | C | D | E | H | L | (HL) | (IX + d) | (IY + d) |
|---|---|---|---|---|---|---|---|---|---|---|---|
| TEXT 'BIT' | 0 | CB 47 | CB 40 | CB 41 | CB 42 | CB 43 | CB 44 | CB 45 | CB 46 | DD CB d 46 | FD CB d 46 |
| | 1 | CB 4F | CB 48 | CB 49 | CB 4A | CB 4B | CB 4C | CB 4D | CB 4E | DD CB d 4E | FD CB d 4E |
| | 2 | CB 57 | CB 50 | CB 51 | CB 52 | CB 53 | CB 54 | CB 55 | CB 56 | DD CB d 56 | FD CB d 56 |
| | 3 | CB 5F | CB 58 | CB 59 | CB 5A | CB 5B | CB 5C | CB 5D | CB 5E | DD CB d 5E | FD CB d 5E |
| | 4 | CB 67 | CB 60 | CB 61 | CB 62 | CB 63 | CB 64 | CB 65 | CB 66 | DD CB d 66 | FD CB d 66 |
| | 5 | CB 6F | CB 68 | CB 69 | CB 6A | CB 6B | CB 6C | CB 6D | CB 6E | DD CB d 6E | FD CB d 6E |
| | 6 | CB 77 | CB 70 | CB 71 | CB 72 | CB 73 | CB 74 | CB 75 | CB 76 | DD CB d 76 | FD CB d 76 |
| | 7 | CB 7F | CB 78 | CB 79 | CB 7A | CB 7B | CB 7C | CB 7D | CB 7E | DD CB d 7E | FD CB d 7E |
| RESET BIT 'RES' | 0 | CB 87 | CB 80 | CB 81 | CB 82 | CB 83 | CB 84 | CB 85 | CB 86 | DD CB d 86 | FD CB d 86 |
| | 1 | CB 8F | CB 88 | CB 89 | CB 8A | CB 8B | CB 8C | CB 8D | CB 8E | DD CB d 8E | FD CB d 8E |
| | 2 | CB 97 | CB 90 | CB 91 | CB 92 | CB 93 | CB 94 | CB 95 | CB 96 | DD CB d 96 | FD CB d 96 |
| | 3 | CB 9F | CB 98 | CB 99 | CB 9A | CB 9B | CB 9C | CB 9D | CB 9E | DD CB d 9E | FD CB d 9E |
| | 4 | CB A7 | CB A0 | CB A1 | CB A2 | CB A3 | CB A4 | CB A5 | CB A6 | DD CB d A6 | FD CB d A6 |
| | 5 | CB AF | CB A8 | CB A9 | CB AA | CB AB | CB AC | CB AD | CB AE | DD CB d AE | FD CB d AE |
| | 6 | CB B7 | CB B0 | CB B1 | CB B2 | CB B3 | CB B4 | CB B5 | CB B6 | DD CB d B6 | FD CB d B6 |
| | 7 | CB BF | CB B8 | CB B9 | CB BA | CB BB | CB BC | CB BD | CB BE | DD CB d BE | FD CB d BE |
| SET BIT 'SET' | 0 | CB C7 | CB C0 | CB C1 | CB C2 | CB C3 | CB C4 | CB C5 | CB C6 | DD CB d C6 | FD CB d C6 |
| | 1 | CB CF | CB C8 | CB C9 | CB CA | CB CB | CB CC | CB CD | CB CE | DD CB d CE | FD CB d CE |
| | 2 | CB D7 | CB D0 | CB D1 | CB D2 | CB D3 | CB D4 | CB D5 | CB D6 | DD CB d D6 | FD CB d D6 |
| | 3 | CB DF | CB D8 | CB D9 | CB DA | CB DB | CB DC | CB DD | CB DE | DD CB d DE | FD CB d DE |

| 4 | CB E7 | CB E0 | CB E1 | CB E2 | CB E3 | CB E4 | CB E5 | CB E6 | DD CB d E6 | FD CB d E6 |
| 5 | CB EF | CB E8 | CB E9 | CB EA | CB EB | CB EC | CB ED | CB EE | DD CB d EE | FD CB d EE |
| 6 | CB F7 | CB F0 | CB F1 | CB F2 | CB F3 | CB F4 | CB F5 | CB F6 | DD CB d F6 | FD CB d F6 |
| 7 | CB FF | CB F8 | CB F9 | CB FA | CB FB | CB FC | CB FD | CB FE | DD CB d FE | FD CB d FE |

**Table 2.13 Rotate and shift instructions**

| Mnemonics | Opcode | Explanation |
|---|---|---|
| RLC A | CB 07 | |
| RLC B | CB 00 | |
| RLC C | CB 01 | |
| RLC D | CB 02 | |
| RLC E | CB 03 | |
| RLC H | CB 04 | |
| RLC L | CB 05 | |
| RLC (HL) | CB 06 | A/B/C/D/E/H/L/(HL)/ (IX+d)/ (IY+d) |
| RLC (IX + d) | DD CB d 06 | |
| RLC (IY + d) | FD CB d 06 | |
| RRC A | CB 0F | |
| RRC B | CB 08 | |
| RRC C | CB 09 | |
| RRC D | CB 0A | |
| RRC E | CB 0B | |
| RRC H | CB 0C | |
| RRC L | CB 0D | |
| RRC (HL) | CB 0E | |
| RRC (IX +d) | DD CB d 0E | |
| RRC (IY + d) | FD CB d 0E | |
| RL A | CB 17 | |
| RL B | CB 10 | |
| RL C | CB 11 | |
| RL D | CB 12 | |
| RL E | CB 13 | |
| RL H | CB 14 | |
| RL L | CB 15 | |
| RL (HL) | CB 16 | |
| RL (IX + d) | DD CB d 16 | |
| RL (IY + d) | FD CB d 16 | |
| RR A | CB 1F | |
| RR B | CB 18 | |
| RR C | CB 19 | |
| RR D | CB 1A | |
| RR E | CB 1B | |
| RR H | CB 1C | |
| RR L | CB 1D | |
| RR (HL) | CB 1F | |
| RR (IX + d) | DD CB d 1E | |
| RR (IY + d) | FD CB d 1E | |

| Mnemonics | Opcode | Explanation |
|---|---|---|
| SLA  A | CB  27 | |
| SLA  B | CB  20 | |
| SLA  C | CB  21 | |
| SLA  D | CB  22 | |
| SLA  E | CB  23 | |
| SLA  H | CB  24 | |
| SLA  L | CB  25 | |
| SLA  (HL) | CB  26 | |
| SLA  (IX + d) | DD  CB  d  26 | |
| SLA  (IY + d) | FD  CB  d  26 | |
| SRA  A | CB  2F | |
| SRA  B | CB  28 | |
| SRA  C | CB  29 | |
| SRA  D | CB  2A | |
| SRA  E | CB  2B | |
| SRA  H | CB  2C | |
| SRA  L | CB  2D | |
| SRA  (HL) | CB  2E | |
| SRA  (IX + d) | DD  CB  d  2E | |
| SRA  (IY + d) | FD  CB  d  2E | |
| SRL  A | CB  3F | |
| SRL  B | CB  38 | |
| SRL  C | CB  39 | |
| SRL  D | CB  3A | |
| SRL  E | CB  3b | |
| SRL  H | CB  3C | |
| SRL  L | CB  3D | |
| SRL  (HL) | CB  3E | |
| SRL  (IX + d) | DD  CB  d  3E | |
| SRL  (IY + d) | FD  CB  d  3E | |
| RLD | ED  6F | ROTATE DIGIT LEFT BETWEEN THE ACC. AND (HL), CONTENT OF UPPER HALF OF THE ACC.  IS UNEFFECTED |
| RRD | ED  67 | ROTATE DIGIT RIGHT BETWEEN ACC. AND (HL), CONTENT OF UPPER HALF OF THE ACC.  IS UNEFFECTED |

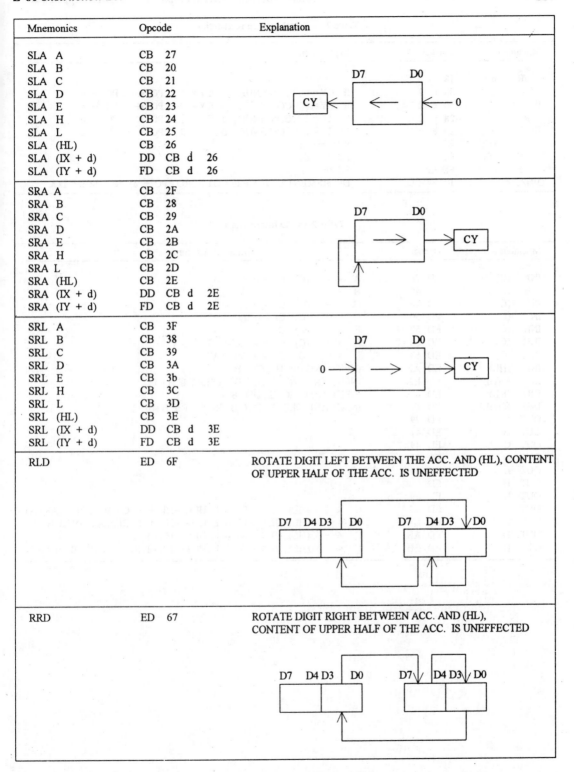

**Table 2.14 Relative jump instruction**

| Mnemonics | Opcode | Explanation |
|---|---|---|
| JR    e    | 18 e - 2 | |
| JRC ,  e   | 38 e - 2 | IF CY = 0 , CONTINUE , IF CY = 1 ,  PC $\leftarrow$ PC + e |
| JRNC ,  e  | 30 e - 2 | IF CY = 1 , CONTINUE , IF CY = 0 ,  PC $\leftarrow$ PC + e |
| JRZ ,  e   | 28 e - 2 | IF Z = 0 , CONTINUE , IF Z = 1 ,  PC $\leftarrow$ PC + e |
| JRNZ ,  e  | 20 e - 2 | IF Z = 1 , CONTINUE , IF Z = 0 ,  PC $\leftarrow$ PC + e |
| JP    (HL) | E9 | PC $\leftarrow$ HL |
| JP    (IX) | DD E9 | PC $\leftarrow$ IX |
| JP    (IY) | FD E9 | PC $\leftarrow$ IY |
| DJNZ, e | 10 e | DECREMENT B, JUMP IF NOT ZERO ( PC + e), e    MEM. LOC. |

**Table 2.15 I/O instructions**

| Mnemonics | Opcode | Symbolic Meaning |
|---|---|---|
| INA  (C) | ED 78 | A $\leftarrow$  (C)  C $\Longrightarrow$ A0 - A7 |
| INB  (C) | ED 40 | B $\leftarrow$  (C)  C $\Longrightarrow$ A0 - A7 |
| INC  (C) | ED 48 | C $\leftarrow$  (C)  C $\Longrightarrow$ A0 - A7 |
| IND  (C) | ED 50 | D $\leftarrow$  (C)  C $\Longrightarrow$ A0 - A7 |
| INE  (C) | ED 58 | E $\leftarrow$  (C)  C $\Longrightarrow$ A0 - A7 |
| INH  (C) | ED 60 | H $\leftarrow$  (C)  C $\Longrightarrow$ A0 - A7 |
| INL  (C) | ED 68 | L $\leftarrow$  (C)  C $\Longrightarrow$ A0 - A7 |
| INI  (HL) | ED A2 | INPUT AND INC HL, DEC B |
| INI  R (HL) | ED B2 | INPUT AND INC HL, DEC B, REPEAT IF B = 0 |
| IND  (HL) | ED AA | INPUT AND DEC HL, DEC B |
| IND  R (HL) | ED BA | INPUT AND DEC HL, DEC B ; REPEAT IF B = 0 |
| OUT  A | ED 79 | |
| OUT  B | ED 41 | |
| OUT  C | ED 49 | |
| OUT  D | ED 51 | |
| OUT  E | ED 59 | |
| OUT  H | ED 61 | |
| OUT  L | ED 69 | |
| OUT  I | ED A3 | C $\leftarrow$  (HL), B $\leftarrow$ B  - 1, HL $\leftarrow$ HL + 1, C [ A0 - A7], B (A8 - A15) |
| OTR  I | ED B3 | C $\leftarrow$  (HL), B $\leftarrow$ B  - 1, HL $\leftarrow$ HL + 1, REPEAT UNTIL B = 0 |
| OUT  D | ED AB | C $\leftarrow$  (HL), B $\leftarrow$ B  - 1, HL $\leftarrow$ HL - 1 |
| OTR  D | ED BB | C $\leftarrow$  (HL), B $\leftarrow$ B  - 1, HL $\leftarrow$ HL - 1, REPEAT UNTIL  B = 0. |

# 3. Some Instruction Sets of 8086 CPU

| Mnemonics | Opcode | Clock | Mnemonics | Opcode | Clock |
|---|---|---|---|---|---|
| ADC AL, # ds | 14 | 4 | ADC AL, CH | 10 E8 | 3 |
| ADC AL, CL | 10 C8 | 3 | ADC AL, DH | 10 F0 | 3 |
| ADC AL, DL | 10 D0 | 3 | ADC AL, BH | 10 F8 | 3 |
| ADC AL, BL | 10 D8 | 3 | ADC AL, (BX) | 12 07 | 14 |
| ADC AL, AL | 10 C0 | 3 | ADD AL, CH | 00 E8 | 3 |
| ADD AL, CL | 00 C8 | 3 | ADD AL, DH | 00 F0 | 3 |
| ADD AL, DL | 00 D0 | 3 | ADD AL, BH | 00 F8 | 3 |
| ADD AL, BL | 00 D8 | 3 | ADD AL, (BX) | 02 07 | 14 |
| ADD AL, AL | 00 C0 | 3 | ADD AL, # d | 04 | 4 |
| AND AL, CH | 20 E8 | 3 | AND AL, CL | 20 C8 | 3 |
| AND AL, DH | 20 F0 | 3 | AND AL, DL | 20 D0 | 3 |
| AND AL, BH | 20 F8 | 3 | AND AL, BL | 20 D8 | 3 |
| AND AL, (BX) | 22 07 | 14 | AND AL, AL | 20 C0 | 3 |
| AND AL, # d | 24 | 4 | CALL d | E8 | 19 |
| NOT AL | F6 D0 | 3 | CMC | F5 | 2 |
| CMP AL, CH | 38 E8 | 3 | CMP AL, CL | 38 C8 | 3 |
| CMP AL DH | 38 F0 | 3 | CMP AL, DL | 38 D0 | 3 |
| CMP AL, BH | 38 F8 | 3 | CMP AL, BL | 38 D8 | 3 |
| CMP AL, (BX) | 3A 07 | 3 | CMP AL, AL | 38 C0 | 3 |
| CMP AL, # d | 3C | 4 | DAA | 27 | 4 |
| ADD BX, CX | 01 CB | 3 | ADD BX, DX | 01 D3 | 3 |
| ADD BX, BX | 01 D8 | 3 | ADD BX, SP | 01 E3 | 3 |
| DEC CH | FE CD | 3 | DEG CL | FE CI | 3 |
| DEC DH | FE CE | 3 | DEC DL | FE CA | 3 |
| DEC BH | FE CF | 3 | DEC BL | FE CB | 3 |
| DEC b(BX) | FE 0F | 19 | DEC AL | FE C8 | 3 |
| DEC CX | 49 | 2 | DEC DX | 4A | 2 |
| DEC BX | 48 | 2 | DEC SP | 4C | 2 |
| CLI | FA | 2 | STI | FB | 2 |
| HLT | F4 | 2 | IN AL, d | E4 | 10 |
| INC CH | FE C5 | 3 | INC CL | FE C1 | 3 |
| INC DH | FE C6 | 3 | INC DL | FE C2 | 3 |
| INC BH | FE C7 | 3 | INC BL | FE C3 | 3 |
| INC b(BX) | FE 07 | 19 | INC AL | FE C0 | 3 |
| INC CX | 41 | 2 | INC DX | 42 | 2 |
| INC BX | 43 | 2 | INC SP | 44 | 2 |
| JC d | 72 | 4/16 | JS d | 78 | 4/16 |
| JMP d/d | EB/E9 | 15 | JNB d | 73 | 4/16 |
| JNZ d | 75 | 4/16 | JNS d | 79 | 4/16 |
| JPE d | 7A | 4/16 | JPO d | 7B | 4/16 |
| JZ d | 74 | 6/18 | MOV AL, (addr) | A0 | 10 |
| MOV AL, (SI) | 8A 04 | 13 | MOV AL, (SI) | 8A 04 | 13 |
| MOV BX, (addr) | 8B· 1E | 13 | MOV CX, d | 89 | 4 |
| MOV DX, d | 8A | 4 | MOV BX, d | 88 | 4 |
| MOV SP, d | BC | 4 | MOV CH, CH | 88 ED | 2 |
| MOV CH, CL | 88 CD | 2 | MOV CH, DH | 88 F5 | 2 |
| MOV CH, DL | 88 D5 | 2 | MOV CH, BH | 88 FD | 2 |
| MOV CH, BL | 88 DD | 2 | MOV CH, (BX) | 8A 2F | 13 |
| MOV CH, AL | 88 C5 | 2 | MOV CL, CH | 88 E9 | 2 |
| MOV CL, CL | 88 C9 | 2 | MOV CL, DH | 88 F1 | 2 |

| Mnemonics | Opcode | | Clock | Mnemonics | Opcode | | Clock |
|---|---|---|---|---|---|---|---|
| MOV CL, DL | 88 | D1 | 2 | MOV CL, BH | 88 | F9 | 2 |
| MOV CL, BL | 88 | D9 | 2 | MOV CL, (BX) | 8A | 0F | 8+EA |
| MOV CL, AL | 88 | C1 | 2 | MOV DH, CH | 88 | EF | 2 |
| MOV DH, CL | 88 | CE | 2 | MOV DH, DH | 88 | F6 | 2 |
| MOV DH, BL | 88 | DE | 2 | MOV DH, (BX) | 8A | 37 | 13 |
| MOV DH, AL | 88 | C6 | 2 | MOV DL, CH | 88 | EA | 2 |
| MOV DL, CL | 88 | CA | 2 | MOV DL, DH | 88 | F2 | 2 |
| MOV DL, DL | 88 | D2 | 2 | MOV DL, BH | 88 | FA | 2 |
| MOV DL BL | 88 | DA | 2 | MOV DL, (BX) | 8A | 17 | 13 |
| MOV DL, AL | 88 | C2 | 2 | MOV BH, CH | 88 | EF | 2 |
| MOV BH, CL | 88 | CF | 2 | MOV BH, DH | 88 | F7 | 2 |
| MOV BH, DL | 88 | D7 | 2 | MOV BH, BH | 88 | FF | 2 |
| MOV BH, BL | 88 | DF | 2 | MOV BH, (BX) | 8A | 3F | 13 |
| MOV BH, AL | 88 | C7 | 2 | MOV BL, CH | 88 | EB | 2 |
| MOV BL, CL | 88 | CB | 2 | MOV BL, DH | 88 | F3 | 2 |
| MOV BL, DL | 88 | D3 | 2 | MOV BL, BH | 88 | FB | 2 |
| MOV BL, BL | 88 | D8 | 2 | MOV BL, (BX) | 8A | 1F | 13 |
| MOV BL, AL | 88 | C3 | 2 | MOV (BX),CH | 88 | 2F | 14 |
| MOV (BX), CL | 88 | 0F | 14 | MOV (BX),DH | 88 | 37 | 14 |
| MOV (BX), DL | 88 | 17 | 14 | MOV (BX),BH | 88 | 3F | 14 |
| MOV (BX), BL | 88 | 1F | 14 | MOV (BX),AL | 88 | 07 | 14 |
| MOV AL, CH | 88 | E8 | 2 | MOV AL, CL | 88 | C8 | 2 |
| MOV AL, DH | 88 | F0 | 2 | MOV AL, DL | 88 | D0 | 2 |
| MOV AL, BH | 88 | F8 | 2 | MOV AL, BL | 88 | D8 | 2 |
| MOV AL, (BX) | 8A | 07 | 13 | MOV AL, AL | 88 | C0 | 2 |
| MOV CH, d | 85 | | 4 | MOV CL, d | B1 | | 4 |
| MOV DH, d | B6 | 12 | 4 | MOV DL, d | B2 | | 4 |
| MOV BH, d | B7 | | 4 | MOV BL, d | B3 | | 4 |
| MOV b(BX), d | C6 | 07 | 15 | MOV AL, d | B0 | | 4 |
| NOP | 90 | | 3 | OR AL, CH | 08 | E8 | 3 |
| OR AL, CL | 08 | C8 | 3 | OR AL, DH | 08 | F0 | 3 |
| OR AL, DL | 08 | D0 | 3 | OR AL, BH | 08 | F8 | 3 |
| OR AL, BL | 08 | D8 | 3 | OR AL, b(BX) | 0A | 07 | 14 |
| OR AL, AL | 08 | C0 | 3 | OR AL, d | 0C | | 4 |
| OUT d, AL | E6 | | 10 | JMP BX | FF | E3 | 11 |
| POP CX | 59 | | 8 | POP DX | 5A | | 8 |
| POP BX | 58 | | 8 | POP AX | 58 | | 8 |
| POP F | 9D | | 8 | PUSH CX | 51 | | 11 |
| PUSH DX | 52 | | 11 | PUSH BX | 53 | | 11 |
| PUSH AX | 50 | | 11 | PUSH F | 9C | | 10 |
| RCL AL, 01 | D0 | C0 | 2 | RCR AL, 01 | D0 | D8 | 2 |
| RET | C3 | | 8 | ROL AL, 01 | D0 | C0 | 2 |
| ROR AL, 01 | D0 | C8 | 2 | INT 0 | CD | 00 | 51 |
| INT 1 | CD | 01 | 51 | INT 2 | CD | 02 | 51 |
| INT 3 | CD | 03 | 51 | INT 4 | CD | 04 | 51 |
| INT 5 | CD | 05 | 51 | INT 6 | CD | 06 | 51 |
| INT 7 | CD | 07 | 51 | SBB AL, CH | 18 | E8 | 3 |
| SBB AL, CL | 18 | C8 | 3 | SBB AL, DH | 18 | F0 | 3 |
| SBB AL, DL | 18 | D0 | 3 | SBB AL, BH | 18 | F8 | 3 |
| SBB AL, BL | 18 | D8 | 3 | SBB AL, (BX) | 1A | 07 | 14 |
| SBB AL, AL | 18 | C0 | 3 | SBB AL, d | 1C | | 4 |
| MOV (addr), BX | 89 | 1E | 2 | MOV SP, BL | 89 | DC | 2 |
| MOV (addr), AL | A2 | | 14 | MOV b (SI),AL | 88 | 04 | 8 |
| STC | F9 | | 2 | SUB AL, CH | 28 | E8 | 3 |
| SUB AL, CL | 28 | C8 | 3 | SUB AL, DH | 28 | F0 | 3 |
| SUB AL, DL | 28 | D0 | 3 | SUB AL, BH | 28 | F8 | 3 |

| Mnemonics | Opcode | Clock | Mnemonics | Opcode | Clock |
|---|---|---|---|---|---|
| SUB AL, BL | 28 D8 | 3 | SUB AL, b(BX) | 2A 07 | 14 |
| SUB AL, AL | 28 C0 | 3 | SUB AL, d | 2C | 4 |
| XCHG BX, DX | 87 D3 | 4 | XOR AL, AL | 30 C0 | 3 |
| XOR AL, CH | 30 E8 | 3 | XOR AL, CL | 30 C8 | 3 |
| XOR AL, DH | 30 F0 | 3 | XOR AL, DL | 30 D0 | 3 |
| XOR AL, 8H | 30 F8 | 3 | XOR AL, BL | 30 D8 | 3 |
| XOR SI, BX | 32 07 | 14 | XOR AL, d | 34 | 4 |
| XCHG SI, BX | 87 DE | 4 | | | |

# 4. Some Advanced Features in 8085A

Several unspecified instructions of 8085A CPU exists which add remarkable strength both in hardware and software. Without these instructions, the 16-bit capabilities of the 8085A cannot be appreciated completely. In this section, a brief summary of these instructions have been described only to give an idea of the full capability of the 8085A chip. Some remarks have been made on the advanced features, a CPU may incorporate within itself.

## 1. MODIFIED PSW

The flag may be shown to be reorganised, associated with more important condition codes as follows:

| | d7 | d6 | d5 | d4 | d3 | d2 | d1 | d0 |
|---|---|---|---|---|---|---|---|---|
| PSW : | S | Z | X5 | AC | - | P | V | C |

where, S: sign bit as specified earlier; Z: zero bit as specified earlier; X5: under flow (**DCX**) or overflow (**INX**)

$$X5 = 01.02+01.R+02.R$$

where, 01: sign of operand 1; 02: sign of operand 2 and R sign of the result.
For subtraction and comparison, replacement of 02 may be made by $\overline{02}$
AC: auxiliary carry as specified earlier; P: parity bit as specified earlier; V: 2,s complement overeflow and C: carry bit as specified earlier.

## 2. NEW INSTRUCTIONS

Some of the most powerful instructions not always specified may be listed as:

### I. DSUB (Double Subtraction)

$$(HL) \longleftarrow (HL)-(BC)$$

Contents of BC pair are subtracted from the contents of the HL pair and the results are stored in HL pair. All conditions flags are affected.

For this instruction.

```
OPCODE : 08
CYCLE  : 3
STATES : 10
FLAGS  : Z,S,P,C,AC,X5,V.
```

### II. ARHL (Arithmetic Shift of HL to Right)

| | | |
|---|---|---|
| H7 $\longleftarrow$ H7 | OPCODE : | 10 |
| Hn-1 $\longleftarrow$ Hn | CYCLE : | 2 |
| Ln-1 $\longleftarrow$ Ln | STATES : | 7 |
| C $\longleftarrow$ Lo | FLAGS : | C |

Contents of HL pair are shifted by to right. The uppermost bit is duplicated and the lowest bit is shifted to the carry. The result is stored in the HL. Only the carry flag is affected.

## III. RDEL  (Rotate DE Left Through Carry)

| | |
|---|---|
| E ⟵ C | OPCODE : 18 |
| E ⟵ E | CYCLES : 3 |
| D ⟵ E | STATES : 10 |
| D ⟵ D | FLAGS : C,V. |
| C ⟵ D | |

Contents of DE are rotated left by one bit through carry. The lowest bit is equal to C and the C is loaded by the uppermost bit. The result is in DE. Carry and V-flag are set.

## IV. LDHI  (Load DE with HL Plus Immediate Byte)

$$(DE) \longleftarrow (HL) + BYTE\ 2$$

Contents of HL are added with the immediate byte and the results are stored in DE. no flag being affected. For this instruction.

OPCODE : 28
CYCLE : 3
STATES : 10
FLAGS : NONE

## V.  LDSI (Load DE with SP Plus Immediate Byte)

$$(DE) \longleftarrow (SP) + BYTE\ 2$$

Contents of stack pointer are added with the immediate byte and the results are placed in DE. No flags are affected.

OPCODE : 38
CYCLE : 3
STATES : 10
FLAGS : NONE

## VI. LHLX (Load HL Indirect Through DE)

$$L \longleftarrow [DE]$$
$$H \longleftarrow [DE + 1]$$

Content of the memory location addressed by DE moves to L and that of the next address to DE goes to H. No flags are affected.

OPCODE : ED
CYCLE : 3
STATES : 10
FLAGS : NONE

## VII. SHLX  (Store HL Indirect Through DE)

$$[DE] \longleftarrow L$$
$$[DE + 1] \longleftarrow H$$

Contents of L are stored in the location addressed by the DE and that of H at the next address. No flags are affected.

```
OPCODE  :  D9
CYCLE   :  3
STATES  :  10
FLAGS   :  NONE
```

## VIII. JX5 (Jump on X5)

If X5, PC ⟵ Byte 3 & Byte 2.

If the X5 flag is set, the control is transferred to the instruction whose address is specified in byte 3 and byte 2 of the current instruction, otherwise the control continues sequentially.

```
OPCODE  :  FD
CYCLE   :  2 or 3
STATES  :  7 or 10
FLAGS   :  NONE
```

## IX. JNX 5 (Jump on not X5)

If not X5, PC ⟵ Byte 3 & Byte 2

If the X5 is reset, the control transferred to the instruction whose address is given to byte 3 & 2 of the current instruction, otherwise control continues sequentially.

```
OPCODE  :  DD
CYCLE   :  2 or 3
STATES  :  7 or 10
FLAGS  :  NONE
```

## X. RSTV (Restart on Overflow)

```
If.  (SP - 1) ⟵ PC
     (SP - 2) ⟵ PC
     SP       ⟵ SP - 2
     PC       ⟵ 40 (hex)
```

If the overflow flag is set, PC is stacked up and then loaded by the address 0040. The SP is decremented by two. Otherwise the control continues sequentially.

```
OPCODE  :  C8
CYCLE   :  1 or 3
STATES  :  6 or 12
FLAGS   :  NONE
```

## 3.  SIMPLE  APPLICATIONS

With a little insight into the instructions, one may visualise that the 8085 CPU is a simple 8-bit CPU having 16-bit computational capabilities, since all the basic operations for 16-bit computations like addition, subtractions, rotations, increment, decrement etc. are available. Moreover, double byte memory-fetching or storing is also possible in indexed mode using DE as the index pointer. These features remarkably raise the status of 8085A and widely increases the sphere of its application. The efficiency in speed and span, one may obtain by using these instructions, have been clarified with some simple examples.

Let us assume that the register pair BC is used as a counter for a subprogram like a DELAY by count down technique. One may achieve this by the old set of instructions as follows:

```
LOOP :  DCX  B
        MOV  A,B
        ORA  C
        JNZ  LOOP
```

In this case, in accordance with the specification made by INTEL, no flag is affected by INX or DCX instructions. Hence, register B and C are required to OR to affect the zero flag and thus the accumulator and the flag registers are affected in a disadvantageous way. But INX or DCX affects the X5 flag and so, one may write the program as follows:

```
LOOP :  DCX   B
        JNX 5 LOOP
```

It is important to note that the same objective is accomplished without affecting the accumulator and important flags like C, P, S, Z etc.

Similarly, let us see how to rotate a double byte by the old set of instructions only. In order to rotate DE left. either of the following programs may be used:

```
A:  ORA  A : (MAY NOT BE DESIREABLE ALWAYS)     B:   PUSH H
    MOV  A,E                                          XCHG
    RAL                                               DAD H
    MOV  E,A                                          XCHG
    MOV  A,D                                          POP  H
    RAL
    MOV  D,A
```

But the same objective may be obtained using instructions "RDEL", Moreover, one may be puzzled to see the difficulty if one needs to affect the carry flag only by this rotation, keeping all other flags and registers except DE unaffected.

The rotation and shift of HL to left may be simple due to the instruction DAD H. In case of rotation of a double byte to right, the same problem is faced with as discussed above. But it is simply performed by one instruction 'ARHL' only. Similarly, it becomes difficult to perform a double byte subtraction by the conventional set of instructions whereas the same task may be completed by using the instruction DSUB only. The double byte handling has been greatly facilitated by the use of DE as the index pointer.

In case of complicated problems, these instructions are of great help indeed. In our concluding example, let us assume that HL pair now contains some value and there exists a table of addresses of some jump programs 80 Hex apart from the content of L. If the CPU needs to N-th jump program and if n be stored in DE register, the program may be as follows:

```
DAD  H
DAD  D
LDHI 80
XCHG
LHLX
PCHL
```

It is really interesting to see how easily these types of programs may be developed by INTEL 8085A

To end this chapter, let us see the following subprogram for multiplication (16-bit × 16-bit = 32-bit):-

SUBPROGRAM :     MULTIPLICATION
                 (HLDE) ⟵— (HL) × (DE)

Registers affected:     A,B,C,D,E,H & L

```
        MULT:   MOV    B, D
                MOV    C, E
                LXID   00 00
                MVI    A, 10
                PUSH   D
                XTHL
        LI   :  DAD    H
                RDEL
                .XTHL
                DAD    H
                XTHL
                JNC    L2
                DAD    B
                JNC    L2
                INX    D
        L2   :  DCR    A
                JNZ    L1
                POP    B
                XCHG
                RET
```

# 5. Standard Peripherals for Motorola, Zilog and Rockwell Systems

## MOTOROLA

| | |
|---|---|
| 6821 | PIA (PROGRAMMABLE INTERFACE ADAPTER) |
| 6843 | FLOPPY DISC CONTROLLER |
| 6845 | CRT CONTROLLER |
| 6847 | VIDEO DISPLAY CONTROLLER |
| 6850 | ASYNCHRONOUS COMMUNICATION INTERFACE ADAPTER (ACIA) |
| 6852 | SSDA (SYNCHRONOUS SERIAL DATA ADAPTER) |
| 6875 | CLOCK GENERATOR |

## ZILOG

| | |
|---|---|
| Z 80 - PIO | PROGRAMMABLE INPUT - OUTPUT |
| Z 80 - SIO | SERIAL INPUT - OUTPUT |
| Z 80 - CTC | COUNTER - TIMER CIRCUITS |
| Z 80 - DMA | DMA CONTROLLER |

## ROCKWELL / MOS TECH. INC

| | |
|---|---|
| 6522 | PIA  (PROGRAMMABLE INTERFACE ADAPTER) |
| 6545 | CRT CONTROLLER |
| 6551 | ACIA  (ASYNCHRONOUS COMMUNICATION INTERFACE ADAPTER) |

# References

1. DV Hall: Microprocessors and digital systems, McGraw-Hill, 1983
2. DV Hall: Microprocessor and Interfacing: Programming and Hardware, McGraw-Hill, 1986.
3. JL Hilburn and PM Julich: Micro computer/Microprocessor: Hardware, Software and Applications, Prentice-Hall, New Delhi, 1981.
4. E Klingman: Microprocessor System Design, Prentice-Hall, New Jercy, 1977.
5. KA Odgin: Software design for microprocessor, Prentice-Hall, New Jercy, 1978.
6. JB Peatman: Microprocessor based design, McGraw-Hill, Kogakusha, Tokyo, 1977.
7. P Katz: Digital Control Using Microprocessor, Prentice-Hall, 1981.
8. RJ Bibbero: Microprocessors in istruments and control, 1977.
9. E Horwitz and S Sahni: Fundamentals of data structures, Galgotia Publications, New Delhi, 1983.
10. JO Ullman: Principles of data based systems, Galgotia Publications, New Delhi, 1985.
11. JJ Donavan: Systems Programming, McGraw-Hill, 1983.
12. Technical Manuals of:
    (i)     Intel Corporation of USA
    (ii)    Zilog Inc.
    (iii)   Motorola
    (iv)    Rockwell
    (v)     Texas Instruments
    (vi)    MOS Tech
    (vii)   Advance Micro Device
13. A.K. Mukhopadhyay and N.C. Das: Microprocessor Based PHESS Meter; IEEE Trans. Ind. Electronics; Vol. IE-34, No. 1, Feb. 1987.
14. Douglas V Hall : Microprocessor and Interfacing Programming and Hardware, Tata McGraw Hill Publishing Company Limited.
15. Hans- Peter- Messmer : The Indispendable Pentium Book, Addition - Wesley Publishing Company
16. Don Anderson, Tom Shanley : Pentium Processor System Architechture Mindshare Inc
17. Microsystem Handbook Volume - I (1984) : Intel Corporation, USA.
18. Microsystem Handbook Volume - II (1984) : Intel corporation, USA
19. Militiary Handbook (1984) : Intel Corporation, USA
20. 8-bit Embadded Controllers (1991): Intel Corporation, USA.

# Index